PRAISE FOR SAID ELIAS DAWLABANI'S

Second Sapiens: The Rise of the Planetary Mind and The Future of Humanity

Second Sapiens is a groundbreaking work that redefines our understanding of human development and its critical role in addressing the existential threats we face today. Said Dawlabani's profound insights into the evolution of human consciousness are thought provoking and transformative, providing a comprehensive framework that integrates developmental psychology, systems thinking, and ecological awareness.

Said's compelling narrative meticulously chronicles the journey from *Homo subsistens* to *Homo magnificus*, highlighting the urgent need for a paradigm shift toward Gaian intelligence. His adept use of the Graves-Beck model, enriched with his own research, brings a fresh perspective to the Spiral-Dynamics framework, emphasizing the importance of ecological alignment in our developmental stages.

What sets *Second Sapiens* apart is its ability to bridge complex scientific theories with practical, real-world applications. Said's writing is clear and engaging, making intricate concepts accessible to a broad audience. His call for a holistic integration of natural and human intelligence is not only timely but essential for ensuring the sustainability of our planet.

This book is a must-read, providing a beacon of light in the face of global challenges. It offers a visionary roadmap that inspires hope and action, encouraging us to embrace a higher order of intelligence that can lead to a more resilient world. *Second Sapiens* is not just a book; it's a manifesto for the future, urging us to evolve and adapt in harmony with the natural world.

—Andrew Cohen
Founder of Manifest Nirvana
Author of *Evolutionary Enlightenment*

In *Second Sapiens,* Said Dawlabani offers a vastly expanded platform that enables us to see through time and make sense of how and why change happens. He addresses what humanity needs to do in order to heal from its self-inflicted wounds in a future which will bring challenges on a vastly higher level of complexity and uncertainty than we can now imagine.

Said calls for reinstating the intelligence that allows us to connect past, present and future. This way of thinking was embedded in many of the world's ancient traditions and mythologies. It entailed the realization that in every moment our actions were creating the future, our *Fate*—which, good or bad, would await us as a result. Fate was the basis for the accountability of individuals within the collective. It could not be controlled or escaped; it could only be prepared for.

Needless to say, this way of thinking is long gone. We think and act as if there is no tomorrow. We believe that through science and objective knowledge we can control whatever challenges lie ahead. Said's fundamental point is that, unfortunately this is not the case.

Critical planetary systems have already reached the tipping point. If humanity is to avoid total extinction, we urgently need to prepare to meet the Fate we already have brought upon ourselves through our collective actions. To do so, we need a very different version of *Homo sapiens* in order to cope with what lies ahead. Hence, *Second sapiens,* which both reinstates ancient wisdom and requires exponentially higher levels of thinking in what Said calls *natural intelligence.* His work is a must-read which allows for a full spectrum view of the "web of Fate" for humanity.

—Bjarni S. Jonsson, PhD
Cofounder of DecideAct

In *Second Sapiens*, Said Dawlabani shows how failure to include Nature has lured *Homo sapiens* into believing it is omniscient and how, nevertheless, She is not convinced. She may even be responding to humanity's destructions with even greater ones of her own through current climate catastrophes. As in his previous book, *MEMEnomics*, Said begins by looking at the practices and ideas behind current attitudes toward international commerce and trade. Drawing on a variety of sources—including economics, systems science, James Lovelock's Gaia thesis, and Ken Wilber's Integral Theory as well as Don E. Beck's Spiral Dynamics—he points to the inadequacies of contemporary and earlier economic, scientific, political, and even spiritual attitudes in a world where climate change is beginning to run riot and will get worse.

Said also suggests ways that the theories used to highlight these problems are themselves still caught up in Anthropocentric attitudes. This includes the thinking of figures such as Clare W. Graves as well as Beck and Wilber, whose ideas originated in times when issues such as climate change were not on the table. Drawing on Graves's unpublished work, Said provides pointers forward that include necessary changes in psychology, technology, spirituality, and religion as well as politics and economics. The key is to work with Nature rather than against Her.

His is, however, no romantic, "back to Nature" approach. It's a journey grounded in gritty reality, acknowledging, as the great physicist Richard Feynman observed in his report on the Challenger space-shuttle disaster, that "Nature cannot be fooled." That acknowledgment comprises the realization that human survival may depend on more people moving from our current impasses to a different level of being. *Second Sapiens* is an invitation and a summons to make that move and to act.

—Graham Mummery
Former investment banker, therapist, poet
Author of *The Gods Have Become Diseases*

With the release of his book *Memenomics* (2013), Said Dawlabani entered my space in the search for the economic-system design that supports all life in balance with Planet Earth. He brought the unique work of Clare Graves and of Don Beck's Spiral Dynamics to introduce his distinctive developmental perspective on sustainability and regeneration. In 2014, he was the keynote speaker at the annual gathering of global sustainability experts sponsored by my nonprofit organization, r3.0 (Redesign, Resilience, and Regeneration).

In *Second Sapiens*, he takes his evolutionary framework one step further and offers additional insight into the needs of human enlightenment if we want to continue as a species. I specifically appreciate his clustering of the problems of the "Age of Acceleration" and the "Great Obsolescence" in part 1 of the book. Unlike many who articulate these issues through a "meta-crisis" perspective, Dawlabani, through his stage-development life-cycle model, provides a deeper layer of connection that exposes the organizing principles underlying today's chaos and collapse.

But that is not the end of the journey, he says. He sees an awakening to a higher stage of human consciousness, a shift in humanity's stages of development from that of the *First* to the *Second sapiens.* Such profound change comes with his acknowledgement of collapse in part 2, specifically in chapter 7, "The Darkness before the New Dawn." His conclusions and shift in focus parallels ours own at r3.0 as we, too, have taken the steps necessary toward collapse resilience.

In part 3, Dawlabani looks at some of the leading-edge, economic-development models. His review includes sustainable development goals (SDGs), doughnut economics, planetary boundaries and alternatives to GDP measurement, not without hinting at shortcomings of their Second Sapiens potential, using criteria of the "Gaiametry economic protocols" to test their ultimate resilience.

I wholeheartedly agree with his summary in chapter 10: "A post-collapse homo sapiens will embrace higher states of awareness that reconnect us to the psychic and spiritual states that have long been sidelined. This is where the road to being one with Nature and cosmic wonder will begin anew. It is in these higher realms that natural and spiritual intelligence reside." Dawlabani's new book is an appreciated and highly recommended contribution to the discussion about humanity's future and role on Planet Earth.

—Ralph Thurm
Managing Director, r3.0
Author of *The Corona Chronicles* (2021)

Second Sapiens

The Rise of the Planetary Mind and The Future of Humanity

Said Elias Dawlabani

Waterside Productions

First Printing, 2024

ISBN-13: 978-1-962984-62-1 print edition
ISBN-13: 978-1-962984-63-8 e-book edition

Waterside Productions
2055 Oxford Ave
Cardiff, CA 92007
www.waterside.com

To Elza, Don, and Clare,
the three sapiens who set my mind and soul on fire

How should spring bring forth a garden on hard stone?
Become Earth, that you may grow flowers of many colors.
For you have been heart-breaking rock.
Once, for the sake of experiment, be Earth!

—Rumi

Contents

List of Figures

List of Tables

Foreword

If I could use Gaia's voice, the first thing I would say about this book is "thank you" to Said Dawlabani for creating the concept of *Second sapiens* and for coining the term to describe the measures that are meaningful to me as the Living Planet that I am. His book introduces the term *Gaiametry*—the metrics for living at a planetary scale. In fact, Said goes one step further and imagines viewing these metrics from Jupiter, giving Gaiametry a context even beyond the planet into the solar system and the universe.

As an author, I have paid special attention to others who take a Gaian perspective, such as physicist James Lovelock, who declared that Gaia is not merely a planet but a living system. Lovelock called humans "Gaia's reflective organs." In my *Integral City* book series, I have imagined further that individual humans are the cells and their organizations are specialized organelles and cities are the reflective organs of Gaia.

At every planetary scale, Gaian energy and intelligence interconnects all living systems as they have emerged through planetary evolution. Gaia has matured from the root condition of consciousness that has spawned the entire universe. Her reflective organs have finally evolved so that they can now express a unitive narrative, a unitive metrics, and even a unitive economics. How inspiring to hear Said use a Gaian language and Gaiametry to express the conditions of life that are reflecting not just a planetary reality but the reality and context of every living system symbiotically evolving on the planet.

How natural that Gaiametry can emerge from the integrated ontologies, epistemologies, and philosophies enabled by Clare Graves's seminal research, Don E. Beck's Spiral-Dynamics framework, and Ken Wilber's Integral Theory model, all of which Said builds on and adapts so clearly to create a developmental guide for the Anthropocene epoch in this book. Said has insightfully reframed Integral City's Gaian intelligences that are reflected at every level of scale: contextual intelligences that integrate the patterns of symbiotic interconnections; individual intelligences for inner and outer agency; collective intelligences for inner and outer relationships; navigating intelligences to steady homeostasis within the planetary body and organs at every scale; and evolutionary intelligence as the spiritual impulse energizing all other intelligences. In doing so, he has insightfully reframed these systems of knowing as a living system, affirming Gaia's (and thus humanity's) evolutionary journey as a never-ending quest.

Moreover, he asserts that this reframing is non-negotiable, saying that "*human intelligence* as we have experienced it must now be nested in *natural intelligence* if we are to survive and thrive as a species in the face of Earth-systems collapse and other existential challenges" (see p. 9). His critique resonates so deeply with planetary intelligence that he can, without flinching, confess the sins that humans have inflicted on Gaia's condition. He enumerates fearlessly the great transgressions that humans have committed through the hubris of imagining that they are separate from Nature, entitled to Gaian gifts without constraint, ignorant of circular planetary life flows, and so dis-eased as to live unconscious of life's principles, waging wars that inflict pain, injury, and destruction against humans, nonhumans, and the planet herself.

Said masterfully traces the history and cycles of human behavior so that readers cannot deny the culpability, immaturity, and lack of integrity of the human species. By mapping the history of *Homo sapiens* on the developmental lifecycle model, he remembers the warning of Dr. Clare Graves, the researcher behind Spiral Dynamics; that is, the "momentous leap of mankind" from what Said calls the *First sapiens's* stages of psychosocial development to that of the *Second sapiens* is likely to be measured in a significant loss of human life.

His work in this book is nothing short of a treatise that not only presents us with the naked truth of climate change but also shows how the human species is responsible for creating the Anthropocene epoch. Every living system on Earth has now been impacted by human behavior. Humans have so unbalanced Gaia's sensitively adapted, key life systems that we are disrupting the benign conditions of the Holocene epoch that has allowed life to flourish for the last eleven thousand years. Now Gaian tipping points are being triggered that destroy the possibility of recovery or redress.

This book, *Second sapiens*, is a catalytic learning cell in Gaia's reflective organs. It mirrors to readers the growing likelihood that generations currently alive may be witnesses to the demise of life as everyone has ever known it. Many will not survive to tell the tale of chaos and devastation. And those who *do* survive will be deprived of the bio-psycho-cultural-social systems that support us because of today's disconnection from Gaia-centricity.

Said tells us that Earth's core systems are moving into more chaotic, unpredictable behaviors as each day passes. This experience is characteristic of the Anthropocene. Human limitations are constricted by stage development that is not equal to the level of intelligence needed to overcome the disastrous impacts with which *Homo sapiens* have encumbered the Earth. Facing these challenges is the work of the next evolutionary stage of humanity, or humans will not be here to witness the outcomes (let alone the solutions) to the problems we have caused.

While Said vividly describes the progression of human intelligence through the first six stages of *First sapiens*, he is extremely doubtful that the leaders in those stages have the capacity to bring humanity through the present chaos into the coherence imagined in the eighth stage of evolution (as proposed by the researchers and authors of *Spiral Dynamics*). Said speaks plainly that the natural progression of human values has been short-circuited by leaders who deny the inextricable (scientifically proven) connection between ecological well-being and human well-being, with all the bio-psycho-cultural-social impacts that connection entails.

Said steps aside from the predictions of the future embedded in the integrative patterns of the Spiral-Dynamics and Integral-Theory approaches that did not know or consider the implications of the science of climate change when they were formulated. He dares to recalibrate those frameworks from a human-centric perspective to a Gaia-centric perspective. He also translates the stages of development into language aligned with anthropologists, geologists, biologists, and historians, thus broadening the discourse beyond developmentalism. In so doing, he exposes the disruptive conditions that are hiding and/or denying the deep entanglement of human-centric activities threatening Gaia's well-being: over-consumption, exploitation, degenerative technologies (including artificial intelligence), globalizations, de-energizing transport systems, infrastructures, wars, and colonizations.

Said realizes that, in Gaia's interconnected living system, we humans are dooming ourselves and all other life by massively skewing behaviors, misinforming expectations, and scrambling life patterns. These insights reveal themselves as he transcends the original Spiral-Dynamics model and includes it in describing the higher order of natural intelligence. He paints vividly with the qualities of Gaiametry the promise that *Second sapiens* could easily manifest an exponentially recalibrated capacity to seek and find evolutionary responses that are complex enough to survive, adapt to, and regenerate life conditions for the well-being of all life.

"*Second sapiens* is in awe of nature and her intelligence and seeks to end *First sapiens's* separation from her" (p. 15), he says. He even suggests that this *Second-sapiens* human will identify with Gaia, thus imagining that humans will finally respond to Gaia's feedback loops and will enable all variations, perspectives, levels, and realms of life to be noticed and examined.

Can humans make the leap beyond the capacities that undermine not only life for *First sapiens* but also any hope of evolving or stabilizing at the level of *Second sapiens*? Said suggests that the hope of the *First sapiens* can murder and prevent the hope of the *Second.* How can Gaia countenance such undermining of her living systems? Said takes us through an incisive journey to consider how the patterns that bring stasis to different stages of evolution change from stage to stage. He examines not just the evolution of stage development but also the impact each stage has in the Coalescence of Authority, Power, and Influence (CAPI), a concept developed by global-management consultant Ichak Adizes. In that process, Said compares the power of states that are *open* (to continuing change and learning) to those that are *arrested* (in which new learning plateaus and does not develop) or *closed* (in which learning is not only stopped but denied and/or rejected). It is in a closed state that meaningful hope perishes, and Said sees many contemporary systems as "closed."

As a planet, Gaia herself is evolving. She has the necessary evolutionary and multiple intelligences to make the momentous leap Clare Graves foresaw. Can the human species actually reflect on/with/as Gaia? Said warns us that to ignore Gaia's principles of healthy living systems is to court human demise. He persistently poses the question: "What would Mother Nature do?" In this musing he contemplates a dark "view from Jupiter"—where the post-apocalyptic world is a post-human one—based on a thema of scarcity with a reduced bio-diversity in all ecological systems that *First-sapiens* humans have taken for granted. He suggests that Gaia will be inured to human pain and suffering until human beings can overcome the misguided, uninformed, small perspectives that have characterized them so far.

With Gaiametry, Said stretches beyond the current dysfunctionality of democracy to sweep in the implications of earth sciences, climatology, ecofeminism, deep ecology, social ecology, environmental philosophy, collapse psychology, and ecopsychology, along with digital economies and the role of artificial intelligence. After meticulously detailing his Gaiametry framework over several chapters, he concludes that unless we urgently deploy the intelligences of *Second sapiens* and empower it to run our institutions, social collapse will become inevitable and that, until that collapse plays out, humans will be at the mercy of Gaia's living systems. Much like Jem Bendell *(Deep Adaptation,* 2018), Said suggests that what we most need is to accept the suffering and despair that will follow from the loss of life and habitat on Earth. Humans will have no choice but to face human mortality, if not come dangerously close to human-species extinction. To that end, Said dedicates an entire chapter to what he calls the processing of the collective shadow of the *First sapiens,* and he does it through the embrace of myth, archetypal psychology, collective grief, and spirituality.

Despite this clear and frightening picture of what David Wallace-Welles has called an *Uninhabitable Earth* (2019), I am somewhat comforted that, in the last chapter, Said's view from Jupiter reveals other possibilities. He is courageous enough to consider the support and guidance humans might access from other realms that embrace the nonhuman energies and intelligences available in the subtle and causal realms. Said conjectures that those who survive the coming cataclysm will have developed residual capacities learned from the encounters with the dark realities of collapse. From the experience of surviving the cataclysm of the Anthropocene, he concludes that *Homo sapiens* will acquire—or more aptly, remember—a new/old era of ontologies and epistemologies that are evidenced in today's Indigenous peoples and shamanic traditions that have been largely ignored, side-lined, or colonized. He suggests that tribal elders may form a brain/heart/soul syndicate to emerge a new circle of wisdom. Will humans perhaps come closer together if they are forced to start over at the tribal stages of development? he muses. Will they perhaps rediscover the faults and mistakes of the *First sapiens* who separated themselves from nature and thus have driven humans to their current situation?

Said imagines that these older, Indigenous *sapiens* will possess a blend of intelligences that combine not just human capacities but also those from nonhuman realities to create a future very different from today. He shows that such a future must be aligned with Gaia's well-being to transition from the Anthropocene into a truly Gaian epoch.

"It is still possible for us to mingle the pure waters of Western thought with the sacred waters of Eastern transcendentalism and emerge fuller humans rising from the ashes of darkness. We can break the shackles of karmic debt, of death and rebirth, and overcome fear and the earthly desires of our egos, knowing that we are part of the cosmic mystery that sprang into being billions of years ago," Said proposes (p. 418). Ultimately, he moves us away from the Anthropocentric delusion that humans are at the center of the universe into "a symphony both of stardust and of newly born stars, all orchestrated by a silent conductor" (p. 419).

Thank you, Said Dawlabani, for serving Gaia as a life-renewing stem cell. Guided by her, humans can evolve and thrive far beyond the disasters and despairs of the *First sapiens*. Your book opens the possibility that a new seed of knowing can be regenerated and nurtured in the Gaian epoch of the *Second sapiens*.

—Marilyn Hamilton PhD, CPA (ret)
Founder of Integral City Meshworks and Living Cities Earth;
author of the *Integral City* book series and the
Tales of the CROFT Regenerators novellas

Acknowledgments

Oftentimes we forget that we stand on the shoulders of giants who came before us. I stand on the shoulders of two: Don Edward Beck and Clare Wray Graves. This book would not have been possible if it weren't for a deeply memorable conversation that took place in the fall of 2016. It was the week before a Spiral Dynamics training session at the Adizes Graduate School in Santa Barbara, and my friend and colleague Don Beck was visiting my wife, Elza, and me in San Diego. This had been the routine for several years: a few days before the training event, Don and his wife, Pat, would come to spend time with Elza and me, and then the four of us would drive together to the training. As we sat in our living room one morning, Don asked if my presentation was going to be about the "view from Jupiter." This was his way of nudging me into exploring new frontiers in the applicability of the Gravesian model. We had both known how difficult it was to address emerging societal and planetary issues through the existing framework when we had first discussed the matter earlier that year.

Dismissively, I responded, "That kind of presentation would require the repurposing of the entire second tier."

Without hesitation, he replied, "So? If anyone can do it, it's you. You don't have to call it 'second tier.' You're standing on Jupiter. Call it something else."

That was the moment that marked the birth of the concept of *Second sapiens.*

In addition, standing on the shoulders of these two giants wouldn't have been possible without the presence of a vast ecosystem of highly collaborative, supportive, and loving communities. And much of my work over the last two decades would have not been possible without the love of my soulmate, Elza, and that of my family. To my daughters, Chloe and Quinn, thank you for your love and patience in continuing to enlighten me on your generation's worldview. To my brothers, Nassif and Nick, my sister, Nuha, and my mom, Jamileh, you are the rock on which I built the foundation that has made me who I am. To my late dad, Elias, who sacrificed so much to put us all through private school, I owe a debt that I can never repay.

I am one of the luckiest people to have lived a life belonging to several pioneering communities, not the least of which is the Spiral Dynamics community that spans the globe. I am thankful to all my colleagues at the different Centers for Human Emergence (CHEs) with whom I have had the privilege of working, and I am especially grateful to those who live in regions of the world that are currently experiencing political unrest, including my colleagues at the CHE Middle East, Neri Bar On in Israel, Nafiz Rifai in the West Bank, and Anatoly Balyaev at the CHE Russia in Moscow. Much gratitude also goes to current and past heads of CHEs—to Jon Freeman at the CHE UK, Roberto Bonilla at the CHE Mexico, Dorothea Zimmer at the CHE Germany, Peter Merry and Anne-Marie Voorhoeve at the CHE Netherlands, and Teddy Hebo Larsen at the CHE Denmark. And my gratitude goes out to other colleagues who use the Gravesian model to augment their work in addressing issues of sustainability and climate change: Robin Lincoln Wood, Ralph Thurm, and Michiel Doorn. Special thanks go to Howard Bloom whose genius has inspired me and thousands of Spiral Dynamics trainees. Special thanks also go out to Nancy Roof, the publisher of Kosmos Journal who brought our work at the CHE Middle East to the attention of the United Nations and for her decades-long advocacy for global transformation. I am grateful to the late Russ Volkmann, publisher of Integral Leadership Review, whose interviews and "Notes from the Field" feature brought our geopolitical and economic applications of Gravesian methodologies to readers the world over.

I'm indebted to the community of supporters from the Adizes Graduate School and the Adizes Institute, to Dr. Ichak Adizes himself, and to his associates and former students Dr. Stephanie Galindo, Dr Bjarni Jonsson, and Dr. Darrell Gooden. I am also blessed to be a member of Ken Wilber's Integral community. While this book is critical of his use of the Graves-Beck model, his remaining body of work is nothing short of a masterful, grand design that continues to integrate and synthesize different world philosophies, religion, psychology, and science into one formidable framework that never ceases to inspire me with its depth and breadth.

Additionally, I am grateful to many members of the Evolutionary Leaders in the Service of Conscious Evolution whose work and support continues to inform and inspire me: Deepak Chopra, Diane Williams, Deborah Moldow, Jean Houston, Andrew Cohen, Bruce Lipton, Elisabet Sahtouris, and David Sloan Wilson. The member of the group who I have known the longest is the one who wrote the foreword to this book: Marilyn Hamilton who walks the walk by practicing evolutionary leaddrship at the Gaian scale. Her generosity and big Gaian heart are a testament to the transformative future of our species.

My gratitude also goes out to other friends and colleagues who have supported my work for decades: Richard Dance, Bruce Gibb, Barbara N. Brown, Phyllis Blees, Kevin Kells, Rica Viljoen, Albert Klamt, Anitta Fuchs, Jim Lockhart, J. Kim Wright, Marc Fabionar, Keith Rice, William Hajdu, Tom Habib, Bence Ganti, Jeff Salzman, Christopher Cooke, the late Gary Stamper, Eric Reynolds, Lisa Celentano, Chuck Robison, Cindy Wigglesworth, Daniela Bomatter, Michael Aschenbach, Adelheid (Heidi) Hornlein, Alain Volz, Eloy Maes, Kabir Kadre, Fred Krawchuk, Graham Mummery, and so many others.

This book would not have been possible without those scientists, systems thinkers, visionaries, climate writers, and activists who appear in the endnotes and the bibliography. They are the foundation on which the ecology of *Second sapiens* is built. They are the ones who continue to speak truth to power and without whom humanity has little chance at survival. Thank you all.

I am eternally indebted to my publisher, Waterside Productions, for seeing the uniqueness of my approach that integrates developmental and social psychology with existential challenges in a sea of books that treat these subjects as separate and distinct fields of knowledge. Your boldness is a testament to the highly collaborative, interdisciplinary, and transdisciplinary nature of the future that awaits humanity.

The last and biggest thanks belongs to my editor and most critical reader, Sharron Dorr, who continues to fan the flames of my fire and make them into a beacon of light. Her acuity and brilliance, along with her subtle prodding and clarity of mind, are the stuff that has made *Second sapiens* possible.

Introduction

Like that rebellious Greek god Prometheus—who stole fire from Zeus and bestowed it upon humankind, Oppenheimer gave us atomic fire. But then, when he tried to control it, when he sought to make us aware of its terrible dangers, the powers-that-be, like Zeus, rose up in anger to punish him.

—Kai Bird and Martin J. Sherwin
American Prometheus

In the history of Western civilization, no other myth has had a more profound influence on art, literature, philosophy, language, and popular culture than that of the ancient Greeks. Their rich and complex stories explore universal themes such as love, loss, good and evil, and the constantly changing human condition. The narratives and interpretations found in these stories have resonated with people for centuries, from the time of the Roman Empire and Early Christianity to the sixteenth-century European Renaissance, in which Greek mythology became a major source of inspiration for artists, writers, and philosophers. Today, it manifests in popular culture in movies, music, theatrical plays, electronic games, and advertising. Its gods and goddesses and human heroes represent ageless truths and archetypes in the human psyche—an archetype, according to depth psychologist C. G. Jung, being a universal pattern or image that is present in the collective unconscious of all humans. Some of these archetypes range from heroes such as Hercules, Achilles, and Odysseus to Zeus—the king of the Gods in the Olympian pantheon who rules over thunder, lightning, the sky, law, justice, and order. Greek mythology, more than any other, has remained relevant to new audiences and continues to speak to the human condition in new and meaningful ways.

Greek myth, as in other world traditions, is intended to provide humanity with a narrative that helps us identify with the dual nature of the binary world, the pairs of opposites that came into existence when the universe was born. These pairs include, for example, the yin and the yang, darkness and light, feminine and masculine, and good and evil, all being the two sides of the same coin that keep the universe in balance.

The central idea behind pairs of opposite is crucial to the narrative in this book. Whether you believe in the scientific big-bang theory of the universe's origin or in the diverse narratives of creation offered by world traditions, there seems to be general agreement that time and space and all other dualities that keep everything in equilibrium were triggered into existence in one momentous act. The scientific narrative of the birth of the universe, like that of the mythological and religious narratives, begins by asserting a formless nonduality.

As Charles Francis, author of *Light after Dark*, writes, "In the beginning there was nothing; a vast expanse of emptiness lay dormant, a canvas devoid of light, matter, and time itself. Then, in a singular, explosive moment, the universe burst into existence, a symphony of energy and particles, marking the event known as the Big Bang."[1] The theory goes that the big bang occurred around 13.8 billion years ago, when all matter, energy, space, and time emerged from an infinitesimal singularity and instantaneously expanded, releasing a burst of energy that ignited the universe's rapid expansion. This colossal event is mirrored in the creation myths of many cultures in which a divine being, a cosmic egg, or primordial waters burst forth, giving rise to the cosmos.

While explanations of the event differ in language and symbolism, a common thread of transformation and origin runs through both scientific understanding and cultural beliefs. The only significant difference is in the nature of the pairs of opposites. Scientific studies of the cosmos include phenomena such as dark energy, or dark matter, that are not fully understood but are believed to be essential for keeping the observable universe in balance. Even before the big-bang theory was brought forth, Sir Isaac Newton had uncovered a scientific basis for the nature of the pair of opposites in his third law of motion, which loosely states that for every action there is an opposite and equal reaction. In our human imperfection, we usually remain unaware of whatever opposite reactions our actions create. Nevertheless, this scientific dynamic is in constant play, and our lack of consciousness about it often contributes cumulatively to states of imbalance.

It is also human imperfection that minimizes the importance of the pairs of opposites told in stories in different world traditions. In Hindu cosmology, the Rig Veda speaks of a cosmic golden egg, Hiranyagarbha, which splits into halves, forming the heavens and the Earth, the first pair of opposites in many traditions. Similarly, in Norse mythology, the giant Ymir is created from the drops of water that form when the cold mists of one realm meet the heat of another, and his body becomes the foundation for the world that emerged from the soup of chaos. Across most cultures, creation myths often feature a cosmic interplay between order and chaos, the pair of opposites that permeates all existence at every level and throughout time. The Babylonian creation epic, Enuma Elisha, tells of the victory of Marduk, god of order, over the goddess Tiamat, symbol of the chaos of creation, leading to the formation of the world from her divided body. In the Christian tradition, the Book of Genesis describes God creating the world as an agent of the good, associated with order and human decency, in opposition to the bad, associated with chaos and human perversity.

We saw the light, and we saw that it was good and dismissed the darkness. We were cast out of the Garden of Eden as punishment for wanting to know the truth about those opposites when we ate from the tree of knowledge of good and evil. We have spent millennia rebelling against the gods for preventing us from fully understanding the mystery of creation, yet that rebellion has created its own blinders to a uniquely human form of the pair of opposites: We have seen the good side of our genius but dismissed its evil opposite. We have built a modern civilization and a global economy based on one side of the coin—the one that promotes order, light, and the good in life—while ignoring the fact that the unexamined opposite side of these matters does not go away. Instead, it becomes part of our collective unconscious that sooner or later will appear in our lives as fate.

This dualistic ontology of human nature has defined our journey through its various stages of evolution and dominated cultural expression, whether religious or scientific. Dualism is universal, and the theme of it has resonated with writers and readers alike for centuries, from John Milton's *Paradise Lost* and Robert Louis Stevenson's *The Strange Case of Dr. Jekyll and Mr. Hyde* to Fyodor Dostoevsky's *Crime and Punishment* and Joseph Conrad's *Heart of Darkness.* The common theme that permeates these and other classic works is that we are all capable of both good and evil; we must constantly strive to choose the right path, to see both sides of the issue, and hold that totality as truth. The conundrum is also expressed in novels that treat the duality inherent in scientific discoveries. Kurt Vonnegut's 1963 novel, *Cat's Cradle*, demonstrates how a brilliant scientist who lacks a moral dimension does not consider the potential consequences of his creation. The novel makes clear that scientific progress does not necessarily equate to moral progress, and that, in fact, scientific developments have the capacity to wreak destruction on the very civilization they are meant to help.[2] This dualism continues to permeate our lives today with worldwide consequences as we contend with the ominous threats that artificial intelligence (AI) represents. The duality here is between those who want to impose a moratorium on AI's development so that we can understand its evil side first and those who, motivated by profit, want to dismiss the moral dimension and move ahead as quickly as possible.

The Gift of Fire

Human rebellion against the Gods is romanticized in the story of Prometheus, one of the most beloved figures from Greek mythology. He is best known for his role in stealing fire from the gods and giving it to humanity in the form of art, science, technology, and innovation, the essential ingredients that define modern civilization and its genius. The name *Prometheus* means "forethought," which among all living species is a uniquely human quality associated with intellect and foresight.

As the story goes, Prometheus was a Titan, the Titans being a race of powerful divine beings that preceded the Olympian gods. The myth is told in various ancient texts, including works by Hesiod, Aeschylus, and others. What keeps the story relevant to the modern mind is Prometheus's rebellion against the gods. When he stole fire from Mount Olympus and brought it down to earth, Prometheus defied Zeus, the king of the Olympian gods. Zeus punished Prometheus by chaining him to a rock on Mount Caucasus, where an eagle daily ate his liver, which regenerated overnight due to his immortal nature. That regeneration symbolizes human resilience. The myth has been interpreted in various ways throughout history, often symbolizing themes of rebellion against authority, the pursuit of knowledge, and the consequences of pushing boundaries. It has inspired numerous works of art, literature, and philosophy and continues to be a significant cultural symbol. It defines the modern creative process by drawing parallels between the act of giving fire to humans and the acts of creating the art that illuminates, challenges, and transforms society and the science that advances human knowledge and enterprise.

Modern authors often employ the Promethean myth as a metaphor to explore contemporary concerns and moral quandaries, especially when it comes to treating the duality within the scientific mind that often lacks a moral dimension. There are many accounts in modern literature that make specific reference to the myth while capturing the essence of the dark side as well as the bright side of human genius, the pair of opposites that keep the universe in balance. Two works, specifically, are most relevant to the concept of Promethean intelligence as a way to describe the evolution of the human mind. The first is a work of fiction, and the other is a biography.

The first work is Mary Shelly's 1818 seminal novel, *Frankenstein: The Modern Prometheus.* This classic work of Gothic literature delves into themes of creation and ambition. It also explores the dark side of these endeavors and the consequences of unchecked scientific pursuits. The character of Victor Frankenstein embodies this theme as his relentless pursuit of knowledge and desire to conquer death leads him to create a monster from different parts of human corpses. His ambition blinds him to the potential consequences of his actions, which ultimately result in the destruction of those he loves and his own downfall. The story has many complex layers that explore the consequences of scientific hubris and the nature of humanity. At the end of the story, the moral is clear: there are two sides to the gift of fire, and one cannot be ignored in favor of the other.

The second work, written by Kai Bird and Martin J. Sherwin, is their 2005 book, *American Prometheus: The Triumph and Tragedy of J. Robert Oppenheimer,* a biographical sketch of the man known as the father of the atomic bomb. Director of the Manhattan Project at Los Alamos, New Mexico, in World War II, Oppenheimer oversaw the creation of the first nuclear weapon that killed between 100,000 and 200,000 people in Hiroshima and Nagasaki in August 1945. The authors' comparison of Oppenheimer to Prometheus highlights the power and responsibility inherent in scientific and technological discoveries as well as the potential dangers that come with them. Awareness of this pair of opposites permeates the narrative of Bird's and Sherwin's book. Oppenheimer was deeply conflicted about the use of atomic weapons. He knew that they could be used to destroy humanity, but he also believed that they were necessary to defeat the Nazis. Ultimately, he decided to go ahead with the development of the bomb, but he continued to struggle with the moral implications of his decision for the rest of his life, voicing his misgivings in a stand that essentially silenced him in the US government.

The Curse of the Burning Embers

One account of the Promethean myth that is less spoken of today describes the god as a supreme trickster. The trickster archetype is a power that appears in the myth of many cultures and has much relevance to this book. Trickster gods are defined as boundary crossers who often break both physical and societal rules and violate the principles of social and natural order, playfully disrupting normal life and then reestablishing it on a new basis.[3] The trickster is also a clever shape shifter who holds a great degree of intellect and knowledge. The fox and the serpent are just a few examples from mythology and folklore. The trickster is known to be the peddler of false prophecy. He lures us into a place of hope and comfort just to see us suffer. This is the side of the Promethean myth that needs to be brought into the light. Our awareness of it requires us to hold the awareness that our actions have opposite and equal reactions. The genius is no longer in the gift of fire alone but in seeing beyond the trickster's falseness to what fire leaves behind.

This book is not about the philosophical, religious, or scientific origins of the cosmos or about the study of comparative philosophies or mythologies. Nor is it about the embrace of human genius in the way it has manifested in the scientific and technological discoveries that were born with the Scientific Revolution in the sixteenth century, carried on in the eighteenth-century Age of Enlightenment, and continue to define our world today. Rather, it is about uncovering the barriers that are preventing us from fully accepting our new reality. These barriers are developmental in nature. They are psychological, institutional, and societal and have enshrined our reality and our worldviews in the modernist virtues for centuries. It is those very views that have shielded us from addressing higher-order existential issues of all types. They highlight the imperfect nature of Promethean intelligence that has forgotten the adage of depth psychologist C. G. Jung that wherever there is light, there is shadow. We have forgotten the shadow. This book is an attempt to provide a window into the psychosocial evolution of our species and show what happens when the modern mind mollifies the dark side of modernity.

Much of the imbalance we see in the world today can be attributed to that mollification. The modern scientific method is associated with the concept of reductionism, which reduces all natural phenomena to their linear, mechanical parts. In the process, it marginalizes the innate qualities inherent in the whole and in nature. Reductionism has given permission to the scientific community to ignore or pacify the dark side of scientific discovery. At the end of the eighteenth century, civilization's answer to modern science was the Romantic era, an intellectual and artistic movement that gave us the works of great writers such as Wordsworth, Shelley, Keats, Byron, and Goethe. This swing of the pendulum was itself an attempt to reach cultural equilibrium by balancing the sciences with the arts, one influencing and informing the other in a seamless dance that showed the full range of Promethean intelligence—its darkness as well as its genius.

Today's reality, however, is quite different. While art and literature remain noble pursuits, the world now runs on much shallower metrics that have sidelined one side of the pair of opposites in favor of the other. Today, the arts hold little power. Instead, it is the sciences that have become an instrument of economic power and prosperity; in their reductive form, science and technology define much of what civilization stands for. While the most intelligent members of society today still identify with both sides of Promethean intelligence, others—especially those who are motivated by profit or driven by reductionism—don't. Even the few who are conscious of the dark side, as was Oppenheimer, are often prevented from speaking about it, especially after their genius inventions and the creation are handed over to those in power. More likely than not, those in control who run our institutions and corporations have no awareness of the dark side of genius or don't fully understand its power.

Modern repression of the dark side of genius is at the heart of how Promethean intelligence in the hands of the powerful became the primary cause of much of the existential problems we face today, not the least of which is climate change. Today, we are dealing with the largest collective shadow in human history. It is the accumulation of the dark side of our binary world that we have ignored and externalized to our environment over the last five centuries. This darkness is so enormous that it has pushed several Earth systems past their carrying capacity, making ecological collapse inevitable and climate-driven events increasingly unpredictable and more devastating in scale. Frankenstein's monster has run amuck. Oppenheimer's fire has gotten out of control, and those who can speak about these dangers have been marginalized. But, unlike in the myth, it is not Prometheus for his gift of fire with whom the gods are angry. Rather, it is us and our misuse of the fire that is triggering the gods' anger. It is the frailty and the imperfection inherent in the human mind that has set the world so far out of balance. And, in doing so, it has particularly angered another Greek deity who is now dictating our destiny.

Prometheus Transcended: Gaia

Controlling Prometheus's fire is what this book is all about. It is a metaphor for how we must keep the universal pairs of opposites in balance. Wherever there is light, there is shadow. Together, they create the wholeness that makes the universe and everything in it complete. They remind us to acknowledge the binary nature of existence made manifest since time immemorial.

What modern-day humans have largely forgotten is that, eons before Prometheus brought us "enlightenment," an intelligence existed in nature that was embodied in another Greek deity named Gaia, the mother of all things. Gaia is the primordial goddess who emerged from chaos and gave form to the air, the sea, and the land. She has evolved her earthly systems for billions of years and given life to billions of species, all the while balancing the totality of the pair of opposites through her *autopoietic* (Gk. self-creating) intelligence and feedback loops that account for the darkness and the light at every fractal level without repressing one side in favor of the other. She is Mother Nature, whose intelligence this book commonly refers to as *Gaian*, or the *natural intelligence* that is unencumbered by human deficiencies. It is this form of intelligence to which we must return in order to save ourselves from ecological and climate collapse.

I say "return" based on how evolutionary biologists, historians, and anthropologists view the impact *Homo sapiens* has had during its time on Earth. According to prominent historian and anthropologist Yuval Noah Harari, the evolution of our species began decoupling from that of nature around 70,000 years ago, and humanity began to view itself and its desires as preeminent on the planet.[4] Ever since then, that decoupling gap has grown wider, but our species still had deep appreciation for nature as recently as the Middle Ages, which lasted in Europe roughly between AD 500 and 1500. At that time, people still considered attempts to control nature as dangerous and even wrong, because nature was seen as part of God's design and its mysteries beyond human capacity fully to understand. The opening lines of the English poet Geoffrey Chaucer's *Canterbury Tales*, originally published in AD 1400, joyfully conveys the sense of harmony in this design between the natural world and humankind as pilgrims embark on a religious journey:

When April with his showers sweet with fruit
The drought of March has pierced unto the root
And bathed each vein with liquor that has power
To generate therein and sire the flower;
When Zephyr also has, with his sweet breath,
Quickened again, in every holt and heath,
The tender shoots and buds, ...
And many little birds make melody
That sleep through all the night with open eye
(So Nature pricks them on to ramp and rage)—
Then do folk long to go on pilgrimage.[5]

Chaucer reflects the view at the time that put nature at the center of life, not human endeavors. Finding new ways to return to that state, in which our engagement with nature becomes a coevolutionary process again, will be a monumental task that requires the transcendence of the ego and its subordination into Gaian intelligence. It will entail what Sigmund Freud called the recognition of the interconnection between the internal world of the mind and the external world of the environment, the former being a shrunken residue of the latter.[6]

At its core, this book attempts to differentiate between *human intelligence*, which, due to its frailty, is made synonymous with Promethean intelligence, and *natural intelligence*, which is synonymous with Gaian intelligence. Its premise is that *human intelligence* as we have experienced it must now be nested in *natural intelligence* if we are to survive and thrive as a species in the face of Earth-systems collapse and other existential challenges.

This approach is based on a human-development model that has been at the heart of my work for over two decades. It originated in the pioneering work of Clare W. Graves (1914–1986), a colleague of Abraham Maslow and a professor of developmental psychology at Union College in New York. Graves developed what he called the "emergent cyclical theory," which posits a series of levels describing human evolution and different stages of psychological maturity. Subsequently, his younger colleague, Don Edward Beck (1937–2022) developed the theory into a model that was brought to the masses under the name Spiral Dynamics.* I worked closely with Dr. Beck for his last two decades of life on different projects, from a macro-systematic approach to the Arab-Israeli conflict to introducing an evolutionary macro-economic model. This work evolved into my 2013 book, *MEMEnomics, The Next Generation Economic System.* Philosopher Ken Wilber created a different iteration of the Spiral-Dynamics model, using selective parts of it to augment his Integral-Theory model. In writing this book, I undertook an expansive effort that involved years of research into Graves's original work. What I discovered was that neither of the two models—Spiral Dynamics or Integral Theory—captures the totality of Graves's work, a shortcoming that I hope to correct here.

The Graves-Beck model is hierarchical in nature and contains a total of eight known stages of development that research has uncovered so far. Just as different Earth systems have limited carrying capacities, each stage of human development also reaches the limits of its proprietary carrying capacities after exhaustive use. It must then recalibrate into a higher stage of psychological development, subordinating the older stages into its new, higher-order system. Each stage has a healthy and an unhealthy side, its action and its opposite reaction in balance. It is when those in power continue to use outdated capacities of lower developmental stages, or force a particular stage past its carrying capacity into its unhealthy side, that we begin to have problems.

Graves described the first six stages of development as "deficient" stages that have defined much of the human journey so far. As chapter 4 discusses, they comprise the stages from the undifferentiated self, the tribal community, and the powerful self to the orderly community, the enlightened self, and the egalitarian community. Stages seven and eight—the ecological and the world centric, as discussed in chapter 5—are described as the emerging virtues of humanity that will save us from ourselves.

---

* To give full credit, Beck's colleague Christopher Cowan was the coauthor of *Spiral Dynamics.* Little information is available about him other than that he passed away on July 15, 2015. Cowan had little influence on my thinking, and I refer to the model as that of Graves-Beck throughout the book.

Graves and Beck divided these stages into two distinct tiers of development: the first tier comprises stages one through six, and the second tier comprises stages seven and eight. The former describes our passage through psychological time since we began to roam the Earth from between 100,000 to 200,000 BCE to where many scientists believe we are today: on the cusp of the sixth mass extinction. (The fifth mass extinction occurred around sixty-five million years ago, between the Mesozoic and the Cenozoic era, eliminating up to 75 percent of all known living species, including the dinosaurs. But that extinction was caused by an asteroid, whereas the sixth will be due to the impact on the planet of humanity itself.)

According to the Gravesian model, the decoupling of *Homo sapiens's* evolution from that of nature accelerated rapidly after we domesticated animals about 8,000 years ago, during the transition between our second and third stage of development. By the end of the twentieth century, we had completely tamed nature and subjected her will to ours—or so we thought. In our dualistic ontology, "Mother Nature" became "ecosystem services," from which we have extracted resources and to which we have externalized the byproducts of these resources. It is only in stages seven and eight—stages which as a species we have not yet reached —that we will become collectively aware of the dangers inherent in this decoupling process. So far, these two ecologically informed stages are present in the minds only of a few visionaries who still have very little power over our institutions and governing structures to affect the necessary healing of the natural world. When viewed from the life cycle aspect of this model, this seems always to be the case with every stage: It is always the wise individuals on the margins who slowly influence change. In this instance, they signal the arduous journey we must make to return again to *natural intelligence,* having learned this single most important lesson for our species.

In the six stages through which humanity has passed, one in particular is more responsible for subjugating nature and causing her collapse than any other: stage five, which has been driven by reductive thinking and the strategic and calculative manipulation of the other and of nature's resources. This stage will be the focus of much of part 1 of this book. Called "The Age of Acceleration and the Great Obsolescence," this part describes our present situation in which the Promethean fire has gotten so far out of control that it has destroyed or made obsolete many human-built systems while simultaneously damaging many of the Earth's systems in ways yet to be fully quantified. Over time, the lack of opportunistic restraint has resulted in vast economic and social inequalities. Humanity has come to be measured by the monetary value of its possessions and by how many resources it could consume. As these virtues spread around the world, they began to deplete Earth's resources and poison its water and air at such an exponential rate that they are now causing the collapse of various planetary systems.

Graves's work reached its zenith in the late 1970s and early 1980s. The '70s are often overlooked as a crucial period in human history when the systems thinking that concerned itself with planetary issues pushed human consciousness to the forefront. This book chronicles the systemic changes the world went through during that time and describes the forces that silenced many forward-thinking voices in favor of models that further burdened our biosphere and Earth's ecology. Unlike Beck and Wilber, Graves was one of many progressive systems thinkers of his generation who sounded the alarm on existential planetary issues and warned of the great dangers we face—from overpopulation to the approaching tipping points of Earth's various resources and everything in between.[7] But as the voices of other systems thinkers were silenced, so was Graves's original voice. This is evident in the work of thousands of practitioners such as I who used Beck's and Wilber's models, selecting parts of Graves's research to address human-built systems. In retrospect, these models were a disservice to Graves's legacy in that they were an extension of Promethean intelligence that believes itself separate from and superior to Gaian intelligence. As I began to research developmental models that uphold Gaian intelligence capable of addressing existential issues such as climate change and ecological collapse, I found myself returning to Graves's seminal work and that of the system thinkers of his generation.

Today, most of the planetary issues those thinkers warned us about five decades ago have come to fruition. Yet, the world remains divided into two distinct camps: the one that believes in the continued existence of the values of the Holocene era—a time that has been defined as the heaven on earth that has lasted for 11,600 years—and the other that believes we are in the throes of entering a new epoch, called the Anthropocene, in which the continuity of life will depend solely on our actions. The models Beck and Wilber created reflect the end of the Holocene era, absent the planetary factors in play that exist outside human-built environments. The former camp still believes that Promethean intelligence and its scientific and technological genius will save us, while the latter camp wants to pry us away from the reductive and mechanical worldview that has defined science for the last three-and-a-half centuries and put our destiny back where it belongs: in the Gaian intelligence that has defined life for billions of years.

This book offers a new iteration of Graves's lifelong work that attempts to recapture his genius and enable its continued use in the new epoch we have entered. It revisits the qualitive, intuitive, and vastly interdisciplinary nature of his work and recasts his research in a new light, away from the academic silos that have sidelined his wisdom for decades. My purpose is to realign its content and change its dynamics better to serve the new higher-order system in an attempt to save it from collapse.

In Beck's original iteration, that higher system was the eighth stage of development, which during the Holocene era was a mostly unarticulated utopian state in a far distant future. It spoke of our planet as an ecologically aligned, single organism; and while that intelligence began to appear in individuals a few decades ago, according to Beck's research it will not manifest in governing systems for yet a few more centuries.[8] This is the nature of fractal structures in life: the larger the system, the longer it takes for change to manifest. Today, our human activities have expedited the appearance of the dark, unhealthy side of that eighth stage, and it looks anything but utopian. My new iteration is an effort to shed light on that dark side and offer possible corrective measures in how we organize our societies and redesign our institutions in the face of our many current existential threats.

The many neologisms in this book are not intended as clever interpretations of existing words or as repackaging of earlier iterations of the Gravesian model. Instead, they mean to simplify the language Beck and Wilber used. To an outsider, their language might sound elitist and cultist, providing a good reason to dismiss the framework altogether. My intention is to bring the framework to a wider audience, possibly to the powers that be who run our economic, financial, and political systems. Toward that goal, my use of more widely known terms is meant as a return to how Graves envisioned his original work, a multidisciplinary approach that integrates psychology, sociology, biology, systems thinking, anthropology, history, and brain science.[9] I also make use of new language and concepts that have emerged in the last two decades around climate change, framed in ways to fit the model. Together, these factors create what I consider a new developmental platform that attempts to address our existential issues in the new Anthropocene epoch.

One of the most prominent changes in this platform is my introduction of the concept of First and *Second sapiens.* This concept renames the stages of development in language more appropriate for anthropologists, geologists, biologists, and historians than it is strictly for developmentalists. In that renaming, I distinguish between the two psychological tiers uncovered by Graves and Beck and used by Wilber: "*First-sapiens*" behavioral systems characterize stages one through six of human development, or tier one in the Graves-Beck model; and "*Second-sapiens*" behavioral systems characterize stages seven or eight, or tier two in their model. An important difference between their work and mine, though, is that the Graves-Beck model conceived of all developmental levels mostly in terms of *human-built* environments. Formulated during the Holocene era, it did not take much of the *natural* environment into account, simply because climate change was not on their radar when they were doing their work.

In light of the accelerating ecological crisis, my purpose is to challenge the idea that their anthropocentric focus alone can save us. It is my new, anthropogenically-informed language, along with my research into natural systems, that has enabled me to differentiate *First* and *Second sapiens* from Graves's and Beck's earlier iterations of first- and second-tier systems and the intelligence that characterizes them.

In the Graves-Beck model, the psychosocial motivations of the first tier remain mostly the same in the Anthropocene as they were in the Holocene: that is, human behavior makes use of whatever systems were designed for it by those who hold power and influence over geopolitics, global economics, and other social systems. In my model, "first tier" is synonymous with "*First sapiens*" in that, while the latter has some awareness of *natural intelligence,* its motivational systems remain deficient and lack the capacity and the power to influence change.

In contrast, "*Second sapiens*" transcends and includes second tier as it nests the *human intelligence* of both the seventh and the eights stages in *natural intelligence* that is in turn informed by changes in natural systems. It replaces Beck's "second tier" with the caveat that, while both tiers in the Spiral Dynamics model presuppose human intelligence as the whole and only intelligence, "*Second sapiens*" describes what happens when the content of these two stages becomes informed by an intelligence of a higher order—Gaian or *natural intelligence*—which in turn is informed by our Anthropogenic reality. *Natural intelligence* includes and transcends the concept of human intelligence on which Spiral Dynamics was built. It refers to the complex, adaptive systems of life and comprises a form of intelligence from which we have separated ourselves as Western civilization ascended. The collapse of Earth systems is an issue caused by *First sapiens,* but the awareness of it appears only in the consciousness of *Second sapiens.* It is this awareness that will guide us toward an ecologically aligned humanity as we navigate an uncertain future.

Based on history, however, *First sapiens,* like his counterpart in Beck's first tier, will attempt to derail the efforts of *Second sapiens* once it sees that our Anthropogenic reality requires deep structural changes to the way we live our lives today. He/she might drive a Tesla and consider him/herself Anthropogenically responsible, but he will not question the sustainability of all the raw materials that go into its production and the environmental impact it will have once its useful life ends. This state of mind underscores the sense that the term "*First sapiens*" is synonymous with "first-tier intelligence."

The *First sapiens* is not a whole person. He does not yet possess the capacity to think in terms of *natural intelligence.* Being in the fifth (Holocene) stage of development, he identifies as separate from Gaia and superior to it. He is the clever work of the supreme Promethean trickster god. The *First sapiens* is completely unaware of his deficient behavioral traits and uses partial brain capacity to fulfill desires and goals.

According to research, the first six stages of human development characterizing *First sapiens* represent 93 to 95 percent of the current human intelligence that holds most if not all the power over human-built systems.[10] *Second sapiens,* on the other hand, is informed by the higher-order system and knows how to mitigate certain aspects of our new Anthropogenic reality. He is fully aware of the limits of human intelligence in its current, dominant form and yet has little power to implement the systemic changes we need to avert existential disasters. He represents a new breed of *Homo sapiens* that began to emerge in the mid-twentieth century at the same time that systems thinking emerged. He uses full brain capacities to express his full humanity. The *Second sapiens* is in awe of nature and her intelligence and seeks to end *First sapiens's* separation from her. He identifies with the primordial goddess Gaia and her feedback loops that leave no dark side unexamined. While the second-tier human intelligence of the Graves-Beck model was gauged at 5 to 7 percent in the Holocene era, no new research has emerged that gauges that intelligence when it becomes nested in natural intelligence. However, according to Beck's pre-Anthropogenic research, the intelligence present in the entire eighth stage of development that identifies with an ecologically aligned planet represents less than 1 percent of human intelligence at present.[11] It holds power in elite and small corners but has little influence over a global ecosystem built and still constrained by the intelligence of the *First sapiens.*

Considering that we are entering a new epoch, viewing the model through the long arc of history and anthropology becomes a necessity. This perspective has necessitated other changes to the model that are the subject of part 2 of the book, "The Sum of All Our Days Is Just the Beginning." This section reintroduces Beck's Spiral Dynamics and infuses it with original Gravesian language and stage designations in addition to new anthropologically informed designations I formulated during my research. It details how all the different stages can be realigned to serve the new model that reflects our new Anthropogenic reality. This process necessitated moving the model from human-built constructs to ones that appear in nature, which required research into the natural systems that preserve the underpinnings of the original framework. The result has been many new discoveries that justify the continuity of the model into the Anthropocene epoch, from the structure of DNA and new findings in evolutionary biology to the evolution of complex adaptive systems as they apply to life, and all the way to a grand model of how Gaia balances her different Earth systems.

The tight grip the *First sapiens* has on the world also led me to revisit Graves's great transition phase from the sixth to the seventh stage of development, or, in my terminology, from *First* to *Second sapiens.* He called it the *momentous leap,* as did Beck and Wilber in their work. The term sounds optimistic, but a closer look at Graves's original writings reveals an untold number of existential challenges we will face before we become empowered with the capacities to take the leap forward. He often referred to these challenges as the "deep chasm" we must cross. While Graves didn't speak publicly of the disasters that will accompany the phase, he did so privately with Beck, who in turn shared those views with me and a few other colleagues. They were made public only in Beck's 2018 book, *Spiral Dynamics in Action: Humanity's Master Code.* My wife, Elza Maalouf, and I each contributed a chapter.

In the book, Beck cites one of Graves's darkest predictions— that, before the intelligence of the second tier can appear, the world will need to process the collective shadow of the first tier. If it fails to do so in time, Graves speculated that the global population will be cut by as much as half.[12] While predictions such as these were dismissed as pure speculation during the Holocene era, the impending climate disasters we are facing today make their fulfillment a distinct probability.

The life-cycle model I discuss in chapter 2—"The Nature of Change and the Life Cycles of Ideologies"—was pioneered by Graves and further developed by Beck. It provides a detailed view of how and when change happens within each stage and why we fail to ascend to higher stages of development. Our new Anthropogenic reality necessitates emphasizing an aspect of the model that was greatly overlooked during the Holocene era. Unlike the six stages of the first tier, which are characterized by competition, stages seven and eight are highly collaborative and share a unifying goal of assuring the continuity of life on the planet. In the past, many practitioners of the model separated the last two stages, using the seventh stage to address human-built systems while relegating the eight stage to the spiritual and philosophical realms. However, the two stages should be considered inseparable as the seventh lays the ground for what the eighth must do to perpetuate life. Both stages are intuitive and complementary with considerably higher degrees of psychological capacities serving this single most important goal. For that reason, I have combined the life cycles of the seventh and eighth stages into one and call it the "*Second-sapiens* life cycle," using the term interchangeably with "Anthropogenic life cycle."

I understand that tragic, real-life scenarios about humanity's future don't sell books or make a person popular. Nevertheless, I wanted to look deeper into why Beck and Wilber avoided addressing these dark issues in most of their teachings. One of my hypotheses comes from the field of positive psychology that has had a pervasive presence during the last few decades. In its ubiquitous, populist form, it became a tool that has repressed the dark side of the pair of opposites in favor of promoting the bright, positive side of Promethean intelligence. It sees a small and obscure positive angle in the darkest of stories and uses it to paint a rosy picture of the whole, creating a modern form of hidden bias masquerading as a positive mental-health model.

With the benefit of hindsight, I revisited Graves's *momentous leap*, looking for language that serves the Anthropocene. As I looked into his various descriptions of the chasm humanity must cross from the sixth to the seventh stages of development—or from the *First* to the *Second sapiens*—it became clear that his various descriptions have not been explored sufficiently. If studied more deeply, they can provide a larger platform capable of addressing the various traumas we are experiencing and will continue to experience more frequently as natural disasters and climate-driven events increase in intensity.

This examination led me to expand the space in the model in which the chasm appears. The result is a full chapter dedicated to processing the collective trauma that has brought us to where we are today. Entitled "The Darkness before the New Dawn," it is the last chapter in part 2 and explores psychological, spiritual, and mythological ways that can help us process the accumulated darkness as a sequential necessity before we can take the *momentous leap* into Gaian intelligence.

My research has also yielded many insights on how the mechanics of Graves's original work, as well as that of my colleague Dr. Beck and my own earlier work on evolutionary economics, can be expanded and made useful. The outcome of this process and its applicability in the Anthropocene epoch is detailed in part 3, entitled "Gaian Intelligence: Empowering What Matters in the Anthropocene Epoch." In this final section of the book I introduce a new concept called *Gaiametry*. As the word implies, *Gaiametry* calls on us to transcend our thinking beyond our human-built systems and begin to design resilient, sustainable, and regenerative systems for a living planet informed by *natural intelligence*. In this much higher-order system, some components will have moved beyond their carrying capacities and others will be teetering on the edge, needing immediate action in order to preserve what remains of Earth's systems and our civilization. Much of this last section addresses issues that first appeared in the minds of visionaries—the systems thinkers who emerged in the 1970s—and follows the evolution of their ideas into the Anthropocene epoch. It is dedicated to the rise of Gaia and includes discussions of the viability of democracy in its current form, ecofeminism, deep ecology, social ecology, and environmental philosophy, among many other subjects. Also, it explores two new areas of psychology that have emerged in the last two decades: collapse psychology and ecopsychology. And it explores the future of the digital economy and the role artificial intelligence plays in it. It examines the different economic models being debated for the Anthropocene epoch, such as circular economies and the donut economies, and places them into a new, *Second-sapiens* iteration of economics that is driven by a Gaian mandate for degrowth. That mandate, detailed in chapter 9, introduces a new concept I call GEP: Gaiametry economic protocols. It is proposed as a possible replacement for the largest measure of economic activity today, GDP (gross domestic product), and is informed by our Anthropogenic reality.

Gaiametry is a platform representing the rise of the feminine aspect of the universe that has long been repressed and silenced. It signifies the return to the Mother archetype, the primordial image of the generative and sustaining mother figure that is ever present within the collective unconscious. According to Jung, the Mother archetype contains all other archetypes. Stories of creation, especially those from the Abrahamic religions, obscured that reality in naming Adam the first member of the human species. By doing so, they tipped Earth's balance away from the ecological order that had made life possible for over 3.5 billion years. Consequently, as our species ascended to the fifth stage of development, that reality became more obscured as we further repressed the feminine aspects of the universe in favor of a world defined by human intelligence. Unlike our species, Mother Nature uses a federalist, decentralized approach when it comes to self-organization. She nests her endless communities of living systems within a flexible and resilient framework in which the whole is more than the sum of its parts. She builds on trillions upon trillions of existing small-scale networks to create bigger and bigger ecosystems; but, unlike in today's human built-environments, each is a little community within itself, naturally adapting and evolving in order to survive and thrive.

Gaia's timescale, unlike ours, is measured in eras and epochs. She can't be rushed as she raises an ecosystem of healthy interdependence far more resilient than any human-built system claiming the same. The challenge for humanity, as we enter a new epoch of our own making, is to choose to assimilate Gaian intelligence consciously and to have a much better understanding of her evolutionary history. Much of that evolution has happened outside human consciousness and over billions of years with the utter moral indifference of our species. It is within the awe and wonderment of this comprehensive ecosystem into which *human intelligence* must now be nested if we are to prevent the extinction of millions of species, including our own.

The final chapter of the book, "The View from Jupiter," explores the question: What if we are wrong, and our efforts to mitigate societal and ecological collapse end up in failure regardless of how inclusive and conscientious our efforts are? It revisits one of Grave's three probable scenarios of the future—a narrative he described as the consequences of our failure to stabilize the world—and considers its ramifications and applicability fifty years later.[13] The post-collapse situation this chapter describes is now within the realm of probability. In this scenario, much of what we have known about modern civilization falls apart, the collective shadow of the optimistic mind becomes visible, and Gaia's feedback loops are on full display. Much of what we have taken for granted about human resilience will be challenged in a time when we are truly at the mercy of nature and her wrath.

Yet, the collapse of civilization may mean not the end of the human journey completely but an opportunity for those of us who survive to learn from our mistakes and choose a different path forward. Post-collapse survival will be defined by a state of continuous scarcity with the threats of instability and extinction hovering over everyday life. Should we survive its first stages, we will be offered the opportunity to stabilize our world again. Based on my new post-collapse model, the likelihood of that survival rising beyond tribal existence will be highly unlikely. Nevertheless, while being dictated by scarcity in the physical world, this existence will be defined by abundance within, an abundance that is now fully aware of the existential dangers inherent in decoupling our evolution from that of nature. It reembraces the wisdom of our ancestors and the spiritual consciousness that existed long before the Western mind negated them in favor of logic and science.

A note on my use of descriptive terms: *Stage, level,* and *system*—or *value system*—all refer to the same thing: the eight stages that make up the model. *Tiers* are the larger containers of stages. There are only two tiers in Beck's model, the first containing six stages/levels/systems, the second containing only stages seven and eight. The number of stages/levels/systems remains eight, only their content changes with my new iteration.

Also, I am aware of the social importance of not using masculine pronouns to represent all of humankind. However, to avoid the awkwardness of saying *he/she* throughout the book, I sometimes say either *he* or *she* indiscriminately at various points in the narrative.

Part One
The Age of Acceleration and the Great Obsolescence

One
Obsolescence and the Modern Mind

The world is not just rapidly changing; it is being dramatically reshaped – it's starting to operate differently in many realms all at once. It is happening faster than we've been able to reshape ourselves, our leadership, our institutions, and our ethical choices.

—Thomas L. Friedman
Thank You for Being Late

On the morning of February 22, 2022, a distinguished, grey-haired man stood silently at the window of his office on the thirty-eighth floor of a high-rise in Manhattan overlooking the East River. It was a warm day by East Coast standards. A few cumulus clouds peppered an otherwise blue, winter sky. The occasional gust of wind that blew through the city's streets and alleys carried with it discarded plastic bags up past the fading skyline toward the heavens. Scaly ripples on the face of the river were visible from a distance as the stiff breeze fluttered across Turtle Bay and made its way over the rest of Manhattan. The ornately assembled flags below at the entrance to the tower—all 193 of them—shook their folds to the wind in a chaotic, splendid dance that left no doubt about what this building represents. It is the world headquarters of the United Nations that sits on eighteen sovereign acres in Midtown. The organization has been a symbol of peace and a beacon of hope since its founding in 1945 when leaders of fifty nations met in San Francisco and unanimously approved its charter. Its preamble, borne of a utopian ideal for humanity, reads as follows: "We the peoples of the United Nations are determined to save the generations of people yet to come from the horrors of war."[1]

But on this balmy February day, peace, hope, and the cooperative spirit of humanity seem to have faded from the world's consciousness, a development that the man standing at the window understood at a far deeper level than most world leaders. As secretary general of the United Nations, Antonio Guterres, he had been a prime witness to the increasing challenges that have befallen the world in the last few decades. Each challenge had tested his organization's resolve in ways that haven't been tested since its founding. The world had become one interdependent global economy built on the ethos of modern development programs that espouse the values of *peace through commerce.*

This noble intent to become one world community has represented the first major form of modern acceleration in human development. What used to take centuries to move people out of a subsistent, agrarian existence now takes less than a lifetime on a much larger scale. We've brought the good life to the less fortunate around the world, cured diseases, and lifted people out of poverty; we've introduced Western models for governance that have set the world on a path toward modernity. Today, it is the dark side of that modernity—the shadow of our success that built a world away from war and through commerce, aided and accelerated by the miracle of the digital age—that is at the heart of our complex problems.

The acceleration of human development as a global goal requires resources of all types, natural, financial, human, and otherwise. And while we continue to chase these endeavors, we have also continued to ignore the byproducts and the consequences of our actions, which today seem to be reaching a critical tipping point. Much of this situation could be attributed to a particular stage of human development that defines itself through a narrow and objective observation of reality. The pursuit of *peace through commerce* and all its peripheral expressions and value systems are grounded in the European Enlightenment of the seventeenth and eighteenth centuries. Those values have brought forth our brilliance, the Promethean fire that has lit our path for hundreds of years. What we're experiencing today is the decline of their most advanced expressions that have shaped our minds and institutions over the last century. The Age of Enlightenment represents a stage of human development that is grounded in the scientific and mathematical observation of all phenomena defined by measurement. We have measured everything by reducing the complexity of the whole into simple and manageable units in order to understand their mechanics. In the process, we have minimized much of the natural world and the very nature of complexity itself. It is this reductive way of seeing the world that is today reaching an inflection point.

The Enlightened mind has relegated much of what it couldn't measure to the unconscious, believing that other worldviews, phenomena, and forms of behavior have little or no impact on modern humanity. While that belief is slowly being replaced by more inclusive ones, the process is not happening fast enough, and forces outside the system are causing it to break down. This falling apart of what we have known to be good, true, and just is at the heart of the trauma that humanity is dealing with today. It is the result of a systemic failure of human-made systems that are reaching different points of entropy all at once, be it in economics, geopolitics, global health, or trade and development.

At the same time, a greater system in which all the manmade systems are nested is signaling that a far larger collapse is underway. Ecological in nature, it is a phenomenon that cannot be fully understood or managed by the Enlightened mind. It points to how our pursuit of modernity has depleted Earth's resources and caused our various planetary systems to begin to crumble. Scientists call this phenomenon the *Great Acceleration.*

It is the coalescence of these two systems—the human-made one and the natural one in different stages of decline—that is leading us to the *Great Obsolescence.* In this crucible of chaos, humanity will witness the completion of the virtues of the *First sapiens* and provide an early definition of the *Second sapiens,* an ecological being driven by higher virtues that acknowledge the interdependence of life and keeps the totality of Earth's systems balanced and conducive for all lifeforms. Unlike the *First sapiens* who thrives on individual merit and discards the costs of his activities to the environment, the *Second sapiens* believes in the collective intelligence of the whole wherein all human activity is accounted for and nothing is reduced or externalized.

The Modern Mind and the Pursuit of Peace through Commerce

The convergence of these two complex systems—the human-built and the ecological—in different stages of their life cycles represent the collective challenge with which all humanity must deal today. What do we do when the collective tools available to the Enlightened mind fall short of addressing this existential issue?

The answer might come from the behavioral-systems model around which my work has long been centered: as our circumstances become increasingly less manageable, humanity will transcend Enlightened values in search of a more inclusive model. Just as the Enlightenment itself transcended the deterministic, collective stage of development that gave us religious order, described by Graves as "absolutistic thinking," we must now transcend the scientific, individualistic stage of "multiplistic thinking" to a higher-order stage. Historically, this has happened as we moved from being cave dwellers to becoming tribes and all the way to where we are today, living in modern cities in a globally interconnected world with layers of complexity and sophistication that bear witness to our genius. It is the *shadow* of that genius that is now manifesting. The Enlightenment represents the fifth stage of development, one in which we have consumed two hundred times more resources than we did when decoupling accelerated 8,000 years ago at the beginning of stage three. Today, the Enlightened mind has completed the decoupling process from nature and must now turn its attention back to the things that have fallen outside its worldview for the last five centuries.

But this will be no ordinary transition from a behavioral system of lower complexity to a higher-order one. That sort of transition has been the endeavor of the *First sapiens*. The new system, in contrast, must reintegrate all the natural systems the Enlightened mind has left out of the reductionist values that have led us here. This reintegration is the hallmark of the *Second sapiens* who, unlike the First, centers its attention around the question, *What would Mother Nature do?* Informed by the answers, it will start to form a new system of behavior that will come to define our future leaders and shape our institutions. This will be no ordinary task as it requires a monumental leap in thinking to do battle with the Enlightened minds that continue to inform our current leaders, define our institutions, and dominate our systems of education. It is because of this historic uphill battle that I call the next few decades of human existence the *Great Obsolescence.* This term represents the period when the values and virtues of the *First sapiens* are coming to an end even while ecological degradation and ecosystems collapse are pointing us in the direction in which we must begin to think as *Second sapiens.*

I am using the work of the United Nations as an example of what institutions created under the leadership of the *Second sapiens* would be tasked with. Our future requires a highly collaborative system of global governance that has the unifying goal of ensuring the survival of life on our planet. The UN has been the first body with the potential to actualize such a goal, but since its inception it has existed in an ecosystem of rules created and greatly hindered by the *First sapiens*. Consequently, there is no institutional global authority that can act decisively to address the unprecedented challenges we are facing. The existence of such institutions will require all humanity to believe in the urgency of solving issues around wars, pandemics, poverty, disease, and climate change and to empower our leaders to create a unified approach toward their resolution. It will amount to the reinvention of the only global body of governance in human history: the United Nations.

This reinvention will entail an advancement in organizational design that gives teeth to the enforcement mechanisms for global governance. But, in order for it to occur, the world has to agree unanimously on the universal, superordinate nature of the threat we face. Otherwise, we cannot set a superordinate goal capable of bringing the world together. We as a collective have created these existential problems without the foresight to understand the complexity needed to solve them. The resolution of the issues will require a monumental leap in thinking that will come to shape our future leadership and our institutions.

The problems we face today require far greater levels of global cooperation and governance than are within the UN's mandate, yet we continue to rely on its obsolete power structure to address existential problems its founders could not have anticipated. Its powers are limited by the very nature of its charter. It couldn't stop wars, for instance, unless all five permanent members of its security council voted unanimously to do so. The UN's presumption that the world community shared its ideals of peaceful coexistence has rendered its effectiveness more obsolete with every passing decade. The utopian paradise of peace promised by humanity for humanity remains elusive to this day. Since its founding, the UN has seen the geopolitical landscape and Earth's ecology undergo unimaginable change, the kind of change that could only be mitigated through a new level of human consciousness and a new alchemy of organizational principles that has so far evaded world leaders. Today, the gap between the ideals of peace and the reality of our current, war-torn world couldn't be bigger.

From War to Commerce

The utopian values of the UN exist in a vacuum within a toxic ecosystem dominated by the values of cultures that have never known peace outside the boundaries of their own ethnocentric and nationalistic worldviews. In its earliest years, the UN helplessly watched as the Cold War split the world into two distinct, ideological divides. "You are either with us or against us" was the line drawn in the sand by the two opposing permanent members of the security council: the United States and the USSR. The ideological grounds positioned America with its Western allies on one side and the Soviet Union and its Eastern European satellite states on the other. These were unfinished sociopolitical battles that the *First sapiens* had been waging for centuries and had very little to do with peace. Each superpower formulated policies that identified the other as the clear enemy. Fear of the known was a decades-long strategy that gave each side an ever-increasing sense of control. We waged proxy wars under the guise of defending our respective ideals. We armed ourselves to the teeth and came close to nuclear Armageddon.

Then, in a final push in the battle for supremacy, the West embarked on a strategy to overwhelm the Soviet Union and roll back its influence. What became known as the Reagan Doctrine was a philosophy that supported anti-communist gorillas and resistance movements everywhere they appeared. It became the centerpiece of US foreign policy that brought the end to the Cold War. The muscle flexing that brought humanity to the brink was over. The peace symbol was sprayed all over the Berlin Wall as an exuberant world ushered in a new era of freedom and prosperity. Capitalism had prevailed over communism, and the virtues of democracy and peace began to define a new era of human values.

> *Capitalism had defeated communism. Now it's well on its way to defeating Democracy.*
>
> —David Korten[2]

But as quickly as the post-Cold War peace appeared, the *First sapiens* defaulted to its subsistent brutal nature in a slightly different form. In the absence of the two ideologies that had defined the world for five decades, many emerging countries fell into a vacuum of nongoverned spaces and became breeding grounds for violence and chaos. This vacuum fueled civil wars and genocides and tribes and warlords who looked to exact revenge for a bloody past instead of to the future to build bridges. Instead of peace and harmony, we defaulted to our savage nature, and the only action the UN could take was to send peace-keeping troops after the killing had stopped. The gap between its mandates and its ability to enforce them were becoming clearer: when it came to assuring world peace, the organization was nothing more than a paper tiger. Its ideals, as in the John Lennon song "Imagine," remain merely aspirational, as illusive today as they were at the end of World War II. It is estimated that since the UN was created, the Cold War and the ensuing war on terror—along with civil wars, proxy wars, and genocides around the world— have claimed as many as twenty-five million lives.[3]

Many good things also happened during the years following the end of the Cold War that showed the positive aspects of a globally connected humanity. For one thing, the number of UN member states swelled. It wasn't limited to former members of the Soviet Union and their affiliates. Countries throughout the world that were former colonies felt the need to belong to a global community that offered hope and the possibility of better lives for their people. This was the period during which the UN development program expanded its reach globally. It introduced several ambitious goals with high aspirations to help the poorest countries address issues of scarcity, hunger, and literacy. In the last few decades, the program has grown in popularity as it encompassed a wider spectrum of goals seeking to address everything from childhood diseases and pandemics to infrastructure development, economic growth, and ecological degradation. For the first time, we began to see fruits of a cooperative humanity and the higher consciousness that comes with the pursuit of global peace and inclusion. The acceleration of human development was quickly reaching its heights, and with it came the acceleration of everything else that the conscious mind of the Enlightened had left out.

From Containment to Outbreak

On that February morning in 2022, as Antonio Guterres, the grey-haired secretary general of the United Nations gazed on the horizon beyond the boroughs of Queens and Brooklyn, several issues were occupying his mind. The world was still reeling from a global pandemic that had killed millions of people and cost tens of trillions of dollars in lost productivity and trade. The pandemic had accomplished something that no political leader or trade organization ever could in exposing the deep, structural fault lines that lay just beneath the surface of what appeared to be a resilient global economy and a peaceful geopolitical landscape. It had shaken Guterres's faith and that of thousands of scientists and epidemiologists around the world in a system that for decades had served us well in controlling the spread of deadly diseases.

In today's interconnected world, a disease discovered anywhere can easily spread everywhere in the shortest time possible. Viruses know no borders, and global organizations such as the World Health Organization (WHO) have had to intensify their vigilance to keep us safe. Invisible and deadly, infectious diseases are very opportunistic. They exploit the smallest gap to spread and grow like wild fire, and we have built the infrastructure for them to do just that. With the explosion in world travel, commerce, and trade, threats to global health have exploded as well. In the last few decades, the world has witnessed some of the deadliest viral pandemics occur in increasing frequency with far-reaching consequences—including the onset of the HIV and AIDS pandemic in 1981, SARS in 2002, Influenza A/H1N1 in 2009, MERSA in 2012, and Ebola in 2013. Government agencies such as the Atlanta-based Center for Disease Control and Prevention (CDC) is on the forefront of discovering and containing these viruses before they spread. The CDC works hand in hand with similar agencies around the world to share data and medical knowledge that keep us ahead in this relentless battle. Its reach provides the ideal model for how to address global-health issues. It engages with foreign governments to help them assess health challenges and provides benefits and collaboration that often serve as entry points for broader diplomatic engagement. The more connected we have become, the more complex and variant these agencies have had to become.

The WHO in collaboration with the CDC are the best examples of a post-World War II model for global cooperation, made possible by the benevolence of the United States and its generous funding of both agencies. It was an outcropping of liberal values translated into policies that have given us a glimpse of what is possible. It was also a preview of how life conditions could be under leadership of a world informed by a higher set of morals that view all human life as one complex organism in need of vigilance and care. But as benevolent as the mission of global health is, its architecture has proven to be fragile in the face of increasing complexity. Our globalized world has taken on the dynamics of a nonlinear, complex system that evolves exponentially with its own hidden undercurrents operating independently from the dynamics of virology and disease. The

COVID-19 pandemic, with its toll that killed millions, was one of the first viruses to escape early detection. It has been the deadliest arrow to pierce the armor of the Enlightenment in the venerated fields of modern science and medicine. Yet, instead of recognizing the structural inefficiencies in the current system, we continue to dismiss these occurrences as anomalies and blame them on a lapse in judgment. The modus operandi is to try to patch the system up instead of to work on a new system that can handle the new, higher complexity.

From Globalism Back to Nationalism

Another arrow to pierce the armor of the Enlightenment has been the pain and suffering of the working class in industrialized countries. That which was ignored by the neoliberals has turned into an infected wound that has permanently hobbled liberal progress. The people who built America and post-war Europe and made them into the economic success stories they are today have been slowly losing power and their sense of purpose as the global economy has downsized and offshored their livelihood. As the world has become one interdependent economy, those workers have been left behind. They have witnessed their once-thriving communities turn into ghost towns and their factories into piles of rust—and no one has been doing anything about it. Their frustration has built over the years until it reached a tipping point in the current movement of right-wing populism that can no longer be ignored, testing primarily liberal virtues such as open borders, cultural diversity, and inclusion. Patriotism associated with past glory has grown and made an enemy of the global elite.

This is a uniquely Western phenomenon that has grown feverishly. The disadvantaged Western worker and those who didn't subscribe to the values driving globalism are finally being heard. Dissent in the form of resurgent populism has been clothed in names such as the Party for Freedom in the Netherlands, one of the most liberal places on the planet. It has caused the United Kingdom to leave the European Union, abandoning the primacy of regional rule and returning the country to British rule.

But nowhere has right-wing populism had a deeper impact on the world than in the election of Donald J. Trump, the forty-fifth president of the United States. In 2016, Trump ran on a platform that promised to undo everything that had defined global cooperation and peace since the end of World War II. This is a man who saw the cost of everything and the value of nothing. He spoke to the anger of the working class in simple language that justified their rage and put them on a path to reclaim past glory. As he promised on the campaign trail, he proceeded to dismantle US engagement from the world immediately after taking office. In a speech to the United Nations, he made clear where this new wave of populism stood: "The future does not belong to globalists. The future belongs to patriots. The future belongs to sovereign and independent nations."[4]

Trump filled his administration with likeminded thinkers who began to make enemies of those who didn't share his worldview. Any agency or international covenant that didn't put America first became a target. The approach was swift and brutal, and it began by cutting funding to most US agencies engaged in global matters. It threatened to undo decades of global cooperation and leadership. It started with China, where the Trump administration implemented a number of policies aimed at stopping what it perceived as predatory trade practices that were harming the US worker.

Nowhere was the impact of these policies felt more severely than in the CDC and its network of global-health organizations. Its office in Beijing became a shell of its former self. Other supporting agencies—such as the National Science Foundation (NSF) and the United States Agency for International Development (USAID), which helped China monitor and respond to outbreaks—were forced to close their Beijing offices.

Significantly, the cuts also caused the US Department of Agriculture (USDA) to transfer out of China the manager of an animal-disease monitoring program. All this, according to the CDC, took place in 2018—a mere year before the COVID19 pandemic began—as the world's scientific community stood by in shock and dismay.[5] The global-health system that had taken decades to establish, with input from over forty thousand scientists and researchers, began to unravel. Its Achilles's heel was in entrusting its funding to politicians representing the values of *First sapiens* whose views of the future are vastly opposed from those who uphold the utopian dream of one humanity living in peace and harmony.

While the world remains divided on who to blame for the mismanagement of the COVID-19 pandemic, much has become clear. The increased connectivity that brought together a world with varying value systems, beliefs, and worldviews needed a multifaceted approach to manage the new complexity. Yet, much of the world still runs on a linear system of thought created by the post-war, neoliberal narrative of world leaders who believed that the more we engage in economic development, the more stable the world becomes. This reductionist view underestimates the possible appearances of deadly wildcards that can destabilize the entire system.

Increased connectivity, whether physical or virtual, proportionately increases systemic risk, a reality that is often lost on a world driven by analog economic principles. As we become one interconnected world, issues of world health need to become the concern of one humanity as well. But today, there seems to be a huge gap between the one and the other. Post-war institutions, while doing much to improve the plight of the poor worldwide, have done little to prevent the decline of the industrial worker and promote the inclusion of the less fortunate in the West. This is yet another form of acceleration that is contributing to the obsolescence of the values of so-called modernity. With the help of global information networks, the rate of this acceleration is increasing with every passing day, making adaptability more challenging and harder to achieve. Metaphorically, we are traveling at the speed of light on roadways built for horse carriages, and we're hitting bumps with increasing frequency and severity. Yet, instead of building more appropriate roadways, we occasionally patch the holes in the existing roads and ignore the dangers that leave us vulnerable to increasingly outrageous risks.

The End of Linearity

The mishandling of the pandemic has proven to be the biggest bump in that road so far, altering the course of much of what we have taken for granted for the last fifty years. It has single handedly accelerated the movement of every manmade complex system by at least a decade. That which was weak, like the traditional retail industry in the United States, came closer to dying. That which usually moves slowly, such as geopolitical realignment, began moving at lightning speed, bypassing traditional diplomatic channels and making the future of global diplomacy and trade less predictable. Ecommerce and virtual tech became indispensable. The need for office space became less of a necessity as remote work became the new norm. Emerging economies in need of revenue from tourism suffered a severe financial setback from which they may never recover. Hourly workers in the West are dictating terms of employment after decades of being at the mercy of their employer. The global supply chain, one of the most sophisticated representations of global commerce, showed a degree of fragility never imagined by those who championed its virtues.

The long-term effects of the virus on the global economy and its financial architecture may prove to be its biggest impact. Bailouts in the trillions of dollars have added to the already bloated balance sheets of the world's central banks, threatening global liquidity and giving rise to the long-forgotten threat of inflation that has not burdened the United States since 1982.[6] All this is bringing us closer to the edge of disaster and to the end of an era that placed economic expansionism and global commerce ahead of everything else. More importantly, it is showing us that the majority of new problems do not respect geographic borders, regardless of how strong or how rich a country appears to be.

Vulnerability to deadly global epidemics is an organizational-design issue. We cannot blame the pandemic all on the fragile ego of one angry leader and his supporters. We must factor in other geopolitical issues that place us at greater risk. China's lack of transparency, its unyielding style of central leadership, and its record on human rights have as much to do with the spread of the coronavirus as the Trump administration had in cutting funding to the institutions that would have contained it. Viruses and manmade conflicts are the manifestations of deeper, structural vulnerabilities that seem to be surfacing in increasing frequency. They exemplify the wider challenge of global governance that the current system cannot handle. Containing a global health threat remains part of a bigger, more complex dance between competing global value systems that have pacified their vast differences in service of the great, neoliberal economic narrative that sees *peace through commerce* as the magic elixir to cure all of humanity's ills. The self-appointed masters of the universe—the ones in charge of our global economic and financial infrastructure—are, in fact, the final and most deadly representations of the *First sapiens.* Whether the challenges we face are economic or geopolitical in nature, they will test the limits of everything we have known and set us on a new journey of discovery for what's next.

From Peace Back to War

As the UN secretary general contemplated the state of affairs on that balmy winter morning in 2022, managing the enormity of the pandemic and its destructive aftermath were not the only existential problems facing the world. What had been a relatively peaceful time in Europe was coming to an end. For months, Russia had been amassing its troops—over 175,000 men on its border with Ukraine in preparation for a massive invasion. That the move stood in clear violation of the UN charter was to Vladimir Putin a matter of pride. The Cold War had been over for decades, and communism in Europe had breathed it last breath, or so it seemed. In its place had risen a formidable European continent, an economic superpower that upheld the ideals of individual freedoms, free markets, and the virtues of democracy. Earlier in his political career as president, Putin had acknowledged the failure of communism as he courted the West to consider Russia's possible membership into the NATO Alliance. The fall of the Berlin Wall had exposed the disastrous economic policies of the Eastern European Block, and he had pleaded for Russia to become part of western Europe, with the security and prosperity that would follow.[7]

For the West, Putin's plea was confirmation that the neoliberal narrative championing prosperity was the modern-day deterrent to war. But, within Putin's half-hearted gestures, one can see the ego of a man who was in fact unwilling to compromise. He wanted no conditions and no waiting in line for Russia. He had thought that *glasnost*—the policy of political openness that Gorbachev had introduced during the Cold War—had given the Russian people enough freedom. To him, the idea of the structural reforms required by NATO and for EU membership were as laughable as his superficial gestures were for the West.

As fate would have it, Putin did not have to succumb to the West's demands. Russia, by virtue of its great size, was rich in natural resources, an advantage that became increasingly indispensable to a growing global economy with a voracious appetite for all types of raw material, including oil and gas. The demand for every commodity needed to keep our world moving increased severalfold during Putin's early years in power, assuring him of far more political and economic sway over the European continent than a measly membership in its elite club ever could have. Europe became dependent on Russian energy as Putin basked in his new-found power. There would be no need for NATO membership, economic diversity, political reform, or a modernized, market-based economy. And all this was fine with the new progressive world order that replaced the complexity of human nature with the single reductive tagline of *peace through commerce.*

There would also be no need to examine Russia's stages of human and cultural development, since what mattered most in a post-World War II world was prosperity. It was all about the measure of productivity that reduced the totality of human existence to a handful of statistical measures created by the new elite who steered the passions of global leaders. The higher ideals of communism that sought to dismantle traditional social hierarchies and build the equal distribution of resources became a thing of the past, and *peace through commerce* became the world's new motto. It paid no attention to what peace meant to dictators and repressive regimes or how they intended to use their new-found wealth. The issues of restrictions on individual freedom and abuses of human rights were sidelined in favor of commerce. This was the same neoliberal, reductionist paradigm that allowed China, Saudi Arabia, and a number of other countries with bleak human-rights records to gain membership into a very elite club.

A new era of Russian prosperity arose in the form of a commodities-based oligarchy that made Putin and members of his inner circle some of the wealthiest people in the world. But this wasn't enough for him. In Putin's mind, the fall of the Berlin Wall and the erosion of communist ideals were the greatest geopolitical tragedy of the twentieth century. He had seen previous Soviet states embrace the virtues of the West and follow the arduous path of economic and political reforms. Stopping the relentless march toward this form of Western modernization became his duty. In his worldview, this march was an unstoppable incursion that would eventually claim the state that mattered to him the most: Ukraine. Ukraine had been on the path of reformation for years seeking Western inclusion. But to Putin, it had been part of the tzars' empire for over three hundred years. Ukraine was where he drew the line as he openly proclaimed it to be the jewel in the imperial crown of Mother Russia.[8] This proclamation sought to impose the values of colonialism inherent in bygone empires in direct contrast to the natural evolutionary process of cultural and political systems. While the world was moving toward more openness and the right to self-determination, Putin's actions sought to do the opposite. His justification for a war of this scale had the potential to disrupt world peace and cause a military escalation that hasn't been seen in Europe since World War II.

From Global Commerce to Universal Pain

In any structural system, when small fractures first appear on the surface, as they push against its limits they tend to weaken the integrity of the entire system. The more the system is pushed, the more frequent and less predictable these fractures become until they form irreversible fault lines.

Eventually, a tipping point is reached from which acceleration toward the death of the system moves at an exponential pace.

Thus it has been with the sociopolitical system of *peace through commerce.* When we collectively put economic globalization ahead of everything else, that "everything else" got relegated to the collective unconscious. In effect, it became the system's shadow that only grew in force with the passage of time. Today, that force has reached a tipping point, breaking through the cracks of the system that has ignored human complexity in favor of the linear simplicity of trade. As the war in Ukraine continues to rage, the brutality of Russian bombardment has turned previously thriving cities into piles of rubble with a death toll that is in the tens of thousands. Increased support for Ukrainian forces, largely from the United States but also from England and Europe, has allowed Putin to project this conflict as a battle against the evils of the entire West and raised the possibility of a deadlier level of engagement involving nuclear weapons.

While the human toll remains the greatest tragedy in this conflict, its secondary effects have reverberated throughout the world. One of the rudimentary concepts in developmental economics, which focuses on improving conditions in developing countries, is the idea of economic specialization. As the words imply, this concept places emphasis on the best and highest use of a country's resources, natural and human. Accordingly, countries and regions of the world rich in natural resources became specialized in them and in the process became a small, but integral part of the mosaic that defined the global economy and its all-important supply chain.

Ukraine has been no exception. The country was considered Europe's breadbasket, and with economic specialization it began also to export its crops to China and many parts of Africa. Before Russia's invasion, it was estimated that Ukrainian farmers fed as many as a half billion people around the world. Combined with Russia, Ukraine accounted for 29 percent of the world's wheat production.[9] Sadly, today we are witnessing in this global system a fragility the potential for which has lain outside the comprehension of modern economics, as the same network that was designed for interconnected prosperity is now delivering systemic pain and punishment. The stockpiles of grain trapped in Ukrainian ports cannot reach parts of the world that need it the most—the starving masses in Africa. But this is just the beginning as the effects of this war create a crescendo of sanctions that will last for years.

Pain and punishment in an economically specialized, interconnected world are not limited to the two parties in a feud. As complex as the post-Cold War world order is, it has a new dichotomy that is only slightly different than the one that existed *during* the Cold War. Only the definition of the enemy has changed. This psychosocial, evolutionary process is in the nature of the *First sapiens* and has defined who we are as a species from the time we were cave dwellers: We exhaust the beliefs and the virtues of one value system until it collapses, then we adopt a new one that seems to be of a higher, more inclusive order. This new, higher order gives us a respite from the old until the new system, too, exhausts its own values and virtues, and we begin to search anew. Just as we made an enemy of communism, today we make enemies out of rogue leaders who disrupt the new world order driven by the virtues of modern economic development. We throw theocracies such as Iran into the enemy camp and impose economic sanctions when they violate our set standards of acceptable behavior.

The idea of economic sanctions became part of Western diplomacy more than a century ago. Its overarching purpose is to achieve diplomatic and foreign policy objectives without the use of military force in a peaceful alternative to bloodshed and destruction. But an assessment over time shows that the use of sanctions has done more harm than good, especially in the last few decades when it has become reactive and repetitive against those who violate the neoliberal global order.[10] In sanctioning rogue governments and their leaders, we impose undue harm on the population under their rule. Rendering a country weak economically and starving its people reflect the shallowness of this approach and the punitive side of global harmony. The most commonly overlooked fact by those who impose sanctions is that the majority of rogue leaders who start wars are intent on imposing a new world order in line with their radical ideology. Their dogmatism transcends what they perceive are temporary measures of economic pain and punishment for their people.

In a world driven by commerce, we seem to have abandoned policies that nudge rogue leaders into higher values of inclusion, individual freedoms, and the guarantee of human rights as conditions for trade and peaceful coexistence. Such abandonment allows the ego of a rogue leader to swell. The non-commerce ethos championing human rights represents a prerequisite stage of human development on which the foundation stones of modern peace-making and democratic institutions are built. This particular stage has historically been the toughest phase of psychosocial evolution in human history, since it entails shifting power from the egocentric leader to the modern institution.[11] By bypassing this essential stage and focusing on trade, we give rogue leaders a seat at the largest commerce table in human history. We also give them license to exploit their own people while at the same time financing their worldview and the threat their value systems pose to world peace.

Permanent peace would have a million moving parts in a tremendously complex human system of which our post-war models represent only a tiny fraction. In our drive to end wars, we've allowed that fraction to be the only solution. Only by transcending the values of commerce and trade and focusing on human needs beyond the profit motive will we gain a deeper understanding of how to achieve long-term peace. As it is, we have gone so deep into the rabbit hole of neoliberal economics and became so complacent that we find ourselves utterly dependent on natural resources that lie within the boundaries of countries led by rogue leaders who have vastly different worldviews than we do. We shine a light on their behavior only when their actions begin to threaten our world order. We impose economic sanctions as a way to punish them, but we don't ask the deeper questions about how we missed early signs of troubling behavior before it presented such a threat to world safety and economic stability. Rogue behavior can manifest on the world stage as rapidly as a virus escapes the initial stages of containment, and by then the actions we take are often too little too late. We have underestimated the degree to which we have deluded ourselves and allowed our reductive values to convince us that we live in a truly interdependent, global economy. It is that delusion—that simple, mechanical view of great complexity—that today is leading the world to a state of interconnected pain and positioning us closer to the tipping point of obsolescence from which there will be no return.

The Sanctioner Becomes the Sanctioned

The current global fallacy of achieving *peace through commerce* shows how, when a concept or an ideology is not built for resilience, it becomes a closed system and the factors it excludes become the very thing that hasten its demise. Russia's war with Ukraine has not only extended pain through the global economic infrastructure, it has derailed years if not decades of progress in combatting the climate crisis. In addition, it has revealed the West's hypocrisy and how our high moral and ethical standards fall by the wayside when rogue leaders threaten our economic stability and the all-important global supply chain.

Nowhere is this truth more visible than in President Biden's reversal of his views on Saudi Arabia after the onset of the war. As a presidential candidate, Biden had vowed to make Saudi Arabia and its de facto leader, Crown Prince Mohamed bin Salman, a "pariah" for the role the prince played in the heinous crime of murdering Washington Post columnist and prominent Saudi dissident, Jamal Khashoggi. (Shortly after the murder, US intelligence implicated the prince directly in the crime.) Biden's stance was an extension of the Western values of civility, human dignity, and the sanctity of life. This is the leading edge of human consciousness that has separated decency from perversity in our species. But all that moral posturing fell by the wayside when gas prices began to rise after Russian sanctions were imposed. The president, fearful of the effects this increase might have on his ambitious agenda and political future, paid a visit to the kingdom, pumped fists with the crown prince, and urged the Saudis to increase oil production to avert a worldwide economic downturn. This tactic became known as Biden's "fist-pump diplomacy." The Brookings Institute's scathing editorial on his visit shows how easily and repeatedly the United States can be manipulated by weak and autocratic regimes that are rich in natural resources but don't share our values and how Western ideals can thus be undermined. It asks if this is the kind of identity we're intent on having on the world stage.[12]

It didn't take long for that question to be answered. A few months after the president's visit, OPEC Plus—the oil cartel whose most influential members are the Saudis and the Russians—voted to reduce oil production in order to keep gas prices high. This was a slap in the face for Biden's desperate diplomatic strategy that shows a new level of disrespect by our so-called Saudi ally. It is also the strongest indication by far of a possible political and economic shift as the Saudis have begun to distance themselves from the United States in the last few years in favor of partners with similar values on human rights and socioeconomic philosophy such as Russia and China. The biggest effect of the OPEC Plus decision, however, has reflected immediately on Biden's poor leadership and his ability to proceed with his ambitious agenda. The OPEC Plus vote happened a month before the midterm elections, and the ensuing increase in gas prices reflects the Democrats' inability to contain inflation and stop the economy from going into a recession. Moreover, the reduced oil production weakens the effect of the sanctions on Russia, as the higher prices it can charge countries that will still buy Russian oil allow Putin to continue to finance his war in Ukraine.

Sanctions-driven moral hypocrisy is not limited to the United States. In the months following the start of the war in Ukraine, the European Union imposed sanctions on Russia's largest economic sector— energy— and promised to cut its dependence on Russian gas significantly within a year. This, however, was easier said than done. Before the war, the EU had been implementing measures to mitigate the climate crisis. Germany, its largest economy, had embarked on a plan to retire all its coal-fired power plants by 2030 and use much cleaner, gas-burning power plants to keep its economic engine running. (Years earlier, the Germans had also decided to retire all their nuclear power plants after the 2011 Fukushima accident and a growing anti-nuclear movement in the country.) But more than half of Germany's gas supply was imported from Russia. With the sudden disruption in Russian gas supply when the war began, the Germans found themselves in untenable difficulties as they searched frantically for alternatives. What emerged was their declaration that they will restart many of the shuttered coal plants and keep several of their nuclear plants on standby as they deal with this new crisis. While such actions might be necessary under the circumstances, the damage they cause the environment may not be reversible.

In a world driven by commerce, Europe's misfortunes under the Russian sanctions quickly became an economic opportunity for US-based oil and gas companies. No sooner had Russian tanks rolled into Ukraine than the fossil-fuel industry swung into action, urging the White House to increase gas production immediately in anticipation of a global energy crisis. In a letter to President Biden dated February 25, 2022, just one day after the Russian invasion began, the largest consortium of liquified natural gas producers in the United States, LNG Allies, noted that the world was reaching a "dangerous juncture." Their demands included approval for more drilling on US public lands, expedited authorization of LNG export terminals proposed in the letter, and expedited approval by the Federal Energy Regulatory Commission (FERC) for pending gas pipelines.[13]

This was a rare opportunity for a dying industry to capitalize on fear in order to give itself a new and lasting lifeline. Studies have showed that, due to our collective efforts to transition to a carbon-neutral economy, within the next two decades more than half the fossil-fuels industry's assets worth tens of trillions of dollars will become worthless. The FERC had been operating from the urgency to curb greenhouse gases for years and hence used delay tactics in approving oil-and-gas exploration permits. But, according to the new narrative by the fossil-fuel industry and its lobbyists, Russia's invasion of Ukraine had the potential to dangerously redraw the world's geopolitical map, so peacetime values and concerns about global warming had to be set aside.

As in so many times in the past, these proven fear tactics motivated by greed achieved their objective. The gaslighting of politicians and an uninformed public succeeded. In response to the largely manufactured "energy crisis," within weeks the White House had adopted the group's demands as policy and granted all the long-term contracts the fossil-fuel industry sought. It paved the way for new pipelines and export facilities and approved hundreds of millions in aid to help build a new gas infrastructure on the European continent.[14] And while the White House spins its actions as temporary measures to ease the pressure on the global economy, the industry's business model and operational history tell us otherwise. The sheer size of the projects and the financial commitment made for the development of its massive infrastructure point to a permanent realignment in our energy policy, one that will undo much of the painstaking work of the last decade to move the world away from fossil fuels. It comprises a reversal of President Biden's promise to do everything in his power to help curb carbon emissions. Along with the European Union's decision to stop using Russian gas, it has created what environmentalists call a new gold rush for fossil fuel. A report by Climate Action Tracker (CAT) claims that these actions challenge the world's commitment to cut carbon emissions from fossil fuels dramatically by 2030 as we risk being locked into irreversible warming.[15]

The war in Ukraine demonstrates how sanctions that might have worked in the past seem less effective, and even harmful, today. Regardless, we still ignore the warning signs that hide just beneath the surface, because their acknowledgment presents a threat to the all-important global economy and the blind drive toward prosperity. The climate crisis brings an entirely new and different dimension to war. Its potential for devastating effects on the entire planet, its inhabitants, and its ecosystems should render the need for any war obsolete. Addressing climate change requires a degree of global cooperation that has never before been seen in human history. This is what the *Second sapiens* will be tasked with, and it is what will define the future of humanity. But, sadly, we still look to the values of a bygone era to punish rogue leaders, find economic opportunities in that punishment, and dismiss our impeding economic and environmental disasters. These newest expressions of modernity and the Enlightenment are bringing us closer to the end of the phase of human development that has been defined by the ego of the *First sapiens* as we search for new ways of being with evolved values and greater awareness and inclusion.

Awakening a Sleeping Giant

In addition to death and starvation and the setbacks in reaching carbon neutrality, Russia's invasion of Ukraine has sent shockwaves through a world defined by commerce. It has reawakened inflation, a destructive mega-force that has been dormant for over four decades and now reappears in a world that is exponentially more complex than it was forty years ago. Battling inflation is a problem of a much higher order than dealing with a recession or managing a business cycle. Similar to policies of early containment, keeping inflation manageable requires a great degree of diligence. Historically, its causes have lain outside the control of economists and policy makers: A war in a faraway land, a sudden boycott of raw materials, or a breakdown in the basic understanding of a certain global financial architecture were the main factors that started the biggest inflationary cycles of the last century. On some occasions, it was the arbitrary printing of money by central banks to fund government programs or stimulate consumer spending that added to inflationary pressures and eroded the purchasing power of currency.

Most of these inflationary factors came into play four-and-a-half decades ago, and with them came the end of the post-World War II economic ideology known as Keynesian economics. John Maynard Keynes (1883–1946), after whom the ideology is named, was a British economist credited for creating the post-World War II economic and financial order known as the Bretton Woods Agreement. It comprised a series of regimented policies driven by mandates for reconstruction, tight controls over the money supply, and the empowerment of government as a partner in economic-policy settings, among other things. The agreement also established the US dollar as the world's reserve currency, linking its value to gold and tying it to a system of fixed exchange rates among the agreement's twenty-nine signatory countries. The agreement also allowed its members to exchange US dollars for gold.

These policies greatly restricted the movement of capital and government spending, which led many of its members to doubt the ability of the United States to maintain the gold standard in the long term. Under the system, tighter monetary policies led to slower economic growth, as the States faced strains on its gold reserves, coupled with funding mandates for social programs and the Vietnam War. All these pressures came to a head in what is known as the Nixon shock. In 1971, President Richard Nixon declared the United States would no longer convert dollars to gold, effectively ending the Bretton Woods Agreement.

What ensued in the aftermath of Nixon's decision was the longest inflationary period in modern, post-war US history lasting over a decade. With monetary restriction all but gone, the US government adopted an expansionary fiscal policy to meet its spending mandates, which in turn allowed the Federal Reserve Bank to increase the money supply and lower interest rates. This new scheme remained in force for years as the focus shifted away from the threat of inflation to promoting growth and employment. Other pressures—such as the devaluation of the US dollar (now no longer backed by gold), the Arab oil embargo, and demands for higher wages—made inflation a chronic issue as it reached double digits in the late 1970s and peaked at over 14 percent in 1980.

Once the battle was over and inflation came under control, a new ideology known as *monetarism* emerged as the replacement for Keynesian economics. Its basic theme was based on a theory developed at the Chicago School of Economics, and its ideological father was the economist Milton Freidman (1912–2006). As the word suggests, monetarism seeks to achieve economic stability through the effective management of the money supply. While this might sound uninteresting to the average person, the changes it brought have altered the way the world has historically viewed the role of money by placing it at the center of macroeconomic policy and making everything else—from industrial policy to trade, fiscal, and labor policies—secondary to it. Monetarism informed President Reagan's economic philosophy, which represented a new era of prosperity that sidelined the role of government, tamed its spending habits, and placed the Federal Reserve, a non-governmental banking agency, in charge of our economy. Monetarism was at the heart the Margert Thatcher's economic policies as well. Its ideas spread around the world and, in a few short years, made Friedman into a modern-day god. His influence informed everyone, from the small business owner to the most powerful CEOs and world politicians. Monetarism became essential in the academic and corporate landscapes that influenced generations of leaders across every segment of society. It instilled the ethos of a three-word phrase of Milton's that came to define his legacy: *only money matters.*

In a world where only money mattered, we began to do things differently. We shifted away from the old moral sentiments of the importance of virtue, justice, and beneficence upon which we had built the wealth of nations to a new world run by individual greed and opportunism. Instead of increasing the *size* of the economic pie to benefit the greater society, monetarism normalized increasing the *price* of the pie and made the corporate stockholder the sole beneficiary of the system. This basic idea revolutionized how we quantify productivity. It moved it from the old measure of industrial output to a new measure of financial output derived mostly from subjective evaluations of financial activities and products.

An Enlightened Thinker

Pollution is not an objective problem. One person's pollution may be another person's pleasure. To some of us rock music is noise pollution; to others of us it is pleasure.

—Milton Friedman[16]

Finance became the primary driver of the US economy as the new ideology penetrated every aspect of our lives. Financial capitalism replaced industrial capitalism and, in the process, money became the tail that wagged the dog of our economy. The all-important measure of productivity was now at the mercy of a financial infrastructure designed by Wall Street bankers and greedy CEOs. The stockholder and those who increased the value of the stock were the primary drivers of this new economy as they sat on one side of the economic calculus and everything else became a cost item that sat on the other side. With the cost side needing to be reduced as close as possible to zero, the monetarists went to work. Businesses large and small were securitized, monetized, and downsized, because only money mattered. Jobs, unions, and workers disappeared.

Manufacturing was offshored, services were outsourced, and as long as inflation remained low, no politician objected and no alarms were set off.

Inflation, the sleeping giant, was forgotten as monetarism moved to the front and center of a globalized economy. As it spread, we set aside whatever remained of our moral compass and extracted natural resources from countries with poor human-rights records ruled by dictators and autocrats. Management gurus introduced concepts that reduced costs and improved efficiency. We expanded global connectivity and set up factories in countries with the lowest labor costs. We made a science out of supply-chain management and mastered concepts such as just-in-time inventory systems. We tamed inflation by removing the cost of volatile goods such as food and energy from the all-important consumer-price index (CPI) calculation. And we did all this while ignoring the simple fact that, in real life, the people and factors that are left out of this skewed agenda don't just disappear. Their exclusion or marginalization contributes to the stresses that eventually push against the limits of the system and cause it to break down.

The first sign of that stress appeared at the onset of the 2008 financial crisis, precipitated by the crash of overvalued financial assets. But instead of acknowledging the fallacy of monetarism and the bubble economies it creates, we doubled down on our delusion. Central banks around the world bought what became known as "toxic assets" created by the same financial institutions that were responsible for the crisis. And they bought these assets without determining their real value, because to do so would have caused a worldwide economic contraction that would have lasted for years, if not decades, and bottomed out only once the real market value of these assets was discovered. This eventuality would have also caused downward pressure on prices of every asset class possible, exposing the unorthodox ways in which we have determined the parameters of productivity as a measure of our new economic reality. Such a development is known as *deflation.* It had the potential to be even more destructive than the inflation of the early 1980s. In the years since, many economists and historians have compared the sequence of events leading to the 2008 financial crisis to those that led to the Great Depression. The cracks in the system based on finance were becoming more visible as the risk began to spread to all sectors of the global economy.

In shifting away from the old stakeholder model of capitalism to a stockholder model, we relegated the ethos of the Industrial Age to the dust bin. We were left only with the two tools of the old monetary policy—control over interest rates and control over the money supply—as central banks deployed desperate measures to stop a repeat of the Great Depression. But the chairman of the Federal Reserve Bank was then Ben Bernanke (1953–). A scholar who had focused his academic career on the causes of the Great Depression, Bernanke had determined that the policies that had tightened the supply of money at the time had been at the heart of the severity and length of the worst economic downturn in modern history.[17] He had deep admiration for Milton Friedman, and the two confirmed each other's biases. Hence, the Federal Reserve, along with the central banks of the world's top economies, *increased* the money supply, giving capital markets the fresh liquidity they needed and hoping that the toxic assets they purchased in return would become marketable sometime in the future. It has been a decade and a half since Bernanke's programs with fancy names such as "quantitative easing" were introduced, but the balance sheets of the world's top central banks have only swelled with additional types of toxic assets for which there seem to be no buyers in sight.

As if the purchase of toxic assets weren't enough of a risk, following the 2008 financial crisis central banks proceeded collectively to employ the only other tool of monetary policy available to prevent economic collapse: They brought interest rates down to near historic lows. The US prime rate, which in December 2007 stood at 7.25 percent, was cut a year later by more than half to 3.25 percent, opening the flood gates for borrowing by corporations, consumers, and governments alike. This was an economic bonanza for a short-sighted policy from which there would be no easy return once deflationary pressures were replaced by their opposing force, inflation. Payments on the largest consumer loans—such as the thirty-year home mortgage loan—were cut by more than one-third, opening the doors to millions of homebuyers who wouldn't have qualified for mortgages earlier. Lower rates also stimulated the refinancing of existing consumer debt, and, with lower payments, the consumer possessed far more spending power. Corporate and government debt everywhere was refinanced. Consumer spending was reignited with cheap borrowing, and a repeat of the Great Depression was averted. Monetarists stood by, assured of their abilities to steer a complex global economy by using the only tools available to them—money supply and interest rates. The end point of these practices became visible within a decade as interest rates reached new historic lows and couldn't be lowered any further. Meanwhile, toxic assets on the balance sheets of the central banks of the world's top economies reached historic highs, backing the world into a corner from which there will be no ordinary escape. Such vulnerability would become much worse if a wildcard from outside the system were to appear unexpectedly.

Conflating Monetarism with Patriotism

When large, exogenous events occur outside the economic and geopolitical radar, they can have devastating effects on economic activity. They give governments and central banks the mandate to do everything in their power to avoid economic collapse. This has happened twice in the last two decades: the first was the following the attacks on September 11, 2001, and the second was during the 2020 shutdown due to the COVID-19 pandemic. These type of events have allowed neoliberal economics and monetarism to gain legitimacy in the last two decades. They tend to exonerate central bankers from their past risky behavior and elevate them as heroes. Moreover, when events of this magnitude take place, our institutions collectively act from a place of patriotic duty—adopting the attitude of "avoid a sudden economic shock, and deal with the consequences later." While, granted, such actions are necessary to avoid disaster, the precipitating events themselves define the enormity of the

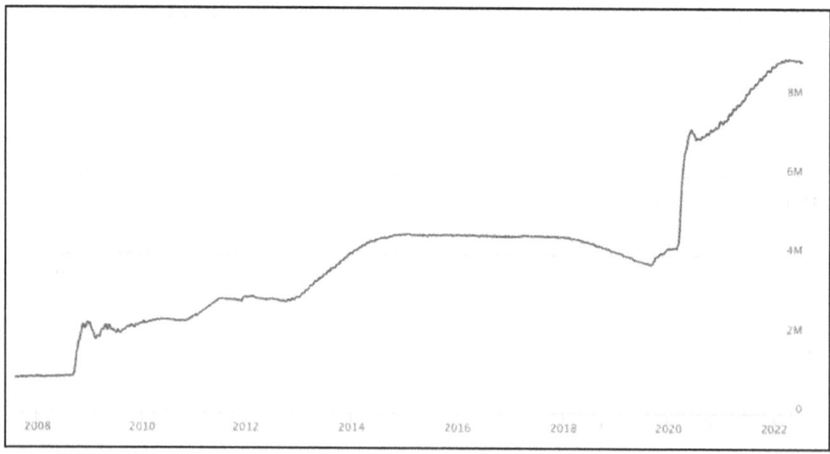

Figure 1.1. The Rise of Total Assets of the Federal Reserve, 2008 to 2022. "Credit and Liquidity Programs and the Balance Sheet," *Board of Governors of the Federal Reserve System*, July 13, 2022; https://www.federalreserve.gov/monetarypolicy/bst_recenttrends.htm.

problems that lie outside the conscious awareness of economists and policymakers. With a weakened monetary system that has struggled to manage the health of the money supply and can't reduce interest rates any further, problems of such magnitude can cause the system to reach the precipice of collapse. That is the point at which central banks throw money at everything, hoping that by some miracle the system will return to financial prudence.

The above graph shows how Federal Reserve policies change around catastrophic events. The policies are represented by the sudden spike in the size of assets acquired in their wake. For instance, by lowering interest rates and adopting an accommodative monetary policy after the events of 9/11, the government planted many of the seeds that caused the financial crisis seven years later. In 2008, the Fed's total assets were around $925 billion in September; by December, they had ballooned to $2.24 trillion.

The size of that bailout pales in comparison to what the Fed did in the aftermath of the pandemic. As the economy shut down in early 2020, the world's top economies stood on a heap of debt that had never previously been seen in peaceful times. With a broad mandate to save the entire US economy, the Federal Reserve made large purchases of government and mortgage securities and supported lending facilities to help households, employers, financial markets, and state and local governments.

Here are the words of Jay Powell, current chairman of the Federal Reserve, when he introduced these measures: "We are deploying these lending powers to an unprecedented extent and will continue to use these powers forcefully, proactively, and aggressively until we are confident that we are solidly on the road to recovery."[18]

So far, these programs have increased the size of the Federal Reserve's assets to $8.9 trillion. Similar actions have been duplicated by the central banks of the world's richest countries as we have again been brought back from the brink. Central bankers have been hailed again as the saviors of the global economy, and stock markets have recovered much of the losses they suffered during the early days of the pandemic.

The financial bailout of 2008 and the pandemic bailout differed not only in size but also in the degree of stress they imposed on a complex system. In 2008, the world trusted central bankers and politicians as they rescued a system that was addicted to high levels of debt and dangerous financial products. However, as I have related, instead of taking structurally corrective measures to bring the system back into a healthy balance, they bought toxic assets, took on high levels of debt, and hoped that at some point the toxicity would subside before another catastrophe took place.

But that 2008 bailout merely empowered an ailing system to become more toxic. The Federal Reserve's massive infusion of fresh capital merely allowed the system to continue to run on automatic just as a new source of fuel would feed a ravenous, out-of-control fire. New financial products were created that upheld the ethos of *only money matters.* Labor and human input on the cost side of the equation were getting as close to zero as possible, and the monetarists loved it. The bailout also made job losses from the crisis permanent, thus adding to economic inequality and creating more tears in the societal fabric. One problem with a complex system in a state of decay is that when we use tools from its own toolkit, without taking the necessary corrective measures, we only add to the chaos and deepen the cracks, bringing the whole system closer to collapse.

According to economic data, since the 2008 financial crisis, this decaying system has operated far below capacity, sacrificing millions of potential jobs in the process. As Nobel Prize-winning economist Paul Krugman argues, this fact alone signals a far greater error committed by policymakers than the passive mistakes of the Federal Reserve in the 1970s that allowed inflation to become so entrenched.[19] And now, the unprecedented actions the Fed has taken in response to the impact of the pandemic have caused the economy to overheat and begin a new inflationary cycle in conditions that are far more complex than those of the 1970s. In addition, unlike the fallout from 9/11 leading up to the 2008 financial crisis, it hasn't taken seven years for the toxicity to work its way through the global economy. While the central bank is being praised for its quick actions in raising interest rates under Jay Powell's leadership, inflation has continued to climb and will remain unpredictable as a result of the enormity of factors that were ignored when we adopted the ethos of *only money matters* and reduced economic complexity to a single variable on one side of the equation.

An important gauge of inflation is the thirty-year fixed mortgage rate. Just as the four-point drop in the prime lending rate in 2008 allowed home borrowers to increase their purchasing power by one-third, the three-point increase since inflationary pressures began in early 2022 has eroded purchasing power by over 40 percent.[20] Similar cost increases on corporate and business borrowing are also affecting the economy as the Fed finds itself fighting many new battles the causes of which it doesn't fully understand, with only one archaic tool remaining at its disposal.

One of the biggest changes that has occurred since the late 1970s is the speed at which information and capital can move in the digital age. While economists and central bankers only saw the positive side of this great innovation in the ease with which they could move capital to fund a business venture, they have completely underestimated its power to spread viral chaos at times of economic uncertainty. This power could be a new wildcard with the potential to spread mayhem and uncertainty in a matter of minutes and bankrupt the largest banks without a single customer ever stepping foot into one. Runs on banks are nothing new, but what has changed is the fact that account holders today don't need to be physically present to withdraw their funds. It all gets done virtually and instantaneously.

For example, consider Silicon Valley Bank (SVB), one the largest banks that failed in spectacular fashion and in the quickest time imaginable in March 2023. The bank catered to digital startup companies and, by extension, to the ecosystem of the digital economy and its venture capitalists. While its customers' deposits were insured by the FDIC for the maximum coverage of $250,000, most customers entrusted far more money to it. When the bank failed, the top ten customers combined had over $4.5 billion on account.[21] Estimates are that as much as $43 billion left SVB in a matter of hours before the FDIC shut it down. Most business pundits blamed the collapse on panicked tweets and messages posted on social media by influencers with large followings. SVB's failure was followed by Signature Bank's failure, which has instilled panic in global finance as fears of a banking contagion has gripped financial markets. This specific form of failure has started a new if overdue debate in the financial industry and among regulators on whether we need to overhaul the current banking system. Its policies and practices remain a relic of the industrial age, when what is needed is a modernized system that protects depositors and businesses in a time when capital moves at lightning speed.

Lost in the current debate, however, is the much larger issue about the corrosive effect that long-term, low-interest rates have had on the culture of banking. SVB had invested the majority of its customers' deposits in US treasuries. This is generally a safe practice as long as interest rates remain low. The yield on treasuries has an inverse relationship to interest rates: When the cost of borrowing money rises (when interest rates rise), US Treasury prices usually fall, and vice-versa. So, when the Fed began to raise interest rates to combat inflation, the return on treasuries turned negative, forcing SVB to sell billions of its holdings at a loss just to remain liquid. This new form of risk was not anticipated by a banking industry that had become complacent and rarely hedged against the idea that interest rates will rise again. It is appearing in a vastly different economic landscape than the one that existed when Ronald Reagan and the new leadership at the Federal Reserve declared war on inflation over four decades ago. The new situation presents a whole new conundrum to policy makers: increasing interest rates is the only way to tame inflation, but continuing to do so after the failure of SVB would place many more banks in danger of failing. The conundrum will contribute greatly to the coming debate among economists and central bankers on whether increasing interest rates will tame inflation or potentially cause another global financial crisis. The traditional question of whether this single lever of monetary policy—increasing rates—will result in a soft landing for the economy has been rendered obsolete. Inflation could run rampant for years if regulators fear that higher interest rates will cause more bank failures. In the larger picture, should there be a soft landing while at the same time bank failures are averted, the bubble economies created under the ethos of *only money matters* will nevertheless continue on their dangerous path toward an inevitable end point.

To get a better idea of how inflationary pressures may play out differently this time, think of finance as the bloodline of an economy. What we've done in the last two decades is ignore the warning signs that our blood is running too rich for the health of the organism. The richness in this case is caused by the abundant availability of money and the low interest rates that come with it. Sooner or later, not catching inflationary signs early enough will manifest in disease leading to organ failure.

The disease of inflation has reemerged after four decades, but now it is doing so in an unfamiliar, interconnected global economy more than eight times the size it was in the early 1980s. Moreover, it is doing so with considerably more variables and a higher number of rich sources supplying a bloodline that has been running too rich for too long. In places like the England and the EU—due to the lingering economic impact of COVID-19, the effects of the war in Ukraine, and economic sanctions imposed on Russia—inflationary pressures have been much worse. The effects of these factors on poor countries around the world could be multiplied several times over.

Reductionists still want us to think that our complex global economy can run on the linear architecture that has streamlined complexity into a few simple algorithms. The *First-sapiens* mind has reduced the greatest variable, the bloodline of the capitalist system, to a simple, linear equation: if prices of anything in the global supply chain begin to rise, you simply find a cheaper supplier. The algorithm reads: cheap and abundant money is the constant in the equation, and everything else is a variable.

But what happens when external forces interrupt that simplistic view after the entire world has adopted it? What happens when the cheapest suppliers cannot deliver due to factory shutdowns caused by wildcards—the two most recent being COVID-19 and climate change—that lie outside *First-sapiens* conscious awareness? While the former has been a temporary problem that shocked the system and exposed its fragility, the latter is a slow-moving crisis that remains highly unpredictable in time scale and size. Sea rise, hurricanes, and wild fires in the last few years have affected suppliers of every type of commodity from China and to Canada, the United States, and Mexico. And while the modern mind searches for new alternatives to keep the supply chain and prices stable, the enormous pressures from these two wildcards are pushing against the limits of the system and causing it to reach a breaking point.

The Great Obsolescence

The *Great Obsolescence* can be thought of as a term that consolidates the different ways the concept of obsolescence itself has been used over the last century. In its widest definition, *obsolescence* refers to the diminished usefulness of an idea, an object, or a concept due to its inability to keep up with the changing times. The Enlightened minds of neoclassical economics have applied the term in various contexts, ranging from functional to technical, architectural, stylistic, and inventorial obsolescence, and so on. The worst of these conceptions is called *planned obsolescence,* which has defined much of the ethos of global trade and contributed greatly to the degradation of our ecosystems by ensuring that products become inferior within a certain timeframe in order for corporations to maximize production and profit.[22]

My use of the term applies to the wider, macro view of the evolution of values systems and ideologies that define complex systems in economics, culture, and geopolitics. When a system the size of our global economy approaches the state of obsolescence, it reaches a nexus point that begins to call on the use of better ideas and concepts. In an *open state* in touch with changes in its environment, the transition happens as part of the normal evolutionary process. But the larger the system, the slower the pace of change. As for a global economy that has adopted the ethos of *peace through commerce*, managing a system of this size and keeping it in an open state becomes a prohibitive task. The entire world becomes a single system operating on specific, centralized assumptions that must remain in an open, evolutionary state to prevent the system from becoming obsolescent.

There are two major forces contributing to the *Great Obsolescence*: the human-built systems and the natural systems that are reaching certain tipping points caused by the human-built systems.

Concerning the first force—human-built systems—there are in turn two contributing factors. One factor is the continued practice of commerce based on outdated concepts. The ideas that inspired the world to move away from war less than a century ago have become less effective and even detrimental in today's complex world. Many of our institutions still use concepts that have reached the point of obsolescence; but, due to the size of the system and the imbedded interests that benefit from the status quo, we keep advancing those same concepts, resulting in decreased marginal benefits that are skewed in favor of the wealthy to the detriment of everyone else and the planet. This collective mindset favoring greed and endless consumption prevents the pursuit of newer, more sustainable economic models. The other factor within the human-built systems contributing to the *Great Obsolescence* is the rise of the digital economy and of artificial intelligence. In just the first three decades since its inception, the digital economy has created enormous disruption in our culture. Tens of millions of jobs have been lost, entire economic sectors have been eliminated, and much of how we relate to each other as human beings has been upended. For better or for worse, experts estimate that, in another two decades, almost half the jobs in the Western world will be automated and that, with the help of intelligent machines, in 120 years all jobs will have disappeared completely.[23]

Along with human-built systems, the second force contributing to the *Great Obsolescence* is the damage *First sapiens* have caused our planet, triggering irreversible damage to Earth's different ecosystems. The *only money matters* ethos, our globalized economy, and our pursuit of modernization have all become endeavors that erode the larger systems comprising all life and make economic activity possible. Those larger systems will be the focus of upcoming chapters.

In the context of this book, obsolescence begins once a complex system passes its nexus point and fails to adopt new evolutionary ideas. It then enters an *arrested state* in which hidden biases become the norm. In this state, leaders live in denial. They become inflexible in their views and protective of the idea that solutions to all our problems should come from within the paradigm that created them. At best, they engage in incremental change that might have worked in the past but that no longer suffice when what is needed are transformational ideas that are systemic and evolutionary. Leaders at every level of the system begin to codify our values and practices falsely as honorable and evolutionary.

An economy can linger in an arrested state for decades until all its virtues are exhausted and the system eventually moves into a *closed state.* Then its practices become toxic, chaotic, and unpredictable, affecting the behavior of other systems. Evolutionary ideas that have waited in the wings gain strength and contribute to many wildcards that repeatedly destabilize the system until it reaches the point of entropy accompanied by despondency, disorder, and disintegration as the surviving systems do battle to define the next iteration.

The two largest complex systems that are in an arrested state today are the interconnected global economy, built on the fallacy of *peace through commerce,* and the monetary system put in place to support it. Given that both systems run on architecture that was not designed or built to handle today's complexity, they have passed the state of obsolescence and are slowly moving us into a closed state. The ideas that have steered our passions for the good part of the last century have been reductive by nature, reducing the complexity behind most utopian ideals to simple mechanical systems. Nowhere is this reductionism more apparent than in the most recent expression of capitalism on which much of the global economy is built.

The ideas behind *peace through commerce* and the monetarism that allowed the global economy to grow originated in the thought of Adam Smith (1723–1790), the eighteenth-century Scottish economist known as the father of capitalism. Smith was considered a "moral philosopher" in that he believed that having a just society depends on the existence of a certain sympathy among the individual and the other members of that society. His blueprint for society takes everyone into account—the least well off as well as the prosperous. His work, as detailed in his books *The Theory of Moral Sentiments* and *The Wealth of Nations*, remains inspirational to this day. Yet, over the years, much of it has devolved beyond recognition, having been reduced and manipulated by economists in order to advance their own views. In their misguided interpretations, they have focused on a narrow aspect of economics driven by consumer behavior with the assumption that in the pursuit of self-interest humans will always be rational actors—an assumption that, needless to say, often proves false. Thus, the world's complexity has been reduced to two major players: the consumer and the producer, and usually without much "sympathy" between them. We are locked in an economic fallacy that ignores everything outside this simple dynamic. Today, it is what most students of economics are still being taught at our higher institutions of learning. The arrested state has not only made the complex system weak through reductionism, it has imbedded itself in our institutions that now operate from a systemwide place of hidden bias.

This simplistic view of human behavior also ignores the very nature of opportunism and greed that develops between the parties—what many philosophers and economists call our "animal spirit." Neoliberal economists have ignored this savage aspect of human nature as they motivated the consumer to pursue maximum gains. The complexity of Smith's philosophy that considered the whole of a society has been reduced to a narrow but false interpretation that defined all of humanity through greed. This is a type of reductive thinking that comes with elegant mathematical models that no one questions. Today, economists who run our global economy make decisions based in mathematical modeling that have nothing to do with moral philosophy or the deeper ecology the determines the fullness of human existence itself. Nor are these economists aware of the systemic bias and the arrested states in which their models are being created.

In our collective desire to maximize our material gains, we have allowed the capitalist system to take on a life of its own while deliberately leaving out the variables that spread its ideals in the first place. But this reductionism didn't start with neoliberal economists. It was born in the Scientific Revolution and the Age of Enlightenment that gave us modern mathematics, physics, astronomy, biology, and chemistry. While these discoveries transformed how we view nature, they also sought to replace it with mechanical models and precise measurement for no other reason than to make the world into a machine in order to dominate and control it. The brightest scientist in this regard was Sir Isaac Newton (1642–1746), whose crowning achievement was the synthesis of the work of those who came before him: Galileo Galilei and his mathematical description of nature, Sir Francis Bacon and his empirical approach to the domination of nature, and Rene Descartes and his certainty of understanding the universe through its mathematical structure.[2] Newton also introduced many of his own advancements in physics and mathematics, allowing his synthesis to dominate scientific thought for over three hundred years. His scientific method remains the standard by which most research is conducted today. The continued success of the Newtonian model has anchored our thinking, our worldviews, and our belief systems in the grand idea that the universe is one huge, mechanical system operating in accordance to mathematical laws.

> *Scientific materialism, taken to its extreme, threatens us with meaninglessness. If consciousness is reducible to the brain and our actions are determined not by will but causes, then our values and beliefs are merely rationalizations for things we were going to do anyway. Most people find this view of human life repugnant, if not incomprehensible.*
>
> —Roy Scranton[24]

Today, one of the most popular models of mechanical systems based on the Newtonian interpretation of the universe is the planetary gearset model, or what is known in industrial manufacturing as "epicyclic gearing." It illustrates what happens when we reduce natural phenomena and whole systems to their mechanical parts. It also provides for a simple understanding of why much of the issues discussed in this chapter are approaching different inflection points that are contributing to the *Great Obsolescence.* While many believe that economics can be studied as a complex system, its complexity is limited to the ideology that created it and the tools put in place to support it. Its centralized nature and its inability to be as adaptive as a natural complex system defaults it to a mechanical system centered around the ideology that made it popular.

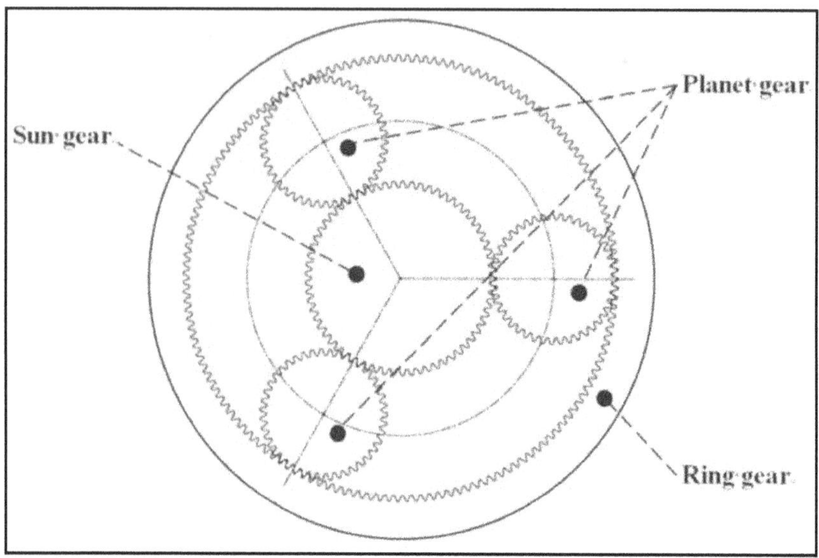

Figure 1.2. Schematic of an Elementary Planetary Gearset. The gearset has three planet gears, based on the Newtonian view of the universe. ResearchGate https://www.researchgate.net. Used with permission.

In the above graph (fig. 1.2), that ideology, or paradigm, can be viewed as the master gear, or "sun gear." This gear is the source of input—or inspiration—and operates independently of all the other gears. The three gears around the sun gear, called "servant gears," represent the planets in any given solar system. In our actual solar system, the behavior of planets is predetermined as they rotate around the sun on different orbital paths and at different speeds. The ring gear represents the outer limits of the entire system.

Consider the values of the Enlightenment as the sun in the model that has provided the energy for keeping the planets going. Then consider neoliberal economics, the values of monetarism, and the misguided pursuit of *peace through commerce* as the three main planets in the system. They can be compared to all the different sectors and forms of output in the global economy. They can also represent the different countries that have embraced the same economic ideologies. Lastly, the ring gear represents the outer limits that contain the spread of these ideologies and stop the world economies from falling out of orbit.

Now, imagine the sun in the model running out of energy. In real life, this could represent the system's tools and ideologies becoming outdated and slowly reaching the point of obsolescence. Also imagine the system overheating as its ideas begin to lay the seeds of its own destruction and move the system from its arrested state to its closed state, causing the outer ring to begin to break down. In this state, the system has reached the entropy stage that brings on disorder and disintegration and can affect much larger systems in which this smaller system is nested. In real life, this could represent the breaking down of boundaries that contain some of the Earth's systems and hold not only our economic activity but all life as we know it.

The mechanical gearset model, like most mechanical models, is by nature a closed system. The gears move in a closed loop in response to input from the master gear in order to achieve the desired movement. However, as much as economists like for us to believe in this Newtonian worldview, economic activity does not occur in a closed system, nor is it mechanical. Yet this is precisely the worldview that has dominated academia, geopolitics, and economic policy setting for most of the last century. Until recently, very few have challenged the idea that endless growth is possible. To speak to establishment economists today about limiting growth is a sure way to end a career or lose a job. It challenges one of the most fundamental beliefs underpinning neoliberal economics that is built on the narrative of *grow or die*. To begin to show that limits to growth is a real issue, one must approach it from outside the system and speak to like-minded people who have the power to affect change. Our global economy does not operate in a vacuum, nor do the byproducts of its activities disappear into thin air. They dissipate into the biosphere and degrade our ecosystems. They pollute our air, our rivers, and our oceans. They cause damage to the greater system in which all life is nested: our planet, the only home we know.

Our task from henceforth should be the preservation and restoration of this home. We must replace the *grow-or-die* paradigm with one based in a reality that discourages unimpeded growth. We must transcend the limitations of the Enlightenment and include its best virtues in a new and evolved definition of the good, the true, and the beautiful. To ensure that life survives beyond our neoliberal economic fallacy will require a monumental leap in thinking—one that challenges the fundamental way in which we perceive reality and thus the way we design our institutions and organize our societies. Many of our institutions today are remnants of an era that catered to the needs of the *First sapiens* who is occupied with matters of his or her own existence absent the full awareness of natural phenomena and higher forms of thinking and inclusion. And, again, issues of planetary degradation cannot be fully addressed by the minds and the institutions that created them. That task will be more effectively handled by the *Second sapiens,* the collaborative humanity that thinks in systems and, unlike the modern mind, does not separate itself from Mother Nature. This is what awaits us on the other side of the monumental leap that must be taken if our species is to survive.

Two
The Nature of Change and the Life Cycle of Ideologies

Modern man does not experience himself as a part of nature but as an outside force destined to dominate and conquer it. He even talks of a battle with nature, forgetting that, if he won the battle, he would find himself on the losing side.

—Ernst F. Schumacher
Small Is Beautiful

On October 31, 1517, a small-town monk marched up to the castle church in Wittenberg, Germany, and nailed a parchment on its door. With that simple act of defiance, he lit a flame that challenged the authority of the Catholic Church and forever changed the trajectory of human progress. The monk was Martin Luther (1483–1546), and the parchment contained his Ninety-Five Theses, which sparked the Reformation movement that became one of the catalysts that ushered in the Age of Enlightenment. Luther was a professor of moral theology and a local preacher who never thought his proclamations would have such a profound effect on Europe and the rest of the world. During his time, the Roman Catholic Church was the only Christian church in Europe, but its practices had become corrupt and outdated. The focus of Luther's theses that took Europe by storm comprised three main critiques of the Church: the financial burden it imposed on its subjects in its *selling of indulgences* in order to finance the building of St. Peter's Basilica; the indulgences themselves, which Luther deemed harmful to their recipients in that they diverted money from charity and impeded salvation by commodifying forgiveness; and his rational argument for why the pope had no power over Purgatory.[1]

Luther was not the first to criticize the Church or the plight of humanity under the rule of religious authority that had become suffocating and grossly outdated, but the timing of his critique, combined with many prevailing ideas of the times, contributed to the transformation of humanity into the way it is today. As his calls for reform gained greater acceptance, the Renaissance, which marked Europe's transition from the Middle Ages, had already begun. This was a cultural movement from the fourteenth to the seventeenth centuries that profoundly affected European intellectual life not just in the perception of religion but also in politics, philosophy, literature, science, and other aspects of intellectual inquiry. It introduced a new method of learning based on human reasoning and empirical evidence.

As these approaches to deeper understanding grew, they gave birth in the mid-sixteenth century to the Scientific Revolution. With advancements in mathematics, astronomy, physics, biology, chemistry, and other disciplines, we began to see the world through a different lens, and this paradigm shift was solidified by Newton's synthesis of the new cosmology. As these three major forces—the challenges to the authority of the Catholic Church—the Renaissance, and the Scientific Revolution—coalesced, they culminated in our ascent to a new era, a stage of psychosocial development that transcended the past and subsumed its best virtues into a new expression of human values. We gained a greater capacity for scientific and quantitative discoveries and for higher degrees of tolerance and inclusion.

This new era, beginning in the seventeenth century, is the period known as the Age of Enlightenment. Marked by the increased awareness of the relationship between the mind and its environment, its doctrines centered on individual liberty, religious tolerance, Newton's scientific method, and the philosophical ideas behind reductionism, which interpret any complex system as the sum of its parts.[2]

Of course, such a generalized description does not cover all the details that made the Age of Enlightenment such an important part of the human story, nor does it account for the emergence of its virtues that have allowed it to evolve and sustain itself for centuries. But in the long arc of history, the era itself represents one of the many stages of human development, each of which comes about according to the system of psychological motivations that are proprietary to that specific stage. The ideas that form these epochal stages are an evolutionary phenomenon that is the creation of the human mind and the environment that shapes it. Once they survive the rigors of the evolutionary process and withstand the test of time, they can spread and dominate our human ecology and our collective thought processes. The fittest of these ideas become imbedded principles and philosophies that have the potential to create an upward shift that can define human virtues for centuries. These paradigm-altering advancements are reflected in new human values and innovations that become superior to the ideas that preceded them. But then, like the ideas they replace, the new values themselves become replaceable as their virtues become outdated and higher orders of thinking begin to emerge and slowly contribute to a new paradigm that eventually replaces the old. This is the nature of the mind in the endless quest of the *Homo sapiens* to uncover the secrets of the universe.

In most human-development models, the Age of Enlightenment is identified as the modern stage that has defined humanity and its institutions for the last five centuries. Cultures that are centered in its values believe that most solutions to our problems should come from the virtues that lay within its vast paradigm, the meta meme that created it and all its supplemental expressions. But what happens when these solutions no longer serve the greater good? What happens when we expand our use of modern tools under the guise of innovation and the outcome makes things worse? What do we do when the mind comes into greater levels of awareness that challenge the wisdom of the current paradigm after that paradigm has imbedded itself in our institutions, our educational and economic systems, and our geopolitical thought? What causes someone like E. F. Schumacher (1911–1977), a prominent, Oxford-trained economist, to articulate a vision that is so scathing and highly critical of his colleagues in the mainstream? Schumacher's most influential work was detailed in his 1973 book: *Small is Beautiful: A Study of Economics as if People Mattered.* It introduced concepts that defy the prevailing centralized ideas on human development and argued for a decentralized economic approach that is energy efficient, environmentally sustainable, and locally autonomous. In the failure to manifest his ideas, what comes next after the world becomes one global economy with a structure so centralized that its mere function ignores basic human and community needs, the very thing that Schumacher warned about? What replaces Adam Smith's vision for the wealth of nations when the pursuit of that wealth is reduced to a few monetary measures that pay little attention to the intrinsic wholesomeness of individuals, communities, and the planet? Can the time have come for a new paradigm shift? Is there a new scientific revolution that will replace the mechanistic and reductive view of the Enlightenment?

Are there other breakthroughs in our perception that are coalescing to move us into a more conscious and evolved stage of human existence?

According to developmentalists Clare W. Graves and Don E. Beck, the answer to the last few questions is affirmative, and to deny the possibility of higher stages of existence is to deny the evolutionary nature of humanity and all living things. Their developmental models reflect the human desire to seek higher psychosocial states of being in a never-ending quest. So far, their research has identified a few postmodern stages of development that have been emerging for decades but have remained on the margins of society and the modern mind. Based on historic data, Graves and Beck have also identified several lower stages that capture the psychosocial characteristics of the past. They put their research into a model that identifies a total of eight stages of human and cultural development, within which the intellectual movements I've discussed have all occurred in stage five. Hence, what most people identify with as the modern stage is designated as level five in the figure 2.1 below, and it is followed by what

Level of Development	First Appeared	WAY OF THINKING Basic Theme for Living
1	100,000 years ago	**SURVIVALISTIC** Do what you must to stay alive. Self is barely awakened.
2	50,000 years ago	**TRIBALISTIC** Keep the spirits happy and the tribe's nest warn and safe. Individual subsumed into the group.
3	10,000 years ago	**EGOCENTRIC** Be what you are and do what you want regardless. Express self fully without regard to guilt or remorse.
4	5,000 years ago	**ABSOLUTISTIC** Life has meaning, direction and purpose with predetermined outcome. Righteous living produces stability and guarantees future rewards
5	500 years ago	**MULTIPLISTIC** Act in your own best interest by playing the game to win. Manipulate earth's resources to create and spread the abundant life.
6	150 years ago	**RELATIVISTIC** Seek peace within the inner self and explore with others the caring dimensions of community. Spread earth's resources and opportunities equally.
7	70 years ago	**INTEGRATIVE/EXISTENTIAL** Live fully and responsibly as what you are and learn to become. Magnificence of existence is valued over material possessions.
8	50 years ago	**HOLISTIC/ECOLOGICAL** Experience wholeness of existence through mind and spirit. Everything connects to everything else in ecological alignment

Table 2.1. Summary of Graves's Emergent-Cyclical-Levels-of-Existence Theory and Beck's Spiral-Dynamics Theory. Said E. Dawlabani, 2024.

is commonly referred to as the postmodern stage, or level six. What comes after reductionism, which characterizes the fifth stage, is the embrace of higher values based in the relativism of stage six and systems thinking of stage seven. What comes after Newtonian physics is Albert Einstein's theory of relativity and Niels Bohr's quantum theory. What comes after neoliberal economic theory that is centralized, insatiable, and unsustainable is a system of postmodern economic principles that are decentralized, altruistic, and regenerative.

Developmental Stages and the Nature of Change

In the Graves-Beck developmental model, the driving force behind any emerging system is to provide for more inclusive solutions than the existing system allows and, in the process, heal some of the damage the old system leaves behind. But, based on history, the ascendence to a higher-level system does not usually materialize merely to advance in a systemic progression of values. Instead, it takes major breakdowns in an existing system to accelerate the ascendence of a new one. For instance, without the brutality of the Spanish Inquisition and the Church's abuse of indulgences, Reformation would not have become such a force for change and taken place when it did. Without the Dark Ages and the Black Plague, the urgency wouldn't have existed for us to seek better ways of understanding ourselves and the universe, and the Scientific Revolution would not have happened when and as it did. In the model, these periods of darkness in human history exemplify the necessary exit phase that is full of chaos and unpredictability in the life cycle of every developmental stage once its virtues stop serving the needs of the culture.

The above examples represent the end phase of stage four, the Absolutistic, which was based in psychosocial structures of rigid and unyielding thinking and characterized by the values of temperance and righteous living. Prohibitively hierarchical in nature, these structures and values brought us monotheism, guilt, and the dogmatism of the One True Way. But, as is the case with every stage, once these values were exhausted, the stage entered into a decline and began to yield to higher orders of thinking.

Moving backward in time, we see a similar cycle in the transition to the fourth stage from the third—the Egocentric—the earlier stage being based in guiltless self-centeredness and defined by instant gratification and brutal conquest. These stage-three values outlasted their efficacy five thousand years ago and led to the transition to stage four that was built on the values of self-control and the ideas of postponing gratification for the purpose of gaining heavenly rewards later. The shift to stage four also symbolized our ascendence to the teachings of the Abrahamic religions in harmony with the values of the system. It healed some of the trauma that had afflicted our species in the previous stage and provided many of the answers to the existential problems confronting humanity at the time.

These upward shifts in values are a function mostly born of existential necessity after existing values and practices become toxic and incapable of generating new ideas. At this worn-out phase of every stage, the system becomes protective of its virtues and closed to new input. In the Newtonian planetary gearset model (fig. 1.2), this is the phase when the planets exhibit the greatest orbital dysfunction and begin to impinge on the outer ring, bringing about the decay and entropy phase of the system. Even then, the emerging system still must do battle with the old, entrenched ideologies that have embedded themselves for centuries in the minds of generations and defined their institutions and styles of leadership. The transition is a slow-moving process that takes decades and includes many false starts and setbacks as smaller and smaller bastions of the old thinking—regardless of its waning efficacy—are fortified through the institutions and societal formations that remain in place. The emerging system must not only win the hearts and minds of people; it must also move those in power who rule over geopolitics, economics, academia, and government. And it must keep spreading its virtues at every level—personal, communal, national, and regional—until the system reaches a tipping point when the old stage of development becomes subordinate to the new.

> *This* [the emergent cyclical theory of adult human development] *is the one theory I know of in operation today that explains the psychological development of the species, the psychological development of a culture, and the psychological development of an individual through this one basic set of conceptions. All three, all at one time.*
>
> —Clare W. Graves[3]

I have been fortunate to witness Beck's genius first hand and work with him on several projects during his lifetime. Whether it was in reframing of Middle-Eastern peace through the model or articulating the world's new geopolitical maps through its lenses, the insights it offers provide for one of the most comprehensive and resilient tools to address the plethora of existential issues we face. As early as 1967, Graves's pioneering work was being called a *theory that explains everything*, and its evolutionary nature was being compared to the work of Charles Darwin and C. G. Jung even though at the time Graves's work wasn't completed.[4] While my upcoming chapters discuss Graves's theoretical framework in detail, an overview of the mechanics of change I offer here provides insights on where we are and why the change we so desperately need doesn't seem to be happening rapidly enough.

While the phases of each stage's life cycle are basically the same, the time frame for change differs greatly depending on the size of the entity. For a theory to apply equally to individuals, cultures, and the species, it must factor in the varying dynamics and levels of complexity within each category. A psychologically healthy individual, for instance, can transition from level one through level eight of the model (see table. 2.1) in as little as twenty years.

The same cannot be said about a group or a community. As figure 2.1 below illustrates, the larger the size of the entity, the more

CONCENTRIC/FRACTAL NATURE OF DEVELOPMENTAL CHANGE

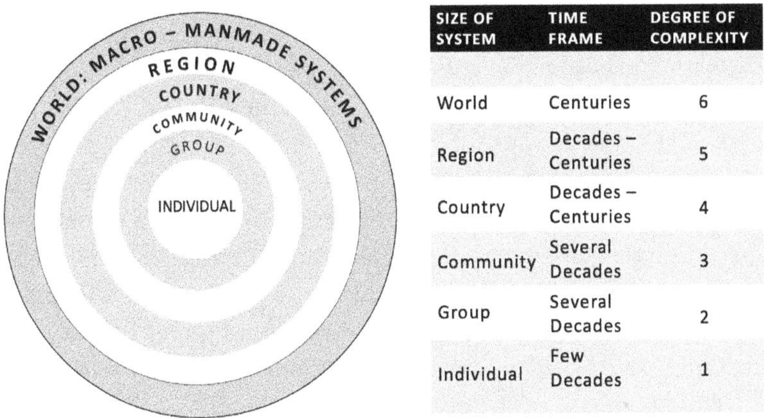

SIZE OF SYSTEM	TIME FRAME	DEGREE OF COMPLEXITY
World	Centuries	6
Region	Decades – Centuries	5
Country	Decades – Centuries	4
Community	Several Decades	3
Group	Several Decades	2
Individual	Few Decades	1

Figure 2.1. The Fractal Nature of Developmental Change. Depiction of degrees of complexity and approximate time needed for developmental change to manifest at different fractal levels on a scale of 1 to 6, wherein 1 has the lowest complexity and 6 the highest. Adapted with permission from the MEMEnomics Group, LLC; https://www.memenomics.com.

complex the factors that play into the dynamics of change and the longer the time frame for that change to define values and virtues at a systemic level.

Beck brought Graves's work to the world through his Spiral Dynamics theory, but his larger legacy lies in his tireless efforts to update the mechanics of the Gravesian conception by applying the newest breakthroughs in the social sciences to its foundational premise. One of Beck's innovations most relevant to our understanding of systems change is the prerequisite conditions needed in order for that change to take place.[5] In a healthy person, an organization, or a culture, the potential for change depends greatly on whether the entity is in an *open*, an *arrested*, or a *closed* state of being. If a person or a culture is in an *open* state and thus sensitive and responsive to the needs of the environment, the potential for change is high. If, on the other hand, the entity is in a closed state and so cannot accept input from the environment, the system cannot change.

An individual in a closed system is generally trapped by neurological, psychological, or environmental limitations that can manifest in disease or anxiety. At the cultural level, the dynamics are characteristic of a complex system that might start off in an open state but becomes more resistant to change as the system grows and spreads its values to wider and more diverse segments of society. In maturity, the culture moves into an arrested state that seeks solutions only from within the system that created it. Eventually, it becomes a closed system that allows little or no input from the environment. Such a closed cultural state can lead to social unrest, revolutions, or civil war. A closed economic system can lead to exploitation, rampant poverty, income inequality, and, in extreme cases, the collapse of social order as a result of its continued use of outdated tools that increasingly serve fewer and fewer members of society. So far in human history, this dynamic has characterized the end phase of every cycle: the system sews its own seeds of destruction that hasten its collapse, allowing for the new system to rise.

Another condition for change in the Graves-Beck model is *dissonance*. In a person or a culture, there must be enough discomfort, enough of a sense that *there has to be something better* than what the current system offers. Only then can we let go and allow for neurological and societal reorganization at a higher level to begin. We start to identify the barriers in the current system that are preventing change from taking place and begin to gain insights into what is causing the current system to fail or become closed.

When a healthy, open-system individual feels this sense of dissonance, the barriers she identifies are oftentimes the very same psychosocial tools she used to help her ascend from the previous stage of development; but with the passage of time and the emergence of higher-order challenges, those tools have become less useful. As often is the case with open systems, different times require different measures. As our evolving problems become more complex, they trigger higher levels of neurological networks that enable the mind to evolve and adjust to new, higher levels of psychological health. In an open-system individual, this is an evolutionary process that happens automatically and naturally, just as a seed germinates or a butterfly emerges from a chrysalis.

But what happens when we apply the model to entities more complex than individuals? In an organization or a small community, we might find people with similar worldviews and value systems who are experiencing

DEVELOPMENTAL STATES & THE POTENTIAL FOR CHANGE

OPEN STATE	ARRESTED STATE	CLOSED STATE
Dynamic. Always open to input from total environment. Changes as conditions change	Dynamism limited to the specific environment within its stage of development.	Always at Equilibrium. No new input to the system. Threatened by change. Fights to stay put.
Plastic. Adaptive. Resilient. Deals effectively with barriers.	Plasticity, adaptivity and resilience limited to the particular its stage of development.	Rigid. Non-resilient. May lack the neurological structures. Unable to recognize barriers.
Constant exchange of ideas and energy with environment.	Ideas and exchanges limited to the environment within the ethos of the particular stage of development.	Little or no interaction with environment.
Fluid and dynamic, able to grow and evolve.	Evolves only to a translational expression within the stage.	Static, stable, threatened by change. Does not evolve.
Evolves and changes into higher order stages in the system.	Only evolves to the nodal phase of the specific stage of development.	Fragile and rigid. Only capable of minor changes just to keep the system alive.
Able to dissipate entropy to environment. The higher the developmental stage, the more it can dissipate entropy and the greater its resilience.	Dissipates entropy of older ideologies within the stage. Resilience limited to the nodal phase of the particular stage of development the system is in.	Cannot dissipate any buildup in entropy. Excess input leads to death of the system.

Table 2.2. Developmental States and the Potential for Change in Open, Arrested, and Closed States. Adapted with permission from the MEMEnomics Group, LLC; https://www.memenomics.com.

a certain level of dissonance and agree there has to be something better, but their opinions might differ about what that something is. This is where the different layers of complexity begin to matter. The larger the system, the more it must account for variables such as cultural expressions, worldviews, motivations, and levels of psychosocial maturity—to name just a few. Once the issue moves beyond individuals, a unifying consensus still needs to exist among the larger social and cultural entities in order for change to occur and for the overall system to remain in a healthy state.

So, in lieu of the individual mind, how do we create a collective mind for the group, the community, the species, and for every entity in between? In the medieval past, we looked to philosophers, saints, and sages to draw inspiration for the answer. During the Age of Enlightenment, we turned to modern science and all the tools of modernity. In the twentieth-century, post-war era, we turned to the mandates of modern development as ways for humanity to pursue *peace through commerce* and move us away from war. All these inspiring ideas culminated in paradigm shifts that brought us collectively to higher levels of psychosocial health. But what happens when the use of past solutions become less effective, or, in some cases, even begins to present an existential threat? What if leaders in charge of larger systems who are supposed to recognize these changes are in a psychologically arrested or closed state and so incapable of understanding change or perceiving threats? What if our institutions are stuck in a business-as-usual mentality due to certain political, philosophical, or religious beliefs or a funding source beholden to an outdated ideology that established them decades or centuries earlier?

If history tells us anything, it is that unless people in charge of the larger, concentric systems take measures to mitigate such threats, they will grow to the point where they become a systemic menace that triggers the collapse of the current system and gradually renders the current paradigm obsolete. Sadly, this dynamic has been the dominant condition for change: instead of emergence to higher values being a function of our natural evolution of conscience, it has become an existential necessity born out of the ashes of the dying system.

As the new system arises from the old, it must search for insights about what went wrong in the previous system and with that knowledge begin to build the safeguards—or *antibodies*— that prevent the end phase of the old system from reappearing and destroying the new.* This new phase of inquiry reveals the higher psychosocial architecture for new approaches that recognize the emergence of new life challenges. This is an essential characteristic of how change happens, but it only represents half of the model. In addition to transcending the values of the previous stage that became toxic and closed, we must still include the healthy expressions of all the previous stages in a subordinate way, lest we forget the healthy virtues of those stages and how they became arrested and closed in the first place. Additionally, we must recognize that different groups and cultures are at different stages of development, and the emerging model must integrate this complexity into its new paradigm if it is to survive and replace the old. The new stage must have greater explanatory powers than the previous stages of development had at their zenith or at their nodal phase. It must also have the capacity to recognize the natural, motivational flows of people and cultures in their different-sized systems and formations and respect the local content of where they are developmentally. And it must serve the purpose of empowering the different groupings to remain in a healthy, open state at whatever their level of development in order to enable emergence to happen naturally. In the Graves-Beck model, this methodology is called *natural design*. It asks the systems designer the question: How does who lead/manage/teach/inspire whom to do what for which people living where?[6] This inquiry seems simple at first glance, but if applied correctly to the proper-sized system with the proper level of development and with the local content of that development stage, it becomes the model on which many modern, complex systems can be built.

Holons and Fractals

Due to the wide range of cross disciplines that Graves covered in his model, critics and academics in the fields of philosophy and the psychology have cast it in the same vein as "general-systems thinking."[7] The scope of his research has contributed as much to phenomenological, existential, and humanistic psychologies as it has to development-stage psychology. Those who saw only the qualitative and subjective observations of his work cast it aside and called it works of prophecy. Much like

* It is important to note that, throughout his career, Beck taught the life-cycle model as one that mimics natural life-cycles consistent with his concept of natural design, using terms such as *safeguards* and *antibodies* interchangeably.

the non-reductionist, whole-systems work of others who were ahead of their time, his five-decades inquiry into the nature of human existence was dismissed by mainstream academics during his life. One of the driving forces behind general-systems thinking is that these wider, cross-discipline approaches have their own models and principles that apply to all the sub-models—irrespective of their particular kind or component elements and the relationships among them. Systems thinkers call this approach the application of universal principles to systems. It removes the discoveries of the *First sapiens* from the reductive silos that created them and places them in an open state within a general-systems framework. Unlike Newtonian science, systems thinking proclaims that a system is far more than the sum of its parts due to the synergistic and emergent behavior that results from viewing the system as a whole.[8]

One of the ways general-systems theory presents itself today is through a model called the *holonic structure,* wherein an entire system, sometimes referred to as a *holon,* is represented as a part inside another entire system. The word *holon* is a combination of the Greek words *holos,* meaning "whole," and the suffix *on,* as in *proton* or *neutron,* which suggests a particle or part. Thus, the word *holon* essentially means whole–part, at once whole in itself and part of a larger whole. While the concept of holons has been sufficiently articulated throughout history, first by the Greek philosophers and then during the Enlightenment by the Germans, it didn't gain much acceptance until Arthur Koestler brought it to the mainstream in his 1967 book, *Ghosts in the Machine.* Koestler's thinking, like that of Graves, strove for a better understanding of the human condition. Like Graves, he saw the need to reintegrate the behavioral psychologies and their mechanistic worldview with the holistic and humanistic worldviews of Freud, Carl Rogers, and Gestalt psychologists and to be able to do so through a natural evolutionary process that applies to the collective as well as the individual. In the model, as we move up in the size and increasing complexity of the structure, the smaller holon becomes the nodal point in the hierarchy that describes the relationship between entities that are self-complete wholes and entities that are seen to be dependent parts.

In Graves's wide body of work, similar characteristics appear in his description of how lower stages in the hierarchy of development become subordinate to and dependent parts of the emerging higher-order stage that becomes self-complete when it is in its nodal phase. In other words, the model begins to behave like a holonic structure in which the new stage becomes the new *whole* and the past stages within it become *parts.* Then, as that new whole matures and exhausts its virtues, we exit its stage of development, and in turn it becomes one of the parts of the new higher stage that has become the whole.

One of Koestler's contributions that makes the model relevant and keeps it in a perpetual open state is his observation that the nature of a holonic, hierarchic organization and all its constituent holons is defined by *fixed rules* and *flexible strategies.*[9] In the Graves-Beck model, the concept of a *fixed rule* applies to Graves's claim that each stage has one *central thema* for existence that can be particularized into almost an infinite number of peripheral expressions.[10] These expressions constitute the *flexible strategies* that come to shape principles, philosophies, scientific discoveries, economic models, models for governance, and so on. As an example, Graves identifies the fifth stage as one of multiplistic and strategic thinking that seeks to uncover the secrets of the universe through rational analysis and the scientific method. This is the central thema of this particular stage and could be regarded as the *fixed rule* in the holonic structure. *Flexible strategies* utilizing this rule in our current fifth stage include the unprecedented advances made in fields such as space exploration, archaeology, and medicine.

Holonic structures that appear in the natural world are often called *fractals.* A fractal is defined as a geometric figure in which each part has the same character as the whole, as in a nautilus shell. Like holons, fractals display self-similarity through repeating patterns; but, unlike holons, which can repeat endlessly, in a fractal the number of structures or iterations that can be reached is limited.

The adoption of a fractal view of complexity is important in understanding the limitations of social and natural systems. It takes the concept of holons out of the theoretical realms and subjects it to the dynamics of natural phenomena. Holonic formations become known as *branching*—meaning a detailed pattern that repeats itself over and over again at any scale, as in the nautilus shell or a tree. This phenomenon of branching becomes especially important when we're addressing issues of how certain man-made systems decline and die off when they reach the limits of their growth, causing a culture either to downshift or to evolve into a higher, more complex fractal that can withstand the challenges the earlier fractal formation could not. A fractal perspective of complex systems is even more crucial if we are to address issues of planetary degradation and have a better understanding of how we're pushing against the limits of natural resources that make life on our planet possible.

In the natural world, fractals do not exist ad infinitum. Like all natural phenomena, they all have their limits in life cycles that follow a natural order with varying functions and sizes. In the biological sciences, this phenomenon is called *allometry*, wherein the degree of branching is determined by the size and the function of the living system or the subsystem within it. An acorn contains an oak tree, and an oak tree contains an acorn. But, once an acorn germinates into a tree, it can only support a limited number of tributaries for large branches called boughs, and boughs can only support a limited number of tributary branches, which in turn can only support a certain number of twigs, which in turn can only support a limited number of leaves and acorns.

Fractals are all around us in the natural world, from the way frost crystals form on cold glass to the way Romanesco broccoli grows and how nerve cells branch out into the body that enable us to sense and feel on the whole surface of our skin. While each natural formation has its limits, the two characteristics of *fixed rules* and *flexible strategies* that apply to holons also apply to fractals. A tree cannot grow from a branch or without having roots. That's a *fixed rule.* But branches and roots, the smaller fractals, can grow in different directions to optimize the absorption of nutrients from the ground and to allow leaves to absorb sunlight for photosynthesis. These phenomena represent the *flexible strategies.*

In the field applications of the Graves-Beck developmental model, these two fractal characteristics of *fixed rule*s and *flexible strategies* have proven to apply in the use of the natural-design formula. Both the model, which will be fully detailed in upcoming chapters, and the concentric degrees of complexity (see fig. 2.1) offer *flexible strategies* that can be as different as night and day based entirely on the answers to the natural-design questions of how does who lead/manage/teach/inspire whom to do what for which people living where. The question constitutes the *fixed rule*, and the answers to it are what define the *flexible strategies* for how to design systems of different sizes with different functions that can serve people at different levels of development informed by the content of the local culture. This is the approach that Graves used to help Beck design appropriate strategies in his ten-year effort to help South Africa transition from the Apartheid system of rule. It is also the approach that several colleagues, including my wife and me, used in collaboration with Beck at the Center for Human Emergence Middle East to help the Palestinians begin an inquiry into how to build their institutions in a way to level the developmental asymmetries that exist between them and the Israelis. The same approach was also used to help Iceland redesign its constitution after the 2008 financial crisis and the Netherlands in introducing new organizing principles to help Dutch society become more accepting of new immigrants.[11]

Dams, Locks, and Spillways

Fractals are important in understanding the life cycle of developmental stages and the natural limits they reach once their virtues, or their *central thema*, become exhausted and spent. Beck had a genius for using physical examples from the natural and built worlds to illustrate certain aspects of the model without reducing much of the complexity that defines it.

One of those examples comes from the design of modern dams. Consider the dam as a stage of development—the *fixed rule*—and the water accumulating in it the various ideologies or modes of thinking that have constituted the *flexible strategies* within the rule over decades or centuries. The continuous flow of water into the dam is a metaphor for the evolutionary impulse of life. The incremental, incoming flows are the smaller ideologies within the largest fractal, and they themselves are fractal representations of the system but shorter or smaller in size and timespan. As the dam fills up with water, these smaller fractals, the ideologies, must become increasingly more evolved. In other words, as the stage of development comes closer to its nodal phase, the new ideas that define it must become more innovative, carry more complexity, and solve more problems than the ones that came before them. As the water in the dam crests—or the ideas within the *central thema* reach a state of maturity—the focus shifts to how to keep it in a stable state for as long as possible. At the cultural level, this is when the highest number of human groupings thrive, and the job of those in charge at every fractal level is to keep the system within the bounds of its *growth* and *maturity* phases. These are also the phases in which new ideas, new waterflows, cannot move the system higher as quickly they once did and become dependent on how quickly the system can dissipate older ideas in order not to overflow the dam. In a well-designed dam, the older flows get discharged into waterways below through an outlet at the bottom of the structure designed specifically for that purpose. In an open state of development, this outlet represents the way an individual or a culture can let go of obsolete ideas in order to allow new ones in and remain in a healthy and well-adapted state. Without letting go of the old, there will be no room for the new.

In the smaller ideological fractals that are in an open state within the system, the fall of older ideas and the rise of newer, more resilient ones represent the evolution of the mind within that stage of development. The older, smaller fractals naturally dissipate through the lower outlet as the overall system reaches higher capacities within the larger fractal. In these lower fractals—or ideologies with shorter lifespans—obsolesce and dissipation are part of the evolutionary process that advances new methods of thinking conforming to the stage's *central thema.* They are incremental in nature and pose minor risk. But what happens when the flow of new water/ideas overwhelm the dissipative capacities of the original outlet created when the dam—the largest fractal—was designed? What happens when the environment in which the dam resides changes faster than what it or the development stage can handle?

When a typical dam reaches its full capacity and water begins to crest, whatever the lower outlet cannot dissipate will overflow into well-designed spillways around the top of the structure that distribute the flow to the environment. Metaphorically, this scenario represents an early warning sign that the entire stage of development itself might be reaching a state of obsolescence. It is a tipping point that begins to expose the limits of the stage's *central thema,* wherein incremental change becomes increasingly ineffective and the search for the next higher stage, the next bigger fractal, must begin.

At the individual level, if a person is in a closed state and can't dissipate bad behaviors or obsolete beliefs, a spillway can manifest as depression, disease, or anxiety. In the worst cases, the individual can become suicidal.

At a cultural level, the new stage is like the building of a new, bigger, more complex dam that will take decades, if not centuries, to build as the current dam enters a phase of decline exposing the obsolescence of the entire system. Solutions offered from *within* its central thema merely add to the problem, causing spillways to happen more frequently and with higher intensity. The 2008 financial crisis was a spillway event that should have focused leadership on the structural flaws in the system and dictated that corrective measures be taken immediately. Instead, those in charge took actions that amounted to nothing more than giving the dam and its spillways a shiny fresh coat of paint that hid the risk of failure, made matters worse, and moved the risk to higher fractals in the system.

When warning signs—such as spillways— are ignored, new forms of stress in the system begin to develop in the form of wildcards that appear from outside the paradigm that created it, and they begin to do so in increasing frequencies. They form cracks in the walls of the dam as a result of stress from persistently higher water pressure that the design engineers did not anticipate. Under increasing stress, these cracks become major fault lines that can result in catastrophic failure endangering the lives and the ecosystems of everything that exists downstream. They represent a closed cultural state at the end phase of that particular stage of development. Historically, for instance, it was the Dark Ages, the Spanish Inquisition, the abuses of the Catholic Church, and a million smaller cracks in the system that together spelled the end of the fourth stage of development. This ending allowed for the building of a new dam—a new

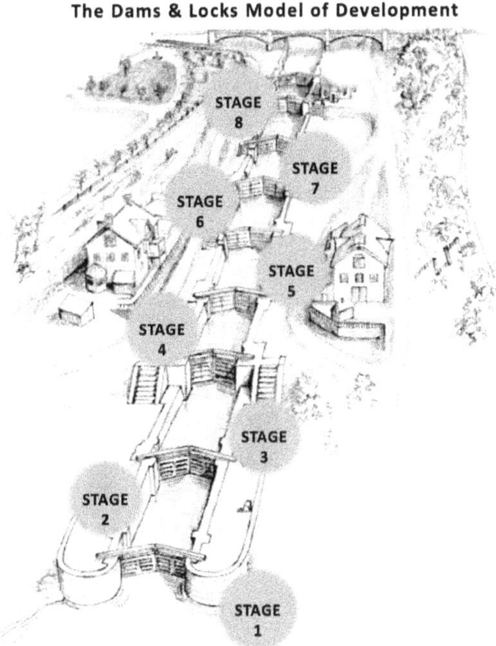

Figure 2.2. The Dams-and-Locks Model of Development. The Netherlands' method of flood control parallels the upward movement from one stage of human development to the next in the Graves–Beck model. Adopted from the Spiral-Dynamics Group and used by permission from Don E. Beck.

stage of development that ushered in the Renaissance, the Reformation, and the Scientific Revolution.

While the metaphor of a single dam might explain one stage of development, in describing the overall model that has eight stages, Beck uses an idea similar to how the Dutch deal with flood control. Because so much of the Netherlands lies below sea level, managing storm surge requires a multifaceted approach that uses a series of dams, dikes, floodgates, and pumps working together to push water levels up and back into the sea. As demonstrated in figure 2.2, all these flood-control systems get activated sequentially. Beginning with stage 1, each flood-control system accommodates the flow of the lower system before it reaches its spillway, and the sequence repeats throughout all eight stages of flood control. This approach parallels the upward movement from one stage of development to the next and is fundamental to how the Graves-Beck model functions. It is also consistent with the hierarchical complexity that defines holonic and fractal formations.

To illustrate in more detail how the shift from one stage to the next happens, or how the movement from a smaller to a bigger fractal happens, Beck uses the concept of locks that accompany dams. At the point where two bodies of water at different levels meet, a dam-and-lock system bridges the gap by creating a contained area that can raise or lower its own water level and step it up or down the waterway. In the physical world, these locks carry boats to higher or lower elevations. In the model, they represent the conduits that carry the new central thema for the higher stage of development that breaks open a new, more complex neurological network. It is the reading of spillways as the early warning signs that signals the need to build a new dam that is more resilient and can handle the complexity the lower dam couldn't. The lowering of boats in the waterway represents the downshift in individuals or cultures that occurs when they are in a closed state or out of necessity to cope with the existential challenges that emerge when the system is in decline.

Neuropsychological Subsystems as Fractals

If we were to map the Graves-Beck model on a chart, it would look like a series of positively skewed distribution waves, each increasing in size with the passage of time. Each would have its own nodal point, and each would connect to other waves at *two* nexus points: one at the lower stage and the other at the higher stage. While the curved lines might look smooth on a graph, each wave is actually far more complex than it appears.

Figure 2.3 below shows the smaller fractal representations within each wave that reflect the incremental movements along the entire stage of development. While each wave itself represents centuries of anthropological and historical data, the smaller fluctuations within it are fractal parts that represent shorter time spans. In terms of individuals, they would be neuropsychological subsystems that arise from our need to cope with the ever-increasing challenges from our environment.[12] In terms of cultures, they would be advancements in science, politics, economics, etc., that bring new ideologies about. They last for a few decades and adhere to the stage's *central thema* of *fixed rules*, but they also employ peripheral expressions as *flexible strategies* at this smaller fractal level that reflect the specific phase of where the overall stage is in its life cycle.

If we are to understand the reasons for why so much in our world is reaching different stages of entropy leading to the *Great Obsolescence,* a closer look at the fractal nature of modern economics and the life cycles of its different ideologies might be helpful. The largest fractal of modern

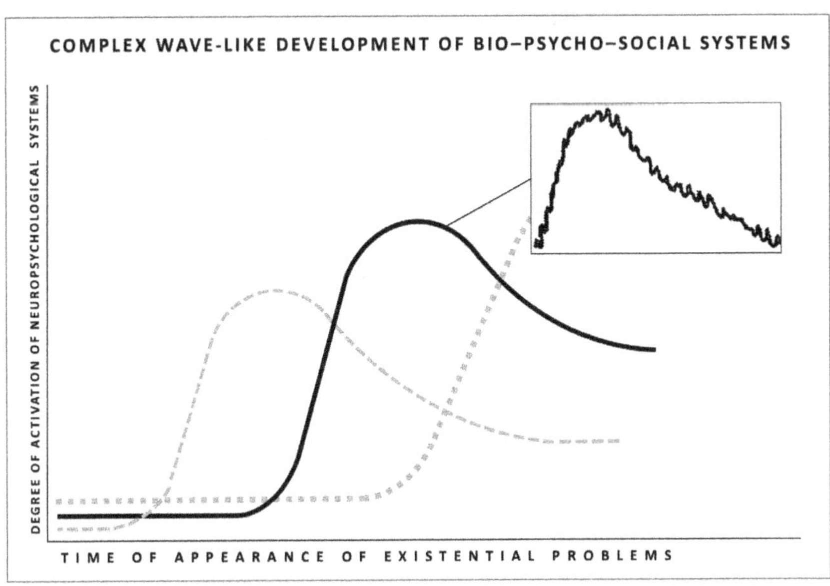

Figure 2.3. Complex Wave-Like Development of Bio-Psycho-Social Systems. This graph shows the fractal nature of ideological life cycles that develop along the contours of the entire stage's life cycle with their unique peripheral expressions that still adhere to the stage's *general thema*. The horizontal axis represents the "socio" aspect of the model as the challenges that must be solved, which appear as a result of our interaction with our environment. Adapted from the work of Clare W. Graves, *Never-Ending Quest*, 177.

economics was born from the *central thema* of the fifth stage of development. At the dawn of the Age of Enlightenment came Adam Smith, whose ideas gave birth to the concept of capitalism and modern economics. Modern economics in turn gave birth to classical economics, which became the primary ideology that defined the virtues of the Industrial Revolution. Classical economics then gave way to neoclassical economics, more commonly known as Keynesian economics. As detailed in chapter 1, Keynes gave us the first global financial architecture and introduced modern macroeconomics that included the role governments play in setting economic policy for a prosperous world away from war. It dominated Western economic policy from the 1940s to the 1970s and put in place the infrastructure on which today's globalized economy was built. Neoclassical, or Keynesian, economics then gave way to neoliberal economics, identified mostly with the ideologies of Milton Friedman and the Chicago School of Economics. A subsystem of this last ideology gave birth to monetarism, which has defined much of US economic policy from the early 1980s until now. It has exploited every corner of the neoclassical-model's infrastructure and combined it with the ethos of *only money matters* to ensure that greed and monetary gain become universal virtues. This is the synthesis that defines global economic activity today.

In applying the Graves-Beck model to economics, the synthesis produces long-wave economic cycles similar in duration and structure to the *K-wave,* named for the Russian economist, Nikolai Kondratiev (1892–1938), who was the first to bring the phenomena to the world's attention.[13] I call them "MEMEnomics Cycles." The meme terminology is adopted from Beck's Spiral Dynamics. He in turn adopted it from Richard Dawkins's original terminology for how ideas and concepts born in the mind spread and come to define values, worldviews, and behaviors. In Spiral Dynamics, each stage of development is referred to as a *value system,* or a *value-system meme,* or ^{v}*MEME* for short. The letter v superscript is how Beck delineated the common use of memes and classified them into meta memes as a way to modernize the use of the term stage. Each ^{v}*MEME* is a stage. Its ideologies—the smaller fractals that ensue from that specific stage—are referred to as *value-system attractors,* or more commonly, *stage attractors.* The field of economics is one *stage attractor,* being a fractal that moves in small waves along the contours of the big wave that defines a specific stage of development. Unlike K-waves or cycles that are mostly determined by technological changes, MEMEnomics cycles are determined by cultural shifts based on the *central thema* of each stage. This theoretical framework examines the long-term effects of economic policy on culture as seen through the whole-systems prism of the Graves-Beck model. In my research, I have mapped a total of four of these cycles in the modern US economy since the end of the Civil War. They are fractal ideologies that are positioned close to the nodal point of the fifth overall stage of development; but, like their greater holonic structure, their own life cycles go through the stages of development as well. The names of these cycles could be considered the *fixed rule* in the smaller ideological fractal.

The graph below (fig. 2.4) depicts these four cycles of modern economic evolution. The virtues of the first—the *fiefdoms-of-power* cycle—were determined mostly by the values of the third stage, when a few egocentric men with vast resources shaped the economy of the time. The second cycle—that of *patriotic prosperity*—was determined by the fourth stage of development, one that believed in the power of the institution

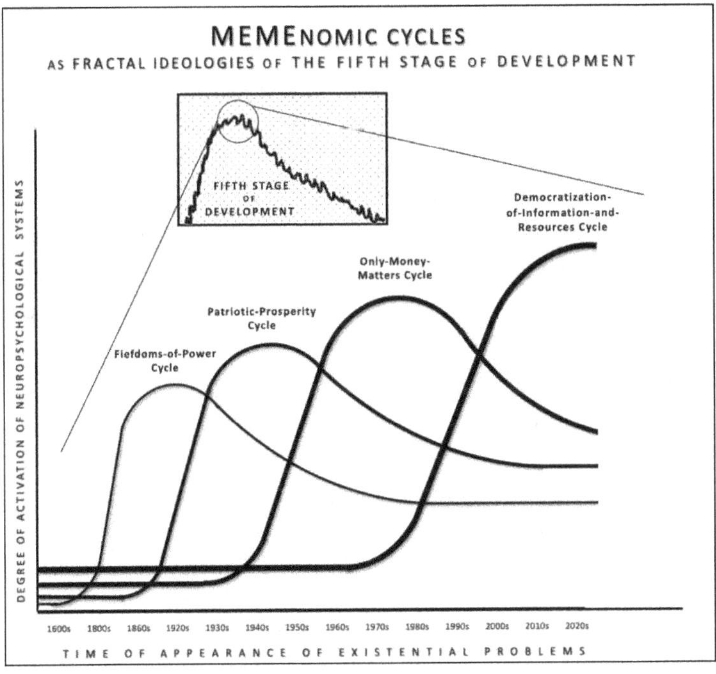

Figure 2.4. MEMEnomic Cycles as Economic Fractals of the Fifth Stage of Development. The ideologies of these cycles have defined the evolution of economic systems in the United States from the end of the Civil War to the present. The inset showing the wave-like nature of the cycles depicts their appearance in the larger, fifth-stage fractal. Adapted from Said E. Dawlabani, *MEMEnomics*, 173.

and the government's ability to shape equitable economic policies. The third cycle—*only money matters*—was determined by the fifth stage, which replaced the fourth-stage ethos of *big brother knows best* with the ethos that the *invisible hand of the market knows best.* The fourth cycle—*democratization of information and resources*—was born with the dawn of the Internet and represents the values of the sixth stage, one that seeks the ubiquitous access to all forms of data in its most transparent form and the equal distribution of economic and financial resources as its primary objective.

The Ideological Life Cycle of Monetarism

The 2008 financial crisis that brought the world to the brink of economic collapse should have signaled the end of the third MEMEnomic cycle defined by Friedman's common refrain of *only money matters.* The end phase of this ideology was a tipping point that pushed the entire economic system beyond its nodal phase where known corrective steps become increasingly less effective. This was a systemic failure that led the system to move into an arrested state from which its movement accelerates to a closed state. In general, right before a system reaches the point of collapse, it reaches its nexus point in a life cycle in which the dying fractal automatically yields to a new, higher-order one as part of the normal evolutionary process. If the architects of the 2008 bailout had been in an open state, they would have enacted into law certain dissipative measures that would have wound down many of the fringe toxic practices within the system that led to the crisis. Such action also would have signaled our ascendence into the fourth cycle—*democratization of information and resources*—an economy defined by the disruptive nature of the digital age. This is a stage of economic evolution that seeks to disrupt everything the dying system considered proprietary and secretive and distributes that knowledge through information networks. It thrives on deconstructing the old system's centralized, revenue-generating model by digitizing it and making it available to the masses as a way to ensure a more equitable economy.

These virtues are in harmony with the sixth stage's *general thema* of spreading Earth's resources and opportunities equally. But the bailout of insolvent institutions by politicians who fully believed in the apocalyptic narrative of those who created the problem demonstrated how deep and systemic the arrested/closed state of the system was. Risky banking activities have gone undetected for so long due to the ethos of *free market knows best* becoming a systemic, hidden bias in government over several decades.

The bailout not only brought the dying system into the *decline* and *entropy* phases of its life cycle, it also helped it monetize the entire emerging system and fundamentally changed its trajectory. The democratization of economic models representing the sixth stage of development was seriously shoved backward and at exponential speed. It transformed startups like Facebook and Google into Meta and Alphabet, two of the largest corporations in history that became that large in the shortest period of time in history. Like many corporations in the digital economy now, they both answer to the same bankers responsible for the financial crisis and still believe in Friedman's ethos of *only money matters.*

The ideology that simplified the complexity of global economic activity to mere financial representation proved to be the greatest example of reductive thinking since the dawn of the Enlightenment. It opened the floodgates to greed and the debauchery of currency and, in the process, brought its ethos to every part of the world. It redefined the historic role that money had played as a store of value and a representation of human productivity in terms that favor bankers and stockholders. But, from a complex-systems perspective, the worst thing monetarism did, metaphorically, was to reverse the relationship between the planets and the sun in the Newtonian gearset model. That is, monetarism sought to make itself the master cylinder—the sun—the source of input around which the planets—the different economic sectors—operate. This is a classic case of the tail wagging the dog that has defined many of the operational fallacies adopted by the world's leading economies. It was just a matter of time until the system began to break down, showing the dangers that come when all economic activity is expressed primarily through the narrow function of finance.

In my 2013 book, *MEMEnomics: The Next-Generation Economic System,* I spent an entire chapter chronicling the role Federal Reserve Chairman Alan Greenspan played in leading the world to the edge of financial collapse. The chapter chronicles the life cycle of monetarism and how ideas are born and develop into larger ideologies that become virtues that define cultural expression. It also shows how these virtues eventually fall out of favor and become replaced by more resilient ones that meet the needs of an ever-evolving culture. Greenspan, the poster child for the neoliberal, monetarist ideology, implemented Friedman's *only money matters* ethos at the highest levels that, over time, led to the creation of a global economy based on finance.

That chapter in my book was entitled, "The Last Son of the Enlightenment." It was intended to show what happens when we don't scrutinize the peripheral expression—the *flexible strategies*—of values that are driven by the objective scientific method, mathematical modeling, and the removal of regulatory structures, all of which together have the power to seduce our modern world. The Enlightened are always on a quest to tame the universe through scientific discovery, research and development, and an endless array of measurement. As noble as these pursuits are, by their very nature they are reductive. They leave out the immeasurable and that which is deemed irrelevant in their worldview, and in doing so they falsely paint a picture of optimism and safety. The Enlightened economist at the nodal phase of the fifth stage of development is defined by cold empirical facts and figures. He express himself distantly and in absolute specificity. She believes her models are unassailable. Such people are the true believers in the ethos of *only money matters.* Their god is Milton Friedman, and they offer their complex models and algorithms as sacrifice to please him and his fallacy without shame or deviation. They rarely acknowledge the fact that the things they leave out of their reductive worldview don't just disappear. Sooner or later, they reappear as fate, which in Jungian terms represents the manifestation of the shadow of all that has not been consciously processed. But to the Enlightened economist, fate is nothing more than a new opportunity to create a new reductive model and call it a study in evolutionary economics.

> *One of Milton Friedman's most cited quotes is this: If you put the government in charge of the Sahara Desert, in five years you will run out of sand. Here we are 30 years later and we are running out of sand, but it's not the government that's doing it. It's the insatiable appetite of the free market.*
>
> —Brian Nitz[14]

At the heart of neoliberal economic thought is the belief that the world could be a much better place if we just throw enough money at it through development programs and economic growth. Monetarism has been this belief's largest and most dangerous peripheral expression of values. Today, it remains the leading edge of economic expression that depicts one of the last stages of the psychosocial development of the *First sapiens.* In the rest of the book, *MEMEnomics,* I tracked the dangerous road we have been put on by the ideology of free markets, low interest rates, and the debauchery of currency. While we haven't seen *complete* economic collapse after the 2008 financial crisis and its subsequent bailout, the global financial architecture that Dr. Greenspan helped put in place has been on life support ever since. In the life cycle of a complex system that remains a fractal expression of the Age of Enlightenment, this is a position of extreme vulnerability in which the appearance of wildcards takes on a greater magnitude and can bring the entire system even closer to the collapsing point. It is the spillways on the dam that trigger the early warning signs of system failure and that signal that many more spillways of increasing intensity and frequency will take place if structural issues are not addressed. Since 2008, the spillways have given us the COVID-19 pandemic and the economic fallout from the war in Ukraine. These are the two largest examples of dangerous wildcards that have appeared and have had systemic repercussions. The cascades from these two events continue to place pressure on a global economy born from the ideology of monetarism that seems to be in its final state of decay.

Phases of a Developmental Life Cycle

The life cycle of monetarism is similar in structure to economic life cycles that preceded it. It is a fractal representation of stage development as well. Each cycle at each fractal level has distinct phases that define its life; only the content, the size, and the time span are different. What is important in determining if a stage or an ideology is in harmony with its environment is its ability to change and adapt. Knowing whether it is in an open, an arrested, or a closed state is a critical task that falls on those who understand the system well but are no longer tied to it through employment or any other ways that would bias their opinions. Whistleblowers who sound the alarm about fraud and/or unfair or unsafe practices in business or in government make for the ideal candidate. Often individuals who are in an open psychosocial state naturally transcend a stage or its fractal ideology, which enables them to view the different phases of a cycle from an objective perspective. The higher the holonic structure, the longer the life cycle and the slower the movement along its contours.

The graph below (fig. 2.5) shows the phases of a life cycle in a complex system as I have adopted it from both the work of Graves and Beck and my own research. The descriptors for every phase on the graph are representative of the actual movement of the monetarist ideology over the last four decades and of actual events as seen through the evolutionary lens of a whole-systems perspective. Following the *fixed rules* and *flexible strategies* of holonic structures, an entire stage of development at the macro level such as the Enlightenment can also be mapped on this life-cycle model.

The Inquiry and Identification Phase

This phase represents the incubation period of ideas when the initial elements of the new cycle begin to appear in the minds of futurists and oracles. Much of it remains hidden from view, just as a dormant seed does under the winter snow. It is nourished by the inevitable forward march of progress and the evolutionary impulse. It carries within it some of the DNA

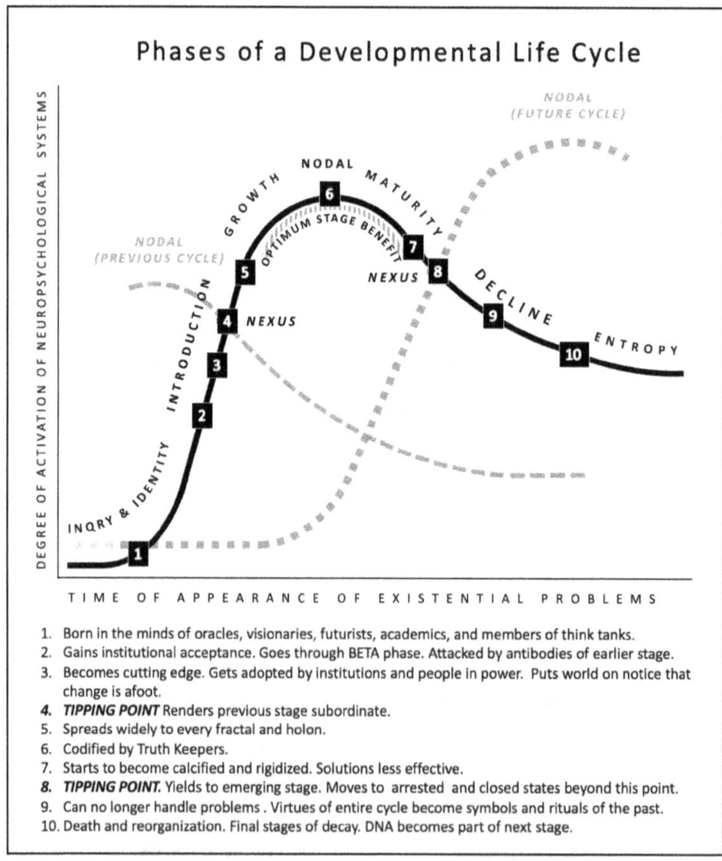

Figure 2.5. Phases of a Developmental Life Cycle. This graph depicts the different phases of a developmental stage life cycle—from *inquiry and identification* to *entropy*—that apply to all fractal levels, including ideologies within the stage. Based on the work of Graves, Beck, and Dawlabani. Said E. Dawlabani, *MEMEnomics*, 77.

of past ideologies, but it must evolve to a new and more advanced form of expression in order to be the fittest of all competing ideas. Evolution at this stage mirrors Darwin's concept of natural selection in which ideas fight for survival to have a chance at defining the next ideology. The longer the current ideology remains within the bounds of the *growth* and *maturity* phases, the longer the new ideology remains in the dormant *inquiry* phase. It continues to develop antibodies that will be needed to fight off attacks from the current system when that system starts to decline. Historically, the *inquiry* phase has consisted of a set of embryonic ideas that gestate for years or even decades in the minds of visionaries before becoming the shared values of the mainstream. Those who pioneer its guiding principles and influence its progress represent its core intelligence and are known as its inner collective. This is the phase in which Adam Smith cultivated his thinking on the virtues of capitalism before they jelled into *The Theory of Moral Sentiments* and *The Wealth of Nations.* This is when John Maynard Keynes added to his thinking over the years before it became the model that rebuilt the world economies after World War II and defined neoclassical economics the way we know it today. It also describes the period of time that Milton Friedman spent at the Chicago School of Economics refining different aspects of the monetarist ideology while waiting for the Keynesian economic cycle to enter its *decline* phase.

The Introduction Phase

The chapter on Dr. Greenspan in my book *MEMEnomics* offers an in-depth analysis of Federal-Reserve policies under his leadership and points to the different phases the current long-wave system has gone through. While all systems have their own unique life cycles, neoliberal economics is a complex system of higher order that requires a higher level of diligence and a greater degree of scrutiny in order to remain adaptive. At the height of his career, Dr. Greenspan's thinking was considered the leading edge in shaping the future of global banking. His thoughts on how to bring finance out of its archaic past were revolutionary and reshaped the fundamental purpose of central banking around the world. Since many of the world's leading economies follow in the footsteps of US economic policy, no one on the world stage challenged the wisdom of what Dr. Greenspan was about to create: a world economy based on finance. This was a new ideology put in place at the highest levels that quickly began to take on the characteristics of a complex system.

The *introduction* phase of an ideology is also what's known in the digital economy as the beta phase, a time when the system gets vetted by early adopters. During this phase, the culmination of knowledge from the *inquiry-and-identification* phase begins to find harmony with other futuristic thinkers in politics, technology, science, and culture. These are the power-brokers who represent the outer collective capable of moving these embryonic ideas beyond their experimental phase and into much larger fractals. The outer collective is made up of key progressive people in power who hold the key to making change happen. They join hands with the inner collective to move the system forward and empower it as the catalyst for systemic change. This is when humanity is given notice that major change is afoot. In the early phases of the monetarist cycle, all that was visible were the success stories that enticed more nations to join in this new and unproven direction. The *introduction* phase is also when the new system is able to absorb and dissipate anything that falls outside the parameters of success, which in this case made Dr. Greenspan and Milton Freidman the stars of a new economic reality.

The Growth Phase

Once the new cycle expands beyond early adopters and becomes the cutting edge of socioeconomic expression, it passes the nexus point of the prior system where power begins to shift to the new system and the virtues of the old system become subordinate to the new. This is where thought leaders who brought the new system into being become heroes and icons of progress. After a decade of stubbornly high inflation and interest rates under his predecessor, Paul Volker, Dr. Greenspan in his early years as the head of the Federal Reserve was being credited for bringing inflation under control and, in doing so, was praised as the hero who saved America and the world's ailing capitalist system. At this phase, just as is true of every ideological cycle due to its pioneering nature, monetarism showed only its positive attributes. The undesirable results it produced at this phase had little impact on its growth, given its young age and its ability to absorb unwanted outcomes as it continued to expand. This *growth* phase is also when a system gets adopted by others, as in this case monetarism did by the European Union that styled its central bank policies in harmony with the Fed's and staffed its top positions with leaders who believed in similar virtues. Soon thereafter, other central banks seeking the greater promise of economic prosperity shifted their monetary policies to accommodate the change from industrial and service economies to ones based on finance.

In spite of all the innovations that were introduced under Dr. Greenspan's watch, the basic facts about the duties of a central bank never changed. While it is responsible for addressing numerous macroeconomic issues, it has only the two main tools mentioned earlier at its disposal: how to exercise prudent control over an economy's money supply and how to determine the interest rates it charges in that economy. This has always been the historic and, by necessity, the boring role of central banking. These two tools provide the lifeline to the complex system called the economy. Due to their fundamental nature, they must remain on the periphery of the complex system regulating them and not become a part of its collective behavior. But since the States moved away from an industrial economy and embraced the virtues of monetarism, the financial sector has done everything in its power to alter this historic reality, and Dr. Greenspan was the facilitator-in-chief of this unorthodox movement.

In its *growth* phase, the monetary system shifted away from funding all sectors of a traditional economy that benefit most stakeholders and began to focus on the financial sector as the driver of prosperity. It created an endless product line of debt-and-equity instruments with sophisticated names such as Collateralized Debt Obligation, Credit Default Swaps, Mortgage-Backed Securities, and an entire alphabet soup of financial investments that temporarily increased the value of everyone's assets and legitimatized financial capitalism. In a little over a decade, these practices became ubiquitous as the world partook in investing and trading in them, which helped the system reach its nodal point, a critical apex in the life cycle where its ethos becomes codified throughout the economy as the "only ideology" that matters to a capitalist system. The codification is spread by those known in the cycle as *truth keepers*, financial leaders who have tested the system and benefitted from it repeatedly. They become absolutists in their beliefs as they reinforce the "truth" about the benefits of the ideology of the cycle and dismiss all other economic cycles as "untruths" or fallacies.

The Maturity Phase

In this phase, problems become more visible but remain manageable; skepticism disappears and the system's values dominate cultural expression. This is also the phase—as in monetary economics—in which the ideology's practices become aristocratic in nature. As its focus shifts away from long-term viability to short-term stability and profit maximization, it exploits innovation and financial products that deliver high returns while increasingly ignoring the potential long-term structural threats to the entire system.

In order to keep a complex system viable, the leaders in charge must do everything in their power to extend its *growth* and *maturity* phases. These phases are when the system serves the greatest good. They are also the phases in which the system's capacity to absorb toxicity begins to diminish due to the maturity of its practices and the saturation of the values it represents. Its feedback loops become increasingly smaller and louder, the early warning system from the spillways gets increasingly ignored, and the tools to keep the ideology viable become less effective.

For example, consider the period of time that preceded the 2008 financial crisis: Between 2003 and 2006, mortgage brokers and investment bankers created an array of questionable financial products in order to maximize their profit margins, remaining complacent about these products despite the systemic risk they presented to the entire financial system. The most prominent of these financial schemes were the subprime mortgage loans and the NINA (no-income-no-asset verification) loans that allowed people who would not have qualified for traditional mortgages to borrow money to buy homes. To add to the risk, investment bankers packaged these low-grade loans with investment-grade financial products and sold them as high-grade securities, which muted the appearance of risk in the short term. These actions represented the disappearance of skepticism from the system, allowing further complacency to set in. The fees both mortgage brokers and investment bankers collected on the sale of these products were multiple times higher than the ones collected from the sale of traditional products.

Initially, these problems were manageable, and the risks were absorbed as capital markets around the world, fearing the loss of opportunity on high-return investments, bought them as securities—proving the resilience that comes with being in the *maturity* phase of the cycle. But within a few short years, these same financial products contributed to major financial insolvencies and became the leading cause of the 2008 financial crisis as the system couldn't handle additional risk and moved past its *maturity* phase.

The Decline Phase

Ignoring problems that move the system past its *maturity* phase does not make them go away. They grow into toxic structures that drive the system closer to a tipping point where intervention becomes less effective as the dynamics of the system itself take over and accelerate its movement toward the *decline* and *entropy* phases. In an open system, moving past the *maturity* phase in a cycle represents the natural evolutionary process that brings us to the nexus point at which the values of the emerging system begin to supersede those of the current one. The critical period between maturity and decline is the last one in which those in charge of the system have a chance to keep it viable. Introducing larger, dissipative measures that prevent it from falling into complete chaos becomes more crucial. These dissipative measures are characteristic of the evolutionary patterns in both natural systems and most man-made open systems. They are, so to speak, the outlets at the bottom of the dam that get rid of old ideas to make room for the new that keep the system in a stable state. They exemplify the way in which a system naturally rids itself of entropy and dissipates it to its environment. This function allows the system to remain healthy and helps it evolve into a more complex state able to absorb new input that will extend its life and keep its practices innovative.

One dissipative element in a US-economic system emerged after the 1980s failure of the savings and loans industry before the banking sector was fully deregulated. The government at the time placed insolvent institutions under its receivership and disposed of their assets in ways it deemed equitable through agencies such as the Resolution Trust Corporation (RTC), established in 1989. Thus, the government, in essence, acted as the dissipative agent that removed toxicity from the system and transformed it into benefits for the environment outside it. It did so by managing the failed real-estate holdings of over seven hundred lending institutions and distributing these holdings to minority-owned businesses, first-time home buyers, and a number of other stakeholders to which the savings-and-loan industry would not normally cater.[15] This exemplifies the role that dissipative structures play in keeping systems healthy and in a stable state within the bounds of the *central thema* that created it. In natural systems, dissipation occurs automatically, unlike in man-made systems that, without conscious intervention, can easily fall into arrested and closed states and allow toxicity to build to the point of collapse.

Neoliberal economists asserted that there was no need for government agencies like the RTC to ensure the viability of a system and that the forces of a free market play the natural role of dissipative structures. They also asserted that market competition promoting the survival of the fittest is as natural as Darwin's idea of the transmutation of species that allows the life of a system to evolve into new forms. But the disappearance of regulation constitutes the disappearance of checks and balances that guard the health of any given system. Such regulation represents the important operation of the locks at the bottom outlet of the dam. With monetarism, the guarding of that outlet was handed to the private sector, more specifically, to the bankers. The fox was now guarding the hen house. The early warning signs that dissipative structures provide had been silenced. The focus on long-term threats diminished as the system gave birth to other riskier financial instruments that escaped the scrutiny of a weakened regulatory structure and industry watchdogs.

The derivatives market was the prime example of this phenomenon that hastened the movement of the system into the *decline* phase. Derivatives were nothing more than contracts made against certain economic assumptions, but they were valued in the trillions of dollars. Dr. Greenspan and a cast of other prominent economists, including Lawrence Summers, President Clinton's treasury secretary, were masterful in hiding the risk inherent in such dangerous betting games every time they testified in front of Congress. By the early 2000s, the false sense of security they engendered moved the system into an arrested state, unable to dissipate any entropy. Their cleverness in hiding risk allowed the value of the derivatives market to eclipse that of the world's annual productive output by several fold, bringing the possibility of catastrophic risk closer to reality.[16] This form of financialization became known as the "casino economy," and the voices of critics in the *inquiry* phase of the next system began to turn the tide against the current one.

In the *decline* phase, cracks in the system become quite visible to a wider segment of society, and the investment world begins to question the fundamental assumptions underlying the entire ideology. Spillway events happen more frequently and with increasing intensity, but these early warnings are never heeded. The dam itself begins to show signs of distress that everyone can see, and new voices begin to warn of the impending disaster. Concerns about the continued viability of the system become wider, and attention turns to identifying what caused the cracks and who were behind them. But instead of looking to shift strategy, these new voices look for someone to blame. The worse the cracks become, the louder the voices of recrimination until they begin to cause panic in the markets, leading to early signs of economic downturn.

When a closed-state system reaches the *decline* phase, its own toxic behavior takes over, and, more likely than not, it will go through entropy and final collapse. The larger the interventions at this phase, the more they contribute to the toxicity that hastens the system's demise. The subprime loan crisis that started in 2006 announced our entry into this phase, when cracks began to manifest in the failure of investment banks followed by insolvencies of smaller commercial banks that threatened the collapse of the entire financial system. The writing was on the wall, and systemic failure was inevitable as the house of cards that had been built on the fallacy of monetarism began to fall. The heroes who had saved America in the *introduction* phase of this brave experiment just a few decades earlier were now the ones responsible for its unmitigated collapse.

In October 2008, Dr. Greenspan was called upon to testify in front of Congress about the causes of the financial crisis. The part of his testimony most relevant to how ideological life cycles rise and fall is the following exchange he had with California Congressman Henry Waxman:

> Congressman Waxman: Do you accept any responsibility for the impending economic disaster?
>
> Dr. Greenspan: Those of us who have looked to the self-interest of lending institutions to protect shareholder's equity—myself especially—are in a state of shocked disbelief.
>
> Congressman Waxman: Could you please elaborate further.
>
> Dr. Greenspan: I have found a flaw. I don't know how significant or permanent it is. But I have been very distressed by that fact.
>
> Congressman Waxman: In other words, you found that your view of the world, your ideology, was not right, it was not working, correct?
>
> Dr. Greenspan: Absolutely, precisely. You know, that's precisely the reason I was shocked, because I have been going for forty years or more with very considerable evidence that it was working exceptionally well.[17]

Those few sentences made under oath speak volumes to the nature of monetarism and to neoliberal economics in general. The self-interest of banks and the financial wellbeing of their shareholders were the exclusive focus of policy makers with little regard to the systemic damage their practices caused. The "considerable evidence"—or readily evident prosperity—of which Dr. Greenspan spoke is indicative of the very nature of the manipulative minds that have driven Enlightened values: the dualistic ontology that excludes everything that falls outside its worldview. To confirm that an overlooked, ideological flaw brought the world to the edge of economic collapse was equivalent to confirming that the largest complex system dominating the world for the last half century has been a highly dangerous, closed ideology at best.

When viewed from the ideological life-cycle perspective, the fall of 2008 represented a crucial opportunity for governments around the world to introduce dissipative measures like those the RTC introduced in the 1990s. Such action would have allowed for transparency and for real market forces to determine the real value of every segment of a global economy that had previously been driven by the ethos of *only money matters*. It would likely have exposed the fallacy of that dangerous ideology and led to a substantial loss in the valuation of global assets of all types and sizes, hastening that economic system's demise and ushering in a new, more inclusive one. But instead, in the bailouts our government gave to banks, it did the opposite. It enabled them to purchase a substantial number of distressed residential properties throughout the country. By 2022, these investments acted like local monopolies in setting rents and home prices.[18] Housing being the largest single monthly expense of an average family, the government's failure to act as dissipative agent contributed further to systemic economic inequality. Moreover, in addition to the housing bubble we're in today, the bailout has contributed to the formation of many other bubbles in different segments of the economy that are moving the whole system into its *entropy* phase.

What gave neoliberal economics its impetus was the idea that government is the enemy of business, an idea that penetrated the American psyche and became a meta-meme shortly after Ronald Reagan uttered it in his 1981 inaugural address. Like Friedman and Greenspan, Reagan was one of the heroes. He was the patron saint who saved America in 1981; and, by 2008, the ideology he espoused had achieved its goal of having a greatly diminished regulatory system in place. As a result, however, our diminished government was unable to introduce any of the structural measures needed to bring sanity back into economic policy. All it did was listen to those who had created the problem warning of apocalypse should the system be allowed to reach a natural state of entropy and collapse. By then, monetarism had become global, and it is true that an economic collapse would have triggered a global depression and possibly contributed to geopolitical instability. But, for a government to grant the wishes of a banking system addicted to toxic practices without requiring substantive reforms amounted to the very definition of incompetence and only moved the risk to a higher fractal. Instead of doing the things required for effective systems management, by bailing out highly leveraged banks and failed insurance companies, the Federal Reserve exchanged the banks' toxic assets at highly inflated prices for fresh cash. This historic failure enabled banks to return to their activities with a higher degree of impunity, not just in the housing sector but in every segment of the economy, including the digital economy. And while the Enlightened economist points to new regulations that were introduced in the aftermath of the crisis in order to quiet the critics of the system, an outside observer only sees how the banking industry has lobbied the US Congress to postpone the implementation of these new regulations in perpetuity.[19] As this toxicity moves the system past its nexus point and into its *decline* phase, it becomes less and less predictable.

The Entropy Phase. Toxicity became exponential in the post-bailout years as the monetary system moved to the final phase of *entropy* while increasingly contributing to income inequality and social disparity as an automatic function of its state of decay. Before the onset of the pandemic and the start of the war in Ukraine, the global economy seemed to have recovered from the 2008 crash. But that recovery has been mostly attributed to an extension of central banking policies that have continued doing what they must do to prevent collapse. The tools that keep monetary policy viable have been exhausted, and all central bankers have done is to keep the system on life support, hoping by some miracle that prudence will return on its own. During the *entropy* phase, Enlightenment's last son was replaced by several caregivers who claimed to be experts on rescuing economies teetering on the edge. Dr. Greenspan's first replacement was Ben Bernanke, who was the opposite of what a new system needed. Bernanke was considered a god sent by the demigods of global finance;

he built his entire career on the philosophy of liberating money from its archaic past in favor of an unproven ideology that replaced human productivity with financial innovation. The shadow of Milton Friedman had never loomed so large as Bernanke unabashedly proclaimed his love and loyalty to the man and his superior thinking among economic scholars.[20] Other successors since have only presided over the end phase of Friedman's creation that hasn't yet stopped. In this last phase, there's always an untamable beast who runs the system. He prints money out of thin air and gives it clever names that help him avoid scrutiny. He creates innovations that only hasten the system's demise. He's the Frankenstein of the system with whom everyone has to dance until the music stops or the lights go on.

The easiest way to understand the nature of monetary policy and the severity of the condition our global financial system is in is found in the philosophy of William McChesney Martin, Jr. (1906–1998), the longest-serving Federal-Reserve chairman in its history. Martin represented the pre-neoliberal prudence that a central banker should always exercise, which he summarized as follows: "The job of the Federal Reserve is to know when to remove the punch bowl at the party."[21] In other words, if the punch bowl—a metaphor for cheap and unrestrained money supply—isn't removed at the right time, the entire economy begins to behave in an irrational, drunken way.

Monetarism flipped that historic reality upside down. Dr. Greenspan, instead of removing the punch bowl, decided to keep it in perpetuity and see what happened. Bernanke, instead of mitigating the damage caused by systemic drunkenness, decided to bring the entire liquor store to the party. His successors since have struggled to manage the drunken aftermath, while needing everything in the liquor store to avoid collapse brought about by the high costs of the bailouts of the 2008 financial crisis and the 2020 pandemic.

Monetarism and the global economy that neoliberal thought created are today the two, intertwined systems that form the largest human-made complex system of the twentieth century. But, due to our inability to manage complexity the way it should be managed, the system has become a logical fallacy that ignores the greater complexity in which it is nested. It has become a corrosive catalyst that has destroyed whatever remains of modern economic theory, finance, and the historic virtues of money. It is a fractal that has gone rogue and a deep delusion that ignores human and cultural complexities in favor of the trade and prosperity that enrich only the few while contributing to social and environmental degradation. Now in its final phase, it has been clinically dead for over two decades, and no one has yet had the courage to pull the plug.

Chronicling our journey through the life cycle of monetarism and its different phases may provide for a better understanding of how precarious the global economy is today. We have become one, globally interconnected economy built on the faulty and dangerous architecture that has replaced human productive output with money. The system has passed its tipping point by a few decades, and the call for more resilient design is too late to save it. Its encompassing size might provide an explanation for why so many smaller nested systems—the various-sized fractals—are reaching an inflection point all at the same time, thus contributing to the *Great Obsolescence.*

Nevertheless, should that happen, it will not mean the end of our human journey. Rather, it will signify that the *First sapiens,* who has evolved through the Holocene era in the first six stages of development that are driven by subsistence needs, has exhausted every possible tool available to him. These are the same tools that have sought to tame nature and reduce its complexity to serve our insatiable human needs, leading to the ecological crisis we face today. All this has taken place within the greater complex system in which all stages of development are but a fractal. A collapse of these lower systems will signify the failure of the *First sapiens* and his inability to acknowledge the interdependent nature of life on our planet. It will also signify the dawn of the *Second sapiens,* who has been with us for decades but has been ignored, scorned, and dismissed.

Three
Turtle Bay and the Battleground for the Future

The new paradigm may be called a holistic world view, seeing the world as an integrated whole rather than a dissociated collection of parts. It may also be called an ecological view, if the term "ecological" is used in a much broader and deeper sense than usual.... Deep ecological awareness recognizes the fundamental interdependence of all phenomena and the fact that, as individuals and societies, we are all embedded in, and ultimately dependent on, the cyclical process of nature.

—Fritjof Capra
The Systems View of Life

On that morning of February 22, 2022, as the secretary general of the United Nations withdrew his wandering gaze from the boroughs of New York, his focus returned to the day's meeting. The existential issues that ailed the human condition on that morning—the impending war, the ongoing pandemic, the threat of inflation, and a possible global recession—all paled in comparison to what was on the agenda for discussion. Seated around the large conference table, his staff sifted frantically through countless tables and graphs contained in the Sixth Assessment Report of the Intergovernmental Panel on Climate Change (the IPCC) as they searched for evidence of progress in addressing the monumental issue of planetary degradation. As the secretary general expected, the news was grim. There would be nothing positive he could report to the world in the form of a 280-character Tweet later that day.

The IPCC is a UN agency created in the 1980s for the sole purpose of advancing knowledge on human-induced climate change. It is governed by its 195 member states who pick a panel of scientists from every technical area in order to provide the most comprehensive information about the state of our planet. Each panel serves for the duration of an assessment cycle, which is usually six to seven years. Its authority is recognized by the global scientific community and world governments alike. The assessment reports it produces have been described as the most extensive peer-reviewed process in the history of the scientific community.[1]

The research covered in these reports since they were first generated in 1990 has shown a steadily increasing certainty that human activity is affecting the climate. This is what the scientific community has dubbed as "Anthropogenic" climate change and what has given this new era the name "Anthropocene." Coined in the year 2000 by chemist Paul Crutze, the term comes from the Greek root word for human, *anthropos*, and refers to the current human age, a new geologic epoch in which the future of life on the planet is entirely dependent on our actions.

The collective power of these scientists gives us a glimpse of what the *Second sapiens* is capable of doing in uncovering issues of this great magnitude. The failure to heed their warnings also gives us a glimpse of the power the *First sapiens* still holds to stop progress if solutions call for too much disruption in his understanding of reality. Since 1990, the more certain the IPCC reports have been about our role in climate change, the more evasive we have become in taking full responsibility, which today explains the critical state of mind of the UN secretary general and millions of frustrated scientists and climate advocates.

The Modern Mind and Seventy Years of Acceleration

Before we entered the Anthropocene epoch, the Holocene era that spanned 11,600 years was known as a paradise on Earth described as the sweet spot for all life. It included everything the *First sapiens* has created as he moved through the different stages of development characterized by the invention of written and spoken language, the emergence of different dynasties and civilizations, the occurrence of the industrial and technological revolutions, the profound transition toward urban living that defines the physical environments in which we live today, and the digital revolution that has connected us all to one another. All these major changes happened in a place of bliss in which we stayed within the boundaries of the Earth's different ecological systems that make life on the planet possible.

Then came the post-World War II mandates that sought to develop the world and modernize its virtues through the ethos of *peace through commerce*. At the same time we decided to end all wars against one another, we inadvertently came together to start a slow but deadly war against Mother Nature's key ecosystems. As more and more countries chose this path, we began to test the limits of this heaven on Earth. In the 1960s and '70s, the world started adopting the American lifestyle and everything that came with it. From the development of a modern infrastructure and transportation systems, to animal-based, high-protein diets, emerging economies as well as the industrialized world adopted this new and insatiable appetite for unbridled consumption. With these changes, the acceleration to test the limits of the Earth's ecosystems went into high gear. The next change was the explosion in world population and having the newly industrialized countries such as China, India, and Brazil become a formidable force in the global economy. In the span of a mere two decades, the size of the worldwide consumer class practically doubled, pushing the boundaries of all Earth systems closer to a highly dangerous tipping point, the return from which will become exponentially harder.

The idea of tipping points in the Earth's systems was first articulated in the late eighteenth century. The most coherent of these arguments, which remains valid to this day, was published in 1798 and entitled *An Essay on the Principle of Population*. In it, the author Thomas Malthus (1766–1834), an English economist and political scholar, theorized that population growth is potentially an exponential phenomenon, while the growth of the food supply and other resources is finite. This reality, he claimed, will eventually reduce living standards to the point of causing famine and war resulting in poverty and depopulation.[2] His proposition, along with his analysis of its social and economic impacts, came to be known as the Malthusian theory, and the event in which population outpaces agricultural production and resources became known as the Malthusian catastrophe. Such an event, he argued, will come as a result of the absence of processes governing unchecked growth, and it will happen quickly with severe and unpredictable results.[3]

To the modern, scientific mind, the Malthusian catastrophe was nothing more than a technological challenge to overcome. Since the publication of the book, and up until the time before World War II, innovations in technology and modern farming techniques expanded our agricultural output and brought forth innovative ways to support higher levels of population. Critics of the Malthusian catastrophe were proven right, and worries about growth—whether in population or in economic activity, along with factors that affect the Earth's systems—were sidelined in favor of technological innovation. After the end of the war, the era of accelerated growth is what led us to the *Great Obsolescence* and into the new, Anthropocene epoch. While Malthus's definition of finite resources has been greatly expanded, his assumption about the absence of governing processes remains salient, as the lack of such processes limiting growth have become the primary cause of the catastrophic climate events we are experiencing today.

Scientists still can't agree on when we entered the Anthropocene epoch. Some believe it started with the dawn of the Industrial Age. Others, such as anthropologist Yuval Noah Harari, believe it started 70,000 years ago and began to accelerate with the emergence of the Abrahamic religions that subjected all life to the dominion of *Homo sapiens.*[4] Others remain in denial about its existence and relegate all the ecological and atmospheric changes to Mother Nature's powers that remain beyond human comprehension. Shifts of epochal proportions don't happen overnight, and while there is still disagreement on when we entered this new epoch, scientific research that is in harmony with the ecological virtues of the *Second sapiens* leaves no doubt as to when human activity became a major force in shaping the future of our planet. Having been sidelined by the reductionist minds, this is the science that is now becoming necessary. It tracks much of what has been externalized by the ambitious post-war development and economic goals and brings it back into the fold as part of a complex system of higher order. The Anthropogenic sciences—the ones that study the changes in Earth's systems from oceanography to climatology and biogeography—represent that highly collaborative, higher-order system of sciences. They study the effects of human activity on a number of Earth-system parameters including population, water usage, food production, use of natural resources, transportation, technology, greenhouses gases, surface temperature, and economic activity.[5]

In a landmark study published on March 2, 2015, in the journal *Anthropocene Review,* some of the world's leading climatologists showed convincing evidence that our globalized economy has become a planetary-scale geological force that can no longer be ignored.[6] In research covering decades of data, they established that there are several highly correlated relationships that tie modern socioeconomic activity to the decline of many of the Earth's ecosystems, as seen in figures 3.1 and 3.2 below. Many of these scientists agree that we have reached a point at which we have clearly moved beyond the physical boundaries of the Holocene era in some of the Earth's systems and are coming dangerously close to exceeding the boundaries in others. It is this research that brought the term the *Great Acceleration* to the mainstream scientific community and enabled other scientists who study complex systems to conclude that the Earth's systems are entering what is called the "second half of the chessboard." This is a statistical reference to a stage in the life of a complex

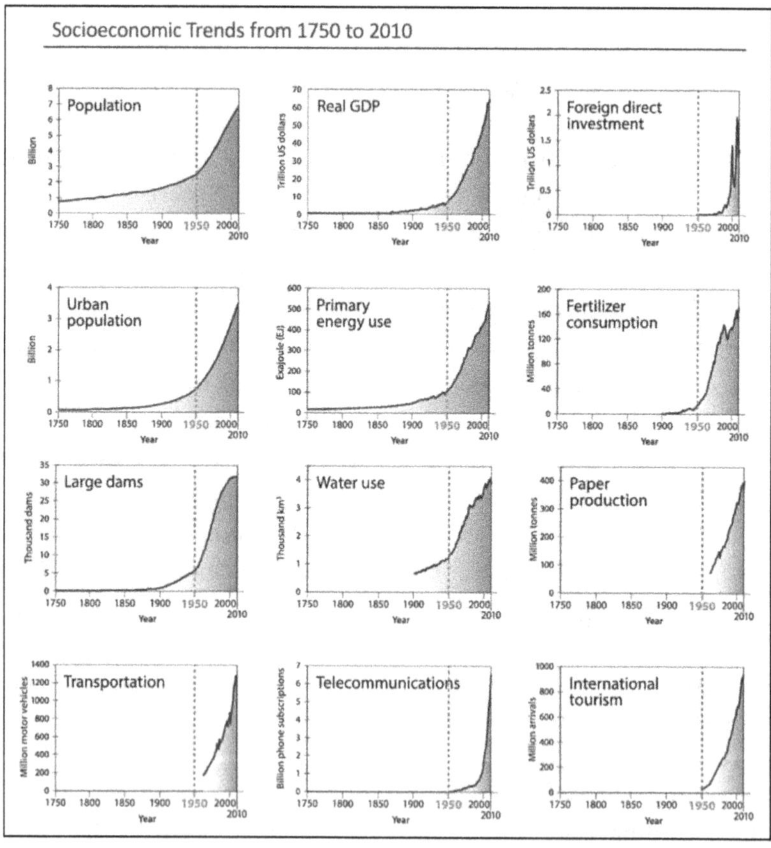

Table 3.1. Socioeconomic Trends from 1750 to 2010. These graphs show the sharp upward trend in human activity beginning in the 1950s, from economic expansion and population growth to modern infrastructure development that are impacting Earth's systems. Will Steffen et al, "The Trajectory of the Anthropocene: The Great Acceleration." FutureEarth Organization, January 16, 2015; https://futureearth.org/2015/01/16/the-great-acceleration/.

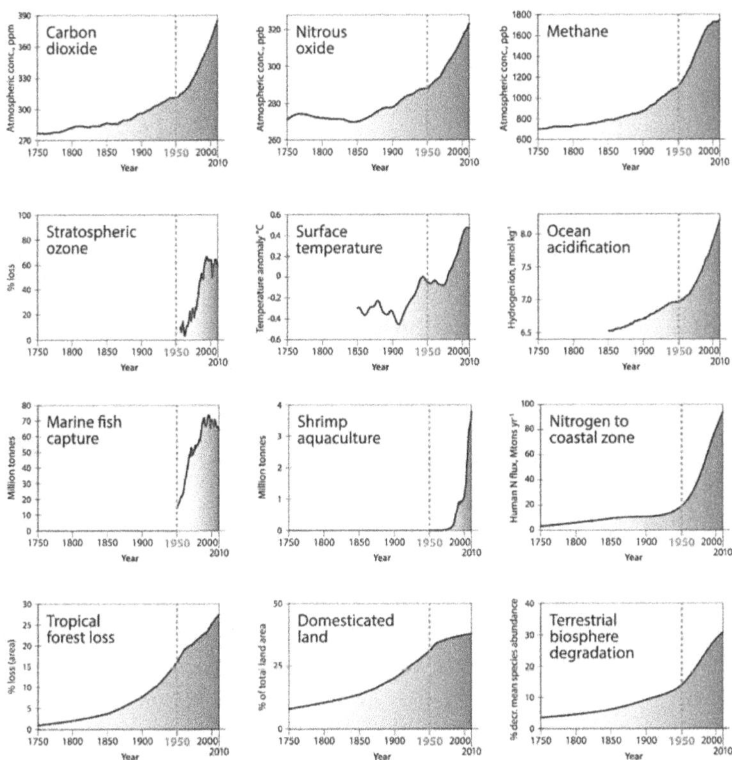

Table 3.2. Earth-System Trends from 1750 to 2010. These graphs show the strong correlation between human activity and its impact on Earth's systems. Will Steffen et al, "The Trajectory of the Anthropocene: The Great Acceleration." FutureEarth Organization, January 16, 2015; https://futuree-arth.org/2015/01/16/the-great-acceleration/.

system in which change moving forward becomes exponential and the possible outcomes become exponentially more difficult to predict. In other words, the *Great Acceleration* itself is accelerating, making it impossible for the scientific community fully to predict the fate of our planet with a great degree of certainty.

Is it possible that we have reached the point of no return and that the ideal conditions for life on Earth that we've enjoyed for the last 11, 600 years are coming to an end? If environmental damage is happening at such an exponential rate, is it possible that the 2015 sets of data, which partially rely on research done more than a decade earlier, are already outdated? Recent changes in the Earth's systems seem to confirm just that. In 2021,

Johan Rockström, the head of the Potsdam Institute for Climate Impact Research and the scientist who pioneered the planetary-boundaries framework, has moved up the timeframe in which we must act if we're to prevent the loss of a million species. Rockström was emphatic in describing the planet's precarious state: "We must halt the loss of biodiversity now, not in 20–30 years, and we must cut CO_2 emissions by half in the next nine years for us to have any chance at keeping global warming to 1.5 degrees."[7]

Increasingly, more scientists are sounding the alarm bells on planetary collapse as the gap between scientific projections and actual events narrows. In some cases, the increased frequency in natural disasters attributed to changes in the Earth's systems have surpassed estimates as we continue to breach the planetary limits on several fronts. The diagram below demonstrates the latest updates on these different boundaries as they were updated as of November 2022. Darker areas contained within the dotted circular line represent the safe operating space for the conditions that existed in the Holocene. Areas outside the dotted line represent the boundaries that have already been breached. By nature, planetary systems are highly interdependent, and the fact that some areas remain within the bounds of the Holocene should not be a source of comfort. According to the Stockholm Resilience Center, transgressing even a few boundaries may be catastrophic due to the risk of crossing thresholds that will trigger nonlinear, abrupt environmental change within continental- to planetary-scale systems.[8]

The question is, Why have our leaders been ignoring these warning signs? Are the issues so large that we are simply sticking our heads in the sand, hoping they will go away on their own? Or are they so removed from our current global socioeconomic and political consciousness that the mere realization of their impact has the potential to uproot many of the belief systems we've known for the last half millennium? Or is it that planetary-systems collapse happens on such a vast timescale that we simply cannot comprehend its immediate effects?

The boiling frog is a metaphor that is often used by environmentalists such as vice president Al Gore to describe this phenomenon. The premise is that if a frog is put into a pot of lukewarm water that is brought to a slow boil, it will not perceive the danger and will remain in the pot to be cooked to death. If, however, the water is boiling from the start, the frog will immediately sense the danger and jump out. The allegory describes our inability—or unwillingness—to react to or be aware of sinister threats that arise gradually rather than suddenly. Before this phenomenon was given a name,

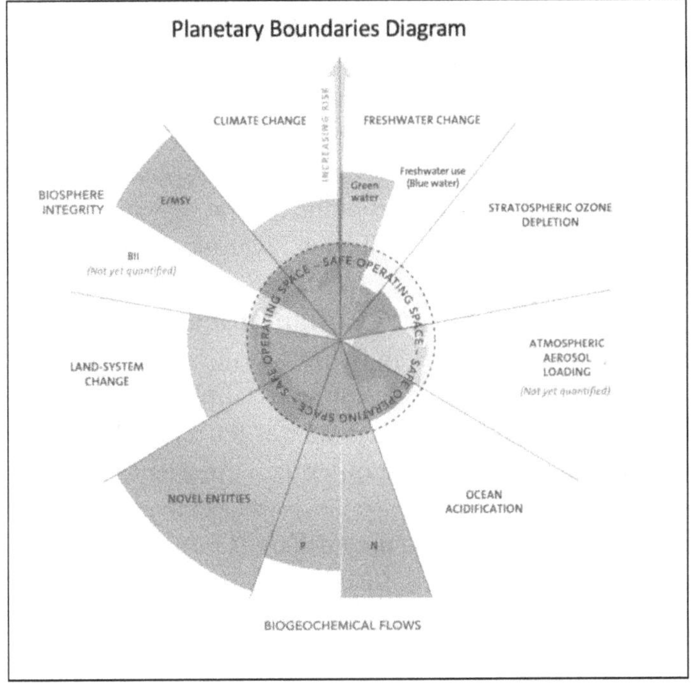

Figure 3.1. The Planetary Boundaries Diagram. In the upper left, "BII" stands for Biodiversity Intactness Index. It is a metric that measures how well a region's biodiversity is preserved compared to its natural state. A higher BII indicates a healthier and more functional ecosystem. Just above BII, "E/MSY" represents Extinctions per Million Species–Years. It is a measurement of the rate of species extinction. A lower E/MSY signifies a slower rate of extinction and a healthier biosphere. "P" in the biogeochemical-flows segment stands for phosphorous and "N" for nitrogen. Figure designed by Azote for Stockholm Resilience Centre, based on analysis in Wang-Erlandsson et al, 2022, Persson et al, 2022, and Steffen et al, 2015; updated November 2022. Used with permission from the Stockholm Resilience Centre, Stockholm University; https://www.stockholmresilience.org/research/research-news/2015-01-15-planetary-boundaries—-an-update.html.

it was described in anthropological terms in the 1980 book, *Overshoot: The Ecological Basis of Revolutionary Change* by William Catton, one of the founders of the eco-sociology movement who put the current time period in the context of the ecological evolution of our species. Catton declared that we are no longer mere *Homo sapiens* with little impact on the environment; instead, we've become *Homo colossus,* each of us having the energy impact of several hundred slaves once controlled by lords and kings. Catton challenged the Western notion of human exceptionalism and saw beyond the accelerated use of energy and natural resources. He warned that we must expect a crash of sorts as a natural sequel.[9] It is this natural sequel that we are choosing to ignore, with grave consequences. The acceleration of the timeframe for the *Great Obsolescence* only seems to increase in magnitude with every passing day. Since Catton's book was published, the footprint of *Homo colossus* has grown several times as many parts of the world have developed their modern economies and adopted the Western lifestyle that uses enormous levels of energy and resources to sustain itself—ignoring the feedback loops coming to us from the natural world while touting our superiority over its resources and all other lifeforms.

The Silos of Enlightenment

Like many other systems born in the minds of oracles and innovators, climate science, and by extension the study of planetary habitability, is part of a complex system of a far greater order than all man-made systems and of a considerably greater order than the science that follows the Newtonian method. This greater system is what systems thinkers call the complex systems of life. It runs on a different form of intelligence that keeps all living systems at every fractal level in an open state that automatically dissipates entropy to the natural environment in order to adapt to the planetary order. This form of natural intelligence has defined life forms for billions of years. It is completely unlike the thinking of the Enlightenment scientist. Those who follow the Newtonian scientific method approach problem solving with a reductive and mechanical mindset that is often focused on singular areas of research that are exclusionary and resistant to integration with other disciplines. *Reductionism* is the term for the idea that complex phenomena can be reduced to simpler ones and higher levels reduced, if need be, to lower levels. The use of levels of understanding in part expresses our human limitations in remembering details and our narrow ability fully to grasp reality outside human perception.

Yet, the Enlightenment scientist who sits in the ivory towers of academia still considers his thinking the leading edge of human emergence. He uses the mechanical mindset that sees the beauty of the part and its relationship to other parts while ignoring the magnificent splendor of the whole. He digs deeper and deeper into understanding the dynamics of each part until he fully grasps its macro, micro, and nano properties while dismissing any negative feedback coming from the whole or its environment. Thus, the mechanical view of all phenomena remains the norm. It garners accolades for the scientist and his peers who engage in a review process born of the same ethos that perpetuates the reductive paradigm, enabling the entire cottage industry of academic research to live in perpetual bliss, ignorant of science of higher order.

Enlightenment philosophers such as Emmanuel Kant (1724–1804) and Edmund Husserl (1859–1938) advised against the use of reductionism in areas such as phenomenology and transcendentalism. They warned that these areas are philosophical in nature and require the suspension of judgment of the natural world, in that judgment strips away every meaning and assumption made about an object while focusing on the narrow analysis of experience.[10] That argument should have been extended to the natural sciences as well. Complexity in natural systems requires a higher-order science, especially when it comes to living cells, neural networks, and, at the macro level, ecosystems, the complexity of which defies linearity. As the urgency to address planetary issues increases, the need to abandon the Newtonian mechanical model in the study of Earth-systems science has become a clarion call. Experts who study climate change and ecological collapse argue that the use of reductionism limits our understanding of complex systems and that there is an urgent need to develop techniques to study ways in which larger scales of organization influence smaller ones with feedback loops that create their own structure at different levels, independent of details at a lower level of organization.[11]

> *In the early 1900s, scientists such as Niels Bohr and Albert Einstein said you can't explain things by Newtonian physics anymore. You have to begin to use the idea of relativity. The concept of relativity appeared then, and it had never been in existence before that time. Five decades later, what you hear so much about today is systemic thinking. The idea that there were systems of behavior was the prime idea that developed right after World War II.*
>
> —Clare W. Graves[12]

Complex Systems

The size of the system and the dynamics of change in climate change are not linear or predictable, nor can they be studied in isolation from other factors. Understanding complexity of this magnitude requires a monumental shift in thinking that is by nature transcendent and inclusionary. The term *complex systems* refers to a scientific approach that investigates how relationships among a system's parts give rise to its collective behaviors and how the system interacts and forms relationships with its environment.[13] The study of complex systems regards collective, or system-wide, behaviors as the fundamental object of study. Consequently, it can be considered not an incremental evolution of reductionism but rather a monumental leap from it that can help us develop a more holistic understanding of the complexity of the world we live in. The purpose of science shifts from improving our ability to predict and control events to the ability better to understand the dynamics and relationships of the systems in which we participate so that our participation can be more appropriate. The reason the behavior of a complex system is difficult to predict is due to the distinct properties that arise in the interactions among its different parts and its environment. The fundamental characteristics of a complex system are nonlinearity, adaptability, spontaneous order, chaos, interconnectedness, unpredictability, uncontrollability, and the presence of feedback loops.[14] The field has given rise to complexity studies in many human-built environments such as information theory, computer science, psychology, sociology, and economics.

An advanced form of complex-systems study is known as "complex adaptive systems." As the name implies, these are systems that have the capacity to change and learn from experience; they have been used better to understand both built and natural environments. They are adaptive in that the individual and the collective behavior mutate and self-organize in response to changes affecting any level in the system's holonic structure. While the model has been used better to understand the behavior of stock markets and social and political systems, it has yielded tremendous benefits in the study of natural systems as well—from the study of immune systems to the study of ecosystems and the biosphere. Although this book does not exclusively focus on the study of complex systems, there are scientists in this field who are very relevant to its premise: Ilya Prigogine and his work on dissipative structures, Donella Meadows and her seminal work in the book *Limits to Growth*, William Catton Jr. and his work on social paradigms, James Lovelock and his work with Gaia Theory, and many other systems thinkers as well.

Complex Systems of Life

The study of complex systems as they relate to human-built environments, and those that are considered adaptive, are the stepping stone into a new pioneering field of complexity called the complex systems of life.

THE GRAVESIAN VIEW OF THE EVOLUTION OF SYSTEMS THINKING

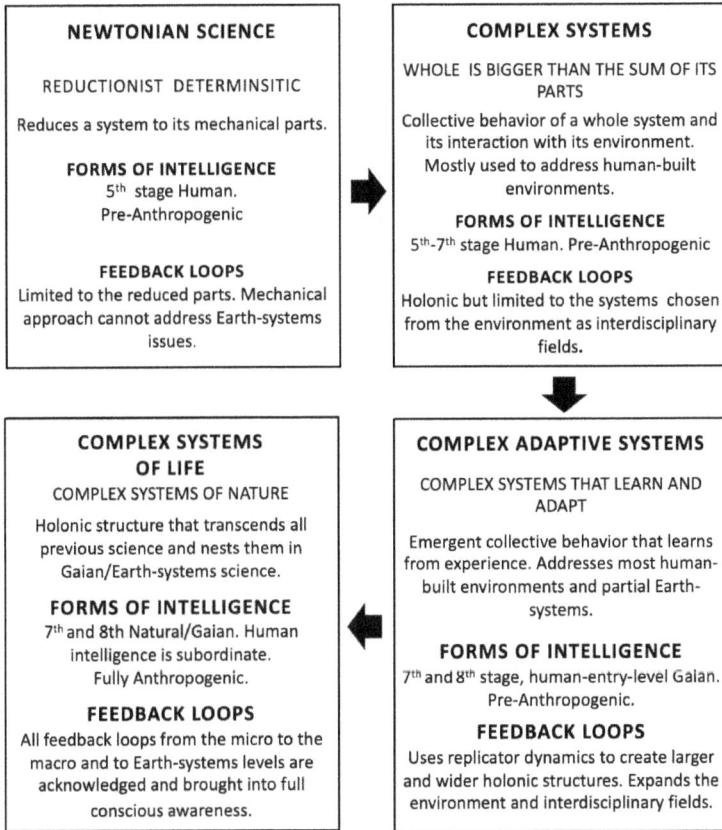

NEWTONIAN SCIENCE

REDUCTIONIST DETERMINSITIC

Reduces a system to its mechanical parts.

FORMS OF INTELLIGENCE
5th stage Human.
Pre-Anthropogenic

FEEDBACK LOOPS
Limited to the reduced parts. Mechanical approach cannot address Earth-systems issues.

COMPLEX SYSTEMS

WHOLE IS BIGGER THAN THE SUM OF ITS PARTS

Collective behavior of a whole system and its interaction with its environment. Mostly used to address human-built environments.

FORMS OF INTELLIGENCE
5th-7th stage Human. Pre-Anthropogenic

FEEDBACK LOOPS
Holonic but limited to the systems chosen from the environment as interdisciplinary fields.

COMPLEX ADAPTIVE SYSTEMS

COMPLEX SYSTEMS THAT LEARN AND ADAPT

Emergent collective behavior that learns from experience. Addresses most human-built environments and partial Earth-systems.

FORMS OF INTELLIGENCE
7th and 8th stage, human-entry-level Gaian.
Pre-Anthropogenic.

FEEDBACK LOOPS
Uses replicator dynamics to create larger and wider holonic structures. Expands the environment and interdisciplinary fields.

COMPLEX SYSTEMS OF LIFE

COMPLEX SYSTEMS OF NATURE

Holonic structure that transcends all previous science and nests them in Gaian/Earth-systems science.

FORMS OF INTELLIGENCE
7th and 8th Natural/Gaian. Human intelligence is subordinate.
Fully Anthropogenic.

FEEDBACK LOOPS
All feedback loops from the micro to the macro and to Earth-systems levels are acknowledged and brought into full conscious awareness.

Table 3.3. The Gravesian View of the Evolution of Systems Thinking. Based on Graves's ECLET model and subsequent research conducted by the MEMEnomics Group, LLC. Used by permission from the MEMEnomics Group; https://www.memenomics.com.

Its origins are grounded in our recognition of the creativity, complexity, chaos, and interdependence present in the natural order, from the smallest organisms to the entire biosphere. This is the new science that pries the study of nature out of the sterile hands of the Enlightenment and reintroduces natural intelligence back into complexity studies. It also reaffirms the perspective of natural philosophers who believe that we can't achieve any real theoretical comprehension of specialized sciences without a broad grasp of interdisciplinary and philosophical views of nature and of life.[15] In contrast to the reductive practice of modern science that viewed natural phenomena in a sterile lab, the new science studies entire ecosystems with their full feedback loops that contribute to whole models of nature that are more intricate and resilient. It returns us to a state of mind in which we are in awe of Mother Nature, looking to better understand her complexity away from the mechanical models that would tame her. The endeavor is holonic in nature in the sense that each holon must adapt to the change dynamics coming from the natural environment in order to keep a given system viable. Both individual and collective behaviors adapt, mutate, and self-organize around a natural form of intelligence that reflects the totality of change within the environment of the whole in order to increase its adaptability and survivability as one macro-structure.[16]

Complex adaptive systems help us better understand how human-built environments can adapt to issues of planetary degradation and how we can mitigate the damage stemming from the various Earth systems that have passed their tipping points. However, if we are to understand the developmental barriers preventing us from fully addressing planetary collapse, we must focus both on human-built environments and on the Earth systems in which they are nested. That is the larger holon to which all human pursuits must be realigned. It is essentially the design of a system defined by Anthropogenic awareness that reshapes all human-built environments, from physical structures to economic systems and technologies that cannot interfere with nature's inherent ability to sustain life.

One prominent scientist in this new area of study is Fritjof Capra, who spent a lifetime synthesizing the work of several systems theorists into a vast body of work called *ecoliteracy*. It constitutes a new paradigm that seeks the wellbeing of the Earth by making sure that we have a deeper understanding of the natural systems that make life possible. In the 2014 book *The Systems View of Life: A Unifying Vision*, which Capra cowrote with Pier Luigi Luisi, the authors offer a conceptual framework that takes a wide-ranging sweep through history across a multitude of scientific disciplines, from the natural sciences to human-built constructs. They examine certain key concepts that have vast implications on how we view a world in crisis. According to their findings, in order for a complex system to be considered truly alive, it must meet three distinct levels of organization, which they summarize as follows:

> The first [level] is self-organization, the capability of assuming an organized structure thanks to the inner rules of the system. The second level is autopoiesis, when the self-organization is such that

> it can regenerate from within all its own components (this is the necessary condition for life itself). Finally, there is a level of living organism when autopoiesis becomes associated with cognition, and therefore both the necessity and sufficient conditions for life.[17]

The term *autopoiesis,* or "self-creation" in biological systems, was introduced in 1972 by Chilean biologists Humberto Maturana and Francisco Varela to define the self-maintaining chemistry of living cells as well as cognition and autonomy in living systems.[18] Their work on this matter is known as the Santiago theory of cognition. The concept of autopoiesis has unleashed many philosophical debates about the origins of life. While those debates are beyond the scope of this book, the concept switches the focus from Newtonian science and the study of complex systems in man-made structures to a more complex, whole-systems approach that will add to the general understanding of life on the planet and our role in it.

> *The entire range of living matter on Earth from whales to viruses and from oaks to algae could be regarded as constituting a single living entity capable of maintaining the Earth's atmosphere to suit its overall needs and endowed with faculties and powers far beyond those of its constituent parts.*
>
> —James Lovelock[19]

We think of modern political and economic systems as macro structures that are complex in nature, but they pale in comparison to the complexity and size of the Earth systems. When considering climate change in the life-cycle model I use, every stage and state, every point of input along the entire cycle, grows exponentially and unpredictably. The bandwidth from which input is derived is exponentially larger, allowing for diverse sources of knowledge and their feedback loops either to emerge or to die off in a normal evolutionary process. The fragility of the less complex systems born in single ideologies that survive the evolutionary process dissolves into the crucible of the greater resilience of the whole. Unlike the complexity needed to address climate change, macro structures of lower complexity, such as politics and economics, follow a single thought leader and eventually take on less complex forms that often exhibit straightforward simplified characteristics.

For example, over the last century, the two main schools of economic thought—the neoclassical school of Keynesian economics and the neoliberal school driven by the ideas of Milton Freidman—have comprised some of the largest human-built complex systems of the modern age. They have generated worldwide paradigm shifts that have upheld the ethos of the thinkers who created them. Generally, once a system moves past the *introduction* phase, most input into it is limited to minor variations that either support its advancement or disparage it but that do not alter the paradigm as a whole. Accordingly, in this case, neither Keynes's or Freidman's ideology was replaced by a newer paradigm until the system they put in place reached a natural state of decline. These types of systems surrender their destiny to the genius of the single individual. With the passage of time, they become ubiquitous and begin to define institutions and policies on a large scale where the pace of change slows considerably and new input becomes less effective, making the entire system less resilient. They limit systems thinking to the ideology within the profession that created them to the exclusion of the complexity of the greater environment in which that profession lies.

The Ecology of the Greater Self

The complex study of Earth systems, the biosphere, and climate change do not involve an ideological figure to worship. The individual ego is subsumed into the Greater Self that represents the collective intelligence of Mother Nature of which human intelligence is but a part. It is an ecological form of intelligence that sees life on Earth as one interconnected whole in which everything matters and nothing is externalized or ignored. It replaces hero worship with the awe and the humility that come from the deep understanding of the natural world and how it operates. It inspires one of the bravest acts our species must undertake: our need to subordinate as a conscious act our own intelligence to her greater intelligence.

Prometheus must become aware of his dark side and begin to think in terms of how nature thinks before it's too late. That is the biggest problem of the *First sapiens.* To him, there is no greater science than that of the Enlightenment that seeks to uncover the secrets of our world in order to tame it. Even those with seventh- and eighth-stage intelligence who apply their understanding of complex systems to human-built environments will be only partially successful in addressing ecological collapse. In their healthiest form, the views of the *First sapiens* on matters of sustainability and regenerative processes only scratch the surface when compared to what systems sciences tell us we need to do in order to save our planet. The *Second sapiens*, on the other hand, honors the collaborative intelligence of the human hive while nurturing and aligning new thinking within the individual mind to build a resilient humanity capable of addressing existential problems the likes of which the human race has not encountered.

When I first started using the life-cycles model detailed in the previous chapter to define climate change, the model itself began to break down quickly. I felt the frustration, fear, and despondency the IPCC scientists felt when world leaders failed to implement their recommendations. This realization led me to question the very nature of the developmental models on which I have based my work. It took some time for me to gain a deeper understanding of how my own thinking needed to evolve in order to perceive our new reality through different lenses. What stood out initially was a quote from Albert Einstein that I often use to demonstrate the nature of evolving, more inclusive systems of thinking: "We can't solve problems by using the same kind of thinking we used when we created them."

In the pre-Anthropogenic era, that statement would have called on the brightest minds from the Enlightenment sciences to create a new, higher-order solution that could solve the problem. This is what science has been doing for centuries, focusing on specific areas of interest in which knowledge is cumulative in nature and taking what we've already known to a higher level to solve problems created by lower-order thinking. But to rely on this progressive, evolutionary process to understand climate change again proved to be futile. Eventually, I realized that the answer might not lie in a progression of most of the scientific processes we already know. What might be needed, instead, is the deconstruction—the *repurposing*—of what we know and how we think and the creation of new organizational principles that account for the variables that have been left out in the reductionism inherent in Newtonian research principles. Hence, going forward will entail reverse-engineering the scientific process itself. It entails, not a slow evolutionary progression, but a monumental leap that will take us from *Enlightenment* to *systems thinking*. It examines every aspect of how we think and the necessary expansion of what we think about into systems of life that were left unexamined by Newtonian science.

The *First sapiens* has gotten used to incremental change that disrupts and reorganizes at a higher, more evolved level of thinking. But the dynamics of climate crisis are of a different order, in which incremental change becomes ineffective. In contrast to human systems, the Earth's ecosystems represent a far larger system that could well have passed its nexus point, the point of inflection that sets it on an irreversible path towards collapse. Sadly, we can't be certain about whether we're at this point because the fractal that represents that level of consciousness lies outside the collective awareness of the *First sapiens*, and based on the scientific evidence of the last few decades, data remains insufficient as to when these nexus points are reached with scientific certainty. By the time we near that certainty, it might be too late to deploy mitigative or adaptive measures, incremental or otherwise.

Climate change and the existential challenges that come with it constitute the collective trauma with which we must sooner or later deal. But instead, we seem to continue to create *First-sapiens* narratives that successfully block us from facing reality. The longer we postpone a systems approach to address this issue, the more we engage in denial as a way to protect ourselves from this overwhelming but inevitable trauma. This is the newest form of reductionism, masquerading as a fractal of systems thinking. It defaults us into believing that incremental change is the only way forward. So, we set up a carbon market; recycle our cans and our plastics; take our reusable bags to Whole Foods, where we also plug in our electric cars; shop for sustainably grown organic food; and return to our solar-powered homes, comfortable in the delusion that we're addressing climate change. This is how the *First sapiens* thinks: in silos, where vision is severely limited. He doesn't ask the deeper questions, such as: Did the entire supply chain for the manufacturing process for his electric vehicle and his solar panels add to planetary degradation in a different form and in a different part of the world? Would her noble efforts make the air in her back yard any cleaner when her neighbors' gas-powered vehicles and coal-fired furnaces continue operating? And, on the much larger scale, if the cap-and-trade protocols that went into effect in the 1990s to reduce greenhouse emissions were working, why haven't we seen a leveling off in the carbon footprint?

As I contemplated these questions, I realized that in order for me to place climate change and its monumental challenges on the Graves-Beck model, I needed to gain a deeper grasp of the leap in thinking that would be required to meet these challenges. I began to do research in Earth sciences and climatology to establish a foundational understanding of the causes of climate change. I read books in order to understand different approaches to the problem. The more I thought I had a basic comprehension of the science, the more Mother Nature proved the scientists and me wrong. For instance, no sooner had the scientific community established a working theory of the melting icecaps than new headlines announced that the icecaps are melting at four times the pace that scientists had hypothesized a few years earlier.[20] Also, projections of the widest measure of greenhouse gases were rendered obsolete as a dangerously high level of carbon dioxide (422 parts per million [ppm]) was detected in the atmosphere in a much shorter timeframe than scientists had anticipated. According to IPCC research, once this figure reaches 500 ppm, Earth's regulation begins to fail as temperatures rises by 3°C and begin to kill one of the most important organisms that absorbs the majority of CO_2—ocean algae—and set it on an irreversible course toward extinction.[21] Even more confounding were reports from well-regarded academic institutions such as the Massachusetts Institute of Technology acknowledging that we don't have the knowledge to get rid of a substantial part of the carbon we produce.

These repeated occurrences led me to a state of hopelessness and to the belief that current scientific methods are greatly insufficient. And even if some of them *were* sufficient, the mindsets of leaders who can effectively address these issues are all grossly inadequate in the face of a problem of this enormous magnitude. For five centuries we have been building a

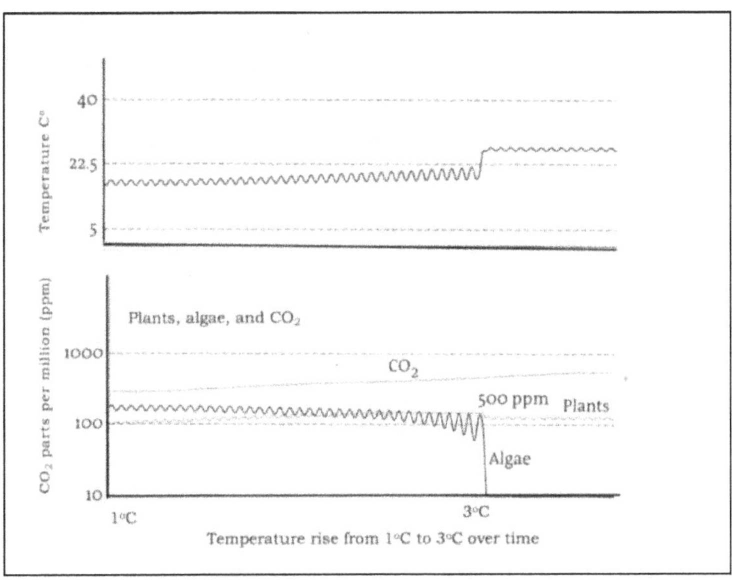

Figure 3.2. Climate Prediction according to IPCC Models. According to IPCC research, 500 ppm of carbon dioxide represents a temperature rise of about 3°C, a point at which the ocean ecosystem begins to collapse. Lovelock, *The Revenge of Gaia*, 33.

system that viewed the complexity within human activities as our greatest challenge. We tinkered with its internal mechanics to make our lives better and to advance the values of the Enlightenment but ignored the greater complexity in which the Enlightenment itself was nested.

Many thought leaders in the world today can identify and address most of the socioeconomic and geopolitical issues discussed in earlier chapters, but these issues all remain those of lower complexity that have obscured the higher complexities that exist outside the proprietary boundaries of the lower. The higher system in which the lower complexities are nested has withstood epochal evolutionary challenges that give it far greater resilience than the human mind in its current form can imagine. The appearance of *Homo sapiens* as a species is but a blip on its timeline. It has operated according to rules vastly more complex than those that run our daily lives. The Earth and her ecosystems run on an independent and often ignored set of metrics that don't care about issues of prosperity or democratic rule. It bends not to our ego and doesn't spare those with a high net worth or those who possess political and economic mastery. Mother Nature's evolution happens unconsciously with utter moral indifference to any single species. Yet, we try to minimize that greater complexity by interpreting it through our existing levels of awareness and in the process minimize the urgency in which we need to act. This is reductionism in its highest and most dangerous form, and it is part and parcel of the *First sapiens's* dangerous worldview.

From Silos to Systems

While I struggled to gain a better grasp of the science, a far bigger question emerged: are world leaders and their institutions *ready* to take the monumental leap in order for the needed change to happen? This is the point at which my life-cycle model began to break down. On the model, I had attributed climate science before the formation of the IPCC to the *inquiry-and-identification* phase. In that phase, climate science remained in the minds of scientists and visionaries who represent the leading edge of evolutionary values. The phase constitutes a gestation period in which decades are spent differentiating various properties, its phenotype and genotype, in order to gain credibility.

Throughout this phase, the model held. I then attributed the scientific findings in the IPCC reports from 1990 to 2007 to the end stage of the phase, readying the system to move into the *introduction* phase. Entry into this phase indicates that the best ideas that fought the evolutionary battles to define the next system have survived the gestation period as they begin their long journey to define the next cycle in waiting. This is where we have a first look at the phenotype of the emerging system.

Then came the IPCC's Fifth Assessment Report in 2014. This report represented the arrival into the all-important *introduction* phase of the new cycle and propelled the new system forward with great anticipation. The level of excitement as we entered this phase was palpable. Think, for example, of how revolutionary the ideas of monetarism became when Alan Greenspan, representing the inner collective of the cycle, joined hands with the outer collective that formed what became known as Reaganomics. Or of how Steve Job's introduction of the first MacIntosh computer in 1984 revolutionized personal computing. Such fresh and pioneering inventions gave the global economy notice that change was afoot and began to render past practices obsolete. They comprised the tipping points that held the promise for collective evolutionary change.

Similarly, the IPCC's Fifth Assessment Report was the catalyst that informed the 2015 Paris Climate Conference (COP21, or the "twenty-first Conference of Parties"). This was when the decades-long scientific research made by the inner collective had its first chance to test the power of the outer collective and together move the system beyond the *introduction* phase. For the first time since climate change had become an issue, and after decades of UN negotiations, the COP21 generated a binding and universal agreement on climate that has been ratified by 194 member nations. The single most important aim of the agreement was to pursue efforts to limit the global temperature increase to 2.0°C above pre-industrial levels in order to reduce the impact of climate change, while aiming for an even more ambitious goal of 1.5°C.[22] This was the greatest, most comprehensive agreement in the history of humankind, and it gave us a glimpse of what global governance driven by a singular existential threat looked like. It was also a preview of what the *Second sapiens* is capable of accomplishing when individual countries with different challenges and ambitions believe in the higher goal of the well-being of all humanity, allowing the behaviors of both individual countries and the global community to mutate and self-organize for the greater purpose of increasing the adaptability and survivability of the entire planet.

But alas, as soon as the aims of the COP21 were ratified, cracks began to appear in its armor. The late stages of the *introduction* phase failed to move into the *growth* phase, the critical phase that begins to subordinate all past cycles into the virtues of its higher order. This was humanity's first test to see if it could act from the virtues of the *Second sapiens.* All signatory countries were given five years to submit their roadmaps to slash greenhouse-gas emissions, and, despite a twelve-month extension due to Covid-19, most countries have still struggled to translate the promises of the agreement into concrete measures.[23] The outer collective has bitten off more than it can chew, and the gap between what needs to be done and our capacity to do it has become utterly visible.

As the research for the next IPCC Report ramped up, it warned that, without substantive commitments to reduce greenhouse gases, temperature rise will be in excess of 3°C this century alone. Further, emissions will rise by 16 percent by 2030— far beyond the goals set by the COP21. The systemic die-off of ocean algae and the collapse of Earth's systems have come closer to being a reality. By the time the first segment of the next IPCC report was issued in August 2021, droughts, wildfires, storms, and the melting of glaciers and sea ice had all intensified. According to the World Meteorological Organization, the eight years since the COP21 treaty was signed have been the hottest years on record.[24]

A closer examination of the nature of the Intergovernmental Panel on Climate Change might give us an idea of why we have failed to begin the structural change needed to save the planet. The IPCC represents the early appearance of a whole new iteration of systems thinking, the largest fractal we'll ever be tasked to understand. It takes all the systems thinking in all the lower fractals that define modern complexities in medicine, science, economics, global trade, governance, and culture and plugs them into its new motherboard, one that is driven solely by the question of how we can keep temperature rise under 3°C. In the holonic model, it represents the movement up in size to the higher structure where the smaller holons that define systems thinking today become the nodal point that redefines the relationship between the higher holon made up of self-complete wholes and the smaller holons that become the dependent parts of the new system. The new holon that represents the IPCC characterizes the emergence of that holon's new *fixed rule,* and the lower holons representing current systems thinking are its *flexible strategies.* In the Graves-Beck model, it represents a new *central thema* that remains in its embryonic phase and uses its derivative expressions to help it move along the critical evolutionary path where it build resilience as it fights off attacks from the current system. Without acknowledging this new holonic formation, systems thinking itself will become the newest reductive tool of the *First sapiens*, resulting in our utter failure to address climate change.

The IPCC Report consists of three segments divided into what are called working groups. *Working Group I* focuses on research and findings from the physical sciences and was summarized as follows:

> Climate change is widespread, rapid, and intensifying, and some trends are now irreversible. It is already affecting many weather and climate extremes in every region across the globe. Scientists are also observing changes across the whole of Earth's climate system; in the atmosphere, in the oceans, ice floes, and on land.[25]

As the gap grew between the new, higher-order scientific findings and our ability to address them, the picture became much clearer: the global governances in place have no enforcement mechanisms to make member countries honor their commitments. Even for the countries that can do so, to meet the goals of the COP21 would require a significant departure from the most advanced iterations of the current economic and governance models to which we have become greatly attached, if not outright addicted (just think of our dependency on oil!). Further, change of this magnitude is not of the incremental nature to which we have become accustomed in modern history. Rather, it requires the reassessment of all we have taken for granted—while collectively we *resist* change, especially *rapid* change.

Because of our inability to take appropriate action on this greatest existential issue facing humanity, the only thing the UN secretary general could do after COP21 was to become the town crier for the entire global community. Right before the COP26 meeting in Glasgow that took place in November 2021, he warned participants that the meeting would be their last chance to ratify what had been agreed to in COP21. This was a code red for humanity, he said. The alarm bells were deafening, and the evidence was irrefutable. At the conclusion of the meeting, a new pact was signed; however, experts were still unclear on how much and how quickly each nation should cut its emissions. There was still no workable plan to limit warming to 1.5°C or even 2°C, and not enough was being done to help vulnerable countries.

February 22, 2022, represented the inflection point from which there would be no return in the minds of the IPCC scientists and the office of the UN secretary general. Their frustrations and their angst only got worse as the world inched closer to COP27 and the more damming news on the growing gap. In his opening remarks in Sharm Elsheikh, Egypt, in November 2022, Secretary General Guterres made it clear on where we stood in this existential fight for survival: "We are on a highway to climate hell with our foot on the accelerator. Humanity has a choice: cooperate or perish. It is either a Climate Solidarity Pact— or a Collective Suicide Pact."[26] Absent from this gathering were two of the top five polluters, China and Russia, and while there was a last-minute agreement to establish a fund to help vulnerable countries, a wider commitment to curb the use of fossil fuels remained elusive. The richest economies in the world responsible for most of the greenhouse gas emissions gave humanity a false sense of hope even as they further pressed their foot on the accelerator.

By now the world has a clear picture on where things stand. Those who believe we need to take immediate action on climate change have become despondent and frustrated. Their cries of desperation are heard in every corner of the planet. They can barely cope with the collective trauma this existential crisis represents. As they unite in solidarity, the younger generations voice their frustrations to the old for the older generation's lack of urgency and failure to act. Other than the youths' engagement in peaceful protests and desperate appeal to their politicians, there is nothing they can do to move the passions of those who can effect change on this critical issue. Guterres's opening remarks at the COP27 painted a clear picture on what separates the *First sapiens* from the Second. By doing little to address this existential problem, we are effectively signing a collective suicide pact for all humanity.

The UN headquarters are in a neighborhood in New York City called Turtle Bay, located on the east side of Midtown Manhattan. The sovereign eighteen acres where the headquarters stand represent the hopes, dreams, and frustrations of all those who are aware of the existential crisis we face. At the UN 2019 Climate Action Summit, what could be called the "Battle of Turtle Bay" ensued when the frustration of forward-thinking scientists and leaders of poor countries most vulnerable to sea rise, drought, and floods found voice in the fiery speech of then sixteen-year-old Greta Thunberg. This young Swedish advocate shamed world leaders with her three-word question: "*How dare you?*" Her words were a searing testament to the arrogance, indifference, and ineffectiveness of world leaders. Beyond the issues of science and political dysfunction, they highlighted what future generations face in the deep denial of the *First sapiens* who still sees the free market as the solution to all that ails us. Thunberg's searing honesty not only bypassed all political and scientific correctness. It also articulated the battle between the past and the starkly different future we are handing to innocent generations yet to come. It so parallels the theme of this book that I feel compelled to share it below:

> This is all wrong. I shouldn't be up here. I should be back in school on the other side of the ocean. Yet you all come to us young people for hope? How dare you! You have stolen my dreams and my childhood with your empty words. And yet I'm one of the lucky ones. People are suffering. People are dying. Entire ecosystems are collapsing. We are in the beginning of a mass extinction. And all you can talk about is money and fairytales of eternal economic growth. How dare you! You are failing us. ... But the young people are starting to understand your betrayal. The eyes of all future generations are upon you. And if you choose to fail us, I say: We will never forgive you.[27]

While this speech was taking place in 2019, just three miles away in Lower Manhattan the *First sapiens* was busy managing the financial portfolio for the world's carbon-based economy and painting a rosy picture for our future. This section of Lower Manhattan represents the colossal power Wall Street wields in keeping the current system alive. The world was still reeling from the disputes over Brexit. Since Brexit was finalized in January 2020, the markets have lost billions, and Wall Street analysts, those self-described *masters of the universe*, have been advising the world on where to find new economic opportunities. This is where the biggest battle for the future of humanity is being waged—in Manhattan, encompassing Turtle Bay and Wall Street—and nothing is off limits to the executives on Wall Street when an emerging truth challenges their worldview. They joked about how a child with Asperger Syndrome could threaten their very existence (Greta Thunberg has been very open about her condition, calling it her "superpower"). As soon as that laughter dissipated, they began to tear down everything that symbolizes the presence of the UN. They blamed disruptions in their busy lives on traffic jams caused every time a General Assembly meeting takes place. They speak endlessly of how much better their lives would be if the UN left its Manhattan headquarters. They deny the severity of climate change and blame it all on the "socialist" agenda put forth by the UN secretary general.[28] Reductionism with a twist that manipulates the facts is part and parcel of how Wall Street and by extension the global economy is being run today. The betrayal of future generations is being committed by some of the most powerful beings in the world with utter contempt for those who disagree with their outdated and perilous narrative.

World leaders on this issue seem to be suffering from the worst case of cognitive dissonance as they hope against hope that the negative information and scientific evidence magically disappear. The inner collective represented by the IPCC community has met the outer collective of politicians and leaders who have repeatedly proven to belong to a much lower holonic structure that is in a closed state and has no capacity to understand the complexity needed to save humanity. Every time we approach the *growth* phase of this all-important new system, the outer collective, instead of acting as a catalyst that moves us forward, acts like an ostrich when it sees an approaching predator. Sticking our collective head in the sand is the surest and the fastest way to die by the hands of the many approaching predators of our own making. This is where we are today, in the middle of the biggest anthropological, existential, and developmental gap in human history. It is within this gap between the past and a vastly different future that the *Second sapiens* stands. He is at the dawn of understanding what needs to be done to save the planet but is resigned to the reality that the power to change things still lies in the hands of the *First sapiens*. The chasm has never been greater.

Human Development and the Anthropocene Epoch

The more I thought about these two diverging dynamics, the more I found myself having to go back and examine the research behind the original developmental models. Like thousands around the world, when I first became a student of Spiral Dynamics and Integral Theory, I was convinced that these were the models that explain everything. The voluminous work that has been done in applying these models and the books that have been written based on their varying viewpoints provided overwhelming evidence that all the answers one needs were found within their vast iterations. But, with the passage of time and in light of the current planetary and societal collapse that seems to accelerate with every passing day, I began to question the models' validity. Did those theories that were created in the pre-Anthropogenic comfort of the air-conditioned, flood-and-fire-resistant bygone era ignore the greater complexity in which their respective influence lies? Does the intelligence needed to understand Mother Nature constitute a paradigm so different that it nests these two models in the far greater complexity that wasn't fully understood when the models were created?

Much like what the Enlightenment science has to do, I had to suspend what I knew in order to embrace greater possibilities. My search for reference to existential issues in the Spiral-Dynamics and Integral-Theory models yielded only modest results. Then, I turned to the original academic work of the man behind the two models, developmental psychologist Clare W. Graves. After much research, I found myself attracted to one, little-known hypothesis that has been greatly ignored by practitioners of both models. Graves called it the six-upon-six hypothesis, which asserts the notion that *Homo sapiens* goes through six incremental developmental stages before it experiences a monumental shift to the next six stages. As I have explained in the introduction, Graves identified two tiers in all. The tier in the second set of six represents a phase of development characterized by exponentially higher human capacities. According to both Graves and Beck, any stages above the second stage in the second tier remain unknowable. That unknowability is due to the overall mechanics of the model, which will be detailed in an upcoming chapter.

This hypothesis is what gave me the impetus to reframe Graves's research without giving up the decades-long refinements it had undergone since he completed his original work. Both Spiral Dynamics and Integral Theory offer their own variations on what the next set of developmental stages ought to be, and, while both models speak to the expanded psychosocial space that opens up in the second tier of human development, very little in their subsequent research answered my single most pressing question: Do any of these new perspectives address the urgent issues relating to climate change? Among the tens of thousands of practitioners who use both models in their professions, only a few were attempting to answer that question. The new models they created in great part assume that we still have time to avert disaster by deploying resources in the form of capital of all types: human, financial, social, psychospiritual, and otherwise.[29] While this thinking would have been sound coming from the second tier of human development, it came from a pre-Anthropogenic awareness that simply underestimated the power of Mother Nature, the greater complexity in which both these models were nested.

As I delved further into Graves's six-upon-six hypotheses, I came across another aspect that has been ignored: His research had revealed that the theme of each incremental level of psychosocial development and its order in the respective tier repeats as we ascend to each new tier but at an exponentially higher level. So, while the *First sapiens* in his earliest existence was concerned with his *individual* survival, the same survival theme reappears in the first level of development in the second tier, but now it concerns itself with the survival of *all life on the planet.*[30] To understand fully what is needed to save our planet, our psychosocial capacities need to recalibrate at an exponentially higher level from where the leading edge of evolution is today—somewhere between the fifth and sixth levels of the first tier.

Based on Grave's research, today we are at one of the most critical thresholds in human history, one that divides a past driven by what he

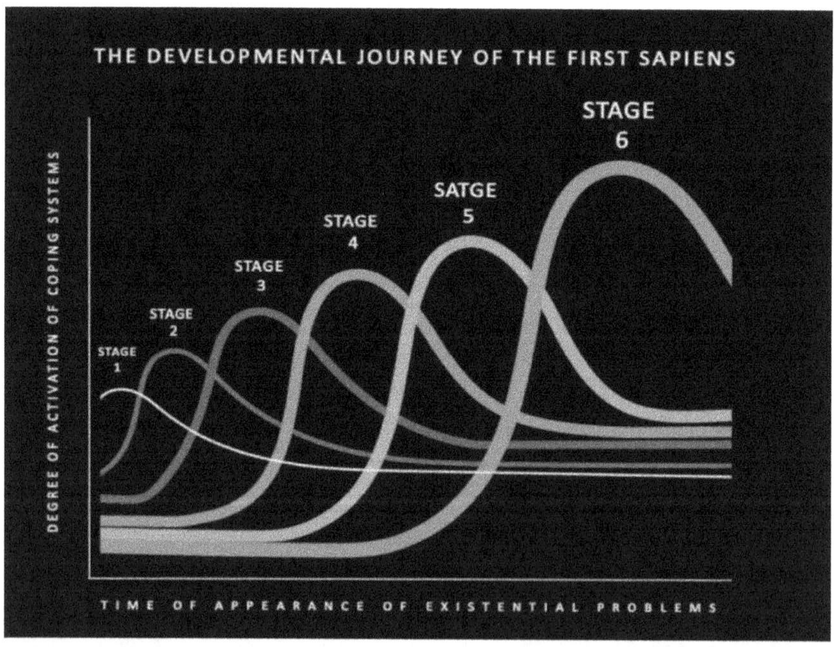

Figure 3.3. The Six Stages of the *First sapiens's* Developmental Journey. Adapted from the work of Clare W. Graves. The two axes—Time of Appearance of Existential Problems and Degree of Activation of Coping Systems—are detailed in an upcoming chapter. Said E. Dawlabani, 2024.

termed the values and the motivations of a subsistent humanity from a future driven by the values that recognize the magnificence of existence and our place in it. This is what led me to classify *Homo sapiens* into the two distinct classifications of First and Second. While the details of the model are the subject of another chapter, I felt it important to try to explain how Graves's little-known six-upon-six hypothesis led to the failure of my life-cycle model so early in its formation. As I further examined Graves's writings, I noticed a distinctive style that seems to be absent from most contemporary literature on climate change and complex systems in general. His writings, in addition to being grounded in objective and quantitative analysis, pay equal attention to the subjective and the qualitative aspects of his findings. And while the Enlightenment scientists who are still caught up in the silos of developmental psychology dismiss the foundational nature of Graves's work, systems science is proving to be all about the reawakening of all the phenomenological and existential narratives that lay outside these silos, placing his writings on the cutting edge of studies about human development today.

Graves argued that for humanity to define itself by the evolutionary values of the next incremental system, the current system must go through a breakdown phase in which much of what we have known and taken for granted experiences some form of collapse. This breakdown will free up the energy needed for the next system to ascend and for us to evolve enough to be able to solve our existential problems.[31] Importantly, though, the critical juncture at which we find ourselves today entails, not a mere *step* from one incremental stage of development to the next, but a monumental *leap*: we must somehow cross a chasm of unbelievable depth of meaning from the *First sapiens's* tier containing the first six incremental stages to a whole new tier that will come to define the *Second sapiens*. This transition is Darwinian in the sense that now is the time when only the fittest ideas from the entire *First sapiens* survive and make it through to the next iteration of humanity. It is also *non*-Darwinian in the sense that we do not have the time for a process similar to that of natural selection that has defined all life in our pre-Anthropogenic existence and the incremental evolutionary intelligence of the *First sapiens*. Evolution of the human mind must be expedited exponentially. That which is an incremental extension of our thinking today will not survive the journey.

To put Graves's writings in language appropriate to Enlightenment sciences, imagine the incremental evolutionary stages of the *First sapiens* as six different petri dishes of the mind in which the strongest ideas and values survive from one psychosocial stage of development to the next. In spite of all the controls set for the experiment, the process itself remains very messy and oftentimes unpredictable. Now, imagine that with the exponentially higher-order problems we're facing, the petri dishes—and, by necessity, the lab and the sterile environment in which these experiments are conducted—can no longer exist. Moreover, the experiment itself is no longer a controlled scientific process that responds to a multitude of linear, predetermined points of input. As the Enlightenment scientist grapples with this new reality, he finds himself on the edge of the precipice. The climb to the next level of scientific understanding that can handle this new level of complexity seems impossible, making the collective suicide pact a real possibility.

This is the point at which we begin to process the darkness that has brought us here. It is the beginning of a collective grieving process that comes after the collective stage of denial ends. The enormous chasm we find ourselves facing today is the new crucible in which the future will be forged. It entails no ordinary breakdown. Rather, it signifies the long psychological journey we must take in order to atone for the actions that have brought us to the edge of disaster. It requires the understanding of how our collective behavior has brought about the decline of the far bigger system in which our thinking is nested. In that dark space, we must find what Jung is known to have called the "gold in the shadow." This term entails the necessity of withdrawing our negative projections from the "other"—the other political party, the other race, the other country, the other ideology—and *owning* the repressed aspects of our own personality that are shameful, ugly, and dangerous. To become a new humanity that is one with all life on the planet, we must first go back and process all that has previously remained unconscious in ourselves. The longer it remains outside our conscious awareness, the more devastating the consequences will be. Only when we withdraw our projections and take responsibility for our own actions can we find the "gold," that is, unlock the positive energy within the shadow that will enable us and the collective to heal. This is the sequential path forward that must be followed now and can no longer be ignored.

Our Anthropogenic reality necessitates exploring a deeper meaning of Graves's chasm. To more fully understand how obsolete, human-built environments and institutions are coinciding with or causing the collapse

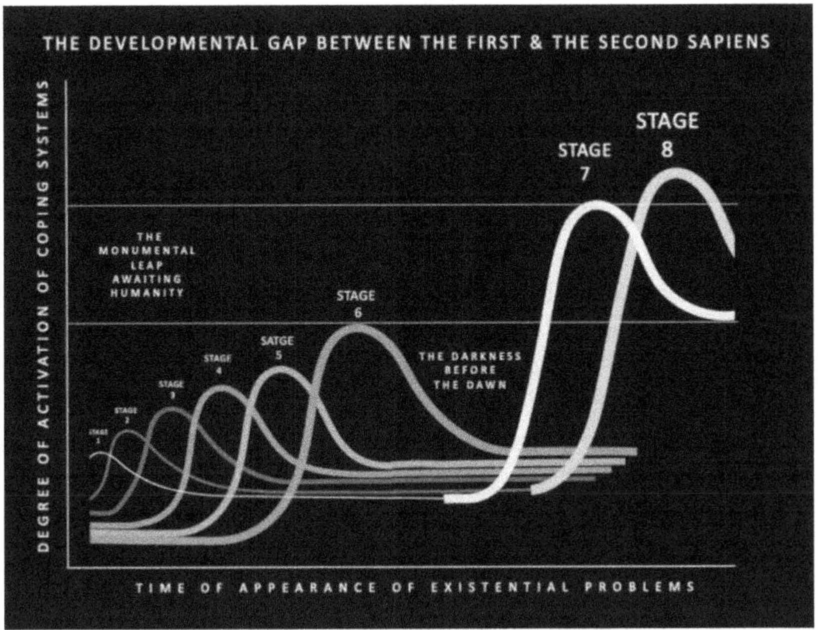

Figure 3.4. The Developmental Gap between the *First* and *Second sapiens*. Based on C.W. Graves's original life-cycles model. With the six-upon-six hypothesis, stages 1 and 2 repeat as stages 7 and 8 with considerably higher psychological capacities, represented in this graph by the wider lines. Said E. Dawlabani, 2024

of planetary systems requires a deeper, more collective approach. This approach must encompass wide areas of human pursuits grounded in psychology, anthropology, mythology, and other meaning-making endeavors that will enable us to process and reinterpret the purpose of our entire species at this critical juncture. I call this juncture the *darkness before the new dawn*. It precedes what Graves called our *momentous leap* and relates to depth psychology in terms of bringing humanity's collective shadow into light. It explores Joseph Campbell's myth of the hero's journey and what it means to be in the belly of the whale. It also looks into the wisdom of many systems thinkers who see beyond the narrow, reductive views of the Enlightenment ideologies that have brought us to the edge of the precipice. My new interpretation of the chasm is depicted in figure 3.6 below. While it is a partial restatement of a minor part of Graves's work, my reinterpretation keeps the model current while preserving its evolutionary nature.

This collective approach is an integration process of monumental proportions that is difficult but necessary. It will amount to humanity's greatest action to help us free the subsistent thinking that has trapped us and our leaders into the lower limits of the mind. That which has been hidden and repressed under the reign of the *First sapiens* must be healed before the *Second sapiens* can fully emerge. It is by processing the accumulated trauma that got us here that we will uncover our own greatness—another meaning for Jung's "gold"—wherein lie the answers to our deeper sense of aliveness, freedom, and vitality. Within this gold is an enormous reserve of hidden energy of which Graves spoke over a half-century ago. It is this energy, trapped and repressed due to the subsistent nature of the *First sapiens,* that has locked us into deficient and often myopic views of the world and kept us in the silos of our own ego. By processing humanity's collective shadow, we shine a light on old patterns of thinking that have shaped our institutions and policies. It is only in seeing our shortcomings that we begin to shift old patterns of behavior that no longer serve us and the Earth. This is how we transform anger, grief, and resignation into power and strength. The freed energy is also what's needed for the mind to begin to absorb the monumental question that the *Second sapiens* faces at the dawn of his reign: How do we ensure the survival of all life on the planet?

This is the question that will begin to dominate the mind of every man and woman and every leader around the world. The more we remain in denial about the existential threat of climate change, the closer we come to the breaking point. In continuing to deny this reality, we accelerate Mother Nature's systems cycles into reaching their various tipping points, from which there will be no return. We see that irreversibility in everyday life: Conditions in dry climates are getting dryer; fire seasons are becoming longer and more ravenous; wet climates are getting wetter and more destructive; hot places are getting hotter and less habitable; and the melting of polar ice has become exponentially less predictable, making it impossible to predict the fate of millions who live in coastal communities.

This breaking point will also be the stage at which man-made systems and institutions begin to collapse, one after the other. The disruption we've experienced in the aftermath of the COVID-19 pandemic and Russia's war on Ukraine will pale in comparison to the coming disruptions of the things we've taken for granted for so long. The collapse of the supply chain and distribution networks, the bankruptcies of entire industries such as insurance and finance, and the dissolution of governmental agencies such as FEMA and the various international aid agencies will be just a sample of what is to come. Even issues of national borders will dissolve into chaos as different parts of the globe become uninhabitable, making the current European refugee-migration crisis look linear and simplistic. The chaos in the crucible in which we find ourselves today requires building a whole new, more resilient architecture for psychological being—all the way from the way we think to how we design systems for global governance, which by their very nature must be highly collaborative and decidedly resilient.

> *The twilight in which we seem to be moving today is the twilight not before night, but before dawn: we are reaching the end of the dark ages of materialism; and the modern mind, without surrendering the tools by which it has achieved its mastery of material nature, will now more fully vindicate its own self-recognition and achieve self-mastery and a more human life, individual and social.*
>
> —Radoslav Tsanoff[32]

As the new stage on the other side of this monumental chasm begins to differentiate itself, its resilient design begins to repel old ways of thinking unless they are devised to be part of the whole. This is the dawn of the new-systems thinking that will enable us to continue our journey forward. Phenomenological in nature, it seems to be appearing in leading-edge research that must be empowered and advanced. It is interdisciplinary and highly collaborative, a phenomenon that is yet to be fully understood and accepted by the Enlightenment sciences that still dominate academia and our institutions. It represents a shift away from Newtonian thought to the far more advanced thinking of physicists such as Albert Einstein and Niels Bohr and uses their scientific discoveries in a new, multidisciplinary approach that addresses all systems at once. It is the melding of epistemology, anthropology, ecology, psychology, and sociology and an array of other fields that must acknowledge the interconnectedness of all human activity and the effects it has on the well-being of the planet. Even the fields of economics and systems management must search for a future built on far greater complexity than what we've known so far in our history; and it must all subsume human intelligence into the greater intelligence of Mother Nature.

Chaos, Randomness, and the End of Certainty

To summarize, the *Second sapiens* is all about the emergence of humanity as a collective force in relation to Mother Nature. This emergence represents the dawn of an era symbolized by systems thinking and the deeper understanding of complex systems, both natural and man-made. Unlike Newtonian science that seeks to tame nature, the *Second sapiens* works to understand and mimic its deeper intelligence; hence, he must reintegrate that which has been ignored by the mechanical models of the *First sapiens.* This is a chaotic and unpredictable process that will render much of our old ways of thinking obsolete. The chaos of its initial stages represents the end phase of the obsolescence of the modern mind that most man-made systems will experience. It will initially present itself as part of the *darkness-before-the-new-dawn* phase in the Gravesian model and of the monumental gap that must be crossed before humanity can emerge to the second tier of development. The more chaos and uncertainty become accepted as the new normal, the more the virtues of the *Second sapiens* become imbedded in the new paradigm that brings us back to being a fractal in harmony with the natural complexity in which we are nested.

As I searched further for reasons why my life-cycles model had failed, I looked for answers for why complex systems move from an open to a closed state. Most research I encountered studied complex systems from a traditional scientific approach that focuses on dissecting our environment in its parts and then establishing cause-and-effect relationships. Chemists and physicists over the last two centuries have followed scientific methods that dissected matter into molecules, molecules into atoms, atoms into positrons and electrons, and so on. Biologists tried to make sense of the environment by isolating it to a single species and then further to single animals, studying their behavior and their physiology. This is how we still approach our understanding of complexity in most of our social constructs, which leave out much of the systems thinking that began to emerge in the 1970s.

As I expanded my research, I wanted to incorporate any scientific findings performed in experiments that had been done as open systems. This led me to the work of physical chemist and Nobel laureate Ilya Prigogine, whose work parallels much of how Graves describes human nature: an open-ended, unfolding, emergent model. In his 1996 book, *The End of Certainty: Time, Chaos, and the New Laws of Nature,* Prigogine contends that determinism is no longer a viable scientific belief: "The more we know about our universe, the more difficult it becomes to believe in determinism."[33] This is a major departure from the approach of Newton and even of Einstein and many other Enlightenment scientists who expressed their theories in terms of deterministic equations. What attracted me most to Prigogine's work was his theory of dissipative structures on which he based his assumptions for the laws of nature.

Prigogine's research was grounded in discoveries made by physicists and chemists who over the years have contributed to our understanding of the laws of *thermodynamics*. The first law says that energy cannot be created or destroyed; it can only be transformed from one form to another. But what has been overlooked for two centuries is that the experiments that proved the theorem were conducted in what are called "isolated systems." In other words, in order to conform to Enlightenment reductionism, our understanding of thermodynamics and the transfer of energy has been grounded in closed-system experiments, leading us to believe that energy, of which most of the universe is made, is in a stable, static state of equilibrium. The simple mathematical formula states that change in the internal energy of a closed system is equal to the difference between the heat supplied to it and the work the system does on its surroundings. In the early nineteenth century, French physicist Nicolas Carnot (1796–1832) tested these rules on real-life models in heat engines and found that some of the energy in the conversion process could not be accounted for. To maintain a constant level of heat output, energy continually needs to be added in. His observations contributed to our understanding of the *second* law of thermodynamics, which placed an upper limit on the efficiency of engines and gave us the rule that, over time, all things begin to break down and become less ordered unless energy is added in some way. The measure of inefficiency is called *entropy*, which has also been described as the measure of disorder, chaos, or randomness.

It is a basic law of nature that the net amount of entropy in the universe is always increasing. Called the *law of entropy*, it describes a movement in the direction of increasing disorder. Entropy applies to all energy systems, from cosmic entities such as stars and planets to systems within a single planet such as weather systems all the way to electromechanical, biological, and social systems.[34] Another way to view the idea that is consistent with the laws of nature is through the concepts of holons and fractals, wherein entropy is at the heart of the *central thema* of all energy systems. Entropy could be considered the largest holonic structure in the known universe—from cosmic entities to cells in our bodies—and each fractal level uses *different strategies* for adaptation in response to conditions present in the local environment. To understand entropy from a scientific perspective is to understand how universal the concept of life cycles is. In complex social systems, the energy lost in the production of heat could be compared to the process of how societies rid themselves of outdated ideas and laws that no longer serve the greater good. The energy added to keep the system operating at optimum efficiency could be regarded as the new ideas generated through the natural evolutionary process that a system acquires from its environment in order for it to remain viable.

> *It turns out that an eerie type of chaos can lurk just behind a facade of order—and yet, deep inside the chaos lurks an even eerier type of order.*
>
> —Douglas R. Hofstadter[35]

While the second law of thermodynamics and Carnot's work contributed to the understanding of increased randomness and disorder, scientists still couldn't explain the paradox of how, in the face of that law, things in the universe nevertheless tended to gravitate toward increased order and less randomness. When viewed from the perspective of how life on Earth began, we see how in the natural world increased order took place: atoms evolved and formed molecules; molecules in turn formed amino acids and proteins; then proteins formed single cells that combined to form multicellular organisms; and multicellular organisms eventually evolved into *Homo sapiens*. Similarly, in the human-made world *Homo sapiens* have evolved to create complex social systems that seem to become increasingly less chaotic and more ordered as they move to higher and higher stages of development.

This scientific paradox wasn't resolved until the 1970s when Prigogine began to study complex chemical reactions subjected to heat in an open system that interacted with its environment. The discoveries he made through rigorous mathematical analysis showed that while open systems *did* become increasingly ordered, they did so by dispersing entropy to their environment, which proved his hypothesis that *order emerges not in spite of chaos, but because of it.*[36] Evolution and growth are products of open systems that temporarily move into a state of chaos and then reorganize at a higher level of complexity, whether that reorganization be in biological, cosmic, or psychosocial systems.

Prigogine's work showed that systems do take energy and matter *from* the environment; but, more importantly, they also dissipate entropy *back to* the environment. His observations proved the second law of thermodynamics of increased entropy to be true but also proved that much of the entropy produced does not take place within the system itself. He called open systems that operate in this manner *dissipative structures*. Unlike classical thermodynamics that viewed the dissipation of energy as waste, Prigogine proved that, in open systems, dissipation becomes a source of order, contributing to a stable state that is far from equilibrium.[37] Ever since his discovery, scientists have confirmed that many open systems in the universe—from chemical reactions and the multiplication of cells all the way to the formation of complex social constructs—follow the natural order of how dissipative structures work.

This understanding provided a significant insight into my research on the change continuum in the Graves-Beck model and how a system moves from an open to an arrested and finally to a closed state. When leaders in charge of complex, man-made systems ignore the basic law of entropy, they place the system on a path toward linearity. The system becomes less resilient as it begins to close itself to new ideas, thus holding on to entropy instead of dissipating it to the environment. These actions move the system into an arrested state that for a while still behaves like a complex system but is running on the limited energy trapped within it. At this stage on the continuum, the longer it holds on to entropy, the more toxic it becomes and the less it allows new energy or ideas into the system. Eventually, the system becomes so out of touch with its environment that it becomes closed and ceases to function in accordance with natural law.

The state of the US economy today gives us a real-life example of this phenomenon. A well-functioning economy with proper dissipative structures in place is supposed to work for the majority of people, including the working class. But, after the monetarists offshored the good paying jobs in manufacturing and made the stockholder the primary beneficiary of the system, it set the working class on the road toward a closed state, slowly holding on to entropy. Within two decades, the system made the stockholder the enemy of the working class. This is evinced today when publicly traded corporations announce massive worker layoffs that simultaneously increase the price of their stock while sending thousands of workers to the unemployment lines. It is this dynamic, among many fractals that define the monetarist ideology detailed earlier, that have made the system toxic, creating tears in the social fabric of America that have given rise to the extreme right now threatening the core of our democratic institutions.

Prigogine's work reinforced much of what the Graves-Beck model on the phases of the life cycle of stage development and its ideological fractals has asserted for over five decades. What is important in both models is the critical phase a complex system reaches that Prigogine calls the "point of bifurcation." In the Graves-Beck model, it is the higher of the two nexus points on the graph in figure 2.5. *Bifurcation* simply means the splitting of something into two branches or parts. Prigogine's research showed that, before a system reaches the bifurcation point, its chemical entity is already determined; but, when the point of bifurcation is reached, new choices emerge and the path becomes indeterminable.[38] This has been his central argument for why determinism is no longer a viable scientific belief.

If we view our modern, post-war era as a complex system that uses these principles and place it on the Graves-Beck life-cycles model, it becomes clear that we still view the ethos of monetarism, globalization, and *peace through commerce* as the predetermined, "chemical" entity before the system reaches the point of bifurcation. But these systems are obviously not chemical reactions, and the belief that we are still at the pre-bifurcation stage is a reductive fallacy that has been in place for several decades. When we prevent a complex social system from reaching the bifurcation point, we interfere with its ability to dissipate entropy to its environment while stopping it from acquiring new ideas that will keep it viable in the long term. By forcing it to become a closed system, we only postpone the inevitable as the system builds entropy that becomes increasingly toxic, making the path of undeterminability more dangerous.

Think of that toxicity as cancer cells that develop past the nexus point in a specific ideological cycle. The further a culture moves past that point without acknowledging that bifurcation has already taken place, the more likely the cancer will spread to other organs and—by the time it is caught—will have reached the point of irreversibility in the form of metastasis that could lead to death. In terms of the fractal model, continuing to use the virtues of a system that has moved past the bifurcation state can be viewed as a cancer that has reached the two, much larger organs we have ignored to keep the current system on life support: the first being our collective emergence into the values of the sixth level of development that champion equality and the fair distribution of resources, and the second being our emergence into the systems thinking that is needed in order to save our planet. Significantly, philosophers of science have described the progression of cancer as a reversion of development and as the evolution of multicellularity.[39] Any man-made system that remains in use past its bifurcation point becomes a cancer that has the potential to reverse human development and spread increasingly to larger concentric circles of communities, nations, and regions of the world, halting human progress.

The nexus point in the Graves-Beck model occurs where the DNA of the current system is passed on to the next system. There, it plays a crucial role in defining the architecture and the virtues of what's to come. Compared to Prigogine's dissipative structures, this DNA uses the entropy from the current system—called waste—that is a source for the new order and combines it with new input from the environment. Graves defined this evolutionary process as both genetic and epigenetic.[40] The genetic aspect could be compared to the order that comes from the system's entropy and the epigenetic to the system's new input from the environment. The nexus point is the bifurcation point where older behavioral systems become subordinate to newer, higher-order systems. Beck referred to this critical phase as the *transcend-and-include* feature of the model that is essential to keep human emergence in an open state. The reference to transcendence could signify the acquisition of new input from the environment, while the reference to inclusion could refer to the entropy resulting from the bifurcation process that forms part of the new order.

The image that best captures the dynamic nature of both Graves's and Prigogine's models is that of a whirlpool in motion. While the whirling water looks static and in a stable state from a distance, a closer look shows it to be in a state of constant change as it dissipates waste water into the drain and simultaneously replaces it with fresh water, achieving a balance of input and output that—far from equilibrium—is in a constant state of flow. This is how all life forms of different types and at different fractal levels operate. Once we fully adopt this open-system view to our man-made social constructs, addressing issues from economic inequality to climate change will become a natural evolutionary process that both honors who we are as a humanity and helps us recognize again that we are but a small fractal in the cosmos operating within the bounds of its universal laws.

Open Systems Meet Social Structures

As did Prigogine's work on dissipative structures, Graves's work came to fruition in the 1970s. This was the time when systems thinking began to appear in the minds of a wider set of visionaries. It constituted the *inquiry-and-identification* phase that follows the natural rules of emergence by expanding the bandwidth that will eventually define the nature of the emerging system. The '70s were also the critical time when the virtues of the ideological cycle that had been in place since the end of World War II were coming to an end. Keynesian economics that had given the world the blueprint for redevelopment. A new global financial architecture was breaking down, and the ideology was undergoing bifurcation. The possibilities of what would have emerged on the other side were, in Prigogine's words, undeterminable.

The zone of undeterminability is where the evolutionary battle in the *inquiry-and-identification* phase of the life-cycle model takes place. The strongest ideas that survive the process play a major role in defining the next system. Much as the monetarist ideological cycle is doing today, the Keynesian cycle remained in place past its nexus point, creating toxicity in the system and limiting the choices of what could define the next system. This toxicity is a smaller fractal representation of the *darkness-before-the new-dawn* phase that Graves identified as the monumental gap we face in reaching the second tier of thinking. On the near side of this gap, though, these lower, first-tier ideological cycles are characterized mostly by incremental steps that fix the damage from the previous cycle and offer binary solutions that focus on preventing the past from reoccurring and providing temporary stability, while sidelining the voices from higher-order systems.

The subsistent nature of the *First sapiens* has prevented systems thinking from defining our future, but it hasn't eliminated it. When a system closes itself from the environment, the ecosystem in that environment develops further antibodies that become stronger as they wait for the next bifurcation event to begin the next stage of chaos and disorder. The less time the system remains in place past that nexus point, the more likely it is for the environment to pick the next higher-order system capable of solving the problems the older system could not. Much like the different phases in the life cycles of the lower six systems that have defined the journey of the *First sapiens*, the first phase of development for the *Second sapiens* has been waiting in the wings for decades building antibodies. So far, though, it has failed fully to manifest due to the monumental change and the deep adaptation it requires. The two major aspects that have kept it in gestation are 1) the need to build a far more resilient bandwidth that can carry systems thinking forward to the *introduction* phase, and 2) the simultaneous need to address the collective issues represented in the *darkness-before-the new-dawn* phase of the entire first tier. Scientific research conducted in silos that inform the *First sapiens* have to yield to a highly collaborative process that answers to a multitude of new challenges. Systems science has to move from the theoretical realms of quantum physics and the theory of relativity to a wider range of sciences that deal with the complexity of integrating the different scientific, political, social, and ecological processes that include and transcend the Enlightenment sciences and all their peripheral expressions of development. This rise in interdisciplinary fields of inquiry was born in the chaos of the 1970s when so many social and geopolitical constructs were reaching various stages of entropy. That stage of bifurcation opened up the psychosocial space in our minds that represents a tipping point in human nature and further defines the *Second sapiens*. And while that stage remains in its *inquiry-and-identification* phase, it has continued to build the wider bandwidth needed for its virtues to reach a tipping point. This is evidenced by the wider acceptance of systems thinking among both the inner and the outer collectives present in the *introduction* phase, which has been accelerated due to our need to address higher-magnitude problems such as climate change and other existential issues.

That acceptance has been well expressed by astrophysicist Neil de Grasse Tyson in his 2022 book, *Starry Messenger: Cosmic Perspectives on Civilization*. In this brief summary, he captures the essence of the tipping point that awaits us:

> The cosmic perspective changes you. If we were to fly all the warring factions in the UN into space and have them look down on earth, all the national borders would dissolve. It's the only way for us to realize how fragile and small we are and what we have to protect. All our arguments, the things we were so deeply

> dug into and thought through, will often crumble under rational analysis informed by a cosmic perspective.... We went to the moon to explore it and we looked back over our shoulder and we discovered earth for the first time. Earth in all its majesty without the color-coded countries we were trained to see to know who our enemies and our friends were. We saw earth the way nature intended it. We saw oceans, land, and clouds, and that changed us.... From 1969 to 1973, during the times we went to the moon, we have created the Environmental Protection Agency, the National Oceanic and Atmospheric Administration; we created the first Earth Day.... There was a firmware upgrade in our perception of earth as a holistic entity that we have to protect.[41]

In viewing Earth from the moon, for the first time we saw the insignificance of our subsistent nature in the face of a much larger reality; it was a superior, holistic view that removed the artificial controls of the petri dish and the lab and placed us back in the cosmic order that holds the greater mystery of existence. Tyson's cosmic perspective is not that different from Graves's as the latter conceives of what it would take for us to start thinking and acting from the second tier of values. Much of Graves's research focuses on the immense difference between the neuropsychology of the *First sapiens* and that of the *Second sapiens*; the *firmware*—as Tyson puts it—gets upgraded considerably. In language similar to Tyson's, Graves asserted that individuals who think from within the second tier find solutions far superior to those from within the first tier. He attributed this skill to their ability to understand systems behavior and to the freedom that comes from an objective understanding of the subsistent motivations that have defined our journey through the entire first tier of human existence. These are the motivations that have trapped the sciences into the very narrow and exclusionary silos that are resistant to integration. Not only did Graves find the solutions of second-tier thinkers quantitatively and qualitatively superior, he also found them to be achieved in considerably shorter periods of time and with less than half the resources used by those in the first tier.[42]

Throughout the 1970s, Graves found his audience in a state of awe and bewilderment as he spoke about the nature of his work and our inevitable need to address existential issues. He often commented that he was answering questions no one in the fields of psychology and the sciences was asking and that the time will arrive when human problems become so unbearable that these questions will be forced upon us. In order to continue our journey, we will be forced to think in terms of second-tier values. His observations put into perspective how other systems visionaries like him have remained on the margins, dismissed by those who hold power over politics, economics, science, and academia.

Due to its open-ended nature, Graves's work was often relegated by Enlightenment academics to the area of general systems theory, philosophy, prophecy, or phenomenology. In other words, it was dismissed—due to its qualitative and subjective aspects, its multidisciplinary approach, and its open-endedness, which made it unpredictable. Graves worked tirelessly to integrate other areas of inquiry in order to answer the simple question: What is human life all about, and what does research show it to be?[43] Such a lofty inquiry might be thought of equally as scientific as well as philosophical or even spiritual and existential. It provided the added proof that Graves's work cannot be contained in one discipline, and therefore, in the worldview of the *First sapiens*, it cannot be taken seriously. That same dismissal was also given to other systems thinkers who at the time began to voice their concerns about our relationship with our planet: the small blue marble on which we live.

Limits to Growth: From Denial to Reality

In addition to the establishment of the Environmental Protection Agency (EPA), the National Oceanic and Atmospheric Administration (NOAA), and Earth Day, our cosmic perspective gave a wider platform to systems scientists concerned with the state of our planet. In 1972, the fields of science, public policy, and economics, run by the *First sapiens*, were shaken by the publication of *The Limits to Growth*. The book was authored by a team of researchers led by four MIT systems scientists: Donella Meadows, Dennis Meadows, Jørgen Randers, and William Behrens III. They analyzed a world system composed of five factors: land, non-renewable resources, capital, population, and persistent pollution. In a summary of their extensive work that began in 1968 with thirty scientists from around the world, their research showed that continued increases in population and industrial output would eventually prove to be unsustainable, leading to possible collapse. The only path to a stable future on Earth was one in which levels of both population and industrial output were deliberately constrained. If growth continued, they argued, change wouldn't be noticed immediately; instead, it would appear as major disruptions to world systems, beginning in the first half of the twenty-first century.[44]

Immediately after the book's publication, the smartest individuals, representing the brightest institutions of the *First sapiens* from the *New York Times* and *Newsweek* to the Chicago School of Economics and Milton Friedman, all called the premise of the book empty, misleading, and nonsensical without ever addressing its core arguments. The *New York Times* charged that the entire premise of the book was motivated by a hidden agenda: to halt growth in its tracks.[45] Such a response can be expected when the science of higher order raises questions no one in the mainstream is asking. The authors of *The Limits to Growth* introduced this science to a system that lacked the psychosocial bandwidth to understand it as well as the urgency to think of issues affecting systems with higher complexity.

In their pioneering research, Donella Meadows et al generated their predictions by using a computer model called "World3" that simulated interactions among the various factors such as population, food production, and industrial growth in relation to the limits of the Earth's ecosystems. What places the book firmly in *Second-sapiens* sciences is that the computer model was designed to account for feedback loops. However, its protocols are different from those of the natural, self-regulating process of homeostasis, and this difference can lead the reader to confuse the nature of feedback under these two complex systems models. World3 has its origins in the systems-dynamics model created by MIT professor Jay Forrester in the 1950s. It provides an approach for understanding nonlinear behavior of complex systems over time. As in all complex systems, it recognizes the correlation among its components—such as their circularity, interlocking behaviors, and oftentimes delayed relationships—and observes this correlation as more important than the system's individual components. The model divides feedback loops into positive and negative: *Positive* feedback loops are often referred to as a vicious circle that commonly defines exponential growth and occurs when a chain of cause-and-effect closes on itself so that increasing any one element in the loop starts a sequence of changes that will result in the originally changed element being increased even more.[46] *Negative* feedback loops, on the other hand, are where solutions to complex problems of this magnitude reside. They tend to regulate growth and seek to hold the system in some stable state. Unlike nature's feedback loops, it is safe to assume that positive feedback loops in the World3 model were being generated by our human-built systems that continue to view growth, even today, as a noble pursuit, while ignoring the negative feedback loops that require us to adjust or even reverse global growth patterns in order to reach stable states. Our dualistic nature has led to the externalization of those negative feedback loops long before *Limits to Growth* was published, and unless we initiate the regulatory processes to bring the different Earth systems—not the least of which is population growth and industrial production—into a state of stability, Mother Nature, through her full accounting of feedback loops, will do it for us as a way for her to reach her own states of stability.

The book *Limits to Growth* was among the first to produce *Second-Sapiens* quantitative analysis on the damage the largest systems built by the *First sapiens* was causing the planet. Its methodologies however, gave critics another angle, known in the digital world as *garbage in garbage out* (GIGO). This is the concept that flawed input results in flawed output. Criticism lasted for decades, continued by those who were entrenched in their mechanistic Newtonian models and the capitalist ideology of *grow or die*. As often happens in the *inquiry-and-identification* phase of the emerging stage, the antibodies from the dominant stage have continued to attack the science of higher order. Such attacks help the current system to move past its nexus point, which in turn affects higher-order fractals and makes outcomes at all levels less predictable and highly irreversible.

It has been fifty years since the initial publication of *The Limits to Growth*, and the bandwidth for the argument it makes has been greatly expanded; sadly, though, it has remained in the *introduction* phase of the stage of development needed to save our planet. While its authors have issued several updates using real-world data that confirm many of their original findings, other scientists haven't begun to validate the research until the last decade and a half as major environmental disasters have increasingly occurred. Awareness of these events has moved the needle in the *introduction* phase of the emerging system to a wider band of the inner collective of scientists and to some in the outer collective of academics, politicians, journalists, environmentalists, and activists. Today, the issue has become critical even for some of the brightest Enlightenment thinkers such as Gaya Herrington, a sustainability expert with the global consultancy KPMG. Acting in a personal capacity, Herrington published her far-reaching findings in the *Journal of Industrial Ecology*, concluding that, unless major changes to resource consumption are undertaken, economic growth will peak and then rapidly decline by around 2040.[47] Her article brought the issue of tipping points in many of our nonrenewable resources front and center to a globalized economy that holds organizations such as KPMG in the highest regard. It was the needed preaching to the choir that allows the ethos of the new system to penetrate the minds of deniers and disbelievers in a nonthreatening way.

As further evidence that awareness of climate change as an imperative issue is gaining more acceptance in the outer collective, a Google search from 2007 through 2022 using the title *The Limits to Growth* and the word *validation* has returned over 124,000 results published mostly by scientific journals, academic institutions, and media outlets. Here's a sampling of these findings: In a comprehensive, fifty-year anniversary assessment, the Post Carbon Institute, a respected think tank on issues of climate change and sustainability, published a critical analysis of all areas of concern addressed in *Limits,* from world population and the depletion of resources to the exponential growth in levels of carbon dioxide and ocean acidification. The institute's analysis found that most of the book's research confirms the standard-run model from 1972 and in many cases has overshot it.[48] The term "standard run" was part of the World3 computer model, with all its feedback loops, that assumed a worst-case scenario, or "business as usual" attitude, in which there is no modification to human behavior in response to the warnings in the book.

In an interview for the piece, Dennis Meadows, one of the original authors, proclaimed that it is not enough to say, "I told you so and now comes doom." He urged us to explore peaceful and equitable ways for managing the upcoming decline and to create ways to strengthen the resilience of all our critical systems. Undertaking these two monumental tasks would have been a lot easier had those in power been in an open state and begun this arduous but necessary journey fifty years ago.

How the collective perceived *The Limits to Growth* fifty years ago confirms Graves in saying about his model that he was answering questions no one was asking. But when someone answers an unasked question stating that we have to reverse what we're doing, it leads to an ideological war fought intensely and unfairly in battles that favor those who hold power to maintain the status quo. The longer in time we have avoided dealing with the problem of climate change, the more it has grown and become unmanageable. Dennis Meadows's retrospective comments acknowledge that it is no longer possible to reverse climate change or stop it.

Irreversibility beyond the nexus point in the life cycle of the Earth's systems has become real. The best we can do is to mitigate the damage as the systems identified in the original research reach their respective bifurcation points and begin to collapse one after the other. Adapting to this monumental change will become the new, highly unpredictable normal and erase much of what we have taken for granted about humanity and its relationship with Mother Nature. Meadows's observations also put into perspective how other systems visionaries have remained on the margins, dismissed by those who hold power over politics, economics, science, and academia. This unfolding reality has sent us scrambling for answers as the existential problems that are causing changes to the higher-order systems increase with every passing day, nudging psychological and planetary sciences further along, making feedback loops central to the study of planetary system, and widening the bandwidth needed for the systems thinking of the *Second sapiens* to take root.

The Last Stand of the Modern Mind

Viewing Earth from outer space in the 1970s gave much-needed impetus for the study of planetary habitability and triggered the pursuit of knowledge about the Earth systems as the new, higher-order science. The firmware upgrade of the human mind began to appear in new areas of interdisciplinary exploration. The era generated the rise of systems thinking, and soon afterward a modern version of *systems theory* was born, signifying the evolution of the Enlightenment virtues long awaited by early visionaries. In a new and fresh direction away from the tribalized areas of specialization, systems theory brought together disparate fields of study in a multi-perspectival way, merging disciplines as diverse as ontology, sociology, political science, biology, computer science, engineering, economics, and many others.[49] It gave us hope that the new systems-thinking approach will save us from Newtonian science and reverse the Enlightenment reductionism that has been at the heart of intellectual thought for the last five centuries.

While all this was happening, the leading edge of development in the Western world was reaching a nexus point—the transition from one ideological cycle to the next that builds on the entropy of the previous cycle. Both cycles were built on the values of the Enlightenment that still viewed the vanguard of humanity in terms of peaceful development rooted in a carbon-based economy. In the Gravesian model, this nexus point is where the true measure of societal change takes place; it is where the leading edge of human intelligence meets social systems. The result is almost always a compromise in the intelligence as it gets applied to the dominant social narrative; the larger the social structure, the lower the common denominator needs to be to avoid major societal and institutional disruptions. Hence, the change becomes incremental and aesthetic instead of structural and transformative. That describes how systems theory was now being applied, that is, to man-made structures that carried the label of *systems* but still served the *central thema* of the fifth stage of development. Although worded in slightly more evolved language, it had little inclusion from theories on natural systems and the physical and ecological sciences.

The net result is a translational evolution of values, not the needed transformational evolution that will save our planet. The systems that have emerged represent a form of intelligence only slightly more advanced than that inherent in the virtues of the Enlightenment. They strategically manipulate human pursuits under the pretense of higher consciousness and inclusion, using a more evolved form of the Newtonian scientific method while leaving out much of the science needed to address real existential issues. These actions are now imbedded in our daily lives, masquerading as "green and sustainable" practices. One of the best examples from the business world is seen in recent changes undertaken by Koch Industries, a conglomerate of more than twenty corporations that operate in more than sixty countries and employ over 120,000 people. Koch is known for pioneering innovative methods to extract oil and gas with revenues that topped $123 billion in 2023.[50] It is one of the highest-valued, privately held corporations in the United States, second only to the food-and-tobacco conglomerate Cargill. In the past decade, Koch embarked on a strategy to improve its public image by investing in renewable energy. Renewables represent a cleaner, higher-order form of environmental awareness when it comes to energy technology. The company claims to have invested over $1.7 billion to acquire businesses focused on renewable energy infrastructure, including battery storage, electric-vehicle charging, and smart-grid technologies. On the surface, these actions appear as the beginning of Koch's divestment from fossil fuels and an evolution in its business practices, but a closer look reveals that they are nothing more than part of a business tactic intended to improve the company's image while diverting attention from its long-term intentions. In July 2023, the Heritage Foundation—a conservative, climate-denying think tank with a close relationship to Charles Koch, the largest stockholder in the company—revealed "Project 2025," a plan to guide the next Republican administration on how to bolster the oil-and-gas industry and gut the Environmental Protection Agency.[51] While this example is extreme, it shows how the mind of *First sapiens* is capable of manipulating our collective perception, using the infrastructure it has in place to silence its critics and present a green-and-sustainable surface image while continuing its business-as-usual practices with impunity.

While the *First sapiens* has rejoiced in his latest success by defining the new parameters of *systems thinking*, those who truly understand the greater parameters of what it means to see Earth from outer space continue to be ignored and marginalized. They are the *Second sapiens* who dedicate their lives and careers to understanding the much larger system in which systems theory and all human pursuits are nested. They are the second generation of systems thinkers whose ideas and worldviews remain in its gestation stage of the new cycle that must move expeditiously and grow exponentially in order for us to redefine our values and our global institutions beyond anything we've yet known and experienced. This difficult journey starts with the rediscovery of the *central thema,* the *fixed rules* of the much larger circle in the holonic structure that has long been ignored. The new *fixed rule* must ask the question: How do we create a system that ensures the survival of *all* life on the planet? To define the system's peripheral expressions or *flexible strategies,* a slightly amended form of the *natural design* formula from the previous chapter provides a good start. Since this is about the future of planetary habitability, the amended formula asks: How does who lead/manage/teach/inspire whom to do what for which living systems in which part of the world in order to ensure the survival of all life?

This question defines the toil of long-term visionaries like the scientists who contributed to the landmark book, *The Limits to Growth.* It is also present in the work of James Lovelock and Lynn Margulis in their 1975 book *The Gaia Hypothesis,* which puts forth the notion that the Earth is a self-regulating, complex system that involves the biosphere, the atmosphere, the hydrosphere, and the pedosphere all working together as one evolving system to find the physical and chemical environment that is optimal for life.[52] Their book, like *The Limits to Growth,* was far ahead of its time. It has suffered the same fate of being dismissed because no one wants to hear the morbid tale of ecosystem collapse and the end of an era that has defined the good, the beautiful, and the true through the narrow lens of Enlightenment reductionism.

The new integral-design formula, while remaining simple, adds the crucial element of the new unifying vision that prioritizes the preservation of *all* life over all other goals. *Homo sapiens* becomes a part of the natural order, not an organism superior to it. The design represents a new landscape that is systemic in nature wherein nothing is externalized or ignored. It is representative of the most complex adaptive system humanity will ever be tasked to devise, in which both individual and collective behaviors mutate and self-organize to serve the greatest good. It is this type of complex engagement that reflects the totality of the change needed to increase the adaptability and survivability of the single most important macro-structure called Earth. It is here that the second generation of systems thinkers concerned with saving *all* life—such as Fritjof Capra and the authors of the original *Limits to Growth* and the *Gaia Hypothesis*—begin to integrate the work of pioneering systems thinkers who have included Gregory Bateson, E. F. Schumacher, David Bohm, C. G. Jung, Clare Graves, and many others.

This new generation of systems synthesizers are the ones who remain in awe of Mother Nature and of all forms of life within her and are humbled by her greater intelligence. They are the recipients of the largest firmware upgrade, the one the Graves-Beck model identified as the highest two stages of development, the seventh and the eighth. In their conceptions, we begin to see the dawn of the *Second sapiens* who views the world as a single, dynamic organism that subordinates systems thinking and all other preceding intelligences into its own collective mind. This is where the latest advancements in information, research, and knowledge are channeled through the greater wisdom that redefines all holonic structures in an ecological alignment that honors the greater complexity in which all life is nested.

Part Two
The Sum of All Our Days is Just the Beginning

FOUR
THE FIRST SAPIENS, HOMO SUBSISTENS*

Human existence can be likened to a symphony with six themes. In a symphony, the composer normally begins by stating his themes in the simplest possible manner. In the existence of Homo sapiens, our species begins by stating in the simplest way those themes which will preoccupy us through thousands of variations. They are the first six levels of existence that comprise the initial statement of the species in its very simplest form.

—Clare W. Graves
"Human Nature Prepares for a Momentous Leap"

On a different February day in a different part of New York state, another distinguished, grey-haired man stood quietly in the middle of a field contemplating the wonders of Old Man Winter. A thick coat of virgin snow covered the trees that bowed their branches with their heavy load toward the ground. The wide expanse of slumbering prairies stretched in all directions as far as the eye could see. Silhouettes of grey smoke rising from distant chimneys animated an otherwise still canvas of white gently fading into a blue horizon. The air was pure and fresh as the gentle breeze swept in from the nearby banks of the Mohawk River,

* *The First sapiens* is my iteration of what the Graves-Beck model refers to as the *first tier*, and *Homo subistens* is the latinized translation of the first tier's *general thema*: the values of a subsistent humanity. Similarly, the *second tier* is renamed *Second sapiens*, and its *general thema*—the value of magnificence—is renamed *Homo magnificus*.

carrying with it the wet smell of pine. Everything seemed quiet, almost muffled. The sun was bright, and the cold was biting. The occasional screeching of birds of prey pierced the deafening silence of an otherwise tranquil winter, reminding the man of the long, hibernal season that made this picturesque hamlet of Rexford home.

I can go another mile, he thought to himself as the steam rose from the top of his sheepskin Cossack hat. His stallion, who had stopped behind him, had other ideas as he tugged back on his reins to remind his keeper of his physical limitations. The Morgan horse and the man had been friends for years. This particular breed is known as the "horse that chooses you," and this horse had chosen his keeper from the time he was born in the stables on the man's property. A few years earlier, the man's imposing physical presence had been compromised when he suffered a stroke and several heart attacks that impaired his eyesight and balance and made reading and writing difficult. He was a prominent professor of psychology and a leading researcher into all matters of human inquiry, and these health issues had derailed his pioneering academic career. He could no longer engage in the rigorous demands of his revolutionary research and experimentation as he had done in years past. He had returned to a light teaching schedule at the nearby college after taking time off to recover as he bemoaned his fate. His health problems had taken their emotional toll, and while his family played an important role in his recovery, he always relied on the nonhuman connection he had with his horse to overcome the lingering effects of his trauma. After a deep, silent pause, man and horse came to an understanding as they both headed back to the nearby stables, each anticipating the other's return in the dawn of a new winter day.

The Oracle in Hudson Valley

As Clare Wray Graves shook off the cold in his warm study that morning in 1974, a million thoughts were going through his mind. Books were piled on every surface of the room, outnumbered only by yellow-paper pads filled with handwritten notes. His secretary at the old psychology building at Union College had been transcribing his writings for years, but she never seemed to catch up. As a professor of psychology, Graves's knowledge was rooted in the theories of Sigmund Freud, John B. Watson, B. F. Skinner, and Carl Rogers.[1] Over the years he often found himself conflicted when at the end of every semester his students asked him which theory was right. His frustration in justifying an answer almost led him to leave the academic field altogether.

But, instead, he began a life-long quest to provide a better understanding of human nature—a quest to uncover who we are and what we are to become. In the course of this journey, much of the proprietary hold on knowledge and the fragmentation that exited in the silos of psychological research, academics, politics, economics, and other human pursuits became apparent. In laying down the foundations of his work, he started to see interconnected systems where others only saw division. Much like the systems thinkers who were emerging at the time, Graves sensed a deeper layer of connection, a set of organizing principles that could integrate prevailing ideas and viewpoints without eroding much of their merits. This was the dawn of a form of thinking in the field of psychology that saw beyond the Newtonian mechanical view that a system is the total sum of its parts. Graves was among the early pioneers who conceived of human development in terms of systems thinking and believed in the synergistic and emergent behavior of complex systems that transcended the dominant narratives defining psychological research at the time.

His groundbreaking approach to research found common ground with the work of psychologist and philosopher Abraham Maslow (1908–1970). The two became trailblazers in the field of developmental psychology that explored the hierarchical nature of human development. Maslow, while developing his own conception that eventually led to the *hierarchy-of-needs* model, was teaching at Brandies University, less than a three-hour drive from Union College. The two men shared their research findings and would often cover each other's classrooms.[2]

Over the years, they engaged in friendly debates about the differing ramifications of their conceptions. While Maslow hypothesized that, once a need is met, a person automatically jumps to the next level of motivation, Graves believed that there is no guarantee that the next motivational system will appear. He argued that neurobiology and social factors play as much of a role as psychology does in determining the emergent nature of a psychologically mature individual. Over the years his work expanded to include the newest developments in neurobiology and the social sciences, but his framework continued to be based on his bio-psycho-social construct, which became widely recognized as the first integral model of its kind. It remains an open-ended approach for defining human nature to this day. The plethora of data and the integrated conceptualization in Graves's model led Maslow to concede that there is no such thing as a final state of self-actualization and that different people self-actualize in different ways.[3] Graves identified this concept as a key distinction in his model, which came to be known as the Emergent Cyclical Levels of Existence Theory (ECLET) and which has the unending nature of human development as its central theme.

> *Briefly, what I am proposing is that the psychology of the mature human being is an unfolding, emergent, oscillating, spiraling process marked by progressive subordination of older, lower-order systems to newer, higher-order systems as an individual's existential problems change. Each successive stage, wave, or level of existence is a state through which people pass on their way to other states of being. When the human is centralized in one state of existence, he or she has a psychology which is particular to that stage. His or her feelings, motivations, ethics and values, biochemistry, degree of neurological activation, learning system, believe systems, conception of mental health, ideas as to what mental illness is and how it should be treated, and conception of and preference for management, education, economics, and political theory and practice are all appropriate to that state.*
>
> —Clare W. Graves[4]

The early stages of this debate between these two pioneering, academic gurus were taking place in the 1950s when conformity ruled the day and ideas that espoused anything outside the parameters of any existing narrative were frowned upon. This was especially true with the American Psychological Association (APA), in which behaviorists and Freudians dominated the scene. It was at an APA conference that Graves witnessed his friend Maslow being torn to pieces by his own colleagues when he introduced his pioneering work. After seeing his friend being lambasted and emotionally crushed, Graves vowed to focus on rigorous research and release his findings only when his theory was ripe and defensible.[5] As he retreated to his academic corner, he began to envision a masterpiece that would stand among the classics—one that would make a revolutionary statement about human nature that would open the mind to new frontiers in psychology. In the years following that fateful event, Graves saw his colleague rise to prominence as Maslow chipped away at the frozen ideologies of the APA. Maslow's pioneering work exposed the limitations of the behaviorists and the Freudians and led to the establishment of several new branches of study, the most prominent of which are the humanistic, transpersonal, and positive psychology movements that still remain on the leading edge of human development.[6]

On that winter morning in 1974, Graves was putting the final touches on a piece that would provide a comprehensive summary of his life's work. He had drawn parallels between his own life and Maslow's, including the health challenges they both faced. After Maslow suffered his first heart attack in 1966, he knew his time was limited to build the framework that later allowed others to conduct more comprehensive studies that brought the field of psychology out of its archaic past. Four years later, another heart attack claimed his life.

After suffering a heart attack and a stroke himself, Graves knew his time was limited as well. He had spent years trying to prove Maslow's views but had ultimately found them insufficient. In the face of mounting data, Graves was convinced that the Maslowian approach provided only brushstrokes on a much larger canvas of human nature.[7] What filled the crumpled pages of those yellow pads in his study were research findings from decades of work on the never-ending evolutionary nature of *Homo sapiens*. According to Graves, this was and remains an open-ended work in progress. He integrated the disparate fields of psychology, sociology, biology, organizational leadership, systems thinking, politics, history, anthropology, and many other fields in his 1974 essay, "Human Nature Prepares for a Momentous Leap." Unlike his previous contributions to scholarly journals such as the *Harvard Business Review* and Canada's *McLean Magazine*, this piece was published by *The Futurist*, the official publication of the World Future Society that had supported Graves's work for years. It was a masterpiece that covered a plethora of topics in a seamless philosophical, academic, and intuitive narrative, away from the scrutiny of academia that couldn't classify the totality of his work into a specific area of focus.

Sixteen hundred miles away from the biting cold of the Hudson Valley, a young, tenured professor at the University of North Texas was struggling with the same issues Graves had struggled with in his classroom decades earlier. Don Edward Beck had been studying forty-two different models of human development but still couldn't provide his students with a definitive answer about which theory was correct.[8] As the thirty-eight-year-old Beck sat in his office one April morning in 1974, he began to read Graves's thesis in *The Futurist.* Suddenly, it all made sense. Beck had found the Holy Grail in his quest to understand human nature. The piece provided him with the missing links, the organizing principles that seamlessly integrated all the models he had taught for years and brought them together in one optimistic, emergent narrative. For the next eleven years, until Graves's passing, Beck, with the help of his colleague Christopher C. Cowan, committed himself to do what Graves's ill health had prevented him from doing: bring his revolutionary model to the masses. At the time they met, Graves had stopped working on the manuscript for his masterpiece, a book he had tentatively titled *The Never-Ending Quest.* He had wavered between that title and the one I chose for this section of the book: "The Sum of All Our Days Is Just the Beginning." In both titles one can sense Graves's optimism gained from the results of his research. They point to the resilience of human consciousness and its ability to find ways to evolve and reorganize at higher levels of neuro-bio-psycho-social development.

As optimistic as Graves's outlook was in his 1974 piece, "Human Nature Prepares for a Momentous Leap," it included a significant caveat—one that caused alarm among academics, thought leaders, futurists, and whoever else read the article: Graves proclaimed that the leading edge of evolutionary thought is one that seeks the preservation of all life on the planet and that, in order for us to accomplish such a goal, we must move at exponential speed to seek the radical reversal of the entire history of human progress.[9]

In later years, the article became known by Gravesian practitioners as the piece that launched a thousand books. In it, he urged readers to start reorganizing the way they think about their problems to include the fact that there is no ultimate set of morals, ethics, and values to be discovered. Instead, all these human virtues and pursuits fall into a hierarchically ordered, ever-changing process that is always open to change, and our task as a species is to learn how to live with that change. The 1974 publication came out during an era when the leading edge of systems thinking was on the rise and we began to develop a cosmic view of life after we saw Earth, the blue marble, from outer space. As Graves laid out his model that contained the hierarchically-ordered eight levels of existence he had uncovered in his research, he began to describe the nature of the *momentous leap.* To him, the changes that were taking place in the world—from our discovery of the cosmic view of life to understanding the limits to growth and everything in between—represented the dawn of the seventh psychosocial stage of development, the first rung in the second tier he had conceived of years earlier. This defined a distinctly new level of human existence in which humanity transcends all the previous six levels that had defined it. Graves labeled those lower levels in terms of the values of a subsistent humanity and the *momentous leap* as the necessary phase we must undertake in order to overcome our deficiencies and begin to identify with the values of the second tier so that our journey can continue.

To Beck and Cowan, these revelations were life altering, and they both worked earnestly with Graves to gain a fuller grasp of his genius. Beck studied much of what Graves had published in addition to his lectures transcribed by Cowan and Graves's archivist, William R. Lee. Their efforts resulted in two books that were published decades after Graves's passing: *The Never-Ending Quest: Clare W. Graves Explores Human Nature,* edited by Cowan and his associate Natasha Todorovic and published in 2005; and Lee's book, *Clare W. Graves: Levels of Human Existence,* published in 2009.

The Never Ending Quest represents the most complete assembly of Graves's research, but, sadly, it only partially reflects his full body of work. According to Cowan, in order to make room for harnesses from the barn Graves had decided one day to clean up the mud room where he kept much of his research material, and when he was finished all that remained were personal papers, articles, and a few chapters that Cowan later reconstructed for his 2005 book.[10]

These limitations, however, did not deter Beck from wanting to tap into Graves's reservoir of knowledge to reconstruct as full a picture as he could of the man's genius until Graves's health issues had prevented him from completing his masterpiece. In 1978, Beck invited Graves to speak at the business school at the University of North Texas. The auditorium was standing room only as Graves disclosed further refinement of his framework. In an effort to express the dynamic complexity of his model, he had renamed it *the emergent-cyclical, phenomenological-existential, double-helix-level-of-existence conception of adult human behavior.*[11] The two-hour lecture filled in much of what had been missing in Graves's earlier work and inspired Beck to begin to think of ways to apply Graves's findings to real-life applications.

Beck described to me a life-altering conversation he had had with Graves regarding practical applications of the model. It came only after Beck had worked for years to prove the underpinnings of Graves's research, including much of what remained in Graves's personal files, all that had been published and transcribed, Graves's own notes on consulting work he had done in the fields of mental health and with the prison system, and the rich conversations the two of them had had over time. Beck had known that Graves yearned to apply his model to large-scale change, to the much larger concentric circles of human development that concerned macro systems such as nations and possibly the entire human species.

"His eyes lit up every time he talked about mapping the psychosocial developmental stages of an entire culture," Beck said. When he asked what Graves wanted him to do with all the knowledge he had acquired, the answer came quickly and unequivocally: "I want you to apply it in the wickedest places in the world!"

After much discussion over many visits to Graves's horse ranch, the two had agreed that South Africa, which was plagued by the Apartheid system of institutionalized racism at the time, would be the ideal place. They had hypothesized that the country demonstrated the *growth* phase of every stage of development on the life-cycle model happening all at once. Soon after that conversation, Beck resigned his position at the university and began a ten-year odyssey working with South Africa's business leaders and designing models to integrate the workplace in preparation for the dismantling of the Apartheid system. He also worked closely with the South African politician F.W. de Klerk and Nelson Mandela, while Mandela was still in prison, to prepare the country for the transition of power.

Beck's advice on how to build national cohesion was summarized in the movie *Invictus*. In real life, he counseled the coach of the South African rugby team, the Springboks, on developing the winning strategy that brought the country together.[12] This work came naturally for Beck, who loved sports. For a period of time, he had been the team psychologist for the New Orleans Saints of the NFL and for years had written a sports-values column for the *Dallas Morning News*. Beyond *Invictus*, the proof that the Gravesian model could be applied to entire cultures appeared in a book Beck wrote with South African journalist Graham Linscott in 1991 entitled *The Crucible: Forging South Africa's Future*. Linscott had chronicled Beck's work in South Africa from the beginning, and the book confirmed that, not only was the mapping of entire cultures on the Gravesian model possible, it was key to understanding the psychosocial motivations of leaders and the needs of their constituents at every level of development in order to design effective models for leadership and change. The book mapped the entire country in accordance with each region's dominant stage of development. It also profiled the social and economic philosophies and the policies of every political party to determine their ability effectively to serve a post-apartheid system of rule. To Gravesian practitioners today, the book is a classic, but it was written from an academic perspective that sought to preserve much of Graves's original work. As a result, it did not receive the attention it rightfully deserved. This lesson was not lost on both Beck and Cowan, who saw the urge to recreate the model in more accessible language. The result was their groundbreaking book, *Spiral Dynamics: Mastering Values, Leadership, and Change,* published in 1996.

Bringing Graves's Work to the Masses

In order to make Graves's pioneering discoveries more accessible without eroding the underpinning of the model, Beck and Cowan sought to simplify much of his terminology and augment it with contemporary research and popular scientific concepts that were on the leading edge of our culture at the time. From Graves's description of the model, Beck had conceptualized that the "upward-spiraling" aspect of the framework is best represented by the word *spiral,* and, due to the framework's open-endedness, *dynamic* was an apt description for completing the term. This two-word title replaced Graves's last stated term containing fifteen sterile words derived from research, which made audiences break into laughter every time he said them.[13] *Spiral Dynamics* became an instant global success as its modernized language informed the essential go-to toolkit for reinventing businesses, regenerating vitality in townships and villages worldwide, addressing inner-city violence, diffusing age-old conflicts, creating inclusionary models for migrants in Europe, and overhauling ailing educational systems in the United States. Many books in publication today detail the entire Spiral-Dynamics framework and its various applications, including my 2013 book, *MEMEnomics.* Instead of reiterating much of the Spiral-Dynamics theory, I will introduce aspects of it throughout this book and integrate them with Graves's original work and my own applications of it, the aim being to present an applied, experience-based narrative that is solidly based on five decades of research. At this point it is important, however, for the reader to gain a basic understanding of the entire model before moving forward.

While the majority of practitioners and certified trainers use the model for personal growth and organizational consulting, very few use it the way Graves intended it to be used: to provide solutions for the wickedest problems in the world. In this book, I explain the most relevant Gravesian concepts as they apply to the macro applications of the model. My discussion refines some of Beck's and Cowan's findings, offers updated analysis of Graves's original work, and, in staying true to the everchanging nature of the model, updates my own writings from 2013. In so doing, I apply the theory to what Beck called "psychology at the large scale," the practitioners of which number less than twenty around the world. They include the heads of the Centers for Human Emergence (CHE), a global constellation of think tanks that dot the globe from Canada and Mexico to the Netherlands, the United Kingdom, the Middle East, and South Africa.[14] This organization is what attracted my partner, attorney Elza Maalouf, to set aside her consulting career and work with Beck to bring peace to the Middle East. The three of us formed the CHE Mideast in which we offered the Gravesian model as an alternative way forward in achieving this goal. The macro-systems application of the model is also what motivated me to set aside a career in real estate development and apply it to geopolitics and macroeconomic systems. This book also offers insights into the comparisons between Graves's ECLET and Beck's and Cowan's Spiral Dynamics and attempts to frame them in terms that address the current manifestations of what Graves called the world's "wickedest" problems.

My hope is that the reader views this model, not just as a tool for personal growth or organizational consulting, but as the largest fractal for understanding our current global existential problems. This model will allow us to reframe our challenges with much more efficacy. It integrates ECLET, Spiral Dynamics, and MEMEnomics all at once, reinterpreted through the lens of large-scale change that factors in the largest existential challenges that have surfaced in the last few decades. It pays homage to Graves, Beck, and Cowan, while updating my own work and recasting it in the dynamics of a never-ending quest.

The section below introduces the reader to what I consider the most relevant aspects of Spiral Dynamics that apply to large-scale change:

- Spiral Dynamics preserved much of Graves's original description of the framework as a human-development model that is hierarchically ordered; always open to change in terms of morals, values, motivations, and worldview; and comprises a self-organizing principle to define an individual, a group, a culture, and our entire species.

- Due to the academic and social resistance to any concept that espouses the use of hierarchy, Beck and Cowan assigned a color to each stage of development according to its numbered level in the upward flow within the spiral. The colors chosen have no particular meaning or historic relevance other than to distinguish each level from another on the model (see fig. 4.1 below).
- Beck's and Cowan's model preserved Graves's description of the oscillating nature of how psychosocial systems evolve to indicate the two types of systems, individualistic and sacrificial. Graves had assigned the odd numbers in the hierarchy to the individualistic systems and the even to the sacrificial systems and labeled the first

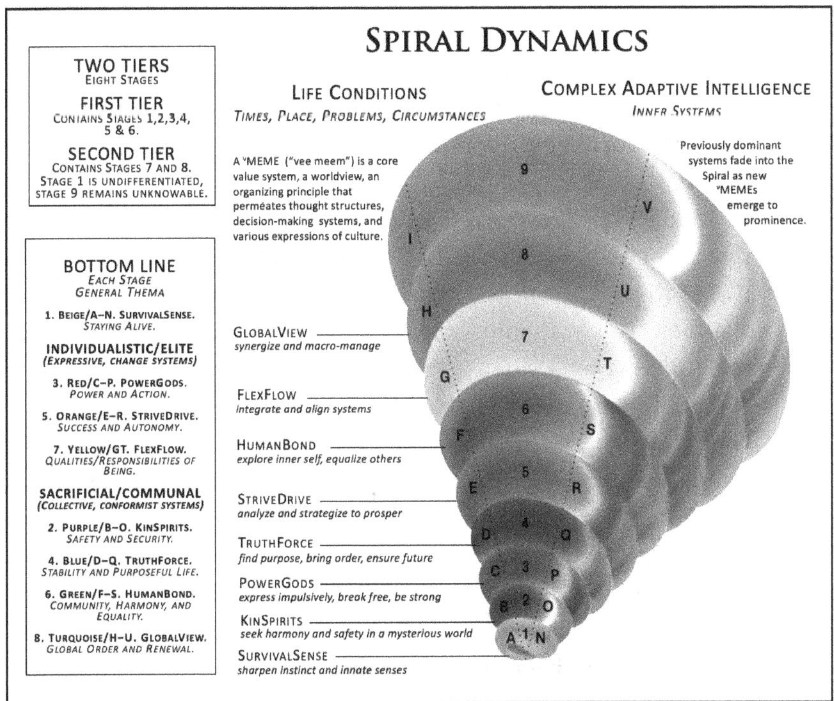

Figure 4.1. The Spiral-Dynamics Model. Adapted and used by permission from the Spiral-Dynamics Group and Don E. Beck.

level as an undifferentiated system. Beck and Cowan also adopted Graves's research indicating that, in the even-numbered systems, the brain's right hemisphere has cerebral dominance and, in the odd-numbered systems, beginning with the third, the left hemisphere has cerebral dominance.[15] In the Beck–Cowan color scheme, the warm colors (red, orange, and yellow) represent the individualistic systems, which are change systems, and the cool colors (purple, blue, green, and turquoise) represent the sacrificial systems, which are conformist systems. The communal systems are commonly referred to in Spiral Dynamics as "we/us/our" and the individualistic systems as "I/me/mine." Movement up the spiral oscillates between individualistic and sacrificial-communal systems.

- Beck and Cowan separated what Graves called the developmental *stages of a subsistent humanity* from the *stages of being* (which he also referred to as the "values of magnificence") and placed them onto two tiers in the model. The first tier contains the first six stages, and the second contains the last-known stages—levels seven and eight. Beck and Cowan also speculated that there might be a ninth stage on the horizon that is yet to be fully articulated.
- They also replaced *human adult psychosocial systems,* which was Graves's short-hand reference to the model, with the term *value systems.*
- To modernize Graves's reference to each stage as having an infinite number of peripheral expressions, Beck and Cowan borrowed the word *meme* from the work of evolutionary biologist Richard Dawkins. Today, the meaning of the word is limited to its use in social media as a video or a tweet that goes viral, but Dawkins originally used it as a cultural analogue to the DNA that carries genes. Memes are capable of self-replication and use the human mind as a host. The viral nature of how values spread was key to the success of Spiral Dynamics. It provided the means to understand how concepts such as capitalism or socialism can spread and come to define the minds of individuals, the driving force behind political and economic ideologies, and the worldview of entire cultures. The term *value system* became *value-system meme*, or ᵛ*MEME* for short, and it replaced the term *stage of development.*
- While Graves articulated a description of each system's organizational structure, it was Beck and Cowan, borrowing from

the management sciences and industrial psychology, who fully depicted the organizing codes and principles of each system and gave each a title that expressed its primary preference for management, as shown in figure 4.2.

- To express the holonic and fractal nature of the model that employs different strategies, Beck and Cowan further divided a ᵛMEME into what they called the *value-system attractor* (fig. 4.3). In the biological analogy, this *value-system attractor* is represented by the amino acids, the informational codes that make up our psychosocial DNA. Each value system or stage of development has an organizing principle, a center of gravity that is a self-replicating force made up of content-specific, geometric fractals forming a magnetic field that determines the totality of the stage's expression.[16] Historically, these fractals have represented vast areas of human inquiry, including economics, philosophy, technology, archetypes, psychology, religion, and politics. Since each *value-system attractor* is a fractal in itself, its content can be further broken down to contain smaller fractals. For example, the psychology fractal can be broken down to a variety of smaller attractors appropriate to each level of development, such as the structural, behavioral, psychoanalytic, and humanistic psychologies, and so on. One can follow this logic all the way down to the lower order of all the other fractals, and up or down the levels of complexity identified in chapter 2 to determine the appropriate attractor

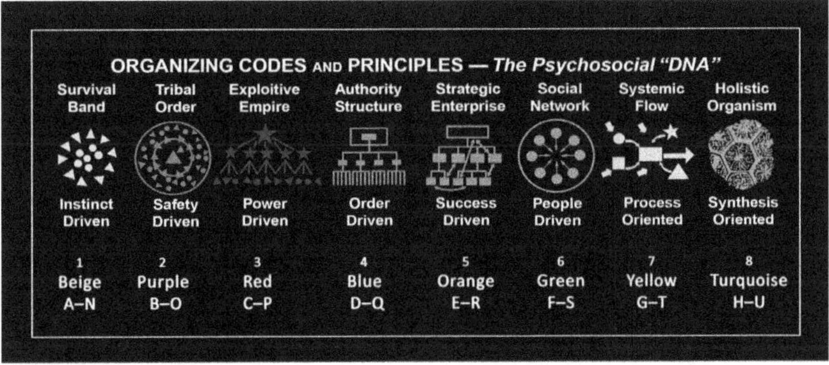

Figure 4.2 The Organizing Codes and Principles of the Eight Value Systems. These codes and principles define the spiral along with number, color, and alphabetical-coupling designations. Adapted and used by permission from the Spiral Dynamics Group and Don E. Beck.

THE VALUE-SYSTEM ATTRACTOR

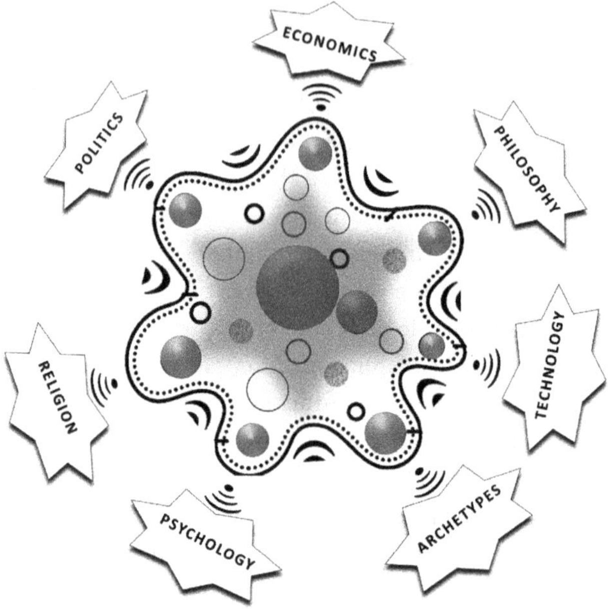

Figure 4.3. The Value-System Attractor. Adapted from Spiral Dynamics and used by permission from Don E. Beck.

mix that defines a region, a country, a community, a group, or an individual.

- Beck and Cowan simplified the neurobio-psycho-social aspect of Graves's model to identify the three aspects that make emergence possible. While Graves's term *core adaptive intelligence* appeared in the original book, in practice Beck changed it to *complex adaptive intelligence*, the term most commonly used by practitioners. *Complex adaptive intelligence* further replaced Graves's term *neurobio-psycho* (to which Graves also referred as *neuropsychology*). And Beck's term *life conditions* replaced Graves's term *social* (to which Graves also referred as *existential problems*). This simplified version of the double-helix aspect of Graves's original work keeps the model viable to this day (see fig. 6.1). The Spiral-Dynamics articulation of the two strands of the double helix are as follows:

  — ***Life Conditions*: Our external reality awakens latent vMEMEs and different stages of development.** The importance of *life* *conditions* in the model cannot be overstated. Our psychological response to our environment is what metaphorically triggers the switching on of lights in a room and the opening of higher-order software programs on a computer. It is what provides the framework, along with continuous adaptability, that defines the very nature of human and cultural evolution. The interaction between our internal states and our external worlds is what needs to be understood in order to provide robust solutions to the problems that face the world today. There are four important aspects to *life conditions* that determine the patterns of psychosocial and cultural emergence: time, place, problems, and circumstances.[17]

1. **Time:** Time is a factor along the overall line of human development. In any given Western community today, one finds people living alongside one another whose thinking is rooted in very different eras. Different people develop their own bundle of ᵛMEMEs designed to fit the time in which they live. While in the West, we view the 1990s as completely different from the 2010s, the times in traditional cultures have remained extraordinarily unchanged for generations.

   Time plays a crucial role in defining *life conditions.* In the historic analysis of geopolitical and economic models, it is when the policies behind these models become misaligned with the changing times that the failure of many governance and economic systems occur. On the life-cycle model discussed earlier, it is *chronic* misalignment that moves a value system to its nexus point where old ideas become subordinate to new ideas from the next value system in a process that keeps emergence healthy.
2. **Place.** *Place* refers to the geographical location and physical conditions under which individuals and groups live. Where we live has a direct impact on the levels of capacities within the brain that can be activated. External stimulation affects an urban dweller far differently than it does a suburban dweller and even more differently than it does the dweller of the rain forest or desert. Place affects the air we breathe, the food we eat, the architecture of the dwellings we design

to work in and inhabit. This aspect of the model has become a bit less relevant in the digital age, since anyone who has an Internet connection can tap into the vast networks of knowledge that bypass the limitations imposed by the absence of knowledge in a particular place.

3. **Problems.** The word *problems* signifies human challenges in terms of needs, priorities, concerns, and requirements for a particular individual, group, or culture that are common at every stage of development. Much of Maslow's *hierarchy-of-needs* framework addresses these aspects of *life conditions*, which involve survival, safety, belonging, and so on. It was Graves who uncovered that when problems overwhelm the existing coping mechanisms, they trigger new systems in the brain that can more accurately perceive the problem and deal with it appropriately.[18]
4. **Circumstances.** Circumstances are understood as the cultural placements within hierarchies of power, status, and influence. One's socioeconomic class, level of education, race, gender, and family lineage play a crucial role in defining this element of *life conditions*. It acts like a set of blinders that prevents an individual centered in a given ᵛMEME from seeing the rest of the levels that exist in reality. Understanding this last aspect of *life conditions* allows a value-systems expert to design strategies that naturally help people or cultures transcend the obstacles created by those blinders and advance to the next level. As an example, a leader in a tribal culture (the second stage of development) may view an outsider with skin of a different color as an enemy, but if that outsider possesses scientific knowledge (the fifth stage of development) and offers a solution to a problem no one in the tribe can solve, then the tribe may begin to lose its prejudice about what the outsider represents and begin to embrace the values of the fifth stage. The digital age has disrupted some such historic barriers and made them more visible; but, in many cases, the barriers have only changed from physical to digital form and cast the human-emergence process in a slightly different light. With Internet access, that same tribal leader can have someone from the tribe who is Internet savvy search for

the needed scientific knowledge online and be able to solve the issue at hand without consulting anyone else. The net effect is that the tribe's interaction with the outside world has changed from a human, face-to-face one to a digital one, giving the tribe the false sense that it can solve its own problems and doesn't need to have physical interaction with the outside world. This process reinforces the tribe's prejudices and other biases towards outsiders. This phenomenon is the primary cause of the tribalization we see in the Western world today.

— *Complex Adaptive Intelligence:* **Humans possess the capacities to create vMEMEs and different stages of development.** This is what the model commonly refers to as the different levels of our neuropsychological equipment that, when activated, can create a "new brain system" capable of handling the complexities that life throws our way. We have within us the capacity to exist at different levels of psychological development that reflect different perspectives of the world and the different complexities that exist in it.[19] I've heard Beck compare this aspect of the model to a personal computer, with the neurobiological aspect represented by the operating system and the psychological aspect represented by the various software programs that are present in latent forms just waiting to be turned on. Graves himself used even more common language, comparing the neurology to electrical wiring in a home and the psychology to the lights in a room that get activated when we turn on the light switch.

Graves explored the field of epigenetics as early as 1959 in an effort to disprove the prevailing deterministic view at the time that we are a product of our genes. He had written extensively about the role the environment plays in affecting who we are and what we are to become.[20] In the end, he couldn't dismiss the genetic—the bio-neurology—aspect of the model entirely. When asked why certain people fail to move into higher stages of existence, even when their environment is very supportive, he would simply answer: "It's the lottery of the brain."

- It is rooted in both models that different value systems, or stages of development, can coexist at the same time in a person or in a society.[21] Yet each will have a center of gravity or default position. For example, an individual might act from one level when she is with family and from a completely different level when at work. In the same way, groups or whole societies can operate from one or another stage of development. No single stage exists on its own; it is the total composite of present systems, sometimes calls the vMEME stack, that determines the totality of what's important for an individual or a culture.
- When determining the capacity for change in an individual, an organization, or a culture, each stage can be described in terms of the three conditions discussed in an earlier chapter: open, arrested, or closed.[23] A more detailed discussion of how to determine capacities for change will take place in other parts of the book.

— Each stage or value system can exhibit both healthy and unhealthy expressions.[22] In most developmental models, including Ken Wilber's integral-theory model, this characteristic is known today as a *growth hierarchy* versus a *dominator hierarchy*. The *growth hierarchy*—the healthy expression—is one that remains in an open state, accepting input from its environment and dissipating entropy to it. Conversely, the *dominator hierarchy*—the unhealthy expression—occurs when the life cycle of a particular stage or any of its fractal ideologies move past their nexus point and enter a closed state that can negatively affect the expression of all stages on the spiral. The closer the system moves to becoming closed, the more toxic its expression.

— One could argue that, within the fifth-level system, Tesla's business practices are a healthy expression that invites other businesses to assimilate its practices, while Exxon Mobil—and, by extension, the fossil-fuel industry—is an unhealthy expression that is in a closed state and wields financial and political power to keep its dying business model relevant. In the process, it contributes to an unhealthy *dominator hierarchy* along the entire spiral. The general rule is, the higher the stage of development from which the unhealthy expression comes in the hierarchy of the entire model, the more systemic damage it can cause a person, a group, an industry, or a culture.

- As a person or a culture moves up to a higher-level system, they transcend and include all the lower-level ones.[24] This is what Graves described as the subordination of earlier stages. It is a natural phenomenon; for example, molecules transcend atoms and cells transcend molecules, but all these structures express themselves in a harmonic mosaic that represents the fractal and holonic nature of the model. Individuals and cultures that transcend and include tend to experience a healthier existence on the spiral than the ones who reject the lower stages. Exclusion, or the skipping of a stage in the hierarchy, can manifest in pathologies or deficiencies when situations arise that call on the use of capacities proprietary to the stage that was excluded.
- When a people or cultures solve the problems of existence within their stage of development, they trigger the emergence of the next developmental stage and begin to work on solving the new problems that are unique to that stage. One shouldn't think of problems as negative attributes but more as life equations in the form of mathematical equations that need to be solved: if the world is thus, then appropriate behavior is so. Think also of the increased complexity of problem solving in terms of mathematics: the brain system that is activated at the second stage might be compared to simple arithmetic, while at stages seven and eight it could be compared to advanced calculus, differential equations, and complex algorithms. These problems can be positive, negative, or neutral; what they represent are new factors and of higher complexity in the equation of living. In this sense, problems are growth producing.

Importantly, the interaction between the two strands in the double-helix model—*life conditions* and *complex adaptive intelligence*—is what constitutes the emergent nature of this framework in defining the coupling of the eight stations as value systems or stages of development. The Gravesian representation of this is shown in figure 4.4 as the coupling of capital letters at every level. Graves arbitrarily picked sequential letters (A–H) in the first half of the alphabet to represent the *existential-problems* half in the ECLET model, or the *life-conditions* half in the Spiral Dynamics model; both models denote the challenges that have emerged from our environment or the problems that need to be solved. As higher-order problems

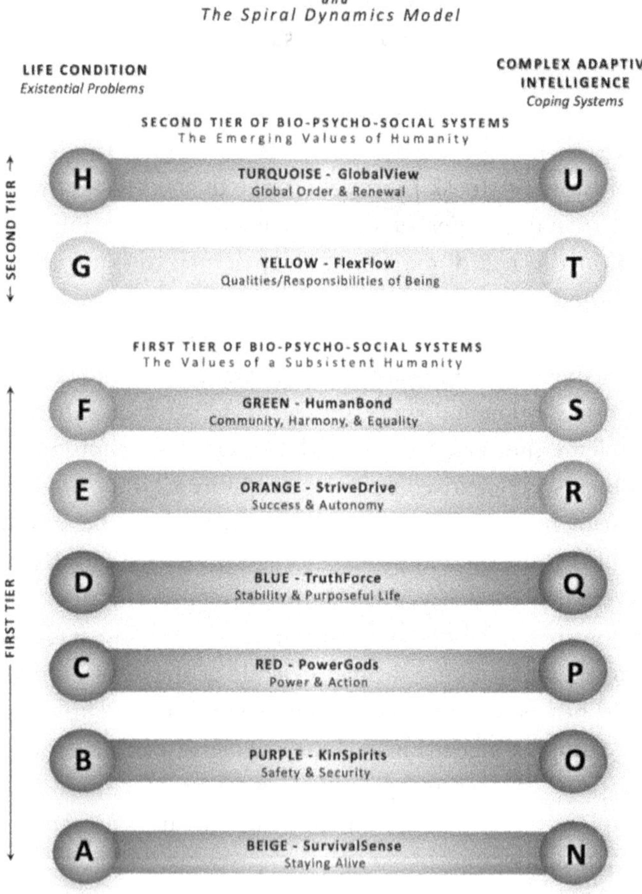

Figure 4.4. The Gravesian Alphabetical-Pairing System Coupled with the Spiral-Dynamics Model. A through H represent the *existential-problems* half of the ECLET model—or *life conditions* in the Spiral-Dynamics model—that have emerged so far. N through U represent the brain-tissue half of the ECLET model, or *complex adaptive intelligence* in the Spiral-Dynamics model. Used with permission from The Spiral-Dynamics Group and Don E. Beck.

appear in the environment beyond the letter H, they will be labeled I, J, and so on.

The second half of the alphabet represents what Graves informally referred to as *brain tissue* in his model, which is the *complex adaptive intelligence* in the Spiral Dynamics model. These neuropsychological systems—what Graves also referred to as coping systems—are unique to every stage and present in the brain, but in latent form. They become activated once a person or a culture is presented with any of the A through H *life conditions.* They are N, O, P, Q, R, S, T, and U. Similarly, as higher-order problems of existence appear, brain tissue V, W, and so on will be activated. This is the open-ended nature of the framework that led Graves to describe it as a never-ending quest. The alphabetical coupling of designations for the eight stages that have appeared in the model so far are A–N, B–O, C–P, D–Q, E–R, F–S, G–T, and H–U. Beck often describes this fundamental aspect of the model in his writings and lectures as a stratified approach to solving personal and cultural problems effectively: For instance, to solve the problems of existence of the A nature (staying alive), we need the N brain tissue (neuropsychological) system. To solve the B problems of safety and security, we need to activate the O brain tissue. The C problems of power and action activate the P brain tissue, and so on up the emergence ladder, coupling the *life-conditions* half of the stage of development with the *complex-adaptive-intelligence* half.[25]

Graves sometimes used two different forms of alphabetical ordering to make room for his *six-upon-six hypothesis* discussed in chapter 2. His research had shown a strong correlation between each level at every tier where the *general thema* of every level repeats in the following tier but at an exponentially higher level of psychosocial complexity.[26] Graves expressed the repeating aspect of the model with a prime designation in the lettering system resulting in A prime, N prime, B prime, and O prime, or in the coupling, A^1–N^1 in place of G–T and B^1–O^1 in place of H–U. The prime numbering should not be confused with his claims about a higher tier being an exponent of its predecessor. Were that the case, A^1–N^1 would have been expressed as A^2–N^2 and B^1–O^1 as B^2–O^2. Graves believed that in the first six stages of existence *Homo sapiens* seeks to satisfy his or her deficient needs in preparation for becoming a full human being in the second set of the six stages, which is why he called the second tier the *stages of being* and used it interchangeably with the *stages of magnificence.*[27]

> *Take anything* Homo sapiens *has strongly valued in the first ladder of existence,* [the first tier representing the first six stages of development], *reverse it, put it in higher-order form, and you have the key to what this theory says. Study the Tasaday tribe of the Philippines* [first stage in the first tier], *put their values and their ways into a technologically complex world, and you have the immediate future of a G–T world* [first stage in second tier, seventh stage overall]. *Then follow this new state of existence into an H–U form* [second stage, second tier, eighth stage overall], *and so on, and you can develop a general picture of the remote future of man.*
>
> —Clare W. Graves[28]

The Genesis of the *Sapiens* Iteration

Since the publication of my book *MEMEnomics,* Beck and I have had several discussions around the idea that chaotic change in the world was happening at such exponential speed that not enough of our collective *complex adaptive intelligence* was being triggered to identify its causes and so begin finding effective solutions. Based on research I began in 2016, I identified three major areas that define some aspects of this vast crucible of chaos.

The first is a general-systems conception I came to call the *Great Obsolescence* as discussed in the first section of this book. It is characterized by the ideologies behind our first-tier systems of subsistence and driven by the blind pursuit of global commerce that has been reaching different points of inflection resulting in a slow movement toward collective collapse.

The second source of chaos has been the disruption caused by the digital age that has rendered entire industries obsolete. It has deeply altered how *Homo sapiens* relate to each other, leaving nothing but mayhem in its wake, from political polarization and tribalization to online terrorist recruitment and everything in between. The most significant problem to arise from the digital age recently is the refinement in artificial intelligence, which has the potential to accelerate all the chaos the digital world has already created and threatens to eliminate whatever jobs and livelihoods the previous wave of digital disruption hasn't been successful in doing. The current iteration of AI is what the industry calls Large Language Models (LLMs) that define Microsoft's Bing, Google's Bard, and Open AI's ChatGPT. While industry leaders consider this iteration of technology their industry's crowning achievement, technology ethicists such as Tristan Harris believe it represents a new danger and a further departure from humanity's best interest. Harris represents a new breed of individuals who see the simplicity beyond the complexity that defines the digital age. In an open letter in March 2023, he and 1,100 of the most prominent tech leaders called on government to impose a moratorium on artificial intelligence with the concern that these systems are developing nonhuman minds that cannot be fully understood or controlled and will make us replaceable if not outright obsolete.[29]

This type of statement, as worrisome as it is, doesn't fully explore the range of damage AI can cause should it fall into the hands of rogue leaders and groups intent on fighting ideological and existential wars. We have already seen some of the damage the algorithms in these models can cause. In just the few months since LLMs became available to the public, a phenomenon known as AI hallucinations have become a wide concern. As the name implies, an AI model "hallucinates" an answer when it incorrectly translates input and its algorithms produce outputs that are not based on its training data or that follow an identifiable pattern of logic. When this happens, the output of misinformation moves at the speed of the Internet.

These recent advancements are the most currently relevant examples of the binary nature of Promethean intelligence. The exception is that we have added an accelerant to the fire that is causing it to move at the speed of light, and very few know how to control it. The issue of AI urgently needs to trigger our *complex adaptive intelligence* if we are to save humanity from the chaos and destruction brought about by the digital age.

The third area of chaos I identified are the various pressing issues regarding climate change and other areas of the Earth's systems that are reaching beyond their carrying capacities, which seem to increase in complex and chaotic ways with every passing day. This is the far greater problem in which all our other problems are nested, and it requires the triggering of the highest *complex adaptive intelligence* Graves, Beck, and Cowan had identified but hadn't fully articulated during their time. While possible solutions to the other two areas of chaos can come from incrementally higher levels of human intelligence, this problem in particular requires an entirely different approach. Climate reality has changed everything we've known about the application of the model. In our myopic pursuit of commerce, digital and otherwise, we have triggered the collapse of Earth's ecosystems, a *life-conditions* problem that requires humanity to subsume its collective intelligence into that of Mother Nature and return to being part of its deep ecology. That is, we must begin to think like Mother Nature in order to prevent the collapse of life on the whole planet. As environmental disasters have increased in size and our scientific models have failed fully to identify their causes and the magnitude of their damage, the *complex-adaptive-intelligence* part of the model has been rendered insufficient, and the capacity for a higher, even more complex science needs to be triggered. According to Graves, *human* intelligence has been around for a few hundred thousand years and, with all its scientific discoveries of the last five centuries, has held all the power in human-built systems. Imagine, then, the irony that, in less than the last mere fifty years, human intelligence has again become secondary to natural intelligence, the intelligence that has defined all life on our planet for the last *three billion* years.

> *We have no evidence, whatsoever, that the* Homo sapiens *who was born this morning is generally any different than the* Homo sapiens *who was born 100,000 years ago. We are but one biological organism, but we have evidence that seven times in our history we have started to think differently as a human being. We are one biological being; we are an infinite number of psychological beings.*
>
> —Clare W. Graves[30]

Every time I discussed these issues with Beck, a genius in his own right, he remained undeterred while reminding me that my focus was too close for me to see the full picture on the long arc of history.

"These are epochal times; you need to stand on Jupiter and look back," he would say, and then he would refer to Grave's work in brain research, anthropology, phenomenology, systems thinking, and other fields that could not be contained within one area of academic study. Beck spent a lifetime proving the totality of the Gravesian conception through modern scientific and academic research and in geopolitical applications and was in awe of Graves's prophetic and intuitive nature. As part of the first generation of systems thinkers, Graves's ability to integrate so many fields of study allowed him to put the history of humanity in proper context and project a future that is remarkably accurate. It was his less-known work overlooked in Spiral Dynamics which reminded me that, in our human journey so far, we have used very little of our brain capacity, and that—as the title of this part of the book implies—we are only at the beginning of discovering who we are.

According to Graves, as *Homo sapiens* we are one biological being, but we represent an infinite number of psychological beings. In viewing our current reality from Jupiter, I remembered Graves's original classification of the two tiers that Beck and I dared not use in our work due to its political incorrectness. That is, Graves often referred to the first tier as *animalistic*, wherein human behavior has remained deficient and much like that of the animals; he said that *Homo sapiens* will begin to realize his full potential only as he enters the second tier, which Graves called the *being* tier.[31] It is from that classification I realized that *Homo sapiens* the human *being* is on the threshold of tapping into the neurobiology of *being* and that our existence so far has been the prerequisite journey through psychological development that has brought us to this critical stage in history. We as human beings might be distinguished from other primates by our exceptionally large brain, but, in our existence until now, we have used only our smallest cognitive capacities to differentiate ourselves from other primates and the rest of the animal kingdom. So, while biologists and anthropologists still classify us as *Homo sapiens*, developmental psychologists such as Graves have classified us in terms of how much of our latent capacity in our big brains has been activated. In creating the *sapiens* terminology, I wanted to integrate the biological, anthropological, and psychological aspects of our development in terms of a much larger holon than the one for which the Gravesian framework has so far been used. This new terminology provides a mega view that transcends and includes the world fractal-level view on geopolitics and economics, the group fractal-level view on organizations, the community fractal-level view on communities, and the individual fractal-level view on personal growth. These are the various-sized fractals that are depicted in fig 2.1. It nests them all in language that reminds us that we are an integral part of the greater intelligence, the natural intelligence of the biosphere, the atmosphere, the hydrosphere, and the pedosphere all working together to ensure that all life on Earth is preserved.

This view on the interdependence of all life is what allowed me to label the Gravesian stages in language and stage numbering that is anthropological in nature, while staying true to both Graves's ECLET and Beck's Spiral Dynamics. The result is the table below (4.1) that honors those who came before me while giving the reader a wider, more mainstream iteration of human nature. This new terminology will be integrated into the two previous conceptions and used interchangeably with them throughout the remainder of the book. While the previous models caused some confusion when the colors or the *general thema* of a stage were applied to all the holonic structures in the model, I designate the latinized names of the stages to the development of the individual *Homo*

STAGE OF DEVELOPMENT Time First Appeared	GRAVESIAN ALPHABETICAL PAIRING ECLET Designation	SPIRAL DYNAMICS Color Designation	HOMO SAPIENS Name	HOMO SAPIENS Numeral Designation	MODE OF THINKING	BASIC THEME & CHARACTERISTICS Personal, Organizational, and Cultural Manifestations
THE SECOND TIER OF BIO-PSYCHO-SOCIAL DEVELOPMENT: THE MAGNIFICENT HUMAN, *HOMO MAGNIFICUS*						
8 50 years ago	H–U, B1–O[1] Experiential	Turquoise	*Homo universalis*	*Sapiens* 2.2	Holistic Planetary	The Regenerative Community Sees Earth as single dynamic organism with its own collective mind. Intuitive and holistic. Fully integrated right and left brain. Driven by Earth's changes. Ecologically aligned humanity and global governance.
7 70 years ago	G–T, A1–N[1] Existential	Yellow	*Homo ecosistamus*	*Sapiens* 2.1	Ecological Systemic	The Integrated Self Values the magnificence of existence. Integrative & ecological. Accepts chaos and change as normal. Big-picture views. Left brain with intuition. Thinks in natural systems. Lean knowledge. Self-principled. Deals with multiple realities.
THE FIRST TIER OF BIO-PSYCHO-SOCIAL DEVLOPMENT: THE SUBSISTENT HUMAN, *HOMO SUBSISTENS*						
6 150 years ago	F–S Relativistic	Green	*Homo consonus*	*Sapiens* 1.6	Humanitarian Pluralistic	The Egalitarian Community Seeks consensus, inner peace with self and others. Equal distribution of resources. Communitarian, egalitarian, harmonious, authentic, sharing, caring, free of greed and dogma.
5 500 years ago	E–R Multiplistic	Orange	*Homo prudentus*	*Sapiens* 1.5	Strategic Manipulative	The Enlightened Self Uncovers the secrets of the universe through the scientific method. Manipulates Earth's resources for the good life. Acts in best self-interest. Driven, optimistic, materialistic, reductionist. Consumer and success oriented.
4 5,000 years ago	D–Q Absolutistic	Blue	*Homo virtus*	*Sapiens* 1.4	Authoritarian Conformist	The Orderly Community Emphasis on meaning, direction, and purpose. Seeks the righteous pathway through truth and the transcendent cause. Discipline, traditions, morality, the rule of law. Lives for later.
3 10,000 years ago	C–P Egocentric	Red	*Homo victoris*	*Sapiens* 1.3	Exploitive Impulsive	The Powerful Self Feels no guilt. Expects attention. Demands respect. Breaks free of domination. Fulfills personal desires. Stands tall. Seeks instant gratification, glitz, conquest, and violence. Lives for now.
2 50,000 years ago	B–O Animistic	Purple	*Homo domestitus*	*Sapiens* 1.2	Ritualistic	The Tribal Community Allegiance to chief, elders, ancestors, and the clan. Obeys the spirits. Rites, rituals, taboos, superstitions, tribes, folkways, and lore.
1 100,00 to 200,000 years ago	A–N Autistic	Beige	*Homo naturalis*	*Sapiens* 1.1	Instinctive	The Undifferentiated Self Driven by instinct and habit. Seeks food, water, procreation, and protection. Staying alive.

Table 4.1. The First and Second Tiers of Bio-Psycho-Social Development. Adapted in part from the work of Clare W. Graves and Don E. Beck and used by permission.

sapiens, and the *sapiens* numbering to all the larger holons. All new terms that refer to these new designations are shown in italics.

The First Tier: Stages of the Subsistent Human

Stage 1: A–N Autistic, Beige, *Homo naturalis, Sapiens 1.1,* Instinctive; The Undifferentiated Self

At the Beige stage of development, *sapiens 1.1,* all energy is directed toward survival through innate sensory abilities and instinctual reactions. At this stage, humans form herd-like, survival bands that are loosely organized with little structure.[32] This is the first emergence of humans from their animal nature. *Homo Naturalis* inhabits caves and whatever crawl-into space Mother Nature has carved out. Food, water, warmth, sex, and safety are the primary focus of attention. At this stage, *Homo sapiens* cannot differentiate him- and herself from other objects in their surroundings.

This stage rarely exists on its own today, but it is seen in newborns, individuals dealing with late-stage Alzheimer's disease, and mentally-ill street people. Beige's motto or general thema is, *Express self now in order to survive.* At this level, there is no attention available for anything but survival. The 1981 movie *Quest for Fire* provides a good example of the *sapiens 1.1* stage of development. And a contemporary manifestation of

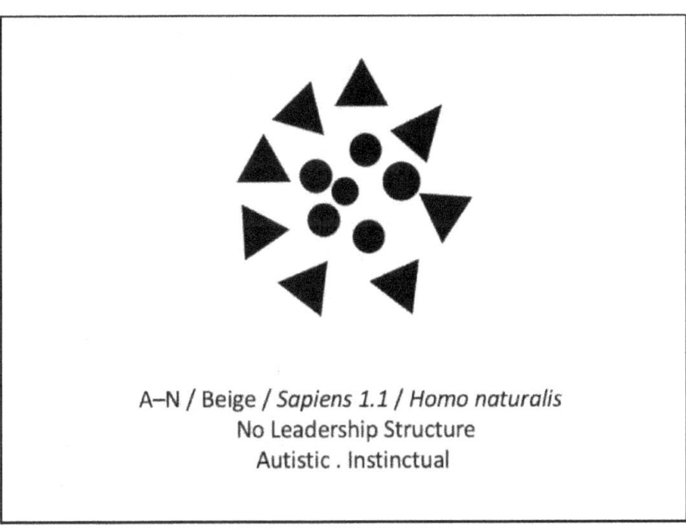

Figure 4.5. Leadership at the Stage 1 Level of Development. Survival band, instinct driven. Adapted from Spiral Dynamics and used by permission from Don E. Beck.

this stage is depicted in the 2000 movie *Cast Away*, in which the character played by Tom Hanks goes through a harrowing journey of survival after his plane crashes on a remote island. In this stage, there are no economic or governance models or the existence of any sort of barter or trade. As food becomes scarcer and the habitat for this first level of existence no longer supports survival bands, *Homo Naturalis* gives way to the second-level stage.

Stage 2: B–O Animistic, Purple, *Homo domesticus, Sapiens 1.2,* Ritualistic; The Tribal Community

This is the value-system level of kin spirits and the tribe.[33] The thinking of *Homo domesticus* is magical and in response to a mysterious and threatening world: Nature is powerful and must be feared, and we must band together to survive. Although the emphasis is still on survival, unlike in the *sapiens 1.1* system that has no permanent organizing structure, in the *sapiens 1.2* system survival is achieved through the banding together of the tribe. It takes an entire hunting party to kill the beast in order for the tribe to eat and survive. *Homo domesticus* is a group-oriented system, in which people sacrifice individual needs for the needs of the tribe, the elders, and the ancient ways and show allegiance to the chief and the clan. Pleasing the gods and spirits, maintaining tribal traditions, and keeping the tribe's home warm and safe are the highest priorities. At this stage, there is no room for individual thinking or action; the ego is subsumed into the group. The group preserves sacred objects, places, events, and memories; it also observes traditional rites of passage, seasonal cycles, and tribal customs. Accordingly, the color of this stage is purple, the color of magic and mystery.

There are many places in the world where *sapiens 1.2* remains the predominant value system, including Africa, many parts of Asia and South and Central America, and on tribal Native American land in the United States. The Middle East, in spite of the sudden appearance of oil wealth over the last hundred years, also remains predominantly in the *sapiens 1.2* value system. Many aspects of this stage are found in highly developed, first-world societies as well. Beliefs in guardian angels, blood oaths, good-luck charms, and family rituals or superstitions are all signs of this value system. Fraternities and sororities, fraternal lodges, professional-sports teams, and certain corporate tribes are all manifestations of this stage of development. Labor unions around the world carry some of its

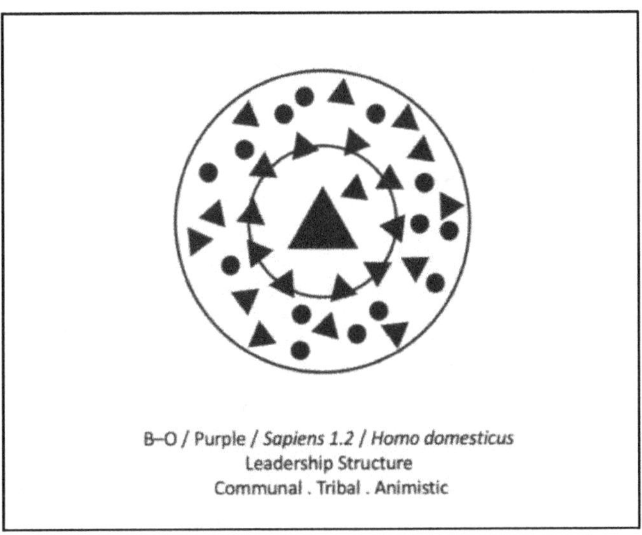

B–O / Purple / *Sapiens 1.2* / *Homo domesticus*
Leadership Structure
Communal . Tribal . Animistic

Figure 4.6. Leadership at the Stage 2 Level of Development. Tribal order, safety driven. Adapted from Spiral Dynamics and used by permission from Don E. Beck.

undertones. Much of religious thinking in less-advanced cultures, regardless of faith or denomination, is rooted in the *sapiens 1.2* stage.

Decision making in this second-level system is based on custom and tradition and is made by a council of elders, often relying on mystical information supplied by a shaman. The average tribal member is uninvolved in much of the decision-making process. Attempts to introduce democratic thought into tribal groups do not work since the idea of individual decision making does not exist at this stage of development. Wealth is divided in a communal manner, regardless of who may have actually created it. A good example of this practice is how Native American tribes distribute gambling revenues from casinos among tribal members. In oil-rich countries of the Middle East, tribes believe that God placed the oil under their feet and that therefore it should be shared.

The nature of thinking at this second-level stage is fearful and mystical. Tribal members must behave in the traditional ways. The taboos must be obeyed and tribal leaders must be honored with absolute obedience and conformity, with a reverence for seniority and ancestors. Education is paternalistic and relies heavily on rituals and routines. Learners are passive, and individual creativity is not possible. The family is one of extended kinships marked by strict role relationships. Rules and traditions are designed to protect kin bloodlines. Ritualistic rites of passage are an important aspect of each stage of life.

The *sapiens 1.2* economic system existed for thousands of years before the Industrial Revolution. Today, it represents 2–3 percent of global Gross Domestic Product (GDP).[34] Localized, tribal, and primarily agricultural, this stage's economic expression is defined by simple production, agricultural trade, or barter. Subsistence was the order of the day if not the century. Life was lived from one harvest season to the next and at the mercy of nature and the gods. Tribes remained in the same geographic location for centuries cultivating their ancestral land. A grandfather's income varied very little from his grandson's. Technological advancement amounted to fashioning a better hand tool to till the ground or a better harness for the oxen. Occasionally, tribes exchanged food or grain with other tribes in an early sign of the emergence of trade.

Land and territory have sacred meaning in this value system, and tribes will fight bloody battles to regain and protect ancestral land. Since there is little individual thought at this stage, a leader who has ascended to the next stage can easily control the group. The subjects of many dictators past and present have been at the *sapiens 1.2* stage of development. But with the passage of time and as *life conditions* change, younger and stronger members of the tribe start to develop individual thinking. This independence emerges when the fear of nature diminishes, tribal bonds weaken, traditional offerings and rituals fail to fend off evil spirits or bring the desired benefits, or the tribal order for some reason begins to collapse.

When the tools of tribal existence no longer serve the *life conditions*, or when *Homo domesticus* loses his or her fear of Mother Nature, is when we move to the next level of existence. The 2007 movie, *Mongol: The Rise of Genghis Khan*, depicts this transition. In it, Khan overcomes his fear of nature after suffering a long imprisonment fully exposed to the elements and emerges to the *Homo victoris* stage, at which point he changes history.

Stage 3: C–P Egocentric, Red, *Homo victoris*, *Sapiens 1.3*, Exploitive/Impulsive; The Powerful Self

Homo victoris is the stage at which we see the first appearance of the individual ego in its raw form. It is an expressive, individualistic stage and represents the first emergence of real and effective individual action. Red

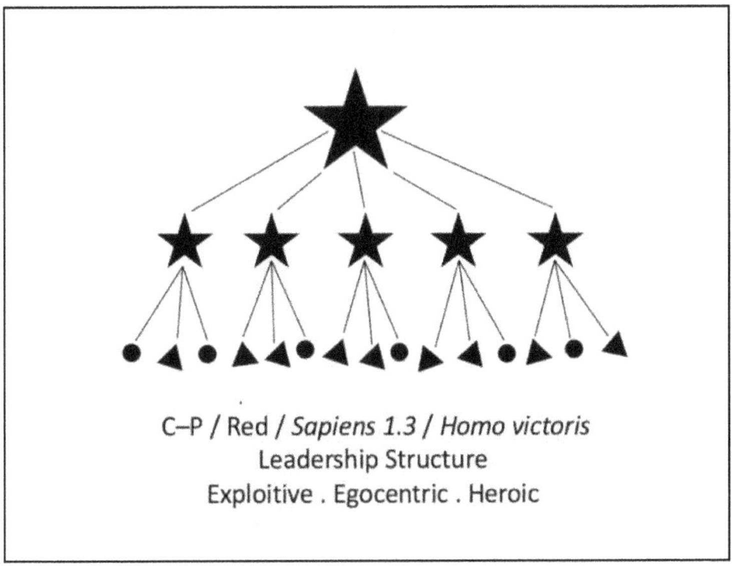

C–P / Red / *Sapiens 1.3* / *Homo victoris*
Leadership Structure
Exploitive . Egocentric . Heroic

Figure 4.7. Leadership at the Stage 3 Level of Development. Exploitative empire, power driven. Adapted from Spiral Dynamics and used by permission from Don E. Beck.

is interested in power and enforces it over self, others, and nature through exploitative, independent action.[35] The motto of *Homo victoris* is, "Express self now and impulsively and to hell with others!" Red grabs what it wants with no guilt and no compassion. To a person at this stage of development, the world is a jungle full of threats and predators. *Homo victoris* wants to break free from domination or constraint. He or she stands tall and makes statements such as, "After me the deluge," or, "I'm the only one who can fix it." She demands attention and respect from others and calls the shots. He acts without conscience and enjoys life to the fullest without remorse. Individuals at this stage of development operate totally in the "now," with no sense of future consequences or any desire or ability either to delay gratification or to make personal sacrifices. Examples of *Homo victoris* include children in the terrible twos, rebellious teenagers, those with the frontier mentality, those in feudal kingdoms, soldiers of fortune, rap musicians, those in the prison culture, dictators, and gang leaders. The mob mentality represented in movies and on television is a good depiction of this value system in modern Western cultures.

In this stage, decisions are made by the most powerful person and are based on what creates the most respect or what feels good in the moment. The leader must give his followers immediate gratification, and absolute loyalty is demanded. All information flows downward from the leader, and little if any information flows upward. Participatory democracy is not possible in Red. While it may use the appearance of the equal, participatory process, Red will corrupt the vote. The most powerful gets the spoils and decides how they are distributed, if they are distributed at all. Education is based on tests of worthiness and tough-love tactics. The community is one in which predators are in control, outsiders are in danger, fiefdoms are formed, and turf wars are constantly being fought. *Homo victoris* includes exploitation of women, children, and the weak and evinces total reliance on the power principle.

In terms of societal structures, *sapiens 1.3* is the level of the empire, examples of which include the Sumerian Dynasty, the Babylonian Dynasty, the Persian Empire, and the Roman Empire. Its value system ranges in functionality from the vicious to the heroic and can contain healthy aspects. Wars cannot be fought without soldiers who have healthy *sapiens 1.3* courage. This stage of development takes society out of the *sapiens 1.2* system and creates the first individualists and proactive humans. Its unhealthy expression is selfish, predatory, and violent, and it refuses to recognize the limits of individualistic capacity. People in this stage have an unrealistic view of their own abilities and knowledge and an unrealistic sense of invulnerability.

Viewing the modern economic history of the United States through this framework, the *sapiens 1.3* economic cycle was the first large-wave cycle of its kind that I had mapped and researched for *MEMEnomics*. It represented economic activity from the period immediately after the Civil War to the middle of the Great Depression. In my work with economic systems, I have labeled this cycle the *fiefdoms of power* to describe the time when a handful of men in the industrial and financial sectors were responsible for the majority of America's productive output.[36] A modern-day *sapiens 1.3* economic system is evident in countries whose overall stages of development have remained in the *sapiens 1.2* stage prior to the discovery of natural resources. They include most of the OPEC members as well as parts of Africa and South America, and they account for 4–7 percent of the global GDP.[37] A contemporary manifestation of this system's economic and governance method is present in Russia, where a few oligarchs who were members of the Communist Party before the collapse of the Soviet Union now control the country's resources. True to the dominant nature of the system's leadership structure, no oligarch has dared to challenge Putin even after he invaded Ukraine, fearing his wrath more than the possibility of losing their financial power should he lose the war and a new form of Russian leadership arise. *Sapiens 1.3* economic activities in advanced Western economies are primarily known for their exploitation, if not for their outright illegal activities. Today, much of the use of crypto currency supports the economic activities of *sapiens 1.3*; those activities are done on the dark Web and represent billions in unsanctioned trade and criminal activity daily. In popular culture, *Homo victoris's* psychological profile is depicted in many of the mob movies such as *The Godfather* trilogy, the 1983 movie *Scarface*, the 2019 movie *The Irishman*, and the HBO series *The Sopranos.*

Homo victoris can transition to the next stage when there is a questioning of personal power and a need for structured discipline. The "I-want-it-all-and-now" ethos that has caused so much bloodshed, destruction, and mayhem begins to give way to a more tempered, long-term view of life and purpose. A healthy leader in this stage of development who is in an open state would recognize when a community or a culture is ready for the transition to the next stage. In most cases, however, *Homo victoris* desperately holds on to power and must be removed by force in order for the next system to emerge.

Stage 4: D–Q Absolutist, Blue, *Homo virtus*, *Sapiens 1.4*, Authoritarian/ Conformist; The Orderly Community

The Blue value system characterizes the beginning of what most people think of as civilization since it is organized around an absolute belief in one right way and obedience to its authority.[38] This is the *sapiens 1.4* stage of development, and some of its examples include the Abrahamic religions; God, Country and Apple Pie; the Communist Party; and the armed forces of a nation. The basic theme of *Homo virtus* is that life has meaning, direction, and purpose, with predetermined outcomes. If the *true meaning* is found and followed, everything will be okay. This is a communal sacrificial system, in which individuality is sacrificed to the transcendent cause, truth, or righteous pathway. In a *sapiens 1.4* system, the order enforces a code of conduct based on eternal, absolute principles. Regulatory structures within governments at various levels fall into the *sapiens 1.4* stage of development. The police, the local zoning board, the Securities and Exchange Commission, the FDIC, and the Office of Thrift Supervision are all examples of *sapiens 1.4* in government, and so are the FBI, the IRS, NOAA, and the EPA.

Homo virtus believes that righteous living produces stability now and guarantees future rewards; that impulsivity is controlled through guilt; that everybody has his or her proper place; and that laws, regulations, and discipline build character and moral fiber. A *sapiens 1.4* society is highly stratified, with each person having his or her role; upward mobility is seniority based and in many cases slow or nonexistent. This stage of development is about law and order in reaction to the lawlessness of *Homo victoris.* Because right and wrong are guiding forces, the spoils at this stage go to the righteous. Whatever the organizing truth is within the system, there is only one right way, and that right way is enforced with laws, punishments, and guilt. Adherence to the Truth is rewarded with guaranteed retirement and the hope of a better future or afterlife.

Education is seen as Truth handed down from authority and accomplished in traditional and hierarchical stairsteps. It often takes the form of moralistic lessons reinforced with punishment for errors. Teaching is strict, punitive, and black and white. The motto is, "Spare the rod and spoil the child." The family is the seat of Truth and values, responsible for teaching moral values and codes of conduct. The community ideals are peace and quiet, law and order, and compliance to rules. The best citizen is a law-abiding citizen who knows his place.

Though the theme of *sapiens 1.4* is the One True Way, the exact nature of this truth can vary widely. The Cold War, for instance, was a struggle between two different *sapiens 1.4* truths—the American Way and the Communist Way. The conflict between the West and Islam also comprises two opposing truths. They can be as divergent as the ideologies behind the Christian Right, Islamic fundamentalism, Communism, the Catholic Church, or right- or left-wing causes. A Western advanced culture might view Islamic fundamentalism as a false or outdated expression of the *sapiens 1.4* value system, while, for the culture practicing it, it might be the only truth it knows. At this stage of development, there are no shades of gray. Everything is either right or wrong, and it is much easier to perceive truth through this black-and-white worldview.

Home Virtus deals with an almost perpetual burden of guilt. It is a sacrificial system that supplants individuality for communal acceptance. Its motto is, "Sacrifice self as authority dictates to obtain the reward later." This is a move from the *now* awareness and instant gratification of *Homo victoris* to an awareness of future consequences. At this higher stage, the reward is often so delayed that it sometimes comes only in heaven, as with fundamentalist Christianity and Islam. The system comes into being to deal with the excesses of *sapiens 1.3* and its lawlessness. Law and order and punishment are major aspects of this fourth stage of development. Rather than managing *sapiens 1.3* and guiding it to the next level, its strategy is to educate, reform, and shape it with either the design of a "good authority" apparatus or, if necessary, the use of more punitive measures. A robust system at this stage of development runs the trains on time, provides safety and security to society, and imposes a form of justice and stability. With individuals and cultures that are in an open state, surrounding *Homo victoris* with *sapiens 1.4* institutions often contains its raw energy and impulsivity and sets it on the right evolutionary path forward.

At the macro and geopolitical levels, the *sapiens 1.4* stage of development represents the foundation stone for a functioning democracy. It removes the power from the hands of the egocentric, charismatic *Homo victoris* leader, who is often male, and vests it in the institutions of a nation. Much of the failed-states phenomena we see in cultures around the world is due to a misalignment between governing structures imposed by Western colonialists and the local *life conditions* in that culture. Western

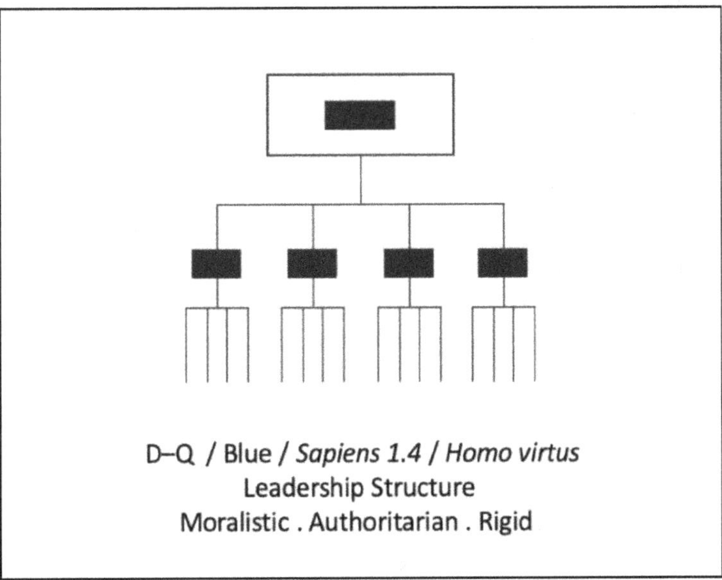

D–Q / Blue / Sapiens 1.4 / Homo virtus
Leadership Structure
Moralistic . Authoritarian . Rigid

Figure 4.8. Leadership at the Stage 4 Level of Development. Authority, structure, and order driven. Adapted from Spiral Dynamics and used by permission from Don E. Beck.

democracy was born from the *sapiens 1.4, sapiens 1.5,* and *sapiens 1.6* stages of development, with dense Western content shaped by the colonialists' own unique histories and experiences. But, when the model is imposed on cultures that have remained in *sapiens 1.2* and *sapiens 1.3* with *their* own unique indigenous content, the *sapiens 1.4* structure that holds the new institutions becomes vacuous and subject to great exploitation. It enables *sapiens 1.3* leaders to use these institutions to extend their reign of terror and persecution over their historic enemies within the territories of the newly created nation, while masquerading as leaders of a sovereign and modern entity on the world stage, exploiting all the benefits the modern designation of "nation" gives them.

The *sapiens 1.4* organizational structure is a passive hierarchy, as in the Catholic Church or the military, with rigid rules for structure and rank and a strict adherence to the organizational chart. The person with positional power makes decisions, and power accrues to the position, not the individual. The *system,* rather than the individual, is of prime importance; and the *system,* not the individual, is promoted, preserved, and maintained. Communication is downward but also horizontal—unlike in *sapiens 1.3,* in which there is no horizontal communication within an organization. This stage of development strongly supports the seniority system, one of delayed gratification in which everyone has his or her place. The result is a stratified society with little upward mobility and many bureaucracies. Generally, the only way to move up in the organizational chart is for someone to retire or die.

The healthy aspects of this stage include the control of violence that defines the previous stage and the creation of a more stable society based on the rule of law. The emphasis is on fairness, equity, and uniform treatment. Laws are applied equally, the motto being, "A country of laws, not of men." This stage also creates meaningful progress over the previous two stages in eliminating human suffering and ending historic sectarian wars fought by tribes with *sapiens 1.3* leaders.

One of the unhealthy aspects of this stage is its punitive and inflexible nature, seeing everything in black and white. It gave us the Salem Witch Trials, the Spanish Inquisition, and McCarthyism. It gave us fundamentalist religions, racism, and totalitarian Communism.

In popular culture, the psychological profile of *Homo virtus* is depicted in the 1989 movie *Dead Poets Society* where, in 1950s America, nonconformity to the One True Way is not tolerated and can result in tragic consequences. It is also depicted in the frontier mentality of Lieutenant John J. Dunbar, played by Kevin Costner, in the 1990 movie *Dances with Wolves*, in which he adheres to the Union Army's rules and procedures even when he hasn't been part of the system for some time. He rations his provisions and uses *sapiens 1.4* weapons in *life conditions* dominated by an indigenous form of *sapiens 1.2, Homo domesticus*—the Lakota Sioux—into which he eventually assimilates. In the process, he comes to understand the punitive nature of a system organized around the Western virtues of absolutism that viewed Native Americans as enemies.

Sapiens 1.4's inflexibility in the economic regulatory fractal within an advanced culture will keep out the new talent and innovation needed to detect fraud, especially when the fraud is perpetrated from within a higher value system. Inflexibility over time leads to that fractal becoming a closed system as incompetence within it grows. A good recent example is our inability to detect the $9 billion fraud perpetrated by Elizabeth Holmes, founder and CEO of Theranos, a company that promised to revolutionize blood testing but failed to deliver on its promise. Holmes was arrested and charged with fraud in 2018 but only after a whistle blower sounded the alarm. Another example—one that could represent the faulty grounds on which the entire cryptocurrency industry stands—is the $32 billion fraud perpetrated by Sam Bankman-Fried, founder and CEO of FTX, the world's third-largest cryptocurrency exchange, which filed for bankruptcy protection in November 2022. In this case, it wasn't a whistle blower who alerted the authorities but an investor who couldn't convert his holdings to cash. In March 2024, Bankman-Fried was sentenced to twenty-five years in prison and ordered to pay eleven billion dollars in forfeiture for his crime.

Both these examples show the deterioration of the *sapiens 1.4* value system in the economic fractal resulting in its inability to detect fraud. The weakening of our economic regulatory structures and institutions began with the first Raegan administration and—over time—moved into arrested or closed states. Had we maintained appropriate regulation of the financial sector, both above crimes would have been caught by regulators and dealt with in their earlier stage. *Sapiens 1.4*'s inability to keep up with how to regulate in changing times, and its inflexible nature in an ever-evolving world, can make it ineffectual, stuck in outdated fault-finding outlooks while at the same time missing the bigger picture.

Most points of view in this fourth stage of development provide an automatic defense of prejudices. Its wars are fought to promote or defend true beliefs and ideology. In many ways, this characteristic makes *sapiens 1.4*–inspired wars more vicious and destructive than those of *sapiens 1.2* or *sapiens 1.3*. Battles for territory at any stage seek to conquer both natural and human resources and subject them to the will of their new masters. The approach of *sapiens 1.3* to war, although violent, is often based on principles of honor, and its warriors show great respect for their opponents. *Sapiens 1.4* armies, on the other hand, demonize their opponents and are quite willing to wipe them out. Evil becomes imbedded in the institutions created the *sapiens 1.4* ideology and can last far beyond the lifetime of a single *Homo victoris*, whose power vanishes upon his death.

A *sapiens 1.4* economic system is one dominated by central planning and production. Its historic manifestation in the United States began as a reaction to the Great Depression and took root at the outset of World War II and ended in the late 1970s. It is the second large-wave cycle, which I call the *patriotic prosperity cycle*, that gave us all the institutions resulting from FDR's New Deal policies that remain with us to this day.[39] In its purest form, a *sapiens 1.4* economy has no room for individuality. A financial system could be well developed, but its purpose is to serve the One True Way as determined by its leaders. This was the economic model romanticized by the communist ideology and quickly proven to be susceptible to corruption and obsolescence if policy makers were out of touch with the needs of the people. The only modern-day economy that uses this model is China, which today represents 14–17 percent of global GDP.[40] It is the ethos of central planning and the command-and-control structure proprietary to the *sapiens 1.4* economy that allowed China to become such an economic superpower in such a short time.

Economic policies at this stage of development, although necessary, should remain transitory. They are designed to build the infrastructure of nations: the physical ones such as highways, dams, airports, and seaports as well as the institutional ones such as the central banks, stock exchanges, and all accompanying institutions that regulate and guide them in spreading the values of a culture built on a *sapiens 1.4* foundation. Many of China's economic woes today can be blamed on its inability to see the transitory nature of the *sapiens 1.4* economic stage of development, which erects entire cities built by elite developers and bankers with close ties to the Communist Party without ever gauging market prices and supply and demand. The rigidity of this value system and its policies allow for very limited free-market mechanisms that determine the true value of the Chinese economy, which has gotten more protective and far less transparent in the aftermath of the COVID 19 pandemic.

sapiens 1.4 economic policies helped the allies win World War II after US president Franklin D. Roosevelt imposed what became known as the Defense Production Act. It gave him significant emergency authority to control domestic industries, which was needed at the time. It created a government-industry partnership to mobilize industrial production in the cause of the war and provided the command-and-control structure to meet the production challenges. This is the ad hoc nature of *sapiens 1.4* economic tools that a free democracy can invoke at times of national emergencies. More recently, Presidents Donald Trump and Joe Biden have both invoked the Defense Production Act in response to the COVID-19 pandemic. Trump used the act to crack down on hoarding, limit exports of medical goods, and increase production of critical supplies. Biden has used it to speed up vaccination and testing efforts.

Homo virtus can transition to the next, higher-value system when society has been stabilized through the spread of effective institutions and after the heroic archetype of *Homo victoris* has been subsumed into the edifice of the *rule of law.* When there is a hunger for autonomy and little purpose found in the One True Way, or if guilt becomes too paralyzing, an individual or culture can be ready for transition. If the truth no longer guarantees order and the future is in doubt, skepticism and new options appear. Smarter members of society, regardless of their position in the social hierarchy, begin to say: "Why wait for social advancement and material abundance? I am smart enough and have enough drive to create rewards for myself." This leads to the emergence to the fifth stage of development, which, once again, is an individualistic, expressive system that seeks change.

Stage 5: E–R Multiplistic, Orange, *Homo prudentus*, *Sapiens 1.5*; Strategic/Manipulative; The Enlightened Self

The Orange stage appears when conditions change in such a way that Blue methods of dealing with existential conditions no longer work as effectively, and when the idea of group sacrifice for the One True Way loses its luster.[41] At this point, the smarter and more enterprising members of the group begin to realize that adhering to the group's rules and procedures is holding them back and that they could create better results through individual action. *Homo prudentus* believes in better living through technology and the scientific method. It wants to uncover the secrets of the universe through science, technology, research and development, mathematical and algorithmic modeling, and medical discoveries. It wants to create an efficient trade system with enlightened self-interest at its core. The changeability of technology and innovation is the hallmark of this value system. Its main idea is that we can shape, influence, and promote progress and generally improve things through the use of scientific methods, quantification, trial and error, and the search for the best and most efficient solutions.

The spread of the ideas of this value system, as discussed in chapter 2, started with the Age of Enlightenment and reached its *growth* phase with the dawn of the Industrial Age. *Sapiens 1.5* gave us Adam Smith and capitalism as well as classical music. It gave us neuroscientists James Watson and Francis Crick and the Human Genome Project. This value system's scientific-research capabilities played a critical role in providing the world with the COVID 19 vaccines that saved millions of lives.

Scientific discoveries are a significant hallmark of this stage and have brought the quality of human life to unprecedented heights in a very short period of time. They have popularized the idea that *Homo sapiens* can control his or her own destiny, leading *Homo prudentus* to believe he or she is our modern-day God. This belief is reflected in the views of many of the scientists who worked on sequencing the human genome and in the views of historian and philosopher Yuval Noah Harari in his recent book, *Homo Deus.* It is also present in the worldview of the Silicon Valley culture that sees its work as representative of godly powers, our institutions as remnants of the Middle Ages, and our intelligence as characteristic of Paleolithic brains dating back a few million years before the *sapiens 1.1* stage of development began.[42] *sapiens 1.5* gave us the concept of human exceptionalism, or *anthropocentrism,* which separated humankind from nature and made it superior to it. Today, many environmentalists believe that human exceptionalism is the central problematic concept behind ecological collapse since it represents a systematic bias in traditional Western attitudes toward the nonhuman world.[43]

In this value system, progress is the natural order of things. The goal is constantly to innovate by learning nature's secrets and seeking the best solutions to the problems of better living. *Homo prudentus* seeks to manipulate the world's resources in the most efficient and effective manner in order to spread the good life. It is an optimistic stage of development that is risk-taking and self-reliant and believes that those with such qualities deserve success. *Sapiens 1.5* is the home of meritocracy, in which much of one's advancement in life is based on the ability to distinguish oneself from the rest. At this stage, a society prospers through science, technology, competitiveness, and the execution of good strategies. One of its driving forces is to create material abundance for everyone, and those who contribute the most garner the greatest share of the spoils. The basic rule is to *act in your own self-interest by playing the game to win,* to express yourself in a calculated way to get the result you want.

Homo prudentus believes there is a job to be done, money to be made, products to be created and sold, and a world to be tamed. On the healthy side, it will compete within the bounds of fair play. One of the ways it differs from *Homo victoris* is in creating tremendous material rewards and progress based on the latest science and technology. It does not act rashly but weighs the various options to create the best possible outcome, using the minimum resources to get the maximum benefit. Status comes not from being from the right family but from success in this life. While *Homo virtus* often looks to the past, *Homo prudentus* looks to the now and to the future.

The *sapiens 1.5* organizational structure is an active hierarchy, wherein authority or positional power can be delegated. Communication can be up, down, or horizontal. Power, while still related to position as in the *sapiens 1.4*

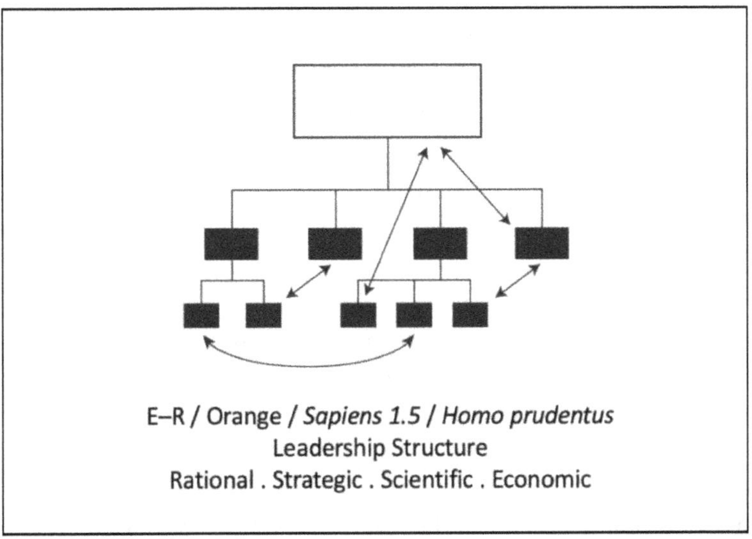

E–R / Orange / *Sapiens 1.5* / *Homo prudentus*
Leadership Structure
Rational . Strategic . Scientific . Economic

Figure 4.9. Leadership at the Stage 5 Level of Development. Strategic enterprise, success driven. Adapted from Spiral Dynamics and used by permission from Don E. Beck, PhD.

system, can be much more easily attained through moving up the hierarchy and by demonstrating the ability successfully to create desired results. Decision making at this stage is based on bottom-line results. Options are tested to see what works best. Achieving the desired outcome is of prime importance, sometimes at the expense of the people involved, and—as has become apparent in the last few decades—at a tremendous cost to the environment. Experts are the most important people, especially those with scientific or entrepreneurial expertise. The *Homo prudentus* family is child centered, with the expectation that each generation could and should do better than the last. Expectations are high, image is important, and upward mobility is encouraged and expected. The community caters to and admires the more prosperous, proudly displays its affluence, seeks material things as a measure of success, and honors competition. Success is measured by material abundance: *He who dies with the most toys wins.*

A *sapiens 1.5* economic system is symbolized by the capitalist ideology in the West wherein individual property rights and the private ownership of resources provide the basics of its foundation. Wall Street and the banking system have a formidable presence. The industrialists in Ayn Rand's *Atlas Shrugged* and economists such as Dr. Greenspan and Milton Friedman, who shaped the ideologies of the most powerful policy makers of the last half century, reside in this value system. A *sapiens 1.5* economy has a robust private sector that seeks to reinvent itself through innovation and often does so with the help of a cast of collaborators from investment bankers and scientists all the way down to the consumer who seems to have an insatiable appetite for anything and everything the system produces. Most institutions in this fifth-level system are geared to accommodate the advancement of a better life but mainly for those with the meritocracy to participate in it. The ones who seem to advance the most do so by manipulating resources and bending the rules made by a lower, fourth-level system with little capacity to detect "white-collar" crimes. This stage of economic development in the United States moved into its *growth* phase with the election of Ronald Reagan. He brought in a cast of economists and policy advisors who systemically deregulated the US economy and allowed the *financialization* expression of capitalism to replace the ethos of Industrial-Age capitalism. In my work on large-wave economic cycles, this stage is represented in the third MEMEnomic wave I call the *only-money-matters* cycle, which occupied much of the discourse in previous chapters. This system today claims the lion's share of global productive output at 50–55 percent.[44]

Some of the unhealthy expressions of the *sapiens 1.5* system are that it can place too much emphasis on the end result at the expense of the people involved and of the environment. It can rationalize exploitation of individuals and the environment in the service of goal achievement. This form of thinking created the idea of planned obsolescence that was born out of the initial ideologies of thinkers such as economist Joseph Schumpeter but eventually got corrupted by reductive economists and is now leading us into the *Great Obsolescence.* The use of many hazardous and nonbiodegradable materials are other rationales *Homo prudentus* uses in his quest for financial success and efficiency. This level of thinking considers more money or more technology as the solution to every problem, whereas *Homo virtus* thinks the solution is more law and order and more rules, and *Homo victoris* thinks the solution is more power and aggression. Though *Homo prudentus* will work a long-range plan and delay gratification, there is also a strong desire for here-and-now results.

Like all other value systems, the fifth stage of development has a healthy and an unhealthy expression. In its unhealthy expression in the United States, it works on weakening the *sapiens 1.4* system from behind the scenes and through political lobbying in order to pacify its regulatory structures and institutions. It can act much like *sapiens 1.3* and manipulate all the lower systems but does so strategically, with an eye on the long term without ever being detected. The unhealthy expression of activities on Wall Street and in the banking sector that escaped the detection of regulators is what brought the world's financial markets to the edge of collapse in 2008. The absence of a robust *sapiens 1.4* system of regulations at the time allowed bankers to dictate terms for the government bailout, which in turn allowed the system to move past its *nexus point* and spread the economic inequality we see today. Once any system passes the *nexus point* in its life cycle, it begins to spawn the seeds of its own destruction. Due to the reductive nature of *sapiens 1.5,* it continues on its endless quest for better innovation, lower regulation, and higher efficiency while rationalizing everything it externalizes and ignores.

When viewed from the perspective of Anthropogenic awareness, the *sapiens 1.5* stage becomes the primary cause of the *Great Acceleration.* It moves into a closed state, and its unhealthy expression becomes a *dominator hierarchy* that negatively impacts the behaviors of most first-tier stages. More than any other stage, once *sapiens 1.5* moves past its nexus point its corrosive effects are no longer limited to human-built systems. Its insatiable appetite for resource consumption begins to affect planetary systems in ways that are not yet fully understood.

This post-Holocene interpretation of the Graves-Beck model made it necessary for me to emphasize the severity and the long-lasting effects this resource consumption continues to have on our planet. *Sapiens 1.5* in the Anthropocene epoch will be known less by his full designation of *Homo prudentus* and more by his post-Holocene unhealthy expression, the label given to him by Catton: *Homo colossus.* My use of Catton's designation is intentional as it captures our species' exponential rise in resource use in its transition from its earlier *sapiens 1.2* stage that consumed less than one two-hundredth (0.05 percent%) of the resources we use today; the term *Homo colossus* also deftly expresses how such irresponsible use of resources will end up in a crash as a natural sequel.

Homo prudentus and his effects on human-built systems absent Anthropogenic awareness is portrayed in several movies that show its unhealthy expression and the evolution of that expression as *life conditions* have evolved. The 1976 award-winning film *The Network* gives us a glimpse of its worldview through the CEO character Arthur Jensen, played by actor Ned Beatty, in the boardroom scene where he explains how the world is a corporation. The 2003 movie *The Crooked E* exposes the fraud perpetrated by the executives at the energy conglomerate Enron. The movie exposes an array of betting games hidden in marketable financial instruments that were designed to predict the future value of energy. The scam was worth billions of dollars. It hid behind complex algorithms that no one understood. Enron was the canary in the coalmine on the use of derivative energy contracts that opened the floodgates to the use of derivatives in the selling of subprime mortgages and other securities that were the primary cause of the 2008 financial crisis. The prelude to the financial crisis itself was depicted in the 2011 movie *Margin Call,* which portrays the failure of an investment bank that is heavily invested in derivatives rooted in the subprime mortgage market. More recently, the 2022 movie *The Social Dilemma* depicts how a much younger and more dangerous *Homo prudentus* can ubiquitously manipulate the behavior of billions around the world by creating addictive algorithms programed into the different social media apps on our smart phones and electronic devices.

Somewhere along the journey through *Homo victoris,* some members begin to ask, "Is this all there is to life?" In a technologically advanced society, an evolved form of that question today might be: "What is in store for our species after we reach technological singularity where artificial intelligence exceeds human intelligence?"

The attainment of significant material abundance and the digitization of everything we have known and created makes for easy living, but something is missing. Questions arise about the existential or spiritual elements of life that are beyond the quantifiable and material worldview. The unrest is a result of a growing need for existential significance, contribution to society in a human way, and a desire for internal rather than merely external fulfillment. The world has been "conquered" through the strategic gods of technology and competition, but this "good life" is somehow unfulfilling. In the pursuit of achieving all of our *sapiens 1.5* goals, a certain cost has been paid in terms of the human element. The consequences of not caring for the environment have begun to come to light, and the absence of the spiritual element has become more apparent. This existential questioning defines the exit stage of this value system and is observable in the transformation of powerful billionaires such as Bill Gates, Warren Buffet, and Ray Dalio. These men have emerged into higher stages of development and are now dedicating their vast resources to address issues such as climate change, world health, war, and poverty. Such vision is present in the advocacy of Apple-Computer cofounder Steve Wozniak and in the post-singularity intelligence of Tristan Harris, cofounder of the Center for Humane Technologies. The rise of this type of intelligences is part of the *Homo sapiens's* evolutionary process when it is in an open state. It is a healthy *Homo prudentus* exiting that stage of existence who is most capable of addressing issues that his own earlier presence in the *sapiens 1.5* stage of development helped to ignore and weaken. In the process of exiting this stage, these individuals expose the limitations of the stage's proprietary values and set an example for other healthy individuals in the system to follow in their footsteps. The exit phase comes in different forms to different cultures and individuals, and, as in every values system, creates chaos and uncertainty; but it is an essential transition phase that moves us to the next stage of development.

Stage 6: F–S Relativistic, Green, *Homo consonus*, *Sapiens 1.6*, Humanitarian/Pluralistic; The Egalitarian Community

The *Homo consonus* stage of development is the last in the first tier of stages; it appears after we transcend the noncaring, materialistic nature of the *Homo-prudentus* stage and when the search for inner peace and human connection begins. The human bond and the well-being of all the people, not just those who are willing to risk and compete, become the highest priority. The motto for this Green value system is, "Sacrifice self now for the needs of the group."[45] Like all the sacrificial-communal levels that precede it, *Homo consonus* wants to sacrifice self but this time does not want to postpone gratification; these people want to obtain it now for themselves and others. They understand the ineffectiveness of stage four and the manipulation of stage five and begin to advocate for solutions that bypass the lower systems, as in some respects the hippie counterculture movement did in the late 1960s. The system responds to the lack of internal fulfillment characteristic of the previous stage by seeking peace within the inner self and by exploring the more caring and spiritual dimensions of humanity. To an individual centered in the *Homo consonus* system, feelings, sensitivity, and caring supersede results and efficiency. Attention turns away from material goods and greater productivity and technological efficiency to the inner subjective dimension of feelings.

When outer-directed, the ideal *sapiens 1.6* organization is the social network, governed by consensus decision making. The system assumes that each person's input has equal value. Though well intentioned, this assumption is often shown to be untrue, and much time can be wasted

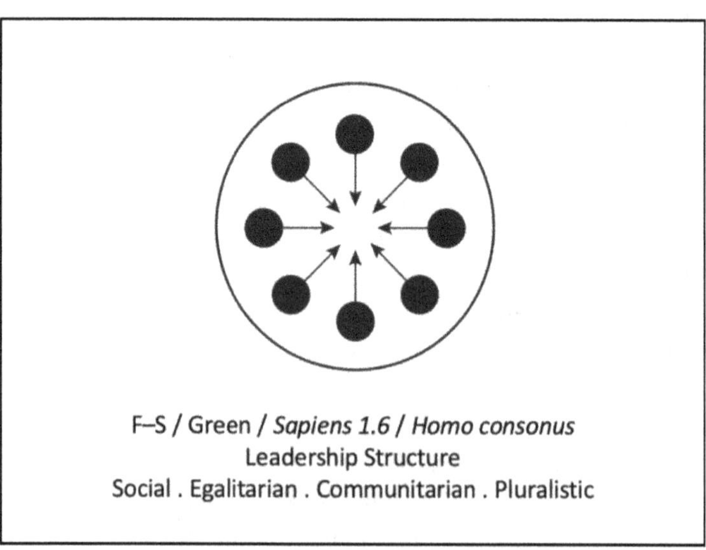

F–S / Green / *Sapiens 1.6* / *Homo consonus*
Leadership Structure
Social . Egalitarian . Communitarian . Pluralistic

Figure 4.10. Leadership at the Stage 6 Level of Development. Social network; people driven. Adapted from Spiral Dynamic and used by permission from Don E. Beck.

on hearing everyone out. The general thema for the *sapiens 1.6* system is, "Egalitarianism and humanitarianism."

This value system believes that resources should be shared equally and that decisions should be reached through consensus, rather than by the chief and elders, as with *Homo domesticus*; by the most powerful, as with *Homo victoris*; by the strict rules of the orderly community, as in *Homo virtus*; or by experts and entrepreneurs, as in *Homo prudentus.* The role of this stage is to renew humanity's spirituality, to bring harmony, and to focus on the enrichment of human development. It exposes the unhealthy practices of the *sapiens 1.4* and *sapiens 1.5* systems. Its worldview can be seen in the music of John Lennon and in the values of Doctors without Borders, Greenpeace, the Sierra Club, the ACLU, and corporate-sensitivity training. In popular culture, its humanistic nature is seen in movies such as the 1982 film *Gandhi*, which shows Gandhi's nonviolent approach to change through the peaceful protest that exposed the discriminatory nature of colonial rule, first in South Africa and then in India. This value system is similarly present in the 2014 movie *Selma*, which is about the life and struggles of Dr. Martin Luther King in his peaceful efforts to bring racial equality and civil rights to minority groups in a 1960s America.

Sapiens 1.6 is organized around community. Its important values include inner peace, equality, inclusiveness, the relativity of all moral positions, group harmony, the exploration of feelings, shared experience, and cooperation rather than competition. There are no losers in a sports competition run by *sapiens 1.6.* Everyone gets a participation trophy as an attempt to humble the winner in thinking of the deeper human connection shared with his or her opponent. This value system's thinking is behind "political correctness," socially-responsible investing, victims' rights, and social safety nets. It is the driving force behind the MeToo and the Black Lives Matter movements. *Sapiens 1.6* is closely identified with the Woke movement that brings attention to racial prejudice and discrimination and other issues of social inequality. In terms of its ability to create results, this system is diametrically opposite from *sapiens 1.5* in its approach. Instead of sacrificing the human element to get a desired result, it will sacrifice the desired result to preserve group consensus and the human element. This emphasis on feelings and harmony is certainly a positive development, but the outcome is often at the expense of productivity and actually accomplishing something.

Under a classical *sapiens 1.6* economic system, policies and institutions are geared toward "equal economic opportunity for all." Although ownership of resources is private, it is heavily taxed and regulated. As a result, it exercises considerably more restraint than does the fifth-level economic system in terms of good corporate citizenry. Awareness of the environment and the health of the planet, as well as the worker, is woven into every private- and public-sector decision. Allocation of capital for an advanced fiber-optics research center is as important as setting aside funding programs for empowering businesses in poor urban areas. Government spending on social programs is the hallmark of this sixth-level economic system. The European Union is a good example of a system that champions *sapiens 1.6* economic policies as evidenced by their generous social-welfare programs. The system's corporate practices have helped bring pay equality to the worker and transparency in issues of sexual abuse at the workplace.

The most common business formation in this value system is mutually-owned enterprises and community cooperatives that represent local business interests catering to the community. The recent emergence of the benefit corporation could also be considered a form of *sapiens 1.6* business organization. According to its online portal, a benefit corporation is described as a new legal tool to create a solid foundation for long-term mission alignment and value creation. It protects its mission through capital raises and leadership changes, creates more flexibility when evaluating potential sale and liquidity options, and prepares businesses to lead a mission-driven life after the initial public offering.[46] In short, this type of corporation takes the healthy corporate expressions of *sapiens 1.5* and formalizes them into the next-level formation that replaces the stockholder model with the multi-stakeholder model. It imposes a new standard for corporations that takes their general public benefit seriously while still maintaining access to capital markets. The only exception is that this model forces capital markets to adopt *sapiens 1.6* standards and virtues that have the potential to disrupt current short-term practices. By requiring its officers and directors to consider the impact of their decisions on society and the environment as well as on the shareholder, a B corporation can begin to address many of the shortcomings of past corporate models. The lack of transparency that has been the source of so much popular anger toward the old corporate model can potentially disappear under a B corp as the law requires it to publish annual benefit reports of its social and environmental performances.

At the macro level, a contemporary manifestation of a *sapiens 1.6* economic system has been the digital economy in its earliest appearances. Rooted in the World Wide Web's undeclared mandate to democratize access to information and resources, its intent was to redefine the purpose of the sixth-level stage of development by systemically disrupting the pervasive practices of the *sapiens 1.5* system in the *only money matters* era. *Sapiens 1.6* was suddenly clothed in digital bits and bytes, and the system's new narrative was to bring systemic equality through innovation, disruption, democratization, and decentralization of everything that defined *sapiens 1.5*'s capitalist virtues. As these new values matured, they began to represent an existential threat to the livelihood of the *sapiens 1.5* system. Staying true to its manipulative and strategic nature, and with an endless supply of capital at its disposal, *sapiens 1.5* investment bankers have been able to monetize much of what the digital economy created and, in the process, thwart much of the digital age's promise of economic equality. Nevertheless, the digital footprint in a *sapiens 1.6* economy remains strong. In both digital and nondigital forms, its economic virtues represent the fourth large-wave economic cycle in my work, which I call the *Democratization of Information and Resources*. Today, it accounts for 10–12 percent of global productive output.[47]

Despite its concern for the human element, this stage of development has many unhealthy aspects. Once consensus is reached, everyone must comply, and there is no room for individual expression or action. In fact, *sapiens 1.6* leaders often do not care what the majority wants. They may manipulate the group to gain consensus for their idea and then disregard what the group wants, or they may decide that the group just isn't "conscious enough" if it doesn't adhere to their politically correct point of view. Today, this dynamic is seen in the *cancel culture*, an extreme expression of *sapiens 1.6* in which the believers become as absolutistic and punitive as in *sapiens 1.4*. The only difference is that the authoritarian power has moved from the traditional institutions such as the Church and the government to the radical liberal left, which masquerades as equality, wields its powers indiscriminately, and no longer has the patience to wait for traditional institutions to deliver results.

One of the big problems in this value system is its reliance on consensus decision making. The energy required to reach consensus takes too much time. The process of coming to consensus often amounts to wearing down those who disagree rather than actually changing their minds.

As a result, little if anything of substance is ever actually accomplished. *Homo consonus* is well known for being overly permissive, especially with *Homo victoris,* and has trouble dealing effectively with the harsher realities of life. It allows *Homo victoris* to be "part of the circle" and treats it equally while blaming its behavior on unfair circumstances created by *sapiens 1.4* and *sapiens 1.5.* It believes that if we were only nicer to those who are at the sapiens 1.3 stage, they would stop being so aggressive, selfish, and cruel.[48] *Homo victoris,* of course, doesn't *want* to be part of the circle; it sees this attitude as insane but is happy to take advantage of it.

The United Nations as an organization operates primarily from the values of the *sapiens 1.6* system. This global agency gives us a glimpse of what a world organized under the sixth stage of development is capable of delivering for humanity, as well as the things that it can't deliver. It has brought many parts of the world out of poverty and helped with issues of health and literacy. It is behind many sustainability programs and is tasked with addressing many of the global issues we face. But it has also proven to be equally ineffective in stopping rogue leaders when they commit crimes against humanity. Much of the criticism of the agency in the first section of the book is because of some of the false utopianism that drives its virtues. It places egalitarianism above all else, and while this is a noble mission, it ignores the very hierarchical nature of the world's value systems. It allows murderous leaders—such as Bashar Assad of Syria who is centered in the *Homo victoris* system and has destroyed his country—to remain in power and be on the UN's Security Council. Further, the UN cannot impose any sanctions on rogue warlords unless all five permanent members of its Security Council agree unanimously to do so. As a result, a resolution in February 2022 demanding that Moscow immediately stop its attack on Ukraine and withdraw all troops failed to be adopted because it was vetoed by Russia, a permanent member of the UN Security Council. Because of the limitations of *sapiens 1.6* organizational structure, death and destruction in Ukraine continue unabated.

The organizational configuration of the UN is also proving ineffective in combatting climate change. The absence of enforcement mechanisms that hold its member countries accountable to the goal of limiting Earth's warming to 1.5°C is indicative that *sapiens 1.6* intelligence will not suffice to save our planet.

On the healthy side, *sapiens 1.6* has done the world a service by bringing attention to the damage *sapiens 1.5* has caused to the environment, exposing social, racial, and economic inequalities and bringing holistic and spiritual thinking back on stage. Emphasizing humanistic rather than materialistic and technological goals, valuing inner peace and the spiritual dimension, and seeing humanity as a universal family are all positive contributions. But in seeing all experiences, all opinions, and all points of view as equal, the system produces a false sense of utopianism that inherently creates complacency and so leads to decay. In a complex global society in which egalitarian *sapiens 1.6* has a blind spot to *sapiens 1.3* who has access to nuclear weapons, annihilation of the human race becomes a distinct possibility. Graves alluded to this in 1974 as one of three scenarios that await us in the future.[49] With Putin's ongoing war with Ukraine counterpoised with a global governing body centered in *sapiens 1.6* values, the manifestation of Graves's scenario becomes all the more probable.

sapiens 1.6 transitions to the next level of existence when some of its members begin to realize that, in spite of all their work, not much has really changed. The warm, human aspirations begin to wear thin as the realities of complex social problems and the system's limited ability to solve them become apparent. Feelings give way to knowledge as the system is confronted by chaos and disorder. The economic and emotional toll of caring becomes overwhelming, and the need for tangible results and functionality begins to emerge. Although Graves predicted that the duration of this stage will be the shortest among the subsistent systems, those who believe in its utopian aspirations prolong its presence by falsely believing that human existence cannot evolve to higher stages. *Homo subsistens* reaches the top rung in this first tier and, after failing to change the world, turns his or her focus to inner peace and harmony. He or she erroneously believes that care for the self is all that matters, while the world all around is falling apart. Graves identifies the "world falling apart" at this stage as the onset of the *problems of existence* in the G–T, A^1–N^1 coupling in table 4.1, characterized by the ecological crisis, the energy crisis, the population crisis, the limits to growth, and an array of other existential challenges.[50]

What Graves couldn't foresee during his lifetime was how the use of technology in its current ubiquitous form can contribute to the list of existential challenges we face as well. *Sapiens 1.6* is a stage of human development in which hierarchy comes to die. When this particular overarching virtue gets distributed to billions of people through technological advancements such as social media, it leaves one of the widest paths of destruction we have ever known in its wake. Suddenly, the hierarchical nature of the *sapiens 1.4* system that appeared five thousand years ago with its rigid formation and sharp elbows, designed to give life meaning and purpose, begins to dissolve. Similarly, the less-rigid hierarchy created five centuries ago by the *sapiens 1.5* system based on meritocracy begins to dissolve as well. But these structures have not been listed in arbitrary organizational charts on the wall of a government agency or a corporation. These have been structures under which entire societies have been organized, and the sudden removal of the organizing principles that have contained them for centuries has created much of the chaos we see in the world today. In its blind pursuit of seeing everything as equal, *sapiens 1.6*, with the help of a well-developed digital and knowledge infrastructure that spans the planet, has created chaos of such magnitude that no stage of development in the first tier can fully comprehend or quantify it. As these *problems of existence* or *life conditions* press up against the limits of the system, our *complex adaptive intelligence* will need to recalibrate at a much higher level of neuropsychology, one that will propel us into the second tier of existence where the *Second sapiens* dwells.

At the exit stage of the *sapiens 1.6* system, many individuals become frustrated and alienated from the group approach. They decide they could accomplish more if they leave this communal-sacrificial system of the highest order in the first tier to bring about the necessary global change. This is when *Homo sapiens* realizes she needs to become a *systemic being* instead of remaining an individual with deficient needs vacillating between two extremes: the individualistic stages wherein she seeks change and the sacrificial stages wherein she subsumes her individuality into the group.[51] The existential nature of the problems that Graves identified as the world falling apart represents the dynamic part of the model, the *life conditions* that trigger the *complex adaptive intelligence* necessary to begin to make the essential changes. But, due to the complex nature of the existential problems we face today, these changes will not be ordinary ones or comprise an incremental movement up to another subsistent stage of existence. Instead, they will be part of a radical shift moving toward an entirely new tier of psychosocial systems. It is at this transition point that our consciousness is poised to take a monumental leap forward and our species evolves from the first tier of *Homo subsistens* to the second tier of *Homo magnificus*.

This second tier is where the *Second sapiens* dwells. It is where psychological freedom grows exponentially and where our broadened humanness begins to heal the damage our subsistent existence has caused. It is where we begin to build structures that ensure the stability of *all* life on the planet and make sure that this new balance of life is never again squandered by the narrow mindedness of the *First sapiens* who fails to see beyond his excessive and self-indulgent behavior.

FIVE
THE SECOND SAPIENS, HOMO MAGNIFICUS

If ever man leaps to this great beyond, there will be no bowing to suffering, no vassalage, and no peonage. Man will move forth on the crests of his broadened humanness rather than vacillate and swirl in the turbulence of his animalistic needs. His problems, now that he has put the world back together, will be those of bringing stabilization to life once again. He will need to learn how to live so that the balance of nature is not again upset, so that individual man will not again set off on another self-aggrandizing binge.

—Clare W. Graves
"Human Nature Prepares for a Momentous Leap"

The monumental shift we face in human awareness will alter all that we have known. Our consciousness is poised for a quantum leap forward. The future will be vastly different, and nothing will look or feel the same. Rhetoric of this nature has been with us throughout history, spoken by saints and sages as well as by opportunists and thieves who insert themselves into the chaos of major transitions and attempt to predict the unpredictable and define the world emerging on the other side. *Homo sapiens* are a species that craves stability. At times of uncertainty, we look for wise leaders and prophets to give us salvation and assure us that order will be restored and uncertainly will disappear if we only believe in their worldview. While a few in history have been able to predict some version of the future, the vast majority of futurists have not. Graves was no exception, at least partially. Because his early work was mostly contained in academic silos, it didn't garner much attention until he began to speak about its real-life applicability and its predictive powers. This allowed him to produce his best and most visible work; and it all happened in the 1970s, in the crucible of chaos shaped by two major forces: a dying system and the one that was being born. Here is what I consider the most prophetic quote from his landmark 1974 piece that garnered him so much attention:

> The present moment finds our society attempting to negotiate the most difficult, but at the same time the most exciting, transition the human race has faced to date. It is not merely a transition to a new level of existence but the start of a new "movement" in the symphony of human history. The future offers us, basically, three possibilities: (1) Most gruesome is the chance that we might fail to stabilize our world and, through successive catastrophes regress as far back as the Ik tribe has. (2) Only slightly less frightening is the vision of fixation in the D–Q/E–R/F–S societal complex. This might resemble George Orwell's *1984* with its tyrannical, manipulative government glossed over by a veneer of humanitarian-sounding doublethink and moralistic rationalizations, and is a very real possibility in the next decade. (3) The last possibility is that we could emerge into the G–T level and proceed toward stabilizing our world so that all life can continue.[1]

The *life conditions* that informed Graves's first two possibilities either were at their *maturity* phase in their life cycle heading toward different nexus points or had already passed it, contributing to more chaos and uncertainty. They were fractals of the larger ideological cycle that began after World War II and was reaching its *decline* phase in the 1970s. They included the specter of the Cold War and the possibility of nuclear Armageddon—a menacing public policy defined by the US military and the defense industry; the collapse of the post-World War II Keynesian economic and financial order; the Arab oil embargo; inflation; and the ongoing war in Viet Nam. Interpreting the totality of what was happening, Graves's scenario was quite accurate in terms of what has unfolded in the last five decades. In my conversations with Beck about what Graves might have shared with him about the first scenario, it became clear that armed conflict, with or without nuclear weapons, could lead to a series of events that could take humanity back to the *sapiens 1.1* stage. The Ik tribe Graves mentioned in the above quote is discussed in a 1972 book by British anthropologist Colin Turnbull entitled *The Mountain People.*[2]

He chronicles the tribe's descent into savagery after the government of Uganda forced them out of the lush valley in which they had lived for thousands of years and into a mountainous region. In the harsh arid conditions, they began to starve to death due to droughts and crop failure. As unlikely as it may seem, a catastrophic event of this type in a Western context today is not out of the realm of possibility. Should the ongoing war between Russia and Ukraine get worse, it could involve a wider conflict with the potential of making Graves's most gruesome scenario about the future a probability.

Graves's description of the second scenario as being only slightly less frightening than an existential war describes precisely how the *First sapiens* has evolved over the last five decades. The only difference is that the developmental stage that wielded Orwellian power was the E–R stage, *sapiens 1.5* in what he called the D–Q/E–R/F–S societal complex (see table 4.1). Instead of a tyrannical government, what evolved was an era defined by the systemic weakening of governmental institutions in charge of regulating our economy. It was the unbridled empowerment of the private sector that I describe in my work as the third MEMEnomic cycle—the *only money matters* cycle—which has contributed significantly to the *Great Obsolescence.* This reality, when applied to the model, can be viewed as a transition from *sapiens 1.4* to *sapiens 1.5* economic policies, a sequential movement up the spiral for at least the economic fractal within it. Graves correctly described the immediate future as being tyrannical and manipulative, but it hasn't been the government that made it so. It has been the private sector, allowed to run amuck, that is now proving to be tyrannical. And it is doing so in a system in which strategic manipulation by *sapiens 1.5* has become a collective bias of the entire D–Q/E–R/F–S societal complex as the life cycle of the monetarist ideology has moved past its nexus point, bringing with it the entire global economy. This new societal complex with E–R being the dominant stage that has pacified the D–Q and F–S stages is what defines Western culture today, and, by extension, the global ethos of *peace through commerce* that shields the *First sapiens* behind a dangerous veneer of humanitarian doublethink and moralistic rationalization. The situation is Orwellian in the sense that it automatically spreads economic inequality, allows Big Tech to legitimize surveillance of every citizen in the pursuit of profit, and contributes greatly to the biggest tyranny: the blind drive for global economic growth that is causing the destruction of Earth's systems.

In light of the severe ecological challenges that have emerged in the last fifty years, Graves wasn't far off in calling his second scenario only slightly less frightening than an existential war. Even when *First sapiens's* intelligence is in an open state, it can enact only incremental change, not the systems-wide, structural change currently needed.

Incremental change is known as a translational variation of the same stage or of several first-tier stages that form the societal complex. It provides surface-level remedies that keep the *First sapiens* in a state of ignorant bliss.

This ignorance pervades the ways in which we have addressed climate change so far—by setting up tradable carbon credits, for instance, and following instructions to recycle our cans and plastics and shop with reusable bags. Even the pride we feel in shopping for sustainably grown foods, driving electric cars, and heating our homes with solar panels is blissfully ignorant. While these activities might appear congruent with the virtues of the second tier, they remain market-based solutions that are a slightly healthier expression of the *sapiens 1.5* stage that seeks scalability and profitability while addressing surface problems only. They rarely examine the sustainability of the entire supply chain, not to mention the health of the entire ecosystem from which each supplier extracts their raw materials. The ignorant bliss of Graves's societal complex could lead to the outcome T. S. Elliot describes in his poem *The Hollow Men*:

This is the way the world ends
This is the way the world ends
This is the way the world ends
Not with a bang but a whimper.

The "bang" is Grave's first scenario; the "whimper" is the second, wherein we drive our electric vehicles into their charging ports in our solar-powered homes, eat our organically grown meals, and give each other high fives for how well we're addressing climate change while remaining completely ignorant that our collective behavior is leading us to the end of the world—at least as we know it.

But while incremental change largely maintains the status quo, systems-wide, structural change is *transformational.* It is indicative of a higher-order, ecological intelligence system; and the ones who can bring about such change have a far larger view of reality that discerns the dysfunction in all the first-tier systems and works to transform the habits and virtues of those systems to serve the larger view. This form of transformational intelligence is nested in the model's second tier—representing the *Second sapiens* and comprising stages seven and eight—and characterizes Graves's third scenario for our future.

Graves's third scenario, also born in the chaos of the 1970s, was the more hopeful one that signaled the beginning of our return to being one with nature. It was based on the dawn of systems thinking that represented the early stages of the *inquiry* phase in the life cycle of a much higher-order system, one that seeks to restore the damage caused by the *First sapiens.* This shift gave humanity the earliest glimpses of the new science represented in, for instance, Ilya Prigogine's work on dissipative structures presented in the *Limits to Growth* and in Lovelock's and Margulis's *Gaia Hypothesis.* It also gave us the life-altering experience of a cosmic view of life after we landed on the moon as well as many other phenomena that put forth the notion that we are more than our subsistent existence.

Graves's uncanny predictions about the future of humanity identified the nature of the problems that *Second sapiens,* with its second-tier intelligence, will be tasked with resolving. His perspective concerned the dawn not just of a higher-order science but of new higher-order *systems* of thinking and being. These systems are highly collaborative and will form completely new foundations for organizing our institutions, our governing bodies, and our principles for conducting education and trade. They will also transform the fundamental ways we relate to each other.

Graves described our ascendance into this entirely new tier of being as humanity's greatest challenge, not the least because it has to emerge in the face of great resistance from the first-tier thinking that has little capacity to understand the totality of our problems and how to address them. Consequently, we will continue to do more damage to our environment and to advance many of the life cycles of Earth's systems beyond their nexus points, allowing Mother Nature to dictate the terms of our species' future. Whether we are forced to change through major natural calamities or do so voluntarily, there is no way to avoid the *darkness-before-the new-dawn* phase that is rapidly approaching. The multiple existential crises that we have created for ourselves are what have led us to this phase, and now we must bring the collective shadow of the *First sapiens* into the light. If we are to become a new humanity that is one with all life on the planet, we must first process all that has remained unconscious in our behavior thus far. This is a sequential path forward that must now be followed and can no longer be ignored. It is what will free us and our leaders from the subsistent thinking that has trapped us in our deficient needs and motivations. What has been repressed under the reign of the *First sapiens* must be healed before the *Second sapiens* can fully emerge. This is the reality Graves was talking about when he referred to the huge chasm of *unbelievable meaning* that we must cross. Using this subjective and highly charged term was Graves's way to show *First sapiens* how restrictive his meaning-making capacities were and how vastly different things will be if he evolves into the *Second-sapiens* stages. Processing the collective shadow and other aspects of the *darkness-before-the new-dawn* phase will be the focus of an upcoming chapter.

> *We don't give man or woman a fish. We don't teach them how to fish. We show them how to create a sustainable habitat for fish to thrive. This is the essence of the natural-design process that ends dependency, creates resilience, and acknowledges the interdependence of all life within all ecosystems.*
>
> —Don E. Beck[3]

Graves's third scenario for the future called on us to begin thinking in ways we had never thought of before. To give an impression of how different the *Second sapiens* is from his predecessor, he proposed that we begin by reversing much of what we have known and taken for granted in our journey through the six stages of subsistence, use those stages' best technological and cognitive advancements, and put it all to the power of two.[4]

We see the contrast in the battle that is taking place between the First and the *Second sapiens* in Manhattan, symbolically represented in the conflict between the IPCC scientists at the UN and the investment-banking community on Wall Street. We see it in the debate between the ecologist and the banker and between the climatologist and the engineer, the latter of whom thinks in terms of *sapiens 1.5* climate mitigation and doesn't ask the deeper questions about the causes of the decline in all Earth's systems. And we see it most generally in the debate between a humanity steeped in the reductive values of the *First sapiens*, who thinks the technology proprietary to his or her stage of development can save us from unmitigated disaster, and the higher-order sciences, which comprehend the great, interconnected web of Earth's systems of which the science of the *First sapiens* is but a small part.

The *Second sapiens* constitutes a stage of human development that involves the rise of systems thinkers who are first and foremost concerned with the health of the entire planet. This perspective empowers them in a highly collaborative effort to create synergistic modes of thinking that in turn create new institutions looking like nothing we have known in human history. The *general thema* of both the last two known stages in the model—again, seven and eight—includes the terms *collective individualism* and *individual collectivism*, used interchangeably. They describe a future in which humanity collaborates globally to create the necessary systems and virtues to save what remains of life on the planet.

Graves's intuition in 1974 about what humanity faces was not that different from what the new discoveries were telling us at that time. The same story was being told through different lenses, but the theme was one: in our subsistent existence, we have ignored much of the greater habitat in which all life, including ours, exists. As the pursuit of economic prosperity and the values of *peace through commerce* dominated human activity in the last century, we externalized the byproducts of the world's annual hundred-trillion-dollar economy to our environment. The result has been the *Great Acceleration* that has depleted many of our natural resources, polluted our air and water, and triggered the sixth extinction. What is following is the *Great Obsolescence*, which bears witness to the atrophy of much of what the modern mind has created. The obsolescence in human realms is happening simultaneously with the collapse of different parts of a much higher fractal, Mother Nature's Earth systems. Graves's warning to humanity was clear: unless we begin to behave from the planetary and holistic perspective of the *Second sapiens*, our species, like millions of other species, will be in danger of becoming extinct.

The Second Tier: Stages of the Magnificent Human

Much of the original description of the second tier of intelligence remains the same since Beck and Cowan first defined it in 1996. In 2000, integral philosopher Ken Wilber, in collaboration with Beck, incorporated the Spiral-Dynamics model in formulating his Integral-Theory framework. Wilber in his later iterations added the spiritual dimension, which allowed him to expand his work beyond both Graves and Beck, but such expansion came at the cost of abandoning many of the underpinnings of

Gravesian thought. While Wilber still refers to Graves's work as essential, very little of Wilber's model adheres to Graves's fundamentals. His creation of a third tier not only violates one of Graves's fundamental tenets about sequential stage development, it also represents a purely speculative notion about the future of humanity and relegates most of the integral framework to the philosophical and spiritual realms. I don't intend to dimmish the importance of these two areas. They would be perfectly valid if our *existential problems* had remained unchanged for the last two and half decades, unburdened by the threat of planetary collapse.

Graves was a practical man who spent his career identifying how the environment influences the mind and how the mind recalibrates to adjust to the changing environment in order to solve the problems of existence at its particular stage of development. Due to the absence of substantive data, he was hesitant to offer a full description of the eighth stage of development and referred to it only sparingly. When Beck and Cowan conducted their own research into second-tier intelligence, they were able to articulate some aspects of it. They also projected the birth of a *ninth* stage on the horizon. In 2016, at a twentieth-anniversary conference celebrating the release of the book *Spiral Dynamics*, Beck acknowledged that the articulation of the eighth and ninth stages might have been premature in that it violated one of the basic tenets of the model: it is only when our neuropsychological capacities can no longer solve our *existential problems* that the brain activates the next-level system. In research conducted in subsequent years since the initial publication of the book, data has shown no evidence of the existence of ninth-level intelligence. In fact, it has shown only less than 1 percent of eighth-level intelligence and only 3 percent of the world's population that is currently capable of thinking in a seventh-level manner.[5]

Research conducted by other entities using the Spiral-Dynamics model in organizational settings showed seventh-level intelligence to be prevalent in 5 to 7 percent of the people surveyed. Beck acknowledged that while some individuals might have second-tier intelligence and first-hand knowledge of what is becoming obsolete in their thinking, the vast majority of humanity remains somewhere between the stages of *sapiens 1.2* and *sapiens 1.6*, rendering the data and the size of the samples scientifically insufficient. And while seventh-level intelligence has seemed to be most prevalent in business organizations that are always searching for strategic advantages over their competitors, it remains greatly absent from other areas of leadership that are critical for addressing our existential problems as the Anthropocene epoch becomes an undeniable reality. Those areas that have remained immune to seventh-level intelligence are the institutions that formulate policy for national and regional governance, the United Nations, and geopolitics in general. If humanity is to survive beyond the *First sapiens*, it must empower a different form of global governance that can effectively address our existential challenges.

Stage 7: G–T/ A^1–N^1, Existential, Yellow, *Homo ecosistamus, Sapiens 2.1,* Ecological/Systemic; The Integrated Self

This is the first stage of development that Clare W. Graves identified as the point at which humanity arrives after it crosses the great chasm of *unbelievable meaning*. That chasm is being reinterpreted in this post-Holocene iteration of the model as the gold, the new dawn on the other side of emergence once we collectively pass through the darkness and process all the trauma of the *First sapiens*. Stage seven is the first level of human existence in the second tier and what Graves described as the first level of *being*, or the first level of *magnificence*. In accordance with his description of the *First sapiens* as "deficient," Graves believed that we become full human beings only when we emerge into *Second sapiens*, This explains his use of the term *being* to describe *Second sapiens*. It is where we begin to understand where we've been and what we might come to be. Beck and Cowan labeled this stage of development with the color yellow and modernized its *general thema* by giving it the designation, "flex flow." It is primarily interested in the healthy functionality of the entire first tier.[6] In their 1996 version of the model, they conceived of this stage as integrating many of the healthy expressions of Green *sapiens 1.6*, Orange *sapiens 1.5*, Blue *sapiens 1.4*, Red *sapiens 1.3*, and Purple *sapiens 1.2* into a separate, more effective individualistic, psychosocial system. This new *sapiens 2.1* stage of development holds the sapiens of the lower stages to a better expression of themselves while contributing solutions to our existential problems that it now identifies from its much higher level of consciousness.

Homo ecosistamus has a big-picture view of matters that challenge the existence of all life as he or she sees them from the much higher fractals of complexity. He or she creates systemic approaches to problem solving and has the ability to handle considerably more variables than all the six levels of the *First sapiens* put together. Graves had uncovered two essential psychological qualities about this stage: the loss of fear and the loss of compulsivity.[7] He attributes these two factors to the exponential increase in psychological freedom with which our species will be endowed once it reaches this stage. While the *First sapiens* has proven to be incapable of solving problems of a higher order due to his attachment to subsistent ideologies and virtues, the loss of which can be a source of fear and attachment, *sapiens 2.1* can freely navigate around all *First-sapiens* ideologies absent any fear and compulsivity. Fear of losing status, economic prosperity, and the understanding of our traditions and history prevent us from embracing the chaos and the uncertainty inherent in higher-order problems such as planetary ecosystem collapse, depletion of Earth's resources, and all other issues that ail the planet. These are the issues with which *sapiens 2.1* must deal.

Free of the attachments of the *First sapiens*, *sapiens 2.1* sees the world as a complex system in danger and explores ways in which to act responsibly. He or she recognizes the various evolutionary stages of the *First sapiens* and works to unblock the hurdles standing in the way of a healthy systemic flow for all humanity, understanding that change is a natural part of the process. She listens to members of all the first-tier systems with deep empathy and gains their trust by acknowledging where they are in their developmental journey while at the same time showing them a larger, healthier version of who they are and who they can become. He intuitively sees how all first-tier stages can work together. In this respect, *Homo ecosistamus* is unlike *Homo domesticus*, who relies on superstitions and is at the mercy of the tribal leader; *Homo victoris*, who sees the world in terms of brutal conquest; *Homo virtus*, who sees everything in absolutistic right-or-wrong terms; *Homo prudentus*, who seeks to understand the world in order to manipulate, monetize, and tame it; and *Homo consonus*, who sees the world's greater complexity through relativistic and egalitarian lenses but has no effective methods of getting things done.

While many characteristics of first-tier human development outlined in chapter 4 still apply in the second tier, with the passage of time and the emergence of additional, second-tier intelligence and research in brain science, some elements have evolved to provide further definition and clarity. The most significant discoveries apply largely to the original-model's conception that movement up the spiral oscillates between individualistic, psychosocial systems with left-hemisphere dominance in the brain and sacrificial ones with right-hemisphere dominance. After the publication of his original book, Beck conducted additional research revealing some essential characteristics that define second-tier intelligence: at the seventh stage, *sapiens 2.1,* the left hemisphere, which is now endowed with an exponential increase in psychological space, begins to mesh with the right hemisphere. By the time emergence reaches the eighth stage, *sapiens 2.2,* both hemispheres operate as one collective-intelligence unit capable of addressing issues of far greater complexity from both the left and right parts of brain seamlessly and simultaneously. Beck reflected these changes by characterizing the yellow *sapiens 2.1* as having knowledge with systemic intuition and the turquoise *sapiens 2.2* as having holistic intuition with knowledge.[8]

In returning to Graves's lesser-known research, I uncovered similar observations. Although he hesitated to articulate much of the eighth stage of development due to the absence of substantive data, he did construct several visual models that show the expansion of the psychological space in the yellow, N^1, *Homo ecosistamus* brain. Figure 5.1 below from his original work demonstrates how, in response to *existential problems* of the seventh level that are present inside the broken elliptical line and designated by A^1, the brain recalibrates to use whole-brain capacities in order to address these problems effectively. In the diagram, the entire brain is nested within the seventh-level ecosystem, the environment that enables it to address chaos and uncertainly of far a bigger order and with far greater capacity than is now available to it. Although Graves's ill health prevented him from doing further research to corroborate these findings, much research in the fields of neurology and psychophysiology today points to higher brain functioning as a product of a super-synergistic integration process that engages the whole brain.[9] While such research suggests how optimization of brain function can be achieved, in the second tier of the Gravesian model, whole-brain capacities that exhibit the exponential growth in psychological space are achieved only after *Homo sapiens* has journeyed through all six systems of the first tier, experiencing both the individualistic and sacrificial systems fully with their increasing complexity. These are sequential evolutionary stages that build brain capacities that enable ascendance to the second tier, where they are included in their mature, healthy state, absent fear and compulsivity. The figure also shows how incremental brain capacities are activated in *Homo sapiens* as the individual moves through the six lower stages designated by Graves's alphabetical coupling A–N through F–S.

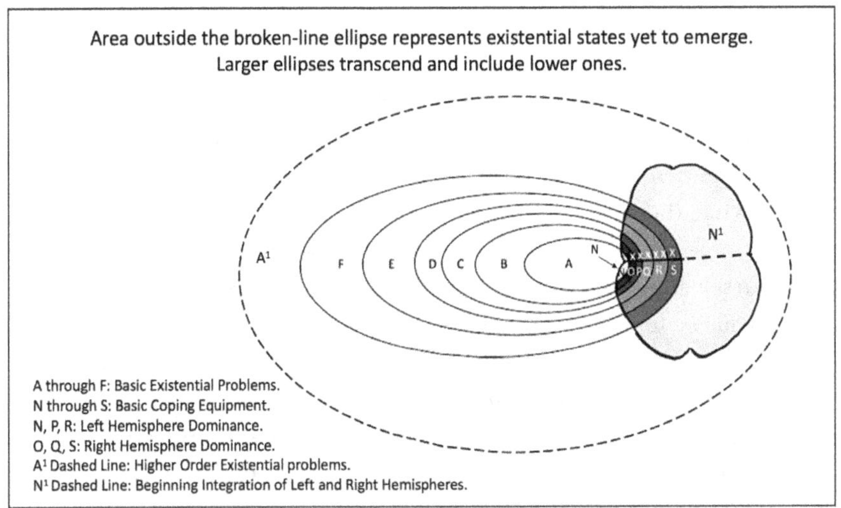

Figure 5.1. Basic Conceptualization of Psychological Life Space of the Species, Sub-Groups, and Individuals. The A^1–N^1 stage occurs when the left hemisphere begins to integrate with the right hemisphere and the two hemispheres become fully integrated at the B^1–O^1 stage. Adapted from the work of Graves, *Never Ending Quest*, 193.

A current example of what the nesting of the whole brain in the entire environment means appears in the research of evolutionary biologists such as Bruce Lipton and Elisabet Sahtouris. Both were Beck's colleagues in the organization entitled Evolutionary Leaders: In Service to Conscious Evolution, a global society founded by Deepak Chopra and Diane Williams. What they discovered were patterns in the evolution of life similar to the evolution of stage development in the first-tier systems, with the switching back and forth between individualistic and communal existence increasing in complexity throughout the evolutionary process for 3.5 billion years. Lipton and Sahtouris believe that humanity today is at a critical juncture where we can no longer evolve in these same oscillating patterns. Instead, the next stage of evolution will be an entirely different one that replaces strict duality with a highly intelligent community that fully integrates the individual into a superorganism called humanity.[10] That full integration could be compared to the N^1 brain in figure 5.1 above that is nested in the largest representation of the environment—the planetary environment designated by the broken elliptical line labeled as A^1. In the Gravesian model, the movement from the first to the second tier essentially represents the movement from a single human to humanity as the leading edge of evolution.

Howard Bloom made a similar statement in his book *The Global Brain*. Bloom has been called the next Stephen Hawking and the Einstein, Newton, Darwin, and Freud of the twenty-first century.[11] He was also a close friend of Beck and a frequent guest speaker at Beck's training seminars. Bloom describes the term *global brain* as a phenomenon that is far beyond what the techno prophets of Silicon Valley tell us it is. Rather, the phenomenon is one in which, were we as humans better to understand ourselves, we would have to acknowledge that we are the neurons in the nervous system of the planet's interspecies mind that has been eons in the making.[12] Bloom's argument describes the essence of the transition we face as we must subsume our *human intelligence* driven by the ego expressions of the *First sapiens* for the last two- to three-hundred-thousand years into the greater *natural intelligence* of the planet's entire evolutionary process—what James Lovelock called the Gaia intelligence that has been billions of years in the making. To relate this to Graves's work, empowering the N^1 brain with exponential capacities and nesting it within the full environment of A^1 confirms his six-upon-six hypothesis wherein *Homo sapiens* returns to what remains of the natural environment that existed during the *sapiens 1.1* stage and begins to reintegrate *human intelligence* with *natural intelligence* in order to understand what it takes to preserve all life on the planet.

To avoid confusion between the mandates of Graves's seventh stage and Spiral Dynamics's eighth stage, Beck and Cowan further differentiated the seventh stage and endowed it with a dual mandate. The first mandate is to unblock the barriers in all the first-tier systems that keep them arrested. In other words, as depicted in the graphic below (fig. 5.2), it is to detect where all the ideologies that run all the first-tier systems have their healthiest expressions, which are often represented by the *growth* and *maturity* phases in the life cycle of each ideological fractal in all the lower systems before they reach the nexus point. The second mandate is to place all the first-tier systems into a functional flow toward a long-term sustainable trajectory informed by the values and the virtues of the eighth stage. Yellow, or *sapiens 2.1*, has one foot in the first tier, helping it detach from its deficient needs, and the other foot at the doorstep of the turquoise *sapiens 2.2*, shaping its ecologically aligned, holistic virtues into lean information to design new institutions for governance that enable the long-term stabilization of all life forms. Beck adopted the use of the term *lean information* from the concepts behind lean manufacturing, which were first defined in the 1990 book, *The Machine that Changed the World,* by James Womack and Daniel Jones. It describes the ways in which the Toyota Motor Corporation gained a competitive edge by organizing its production systems efficiently. The practices were then popularized by management consultants. Beck's use of the term applies to the principles of information management intended to minimize unnecessary data, streamline information flow, and ensure information accuracy to support efficient decision making relevant to the *sapiens 2.1 general thema.*

In figure 5.2 below, the alignment to the *sapiens 2.2* stage is represented by the two thick white lines. The bottom line represents *sapiens 2.1* having one foot in the first tier to help it detach from its deficient needs and keep it from moving past each stage's nexus point, and the top line represents *sapiens 2.1* cultivating the healthiest expressions of the first-tier systems.

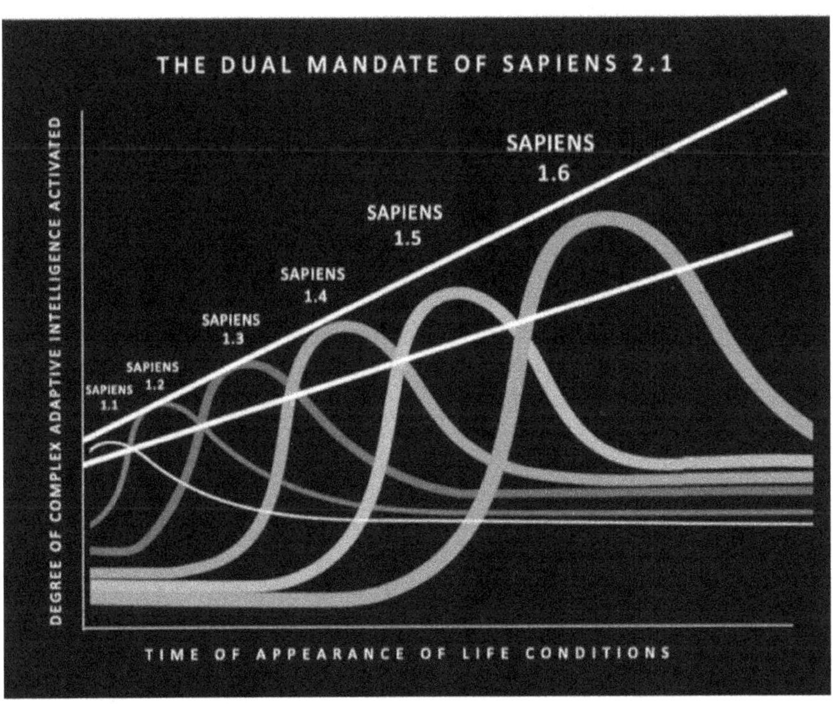

Figure 5.2. The Dual Mandate of *Sapiens 2.1.* The tasks are to unblock the dysfunction in the first six stages and place them on a long-term sustainability trajectory. Adapted from the work of Clare W. Graves, the Spiral Dynamics Group, and the MEMEnomics Group. Used with permission from the MEMEnomics Group, LLC; www.memenomic.com.

In the macro application of *sapiens 2.1*, its dual mandate is to unblock the barriers in all institutions and other large holonic structures created by the first-tier systems and then to place them on a long-term, ecologically aligned trajectory into the future. It relies on lean information and is steered by people with high competencies who fully understand the motivations of leaders and actors in all the lower stages and the design flaws in the systems they create. The person with the most knowledge of a specific issue leads and makes the decisions, and, as the situation changes, leadership changes. Good leadership is based on the ability to handle complexity. In the quest to create real solutions, knowledge and competency supersede rank, power, and status. The organizing intelligence structure capable of addressing a multifaceted, whole-systems approach to existential problems is a constellation of *sapiens 2.1* thinkers, a brain syndicate of highly competent individuals who are proficient in their area of specialty. More importantly, they fully and consciously recognize the limits of their specialized intelligence and respect and trust in the competencies of all the other individuals that form the brain syndicate. Recognizing the limits and the non-transferability of specialized intelligence at this stage of development is more important in today's culture full of *sapiens 1.5* biases that conflate the net worth of an individual with his or her overall ability to handle other specialized *sapiens 2.1* intelligences.

> *Those centralized in this cognitive existential state truly learn that life is interdependent. The world is seen kaleidoscopically with different views demanding different attentions. Knowledge in* A^1–N^1 *thinking exists in different settings; knowers think in different ways. Thus, thinking is in terms of several legitimate different interpretations of the systemic whole, and thought is about many different wholes in different ways.*
>
> —Clare W. Graves[13]

Elon Musk, who is one of the richest and most powerful people in the world, provides a real-life example. He belongs in a very narrow and specialized area of the *sapiens 2.1* brain syndicate, the engineering intelligence area. He single-handedly brought electric vehicles to the forefront of addressing CO^2 emissions and in the process disrupted the entire auto industry and aligned it on a sustainable *sapiens 2.1* trajectory.

His actions outside his engineering intelligence, however, point to deficient *First-sapiens* views in areas of politics and matters concerning free speech. In his misguided $44 billion purchase of Twitter, Musk, a self-proclaimed free-speech absolutist, stated that, above all, his decision to purchase the social-media giant was to stop its pervasive censorship of conservative causes. Six months into his ownership, a reversed censorship has occurred on the platform that now represses liberal-leaning causes. Observers argue that it is an extension of his business practices and his treatment of union organizers and whistleblowers that makes his free-speech absolutism code for a high tolerance of bigotry.[14] His support for a conservative political party that denies the existence of climate change negates everything his engineering intelligence has contributed to a *sapiens 2.1* brain syndicate tasked with addressing existential planetary issues.

In spite of his or her desire to obtain lean, unbiased information, Homo ecosistamus listens with deep empathy. It is a quality that allows one to move past the surface manifestation of behavior and dig deep into understanding the mindsets and motivations that produce that behavior and the systems that shape it and prolong its existence in an arrested or closed state. The need to hear all points of view, which is characteristic of *sapiens 1.6,* gives way to a practical desire to listen only to those with knowledge and expertise. This does not signify the reappearance of the hierarchical structures that define *sapiens 1.3, 1.4,* and *1.5*; nor does it signify a rigid ideological way to get things done. Rather, *sapiens 2.1* is interested merely in finding the right solution for the existential problem at hand at certain given times, which makes it a highly functional system that uses the intelligence of any of the lower stages to achieve its goals. This characteristic gives it the ad hoc, nonideological resilience it needs to handle chaos and uncertainly. If a given situation requires the raw courage of *sapiens 1.3, sapiens 2.1* empowers it to take the lead, but only until that particular task is achieved. If it needs to understand a specific scientific concept in order to address another existential problem, it taps into the *sapiens 1.5* intelligence, but only to attain the lean information that becomes part of the decision-making process of its higher-order system. This is the synergistic synthesis that characterizes this stage of development, which allowed Beck and Cowan to further interpret its *general thema* as an intelligence concerned with the *natural design and functional flow* of systems wherein design and function come together to serve its dual mandate.

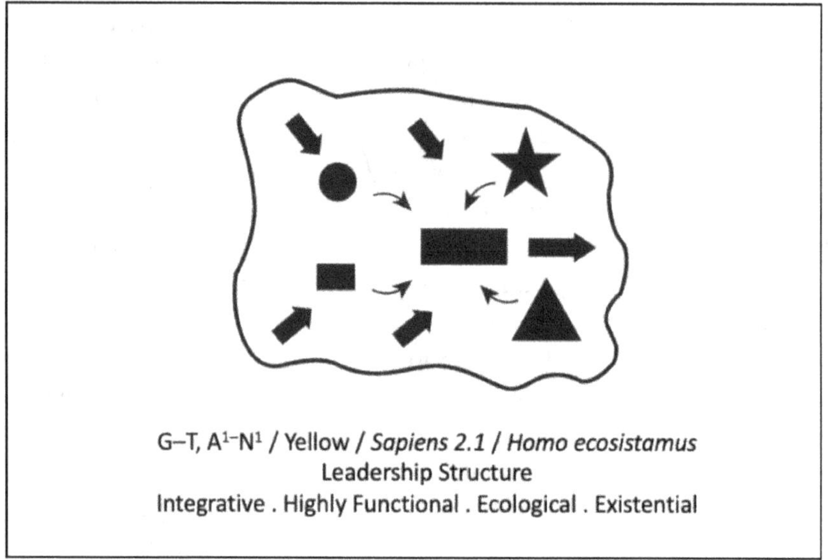

G–T, A1-N1 / Yellow / Sapiens 2.1 / Homo ecosistamus
Leadership Structure
Integrative . Highly Functional . Ecological . Existential

Figure 5.3. Leadership at the Stage 7 Level of Development. Systemic flow, process oriented. Adapted from Spiral Dynamics and used with permission from Don E. Beck.

Decision making at the level of *sapiens 2.1* is highly principled and centered in knowledge and data derived from the paradigm that there is an existential urgency to manage the chaos of human existence. The brain of *Homo ecosistamus* has the innate ability to filter out data that is tainted or heavily influenced by any of the lower, first-tier stages of development. This quality becomes increasingly important in today's post-truth reality of left and right political polarization, the tribalization and fragmentation in our culture caused by the digital media, and the digital deep fakes that can sew mayhem. One of the current challenges is to address the advancements in artificial intelligence that are accelerating all the chaos the digital world has created as it moves at warp speed to quantify and disrupt whatever remains unquantified in human pursuits. Much of that quantification requires human-led, *Second-sapiens* scientific research to emerge fully before an algorithm can mine its content. The scientific fractals in *Second sapiens*, like the intelligence of the entire tier, remain in single percentage points fighting the antibodies of *sapiens 1.5* sciences.

Sapiens 2.1 thrives on competence in all areas that present a threat to life on the planet. He or she understands complexity and is self-directed but bases his or her approach on existential conditions that are continually shifting and changing. Such people build on advanced research methodologies developed by *sapiens 1.5*. Both stages seek to understand the secrets of the universe through scientific discoveries and mathematical modeling. But, unlike *sapiens 1.5*, who uses the research to monetize discoveries and degrade Earth's systems, *sapiens 2.1* uses all known capacities from other disciplines concerned with the biosphere, the atmosphere, geology, sociology, oceanography, climate change, and all other areas of science representing the *natural intelligence* that *sapiens 1.5* deemed less relevant through its reductive values. It is this systemic approach that can reverses the damage that the *First sapiens's* Orwellian societal complex has caused the planet. At this *sapiens 2.1* stage of development, chaos is determined by the coalescence of two major factors: the first concerns the mandate to mitigate or reverse the unhealthy expressions of all the first-tier systems, and the second concerns the necessity to integrate *natural intelligence* into the mind and make all previous intelligences subordinate to it.

Homo ecosistamus does more with less and uses appropriate technologies to get the job done with less waste and fewer ecological problems. He or she is not deterred by political correctness but uses it when it is absolutely necessary. Since power flows to the most competent in each situation, it is less concentrated. This factor is not to be confused with a distributed system of management. By recognizing the chaos present at this stage of development, *sapiens 2.1* can resort to strict hierarchal decision making when the situation so warrants.

This flexibility is shown in figure 5.4 above, which depicts the structures of three communication-distribution networks, all of which *sapiens 2.1* can use as needed. For instance, the rigid network of *sapiens 1.4* appears in the first configuration to the left, labeled "Centralized (A)." *sapiens 2.1* can use the sharp elbows of this organizational structure to deploy the army, the national guard, or any other governmental force to address natural disasters, which have increased in size and frequency in the last few decades. The middle network, labeled "Decentralized (B)," could be considered an extension of the *sapiens 1.5* organizational structure that empowers leaders with meritocracy. *Sapiens 2.1* uses this structure when it calls on those who exhibit competencies in the specific areas of expertise deemed necessary for the specific situation at hand. Finally, if the milieu calls for an egalitarian style of communication absent hierarchical structures, then *sapiens 2.1* uses the distributed form of communication

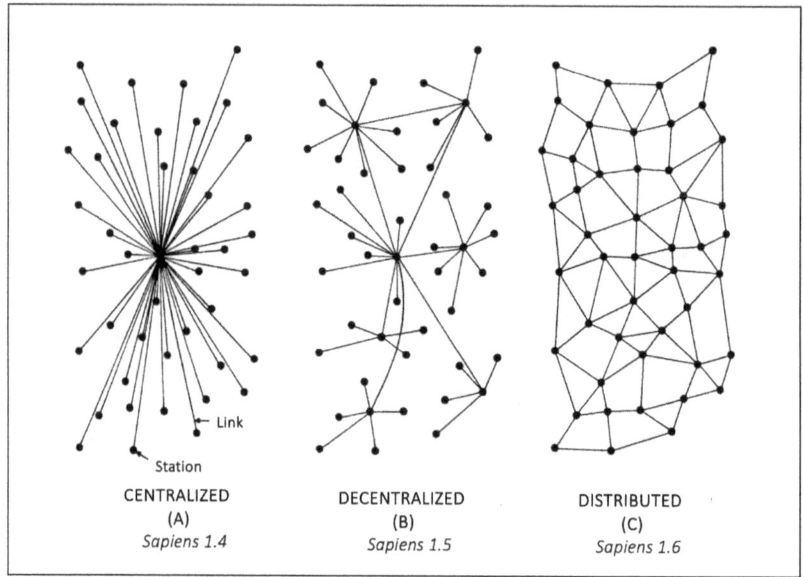

Figure 5.4. Communication-Distribution Networks. In the drawing on the far left, the label "Link" refers to the physical communication channel—such as a cable, a radio wave, or any other medium allowing data transmission—that carries information between stations. "Station" represents a device on the network—such as a computer, a router, or any other node participating in communication—that can send and receive information. Paul Baran, *On Distributed Communications: I. Introduction to Distributed Communications Networks.* Memorandum RM-3420-PR (August 1964); http://www.rand.org/content/dam/rand/pubs/research_memoranda/2006/RM3420.pdf.

shown in the configuration on the right, which is harmonious with the organizational structure of *sapiens 1.6.*

While our modern and postmodern societies believe the return to the brutality of *sapiens 1.3* is highly unlikely, *sapiens 2.1* will consider deploying its virtues in an effort to save the planet. This will be the first in a kind of global martial law that combines the ruthlessness of *sapiens 1.3* with the absolutism of *sapiens 1.4* to suspend civil liberties, enforce *right behavior,* and wage war against the nonconformists in a world facing extinction and ravaged by natural disasters as we inch closer to the *Great Obsolescence.* The key concept in a *sapiens 2.1* management system is that the most competent people from different areas of knowledge spanning the range of the entire first tier are plugged into a motherboard with a higher level of neuropsychological development, resulting in considerably higher levels of agility, resilience, and adaptability capable of addressing existential problems as they appear. This is the stage that concerns itself with the survival of all life on the planet. Similar to that of *sapiens 1.1,* its *general thema* is survival; but instead of being confronted with beasts and the elements, *sapiens 2.1* is confronted with exponentially greater threats of the collective beasts comprised of dangerous and toxic elements of our own making. It is the collapse of all the planetary systems caused by the numbness we have created for ourselves that Graves described as the Orwellian societal complex that shields us from knowing too much about what lies outside the world of the *First sapiens.*

In aligning the healthy expressions of the lower six systems on its platform, *sapiens 2.1* empowers the human element of *sapiens 1.6* and its apprehension about the effects of human activity on the environment, as well as placing greater emphasis on the spiritual nature of humanity and less emphasis on status and materialism. Also, *sapiens 2.1* cannot build much of its resilience without empowering a healthy expression of *sapiens 1.4,* the cultural stage that forms institutions that are the foundation of a functioning democracy. This issue is essentially one of how to transform weak governance with newly empowered institutions capable of enacting new laws that can address our existential problems effectively. Much of my work in the last decade has focused on exposing how the weakening of *sapiens 1.4* institutions is at the heart of many of our problems, from economic inequality to environmental degradation. A *sapiens 1.4* redesigned and re-empowered by *sapiens 2.1* is what I called *Smart BLUE* in the language of Spiral Dynamics and will call *Smart sapiens 1.4* in this iteration.

Among the very few politicians I've identified as possessing these *Second-sapiens* capacities is Massachusetts Senator Elizabeth Warren, who has the uncanny ability to see through all the first-tier systems and expose their closed or arrested states that are preventing the effective regulation of our economy. My 2013 book *MEMEnomics* and several subsequent writings analyze situations in which Senator Warren, along with nonpoliticians who have a big-picture view of our economy, have exhibited *sapiens 2.1* leadership qualities that expose the toxicity that *sapiens 1.5* in the *only-money-matters cycle* has caused in our government and in our economic system. In 2018, the *Washington Post* considered Senator Warren a top contender for the 2020 Democratic nomination for president. To demonstrate how prohibitively difficult the transition to a *Smart sapiens 1.4* system of regulation will be and how much *sapiens 1.5* fears and despises *sapiens 2.1* intelligence, shortly after Warren announced her candidacy the leaders of Wall Street summoned the top officials in the Democratic National Committee. Their purpose was to inform the DNC of their decision to stop all contributions to the entire Democratic Party should she become its nominee.[15]

Similar patterns of *sapiens 1.5* behavior occurred in the early days of the Obama Administration. In November 2008, President-Elect Obama formed the President's Economic Recovery Advisory Board with Paul Volcker at its helm. Volcker was mostly known for taming runaway inflation in the 1970s and early '80s when he was the head of the Federal Reserve. But in the Gravesian framework, he was a smart regulator within the economic fractal with *sapiens 2.1* intelligence. Volcker was a non-ideologue, which is a necessary quality for the *sapiens 2.1* stage. He confronted the limits of Keynesian economics defining the *patriotic prosperity cycle* that had lasted from the end of the Great Depression to the late 1970s; he also resisted Friedman's *monetarism*, which has been the *general thema* of the *sapiens 1.5, only-money-matters* cycle. He persistently spoke against the financialization of our economy and the corrosive toll it was taking on the American middle and working class.[16] Volker was slated to be the new White House Head of Economic Advisors, but, unfortunately, that was not to be. Both he and President Obama had underestimated the degree to which the toxicity of *sapiens 1.5* has permeated the sociopolitical fabric of America. Under pressure from bankers and Wall-Street lobbyists, the day President Obama took office, Volcker was replaced by Larry Summers, economic advisor to the Clinton Administration. It was on Summers's watch in the 1990s that the deregulation of banks was completed. Summers also advocated for Congress not to regulate the trading of financial derivatives, which became the primary cause of the 2008 financial crisis.[17]

The *sapiens 2.1* view of our sociopolitical reality is that a diminished *sapiens 1.4* system of regulation has relinquished its responsibilities to the *sapiens 1.5* system and in the process eroded the foundation of fairness and opportunity for those who don't share its proprietary and corrosive worldview. The degree of difficulty in exposing the current arrested state of affairs becomes exponentially greater as our existential problems shift the focus to the Earth's systems, a much higher fractal of complexity. In the light of climate change and ecological collapse, and re-enabled by *sapiens 2.1, Smart sapiens 1.4* becomes *resilient/existential sapiens 1.4,* an open system made up of regulatory structures that transcend the focus on economic regulation and include them as a smaller fractal in the wider system equipped with institutions capable of ensuring the continuity of life on the planet.

A *sapiens 2.1* economic system is one of intuitive intelligence and functionality. In *MEMEnomics,* I spent several chapters defining a new economic-sustainability platform based on the virtues of this level of development. Much of what I articulated then remains true today with the exception that, given how quickly Mother Nature seems to be dictating our future, the *platform for sustainable capitalism* I created then has become nested in a new, higher-order framework. This new framework accounts for the emerging *existential problems* identified at the *sapiens 2.2* stage, in which *sapiens 2.1* has one foot. It is the resilience and functionality inherent in the highly collaborative nature of these two last-known stages of development that represent the *Second sapiens.* If the higher-order science informing *sapiens 2.1* suggests a reversal of current economic practices in order to preserve all life on the planet, then this becomes the obligatory systemic task. Economic philosophies of the *First sapiens* that emphasize growth at any cost would have to go through a major reconning in order to adopt economic policies of degrowth that look nothing like the *First sapiens* has encountered in the last five centuries.

> *To demonstrate the highly collaborative nature of the second-tier systems, imagine the seventh-level yellow as the surgeon who stiches together a wounded world and the eighth-level turquoise as the physician who applies the healing ointment that ensures the world's long-term resilience.*
>
> —Don E. Beck[18]

Today, *Homo ecosistamus* is tasked with the most difficult mission in human history. Not only does he or she have to align the virtues of the all the previous stages of development onto a healthy, sustainable, long-term trajectory, he or she must also guide it through the grim task of processing its collective shadow before it is freed to take the *momentous leap* forward. Based on the six-upon-six hypothesis, and as I have said, *sapiens 2.1* will repeat the survival theme of sapiens *1.1* but at an exponentially higher level of psychoneurological capacity and with access to all the good and healthy things the *First sapiens* has created. Just as sapiens *1.1* was the longest stage of existence in the first six stages, when most of our time was spent mastering our individual survival skills, *sapiens 2.1* will spend an inordinate amount of time mastering the skills needed to ensure the survival of all planetary life. While the time needed at this stage might be reduced by a factor of two from that of *sapiens 1.1,* the ecological systems that preserve all life are signaling a state of collapse that respects no timeframe set by any *Homo sapiens.* Should *sapiens 2.1* fail to stabilize the world, the *Great Obsolescence* that entails the transcendence of the *First sapiens* will become the *Great Extinction.* However, if Mother Nature affords us the time to spread the virtues of *sapiens 2.1,* we will have a chance to stabilize the world at a new stage of existence that looks completely different from anything we have known before.

Stage 8: H–U/B^1–O^1, Experiential, Turquoise, *Homo universalis, Sapiens 2.2*, Holistic/Planetary; The Regenerative Community

Sapiens 2.2 shares *sapiens 2.1's* global view and its ability to think systemically. This stage of development uses physics and metaphysics together to explore the problems of all life forms. It combines the objective with the subjective, the intuitive with the logical, and the material with the philosophical and the natural. And it takes the exponential growth in whole-brain capacities achieved in the arduous work of *sapiens 2.1* and begins to shape it into organismic, regenerative ecological units that form a new world order behaving as a single, dynamic organism with its own collective mind.

The self is at once distinct and a blended part of a larger, compassionate whole.[19] Everything connects to everything else as one holonic structure that is holistic and intuitive, wherein synergistic and cooperative actions are a normal reflection of the stage's virtues and ways of thinking. Evolutionarily, this is what comes after we fully realize the cosmic view of which astrophysicist Neil de Grasse Tyson spoke and Beck's stitching together of a "wounded world" (see boxed quote on p. 203). Observations such as these trigger *sapiens 2.1* intelligence to widen psychosocial capacities in preparation for the long-term resilience and sustainability of the *Second-sapiens* virtues needed for the building of a new civilization.

> *There is a serious, stable cast to the values of the eighth level man who perceives the world as somewhat beyond his ken. At the B^1-O^1 level, man values wonder, awe, reverence, humility, fusion, integration, unity, simplicity, the poetic perception of reality-non interfering perception verses active controlling perception, enlarging consciousness and the ineffable experience. He values the marvelous rich world of context and sheer fluid beauty and the fearless face-to-face awareness of now-naked life.*
>
> —Clare W. Graves[20]

This eighth stage of development is known to be highly integrative. It behaves as one living organism as it blends and harmonizes a strong collective of individuals into a holistic field that intuitively senses how the behavior of any element in the universe immediately impacts all the others.[21] It is the ultimate stage of human development that recognizes our species as one superorganism called humanity, which is also a fractal representation of Bloom's global brain and Lovelock's Gaia intelligence that has been 3.5 billion years in the making. It is Beck's metaphorical healing ointment that is the alchemy of the entire evolutionary process, the evolutionary intelligence of all life. *Homo universalis* uncovers the connections and principles that underlie the entire living process and, in the process, becomes fully endowed with *natural intelligence.* He acts on the behalf of Mother Nature and makes the difficult choices that previous stages wouldn't make due to the absence of awareness about the severity of our existential problems that have become epochal in nature.

At the macro level, *sapiens 2.2* is charged with maintaining global and planetary systems in an ecologically aligned, sustainable, and regenerative state. This governing structure is yet to manifest but will emerge as a holonic form of democracy that is a distributed system of *natural intelligence* with a primary focus on the preservation of all life. The things we have taken for granted—such as global commerce, current forms of democratic rule, untamed population growth, and the exploitation of natural resources—will alter significantly if not be sacrificed outright under this governing system.

Sapiens 1.6 often thinks she is operating at the *sapiens 2.2* stage, but there are some key differences. *Sapiens 1.6*'s inclusiveness and belief that everything and everyone is of equal value keeps her from making difficult choices. She does not want to sacrifice anyone because everyone is equally treasured. An example that illustrates the confusion between these two stages is that of the United Nations. While many believe the organization is the first manifestation of global *sapiens 2.2* institutions, the fact that it has no enforcement powers to stop wars, or to stem the causes of climate change and ecological decline, defaults it to a *sapiens 1.6* institution. It falsely assumes we all share the same utopian values that make us behave like one superorganism. So far, this state of being has proven to exist only selectively in a world ruled by first-tier systems. Like *sapiens 2.1*, the *sapiens 2.2* stage of development is interested in results, but unlike *sapiens 1.5* that seeks to manipulate results for its subsistent needs, *sapiens 2.2* seeks

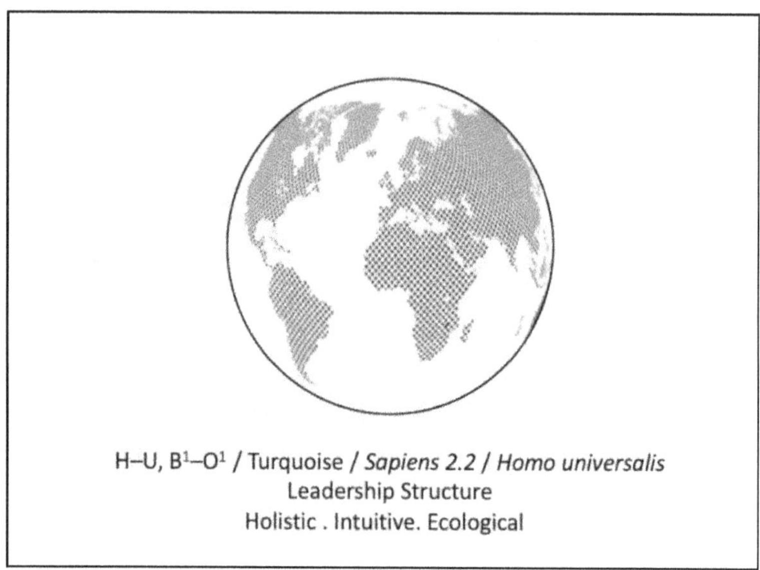

H–U, B¹–O¹ / Turquoise / Sapiens 2.2 / Homo universalis
Leadership Structure
Holistic . Intuitive. Ecological

Fig 5.5. Leadership at the Stage 8 Level of Development: Holistic organism, synthesis oriented. Adapted from the Spiral Dynamics Group and used with permission from Don E. Beck.

results through a synergistic organic process that ensures the continued stability of all life in the pursuit of a safe and orderly world that must maintain ecological balance at all times.

One real-life example of large complex structures behaving as a single organism in accordance with *sapiens 2.2* characteristics comes to us from a grove of aspen trees in the Fishlake National Forest in Utah. Known as Pando, this forest covers 106 acres of land on the southwest bank of Utah's Fish Lake. In 1976, scientists identified the forest as the largest single living organism on Earth with a massive, interconnected underground root system.[22] What appears to the casual observer as single trees are in reality stems or shoots, and Pando has over forty thousand of them in different stages of life. Because these are shoots and not individual trees, they don't have tree rings, which makes it impossible for scientists to determine the forest's exact age, but estimates range from eighty thousand to one million years old. The forest is an exquisite embodiment of the collective individualism characterized by the *Second sapiens*; what appears as an individual tree is part of a much deeper, ecological collective comprising a fractal representation of the Earth's different systems that make life possible.

If *sapiens 1.5* visits Pando, he will see only trees and dismiss much of the complexity of the whole organism. His limited perspective leads him to think that he is separate from Mother Nature and doesn't have to be part of her interconnected web of intelligence. Pando is a powerful symbol for civilization as an ecologically aligned, single organism. It nests what appears to be independent trees in its *natural intelligence* that includes the millions of different stems and fibrous roots going through countless life cycles that define the greater complexity of all life characterized by interdependence, chaos, and natural creativity that is present at every fractal level, from the smallest to the largest organism.

As a *natural-intelligence* system, Pando automatically recognizes the limits to growth. It has done so since prehistoric times. When its expansive root system cannot find enough resources such as water and minerals, it slows the rate of expansion of new shoots.[23] This is the kind of innate intelligence needed if we are to prevent the various planetary systems from crossing certain thresholds beyond which life cannot be sustained. Our failure to subordinate *human intelligence* to this form of *natural intelligence* will trigger nonlinear, planetary-scale catastrophes. Preventing these catastrophes is the awesome responsibility with which *sapiens 2.2* is tasked.

In *MEMEnomics,* I speculated that a *sapiens 2.2* economic system would look like nothing we have known or experienced. In the absence of full Anthropogenic awareness, I had believed that the normal evolutionary process of stage development would continue and that—since a *sapiens 2.1* economic system was just beginning to emerge—it would take decades if not centuries for it to stabilize the world's first-tier systems before it reached its nexus point, at which time the virtues of a *sapiens 2.2* economic system would take over. Based on the ecological nature of the stage, what I articulated then remains true today. It just needs to happen with a far greater sense of urgency. Below are two paragraphs from that section of my book:

> At this stage of development, groups that are taxing the precious resources of the planet, whether it is Wall Street, OPEC, Russian Oligarchs, or Chinese Central Planners, will simply not exist. Waste and inefficiency will be eliminated through a process akin to natural selection and confirmed by a committee of highly-evolved world leaders, a Yellow brain syndicate that informs, empowers, and enforces a network of distributed intelligence that seeks the ecological alignment of our species. There will be elements of

> Marxism that will distribute resources equally combined with the best elements of capitalism that empower innovation in research and development with the overall goal of guarding our precious global resources and regenerating nature. A full merit system of exchange that recognizes the totality and efficiency of serving the biosphere will replace all monetary forms of exchange. Every productive member of society from the landscaper to the healer and the nonmonetary banker will perform his or her job knowing he or she is a highly specialized, efficient, and indispensable member of an ecosystem that naturally reciprocates in providing for all his or her needs.

> The emerging science of biomimicry and its construct of an economic ecosystem provides an early glimpse of what a future under a Turquoise economic system would look like. Without a doubt, this is a distributed intelligence that is intuitively prudent. If boundaries still exist by the time Turquoise appears, nations with natural resources will place priority on their efficient distribution to keep the ecosystem functioning over their need to build the wealth of a nation. Intelligence of all types will be distributed to the widest degree possible. Global villages that use the highest, best, and newest forms of technology with the smallest environmental footprint will become the norm. Commodities and futures markets will disappear. Efficiencies in markets of all types will be naturally built in as a reflection of the *life conditions* of the value system that recognizes the seriousness of what it is to be alive on a planet with limited resources.[24]

Since the Turquoise *sapiens 2.2* stage was first conceived by Beck and Cowan, its mandate has been fully to integrate the *Homo-sapiens* brain and align it with *natural intelligence*, a state of being that is in harmony with Mother Nature. While Wilber has moved past this eighth stage of development in his work, Beck, until the time of his passing in 2022, still asserted that its full characteristics remain beyond our knowledge. Since ecological collapse, which represents B^1 in the B^1–O^1 coupling in the *sapiens 2.2* stage, was not as visible a decade and a half ago as it is today, both Beck and I had speculated that any specific timeframe for the emergence of the eighth stage and the nature of its content remained highly speculative. That speculation ranged from the stage being charged with rebuilding what remains of life after the ravages of ecological collapse to it coming about in a Utopian existence in which humanity acts as one superorganism connected to its evolutionary intelligence in ecological alignment with all life. While awareness of environmental degradation began to seep into the consciousness of several thinkers in both the Spiral-Dynamics and the Integral-Theory camps over a decade ago, fully placing the Anthropocene into our respective evolutionary models has been only partially successful.

Anthropogenic *life conditions* take everything that has been known and articulated in the last three decades about this eighth stage of development and pushes it further up the bell curve in its life cycle. It is no longer on the far horizon where its virtues first appeared in the minds of prophets and oracles. Those were the systems thinkers such as Graves who emerged in the chaos of the 1970s and warned us about what was to come. In spite of all the scientific research proving their claims, we have collectively ignored the warning signs. Consequently, *Homo sapiens* has ceded his destiny to a far greater system than the one he controls—that greater system being the one that contains all the planetary systems in which all life is nested. This fact not only requires a new, post-Holocene interpretation of both models, it has forever disrupted the nature of what second-tier intelligence has to address.

Six

Homo Magnificus and the Anthropocene

It is a pity we're still officially living in an age called the Holocene. The Anthropocene—human dominance of biological, chemical, and geological processes on Earth—is already an undeniable reality.

—Paul J. Crutzen
Winner of Nobel Prize in chemistry, 1995

At the time that Beck's and Cowan's work gained popularity, the leading edge of the first strand of the double helix, that being the one that identifies the *existential problems* (*life conditions*), was not identifying climate change, ecological degradation, the loss of biodiversity, and the limits to growth as immediate threats. Even though Graves had identified these future challenges as existential in nature, both strands of the double helix—the *life conditions* and the *complex adaptive intelligence*—remained dormant on this issue. The reason for this dormancy could be that the source of these challenges was coming from a fractal so advanced and complex that it couldn't possibly trigger enough neuropsychological awareness to become our species' main focus. The particular warning signs such as climate change were telling us to look to Mother Nature's *natural intelligence*—the *complex-adaptive-intelligence* half of the model in that advanced fractal—to begin the search for effective and sustainable solutions. But instead of doing so, the leading edge of human emergence that identified with the second tier absent Anthropogenic awareness defaulted to addressing problems within humancentric, man-made systems that use the smaller fractal of intelligence: *human intelligence.* The stage of development that can handle the complexity of the existential threats of the

Anthropocene epoch is one that must transcend all the lower fractals of complexity from individual, organizational, communal, regional, and macro systems and nest them in a new mega system capable of addressing the new *life conditions* being dictated to us by our current conditions. If there had been no greater threats than issues of geopolitics, economics, governance, and the like, the original content of the second tier that Beck and Cowan envisioned would have been sufficient.

Defining the Post-Holocene *Second Sapiens*

To summarize the point, due to the absence of Anthropogenic awareness, Beck, Cowan, and, by extension, Wilber had defined the values of the second tier from within the Holocene era at a time when issues of planetary collapse were not at the forefront of either the Spiral-Dynamics or the Integral-Theory model. Practitioners of both models have created a large body of work that attempts to define the future of humanity. Yet very few in both camps have identified the role *natural intelligence* plays in shaping the *complex-adaptive-intelligence* half of the model at the two highest levels of human development that define the second tier. Even for those who have done so, very few have been able effectively to translate the foundation of both models into post-Holocene frameworks capturing the essence of *natural intelligence* that defines Anthropogenic living. This is the intelligence of Mother Nature, from which *Homo sapiens* has defined himself as separate but to which he must now return. The difficulty with followers of both frameworks is the presence of huge egos, pure and simple. When Graves's work was called the "theory that explains everything" in 1967, there was no mention of how the theory would deal with the colossal and pervasive issue of climate change and ecosystem collapse. Yet this didn't stop Beck and Wilber from making similar claims about their own theories. Today, both camps still believe that *Homo sapiens* is still in charge and that his/her own spiritual and psychosocial evolution will save us and the planet. Although the death of the ego, which symbolizes the exit from the first tier, plays a significant part in Wilber's articulation of transcendence in the second tier, reference to how this new state of awareness can influence the design of new mega systems for governance and the effective management of all life in a post-Holocene reality remains greatly unaddressed.

Today, Wilber arbitrarily continues to claim that humanity's transition to the second tier will reach a tipping point once 10 percent of the population reaches the A^1– N^1 stage, the first level in the second tier (see table 4.1).[1] Absent any reliable data, he continues falsely to compare this transition to the one from the blue *sapiens 1.4* stage to the orange *sapiens 1.5* stage, wherein the values of the Enlightenment became the leading edge of human development. While Wilber's reference to Graves has become more frequent in the last decade, very little of what he says falls within the parameters of the Gravesian framework. Wilber is missing the mark in three different areas in continuing to make unfounded claims about our transition into the second tier:

1) First, he seems to be completely unaware of the degree to which the unhealthy expression of the orange *sapiens 1.5* stage has become pervasive and toxic. This is the dominator hierarchy that has moved far beyond its nexus point and ensnared the entire world in the *peace-through-commerce* ethos, the one Graves called the Orwellian societal complex that shields us from knowing much beyond the *First sapiens.* This ethos has gotten a stranglehold on all of the world's institutions—academic, political, and otherwise—rendering the barriers to higher stages far more prohibitive. It has monetized the only hope the green *sapiens 1.6* stage had to spread its virtues of equality and the human connection by enslaving the digital economy and its globalized social networks. In so doing, it has made this economy into the largest, most addictive business model in human history and cemented the grip of *sapiens 1.5* on the world. It has introduced new forms of chaos that neither Graves, Beck, nor Wilber ever envisioned in shaping the *life-conditions* half of the model, a critical precondition that determines the content of what second-tier intelligence—the *complex-adaptive-intelligence* half—has to address.
2) Secondly, Wilber seems to be unaware that, unlike the transition from blue *sapiens 1.4* to orange *sapiens 1.5,* the current transition does not comprise an incremental movement up the spiral to another stage of deficient human needs. Rather, it comprises a monumental, upward shift that must be preceded by a prolonged downshift into all the issues that have remained unresolved during the whole previous presence of *Homo sapiens* on the planet. This is the gap of unbelievable meaning of which Graves spoke, and we can only get to the other side of it after we pass through the *darkness-before-the new*-dawn phase of the entire first tier. Many of the

examples Wilber uses as tipping points that will move us to the next stage of development are rendered moot when our new reality dictates that much of what we have known to be good and true must be reversed if we are to emerge successfully into a global society organized under second-tier principles with Anthropogenic awareness. Wilber's analysis seems to have greatly overlooked this sequential but important stage. Perhaps it is because his view is from a place beyond Jupiter or any physical realm that lies in the third tier—a set of stages that in the Gravesian model cannot yet manifest and remain in the philosophical and spiritual realms, making their predictive capabilities for the physical realms far less reliable.

3) The third point missing from Wilber's argument is that he seems to have little awareness that we no longer live in the comfort of the Holocene era. Issues of planetary degradation have triggered the collapse of a much higher-fractal order that changes Wilber's iteration of the Gravesian model. In Graves's words, the roof is collapsing in on us as we sit in our meditative states seeking higher realms of consciousness. His words are echoed today by the UN secretary general when he proclaims that our failure to limit CO_2 emissions to the target date set by the IPCC to be a *code red for all humanity*. The integral model seems to have remained greatly uniformed by this new reality. As do many in the human consciousness movement, most of its practitioners continue to indulge in a view with a new, glossy veneer and a fixation on a societal complex that includes the uses of some of Wilber's own second-tier and third-tier concepts, giving little heed to the fact that the *life-conditions* half of the model constitutes a different set of existential threats than the ones Wilber conceived in the comfort of the Holocene era. This reality was evinced in the largest gathering of Integral-Theory practitioners—the Integral European Conference, which in 2023 brought several dozen speakers together under the banner of Planetary Awakening 2.0.[2] With only two or three exceptions, the majority of speakers remained uninformed of the urgency we now face in the Anthropocene era, defined by the new content of the second tier driven by *natural intelligence* that transcends the current content that has placed *human intelligence* in charge. A worldview dominated by *human intelligence* is how both Wilber and Beck conceived it in a pre-Anthropogenic era.

After Beck ended his collaboration with Wilber in the mid-2000s, Beck became increasingly critical of how the integral movement as a whole was ignoring one vast, fundamental aspect of Graves's model that made it evolutionary—the environmental influence, the effect of *life conditions* on stage development. This half of Graves's model can be compared to the sun gear, the master cylinder in the planetary gearset model (fig. 1.2) that determines the movement or the recalibration of the servant gears, represented in this case by our *complex adaptive intelligence* that exists in us in latent form, waiting to be triggered by *life conditions.* Integral practitioners who acquire their knowledge of Spiral Dynamics through Wilber's framework have little awareness of how Graves's *life conditions* shape the entire evolutionary process.[3] And while pure Gravesians have considered this second strand of the double helix essential to the evolutionary process, both models have rarely identified Earth's systems as the source of the *existential problems* that inform *life conditions* in the second tier.

Graves's Double Helix and the Dual Inheritance Theory

My search for evolutionary patterns that can legitimize the use of the Gravesian model in the Anthropocene era began with a search for models in the field of social psychology that mimic Graves's double-helix conception. Finding a macro-scale model in culture that is part of the current academic mainstream could extend well-needed legitimacy to Graves's work. One of the most prominent conceptions I found is the dual inheritance theory. It was mostly developed in that yeasty decade, the 1970s. Rooted in biocultural anthropology, the theory is the most-used example of how genes and culture continually interact in a feedback loop and of how genetically evolved psychological adaptations for acquiring ideas, beliefs, values, practices, and mental models can lead to cultural changes that can then influence genetic selection, and vice versa.[4] In a way, the theory confirmed the role that memes play in the evolutionary process that is foundational to the Spiral-Dynamics synthesis of ᵛMEMEs. It also confirmed many of the mechanical and dynamic underpinning of the Gravesian model. But, like other models, it remained largely limited to the dual interaction between human-built environments representing culture and the phycological adaptations reflected in *human intelligence.*

What I eventually realized is that I was searching for models that explain far greater complexity but was doing so from within a dominant social-sciences narrative that limited the search process to the scope and methods of the *First sapiens.* Fields that study human pursuits, such as biocultural anthropology, are interdisciplinary in nature, but they are not approached in the context of naturally occurring, complex adaptive systems that are full of synergistic syntheses and thrive on the living process and the chaos, creativity, and complexity inherent in it. I needed to move beyond humancentric models in search of ones that recognize the full range of *natural intelligence,* the evolutionary intelligence that has shaped life for billions of years. The frameworks I needed had to serve two purposes: the preservation of the coevolutionary nature of emergence depicted in Graves's iteration and its validation as a model that can be used to define our Anthropogenic stages of development.

Graves, Darwin, and the Superorganism

In order to justify the continued use of the Gravesian model beyond the dual-inheritance theory in a post-Holocene era, I searched for patterns in nature and in the physical sciences that might mimic the evolutionary process in Graves' model and so justify nesting it in *natural intelligence.* The next area I explored at a deeper level was the work of evolutionary biologist Bruce Lipton. In his groundbreaking book *The Biology of Belief,* Lipton puts forth the idea that Darwinian evolutionary theory and its emphasis on the survival of the fittest is in part responsible for much of today's environmental imbalance.[5] He argues that the Darwinian genetic mechanisms gave scientific legitimacy to the use of power, greed, and violence to advance our civilization. His reasoning against the legitimacy of this Darwinian view is based on the most recent discoveries in the field of epigenetics and from the Human Genome Project; they have to do with cooperation as the primary impulse that guides the evolutionary process. Through decades of research in epigenetics, Lipton built the hypothesis that the cell *membrane,* not its *nucleus,* is responsible for the information processing that controls the cell's fate; he further hypothesized that molecular switches built into the membrane translate environmental information into cell behavior and that, together, they represent the basic building blocks of consciousness.[6] Lipton was able to create a modern scientific basis for the theory of conscious evolution first put forth in 1809 by John Baptiste de Lamarck (1744–1829). At the heart of Lamarck's theory are two forces: the first is an alchemical, complexifying force that drives organisms up a ladder of complexity, and the second is an environmental force that adapts them to local environments through the use and disuse of characteristics, differentiating them from other organisms.[7]

This two-factor aspect of Lamarck's model, when viewed from a fractal perspective, shares the same *general thema* with the underpinning of the Gravesian model. The complexifying force that drives an organism up the ladder can be compared to the neuropsychology—the *complex adaptive intelligence*—that complexifies as an individual, a group, or a culture move up to higher stages of development. Similarly, the local environment can be compared to the *existential-problems/life-conditions* half of the model responsible for triggering the neuropsychology of a higher order that is present but until that point had remained in a dormant state.

I also found Lipton's observation about the cell membrane to be in harmony with the Gravesian model. While the debate about whether the nucleus or the membrane of the cell is its brain, I propose that, based on Graves's earlier conception, the two are inseparable in that they come together to form one strand in Graves's double-helix model. If the cell membrane is responsible for processing information from the environment, then its equivalent in the Gravesian model is the mind, or the psychology leg in his earlier bio-psycho-social, three-legged conception, with the nucleus representing the brain or the biological leg. The two came together to represent the neuropsychological strand of the double helix more commonly referred to as *complex adaptive intelligence.*

Lipton models the membrane-evolution concept using fractals to offer insights into the origins of consciousness and the role cooperation plays within and among species. He proclaims that what is common to all biological evolutionary processes is a repetitive pattern with two phases:

> Phase one starts with the origin of a new organism and proceeds to create the most conscious version of that organism. This phase ends when physical limitations prevent further enhancement of the organism's nervous system. Phase two advances evolution by increasing consciousness through the assembly of individual organisms into cooperative, information-sharing communities. This phase ends when the most conscious communal organization transforms into a new organism. The presence of a new organism initiates the repeat of phase one this time expressing a higher level of evolution.[8]

Lipton's two phases defining the biological evolutionary process are similar to how the Gravesian evolutionary process works in that it also alternates between individualistic and communal psychosocial systems.

Just as in nature, once the individualistic system has exhausted the neuropsychology proprietary to its specific stage of development and can no longer serve the evolutionary process, it switches back to a communal form of existence but at a higher level of consciousness that transcends and includes previous stages. The life cycle of an organism could be compared to the life cycle of a development stage or any of its ideological fractals. What is important to know is when a system, whether individualistic or communal, has reached the equivalence of Lipton's physical limitations. Those limitations in the Gravesian model occur when the life cycle reaches its nexus point. If the system is in an open state, the transition to a higher, opposite, more complex phase happens naturally, and the psychosocial evolutionary process continues. If it is in a closed or arrested state, the system moves into its *decline* and *entropy* phases. This is a societal phenomenon that defies the natural evolutionary process in biological systems; a person cannot stop the cells in her body from multiplying, nor can she stop a seed from germinating.

When formulating the superorganism model, Lipton believes that the process will represent a monumental shift in human consciousness. The current state of membrane awareness, which he compares to the modern mind, has reached its membrane limits, and the next stage of evolution is the assembly of the *human mind* into a larger assembly, the much higher, communal evolutionary stage that serves *all of humanity*. Just as in Graves's shift into *Second-sapiens* consciousness, Lipton acknowledges that the shift to becoming the superorganism called *humanity* will be no ordinary movement up the evolutionary ladder but rather a form of metamorphosis similar to that of the butterfly:

> In the body of the growing caterpillar, the economy is booming and the cellular community is actively employed. This organism's voracious appetite leads to it devouring the leaves of the plant on which it's living. Caterpillar growth slows and eventually comes to an end as available resources are consumed. Cells are out of work, and the highly structured community begins to fall apart. Specialized cells within the ensuing chaos provide organizing information and direction to create a different, more sustainable future. Metamorphosis is complete when the unsustainable caterpillar civilization transforms into the ecologically sensitive butterfly civilization.[9]

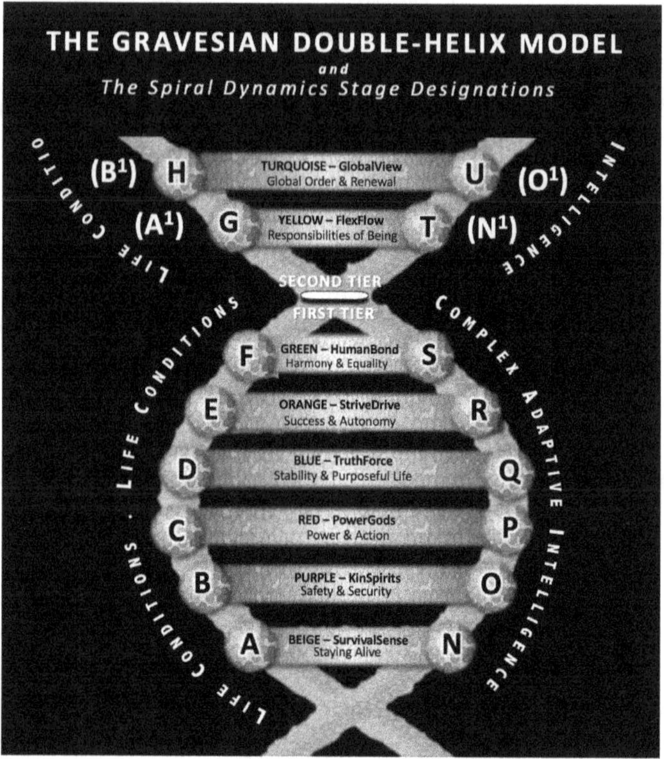

Figure 6.1. The Gravesian Double-Helix Model with the Spiral-Dynamic Stage Designations. Adapted from the work of Graves, Beck, and the MEMEnomics Group and used by permission from the MEMEnomics Group.

The voracious appetite of the caterpillar can be easily compared to the *sapiens 1.5* stage, that of *Homo Colossus* who devours Earth's resources indiscriminately. The consumption of resources and the fall of the structured community is represented in the *Great Obsolescence* that comes after the *Great Acceleration,* leading to the place of metamorphosis, the *darkness-before-the-dawn* stage in the Gravesian model. Also, Lipton's reference to the specialized cells within the ensuing chaos can correspond to the *sapiens 2.1* brain syndicate that will be tasked with transforming humanity into an ecologically aligned civilization.

The Search for Mother Nature's Double Helix

My search for models that can justify the Gravesian model in the Anthropocene epoch didn't stop with Lipton's epigenetic reinterpretation of the theory of conscious evolution. Viewing life and its interactions with its environment and the consumption of its resources, organic and inorganic, had to play some role in determining which species thrive, mutate, survive, or become extinct and how the diminishment of these finite resources affect the evolutionary process itself. I wanted to test that intuition by searching for an all-encompassing model that could represent the leading edge of post-Holocene, *Second-sapiens* consciousness.

My search led me to the book *The Gaia Hypothesis* and the work of its authors, James Lovelock, a chemist by training, and Lynn Margulis, a microbiologist. The word *Gaia,* from Greek mythology, signifies the personification of the Earth. According to the myth, Gaia is the ancestral mother of all life: land, sky, and sea. Lovelock, through his studies of astrophysics, knew that heat from the sun has increased by 25 percent since life on Earth began and that, in spite of that increase, Earth's surface temperature has remained constant, enabling life for four billion years. He proposed the question: What if the Earth were able to regulate its temperature, its atmosphere, its oceans' salinity, and other planetary conditions just as a living organism would? The answer was the Gaia Hypothesis, which advanced the idea that living organisms interact with their inorganic surroundings on Earth in a coevolutionary, synergistic, and self-regulating process that helps perpetuate the conditions for life on the planet.[10] Gaia can be understood as a superorganism made of organisms, just as multicellular life can be understood as a superorganism on a smaller scale. Through their research, Lovelock and Margulis demonstrated that, lacking a conscious command-and-control system, Gaia uses feedback loops to track and adjust key environmental parameters in a process they called "Gaia intelligence." Their all-encompassing, ambitious proposition brought together the biosphere, the atmosphere, the hydrosphere, and the pedosphere, each with its tightly coupled strands of organic and inorganic matter coevolving through feedback loops as one system called *Gaia.*

> *Gaia is a tough bitch—a system that has worked for over three billion years without people. This planet's surface and its atmosphere and environment will continue to evolve long after people and prejudice are gone.*
>
> —Lynn Margulis[11]

While it is not easy to nest stage-development models into this hypothesis, parallels can be drawn regarding the dual interactions between the environment and the organism. The coupling of organic with inorganic matter in Earth's systems could be compared to Graves's coupling of neuropsychology with the environment and viewed as a fractal representation of different double helices that represent the evolutionary nature of all life. The hypothesis is perhaps the most elegant expression of a living, self-organizing system that meets all three of Fritjof Capra's conditions for it to be called a complex living system: self-organization that follows Mother Nature's inner rules; the presence of autopoiesis; and the presence of the feedback loops, the point at which autopoiesis becomes associated with cognition. This is a leap into the science that defines the totality of a post-Holocene interpretation of the Gravesian model, especially the second tier. It takes the organism that contains the *complex adaptive intelligence* from its Holocene environment defined by *human intelligence* and nests it in the *natural intelligence* defined by the dynamic and chaotic feedback loops of the Anthropocene. This simple coupling process, although planetary in scale, shares much of its underpinnings with the Gravesian model. It recognizes that Earth's systems are open systems that are far from equilibrium, an essential property if post-Holocene, *Second-sapiens* intelligence is to be tasked with saving the planet. The similarities in how Earth systems maintain stability is the larger fractal of how individuals and cultures adjust and perpetuate their presence at certain stages of development. The feedback loops presented in the hypothesis, whether negative or positive, correspond to how individuals and cultures in Graves's model adjust to upshifts or downshifts in stage development depending on whether the system is in an open, an arrested, or a closed state and whether the environment in which it is nested is threatened.

These examples illustrate just a few of the similarities that underpin both theories and provide a roadmap to reinterpret Graves's double-helix conception for the Anthropocene epoch (see fig. 6.1). The coupling among all life on the planet and all the inorganic matter within it becomes the exponential expansion of the earlier, second-tier coupling between the *complex adaptive intelligence* and *life conditions*. In order to address Graves's survival of all planetary life in the Anthropocene, the strand in the double helix that represents *human intelligence* must be transcended and included in Mother Nature's *natural intelligence* that has taken billions of years to develop. Similarly, the strand that represents our *life conditions* must transcend manmade constructs and environments that ignore our finite resources and reframe them in terms of the much larger Earth systems, full of inorganic matter from which bacteria emerged as the earliest forms of life.

Lovelock's and Margulis's work, like that of Donella Meadows in the *Limits to Growth* and most systems thinkers who first appeared in the 1970s, represents the *inquiry-and-identification* phase of a far more complex system: the planetary system and its own unique life cycle. It is no surprise that their framework has been heavily criticized by the antibodies of the existing system—the mainstream media and the scientific community that operate in silos. Similar to *Limits to Growth,* the book *The Gaia Hypothesis* was targeted for violating the existing Newtonian scientific paradigm. Stephen Jay Gould, a prominent evolutionary biologist and Harvard professor, dismissed its premise due to the absence of actual mechanisms by which self-regulating homeostasis is achieved.[12] The thought that the "mechanisms" for Gaia to achieve self-regulation have to be an extension of prevailing scientific understanding precludes the possibility that a higher form of science might exist. Similarly, Richard Dawkins, the evolutionary biologist who coined the term *meme*, stated that for organisms to act in concert would require foresight and planning, which is contrary to the current scientific understanding of evolution.[13]

The mechanical metaphor presented in these views is in complete contrast with the organic metaphor informing Gaia. *Gaia* does not refer to a machine built and manipulated by human intelligence. To think of it in such terms leaves out the active qualities of living entities and the natural agency present in life from single-celled organisms all the way to the biosphere. Rather, *Gaia* refers the intelligence of which Lipton, Bloom, and Sahtouris speak when describing the global brain and the superorganism that has evolved over eons. Lovelock has attributed the views of his critics to their lack of understanding of nonlinear dynamics and often used the term *greedy reductionism* to describe their worldview. It is this worldview of Newtonian science steeped in the values of *sapiens 1.5* that must be transcended. In defending the coevolutionary, homeostatic, geophysical underpinnings of the Gaia hypothesis, ecologist and philosopher David Abram compared it to Maturana and Valera's autopoiesis, the theory that pries science out of its Newtonian silos and nests it in the study of complex systems of life.

> *There is a strong current in contemporary culture advocating "holistic" views as some sort of cure-all. Reductionism implies attention to a lower level while holistic implies attention to higher level. These are intertwined in any satisfactory description, and each entails some loss relative to our cognitive preferences as well as some gain. There is no whole system without an interconnection of its parts, and there is no whole system without an environment.*
>
> —Francisco Valera[14]

Since the Gaia hypothesis was introduced, it has gradually become part of mainstream science. It is now known to most proponents of Lovelock's work as the *Gaia theory*; but, due to the early criticism it received from the academic community—especially the biologists—it is now known as the study of Earth-systems science. Much of Lovelock's predictions made over the last four decades have come to pass. In his 2006 book, *The Revenge of Gaia*, he predicted that by 2020 extreme weather would be the norm. He has dismissed the carbon-offset scheme as a joke and a scam and said that renewable energy sources would not be enough to sustain the world's energy needs. All in all, as many as twelve of the major conditions he predicted have occurred, but the scientific community still refuses to acknowledge that his hypothesis can quell all the scientific skepticism that dominates the institutions of the *First sapiens.* When asked about the reasons for our failure to heed his warnings, Lovelock bluntly responded that human beings are too stupid to prevent climate change: "I don't think we're yet evolved to the point where we're clever enough to handle as complex a situation as climate change."[15] Lovelock's observation speaks volumes to the predicament in which those who possess *Second-sapiens* intelligence find themselves when their thinking is dissolved into simpler, less conscious ecosystems and institutions built by the *First sapiens.*

In his 2013 book, *On Gaia: A Critical Investigation of the Relationship between Life and Earth,* Toby Tyrrell, a professor of Earth-system science, gives us a glimpse of what the battle between the sciences of *sapiens 1.5* and *sapiens 2.2* looks like:

> I believe Gaia is a dead end. Its study has, however, generated many new and thought-provoking questions. While rejecting Gaia, we can at the same time appreciate Lovelock's originality and breadth

> of vision, and recognize that his audacious concept has helped to stimulate many new ideas about the Earth and to champion a holistic approach to studying it.[16]

A holistic approach to studying Earth systems and the affect human activity is having on them is precisely the definition of the higher-order science of a post-Holocene reality. It does not reject Newtonian science; it transcends and includes it as a fractal within the *sapiens 2.1* brain syndicate that is informed by the urgency of ecological collapse. Its wider, cross-discipline approach nests lower-complexity models and their principles—regardless of their particular kind, nature, or component elements—into the larger holon of *natural intelligence.* This is general-systems thinking that uses universal principles and intuitively understands that a complex system of this magnitude is far more than the sum of its parts due to its emergent behavior and its synergistic properties. In order for science to become the science of the Anthropocene epoch, humanity has to view Gaia as the largest living organism that is at once a holonic representation of its smallest one, adhering to the *fixed rule*—or the *general thema*—of autopoiesis, the self-regulating chemistry of living cells that defines cognition and autonomy in all living systems.

Subordinating Human Intelligence

If the Gravesian model is to remain relevant, its original conception has to expand far beyond the limits of understanding adult human behavior. In other words, the environment in which the whole brain becomes nested in the second tier can no longer be the one of Holocene bliss and safety. That paradise had been lost. In the words of Lovelock, "Mother Nature is beginning to evict our species from her home due to our schizoid tendencies and destructive teenage behavior, and we seem to be righteously ignorant of her reasons."[17] This eviction process has already begun, and the only way for our species to stay at home is to understand Mother Nature's motivation and to stay in her good graces. This reprieve will require the transcendence of *human intelligence* and its subordination into *natural intelligence.* As we consider the severity of our new problems and move up the life cycle of this epochal-scale fractal, we might discover that the destructive teenage behavior of our species might have forced some of Earth's systems past their nexus points; they might now be entering the "second half of the chessboard" where change occurs at an exponential rate and the possible outcomes become exponentially more difficult to predict. This is in reference to Prigogine's model on dissipative structures being used to understand Earth systems reaching their bifurcation points, wherein the biosphere and the atmosphere can no longer dissipate entropy to the environment. The energy input into the system—that is, our insatiable drive to use up natural resources in the last century—has become considerably higher than Mother Nature's ability to do that work of dissipating energy. It is what the IPCC scientists referred to as our species living beyond the carrying capacity of Earth's systems. The net waste, this living beyond Earth's capacities, is the essence of what will inform *life conditions* in the post-Holocene, Gravesian model. It is giving birth to a new, higher-order system that must address the long-forgotten balance between input and output, production and production capacity, that adheres to the principles of autopoiesis that keep all life in a constant state of flow.

Today, these new realities seem to be missing from the consciousness of most practitioners of the Gravesian model. Until recently, the followers of both Beck and Wilber, including me, were defining second-tier intelligence from the comfort of our humancentric, air-conditioned, flood-and-fire-resistant, bygone years of the Holocene era, ignoring any and all sense of urgency arising from the newly emerging, *life-conditions* half of the model. In other words, since Beck, Cowan, and Wilber first defined the content of second-tier intelligence, the *existential-problems* half of the model—the sun gear (see fig. 1.2) to which our *human intelligence* must adapt—has completely changed as more research points to the epochal shift from the bliss of the Holocene era to the planetary existential threats of the Anthropocene. This shift is what is demanding that the *human intelligence* of the Holocene give way to the *natural intelligence* of the Anthropocene. It essentially constitutes the appearance of the original form of the A^1 half of the model, the *existential problems* of the A^1–N^1 coupling of the seventh stage that Graves identified over five decades ago. The very nature of what the entire second tier has to deal with shifts as our new reality shows no possibility of returning to pre-Anthropogenic *life conditions.*

The more we realize there will be no return to the Holocene era, the more the content of our second-tier reality changes. We have more data from the environment indicating that our new problems need a different form of intelligence in order to be solved. The very nature of this data is unlike any other that has influenced our stage development in the past. The

B^1 half of the B^1– O^1 coupling is no longer undifferentiated or speculative. It is giving content and context to the eighth stage of development faster than our current, pre-Anthropogenic intelligence can process. Unlike Beck's and Wilber's earlier speculations about the nature and urgency of this stage, the newly emerging data is clear: our planet's systems are in distress, and the data we are receiving indicates a higher-order fractal system in collapse. To remain true to the model, the appropriate form of intelligence that must be triggered to solve such problems must expand beyond our humancentric reality. While this notion might be difficult to grasp, just think of the time when *Homo sapiens* declared himself/herself to be God in charge of his/her own destiny in the context of the reductive values of the *sapiens 1.5* stage of development. The needed intelligence today sees all *sapiens 1.5*'s accomplishments from Jupiter and can easily differentiate between their brilliance and their blind spots. The *natural intelligence* of the post-Holocene *Second sapiens* places that brilliance in a far larger mosaic that completes the picture of life in the Anthropocene epoch.

To use the metaphor of the dams-and-locks model of development (fig. 2.3), our early entry into this new geologic epoch represents the early warning signs that are appearing with higher and more intense frequency in the spillways of the largest dam nature has ever built. To fix them requires an entirely different approach, a collaborative intelligence that reintegrates all phenomena ignored by the reductive *sapiens 1.5* intelligence that built the most sophisticated man-made dams. Even Beck's example of the Dutch model—the most complex one with its integrated network of dams, dikes, floodgates, and pumps representing the multifaceted nature of stage development—must all be nested in Mother Nature's dam, meaning the Earth's inherent *natural intelligence* that must now inform the *general thema* of *sapiens 2.1* and *2.2*.

The post-Holocene era also necessitates reexamining the meaning of *existential problems*. Beck and Cowan first articulated them as the mathematical equations varying with different levels of complexity that are needed to solve the equation of living. In this new era, mathematical complexity must give way to the complexity of systems thinking, a highly collaborative process steeped in *natural intelligence* wherein evolution happens *unconsciously*—in a Gaia-like, autopoietic way that defies the current scientific understanding of psychosocial evolution and is utterly indifferent morally to the intelligence of a single species: *us*. This reality needs to become part of both the Spiral-Dynamics and the Integral-Theory models as they inform existential solutions to shape our future. What is required is a new state of awareness that our species can become extinct as Mother Nature adapts to a far greater system in collapse and as an automatic, unconscious, autopoietic way for her to reach balance.

This new reality also changes the very nature of the chasm that must be crossed and what *transcendence* and *inclusion* mean. We are no longer driven by the different expressions of the ego of the *First sapiens,* nor will our transcendence through meditation and the processing of our individual shadow fully address our *existential problems.* The new reality takes the death of the ego out of its psychological, spiritual, and mythological realms and reestablishes it in terms of understanding the massive die-off in our own species and in the millions of other species that will alter all life on Earth as we know it. The only way for us to bridge that chasm and get to the other side of the new, Anthropocene-aware *Second sapiens* is by first passing through the *darkness-before-the new-dawn* phase of the *First sapiens.* Without doing that, our solutions will be greatly influenced by our *First-sapiens* models and may not fully embrace the higher fractal in which *human intelligence* is nested.

The changing nature of our *existential problems,* our post-Holocene reality, dictates changes to how all stages in the model work. The first change might occur in how second-tier thinkers might fashion the acceptance of our new reality in language and action appropriate for each level of development in the first tier. For example, *sapiens 1.2* tribal formations all over the world should be discouraged from pursuing the lifestyle of *sapiens 1.5* and become reempowered by the wisdom of their elders who advocate for a simple, ecologically sustainable lifestyle while also for having access to scientific and technological discoveries that enable them to adapt to Earth's changes. This could entail the planting of drought-resistant crops and the adoption of permaculture, a decentralized approach to land management and design using a whole-system approach to reintroduce natural ecosystems that make the environment capable of regeneration.

Similarly, a religious *sapiens 1.4* community could be empowered by ideas quoted from their own holy scriptures that speak of how we as a species are commanded by a higher authority not to pollute and not to cause other species and the Earth any harm. Or, the genius of *sapiens 1.5* could be put into the right type of scientific research to verify the science of higher complexity, as was the case with Gaya Herrington, the sustainability expert at the global consultancy KPMG who translated *sapiens 2.2* science into language that her corporate clients could understand. Second-tier thinkers could also use the global financial infrastructure put in place by *sapiens 1.5* to bring broader awareness to the limits to growth and offer alternative forms of investment informed by the new Anthropogenic reality. This initiative has already been seen in the monumental shift that BlackRock, Inc., has recently undertaken under the leadership of its cofounder Larry Fink. The firm is the world's largest asset manager, with eight trillion dollars in assets under management. In 2020, Fink announced that environmental sustainability will be at the core of his firm's investment decisions as climate change becomes the driving force affecting all aspects of our global economy.[18]

All these adaptive changes along the contours of the entire first tier point to a new, superordinate narrative informed by the appearance of the *existential problems* of both *sapiens 2.1* and *sapiens 2.2*; but the narrative must be translated carefully into each stage's own unique way of understanding the problem so that its constituents won't be overwhelmed by the complexity of it. A post-Holocene economy must acknowledge that the Earth's carrying capacities and its finite resources have reached a tipping point and that degrowth is the only way forward. The pursuit of environmental sustainability purely as an investment vehicle that keeps the old global financial infrastructure intact is an incremental solution, an extension of *sapiens 1.5* virtues that do not promote degrowth but instead have a new veneer of green-sounding doublespeak. Without collective, global leadership informed by Anthropogenic awareness, there is no guarantee that such ad hoc, uncoordinated efforts will stabilize the planet's systems if those systems' life cycles have moved beyond their nexus points and if—because the understanding of such phenomena is nested in higher-order science—we are simply unaware of it.

Beyond Macro Systems

The shift to a post-Holocene iteration also necessitates revisiting the application of the model to the different-sized holonic structures that can be affected by it. Before Anthropogenic awareness was introduced to the model, the largest fractal in it was its application to human-built macro systems. This characterizes the work that Beck and the global constellation of leaders at the Centers for Human Emergence attempted to do in various regions of the world. It also characterizes the work of Sean

Esbjorn-Hargens, who expanded his work with Integral Theory to create the Wisdom Economy based on his ten-capitals model.[19] Similarly, it has defined the work of Daniel Schmachtenberger and his associates at the Consilience Project, who attempt to address the existential threats facing humanity, and my own work on evolutionary economic systems. Without full Anthropogenic awareness, this collective work has represented the leading edge of human emergence. At the heart of it has remained the idea that *human intelligence* still has the time it needs to borrow selectively from *natural intelligence* to design adaptive and mitigative measures that can save humanity.

Our new Anthropogenic reality takes all these forms of intelligence on the leading edge of human emergence a step further and nests them in the higher fractal of Earth's different systems. It charges all our actions with urgency so that we become fully aware that something bigger than addressing economic and geopolitical macro systems deserves our full attention. We must now focus on the planetary boundaries that make up our biosphere, atmosphere, hydrosphere, and pedosphere—all the spheres that allow for all the smaller formations to exist on Earth. They are what now replace the content of

POST-HOLOCENE ITERATION
CONCENTRIC/HOLONIC NATURE OF DEVELOPMENTAL CHANGE

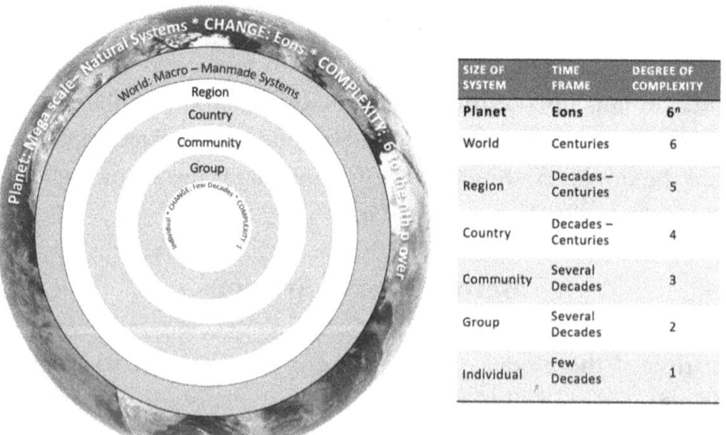

SIZE OF SYSTEM	TIME FRAME	DEGREE OF COMPLEXITY
Planet	**Eons**	6^n
World	Centuries	6
Region	Decades – Centuries	5
Country	Decades – Centuries	4
Community	Several Decades	3
Group	Several Decades	2
Individual	Few Decades	1

Figure 6.2. Post-Holocene Iteration: Concentric/Holonic Nature of Developmental Change. Adapted from the work of Clare W. Graves, Don E. Beck, and the MEMEnomics Group, LLC; https://www.memenomic.com. Used by permission from the MEMEnomics Group.

the second-tier stages in our new Anthropogenic reality as the largest fractal. I call them *mega systems*. The term is derived purely from the common metric-system prefixes that show the exponential increase in size and complexity of natural systems when we move beyond the bounds of the Holocene era. In figure 6.2 below, it signifies the difference between what is labeled as the sixth degree of complexity that addresses issues with human-built macro systems in the world and the exponentially higher degree of six to the power *n* that is intended to address the mega issues of our planetary systems. How effectively we deal with the Anthropocene and how we determine the lowest number the exponent *n* represents is a direct function of how quickly *natural intelligence* becomes the leading edge of the evolutionary process that informs our solutions.

A Post-Holocene, Three-Legged Model

A post-Holocene reinterpretation makes it necessary to revisit the original conception of the Gravesian model, the content of which Graves himself said will change as our existential reality changes. This is the essence of what keeps his work current and on the cutting edge for those who understand its dynamic underpinnings. In Graves's own words, the model asks the simple question: "What is adult psychological development all about and what does research show it to be?"[20] Today's research in a post-Holocene reality points to planetary collapse and our inability fully to understand it, which moves the needle considerably in how we determine psychological development. The initial conception of the model was defined by three main aspects summarized in most of Graves's work as the *neurobio-psycho-social* conception of adult human behavior. It is a three-legged stool that describes how and when different worldviews emerge and how they form themselves naturally into hierarchical levels of complexity.

This concept has remained part of the Spiral-Dynamics iteration throughout the years, the three legs of the stool having been referred to as follows:

- The first leg represents the neurobiological equipment with which each individual is uniquely endowed. It is what Graves described as the lottery of the brain that is the determining factor in psychological growth. He compared it to the electrical wiring in a home.

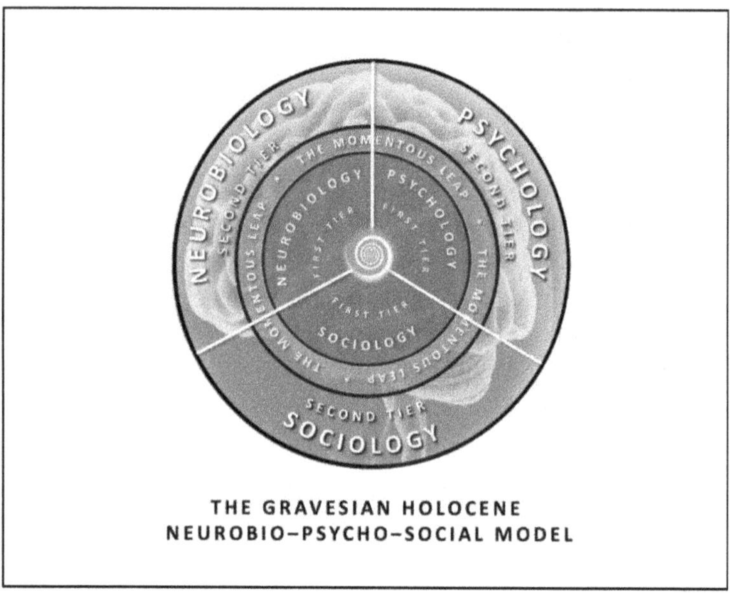

Figure 6.3. The Gravesian Holocene Neurobio–Psycho–Social Model. Adapted from the work of Clare W. Graves and the MEMEnomics Group and used here by permission.

It could also be compared to an operating system or the firmware of a personal computer.

- The second leg of the model represents the psychological part of the brain that remains in latent form. It could be thought of as the light switch in a new room that turns on the appropriate level of psychological development capable of solving higher-order problems. It could also be compared to the computer software that activates certain programs, enabling us to write various scenarios and critical analysis and to apply different mathematical combinatorials addressing our external *life conditions* so that we are able to attain higher levels of psychosocial health.
- The third leg of the model—that of sociology—represents the challenges coming to us from the societal field that trigger the recalibration of our abilities in order to solve our problems of existence. It is the call for us turn on the lights that haven't been turned on before in that new room. In the computer example, it could be represented by our need to access certain new programs enabling us to address *life conditions* coming to us in the form of

external demands such as work projects or school assignments that are more complex than usual.

Figure 6.3 above represents how the neurobio-psycho-social model was brought to the world through Spiral Dynamics and its worldwide constellation of practitioners. Graves and Beck often considered neurology and biology as a single leg. Wilber's iteration divided the sociology leg into two legs—one for the smaller social formations such as institutions and organizations and the other for society at large—for a total of four legs altogether. These four legs in Wilber's model came to be known as the four quadrants. The more accurate representation of the Gravesian model in the Anthropocene epoch is yet another iteration that transforms the original three-legged model and nests it in ecology, an essential requisite for the model's survival beyond the Holocene. That new Anthropogenic interpretation yields a new neuro-bio-psycho-socio-ecological model.

With the existential threats of the Anthropocene era, the social-factors leg of the model that triggers the appropriate brain capacities for psychological health is pointing to an epochal shift away from the bliss

Figure 6.4. The Gravesian Model: Post-Holocene Iteration. Adapted from the work of Graves, Beck, and the MEMEnomics Group and used by permission from the MEMEnomics Group.

and rapture of the Holocene. In this new iteration of *Second-sapiens* intelligence, the very nature of the three-legged model changes in order to reflect the monumental shift in focus that must be addressed. The modifications needed to accommodate this new iteration are depicted in the diagram below as follows:

- **Graves's *momentous leap* is replaced by the *darkness-before-the new-dawn* phase**, as represented in the graph by the second circle labeled, "The Collective Shadow of Humanity." This is a necessary sequential stage that has to process the collective trauma of the *First sapiens* before the *Second sapiens* can be endowed with the exponential level of psychological freedom that enables him or her to address post-Holocene *life conditions*. The *momentous leap* becomes the byproduct of *First-sapiens* processing that can no longer remain in the collective unconscious. The *darkness-before-the new-dawn* phase is the focus of an upcoming chapter.
- **The leg of psychology becomes that of ecopsychology**. This is an area of human pursuit that brings *human intelligence* back into the fold of *natural intelligence*. It is what Freud called the recognition of the interconnection between the internal world of the mind and the external world of the environment, the former being a shrunken residue of the latter.[21] It is also what Graves termed as *existential psychology*, which is part of the *general thema* of the *sapiens 2.1* stage that must develop capacities to ensure the survival of what remains of life on the planet in all its forms. The field of ecopsychology will be discussed in further detail in an upcoming chapter as well.
- **The neurobiological leg becomes that of the neurosphere and the biosphere**, in that the Post-Holocene model differentiates between neurology and biology. Both these spheres have been discussed in earlier chapters. The neurosphere in this developmental model is not the one that exists in the arrays of stem-cell experiments that mainstream science has conducted in petri dishes. Rather, in the Gravesian model, the neurosphere is embodied in Lipton's and Sahtouris's superorganism as a representation of both brain neurology and membrane awareness that have defined the evolutionary process throughout time. That intelligence is poised to become the neurosphere when it moves from the organism called *human* to the superorganism called *humanity*. The neurosphere is

also present in Bloom's global brain. It is the evolutionary process itself that calls on us to acknowledge that we are the neurons in the nervous system of the planet's interspecies mind that has been eons in the making.

- The biosphere and the neurosphere become one in Capra's definition of the complex system of life (i.e., the *neurobiosphere*) and in Maturana's and Valera's autopoiesis. Self-creation in biological systems that define the self-maintaining chemistry of living cells as well as cognition and autonomy in all living systems is the very definition of a neurobiosphere that defines *natural intelligence.* Lovelock's and Margulis's work with Gaia theory brought autopoiesis into the heart of the Earth-systems sciences that must now define the *Second-sapiens* intelligence that will be tasked to save the planet.
- **The sociology/social leg becomes that of ecosociology**. It transcends all man-made social conceptions and built environments and nests them in natural environments. It expands on a concept that was formulated in the 1970s by sociologists Riley Dunlap and William R. Catton Jr. They created a new theoretical outlook in the field of sociology called the new ecological paradigm (NEP), which gave birth to the idea that human exceptionalism has failed to create linkages between ecosystems and social systems.[22] NEP will also be the subject of a detailed discussion in an upcoming chapter.

> *As numerous and as technologically advanced as mankind on the average had already become after four centuries of exuberance, we had besieged ourselves. Each of us was now doing damage, just by living, to the life-support systems of our finite planet.*
>
> —William R. Catton Jr.[23]

The Anthropocene Epoch and Its Fractal Attractors

Similarly, a post-Holocene iteration of the model necessitates revisiting Beck's and Cowan's conception of the stage-attractor principle. This is the self-replicating, self-organizing force that makes up the content-specific geometric fractals forming the magnetic field that determines the totality of the stage's expression. The Anthropogenic shift that utilizes the exponential expansion of psychological freedom on after the new dawn affects the model just as it did in Graves's original neurobio-psycho-social model; it nests it in *natural intelligence.* This creates a highly interdependent, unifying model that transforms the content-specific nature of the stage-attractor fractals into a highly collaborative, interdisciplinary, interconnected magnetic field that determines the synergistic totality of its virtues. Its organizing structure takes the *general thema* of *sapiens 2.1* concerned with ecological and existential issues out of the hands of humancentric systems and imbeds it in planetary systems. Once the *First sapiens* is aligned with these new virtues, *sapiens 2.1* yields to *sapiens 2.2,* who is charged with the long-term stabilization of life in the Anthropocene age. In addition to the psychology fractal becoming ecopsychology, neurobiology becoming the neurosphere and the biosphere—what Capra termed as the neurobiosphere—and sociology becoming ecosociology, all the remaining fractals become nested in a single planetary ecosystem that defines the challenges of the Anthropocene. As depicted in the graphic below (fig. 6.5), the cell-like diagram represents the stage and its attractor fractals dissolving into the *natural intelligence* of Earth. The result is a new unifying model that

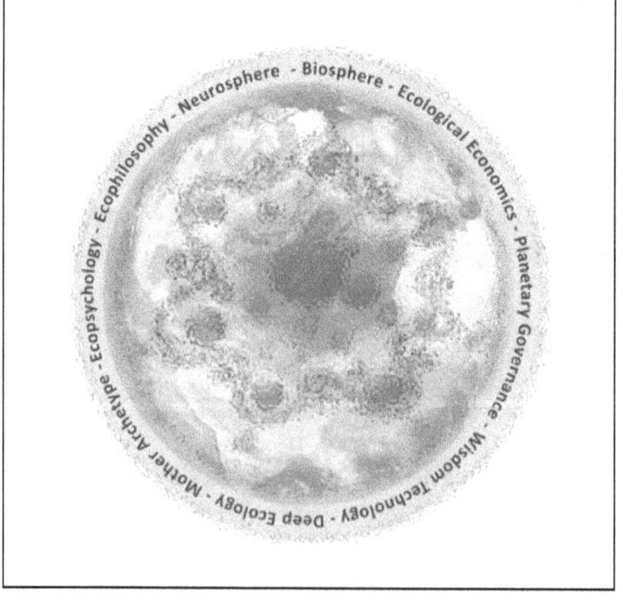

Figure 6.5. The Stage-Attractor Model Nested in Natural Intelligence. Said E. Dawlabani.

has the superordinate goal of ensuring the stabilization of life in all its forms within our ominous, post-Holocene realities.

This is how the post-Holocene, stage-attractor fractals transform on the other side of the *darkness-before-the new-dawn* phase and become part of the *momentous leap* into *natural intelligence*. Collectively, they represent the mega-scale, whole-systems approach that this book attempts to address and that upcoming chapters will discuss further. It comprises the platform for a post-Holocene Gravesian model that I call *Gaiametry*. Its *general thema* is the empowerment of what matters in the era of the Anthropocene. Below are brief descriptions of each fractal's peripheral expressions that form the totality of the Gaiametry framework, the largest fractal formation that *Homo sapiens* will ever be tasked with overseeing:

- **Economics becomes nested in ecology and anthropology.** This is the largest and most important area of focus for the Anthropocene era, the driving force that will determine whether ours and millions of other species survive. Due to its reductive nature, the *sapiens 1.5* stage that gave us modern economics and the ontology of *peace through commerce* must be reversed and returned to a non-reductive state that recognizes the totality of life on the planet. Placing modern economics in an ecologic and anthropologic timeframe gives us a clearer picture of how much planetary damage we have done in such a short time and what we must do to mitigate that damage or adapt to it with a fuller state of awareness on a planet in peril. This area of ecological economics is where the *sapiens 2.1* brain syndicate must focus first, as will be the subject of an entire chapter. It constitutes the reversal of economic policies that gave us *Homo colossus* and his/her insatiable appetite for consumption and the lifestyle needed to support it. It is the sea change from the deficient needs of the *First sapiens* that caused many of the Earth's systems to move past the safe boundaries that are now triggering nonlinear and abrupt environmental change on continental and planetary scales. Ecological economics must deal with the damage its younger kin in the first tier has caused. It reverses the ethos of all the lower economic models that had little or no awareness of the planetary limits to growth and nests them in the reality of the Anthropocene. While the field of anthropology focuses on the scientific study of human behavior—its biology, culture, and society going back to the dawn of the sapiens *1.1* stage—modern economics seems to be a dangerous break, a short-lived malfunction, on the long arc of human history. The reductive circular-flow concept created by neoliberal economists that condensed the world's complexity to the consumer and the producer must now be nested in the economy of the Anthropocene era, in which nothing is externalized and the ethos of *degrowth* and *post-growth* replaces the *grow-or-die* ethos of the last century.

- **Politics and geopolitics become issues of planetary governance.** Of all the fractals that define the Anthropocene, this is the one most intertwined with issues of economics. The *sapiens 2.1* brain syndicate must address both the political and the economic fractals simultaneously. The overarching principle in both is the acknowledgment that many of Earth's systems are reaching their nexus points and that a different form of world order that is ecological in nature is needed. Here, the *general thema* of the eighth stage that Beck and Cowan described as an ecologically aligned humanity is injected with our Anthropogenic reality backed by research conducted by political scientists and economists possessing eighth-level intelligence. As an example, the Nobel Prize-winning economist and political scientist Elinor Ostrom embodied those two areas equally. In her 1990 book, *Governing the Commons*, Ostrom used several case studies to demonstrate how cooperative enterprise at the community level results in better management of natural resources called the "commons" and how that leads to institutional change and reform.[24] The opposite, damaging approach to natural resources is expressed by Garrett Hardin in the quotation below.

> *Therein is the tragedy. Each man is locked into a system that compels him to increase his herd without limit—in a world that is limited. Ruin is the destination toward which all men rush, each pursuing his own best interest in a society that believes in the freedom of the commons.*
>
> —Garrett Hardin[25]

- **Philosophy becomes environmental philosophy.** This is a new branch in the field of philosophy that, along with the new ecological paradigm of Riley Dunlap and William R. Catton Jr., was also born in the 1970s chaos crucible and has grown and evolved significantly. It includes areas known as deep ecology and the resacralization of nature and other approaches that examine what needs to be done to restore the degradation modern man has caused our environment.[26] The field concerns itself with how to value nature and develop ways to promote its aesthetic and intrinsic value in order to preserve it for future generations. It is an all-encompassing approach that integrates areas of study from other stage attractors such as those concerned with natural history and natural religion. Among the considered leaders in the field is James Lovelock. Recent additions include ecologist and philosopher David Abram and biologists Humberto Maturana and Francisco Valera.[27]
- **Religion becomes deep ecology.** This monumental shift transcends monotheism and the Abrahamic religions and nests them in Gaia consciousness, the *natural intelligence* that transcends *human intelligence*. Deep ecology is part of the environmental-philosophy movement. Its core principle is the belief that the living environment as a whole should be respected and regarded as having certain basic moral and legal rights to live and flourish, independent of its benefits for human use.[28] Deep ecology provides a good example of how complex adaptive systems in nature recognize the interdependent and highly collaborative parts of an ecosystem that function as a whole.
- **The archetypes become nested in the Mother archetype.** In Jungian psychology, the Mother archetype is associated with qualities such as nurturing, love, compassion, and protection and is often depicted in myths and religious traditions as a symbol of the feminine principle representing the qualities of fertility, creativity, and abundance.[29] In Gaiametry, the Mother archetype is represented by Gaia herself, the universal mother, the ancestral mother of all life. By necessity, it must pry the control of social systems out of the hands of the patriarchy that gave dominance and privilege almost exclusively to men, the same men who created the largest dominator hierarchy in human history that has defined

our journey through the Holocene era. This male dominance began with the dawn of the Abrahamic religions that ended the worship of the goddess archetypes and gave us the patriarchal, monotheistic religions of Judaism, Christianity, and Islam. Even the Enlightenment as seen by the modern humanism movement is considered an era in which women gained nothing, and in some cases their position in society was seriously degraded.[30] But the greatest damage the patriarchy has inflicted has been by the leaders of industry and their cast of cohorts from economists to politicians who represent the ethos of modern society in the last century. They are the men who are responsible for the *Great Obsolescence* that has placed us squarely at the mercy of Mother Nature. It is the empowerment of her virtues that will restore what remains of our ecological and planetary systems to ensure the continuity of all life.

- **Technology becomes nested in human wisdom.** Technology for the Anthropocene era subordinates what the digital age has created to *Second-sapiens* intelligence. It recognizes the genius that created the digital age but pries it out of the hands of *sapiens 1.5* who made it into the most addictive global-business model in human history. Anthropocene technology places this proprietary brilliance at the service of *natural intelligence* and creates a digital neurosphere and biosphere informed by all the stage-attractor fractals of our post-Holocene reality. It synthesizes the evolutionary intelligence in Bloom's global brain, in Lipton's and Sahtouris's superorganism, and in Lovelock's and Margulis's Gaia intelligence and creates new supermodels to help the *sapiens 2.1* brain syndicate formulate decisions on how to save the planet. Its capabilities will be limited to knowing the content of all that is knowable, but the wisdom of when or where to apply that knowledge will be reserved for the *Second sapiens.*

Much of the argument in this reinterpretation of the Spiral-Dynamics, stage-attractor model and this chapter's reformulation of some of Graves's original concepts gives us a unifying, all-encompassing approach that is informed by our post-Holocene reality. The complexity of what we must deal with in the age of planetary collapse cannot be fully quantified through this model, nor does my area of expertise allow me fully to articulate the specifics of each discipline that makes up the totality of the *sapiens 2.1* brain syndicate—the intelligence that will be tasked with getting us to the other side of the great chasm we face. Like those who classified Graves's work under general-systems theory, I consider my work an attempt to extend the evolutionary mechanism that keeps it relevant. In nesting *human intelligence* in *natural intelligence,* an endless number of human pursuits—including those this chapter articulates—would be transformed, but many of them, like Gaia's autopoiesis, will remain unpredictable and unknowable to the human mind that is just beginning to understand how to transcend its Newtonian stage of knowledge. What is knowable is that we need different but highly collaborative ways to begin measuring our new Anthropogenic reality with an intelligence that mimics nature and learns from her feedback loops. The new system will not only embrace the dark side of our binary views of the universe, it will also fully integrate them as an inseparable whole that keeps the world in balance at every holonic formation.

From Pantometry to Gaiametry

When I was searching for a way to express the journey of the *First sapiens* beyond the limitations of the Enlightenment and the virtues that have defined the *sapiens 1.5* stage of development, I ran across the concept of *pantometry.* From Old English, the term was first used to define the steps the scientific mind had taken in the Middle Ages to measure everything that was deemed measurable. Then came the Scientific Revolution that replaced pantometry with the Enlightenment, which not only quantified the quantifiable but also began to quantify certitude, virtue, and grace.[31]

Pantometry saw a resurgence in use after Alfred W. Crosby's 1997 book, *The Measure of Reality: Quantification and Western Society, 1250–1600.* Crosby, a renowned professor of history, acknowledges the epochal shift from the qualitative to the quantitative perception that revolutionized humanity. In his book, he rhetorically asks if our devotion to break down things such as energies, particles, and perceptions into uniform, measurable parts is in itself reductionism.[32] He then proceeds to lay out the case for measuring reality through the lens of the Enlightenment against the backdrop of measurement during the Middle Ages in areas of astronomy, cartography, mathematics, painting, music, commerce, accounting, and military techniques as well as spiritual and historical time.

Crosby, in the Gravesian model, is someone who is fully realized in the values of the *sapiens 1.5* stage of development, and his intelligences from all his other stages are in service to that stage. He is the quintessential representative of human exceptionalism. What Crosby misses is that while it might be true that everything is measurable, what is important to measure changes considerably as we move up the spiral. The progress he traced in Western society from the Middle Ages to the Enlightenment takes on a different form in higher stages of development. The measure of reality becomes more inclusive and less reductive at the humanitarian *sapiens 1.6* stage and exponentially more inclusive at the *sapiens 2.1* and *2.2* stages. Crosby's analysis fails to see the dark side of measurement at the *sapiens 1.5* stage, which itself becomes measurable only after that which has been exhaustively measured and exploited moves past the nexus point of its own life cycle. The activities of the Enlightened mind that gave us modern commerce, technology, accounting, and the military advancements of which he speaks have all used their reductive virtues to externalize that which didn't serve the *sapiens 1.5* stage. It is that very externalization that has grown exponentially in the last century and is at the heart of planetary collapse. Had we remained in the bliss and comfort of the Holocene era, *pantometry* would have remained a viable term regarding measuring all that is measurable through *human intelligence,* including the virtues of the second tier. But our Enlightened minds have caused the collapse of a much higher fractal that is nested in *natural intelligence,* which in turn necessitates nesting pantometry in that higher-order fractal as well if we are to have a chance at saving what remains of life on the planet.

The nature of this transcendence process naturally extends the concept of Gaiametry from the Gravesian model into the Anthropocene epoch. When pantometry becomes nested in Gaiametry, measuring what matters for the human race transforms into empowering what matters for the survival of the planet. Table 6.1 below is a partial representation of what this monumental shift entails.

Graves and the Anthropocene Epoch

While this book attempts to expand the Gravesian model into areas beyond human development, it nonetheless remains true to many aspects of Graves's body of work and to several concepts in the Spiral-Dynamics iteration, not the least of which is the stage-attractor concept and the

THE JOURNEY OF HOMO SAPIENS Nesting Human Exceptionalism in Gaia's Evolutionary Intelligence	
FROM PANTOMETRY	**TO GAIAMETRY**
Psychology	Ecopsychology
Sociology	Ecosociology
Biology	Biosphere
Neurology	Neurosphere
Egocentrism	Ecocentrism
Human intelligence	Natural intelligence
Quantification & externalization	Quantification & integration
Western philosophy	Ecophilosophy
Technological singularity	Planetary conformity
Democracy	Planetary governance
Patriarchal archetypes	Mother archetype
Monotheism	Deep ecology
Economic philosophy of grow or die	Degrowth philosophy of restore & live
Market feasibility	Planetary habitability
Global GDP	Planetary economic protocols
Scarcity in a world of abundance	Regeneration in a world of scarcity

Table 6.1. The Journey of *Homo sapiens*: Nesting Human Exceptionalism in Gaia's Evolutionary Intelligence. Said E. Dawlabani.

evolutionary change it undergoes with each stage recalibration. In his six-upon-six hypothesis, Graves identified the first stage in the second tier as an existential one with a *general thema* that seeks to preserve all planetary life by reversing much of the deficient behavior of the human race's previous six stages of development in the first tier. Regarding what will be reversed, Graves identified as many as ten concepts that fit into table 6.1 above, from the factors that determine the quality of life and work to the deficiencies inherent in democratic rule and the need for unity with nature to replace unity with God.[33]

When I asked why Graves didn't venture deeper into this type of research, Beck gave me two answers. The first was Graves's poor health, and the second spoke to the very nature of the model: the *life-conditions* half of the double helix in both A^1–N^1 and B^1–O^1 were not fully known to him then. With Beck's academic credentials, he brought the Gravesian model to the masses and created a global *sapiens 2.1* brain syndicate represented by the different Centers for Human Emergence that dot the globe. Beck's work focused on the macro-scale applications of the model. Those were the *existential problems* of his generation—the "second-generation Gravesians," as he would often call Cowan and himself. He made it clear that it was up to the *sapiens 2.1* global constellation of third-generation Gravesians such as I to carry on the Gravesian legacy. It has been five years since my late friend and I had these conversations about the possible obsolescence of our model and whether the leap into *Second-sapiens* intelligence would preserve it in light of ecological collapse. In that time, I have come to understand more deeply what Beck meant when he spoke of experiencing epochal change—that is, standing on Jupiter in order to see our problems through a much wider lens. This was my invitation to venture beyond the macro-systems application that was his life's work to the mega application that this book explores. It is with this new awareness that includes and transcends the work of Graves, Beck, and Cowan during the era of Holocene awareness that I give a much wider Anthropogenic definition to the Gravesian model. It does not render human development obsolete; it pries it out the hands of the *First sapiens* and nests it in a new reality that acknowledges our *existential problems* today to be planetary in nature. Human exceptionalism that created our different planetary crises must now be subsumed in Gaia's self-regulating homeostasis. This is the necessary expansion of the model needed to bring stabilization to all life and to ensure that *Homo sapiens* will not destroy what remains of nature's systems.

SEVEN
THE DARKNESS BEFORE THE NEW DAWN

The first step to the knowledge of the wonder and mystery of life is the recognition of the monstrous nature of the earthly human realm as well as its glory, the realization that this is just how it is and that it cannot and will not be changed. Those who think they know how the universe could have been had they created it, without pain, without sorrow, without time, without death, are unfit for illumination.

—Joseph Campbell
The Power of Myth

In reexamining the entire psychosocial, evolutionary process depicted in Graves's life-cycles model, the gap between first- and second-tier intelligence becomes the new crucible, the womb in which the post-Holocene, *Second sapiens* gestates. It is the starting point at which the DNA of natural intelligence is reborn and wages battle with human intelligence in order to subordinate it. But as, discussed, the gap between the two tiers requires a *momentous leap*, only on the other side of which can we begin to stabilize the world and align human virtues with ecological harmony. It is here that the long-awaited structural realignment of all the lower fractals will take place, from the individual to the largest macro system to Earth's mega systems with the *general thema* that seeks to preserve what remains of life and its planetary support systems. Since this realignment is driven by natural intelligence, it operates within a far more complex system of evolutionary forces and will not favor any person, group, or species. Because of its encompassing size, the system is characterized not only by far more complexity but also by more chaos and unpredictability and will require a considerably longer period of gestation.

In this epochal battle, there is no guarantee that our species will survive. We will be at the mercy of Mother Nature and her autopoiesis, the intelligence that predates human intelligence by 3.5 billion years. This uncertainty, however, should not prevent us from doing our part to help us get to the other side of the darkness. The battle will entail the processing of all that has remained unconscious in the journey of the *First sapiens* so far. Of the things that have remained unconscious and must now be brought into the light are the ethos behind human exceptionalism and Enlightenment reductionism and the ideas of endless economic growth that are leading us to the *Great Obsolescence.*

I don't claim to be an expert in this chapter's various subjects. I did, however, experience my own journey through darkness when in 2018 my wife and soulmate, Elza Maalouf, was diagnosed with frontotemporal dementia (FTD). The diagnosis profoundly changed the trajectory of our lives and sent me into the deep recesses of my psyche. Very few of my skills and knowledge in economics and Spiral Dynamics could help me cope, and I found myself having to go inward, into the vast, subjective spaces, in order to make sense of what I was experiencing. In addition to being an expert on Middle Eastern politics, Elza had had a profound understanding of depth psychology, myth, and spirituality and would often nudge me into incorporating knowledge of these subjects into our lives when I was experiencing difficulty. After she became incapacitated and unable to speak, memories of those rich exchanges and from our accumulated knowledge resurfaced to guide me through what I was experiencing. In the two years that followed, I became obsessed with Jung's work on the shadow, Elizabeth Kübler-Ross's work on the stages of grief, Joseph Campbell's hero journey, and St. John of the Cross's dark night of the soul. What I experienced personally is regarded in myth and spirituality as the death of my former self, and the only way to be reborn was to embrace the transformational nature of my journey through the darkness. These experiences are recounted in my 2021 book, *The Light of Ishtar.* This current book would have not been possible without that journey, for it expanded my consciousness and opened the space for me to move beyond evolutionary economics and to care about the future of all humanity and the planet.

While Graves and Beck rarely ventured into spirituality and myth, parallels can easily be drawn between their approaches and the subjects of this chapter. For example, the chaos and reorganization that take place at stage transitions in the model corresponds to the dark night of the soul, especially when the stage is in a closed state. In the life-cycle model, decline and death are an intrinsic part of the closed state that must occur before rebirth into the higher-order stage can happen. The nature of Graves's gap between the first and second tiers and his description of it over the decades leaves no doubt that getting to the other side necessarily requires processing all the unhealthy aspects of the first tier, which collectively represents the metaphorical death of the *First sapiens* and his rebirth as the more enlightened *Second sapiens* endowed with exponential growth in his/her psychological capacities. Having drawn these comparisons, I nevertheless acknowledge that my treatment of the various subjects in this chapter comes from general knowledge that does not qualify me to dive deeply into their specialized applications.

The driving force behind this exploration is to provide a general, multifaceted approach to how we might address this critical transition stage known as the *gap*. While there's no evidence that either Graves or Beck relied heavily on psychological concepts from other sources—such as Jung's work with the shadow—to explore the depth of this stage, they both spoke in philosophical and existential terms about its meaning and significance. To incorporate Anthropogenic awareness into the Gravesian model, it becomes crucial to give shape to the content of this critical stage of development. I hope this chapter, in the most general terms possible, provides an opening for the reader to explore further into depth psychology, myth, spirituality, and ways to process grief.

It is difficult to imagine how these different areas of inquiry *will* unfold in the future. They are all human constructs intended to give us a better understanding of mental and spiritual health and to help us unlock some of the mysteries of existence and the wonder of being. My interpretation of them here is intended to help us process the centuries of damage we've inflicted on the natural world, and by doing so, to contribute to our ascendance into *Second sapiens*. The scientists who named this epoch the *Anthropocene* made it clear that if we fail to act in an urgent, committed way, our fate will be determined by the breakdown of both human-built environments and Mother Nature's systems that are in different stages of collapse. This dark reality has spun a new area in the study of human behavior called *collapse psychology*. It examines personal and collective collapse in all aspects—including mental, emotional, spiritual, and communal—of the accelerated change we're experiencing and explores how to deal with it.[1] To date, it is too soon to know whether the insights gained from such study will inform those in power in time to reverse, prevent, or partially mitigate the ecological, societal, and economic collapse that is underway; or whether it will emerge as just another tool to help the masses process trauma and grief absent the wise leadership that can successfully shepherd us to the other side.

When scientists speak of the sixth extinction being upon us, they are not predicting a massive asteroid hitting the Earth like the one that wiped out the dinosaurs sixty-five million years ago, nor are they predicting the movement of continents or major shifts of Earth's tectonic plates. They are referring to the Anthropocene—an extinction event brought about by human activity. When mass extinctions are viewed in geologic time, the transition phase is measured in millions of years. It takes that long for Mother Nature to digest what has happened and allow her systems to adjust, evolve, and heal before a new, more resilient epoch can begin. In every past extinction event, the casualties were enormous. Scientists estimate that 75 percent of all living species were wiped out during the second mass extinction and as many as 95 percent during the third mass extinction.[2] The Anthropocene epoch presents us with multiple crises that will batter the Earth and our society—extreme heat, rising seas, fire, and catastrophic storms—that will change our global demographics and cause massive loss of life. Physical survival will become the central question for many communities. But for those who see the Anthropocene in epochal terms that transcend our present civilization, the transition phase takes on an entirely different dimension. Their view is nested in natural intelligence and endowed with the grace and the beauty that embraces darkness, death, and rebirth as inevitable parts of life and renewal.

This transition may not take as long as previous epochal shifts have, but the rebirth on the other side of the chasm cannot occur unless we look back to examine the consciousness of pre-Holocene or even earlier humanity. We must gain a deeper understanding of our beginnings and explore how *sapiens 1.1* learned to live with nature. This time around, *sapiens 2.1,* like *sapiens 1.1,* will fear nature's wrath. But, unlike in the conditions that existed two- to three-hundred-thousand years ago, *sapiens 2.1,* with all that he has become, will understand that the actions of his own ancestors are what is causing Mother Nature to convulse. It is that awareness, along with all that has been learned along the evolutionary ladder, that makes it possible—even necessary—to explore phenomena steeped in modern psychology, ancient mythology, and spirituality. Together, these three areas of inquiry become the midwife, the vessel, that transforms darkness into light and death into rebirth. Examining the different stages of grief and the processing of the shadow go hand in hand with the exploration of mythology, the archetypes, and spirituality. This is where ancient wisdom, instinct, and subjectivity give form to the insight and intelligence of the *Second sapiens.*

It is important to keep in mind that, in common literature, most of the focus in these areas is on the individual. Their application to larger holonic structures takes on greater complexity and uncertainty, which renders their application to the collective less predictable and considerably more challenging. If *Homo sapiens* survives this journey, much of what will be gained will become part of *Second sapiens* DNA in a critical growth stage that will prevent him/her from falling back into the deficient motivations of his/her ancestors.

The Gap and the Collective Unconscious

Introduced by C. G. Jung, the concept of the collective unconscious describes a segment of the deepest, unconscious part of the mind common to all humanity. It is generally associated with idealism and populated by instinct and the ancient, primal symbols of the archetypes.[3] According to Jung, archetypes are universally present images in the psyche that have been inherited from our earliest human ancestors. Jung believed that the concept helps to explain why similar themes occur in mythologies around the world. Although it is transpersonal, the collective unconscious has a profound influence on the lives of individuals, who live out its symbols and clothe them in meaning through their experiences. Well-known archetypes include the Tree of Life, the Great Mother, the Wise Old Man, the Hero, the Trickster, and so on. Of all the archetypes, the one most relevant to our crucial transition phase is the Shadow—the part of our personality that, throughout the course of our life, is relegated to the darkness of the unconscious unless we consciously work to access it.

Processing the shadow plays a large part in Jungian analysis. When we deny an unwanted or unattractive aspect of ourselves, it doesn't disappear; it just fades away from our conscious awareness and becomes part of the shadow that has a life of its own. This form of fragmentation happens at an unconscious level, and the more we are unaware of it, the more we unknowingly empower our dark side. It is through the process of conscious observation that we begin to integrate the shadow into the light and make the unconscious conscious. The shadow goes by many familiar names, including the disowned self, the lower self, and the dark twin or brother in the Bible and in popular myth. In the post-Holocene, Gravesian model, that disowned self manifests as the accumulation of the dark side of all the lower six stages of development that have remained unconscious or that persist in a closed or arrested state. It contains all the inferiorities that we choose not to know about. When these inferiorities remain unconscious, they wreak havoc in our lives. Left unprocessed, this disowned content functions independently of our conscious awareness and takes possession of our being, exerting control over our thoughts, emotions, and behaviors. It can unconsciously drive us into hard times, even as we remain ignorant that these troubled periods have been self-imposed and are not the product of bad luck or fate.[4]

> *None of us stands outside humanity's black collective shadow.*
>
> —C. G. Jung[5]

Collectively, the shadow represents the past and present tragedies and horrors perpetrated by all humankind throughout time and stored at a deep unconscious level. The bigger the fractal scale of human activity, the larger the shadow it creates and the longer it takes to process. As we begin to address global issues such as ecological collapse and climate change, the mega-scale shadow that has been buried in the unconscious gradually becomes visible. It is in that deep darkness where matters such as the *Great Obsolescence* and its various components lie. In the mind of the individual, the shadow contains qualities that seem weak, socially unacceptable or even evil, but when dealing with the collective shadow at the mega-systems level, those inferiorities are recognizable as such in the minds of only a very few people. It seems that when a person comes into Anthropogenic awareness, the vast majority of humanity appears to be acting from that collective shadow and seems to be doing so on automatic, remaining ignorant of its actions and justifying its thoughts and behaviors. That Anthropogenic state of awareness is seen today in the actions of climate activists and scientists and in young people who fear for their future. As vocal as they have been, their voices have not reached anywhere near the state of collective awareness needed to process the darkness effectively. Otherwise, there would have been systemic rebellion against the current world order, its leaders, and its outdated institutions. This mega shadow is so deeply entrenched that merely recognizing it will begin to unravel our reality and everything we have known to be good, just, and true.

When we commit to bringing aspects of our shadow into the light, we begin to recognize the patterns in which the shadow influences our lives. One of these patterns is called *projection.* Jung described projection in the simplest terms as a defense mechanism in which we unconsciously discover our negative traits in other people and disapprove of them accordingly. This unconscious process allows us to avoid taking responsibility for our own faults and misbehavior. Projection is an inevitable and necessary component in our psychological development. It is one of the primary means by which we can gain awareness of what resides in our unconscious. After we project a certain behavior, the healthy thing to do is to recognize its subjective nature, withdraw it from the external world, and integrate it into our conscious awareness. By withdrawing our projections and becoming aware of the faults we previously projected onto others, we can take corrective measures and widen our capacity for psychological growth. However, the process of withdrawal and integration is difficult. The type and the severity of the trauma, the stage of one's development, and whether or not the individual is in an open or a closed state can determine the degree to which one has the courage and the capacity to face up to one's weaknesses and dark qualities.

Jung warned that when we're unable to process individual projection, the problem becomes widespread collectively and war is the likely outcome.[6] At the collective level, those in positions of power driven by their shadow can project societal problems onto others and onto certain groups. In today's life conditions, societal power structures are different from those in Jung's time. Today, we live in a world informed by decentralized media and in a society built on free speech. Individuals who have not examined their shadow issues can become social-media influencers with millions of followers who find kinship and harmony with the influencer. In turn, the groups on whom shadow is projected are empowered to project their own shadow onto other groups, resulting in a collective form of shadow repression and deep societal fragmentation. Projection today has a million channels and can spread like wildfire through a million different online media outlets. The addictive nature of social media reinforces the empowerment of the external world, while the "likes" it generates act as an immediate feedback loop, proffering the instant gratification that prevents us from integrating the shadow and making the unconscious conscious. This collective empowerment of the dark side is subtle as well as decentralized. Its choice of weapon is not an armored vehicle or a nuclear warhead but a fallacy that prevents us from bringing our shadow into the light. Our collective inability to face our own weaknesses and destructiveness out of a passive lack of awareness allows internal battles to manifest on a vast scale in the external world. Today, this reality serves as the main distraction that saps our attention and prevents us from addressing the bigger issues of ecological collapse and climate change.

Anthropogenic awareness is an exponentially larger fractal than the one that accompanied the Holocene era, and therefore the size of its shadow will be exponentially larger as well. To use the boiling-frog metaphor, the pot represents the collective unconscious, and the water represents all the shadow elements of the *First sapiens* that must be processed and brought to conscious light. As the water continues to heat up—i.e., our shadow projections become more destructive globally—the frog, humanity, remains unconscious of the threat because the increase is gradual. For the frog to jump out would represent a new scenario in which a humanity that has processed its shadow is aware of the dangers that lie in the dark recesses of the unconscious. As it is, though, the original scenario prevails: the frog remains oblivious of his immanent mortality as the water continues to heat to the boiling point. That is, the *First sapiens*, acting from his/her shadow in an attempt to repress Anthropogenic awareness, has numbed the frog's ability to sense higher temperatures. Consequently, we remain in the increasingly hazardous pot, and with increasing frequency the major catastrophes that lie outside our collective awareness will come to us as fate: disastrous storms, extreme heat, rising seas, and fires—which, if unabated, will render us cooked.

These catastrophes will act as triggers from the higher fractal that will unleash the pathologies hidden in the collective shadow of the *First sapiens* to help expedite its processing. The hope the *Second sapiens* holds in this new reality of shadow repression is that the *First sapiens* begins to yield to the Second after the natural calamities become untenable. Until then, the largest collective shadow that we have relegated to the deepest realms of the unconscious will continue to possess and direct our conscious awareness and inform our leaders and our institutions.

The Anthropocene epoch requires us to begin to think differently, to recognize the dark side of human exceptionalism and all the unprocessed shadow aspects of the *First sapiens.* This entails exceptional leadership that lies outside our current reality and psychosocial capacities. If there is a way to empower the *sapiens 2.1* brain syndicate with collective abilities, among its first tasks will be to process just enough of what has remained unconscious in our collective shadow to place *First sapiens* in an open psychosocial state. This will be a Marshall Plan for the mind, a necessary sequence of development that enables us the take the *momentous leap* forward by processing the past and putting it into proper psychological perspective. Doing so will face much resistance from the entire societal complex of the *First sapiens* with its rose-colored glasses and a reality glossed over by a veneer of humanitarian-sounding doublethink and moralistic rationalizations that cannot differentiate between darkness and light at this new, higher fractal of awareness. In spite of this stark reality, one of the greatest hopes for a successful transition out of the darkness lies in the younger generation that was born into Anthropogenic awareness. When their time comes and they hold authority, power, and influence in the world, they will enact meaningful change that will bring enough of our collective shadow into the light, pick up the charred remains and destruction left behind the reign of the *First sapiens,* and begin the long journey of aligning *human intelligence* with *natural intelligence.*

Processing Collective Grief

Another area of psychology that might help us process the grief and trauma of transitioning through the collective darkness comes from Dr. Elisabeth Kübler-Ross (1926–2004), a psychiatrist who was a pioneer in near-death studies. Her work was influenced by Jungian psychology and can be applied to the individual as well as the collective. Among the important things for which Kübler-Ross is known is the five-stages-of-grief model that she originally developed to describe the process patients with terminal illness go through as they come to terms with their own death. It was later expanded to include grieving friends and family members, who seem to undergo a similar process. The model first appeared in her 1969 book, *On Death and Dying,* which has since been translated into over forty languages. The stages of grief are popularly known by the acronym

DABDA, which stands for denial, anger, bargaining, depression, and acceptance.

It is important to note that Kübler-Ross's model, like all other models, is intended to give an overall framework for how an idea or a theory works and that each person grieves differently. These stages are not linear, and progression from one stage to the next cannot be gauged. A time frame for reaching the final stage of acceptance varies greatly among individuals and becomes considerably less predictable when the model is applied to larger fractals. Just as in shadow processing, going through these stages depends greatly on one's psychological capacity for handling trauma from loss, one's stage of development, and whether or not the individual is in an open or a closed state. Today, her model is frequently applied to grief situations other than death such as the end of a relationship, a divorce, the loss of a job, and so on.

> *Should you shield the valleys from the windstorms, you would never see the beauty of their canyons.*
>
> —Dr. Elisabeth Kübler-Ross[7]

Significantly, a collective grieving process at a global scale has not been experienced before, nor are there any sure ways for us to know and gauge progress in processing collective grief. What follows is a more detailed discussion of Kübler-Ross's five stages of grief as they apply both to individuals and to the collective:

Denial

This first stage in the model is a common defense mechanism. It is a temporary response that carries an individual through the first wave of pain. Denial helps those who are experiencing loss to create a buffer zone that prevents them from experiencing immediate shock. In the case of a terminal medical diagnosis, the individual believes the diagnosis itself is somehow mistaken and clings to his/her reality that existed before the diagnosis was made. This stage includes fantasizing about alternative scenarios in which, for instance, a person overcomes medical odds, a divorcing spouse comes to his senses and returns to the relationship, or a boss realizes the person's value and gives her back the position she previously held. After this first reaction of shock and denial, a person comes to the realization that life as he/she knew it has changed. At this stage, a person may go numb for a while and feel like nothing matters anymore, making it difficult for him to move on.[8] Eventually, when that person is ready, the emotions and feelings he has denied will resurface, and the healing journey will continue.

At the collective level, denial become denialism. It is the rejection of basic facts and concepts that are undisputed, well-supported parts of the scientific consensus on a subject in favor of ideas that are radical, controversial, or fabricated.[9] It is a systemic refusal to accept reality and truth, a defense mechanism intended to protect the denialists from mentally disturbing facts and ideas. In corporate settings, denialism is a strategic approach to debunk the truth about the danger of certain products. Denialism exists in many different forms, whether the motivation behind it is political, religious, economic, or based in any other ideology that uses half-truths and misrepresentation of facts to promote its own self-interest. Historically, this form of cognitive dissonance was responsible for distorting the truth about the Holocaust, the AIDS pandemic, and, more recently, the COVID-19 pandemic. In issues of world health, the tobacco industry, in the face of mounting scientific evidence, had for decades denied the negative health effects of smoking.

The largest fractal of denialism today is climate change, and the *Great Obsolescence* represents the largest and longest road of it in human history. The entities that are creating this particular form of denialism stand to lose the most if world leaders were to adopt the recommendations of the IPCC or the findings from any of the other scientific entities that study Earth systems and the ecological state of our planet. Corporations that rely on carbon-based activities will engage in systemic but subtle forms of denialism, just as the tobacco industry has in the past. As an example, ExxonMobil, one of the world's largest fossil-fuel corporations, has poured billions into funding a network of fake citizens' groups and bogus scientific bodies that for years have been claiming that the science of global warming is inconclusive.[10]

At the collective level, the size and severity of a potential loss has a direct relation to the size and severity of the denial. If we are to save the planet, much of what got us to the *Great Obsolescence* must be reversed or at least somehow mitigated. Because of the collective shock this will create, many imbedded interest groups will engage in denialism that will only prolong the agony of this stage. It is another manifestation of Graves's Orwellian societal complex of the *First sapiens* hiding behind terms that sound environmentally safe, such as the "green economy." Those who understand the science know that much of what represents the green economy is a veneer of denialism called "greenwashing" that is pervasive and systemic and rarely addresses long-term solutions needed to avert climate disasters.

Anger

In the grieving process, loss is often reflected in anger, which is the next stage in the model. In many cultures, anger is a rejected emotion, and, as a result, it becomes part of the repressed shadow. What is important to keep in mind is that anger is another form of showing and processing pain. It might start with the simple questions of, Why me? and, What did I do to deserve this?[11] An individual might become angry at friends, family members, strangers, and even those who have left or passed away. While this is a form of projection in which a person looks for answers outside himself, it also serves as a way to reconnect with the world after the isolation that accompanies the denial stage.

Anger at the collective level in the Anthropocene era is the starting point that offsets the subtle, systemic denialism underpinning our global economy and informing our leaders. This is part of the gold in the shadow of which Jung speaks. Unfortunately, due to the slow-moving nature of climate change and as depicted in the boiling-frog allegory, collective anger may not reach the tipping point in time for meaningful change to take place.

Collective anger has a legitimate cause that is based in some form of injustice and with time will culminate in some form of collective action. According to a research group that studied over 180 cases of collective action, the phenomenon is grounded in many areas of the social sciences. It attempts to integrate three dominant sociopsychological perspectives—injustice, efficacy, and identity—that explain the preconditions leading to its formation.[12] Here are the main aspects of the model and the difficulties we face in applying them in the Anthropocene era:

- *Injustice*: Collective anger generated during the Holocene era must translate to collective action informed by the Anthropocene. Social justice becomes climate justice, which moves considerably slower and remains in the early stages of its life cycle facing relentless attacks brought on by the antibodies of the current system. While the model might help us understand the causes of social injustice and how to remedy them, it may be difficult to apply it to climate change.

- *Efficacy*: This aspect in the model concerns the availability of structural resources that enable change to take place, whether the resource is an existing legal framework such as a constitution, a well-developed judiciary system, or a financial entity that enables activism. On the other side of our journey through the darkness, efficacy becomes nested in environmental democracy that is based in the rights of nature, and financial resources are directed to accommodate the transition stage. Sadly, neither of those conditions are part of the current global consciousness as they also face the current system's relentless attacks.
- *Identity*. In this aspect of the model, the focus changes from the social identity that distinguishes the disadvantaged group to the entire human race as the disadvantaged species looking to survive climate change and ecological collapse. This level of awareness, while on the rise, will not reach the needed tipping point any time soon as the issues of social identity of many disadvantaged groups are just coming to the surface and will dominate the cultural debate for the foreseeable future.

In order for anger at the collective level to grow and manifest into collective action for the climate, it must be helped by phenomena or forces that lie outside the conscious awareness of the *First sapiens*. Like the forces that exposed the tobacco industry's lies, at some point catastrophic climate events will reach a tipping point and expose the systemic denialism that keeps our global, carbon-based economy in place. This is how collective anger in the Anthropocene era rises and how the collective grieving process continues.

Bargaining

Bargaining is a stage of grief that helps a person hold on to hope in a situation of intense pain.[13] At the individual level, this is a stage of internal negotiations where a person considers several "what if" scenarios in the hope of changing a future dreaded outcome. An example would be, "If

I can survive this cancer, I will never smoke or drink again." All internal dialog of this sort is aimed at bringing things back to normal. An individual might also explore ways he or she might have done things differently to prevent a loss that has already occurred: "If only I had lived closer to my mother, I could have taken better care of her." Such attempts to bargain might be accompanied with guilt as the grieving person thinks they can exert control over a situation that is in the past—while in reality, of course, they can't. As hard and unrealistic as the bargaining stage may be in the grief process, it still helps people heal as they confront the reality of their loss.

At the collective level, in the bargaining stage the emotional battle between activism and denialism subsides, and a shared communal sadness prevails. Anthropogenic denialism is driven primarily by the goal of preventing the monumental losses the global economy will suffer as a result of the *Great Obsolescence.* Economists have a term for this form of loss. It is called stranded assets, and they estimate the share of loss for the fossil-fuel industry alone will be over $30 trillion.[14] Given the increasing frequency and intensity of climate disasters, denialists gradually and reluctantly yield to the truth. This signifies the beginning of *First sapiens* acknowledgment of the obsolescence of his/her values and virtues and the poisoning of the ecosystem in which all economic activities lie. At this stage, "what if" scenarios take the form of inquiry that spurs efforts to avert the worst outcomes of collective loss. Such inquiry also gives the denialists the hindsight to revisit the mistakes they made and to learn from them as they begin to incorporate *Second-sapiens* intelligence into their decision making. The collective guilt that besets them at this stage gradually transforms into the will to save what remains of life as we transition through the darkness.

Today, Anthropogenic awareness remains in the *inquiry-and-identification* phase of Graves's life-cycles model (see fig. 2.6), the equivalent of Kübler-Ross's first stage, denial. The inner collective of climate scientists and other *Second sapiens* are still battling the antibodies from the dying system, represented by the denialists. At the collective level, Kübler-Ross's bargaining stage equates to the early stages of Graves's *introduction* phase, corresponding to the point at which change just begins to occur. This is where the culmination of Anthropogenic knowledge from the *inquiry-and-identification* phase is embraced by the outer collective, the *First sapiens* who are entering *Second-sapiens* stages and who still hold power, authority, and influence over politics, technology, science, and culture. This is the stage where all humanity works at uncovering the damage we have caused our planet as prolonged sadness leads to the next stage.

Depression

At the individual level, Kübler-Ross's depression stage occurs when a person starts facing his/her present reality and the inevitability of the experienced loss.[15] Just as in all other stages of grief, different people process depression differently and at their own pace. The sadness and despair that accompany this stage are a normal response to grief. A person experiencing depression might feel an array of emotions ranging from vulnerability, fatigue, confusion, and distraction all the way to a general loss of joy.

Collectively speaking, the anxiety caused by climate change is another emotion to add to that list. The grief and anxiety over worsening ecological conditions that signal the loss of a stable future especially affect activists, climate scientists, and younger generations.[16] As overwhelming as these feelings can be, going through depression is a necessary part of our healing journey to get us to the other side of the darkness.

Depression at the collective level will be experienced more frequently and at global scale as climate catastrophes intensify. This will happen when the failure of our leaders reaches a tipping point and the human race acknowledges that climate collapse has become inevitable. It is when the weight of our collective past actions will fall on the shoulders of all humanity, indicating the extent of the difficulties we face on the road ahead. While the depression of an individual might be measured in weeks or months and could be helped by therapy and medication, the depression of the collective is characterized by a prevailing and seemingly permanent sense of sadness and hopelessness that is shared by a high proportion of its members.[17] In the pre-Anthropocene world, collective depression has affected smaller fractals in society, groups who have felt trapped with little chance of escaping their exiting reality. The most common are the inmates of concentration camps and prisons. Often, groups who live in urban ghettos also experience a collective sense of hopelessness, which perpetuates the cycle of sadness and loss of hope.

The way to address collective depression is by restoring collective hope, and this becomes the task of all humanity during our transition through this stage of darkness. Once we realize we are our own imprisoners, and that it has been our collective actions that led us here, we begin to take responsibility for our collective future. This is when the *First sapiens* is seated on the therapist's couch, processing all past traumas and identifying the collective triggers that keep us in the state of perpetual hopelessness. This is when the entire mental-health profession identifies with climate trauma as the primary cause of our depression, and the treatment becomes a collective act that supersedes all other acts. It is when the *sapiens 2.1* brain syndicate empowers its members who are mental health specialists and places the needed resources and support from the remainder of its collective at their service. The most difficult aspect of the collective-depression stage might occur when we realize that, in spite of our efforts, we cannot restore matters to the way they were during the Holocene era.

Loss at this fractal level encompasses the loss of entire species and vast areas of our multiple ecosystems. As many scientists have warned, we have exceeded the Earth's carrying capacities in many of her systems. These capacities define the safe boundaries that ensure life, and crossing them may be catastrophic in that they will trigger nonlinear and abrupt environmental change on a planetary scale. In short, processing loss at this larger fractal level will not fully heal our collective trauma. We must acknowledge that, if we make it as a species to the other side of this darkness, we will remain at the mercy of a much larger, complex system in which many of its elements have passed their nexus points. Until these elements reach their own new level of stability, environmental chaos and unpredictability will become the conditions with which we must learn to live. Just as at the individual level, collective depression allows us to process the loss and so leads to acceptance of a new reality. Our Anthropogenic reality commands us to remember the climate trauma caused by the *First sapiens* and to learn to integrate it into our collective awareness as we transition to the next stage.

Acceptance

The final stage of the grieving process in the Kübler-Ross model, acceptance at the individual level is about how a person acknowledges the losses he/she experienced, how to learn to live with those losses, and how he/she readjusts to life accordingly.[18] Like all the other stages of grief, some people reach this final stage sooner than others, and some might linger with residual trauma for some time to come. The so-called triggers of sadness become lessened, and, when they occur, are less impactful; but they will not completely disappear. Sometimes they lead back to earlier stages of grief, which, according to experts, is part of the normal healing process. Triggers serve as a reminder of how things used to be and become subordinate to one's new state of awareness. This is how the human mind transcends trauma and includes it in a processed, less threatening form. Acceptance is relative, and it is not necessarily about being okay with what happened. As it becomes the new state of consciousness, sadness and anger over the loss transform into new capacities that help the individual deal better with his/her new reality in the long term.

In the post-Holocene, Gravesian model, acceptance comprises the acknowledgment that *Homo sapiens* has processed most of the trauma that has remained in the collective unconscious during the journey through the first six stages of development. It is defined by when the *First sapiens* hands over the reign to the *Second sapiens.* Acceptance is in the *momentous leap* that propels us past the darkness and carries with it the trauma of the *First sapiens* as a constant reminder of our past irresponsible and deficient behaviors. At the collective level, this is when humanity begins to transcend the limits of Pantometry and embraces the virtues of Gaiametry. It is a long journey, and the larger the holon, the longer it will take for the trauma to be processed. Acceptance is also what will bring about the dawn of a new renaissance led by a highly diverse, *sapiens 2.1* global brain syndicate, driven by the wisdom and foresight that will ensure the survival and subsequent stabilization and flourishment of all life on the planet. This is the new state of awareness that will make sure that the balance of nature will not again be upset and that *Homo sapiens* will not again set off on another self-aggrandizing binge.

Humanity on a Hero's/Heroine's Journey

Mythology is another approach that helps us process trauma as we transition through the darkness. In the broadest terms, myths are traditional stories about gods, kings, and heroes handed down through generations as powerful tales that embody a collective form of knowledge. Mythology defined world wisdom and its different traditions before the Enlightenment rendered it unscientific and sidelined its crucial role in the human experience. In his work with the collective unconscious, Jung used many common themes and symbols from mythology to identify the archetypes that become central to his work. Then, as we entered the second half of the twentieth century, myth and the use of archetypes witnessed a great resurgence through the work of comparative mythologist Joseph Campbell, and our search for postmodern meaning began.

Mythology, according to Campbell, provides a bridge between one's local consciousness and the universe, "the sheer vast, overwhelming environment of Being. It reconciles local, historical space-time with the transcendent realms and the eternal forms." Most importantly, myth fosters "the centering and the unfolding of the individual in integrity" with him- or herself, the culture, the universe, and ultimately with the creative Mystery that is "both beyond and within" the individual and "all things."[19]

The material focus of the Enlightenment discredited the truth of myth and, in the process, we seem to have forgotten our origins, the universal consciousness in which our enormous, untapped possibilities of mind, body, and spirit are nested. As we approach the *Great Obsolescence,* we begin to recognize that our survival requires more than the objective scientific observation of reality and that our views of human exceptionalism must evolve. This is when a new order begins to emerge on the other side of chaos. But it will be no ordinary transition. It will be an epochal shift that entails gradual societal and environmental collapse of all we have known to be good true and just and a slow and painful reestablishment. Myth tells the story of how this transition might happen as it strips our minds naked and exposes us to the archetypal world of collapse and renewal, of the yin and the yang, and of darkness and light in the dual nature of existence that is eternal. It is full of stories of horror and of beauty that have defined the world. It shows us how we gain a transcendent understanding of life and death and of historic patterns that can hasten, destroy, and transform the human endeavor at any time and at any place along life's journey.

One of Joseph Campbell's most popular allegories that captures this transformational experience is the hero's journey. It is a monomyth that involves the archetype of the hero who goes on an adventure and encounters several obstacles and helpers he/she meets along the way. After enduring many trials and tribulations, the hero returns home changed and transformed, bearing some sort of gift—sometimes called the "elixir," that will benefit the entire community. Campbell describes a total of twelve stages of the monomyth, but not all monomyths necessarily contain all twelve; some may focus on only one of the stages, while others may deal with the stages in a somewhat different order.[20] While this entire book can easily be adapted to the hero's journey using all twelve stages, due to the brevity of this section, I will approach it from the general theme of its three main stages: the departure, the initiation, and the return.

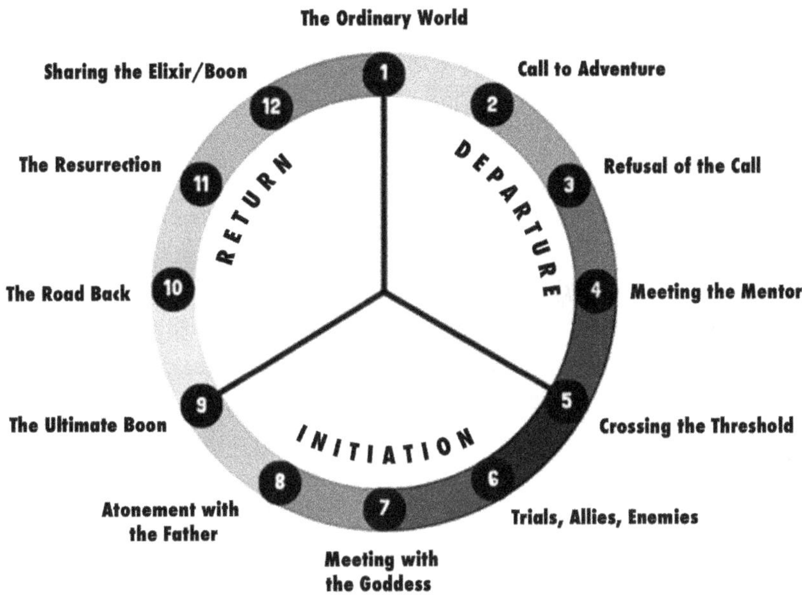

Figure 7.1. The Hero's Journey. Based on Joseph Campbell's conception in the *Hero with a Thousand Faces*, the diagram shows the phases of the journey within the overall structure of departure, initiation, and return. First published by Pantheon Books in 1949. Graph by Said E. Dawlabani.

The Departure

The first phase in the departure is what Campbell calls the "call to adventure." It depicts an event or insight in which the hero receives information that change might be coming in the ordinary life he has lived until now. In the Gravesian life-cycle model, the call to adventure corresponds to the time when all six stages of the first tier, the *First sapiens*, reaches the nexus point. It corresponds the early stages of the *Great Obsolescence* before the beginning of the precipitous drop into the darkness. The call to adventure represents an invitation to systemic change of the way things are and have been. It has the potential to uproot everything the hero has known as his sense of duty and obligation to maintain the status quo becomes threatened. The call also exposes the hero to fear and insecurity and a sense of inadequacy in being able to undertake the journey. As a result, the hero may refuse the call to adventure, sending him into a state of denial as his efforts turn to reinforcing the status quo.

But, as time passes, the call becomes undeniable, and the hero commits to the quest. According to Campbell, this is when supernatural help appears in the form of a mentor: "Having responded to his own call, and continuing to follow courageously as the consequences unfold, the hero finds all the forces of the unconscious at his side. Mother Nature herself supports the mighty task. And in so far as the hero's act coincides with that for which his society itself is ready, he seems to ride on the great rhythm of the historical process."[21] To adapt this phase to the post-Holocene Gravesian model, the forces of the unconscious are represented by the natural disasters precipitated by climate change. Mother Nature herself confirms the views and virtues of the *Second sapiens*, who is the hero that emerges on the other side of the journey. This phase slowly pushes the *First sapiens* into action by exposing him/her to the danger of being stuck in the denial that prevents him/her from undergoing the needed change.

Once the hero leaves the known world and its limits, he/she enters a new stage of the journey in which the new rules and the limits are unknown. This is what Campbell calls the "threshold" that is at the entrance to the zone of magnified power where the hero sees the limits of his/her present sphere of life and what lies beyond it: darkness, the unknown, and danger.[22] In the Gravesian model, the darkness and the unknown represent the difficulty we face in getting to the other side of the chasm between the first and second tier. The threshold is where fear and compulsiveness that have defined the journey and deficient needs of the *First sapiens* come face to face with the exponential increase in the psychosocial space of the *Second sapiens* that expels these vices. The threshold also gives the *First sapiens* a glimpse of how different the world on the other side of it will be. It is, in the words of Graves, a chasm of "unbelievable meaning" that must be crossed.

As the hero crosses the threshold and leaves the old world behind, he undergoes what Campbell calls *metamorphosis*. This is the phase in the monomyth known as the "belly of the whale," and it represents the final phase of the first stage of the journey. It is the heart of the *darkness before the new dawn*. Campbell describes it as a form of self-annihilation:

> Instead of passing outward, beyond the confines of the visible world, the hero goes inward, to be born again. The disappearance corresponds to the passing of a worshiper into the temple—where he is to be quickened by the recollection of who and what

> he is, namely dust and ashes. The temple interior, the belly of the whale, and the heavenly land beyond, above, and below the confines of the world, are one and the same.... Once inside the hero may be said to have died to time and returned to the World Womb, the World Navel, the Earthy Paradise.[23]

The belly of the whale is where the *First sapiens* is finally stripped of his destructive powers. It is in that sacred space that he is shown the limits and the dangers of his subsistent nature and is offered a glimpse of his own magnificence. After repeatedly failing to remedy existential issues, he must now acknowledge that he has run out of tools and strategies with which to move forward. This comprises the point of detachment from the past and the atonement with it and the long-awaited embrace of whatever may come. It is the place where we lose the fear and compulsivity that bind us to our deficient motivations. It is equivalent to standing on Jupiter for the first time and seeing the damage that we have caused our world as we deepen our understanding of who we are in relation to the cosmos and to all living creatures. It is the beginning of a new journey that widens our psychological and spiritual capacities and allows us to embrace new beginnings.

In the Gravesian model, atonement and going inward represent the critical search for the *Second sapiens* and for ways to lose fear and compulsiveness. It is the free fall into the collective unconscious that rids the hero of his subsistent needs and endows him with the exponential growth needed to continue the journey. The death is metaphorical in the sense that the *First sapiens* can no longer use outer objectivity and scientific reductionism to move forward. He is helped by forces outside human intelligence that pry the mind out of the grip of *Homo sapiens's* subsistent needs, represented by the ordinary world. It detaches him from his narrow focus on economic growth and the ideals of human exceptionalism and places him in a vast, open state where he begins to reacquaint himself with *natural intelligence*, the earthly paradise in which all life is nested. As we continue to fail to address ecological collapse, the death may not be merely metaphorical, and the journey into the belly of the whale may be forced upon us out of necessity and desperation, not out of a heroic act.

The Initiation

This stage of the hero's journey is by far the longest. It represents the long-awaited birth of the *Second sapiens* as he/she begins to pick up the charred pieces of what remains from the reign of the *First sapiens.* It is the beginning of the longest life cycle to date—the *sapiens 2.1* life cycle that represents the transition between the two *sapiens.* This is the stage in which the hero is tested in several ways as he/she experiences a range of emotions and setbacks that come when one seeks closure on the past while seeing the hurdles along the road to the future. According to Campbell, the first phase in the initiation process is called the road of trials that "represents only the beginning of the long and perilous path of initiatory conquests and moments of illumination. Dragons have now to be slain and surprising barriers passed—again, again, and again. Meanwhile there will be a multitude of preliminary victories, unretainable ecstasies, and momentary glimpses of the wonderful land."[24] This phase of the journey corresponds to the challenges that *sapiens 2.1* faces in his first mandate, the alignment of the healthy virtues of the *First sapiens* unto a *Second-sapiens* trajectory. Campbell's repeated emphasis for overcoming barriers will be as real in life as it is in myth.

The road of trials also corresponds to Graves's *introduction* phase in this new life cycle, and, just as it is at this stage with every life cycle in the model, the antibodies from the dying system will attack the new system, looking to kill it and prevent its virtues from defining the next stage. The dragons that must be slain are what remains of the deficient motivations of the *First sapiens* that have become deeply imbedded in our institutions and have moved into a closed state. They are the last denialists who continue to see the world through rose-colored glasses and exert extraordinary measures to mask the truth about climate change and other existential challenges. They are the powerful politicians and the corporate leaders of a carbon-based global economy engaged in a final, desperate attempt to stop the evolutionary process.

Repeated victories over the dragons of the *First sapiens* represent the trials the hero overcomes in the first half of the *introduction* phase, represented by the inner collective in which the ethos of Gaiametry begins slowly to replace the ethos of pantometry. Eventually, those victories reach a tipping point, where they attract the attention of the outer collective that holds the power to spread the virtues of Gaiametry and begin to stabilize the world. In the hero's journey, the meeting of the outer and inner collective is symbolized by the hero meeting the goddess. Campbell describes this phase as the place where the hero gains items that will help him in the future:

> The ultimate adventure, when all the barriers and ogres have been overcome, is commonly represented as a mystical marriage of the triumphant hero-soul with the Queen Goddess of the World. This is the crisis at the nadir, the zenith, or at the uttermost edge of the Earth, at the central point of the cosmos, in the tabernacle of the temple, or within the darkness of the deepest chamber of the heart.[25]

In the post-Holocene, Gravesian model, this essentially constitutes the long-awaited reunion of the masculine and the feminine, the latter being the other half of the universal psyche that the *First sapiens* has ignored for centuries. It represents the transcendence of the monotheism that placed the patriarchy in charge of the Earth and subjected all living creatures to its will. It restores the balance between the yin and yang, wherein the voice of the feminine is equal—not subordinate—to that of the masculine. It signifies the return to the archetype of Mother Nature, the primordial image of the generative, sustaining mother figure ever present within the collective unconscious that, according to Jung, is the most important archetype seeming to contain all else. And it signifies the return to the Gaia intelligence that will save humanity on the other side of the *Great Obsolescence.*

To embrace the feminine fully on the journey, the hero must take responsibility for the damage his own patriarchal past had caused along the way. This is what Campbell calls the atonement with the father or the abyss:

> [Atonement] consists in no more than the abandonment of that self-generated double monster—the dragon thought to be God (superego) and the dragon thought to be Sin (repressed id). But this requires an abandonment of the attachment to ego itself, and that is what is difficult. One must have a faith that the father is merciful, and then ... the dreadful ogres dissolve. It is in this ordeal that the hero may derive hope and assurance from the helpful female figure, by [whom] ... he is protected through all the frightening experiences of the father's ego-shattering initiation.[26]

The merciful father is represented by the *sapiens 2.1* brain syndicate that is endowed with empathy and empowered by the reintegration of the feminine and that works tirelessly to bring the shadow of the *First sapiens* into the light. This higher consciousness acknowledges that the dreadful ogre—representing the first six stages of development—can be dissolved only when the feminine aspects of the universe are embraced and become an undivided part of what remains of the human journey.

After progressing thus far, the hero reaches a new state of enlightenment that Campbell calls *apotheosis.* In Gravesian terms, apotheosis would occur in the acknowledgement that the capacities of the *Second sapiens* to enact change have reached their zenith. As a result, the hero gains confidence that the trajectory of the future can be changed. This leads to the final phase of the initiation stage; the ultimate boon. This boon is what the hero went on the journey to get, and all the previous steps serve to prepare him/her for its ultimate realization. In Campbell's words,

> The gods and goddesses then are to be understood as embodiments and custodians of the elixir of Imperishable Being but not themselves the Ultimate in its primary state. What the hero seeks through his intercourse with them is therefore not finally themselves, but their grace, i.e., the power of their sustaining substance. This miraculous energy-substance and this alone is the Imperishable; the names and forms of the deities who everywhere embody, dispense, and represent it come and go.... Its guardians dare release it only to the duly proven.[27]

While this explanation holds much meaning for mythology and religion and the varied manifestations of the god/goddess power in world traditions, it can also describe the nature of *sapiens 2.1* intelligence. The idea that the boons only allow the hero access to godly powers and not to become the Divine itself represents the transcendence of the ego, the enlightenment that comes with the Greater Self that moves beyond the self-centered existence of the *First sapiens.* While *sapiens 1.5* had declared himself God, *sapiens 2.1* is fully aware of the damage caused thereby; he/she seeks to nest that declaration in the far greater intelligence that represents the eternal source of knowledge given to us by the powers that gods and deities have embodied since time immemorial. The transcendence of the self-centered existence is the imperishable energy-substance represented by the *natural intelligence* to which *human intelligence* must realign itself.

Campbell's statement about the sustaining substance being released only to the duly proven represents the rigorous process those who form the *sapiens 2.1* brain syndicate must go through in order to prove their capacities. In the applications of Spiral Dynamics and Integral Theory, absent Anthropogenic awareness the overall level of this form of psychosocial development in the world was gauged at less than 3 percent and as high as 7 percent in organizations. No attempts have been made to measure second-tier intelligence that is endowed with Anthropogenic awareness. Today, based on our collective inability to address ecological collapse and issues of climate change, those who form the *sapiens 2.1* brain syndicate are less than 1 percent and hold little power over institutional change. The 1-percent figure is based on the pre-Anthropocene research cited earlier, in which the *complex adaptive intelligence* capable of dealing with global governance and ecological issues was considered in the far distant future and limited to stage eight in the Spiral-Dynamics model. Our entry into the Anthropocene epoch, out of existential necessity, moved the responsibility of the eighth to the seventh stage in this model. If movement along the different phases of past-stage life cycles is any indication, then the *sapiens 2.1* intelligence, with all the resistance it faces from the *First sapiens*, wouldn't be much higher than that of the intelligence of the eighth stage three decades ago. It will be the *sapiens 2.1* brain syndicate—the diverse group of individuals endowed with exponential levels of psychosocial capacities—who will face the uphill battle to be duly proven. That process itself will be helped by *First-sapiens* people in leadership positions who, after presiding over repeated climate disasters, will find themselves forced to abandon their habitual attachments and embrace the treacherous road ahead. The course is one of the dissolution of the ego into the greater collaborative Self acting as a single organism and serving a far greater purpose.

In order to continue the journey and spread the virtues of Anthropogenic awareness, a *sapiens 2.1* brain syndicate must include those who hold power, authority, and influence over all *First-sapiens* institutions, especially those in politics and economics. This is where we begin to transform our institutions and inject them with *natural intelligence.* It is the longest segment of the journey that has to work systemically at replacing the virtues of pantometry with those of Gaiametry at every fractal level, from the way global governance and commerce are run all the way to how all individuals view themselves as citizens of their communities and the world. This is the road that leads to the permanent stabilization on the other side of the *momentous leap*, which represents the final phase of the hero's journey. It also represents the movement from the *introduction* phase to the *nodal* phase in the *sapiens 2.1* life cycle. This *nodal* phase contains the *growth* and *maturity* phases that work synergistically and collaboratively with the next stage, the *sapiens 2.2* stage, to ensure the permanent ecological alignment of all life and its long-term capacity to regenerate.

The Return

This is the final stage of the hero's journey with several phases. The two most relevant for our purposes concern how to become the master of both worlds and how to gain the freedom to live in both worlds simultaneously. After the hero works on spreading the wisdom gained from the first two stages of the journey and integrating them into societal institutions, the world begins to stabilize at the *sapiens 2.2* level. He/she now has the freedom to move between the two worlds. Campbell writes:

> The individual, through prolonged psychological disciplines, gives up completely all attachment to his personal limitations, idiosyncrasies, hopes and fears, no longer resists the self-annihilation that is prerequisite to rebirth in the realization of truth, and so becomes ripe, at last, for the great at-one-ment.... The hero is [now] the champion of things becoming, not of things become.... "Be sure there's nothing perishes in the whole universe; it does but vary and renew its form."[28]

This quotation sums up the entire nature of *Second-sapiens* intelligence. The prolonged psychological disciplines that allow for detachment from limitations represent the chasm we must cross to access the exponential increase in psychological space on the other side of the darkness. This increased space is where *sapiens 2.1* prepares the world for the realization of the oneness we experience in the *sapiens 2.2* stage. It is the oneness present in the Gaia organism, in the global brain, and in the *natural intelligence* that has been billions of years in the making.

As the hero indulges in his new-found freedoms after his return, he is in a transcendental state of being. In terms of the hero's journey, those are the blessings that constitute his return to the community to share the elixir of wisdom and new knowledge he has received and thereby benefit the entire collective. The planet and all life on it have been set on a course toward ecological stabilization through the efforts of *sapiens 2.1,* and the long-term, regenerative care for that life has been handed over to *sapiens 2.2.* As the hero enjoys the spoils of the journey, he/she is fully aware that the world of the *First sapiens* still exists, but now it is nested in the institutions and the ethos of the *Second sapiens.* It is nested in Gaiametry. This is where the hero finds the freedom to become the master of both worlds. This freedom comes from our collective understanding that the virtues of the *First sapiens* that brought us to the edge of collapse have been transcended. The collective shadow has been processed, and the healthy expressions of the *First sapiens* have now become part of the oneness that defines life after a long, harrowing, and existential journey.

The Dark Night of the Soul

The term *dark night of the soul* originated in a sixteenth-century poem by Spanish mystic Saint John of the Cross. Over time, it was modified and used by religious scholars, spiritual teachers, and psychotherapists to help people through some of the most difficult passages of their lives. It is commonly described as a time when all meaning collapses and a deep sense of meaninglessness erupts in which nothing makes sense anymore and there is no purpose to anything.[29] The events that send people into this state of being have a profound effect on their lives. Such events are often triggered by matters outside their conscious awareness that shatter their worldview and crush the values and virtues within their varied stages of development. At the individual level, the triggers could be the sudden death of a loved one or a family member—or, as in my personal situation, the incapacitation of my partner and soulmate. At the broader level, the triggers often come from our collective shadow, resulting in the existential wars that have punctuated the *First sapiens's* existence for centuries. The biggest trigger of them all, however, remains in the making, but it has grown exponentially in the last few decades. It is climate change.

The dark night of the soul provides yet for another approach for us to understand the *darkness before the new dawn* phase in the Gravesian model. The collapse of meaning today is felt by those who are part of the inner collective: the activists, the climate scientists, and the younger generations who have lost hope for a meaningful future. As does the initiation in the hero's journey, the dark night takes a person from one phase of life to another. But this is no ordinary journey, and no meaning from the past can be carried into the future as a ray of light that gives hope. This state of meaninglessness spares nothing with which a person has identified. It destroys whatever has remained of the ego and thrashes the person into the place of no return until he/she reaches the point at which there is nothing left to lose. It is in this space of surrender that we detach from our ego and become witness to its past actions, seeing our shameful and deficient behavior bare and naked. It is in this place of darkness that we begin to let go of the past. It is here that we are painfully stripped of all our attachments that gave meaning to our world. It is here that we die to our old selves before we can be born again.

When it comes to the rebirth of *Homo sapiens* into the Anthropocene, our journey into the dark night has the potential to be more catastrophic than all the wars we have waged against one another since *sapiens 1.1* began fashioning weapons. The death will not be that of the ego alone but of masses of life due to ecological collapse, the loss of biodiversity, and the effects of climate change. Historians have captured a glimpse of what this might feel like through the words of Abraham Lincoln in the aftermath of one of the worst battles in the American Civil War: The battle for Fredericksburg, Virginia, which took place December 11–13, 1862, left an estimated 18,500 soldiers dead, among whom 12,500 were Union soldiers and 6,000 were Confederates.

When Lincoln heard the news, he moaned, "If there is a place worse than hell, I'm in it!"[30]

This is the place where things cannot possibly get any worse, a place of conceptual meaninglessness and helplessness that forces the person to surrender to destiny. It is similar to being swallowed into the belly of the whale in the hero's journey, which represents the final separation from one's known world. This is also the place where we begin to glimpse a future that is far different than the past. It is the place that served as the ground out of which grew Lincoln's leadership and determination to win the war and preserve the Union. And it will be the ground out of which *Second-sapiens* leadership will come to define our future and preserve what remains of life on the planet.

Today, we are at the mercy of Mother Nature, and our actions in the last hundred years have made her less merciful toward our species. Our collective journey into the dark night of the soul is the crucible in which we acknowledge the obsolescence of the virtues of the *First sapiens*, a place where *human intelligence* yields to *natural intelligence.* Here, the exceptionalism of *sapiens 1.5* is exposed for the damage it has caused the greater system in which all life is nested. By failing to embrace Anthropogenic awareness consciously, the dark night will come to us as fate in which nothing we have known fits into a conceptual framework anymore. It is out of these devastated grounds that our new state of awareness will be born. This awareness will be characterized by the permanent sense of humility that comes with the exponential psychological freedom the *Second sapiens* realizes on the other side of the darkness. In this awareness, we will collectively realize that our species is but a small part of a very complex and interdependent ecological landscape, not one that is superior to it. We will begin to embrace Gaia's intelligence and start our long journey toward a future that ensures the survival of all life on Earth, the only home we have known. The voyage that must be taken is perilous, with resources greatly depleted, but with the resilience, patience, and determination that has made life forms thrive and evolve for billions of years, it can be done.

Part Three
Gaian Intelligence: Empowering What Matters in the Anthropocene Epoch

EIGHT
THE RISE OF GAIA

In my wanderings I once saw upon an island a man-headed, iron-hoofed monster who ate of the earth and drank of the sea incessantly. And for a long while I watched him. Then I approached him and said, "Have you never enough; is your hunger never satisfied and your thirst never quenched? And he answered saying, "Yes, I am satisfied, nay, I am weary of eating and drinking; but I am afraid that tomorrow there will be no more earth to eat and no more sea to drink."

—Kahlil Gibran
"The Plutocrat"

As humanity makes it to the other side of the darkness, it arrives at the doorstep of the *Second sapiens* on its last breath: exhausted, diminished, and spent. The intense journey through psychological, mythological, and spiritual transformation has given us a deeper sense of who we are and of our place in the universal order of things, but it has not restored the physical world that will exist on the other side. It has only expanded our ability to live with that world and accept the consequences and the devastation caused by our past actions. This is how we become the masters of both worlds—the one defined by our behaviorally deficient past and the one that has to pick up after it and make sure we never repeat it.

Understanding what has brought us to the edge of collapse is visible in unmistakable clarity as our surroundings on the other side rarely resemble those that existed several decades earlier. The planet has become increasingly uninhabitable as fires, floods, and extreme temperatures present a continuous and escalating threat to human existence. After failing to keep temperature rise to under 2°C within the time frame in accordance with the Paris 2015 agreement, temperatures are now expected to reach 3–4°C by the end of this century, causing sea levels to rise 100 to possibly

200 cm.[1] Most of the world's coastal regions are expected to be underwater, and millions will be forced to flee their homes. Polar ice will continue to melt at exponential rates and won't recover. Unprecedented droughts will claim larger and larger areas of farm land, making much of the world, including America's bread basket, inhospitable to agriculture. Decades of commercial farming will have left top soil greatly depleted. Most of the pollinator species will have died, and ocean fisheries will have collapsed. The IPCC's warning about the killing of ocean algae will have come to pass, and carbon dioxide in the atmosphere will have grown considerably as we set ourselves on a possibly irreversible course toward extinction. International aid agencies will have reached their breaking point, and desperate calls for help will go unanswered as each nation has to deal with its own existential challenges. With their institutions and governmental agencies extended beyond their capacities, nations one after the other will begin to collapse, unleashing chaos and mayhem as the world order, organized under the reign of the *First sapiens,* continues to unravel.

The *momentous leap* into second-tier awareness during the Anthropocene epoch barely resembles the one that Beck, Cowan, and Wilber articulated in their models a few decades ago. They did so from the paradise of the Holocene era in the comfort of their air-conditioned homes absent fires, floods, and extreme heat, unaffected by the early warning signs from a much higher fractal cautioning us that several of Earth's systems were passing their tipping points. Even Graves's own warnings about the consequences of our failures pale in comparison to what is unfolding on the planetary stage today. The great party of the twentieth century, cleverly disguised by the modern mind as *peace through commerce,* has come to a crashing end. *Homo colossus* has damaged Mother Nature much more than he has himself. As in Gibran's parable, the plutocrat, out of fear and greed, has justified the unjustifiable, having eaten the Earth and drunk its seas far beyond any reasonable need, far beyond the limits of Earth's carrying capacity. Fear and greed are two of the basic building blocks on which an insatiable, *sapiens 1.5* consumer society is built. The plutocrat, *Homo colossus,* and the *First sapiens* are one and the same; they represent a humanity that has long ignored the ecological consequences of its actions, and as a result whole ecosystems have become extinct. This is chaos and disorder that is unpreceded in human history.

Into this reality will walk the *Second sapiens,* battered but endowed with Gaian intelligence, the *natural intelligence* that transcends *human intelligence.* He/she will see glimpses of an eerily new order that lurks inside the eerier chaos, just as scientist Douglas R. Hofstadter has described it (see boxed quote, p. 112). He/she will be tasked with preserving what remains of human civilization and will need to do so from the few remaining habitable regions of the world. And he/she will have to continue these monumental, restorative, and mitigative tasks without ever knowing if such efforts will bring humanity back into Mother Nature's mercy and grace.

Out of Chaos, a New Ecological Order

Understanding how Earth's systems operate makes it necessary for us to frame our existential challenges in geologic time. Earth's history is divided into a hierarchical series of smaller periods, referred to as the "geologic time scale." These divisions, in descending lengths of time, are called eons, eras, periods, epochs, and ages. Life as a single organism first appeared 3.6 billion years ago in the Paleoarchean era, the second of eight eras on the geochronological time scale. What is of interest to the narrative of this book are the smaller time spans within the current era, the Cenozoic. The evolutionary changes that have taken place in this time span have given rise to the Tertiary period, which began after an asteroid wiped out the dinosaurs sixty-six million years ago. The second period is the one we are in now, the Quaternary which began when many large mammals became extinct and the modern *Homo sapiens* fully emerged.

GEOLOGIC TIME SCALE: THE CENOZOIC ERA				
Era	**Period**	**Epoch**	**Major Events**	**Start Date**
CENOZOIC	Quaternary	Holocene	Rise of human population. The last ice age ends.	11,700 years ago
		Pleistocene	Ice ages and warmer periods. Extinction of many large mammals. Evolution of fully modern humans.	2,588,000 years ago
	Tertiary	Pliocene	Climate cools further. Australopithecine hominins evolve.	5,333,000 years ago
		Miocene	Earth has many forests. Animals flourish but later temperatures start to cool.	23,030,000 years ago
		Oligocene	The continents move into their current places.	33,900,000 years ago
		Eocene	The Himalayas are formed as India moves into Asia.	56,000,000 years ago
		Paleocene	India reaches Asia. Mammals evolve into new groups. Birds survive extinction.	66,000,000 years ago

Table 8.1. Geologic Time Scale Chronicling the Cenozoic Era. Adapted by Said E. Dawlabani from Wikipedia; https://simple.wikipedia.org/wiki/Geologic_time_scale.

While the Anthropocene is considered an epoch, many scientists, including evolutionary biologists Bruce Lipton and Elisabet Sahtouris, believe that we have entered the sixth mass extinction. If this is the case—and evidence strongly points in that direction—then the Anthropocene could represent our entry into a new epoch in an entirely new period. Or, at best it will be the last of the eight epochs that have defined the Cenozoic Era.

If we as a species are among the lucky few who will make it through to the Anthropocene epoch and a possible mass-extinction event, it will be due to Mother Nature's autopoiesis, her feedback loops and the greater complexities of her different systems going through chaos and reorganization on a geologic time scale. It certainly will not be due to our own *human intelligence.* It has been Mother Nature's *natural intelligence,* measured in millions of years, that has made life possible again after each mass extinction that has occurred thus far. It was her intelligence using natural selection that allowed mammals to thrive after their primary predator, the dinosaur, became extinct. Here's how the most recent scientific evidence frames that historic transition: While the dinosaurs were extremely large, the much-smaller mammals were better at escaping the heat released by the meteor strike, hiding in underground borrows and aquatic environments. Further, while the majority of the dinosaurs were herbivores, the mammals could survive in habitats nearly devoid of plant life by eating insects and aquatic plants.[2]

If the survival of the fittest is the era-sized stage that repeats with the sixth extinction, the question becomes, What species of plants and animals can survive on a greatly diminished Earth that has lost most of its biodiversity and its fresh-water supply, with its oceans too hot and salinized to support marine life and most of its farm land turned into massive deserts? Unlike in the aftermath of the fifth extinctions, mammals may not be able to crawl into borrows rich with grubs and insects to ensure their survival, nor will there be a guarantee that edible aquatic plants might still exist, given how quickly we seem to be destroying our marine habitats. Even the elite—the billionaires who have built underground survival bunkers stocked with food and water to last decades—may be surprised to find after they crawl out of their bunkers that the Earth has remained an inhospitable place for growing food. It is also likely that all the seeds that are stored in the global seedbanks created to guarantee the world's food supply after major disasters may not serve their purpose, due to the greatly diminished ecosystems of flora and fauna that supported their earlier existence.[3]

Before the appearance of *Homo sapiens*, there were no man-headed, iron-hoofed monsters who destroyed the Earth and drank her seas beyond their need. The rise of the mammals and all life after the fifth mass extinction was made possible through a long evolutionary process that enriched the planet's resources and made her atmosphere conducive to habitation. It took millions of years for her to provide us with the Holocene-era heaven on Earth that we have enjoyed for the last 11,600 years. It took our species less than a hundred years to destroy most of what Mother Nature has given us. But, like Lynn Margulis so bluntly stated, Gaia is a tough bitch, and she will be around long after our species has disappeared. She cannot be rushed because we are in a jam of our own making. Just like she did in the past, she will continue to build her ecosystems very slowly, based on her geologic calendar, not the plutocrat's end-of-fiscal-year calendar or *sapiens 1.5*'s business cycle. If we are to survive as a species, we have to learn to mimic Mother Nature's behavior and understand that her evolution happens over millennia. Through her feedback loops and her autopoiesis, an old form of cognition will be reborn. It is the global brain that includes the Cambrian intelligence that existed over five hundred million years ago. It is the cell-membrane awareness that made evolution possible. It is the *natural intelligence* with unparalleled resilience—absent the human ego and its prejudices—that will allow her to regenerate.

Regardless of what she has to work with, Mother Nature will continue to create billions upon billions of small-scale networks that will form bigger and bigger ecosystems in which she will nest her new communities, which may not include us. Each of these communities, from the smallest to the largest, will form the most resilient holonic structure—one that *human intelligence* alone cannot create. This is how *natural intelligence* nurtures an ecosystem of healthy interdependence wherein the whole is much larger than the sum of its parts. As the *Great Obsolescence* has proven, the absence of holonic resilience that allows local ecosystems to thrive results in an unhealthy form of interdependence—one that spreads failure and toxicity throughout its structure in a much faster and more systemic way, exposing the fragility and the unsustainable nature of the most sophisticated human-built networks.

From Digital Knowledge to Human Wisdom

One of the Gaiametry fractals that must be examined in our movement from *First-* to *Second-sapiens* stages is the use of technology as a catalyst to propel our intelligence into the Anthropocene epoch. The large language models that first appeared in the fall of 2022 have dominated the debate over the future of AI and its purpose in our lives. Technology solutionists today believe that the refinement of these innovations will help us revolutionize that future. However, those who have a planetary-systems view of the future remain skeptical about how much digital technologies in their current form and content can contribute to stabilizing a world defined by mega-scale systems and exponential change. Nothing explains the binary nature of *First sapiens* better than the digital universe it has created. Information, which is the bloodline of the digital age in its elemental form, is binary. Computers store and process data using bits and bytes that can only be in two states: 0 or 1. The binary system has no innate intelligence; it merely allows for efficient manipulation and transmission of information that makes all digital devices from smartphones to supercomputers operate the way they do. Algorithms that run the world—from the largest supply chain spanning the globe to the world's biggest financial trading platforms handling billions of dollars' worth of transactions a day—are all encoded using binary sequences.

The digital age that has disrupted so much of our lives, for better or for worse, is fundamentally built on binary information storage and processing. It is the different combinatorials and iterations, the creative sequential and algorithmic programming, that give us the rich complexity of the world and its ever-expanding technology ecosystem as we know and experience it today. But what happens when the most advanced form of AI perceives patterns or objects that are nonexistent and altogether inaccurate? What happens when the computer models designed to help navigate the Anthropocene must do so with insufficient data from the higher-complexity science that is proprietary to that stage of development? Why do computer models still fail accurately to predict the annual rate of the rise of global temperature and of ecological collapse and how quickly polar ice is melting?

Based on past experience, there is little doubt that we can work out the bugs in the current systems of knowledge. We will find AI-based cures for all types of diseases by expediting the processing of genomic data and creating tailored treatment plans unique to each individual. But how do we know what the bugs *are* in a system in which its data is of a completely different order and remains emergent, changing unpredictably in real time? It took scientists over twenty years to map out the human genome, which makes it possible for AI to mine that data in a fraction of the time it took researchers to uncover it. What Earth-systems knowledge base can programmers use to establish reliable patterns that AI can mine so we can predict our future within reason? Unlike the current ways AI gathers data, will programmers be able to train their models to gather data from the future—data that doesn't yet exist? AI could not create those tailored treatments derived from the genomic knowledge base if it weren't for the extraordinary worldwide commitment to fund and support the Human Genome Project for over two decades. Similarly, AI's role in helping us resolve problems in the Anthropocene epoch must be proceeded by investments and long-term commitments intended to quantify the nature of Anthropogenic sciences.

Much of this new science is yet to be uncovered, and, due to its complex and highly interdisciplinary and collaborative nature, patterns of its emergence remain greatly unpredictable. This becomes a challenge to computer programmers attempting to train their data models to follow identifiable patterns when the science that creates patterns has remained beyond quantification and far beyond the linear and binary grasp of *First-sapiens* intelligence. Due to what remains unknown in the Anthropocene, would computers hallucinate answers the way ChatGPT and other AI generative models do today, and would such hallucinations create more chaos and misinformation that would derail the upward progress we've made in moving the needle on the Anthropocene life cycle? If we acknowledge this as our new reality, then the question for technology solutionists becomes, How can we build predictive training models in the form of machine learning that help address Anthropocene issues from a knowledge base that has been greatly shaped, defined, and constrained by the deficient motivations of the *First sapiens*?

I found two possible answers to that question in the work of two individuals who are not technology solutionists but think in systems. The first is historian and philosopher Yuval Noah Harari, who declared an end to human history shortly after we witnessed the dawn of large language models and generative AI. Harari was quick to qualify what he meant by the end of human history based on his own perception of the evolutionary stages of *Homo sapiens*. In his 2017 book, *Homo Deus: A Brief History of Tomorrow*, Harari argues that we have sidelined deo-centrism, the worship of an outer god, in favor of homo-centrism, the worship of ourselves, and that the next stage of evolution would sideline homo-centrism in favor of data-centrism.[4]

In interviews and lectures he has given since the release of the different large language models, Harari defends his views on the end of human history by claiming that the operating system of human culture is language. It is from language that we have created human narratives such as myth, law, art, and science, and these are the things that build civilizations. By gaining mastery of language, Harari believes that AI has acquired the master code to human civilization. In some sense, this development could represent what has long been feared and debated: a concept known as the technological singularity in which machine intelligence surpasses human intelligence and forever changes the trajectory of our future.

Unlike past narratives depicted in science-fiction movies, large language models are not violent machines that subjugate human civilization through blood and gore. Rather, they do it through soft skills that affect the mind. They do it by telling alternative stories generated by their algorithms that first and foremost seek to maximize profits and valuations for the companies that create them. The end of human history based on this data-centric narrative is far more dystopian than science fiction can imagine. It will be brought about by us, disintegrating from within. Generative AI, like its younger kin, social media, will continue to exploit our weaknesses, our biases, and our addictions. It will continue to assemble language that vastly expands our social and political polarization, undermines our mental health, and unravels our democracies. Without wise regulatory structures that see through the mirage of technology and learn how to transcend and use it wisely, human history could end the way Harari defines it.

In the Gravesian model, however, a humanity that is data-centric, in a free-market economy that monetizes data, is nothing more than an extension of the *sapiens 1.5* ethos operating without government supervision. Before large language models, language spoke to different people and different cultures at all eight stages of development. We fought against the dark forces of the unhealthy side of these stages to unshackle ourselves and move up to higher levels of psychological freedom. This is the nature of the evolutionary process that enables the never-ending quest to continue. It does not signify the end of human history; it is the transcendence of *First sapiens*, more specifically, the *Sapiens 1.5* stage in its unhealthy expression. In order to navigate such transcendence successfully, there needs to be a presence of a wise regulator in the *sapiens 2.1* brain syndicate. The ideal candidates for this crucial transition will be those who see the simplicity beyond the algorithmic complexity. Tristan Harris and Aza

Raskin, the cofounders of the Center for Humane Technologies, along with the 1,100 technologists who in March 2023 asked our government to place a moratorium on AI development, will be ideal candidates that fill the technology regulation part of that *sapiens 2.1* brain syndicate. Becoming part of that complex adaptive system can transform the end of human history into informational units that serve the Anthropocene.

Harari's narrative on the evolutionary sequence of *Homo sapiens* led me to search Graves's work for his views on technology and the role it plays in our psychosocial, evolutionary process. That is where I found the second answer to my question of how we can build predictive training models in the form of machine learning from a knowledge base constrained by the deficiencies of the *First sapiens.* Unlike Harari, Graves was very cautious in predicting the precise details of our future, especially when that future entails our ascendence into *Second-sapiens* intelligence known for its exponentially higher degrees of neurological and psychological activation. However, based on his *general thema* for the A^1–N^1 stage—the survival of all life on the planet—he was able to fashion a narrative that in hindsight seems to be prophetic. Graves believed that human values and beliefs from that stage forth will represent a reversal of first-tier values, the only exception being technology, which will be a quantitative extension of the first tier.[5]

In examining how his hypothesis has withstood the test of time, one might think that advancements in artificial intelligence and machine learning that were beyond Graves's grasp at the time would have rendered his thinking obsolete, but that may not be the case. As complex as the digital world is today, with all its complicated iterations and the various creative programming that gives it form, the best it can do is mine knowledge of our human experience that is part of our present and our past. Even with its predictive powers, it cannot give us a reliable, nonlinear representation of the future, especially if that future represents a partial reversal of the past and is defined by an exponentially higher level of psychosocial intelligence that is nested in *natural intelligence.*

Generative AI and other forms of machine learning will continue to expand our intellectual rigor and raise our cognitive intelligence. They will even help us articulate some *Second-sapiens* concepts, but these improvements are quantitative and will come at a high cost; that is, the more machine learning we rely on, the more we will lose our uniquely human qualities. Virtues such as emotional and spiritual intelligence become diluted in an ecosystem designed for a data-centric society. We are becoming less and less equipped to handle uniquely human problems at a time when we most need to do so. Ultimately, when the time comes to transcend the ideology of data-centrism, we will realize that the idea of technological singularity in which machine intelligence surpasses human intelligence is a fallacy and that AI will reveal to us what *Homo sapiens* is by revealing the things it cannot do. The more our Anthropogenic reality comes into focus, the more it will become necessary for us to reverse the corrosive aspects of our present and past and create new ways of being and thinking. The intelligence that defines those virtues is just beginning to emerge and will eventually serve as the new reservoir of knowledge in which machine intelligence is recognized for what it is—a utility subordinate to the human wisdom that helps all life forms on the planet survive and thrive.

The Return to Gaian Intelligence

As I have emphasized, if our species is to survive through the Anthropocene epoch and possibly through a sixth mass extinction, we must nest *human intelligence* in *natural intelligence* and fully embrace Mother Nature in all her complexity. This is quite a departure from the type of leadership defined by patriarchal values that has dominated modern human expression as it evolved over the centuries from within the Judeo–Christian traditions. When the Abrahamic religions declared Adam the first man of the human species, they tipped Earth's balance away from the ecological order that had made life possible for over 3.5 billion years. A new moral authority was asserted, giving men privileges over women that caused exploitation and oppression. Forgotten was the truth that the feminine and the masculine are the two sides of the same coin—the two primal energies of the yin and yang—that determine the totally of life in balance. Both psychology and ancient mythology have distinguished between these energies in terms of two fundamental dimensions, attributing agency to the masculine and communion to the feminine. *Agency* pertains to traits such as self-assertion, independence, competence, decisiveness, and other qualities geared toward goal achievement and task functionality; whereas *communion*, having to do with the maintenance of relationships and social functioning, pertains to traits such as benevolence, trustworthiness, and morality. During the Enlightenment, the domination of the masculine through modern science, philosophy, and politics is what has eventually brought us to the brink of extinction today. This is when agentic chaos must end and communal healing begin. From now on, agency must come home to its origins. It must again be nested in the principles of compassion, love, and cooperation and in the creativity and abundance that define the Mother archetype.

There is no better depiction of the feminine aspect of existence than the one Jung made about the Mother archetype that is present in the collective unconscious of all humans, and there is no better story that captures the epochal change we're going through than the origins story of Gaia. According to ancient Greek myth, Gaia is the ancestral mother of all life, the personification of the Earth, and the first goddess to have existed. She was born from Chaos, the mythological void state that preceded the creation of the universe. Of all the gods and goddesses revered in ancient Greece, none held as much influence as the great mother goddess herself. Many world traditions give the title "mother goddess" to their most celebrated deities revered as the embodiment of the Earth's bounty and the source of creation, fertility, and motherhood. But just as the first mother goddess emerged as a primordial form of order out of chaos, she must now return to restore us from the chaos of our own making, the one born out of our misuse of knowledge and technology given to us by another god, Prometheus, the god of fire. The chaos from which we must be delivered today is the one left in the wake of reductionism, mastered and spread by *sapiens 1.5* and a capitalist system that has sought to monetize everything in sight and has ignored the greater ecology in which all life is nested. On the other side of that chaos is where we find the emerging order of the *Second sapiens*, defined by the new *general thema* that seeks the survival and eventual flourishment of all life on the planet and embraces the virtues of Gaiametry as the full, systemic, ecological, interconnected, and interdependent measure of our new reality.

Predicting *Second Sapiens's* Capacities for Success

When it comes to planetary systems, holonic resilience must be present at all fractal levels, from the smallest cellular organism to the largest—Gaia herself. As the urgency for action grows, it becomes more important now to focus on the largest fractal first, the one that contains all of Earth's systems and nests all the lower fractals into its *fixed rules* and *general thema.* While Anthropogenic awareness continues to grow, much of what we have seen in the form of solutions has fallen short of being implemented at the highest levels. This is apparent in our failure to mitigate climate change by enacting needed measures such as the one with which most people are familiar: curbing carbon emissions in order to keep global temperature from rising over 2°C. Gaia, through her feedback loops, is increasingly showing us that she has started to evict us and a million other species from her home, but those who hold power at the highest levels, from politicians to corporate leaders, don't seem fully to understand the urgency for mitigating action. The summer of 2023 broke new records for atmospheric temperatures, ocean-water temperature, floods, and fires in most parts of the world.[6] On July 25 of that year, ocean temperature near Manatee Bay in South Florida reached 101°F, triggering alarm bells among scientists and activists who warned of the dangerous effects such heat will have on marine life and the irreversible damage it will cause to many of the ocean's ecosystems. A day later, the planet's crier, the UN secretary general, took to the airwaves and proclaimed, "The era of global warming has ended, and the era of global boiling has arrived."[7]

> *Never underestimate the power of a few committed people to change the world. Indeed, it is the only thing that ever has.*
>
> —Margaret Mead[8]

Could it be that we are in the time when the failure of some of Earth's regulatory mechanisms has entered an advanced stage and change has become exponentially more frequent and difficult to predict? Could those changes have already cascaded into other areas so that the failure becomes planetwide and systemic? Will we look back at the summer of 2023 in a few years and describe it as tame in comparison? Is it too late for us to use a different approach to examine why the needed solutions don't get implemented? Are there ways for us to know ahead of time if *Second-sapiens* intelligence will translate into *Second-sapiens*, planet-wide action? Do we wrongfully project our success in saving a small local ecosystem as a model that can be used to address all of Gaia's systems? Does Margaret Mead's above inspiring quote still work in our post-Holocene reality, or has the power to change the world moved to the hands of those few who simply don't have the capacity or the incentive to undertake this type of change?

In my work with Don Beck at the Center for Human Emergence Middle East, we often answered questions of systems failure with another question: Does the framework have CAPI, the Coalescence of Authority, Power, and Influence? The answer to that question often provides the needed insights into why implementations of recommended corrective measures fail to become part of a lasting solution and what needs to be done in order to design a more resilient framework. The CAPI concept was envisioned by Dr. Ichak Adizes in his work on corporate life cycles. He is the founder of the Adizes Graduate School in Santa Barbara, one of the very first graduate programs in the world to incorporate the Spiral-Dynamics framework into its curriculum. It is also the place where Dr. Beck and I taught Spiral Dynamics and transformational leadership for over a decade. CAPI was incorporated by the different Centers for Human Emergence around the world and became a macro-scale model used in our work in geopolitics and other macro-scale systems, making its applicability possible in different holonic structures. Dr. Adizes proclaims that in order to implement decisions that effectively solve problems, decision makers need a source for managerial energy, and that is where authority, power and influence reside.[9]

Authority

Authority is defined as the right to make decisions and to say yes or no to change.[10] It is an express formal right inherent in a person's job title, whether it is as the CEO of a small organization, the president of the most powerful country in the world, or, in the case of the United Nations, its secretary general representing the global community of nations. When people in positions of authority say no to change more often than they say yes, their organization becomes increasingly more bureaucratic and loses its ability to react to changes occurring in its environment.

But what happens to the yes–no dynamic when change in the environment points to the need to implement change of epochal proportions the likes of which *Homo sapiens* have not encountered before? To say yes to such change requires an unprecedented degree of courage, extraordinary levels of sacrifice, and an unparalleled level of collaboration. Moreover, it must all be implemented simultaneously across all top leadership structures in all institutions that hold the authority to say yes on the matter all around the world. People in a position of authority don't necessarily have to say no. That response is implied in their choice to maintain the status quo. It is also implied when they adopt a translational, *First-sapiens* response to a situation requiring transformational and structural change. Even if we can climb this steep mountain and solicit the necessary yes, securing the authority aspect of CAPI is not enough to implement change successfully.

Power

Power is the second source of managerial energy in the equation. Simply put, power in the CAPI model is defined as the ability to punish or reward. If the implementation of change requires the cooperation of a certain group or individual, and they withhold their cooperation, they have power.[11] The degree of power a person or group holds is directly proportionate to how much their cooperation is needed. If that power is monopolistic, as it seems to be with many of the world's corporations that rely on the continuity of a carbon-based economy for their livelihood, then the power they wield becomes the primary reason for the failure of implementing effective climate measures. In the United States—the world's second largest emitter of carbon—those who hold power in the private sector exercise tremendous influence over those who hold authority in government. The former rewards those who deny the existence of climate change and empowers them to endorse a carbon-based economy. They also punish those who know the truth about climate change and in the process say no to the truth sayers' power and authority.

It is difficult to know who in the private sector withholds power on addressing climate issues since most of these decisions are made by the highly manipulative *sapiens 1.5* in secret boardroom meetings and are often masked through long-term campaigns of climate denialism and political lobbying. In the US Congress, however, those who withhold power on legislative issues concerning the climate are known in the way they vote. Saying no to enacting laws that mitigate climate change becomes a lethal weapon that forces the sponsors of the law into compromises that greatly alter its initial intent. As an example, the 2022 Inflation Reduction Act passed by Congress authorized a record $369 billion in funding for clean-energy projects. But in order for the bill to become law, lawmakers who hold the power to say no had to be offered guarantees for new oil and gas leases, and any language addressing emission reductions had to be excluded from the bill.[12]

Influence

The last part of the CAPI model, influence, is defined as a person's or a group's ability to cause others to act without having to invoke authority or power.[13] Influence resides in people who have independently recognized the validity of the decision that needs to be implemented. They are generally the resilient ones who represent the self-organizing aspects of a complex system. They are the dynamic, nonbureaucratic part of CAPI and are informed by changes in the environment. They have not been coerced by any other forces to think otherwise. When it comes to climate change, they are the IPCC scientists and the systems thinkers who were sounding the alarm on changes in Earth's systems as early as the 1970s. They represent the inner collective in that new higher-order system that has now influenced wider circles of influencers made up of climate activists and the increasing number of nations, groups, and people around the world who are convinced that the collapse of Earth's systems is real and continues to get worse.

In short, when it comes to addressing climate change, those who are telling the truth about it—the ones who hold the *influence* part of CAPI—cannot alone affect change, regardless of how ubiquitous their wider circle of influence becomes. In order to be effective, those who hold *authority* must be moved into a nonbureaucratic, open state to begin to see the existential change taking place in their environment. They need to be shown that, in being passive and saying no, they are effectively saying yes to disasters from which they will not be immune. In addition, those who hold *power* need to move from a stance of withholding cooperation to a state of granting it. They need to be shown that their power to withhold cooperation is in itself the empowerment of their own demise. When not all three aspects—authority, power, and influence—are present, we must search for the lower fractal in which they *are* present. That is where those who hold influence can begin to affect larger fractals. Often climate-related CAPI is present only at the lower-community and some national levels. When it comes to applying it as a measure of effectiveness at the planetary scale, and although the influence aspect seems to be present, we seem to be missing much of the authority and the power aspects, and without them a successful solution for climate change cannot coalesce.

My work with Don Beck, my wife, Elza, and a number of other Gravesian practitioners in the Middle East between 2000 and 2010 provides a real-life example of how we can foster CAPI. One of the first questions we asked when we started our work in Israel and the West Bank was, Where does CAPI exist, and what do we need to do to bring it up

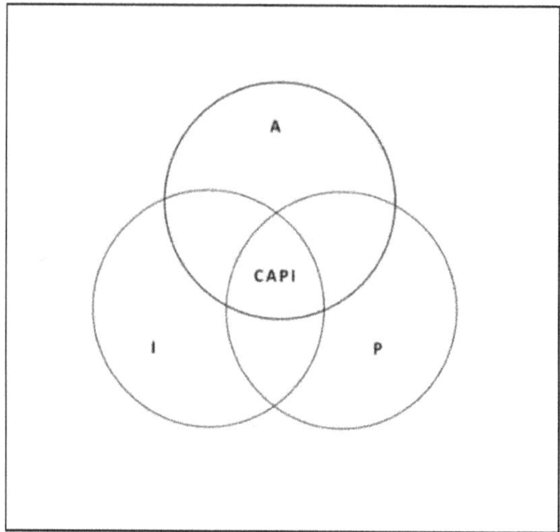

Figure 8.1. The Adizes CAPI Model: A depiction of the Coalescence of Authority, Power, and Influence. From Ichak Adizes, *Managing Corporate Life Cycles*, 265. Used by permission.

to a level at which our mission for achieving peace is possible? The initial answer was that only a very small level of CAPI existed among a few activists on both the Israeli and the Palestinian sides. Both groups were familiar with Dr. Beck's work in South Africa and understood how different the Gravesian/Spiral-Dynamics approach to peace was. Compared to traditional approaches that viewed peace through treaties and bilateral agreements, ours was the only one that viewed it from a perspective of psychosocial-cultural development. First and foremost, we examined each culture's dominant stages of development and worked on leveling the developmental asymmetries that existed between the two cultures as a way to pave the road to peace. In light of how different our approach was, the answer to our question placed our starting point at the grassroots levels, where we embarked on research, education, and activism that grew concentrically over the years, reaching tipping points and attracting larger and larger stakeholders who held larger representations of CAPI on both sides of the peace equation.

Based on our research findings into each culture's stages of development, our efforts turned to addressing the institutional asymmetries that existed between the two sides: Israeli culture was firmly present in *sapiens 1.4*, *1.5*, and *1.6* virtues, while Palestinian culture was struggling to adopt *sapiens 1.4* institutions. The content of these stages on each side was also a factor in determining how much CAPI we held. The content on the Israeli side was mostly influenced by Western values, while the Palestinian side was influenced mostly by Arab values. Our initiative became known as the Build Palestine Initiative, and, by 2008, it had attracted the attention of the top ranks in the Fatah organization, the Israeli Knesset, and the office of Prime Minister Ehud Olmert. Many of these officials were invited to our Nation Building Conference in 2008 in Bethlehem, where over seven hundred community leaders from every corner of the West Bank gathered to share insights on what it takes to build a prosperous and peaceful nation.[14]

Unfortunately, our work could not continue in the long term as our NGO funding sources that allowed for research, staffing, and training began to dwindle after the 2008 financial crisis. The experience, however, still serves as a template for how to expand the reach of CAPI and how to identify sources of vulnerability through the model. The diagram below depicts the holonic structure for the CAPI model that can be used to gauge success from the smallest holon, the grassroots levels, all the way

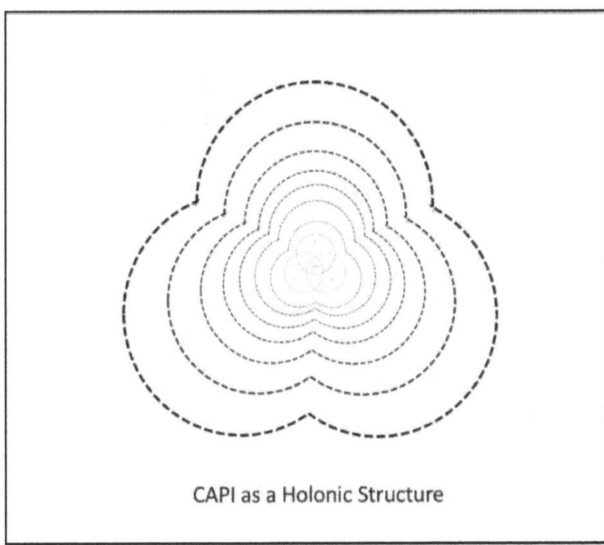

Figure 8.2. The Coalescence of Authority, Power, and Influence (CAPI) as a holonic structure. The model can provide solutions at every level, from individual to global. Used with permission from the Center for Human Emergence Middle East; http://www.humanemergencemiddleeast.org/.

up to the macro systems that define geopolitics and global economics and then the mega systems, the different Earth systems that define Gaia. When designing solutions, asking the simple question of whether or not CAPI exists can save a person or an organization tremendous amounts of energy, time, and resources.

CAPI is yet another tool that makes the post-Holocene Gravesian model more resilient. It adds a new dimension that enables the *sapiens 2.1* brain syndicate to determine which structures at which level in the lower six stages of development are preventing change from taking place and then focuses that specialized part of the brain syndicate on resolving that issue so that forward movement becomes possible. Regarding climate change, an assessment of where authority and power are withheld points to *sapiens 1.4*, *sapiens 1.5*, and *sapiens 1.6* institutions and organizations that are in an arrested or closed state. Even if they *appear* to be in an open state, they continue to believe exclusively in Promethean intelligence, while our new Anthropogenic reality requires a structural shift in the basic way we think. This new reality places Graves's entire earlier model into that Orwellian societal complex with its CAPI highly diminished due to it being nested in *First-sapiens* consciousness that engages only in incremental change instead of systemic transformation. Now, CAPI itself must become nested in *natural intelligence* in which its operation becomes an automatic part of Gaia's autopoiesis, albeit guided as well by *human intelligence* that has transcended *First-sapiens* deficiencies. It is this fundamental shift in thinking that will allow the *Second sapiens* to act on behalf of Gaia to ensure that all life can continue.

Prometheus in Treatment

The expansion of our psychosocial capacities beyond human concerns—or the nesting of Promethean intelligence in Gaian intelligence—is one of the most crucial changes that must take place in the new Anthropocene epoch. Our ability to develop empathy and care for Gaia's other creatures and for her different Earth systems is a critical development that will help us get through many existential issues. This ability will be a permanent part of the bio-psycho-socio-ecological awareness of *sapiens 2.2*, which will come after *sapiens 2.1* has endured the journey through the collective darkness and has put in motion the initial steps to stabilize the world. That stabilization will be the foundation for a new branch of psychology that harkens back to the days before *sapiens 1.5* separated himself from nature and became *homo colossus*, eating and drinking from the Earth at rates more than two-hundred times his earlier predecessor, *sapiens 1.2*.

When viewed from Graves's six-upon-six hypothesis, *sapiens 2.2* is a repeat of *sapiens 1.2*, a stage of development in which all the world's tribal communities identified with what is known today as "indigenous intelligence." The only significant difference is that, today, the tribal formations are interconnected and global in nature. They take the form of ecologically aligned, global villages that nest the healthy expressions of Promethean intelligence in Gaia's intelligence and her feedback loops to create human-built environments that are functional and in harmony with nature. Considering the consequences of our actions for seven generations into the future, as most Native American tribes do, is just one small measure of this new psychosocial state. Once the need to maximize efficiency and profitability—along with other man-made metrics—are transcended, we open ourselves to the much-larger metrics of beginning Gaia's restorative actions that are measured in eras and epochs. The psychological dimension of this transformation is an elemental fractal in the Gaiametry framework called *ecopsychology*.

Like so many other fractals in the framework, ecopsychology is an interdisciplinary and transdisciplinary field that combines ecology and psychology for the purpose of meeting Gaia's mandates for the Anthropocene epoch. Most simply, ecopsychology is the mere recognition that *human intelligence* is part of Gaian intelligence and not a phenomenon separate from her. It comprises a return to the psychology of a pre-reductive world with the full benefit of hindsight that recognizes nature in her fullest and the present danger to her different Earth systems. Its central goals are to heal humanity's alienation from the natural environment and to examine and transform the modes of thinking and behaving that have led to the imperilment of ecosystems globally.[15]

Interestingly, many of the communities and nations around the globe that have managed to bypass the corrosive effects of the *sapiens 1.5* stage have never stopped relying on this integral connection to nature. In indigenous communities worldwide, from Australia and Africa to the Americas, this view of wholeness remains unbroken. Ecopsychology recognizes that the well-being of humans and the natural world are inextricably connected and that our need to heal the human–nature divide is more important now than it ever was. The field focuses on building pathways that newly recognize the ecosystems in which *Homo sapiens's* relationship with nature and with other animals is nested. It aims to open up the psychological space needed for the restoration of habitats and the creation of built and natural environments that follow nature's mandates for long-term sustainability.

One of the earliest twentieth-century references to this dance between the individual and the environment appeared in Freud's 1929 book, *Civilization and Its Discontents.* In it, Freud recognizes the interconnection between the internal world of the mind and the external world of the environment. His most relevant quote from it was cited earlier but is worth repeating here as it is one of the foundation stones of modern psychology that brought forth the field of ecopsychology: Freud viewed the mind and the ego as being the "shrunken residue" of the all-embracing environment in which it lies and asserted that the intimate interplay between the two must not be severed. This observation has since been made in many interdisciplinary studies and has attracted philosophers, anthropologists, biologists, and science writers. One of those writers is the academic Theodore Roszak, who coined the term *ecopsychology* in his 1992 book, *The Voice of the Earth.* In it, Roszak invokes the biophilia hypothesis made by E. O. Wilson, a biologist credited for pioneering the field of sociobiology. The basic premise of the hypothesis is that, as a product of biological evolution, humans possess an innate tendency to seek connection with nature and an urge to affiliate with other forms of life.[16]

Whether it is Roszak's current writings or those of his many collaborators and colleagues in this new and emerging field, the focus seems to be mostly on how to free psychological health from the tight grip of the modern, *sapiens 1.5* mind so that it can focus on the far greater issues of the environment. This uphill, mental-health battle is made evident by the 2016 listings of the American Psychiatric Association in its Diagnostic and Statistical Manual (DSM), which cites more than three hundred recognized mental diseases but contains only one listing remotely connected to nature: seasonal affective disorder, characterized by depressive mood swings occasioned by seasonal changes.[17] Like all other Gaiametry attractors, ecopsychology is a science of a much higher order than the *sapiens 1.5* sciences through which much of our worldview is still defined. Recently, the American Psychological Association has begun to develop strategies for therapists to help mitigate climate change and promote adaptation to its effects. However, as of March 2022 the American Psychiatric Association had not added climate anxiety and other climate-related mental health issues to the DSM, stating that their symptoms are not yet known.[18]

Psychotherapists have exhaustively analyzed every form of dysfunction resulting from us living in a *sapiens 1.5* fashion, from family matters, marriage, work, school, social relations, and everything that comes with an urban industrial lifestyle. But they have ignored much of what lies outside our conscious awareness when it comes to the issue of planetary degradation. That may be due to the enormity of the problem or perhaps because the apocalyptic scenarios our minds envision are too frightening to think about. But whether or not we classify climate anxiety as a mental disorder, nature's Earth systems continue to collapse. This and other existential issues brought forth by the *Great Obsolescence* are now the petrifying eight-hundred-pound gorilla in the room—a beast that we're seeing for the first time. Our new reality—with or without the help of the mental-health professionals—requires us to befriend that gorilla, to learn to live with it and respect its fury for the remainder of our existence. The challenge we face is, How do we do that? How do we bring awareness to the single most important threat to our planet? The answer might come from a shift in how we label these existential threats.

In a March 2019 article in the peer-reviewed quarterly journal *Ecopsychology*, integral psychologist Zhiwa Woodbury put forth the idea that the field of mental health needs a new taxonomy, which he called *traumatology*.[19] He argues that climate change is a quickening trauma that triggers all our other traumas, but it's yet to be acknowledged. In researching other forms of trauma, I found Woodbury's argument compelling. Classifying climate change as climate trauma brings it into the holonic formation that has the *general thema* of trauma that transcends and includes all earlier forms of it: personal, generational, and cultural, all seemingly holonic in nature. Also, the argument brings the issue front and center and expedites the process in which it becomes part of our conscious awareness. And it illustrates how all mental-health issues we dealt with in the Holocene era must now be nested in the greater ecosystem of mental-health challenges in the Anthropocene, requiring interdisciplinary collaboration with other fields to make up the totality of the Gaiametry framework.

In asking whether the new field of ecopsychology has enough CAPI to change the trajectory of how we view and treat our planet, the answer might lie in how quickly we learn to befriend the eight-hundred-pound gorilla in the room. Institutions and leaders who use the field of psychology today to influence outcomes are not necessarily focused on existential planetary issues. They do, however, adhere to CAPI principles but at a much lower fractal, using it to promote the status quo. The branch of psychology that holds power and influence today is behavioral psychology. The field has become ubiquitous, from thinktanks in geopolitics that attempt to gauge the behavior of certain world leaders to the biggest financial powerhouses that use behavioral economics to gauge consumer behavior. The authority aspect of CAPI seems to rest with the two APAs: the American Psychological Association, which seems to be in its early stages of identifying the symptoms of climate trauma; and the American Psychiatric Association, which believes those symptoms remain unknown. It seems that Prometheus will be seated on the therapist's couch for a long time.

From Democracy to Gaiacracy

Gaia cannot speak for herself in a system of laws created by *Homo sapiens* for *Homo sapiens*, but she is capable of speaking in far more powerful ways. Through her *natural intelligence* and feedback loops she can show us the consequences of our actions in devastating clarity. Since she operates on a time scale of eras and epochs, the causation may not appear in time for the human mind fully to comprehend it. But what happens when our collective actions over many centuries reach a tipping point in several of her largest fractals, the Earth systems that point to imminent collapse? What happens when those large feedback loops tell us we must change our ways, and we simply rationalize that information through the narrow and deficient psychology of the *First sapiens*, the one that engages in endless incremental translations of reality that shield and preserve the status quo? What happens when the whole world becomes a marketplace steeped in the capitalist virtues of *sapiens 1.5* that sees Earth's resources—including its air, oceans, lakes, rivers, and natural waterways—as matters of property rights that can be owned, exploited, and manipulated? What happens when social democracy, or *market* democracy, continues to focus on the lives and rights of its constituents to the detriment of Mother Nature's ecology? What happens when the system of laws created by the *First sapiens* no longer ensures the survival of the ecosystems that guarantee life itself?

The answer to all these questions requires us to see Earth from outer space as the blue marble without her artificially drawn borders and market mechanisms. It is Earth without plutocrats and billionaires and without a political system that rubber stamps and encourages their insatiable behavior while hiding behind the virtues of modern development, employment goals, and the endless array of prevailing econometrics. From this vantage point of space, the systems that appear beyond politics and the rule of law are the self-regulating, complex systems that involve the biosphere, the atmosphere, the hydrosphere, and the pedosphere. These systems are what human rule needs to be nested in—the rule by Gaia, or what I call *Gaiacracy*. The framework I'm proposing allows democracy to survive and thrive as a form of rule embedded in the greater rule of Mother Nature. It is driven not by any political ideology or party affiliation but by the greater awareness that *Homo sapiens* should never again go on another insatiable binge causing infractions in the greater governing systems. Just as we recognize our rights to life, liberty, and the pursuit of happiness as inalienable, universal, and nontransferable, we must recognize that these rights are made possible only when Earth's systems are in a state of homeostasis that ensures all life. This is how Gaia's rights become inalienable and must remain so through time. What we must recognize is that her self-regulating systems are now entering or surpassing certain tipping points in their life cycles wherein a new homeostasis may exclude much of human civilization and the millions of species that has made self-regulation on a planetary scale possible.

Earth-Systems Governance

Gaiacracy is a new self-organizing form of global governance that follows the rules of complex systems and holonic structures. Its *general thema* focuses on assuring the preservation of all life. When it comes to complex life systems, fractal formations in nature cannot be rushed. As a result, we might not be able to tell if our Anthropogenic efforts to save the planet will succeed, even if reaching CAPI at the highest fractal levels is possible. However, this form of consciousness is on the rise, and it is attracting *sapiens 2.1* intelligence in all forms of disciplines and in different geographies of the world in a natural, emergent way. It is seen as part of an integrative new paradigm known today as Earth-systems governance, which brings together a variety of disciplines including political science, sociology, economics, ecology, policy studies, geography, sustainability science, and law.[20] This type of global collaboration in so many areas is the quintessential representation of the different stage attractors of the Gaiametry framework that guide the *sapiens 2.1* brain syndicate in laying down the foundation for a new platform for life in the Anthropocene epoch. In 2009, the *sapiens 2.1* brain syndicate that gave birth to Earth-systems governance resulted in the establishment of the Earth Systems Governance Project, consisting of a network of over four hundred experts on the matter, including Nobel laureates, leading policymakers, and the world's most renowned thinkers and experts on global sustainability. In 2011, the group called on world leaders to strengthen Earth-systems governance as a priority for coherent global action. The memorandum was submitted to the high-level panel on global sustainability appointed by the UN secretary general, which informed the 2012 UN Conference on Sustainable Development held in Rio de Janeiro.[21]

Regardless of how pioneering these efforts are and of the transformative potential they hold, the quintessential question that measures their effectiveness must still be asked: Does the framework have CAPI? The answer may not come as a surprise. Had world leaders heeded the advice of the group in 2012, the world would have seen a glimpse of the new, highly collaborative nature of humanity on the other side of the Holocene. It would have given hope to those who believe in the resilience of the human mind and its ability to transcend its *First-sapiens* limitations. But, alas, the most crucial piece of the CAPI puzzle—the political leaders who hold the authority that would have set the planet on a new course—were missing then and are still missing to this day. Without that crucial piece, all *sapiens 2.1* efforts will continue to swim in the toxic ecosystems of the *First sapiens,* unable to achieve meaningful change and leaving us at the mercy of Mother Nature, who has become less merciful toward our species.

Guardians of Nature

On the lower fractals of the Gaiacracy model, many organizations around the world are engaging in grassroots efforts to challenge the supremacy of those who hold power and authority and the institutions through which they embolden their perpetual denial of our Anthropogenic reality. The movement, although at the grassroots level, seems to have taken on the emergent, self-organizing characteristics of a complex system. It attempts to create a system of laws recognizing the rights of nature at the local level that, if successful, will move up the holonic structure and nest power and authority in the highest holon of the Gaiacracy model, making it operational.

One of the first lawsuits ever to be filed on the behalf of Nature in the United States was in Orange County, Florida. In November 2020, with an

89-percent vote margin, Orange County passed an ordinance that recognizes the *rights of nature* for waterways to flow, be protected against pollution, and exist and maintain a healthy ecosystem.[22] The ordinance also allowed for guardians of nature to sue on its behalf. Learning of those plans, lobbyists who hold the power over the state legislature secured the passage of a state law that prohibits local governments from granting any legal rights to a plant, an animal, a body of water, or any other part of a natural environment. The state statute went into effect before Orange County voters adopted the ordinance. On April 26, 2021, Chuck O'Neal, one of the primary advocates of the county's Rights of Nature law, represented by attorney Steve Myers, filed a lawsuit against a housing developer and the Florida Department of Environmental Protection. His aim was to stop the development in the county of nineteen-hundred acres that, if allowed to proceed, would have violated the rights of streams, a wetland marsh, and two lakes.[23] The lawsuit is currently tied up in local courts and has a steep uphill battle ahead of it, but Myers is determine to take the issue all the way to the US Supreme Court.

> *We are on the edge of the Universe here trying to make new law. Today we start a new chapter in this fight going on throughout the world, to recognize that nature must have legal rights and the people must have the legal means to defend her.*
>
> —Steve Myers
> Attorney representing Chuck O'Neal[24]

The idea that nature can sue for its own protection is not new. It was born in the early 1970s after we saw the blue marble of our planet from outer space. That is when law professor Christopher Stone published an article in the *California Law Review* arguing that a legal precedent in recognizing the rights of inanimate objects was established in 1886 when the law recognized the "personhood" of corporations, and thus legal standing should be extended to natural objects as well.[25] Stone called it the legal "Rights of Nature."

Just as with all other ideas that represent the new, higher-order life cycle, Stone's idea was attacked by the antibodies of the current system by everyone from legal scholars and academics to politicians and the lobbyists who hold power over them. The concept of legal standing requires law suits, with plaintiffs to show that they were injured by defendants and a court to provide judgment. Without legal standing, a case is thrown out of court. Since the 1970s, several lawsuits brought under the various Rights of Nature laws in different US localities have succeeded, but their success is not enough to ensure that the millions of threatened ecosystems throughout the country can be protected. In the United States, success at the local municipal or county level does not translate to success at the national level because, in most cases, state or federal laws can trump local laws. As a result, the legal system has fallen short in establishing a national standard, or a constitutional amendment, that makes the Rights of Nature as unalienable as our own rights. The presence of CAPI when it comes to guarding nature's ecosystems seems to break down and becomes more challenging at the nonlocal state and federal levels.

At the global and regional levels, however, other countries have recognized the Rights of Nature at the highest levels of government. Canada, New Zealand, Mexico, India, Columbia, Pakistan, Ecuador, and many other countries, through legislative and judicial decisions and through constitutional amendments, have enshrined Gaia's rights into their legal systems.[26] The question of whether these measures are sufficient to prevent ecological collapse remains unanswerable. While protecting their local ecosystems, most of these countries have fallen short of creating plans to transition into carbon-neutral economies, an essential feat that is monumental and must be global in scale. Meanwhile, global issues such as the increasing amount of carbon dioxide in the atmosphere, polar-ice melt, and rising oceans all affect weather patterns and cause temperature rise that knows no national boundaries and respects no constitution. On the issue of ecosystem governance, CAPI might be present at some national and regional levels, but unless it becomes part of a collaborative, global effort that engages the majority of nations, especially the industrialized ones, efforts to implement Gaiacracy will fall short.

Climate and the Right to Life

As Gaia's feedback loops increase in intensity, so does the urgency to hold those responsible for climate change accountable. On June 12, 2023, the first climate lawsuit in the United States went to trial in Helena, Montana, based on a legal challenge by sixteen young plaintiffs, ranging in age from five to twenty-two, against the state's pro-fossil fuel policies.[27] The plaintiff representing the youth was a legal nonprofit group named Our Children's Trust founded in 2010 by environmental attorney Julia Olson for the purpose of leading a strategic, global campaign on behalf of the world's youth against governments everywhere.[28] The complainants in the case were not acting on the behalf of an inanimate object or of Gaia. They were exercising their own unalienable right to life that will be impacted considerably by climate change and are targeting the fossil-fuels industry for monetary damages. The lawsuit, Held v. Montana, is based on the state's constitutional guarantees to a clean and healthy environment, which were enshrined in the 1970s and which the plaintiffs say the state has violated by supporting the fossil-fuels industry. The legal action was allowed to advance along with many other cases after a recent Supreme-Court decision denied oil companies bids to move the venue of such lawsuits from state courts to federal courts. The decision opened the door for more than two dozen US cities and states to resume their legal actions against big oil, alleging that the fossil-fuel industry had known for decades about the dangers of burning coal, oil, and gas and had actively hidden that information from consumers and investors.

On August 14, 2023, the judge in the case ruled in favor of the youth group, stating that the state's failure to consider climate change when approving fossil-fuel projects was unconstitutional. The ruling means that Montana, a major coal- and gas-producing state that gets one-third of its energy by burning coal, must consider climate change when deciding whether to approve or renew fossil-fuel projects.[29] In response to the ruling, Julia Olson proclaimed the decision to be "a huge win for Montana, for youth, for democracy, and for our climate. More rulings like this will certainly come."[30]

Olson, in the post-Holocene, Gravesian model, represents an indispensable part of the *sapiens 2.1* brain syndicate. Cases such as hers are bringing unprecedented actions against the fossil-fuels industry from every legal angle possible. They allege negligence, product liability, fraud, racketeering, and violation of state consumer-protection statutes, among many other charges. The approach seems to be similar in nature and trajectory to the actions brought against the tobacco industry and can similarly bring the fossil-fuels industry to its knees. It is *sapiens 2.1* intelligence using the existing *sapiens 1.4* infrastructure of law to help Gaia mitigate the damage caused to her different systems. According to researchers, these types of cases have doubled since 2015 and today exceed two thousand in number around the world.[31]

Nonetheless, the question remains: Even if all these actions succeeded, how effective would they be in mitigating climate collapse? The fossil-fuel industry has far deeper pockets than the tobacco industry, and it has poured hundreds of billions into funding a network of fake citizens' groups and bogus scientific entities that continue to claim that the science on global warming remains unsettled. Its financial breadth and depth enable it to drag litigation for decades further than the tobacco industry did.

Should plaintiffs in all such cases emerge victorious in the future and be awarded the financial damages they seek, this alone will not lower emissions or mitigate damage already caused to other Earth systems that have moved past their tipping point. What it *might* do, though, is tip the system in favor of more actions against the fossil-fuel industry as their past deceptive practices become more exposed, opening the floodgates to their financial ruin. In asking whether these recent legal developments hold CAPI at higher fractals, the answer might lie in how effective they will be in forcing the industry to adopt much stricter production and emission standards. To keep global warming under the 2°C may not be possible without significantly lowering global economic output or banning fossil fuels altogether in a short period of time. Sadly, there is no regulatory structure with enforcement mechanisms anywhere in the world today that can accomplish that aim. Even if there were, in a global economy that relies on fossil fuels for over 80 percent of its energy needs, significant reductions will trigger a worldwide economic depression the likes of which modern humanity has not experienced.

It is impossible to explore every Earth-systems issue at every fractal level possible to determine if Gaiacracy can nest democracy in its *natural intelligence.* What is clear, however, is that there is an increasing level of despondency around the world because of the inability of the current political and legal frameworks to address issues of planetary collapse. The current mitigating actions we seem to be taking today might have been effective several decades ago before change in Earth's systems accelerated and reached points of bifurcation. If we had heeded the warning signs from the higher-order systems then, the planet would have likely remained within the bounds of the Holocene, and much of what we have to deal with today could have been averted. But, alas, we are now past that point. Now climate events seem to increase in severity and frequency with every passing day, and the reversal of this trajectory becomes ever harder.

From Monotheism to Deep Ecology

If we are to embrace Mother Nature in all her complexity, we must adopt all the stage-attractor fractals that make up the Gaiametry framework as a full, interdependent, and resilient platform. Nesting democracy in natural intelligence is a beginning step, but without addressing all the other urgent transition topics the shift will not be systemic and will remain susceptible to failure. Gaian intelligence preceded human intelligence by billions of years, and when the latter *did* appear in its A–N *sapiens 1.1* form, it was inseparable from nature. According to Graves's research, *homo naturalis* was a hunter/gatherer who was animistic in behavior and couldn't separate himself from other animals and his environment. The hunting grounds of mountains and valleys belonged to all inhabitants, and they negotiated with one another in an autopoietic, natural way. *Sapiens 1.1* talked to animals, trees, and stones, and out of that web of communication emerged the core of that stage of development with automatic norms that bound humans to animals and plants and to the Earth. A hundred-thousand years afterward, we find ourselves at the cusp of repeating the *sapiens 1.1* experience at the *sapiens 2.1* stage that must bind us again to all living creatures, to the plants, and to the Earth. The only difference today is that we have passed through several additional stages of development that have augmented our arduous journey over the centuries. We have also brought ourselves to where we are today: at the brink of the sixth extinction. Will we be able to transcend all our *First-sapiens* deficiencies and use each stage's healthiest practices to bring us back into the fold of Mother Nature and remain one with her?

Homo Virtus and His God

In examining where in the lower stages *Homo sapiens* began to see him/herself as separate from the environment, the answer is quite clear: after the destructive and bloody rampages of the *sapiens 1.3* stage, the *First sapiens* sought a more virtuous and tempered existence. That was when we emerged into *Homo virtus*, the *sapiens 1.4* stage that sought to bring absolutistic values and beliefs in the One True Way and create ways to maintain obedience to one absolute authority. It included the birth of the Abrahamic religions, the absolute belief in one God. According to the religious scriptures of Judaism, Christianity, and Islam, Abraham was chosen by the only higher authority, God himself, to spread the message of monotheism. Thus, religionists began to argue that Gaia was no longer a parliament of beings but a theocracy ruled by two main characters—man and God. As the first man of the human species, Adam subordinated nature's intelligence to his *own* intelligence and in the process shifted Earth's balance away from the ecological order that had made life possible for billions of years. Monotheism gave rise to the patriarchy and in the process silenced the Mother archetype in which all other archetypes are nested. It became the source of moral authority and gave men privileges over women, making us forget that it is the masculine and the feminine in balance that has defined the primordial aspects of the universe since time immemorial.

Homo prudentus as God

With our emergence into the Enlightenment, *sapiens 1.4* absolutism gave way to *sapiens 1.5* pragmatism and objectivism. The movement up the evolutionary ladder also removed the macro-scale CAPI from the hands of the Church and the dual relationship between man and God to the hands of the scientist as God himself. *Homo prudentus*, through his Enlightened mind, put himself in charge of it all. But instead of reintegrating himself with nature, he completed the task of separating from her. Through the scientific method, he replaced natural complexity with mechanical reductionism. This action enabled him to rationalize his supremacy over natural phenomenon through scientific proof; eventually, he made himself the apex predator, the *Homo colossus* atop a trophic pyramid of his own creation. Reductionism became the primary expression of man as God, the new god who justified the externalization of everything that lay outside the realm of quantification.

The genius of the *sapiens 1.5* stage became the standard by which we measured progress and justified relegating what we deemed unquantifiable and immeasurable as insignificant. Praying to a higher god for good health was replaced by a trip to the pharmacy or the doctor who granted the same thing without the interference of a higher authority. Science alleviated our reliance on tradition, personal experience, and logic. Since it could not reduce to a mechanical model the intrinsic qualities of life such as mystery, spirituality, humility, wonder, and all the other things that make us human, those qualities disappeared from the conscious awareness of the scientific god. Now they are part of the collective shadow of our genius that is appearing to us as fate. In part because that shadow has remained unprocessed, it is now triggering the collapse in the higher-order systems. The deficiencies of these two stages of development—*sapiens 1.4* and *1.5*, which worshipped the Abrahamic God and the scientific god, respectively—is what has sidelined natural phenomenon and allowed for the interpretation of a higher power arbitrarily away from Gaia. This is what the *sapiens 2.1* brain syndicate must transform and attempt to bring back into the fold of *natural intelligence.*

Environmental Philosophy

Following the Holocene era, the monotheist God and the scientific god become nested in *natural intelligence* again. They become part of a far deeper and higher-order system that concerns itself with *Homo sapiens's* place in the natural environment. The question of where we belong in nature has been with us for millennia but became formalized as a branch of philosophy in the last half century. Like so many fields concerned with nonreductive, higher-order systems, it was born in the chaos crucible of the early 1970s. Not surprisingly, those who held CAPI in the existing system described the field as detrimental to economic growth and discounted its relevance as nonscientific, comparing its practices and ethos to archaic and indigenous virtues of the tribalistic *sapiens 1.2* stage that had no place in the modern world. Environmental philosophy attempts to correct humanity's sense of alienation from nature, which has become greater with every stage of development we have gone through. Like all other stage attractors that form the Gaiametry framework, it must work on prying the control of social systems out of the hands of the patriarchy and nesting them in natural systems. Environmental philosophy asks questions such as, What do we mean when we talk about nature, and what is the value of the natural, nonhuman environment to us? How should we respond to environmental challenges such as environmental degradation, pollution, and climate change? How can we best understand the relationship between the natural world and human technology and development? What is our place in the natural world?[32]

In earlier years, the main debate concerned whether nature has intrinsic value in itself or whether its value is merely instrumental to humanity. Others challenged whether there actually *is* such a thing as the wilderness or whether it was merely a creation of the colonial mind.

To frame such debates in broader, Gravesian terms, environmental philosophy asks whether *human intelligence* is superior to *natural intelligence* and whether the approach to solving our existential problems should be eco-centric or humancentric.

While these types of inquiries are essential for our survival in the Anthropocene epoch, the one that takes priority is whether or not nature has its own intrinsic value independent of human values and what we need to do to prevent the *First sapiens's* continued interference with its right to exist. In fact, in recent decades some newer schools of thought have argued again that nature doesn't even exist beyond some self-contradictory and even politically dubious constructions of an ideal that ignores the real effect our human interactions with the environment has on our world. In an article entitled "Environmental Philosophy after the End of Nature," Steven Vogel, philosophy professor at Denison University, says,

> The world we inhabit is always already one transformed by human practices. Environmental questions are social and political ones, to be answered by us and not by nature. Practices are real ... [and] those that acknowledge human responsibility for transforming the world are preferable to those that don't. Environmental harm results when we do not recognize our own responsibility for the world our practices create."[33]

The changes in perspective as Vogel articulates them are described as *postmodern* and *constructivist* and include the most recent term in environmental philosophy: *postnaturalistic.*

Ecofeminism

While heightening the voices of both supporters and descenders, environmental philosophy also gave birth to several branches of inquiry that are becoming essential in helping our transition to the other side of the Holocene era. One of those branches is *ecofeminism.* The term was initially coined in a 1974 book entitled *Feminism or Death* by French author and feminist Francoise d'Eaubonne. According to her views, ecofeminism associates the oppression of all marginalized groups (women, people of color, children, the poor) with the oppression of nature (animals, land, water, air.). She argues that domination, exploitation, and colonization by Western patriarchal societies have directly caused irreversible environmental damage.[34]

Ecofeminism has attracted considerable interest from younger academics and activists in the last few decades as a way to explore connections between women and nature in culture, economics, religion, politics, and literature. They also draw parallels between the oppression of nature and the oppression of women. In a 1993 groundbreaking essay entitled "Ecofeminism: Toward Global Justice and Planetary Health," Greta Gaard and Lori Gruen, both academics and environmental activists, outlined what they called the "ecofeminist framework." Their publication provided a wealth of data and statistics in addition to outlining the theoretical aspects of the ecofeminist critique. The framework is intended to establish a more complex view of our understanding of the world so that we can better recognize how we arrived at where we are now and what we can do better to address our problems. Gaard and Gruen outlined four main pertinent developments in human history congruent with many of the subjects in this book:

- The Newtonian mechanistic, materialistic model of the universe that resulted from the Scientific Revolution and the subsequent reduction of all things to mere resources to be optimized—dead, inert matter to be used.
- The rise of patriarchal religions and their establishment of gender hierarchies along with their denial of immanent divinity.
- The self, its dualistic ontology, and the inherent power and domination ethic it entails.
- Capitalism and its claimed intrinsic need for the exploitation, destruction, and instrumentalization of animals, Earth, and people for the sole purpose of creating wealth.[35]

Gaard and Gruen believe that these four factors, more than any others, have acted as a catalyst to separate nature from culture and are the primary source of our planetary problems today. Other scholars in the field, such as Vandana Shiva and Maria Mies, have challenged the foundation on which modern science is built. They view the dominant stream of modern science not as objective but as a projection of Western men's values that determine what is considered scientific knowledge in a field that is controlled by men and for the most part has been historically restricted to men.[36]

The ecofeminist movement has also given birth to a field of study, called *ecological democracy*, which recognizes what *sapiens 1.5* has ignored and exploited under the traditional guise of democracy. Ecological democracy, based on an informed feminine perspective, uses its understanding of the unjustified domination of women, animals, and nature to reconceive notions of democratic governance, citizenship, and free speech; it recognizes that we all live in both cultural and ecological communities full of socially diverse relationships among people and places, society and nature.[37] The framework expands the definition of what it is to be a citizen living in a democracy to what it is to be an ecological citizen who exercises civic virtues that foster the health of all humans and the planet.

Social Ecology

Another branch of environmental philosophy that has grown in popularity since the 1970s is social ecology. It presents ecological problems as arising mainly from social problems, in particular from different forms of hierarchy and domination, and seeks to resolve them through the model of a society adapted to human development and the biosphere. Like so many of the Gaiametry fractals, it is a holonic framework that is interdisciplinary in nature and draws on philosophy, politics, social theory, anthropology, history, economics, the natural sciences, and feminism. Social ecology advocates a reconstructive approach to social and environmental issues and promotes a direct democratic and confederal form of politics that is decentralized. As a body of ideas, social ecology envisions a moral economy that moves beyond scarcity and hierarchy toward a world that brings human intelligence back into the natural world while promoting diversity, creativity, and freedom. Humanity, in this line of thought, represents evolution's latest iteration in the long history of organic development on Earth.

The field has been influenced by the work of political philosopher and social theorist Murray Bookchin. He presents it as a utopian philosophy of human evolution that combines the nature of biology and society into a third "thinking nature" beyond biochemistry and physiology, which he argues is a more complete, conscious, ethical, and rational nature.[38] His theory emerged at a time when ecological thought, and even ecological and environmental sciences, were widely viewed as subversive. When subsequently the environmental movement began to question the acceptance of a capitalist system based on perpetual economic growth, many in the field of social ecology, including Bookchin, were labeled anti-capitalists or communists. Bookchin, however, went beyond the critics' description of subversiveness and referred to his work as fundamentally revolutionary and reconstructive.

Social ecology takes an anthropological account of a simpler life that might have existed at the *sapiens 1.2* stage and puts it in a modern context. It is made up of small tribal communities, in which we live within a nonhierarchical social nexus. It replaces a market-based economy with a moral economy in which economic as well as political relationships are guided by an ethic of mutualism and genuine reciprocity. It replaces the capitalist ethos of private-property rights and private ownership of resources with the rights of *usufruct*, meaning "open access to all." Unlike a society defined by the capitalist virtues that promote competition, social ecology promotes the ethos of complementarity and cooperation. It also promotes the idea of an irreducible minimum, whereby everyone is afforded the basic necessities of life.

In his work, Bookchin promotes the idea of municipalism, in which everyone can cultivate him/herself within an authentic, caring, loving social relationship that is driven not by power and hierarchy but by ethics, imagination, and utopianism. Unlike many ecologists' views on politics, his embraces the historical role that cities play as potential sites of freedom and universalism. He sees the practice of citizenship in empowered neighborhood assemblies as a means for educating community members into the values of humanism, cooperation, and public service.[39] Given climate change and the fact that more than half the world's population now lives in urban settings, concerns of how to nest all the elements that define social ecology and the complexity of urban life into Gaian ecology must become the driving force behind the field. As a way to heal the damage cause by the *sapiens 1.5* stage, social ecology reignites a philosophical inquiry into the evolutionary relationship between human consciousness and natural evolution and emphasizes the potentialities that lie latent within the evolution of natural and social phenomena. It celebrates the uniqueness of human creativity and intelligence while emphasizing its emergence from the possibilities inherent in Gaian intelligence. This is the evolutionary process described in Lipton and Sahtouris's superorganism and in Bloom's global brain that has been billions of years in the making. It is also Bookchin's "thinking nature" that nests *human intelligence* in *natural intelligence.*

Deep Ecology

Contrary to some worldviews that consider deep ecology a form of organized religion, deep ecological consciousness involves widening the objective inquiry about Earth's systems through active, in-depth questioning that becomes accessible only after the *momentous leap* into *Second-sapiens* consciousness has unleashed an exponential level of psychological freedom. It does not comprise an incremental translation of *sapiens 1.5* science or *sapiens 1.4* religious doctrine. The term *deep ecology* itself was coined by Norwegian philosopher Arne Naess, who was an influential figure in the environmental movement of the late twentieth century. He has argued that while post-World War II environmental groups had raised public awareness of environmental issues of that time, they had largely failed to discover insights into the underlying cultural and philosophical background of these problems. He believed that our ongoing environmental crisis had arisen due to certain unspoken philosophical presuppositions and attitudes that remained unacknowledged within Western developed societies.[40] The core principles behind deep ecology are tied to Gaiacracy and the Rights-of-Nature laws. They view the living environment as a whole full of emergent complexity and interdependence that should be respected and regarded as having certain basic, unalienable moral and legal rights that enable it to live and flourish. The shallow, ecological thinking of the utilitarian and pragmatic *sapiens 1.5* is replaced with that of *sapiens 2.1*, who fully appreciates the complex web of interdependence and resilience of all living systems that guarantee biodiversity and ecological balance.

The foundations of deep ecology are the basic intuitions and experiences of us ourselves in relationship to nature. Many of the questions it raises are of the perennial philosophical and spiritual sort that acknowledges the inseparable aspects of the whole: we are all part of one organism in which there is no separation between the self and the other or between the self, the other, and the Greater Self—Mother Nature herself. This view is in sharp contrast to that of the *sapiens 1.5* stage that sees *Homo sapiens* isolated and fundamentally separate and different from the rest of nature, or superior to and in charge of it and the rest of creation.

Naess developed two perspectives describing his framework that lay outside the consciousness of all the *First sapiens's* six stages of development. He called them the *ultimate norms* and described them as *self-realization* and *biocentric equality*.[41] Self-realization in the Gaiametry framework corresponds to the *sapiens 2.1* stage of development and biocentric equality to the *sapiens 2.2* stage. The two perspectives are, by necessity, sequential. In order for the biocentric-equality aspect to be sustained permanently, humanity—or at least those who hold CAPI in the new epoch—must work on realigning our evolutionary trajectory and infusing it with Anthropogenic awareness. Both perspectives are reached by the deep questioning process that reveals the importance of moving away from reductive measurement into the philosophical and spiritual realms of wisdom, and both are representative of the harmonious and highly collaborative *Second-sapiens* stages of consciousness.

Naess's *ultimate norms* cannot be validated by—nor do they adhere to—modern science and its narrow, mechanical definition of knowledge. Following this wisdom, we know that deep ecology is in harmony with nature, which doesn't allow a single species to dominate it. Adherents believe that Earth's resources are limited and therefore should be cherished and conserved. They believe that technological progress should be directed toward ecologically informed solutions that seek the *reduction* of our carbon footprint, not the incremental expansion of consumerism that adds to it. Deep ecology views nature as having intrinsic rights equal to our own, not as a resource at our full disposal. It limits the pursuit of our material goals to serving the larger goal of self-realization instead of endorsing the endless economic growth that has brought us to the precipice of ecological disaster. Deep ecology asks us to view the nature of our reality and our place in it in a much larger scheme, one that cannot be fully grasped intellectually but is ultimately experiential. In light of how quickly we are moving toward ecological collapse, the only question that remains is, Will we still have the luxury of moving voluntarily into experiential states, or is the ecological imbalance we have created now dictating the terms of our continued existence?

While environmental philosophy continues to attract talent that advances many needed causes, will its feminist virtues expand and reach a tipping point in time to save us from ecological collapse, or is humanity headed—in the words of Francois d'Eaubonne—toward death? Even more relevantly, does the environmental movement hold CAPI at the levels needed to avert climate disaster? CAPI in this field might be present in many academic pockets worldwide and in some of the countries that have enshrined Rights of Nature laws into their constitutions. It is present in most movements involving climate protesters. It is also present in the national consciousness of the countries comprising the global south and of those that are not part of our globally industrialized economy. It has been present in indigenous communities long before academics defined it as a field of study. The influence aspect of CAPI is attracting an exponentially increasing number of groups from different disciplines and at every fractal level possible. It is safe to assume that CAPI is present in many regions of the world that have not organized their civilization around the *sapiens 1.5* ethos.

A few simple questions remain: Will all this progress be enough to make those who hold power and authority at the highest levels yield to a system that sees their power and authority as the primary cause of ecosystem collapse and climate change? Will there come a time in the near future when those who hold power and authority realize that they will have *none* in the absence of a viable living planet? Perhaps time and Mother Nature in her mercy are the only ones who can answer that question.

From Human Exceptionalism to Ecological Homeostasis

Since the Gaiametry framework addresses the survival and eventual thriving of all planetary life as its *general thema,* many of its stage attractors overlap in their coverage of different subject matters. This is the nature of the highly collaborative process of *Second-sapiens* intelligence. It sees each aspect of such synergistic and complementary overlapping as a different facet of the same diamond. While the previous section briefly discussed the subject of social ecology as a specific field, the social aspects of Earth's ecology permeate this book as different facets of this same diamond, which in its entirety is called *Gaia.* One of those facets that preserves the original Gravesian bio-psycho-social model is sociology, which in the post-Holocene iteration becomes environmental or ecological sociology.

The field of environmental sociology was established as a section of the American Sociological Association in 1979 by William R. Catton Jr. and Riley E. Dunlap. Like most stage attractors of the Gaiametry framework, it had been in its embryonic *inquiry-and-identification* phase since the early 1970s, after we saw Gaia from outer space. In 1978, Catton and Dunlap coauthored a pioneering paper that not only established the field of environmental sociology but courageously advocated for a major paradigm shift. The paper identified the current paradigm as the human exceptionalism paradigm (HEP) and the one that we must adopt as the new ecological paradigm (NEP).[42] In the authors' view, sociological research until their time had been fundamentally flawed. The field, they claimed, failed to recognize that human dependence on finite natural resources and fossil fuels—along with our degradation of the air, water, soil, and biological processes on which all life depends—would ultimately encroach on human social systems in powerful, unseen ways.

The HEP theory summarizes five centuries of the evolution of *Homo prudentus* in one eloquent anthropological iteration. It claims that humans are such a uniquely superior species that they are exempt from environmental forces. Shaped by the leading Western *sapiens 1.5* worldview born from the ethos of the Enlightenment and the Industrial Revolution, human dominance, Catton and Dunlap argued, was justified by the uniqueness of culture, which is far more adaptable than biological traits. The paradigm confirms the *general thema* of that deficient stage of development and what has been proven practice: the idea that culture has the capacity to accumulate and innovate, making it an unbounded resource capable of solving all natural problems. This characteristic, they argued, makes *Homo sapiens* an exception, ungoverned by natural conditions.[43] The theory also confirms another *sapiens 1.5* perspective: that human beings are scientific gods endowed with the power to exercise complete control over their own destiny and that any potential limitation posed by the natural world will be overcome by human ingenuity.

NEP turns the tables on these assumptions in that, while it recognizes the innovative capacity of humans, it also asserts that humans are nevertheless ecologically interdependent with other species. In other words, *human intelligence* must again become nested in *natural intelligence*. NEP's premise is outlined in three propositions: (1) *Homo sapiens* is only one species consisting of many dependent species in the biotic communities that constitute social life; (2) a complicated linkage causes impact and feeds back on the natural web, resulting in undesirable consequences that are different from intentional human actions; and (3) potential physical and biological limitations impede economic growth, social progress, and other social phenomena.[44] This theory recognizes the power of social and cultural forces but nests them in *Second-sapiens* intelligence that acknowledges the impact of cause and effect and feedback loops of ecosystems that define natural intelligence, which *sapiens 1.5* has mostly ignored. Unlike the view of some critics, it's approach is not deterministic but rather forces us to recognize Gaia's finite levels of natural resources and her limited capacity to handle the externalization of *sapiens 1.5*'s endless waste to the environment. Thus, the new ecological paradigm forces us to explore vastly different approaches to our problems, ones that are steeped in the study of complex systems of life that negate the definition of determinism by nesting it in Gaia's *natural intelligence.*

In 1980, Catton published the book *Overshoot: The Ecological Basis of Revolutionary Change,* in which he gives a detailed chronology of how *sapiens 1.5* came to dominate the environment through what he called a cornucopian myth of limitless resources. To provide a Gaian perspective on the issue, he introduces the concept of "carrying capacity," which quickly became a pillar on which much of Earth-system sciences relies. He describes the concept as defining the maximum, permanently supportable number of people a given environment can sustain indefinitely.[45] If this number is exceeded, he argues, then environmental damage will occur, and in time the carrying capacity will be reduced. In the past, technological breakthroughs contributed to the growth of carrying capacity and population increases followed. But many of the newer technological breakthroughs, Catton argues, have created problems of their own in terms of their impact on the environment—particularly the use of fossil fuels. The concept of carrying capacity became a way to advance the Malthusian theory to other nonagricultural resources as well as fossil fuels and to show the limits of technology and the unsustainable nature of consumerism given a world population that has increased in size more than seven times and requires exponentially more resources than what Malthus had predicted. In a mathematical projection of catastrophe similar to his, Catton argues that if Earth's carrying capacity is overshot, then the environmental damage that will occur will, in time, reduce that capacity to one that can support only a fraction of today's population.

Catton distinguishes between the technologies that existed before World War II and the ones that emerged subsequently as we turned our attention to building a world based on peaceful trade and commerce. The startling technological achievement that ensued, he argues, led us to believe that whatever the problems are that might confront us there will always be new technology to deal with them. The overreliance on these assumptions proved to be a dangerous delusion, according to Catton. The period of time to which he refers is the same period that marked the beginning of the *Great Acceleration* that placed us squarely in the throes of the Anthropocene. To avoid the disastrous consequences of overshooting the planet's carrying capacity, Catton calls on several changes that must be undertaken to avoid ecological collapse: The first entails a shift away from our current economic paradigm that prioritizes perpetual growth and toward the embrace of sustainable economies. The second entails a revolutionary shift in our behavior and the way we think and organize our institutions and societies. In acknowledging the limits of the planet's resources, we must adopt a more harmonious relationship with the environment that involves the reevaluation of societal values, mores, and consumption patterns. And the third change entails the adoption of an ecological ethic that recognizes the intrinsic value of the environment and emphasizes stewardship over its exploitation, which he says is essential for achieving sustainability and preventing further environmental degradation.[46]

Like so many ideas that were born in the higher-order system in the 1970s after we saw Earth from outer space, the field of environmental sociology has withstood many attacks from the antibodies of the current system. It has evolved and grown tremendously since its founding. The terms *carrying capacity* and *overshoot* have become standard parlance in today's ecological sciences. They apply not only to climate change but to all the remaining Earth systems that were identified in the *Great Acceleration,* from the loss of biodiversity and ocean acidification to the factors that determine the integrity of the biosphere. In a recent article, John Michael Greer, who has written extensively on ecological and planetary issues, describes the concept of overshoot as the core of the entire world of appropriate technology and green alternatives and the essence of the recognition that the principles of ecology apply to industrial society just as much as they do to other communities of living things.[45] Similarly, Richard Heinberg, a senior fellow at the Post Carbon Institute and the author of fourteen books focusing on issues of peak oil, resource depletion, and sustainability, conveyed the concept of overshoot in current Anthropogenic relevance four decades after Catton envisioned it. Climate change is not our biggest problem, Heinberg proclaims: overshoot is. He adds that global warming is but a symptom of ecological overshoot.[46]

Catton is a visionary whose insights have not only expanded the field of environmental sociology. They have also provided a foundational underpinning for Earth-system scientists that enable them to articulate the plethora of challenges facing our planet and a new way to speak about tipping points in Gaia's different systems. The new ecological paradigm and the concepts of overshoot and carrying capacity recapture an important part of the science behind the complex systems of life and provide the feedback loops that *sapiens 1.5* has long ignored. The absence of these feedback loops is what is responsible for our post-war behavior, which Catton has bluntly described as *stealing from the future.* This behavior also defines Gibran's plutocrat, who consumes incessantly of the Earth and the sea far beyond his needs. Like many of the stage attractors that make up the Gaiametry framework, environmental sociology calls for a thorough reexamination of our deficient behavior that normalized the ethos of endless growth under the reign of *sapiens 1.5.* That same ethos created what Catton has called "phantom" carrying capacities, meaning that they are a fallacy limited to the reductive, mechanical views of the Enlightenment that sees endless growth as part and parcel of human exceptionalism. It also created what Graves called the Orwellian societal complex that cannot deal with issues of complexity at the planetary level and glosses over existential issues with a veneer of humanitarian-sounding doublethink and moralistic rationalizations while repressing any feedback loops coming to us from Gaia.

Like all other stage attractors in the Gaiametry framework detailed in this chapter, environmental sociology calls on us to develop a new paradigm that utilizes the virtues of the *Second sapiens* in order to preserve what remains of life on the planet. The question that must still be asked is, Does the field and its cast of collaborators hold enough CAPI to tip the system in favor of survival and preservation? Like so many other attractors, the influence part of the CAPI equation is garnering exponential support throughout the world. But will it be enough to make those who hold authority and power at the highest levels within the paradigm of human exceptionalism yield to a system that sees them as the enemy?

NINE
SPEAKING GAIAN TRUTH TO ECONOMIC POWER

> *We are all heirs of dualistic ontology. We can see it everywhere in the language we use about nature today. We routinely describe the living world as "natural resources," as "raw materials," and even—as if to emphasize its subordination and servitude—as "ecosystem services." We talk about waste and pollution and climate change as "externalities" because we believe that what happens to nature is fundamentally external to the concerns of humanity. . . . Dualism runs so deep it wriggles into our language even when we're trying to be more conscientious.*
>
> —Jason Hickel
> *Less is More*

Two general schools of thought seem to have emerged in the last two decades around the subject of how to deal with climate change and the possible collapse of the different Earth systems.

The first reflects the optimistic nature and scientific genius of the modern mind and its perceived ability to counter the wrath of nature through new technological discoveries and breakthroughs in design. It calls on an elite breed of experts such as Bill Gates, who in his 2021 *New York Times* best-selling book, *How to Avoid a Climate Disaster,* assembled one of the most comprehensive guides to relevant technologies, including the ones currently under development and the ones we still need to implement in order to arrive at the magic number of net zero by 2050. Climate scientists describe the term *net zero* as a state in which human-caused emissions from carbon dioxide and greenhouse gases are balanced by carbon-dioxide removal from the atmosphere over a certain period of time.[1] It is seen as the driver of our collective efforts to keep global warming under 1.5°C. Gates received much praise for his work from the general public as well as from world leaders and politicians, but those who have a systems view of the problem consider his approach insufficient. Many environmental advocates view the book as the work of a technological solutionist who falls short of addressing political obstacles and policy issues, while others accuse him of having a financial interest in most of the technologies for which he advocates.[2]

Gates's engineering genius is on the cutting edge of innovation. It is prevalent in many communities around the world and in elite schools from MIT and Stanford to Harvard and Yale. The new ways of reimagining technology Gates promotes have created new ecosystems of thought that seem to have transcended the scientific ethos of *sapiens 1.5* and are now emerging as the much higher and more inclusive science of *sapiens 2.1,* capable of crafting adaptive and mitigative measures to save humanity from itself. What these new systems of thought seem to overlook, however, is that, in terms of the *sapiens 2.1* brain syndicate, technological innovation is but a small part of the whole. Unless it is integrated into a full *Second-sapiens* platform that includes areas of politics, ecology, sociology, human development, and other sciences concerned with Earth-systems studies, its efforts will fall short of saving us from climate disaster. Just like that of its earlier kin, *sapiens 1.5,* this new form of thinking is eternally optimistic as it views the world through its perpetual ability to create innovation, dismissing the dark side of its creations and their feedback loops, continuing its reductive thinking, and excluding other factors that lay outside its field of specialty.

The second school of thought regarding how to deal with climate change has grown exponentially in the last decade and shows the rapid transformation of some the most advanced minds that now see this issue from Jupiter. They come from every walk of life—from economist Naomi Klein, who sees beyond the fallacies and limitations of her profession, to renowned politicians such as former Vice President Al Gore and UN Secretary General Antonio Guterres, who are both now convinced that the current systems of governance are grossly ill-equipped to address issues of planetary magnitude. These are the individuals who have glimpsed Gaian intelligence in its complexity and its wrath when various Earth systems reach certain tipping points that lay outside Promethean intelligence to comprehend.

The former, "optimistic" school of thought believes that incremental advancements made in scientific discoveries, including those made with artificial intelligence, will save humanity, while the latter school sees this belief as insufficient and inadequate. The former remains in an ecosystem of bliss and optimism habitual to the Holocene era, while the latter seems to be standing on the burning grounds of the Anthropocene, sounding the alarm on existential issues we were warned about five decades ago. The former has resisted a full, integrative approach that relies on the inclusion of other fields of study, while the latter sees the devastation caused by that exclusion and is resigned to the enormity of the problem and our inability to stop it from getting worse. The former forges forward with technology as the guiding light, while the latter understands the limits of technology and human-built systems. Adherents of this latter school use that knowledge as a platform to become modern-day town criers sounding the alarm on the world stage, using recriminations and I-told-you-so scenarios in order to be on the right side of history should things get worse.

While I was researching climate change and its relevance to the Gravesian model, I witnessed myself transitioning slowly from the first school of thought to the second. This shift was due not to pessimism but to two major factors that emerged when I began to see the issue from a systems preceptive. The first was the realization that in order for planetary matters to be understood properly, they require a considerably higher degree of psychological development. They belong to a mega-level system that follows the *natural intelligence* of which *human intelligence* is but a small, subsumed part. Their evolution occurs over eras and epochs and reaches points of bifurcation that move the different parts of Earth's systems into states of chaos—many of which have escaped human detection. Even as we become aware of issues of climate and ecological collapse, we still can't sufficiently predict the behavior of such planetary systems and how close they might be to reaching points of bifurcation. The science that studies these matters is a *Second sapiens*, highly collaborative and interdisciplinary one that remains in the early stages of emergence in the higher-order mega system identified with the Anthropocene life cycle. For five decades, this collaborative science has engaged in a continuing fight with the antibodies of the prevailing system that seek to suppress if not outright kill it.

The second major factor in my change of perspective was my stark realization that those who hold CAPI in the current economics fractal fall into different stages of *First-sapiens* intelligence. While some might be in an open state, once they become nested in the *natural intelligence* of the Anthropocene they move into closed or at best arrested states. They are beholden to an ecosystem of institutions built and constrained by their worldwide deficient virtues and needs that could be summarized and put into the following three general developmental categories:

- In modern capitalist democracies today such as the United States, and in terms of CAPI, Power and Influence at the macro level are vested in those who wield financial prowess gained through the current economic and financial infrastructure. They use these two elements to pacify those who hold Authority, which is vested in government institutions at the *sapiens 1.4* stage of cultural development. There is an inherent danger in pacifying the *sapiens 1.4* regulatory structures responsible for issues of compliance and governance and in trusting that *sapiens 1.5* market forces can act as a substitute for regulation. The absence of rules that regulate the capitalist system, as proven in research I conducted for my 2013 book, corrupts every stage in the *First-sapiens* systems, transforming capitalism into a system of theft and institutionalized inequality.[3] Today, the continued pacification of *sapiens 1.4* institutions makes it necessary for every green-energy innovation to be scalable and economically feasible; therefore, each such innovation must use the existing *First-sapiens* capitalist infrastructure, regardless of how beneficial it might be in the Anthropocene epoch.
- In most OPEC member countries and the ones rich in natural resources, most if not all three CAPI elements are vested in one entity: a *sapiens 1.3* leader such as Putin and bin Salman. There are no institutions that provide a system of checks and balances in their world. The institutions that do exist are vacuous and passive in nature. They create the illusion of institutional presence to legitimize the leader's singular views to a world run by institutions. The *sapiens 1.3* stage of economic development relies heavily on revenue streams from the sale of fossil fuels and nonrenewable resources to finance the leader's worldview and perception of reality, be it to enrich himself and his circle of oligarchs or to finance wars, either directly or through proxies based on outdated and often bloody ideologies.

- In China, the second-most powerful economy in the world, most if not all of CAPI is held in the ideological hands of *sapiens 1.4*, the Chinese Communist Party. Today, China is responsible for 27 percent of global carbon emissions and a third of the world's greenhouse gases.[4] While many believe that central planning makes it easier for China to pivot toward environmentally sustainable economic policies, the nation's current level of economic stagnation unprecedented in its modern history might prevent it from doing so. Much of China's economic slowdown can be attributed to the deficiencies inherent in its *sapiens 1.4* stage of economic development. As detailed in chapter 4, this stage in macroeconomics is the foundation on which modern economies are built, but it should remain transitory for the purpose of building the institutional and physical infrastructure necessary for the economy in question. When the time came to transition from *sapiens 1.4* central planning to *sapiens 1.5* free markets, Chinese leaders resisted the shift. The effect was to move the system past its nexus point, exposing its blind spots and limiting the availability of capital needed for a sustainable energy transition.

These three points describe the fragile and unhealthy interdependence created by the *First sapiens.* It has gaslighted the world into thinking that a globalized economy is the sure path to peaceful coexistence among nations and that technological breakthroughs and other incremental changes can remain the leading edge for solutions without challenging our collective bias that limitless growth can continue unabated.

GDP: The Metric to End All Metrics

In general, the battle for world dominance today is not a gruesome one fought by empires and their armies with the traditional machinery of war and blood shed as it was done during the reign of *sapiens 1.4.* It is not about physical prowess and who can dominate whom as in *sapiens 1.3.* It is not about the conquest of peoples and land and their subjugation to some religious doctrine. Although these things still happen, they do not represent real power the way we have defined it since the end of World War II. Power on the world stage today is defined by a nation's monetary measure of economic output as determined by one globally accepted standard metric called *gross domestic product*, or GDP for short. Briefly, GDP is a monetary measure of all goods and services a nation produces during a certain period of time. The nation with the highest annual GDP is the undisputed champion of this new world defined by commerce and trade, the newest expression of the *sapiens 1.5* stage of development. Countries that have competed and lost are encouraged to increase their economic activity and the wealth of their nation in the hopes of moving up in the ranks the following year. The idea of GDP rose out of the ashes of the Great Depression and the Second World War. It was intended to be the ultimate measure of a country's overall welfare, a forensic view of an economy's heart and soul, the indicator to end all indicators. As the adoption of the *peace- through-commerce* ethos spread across the globe, so did the use of GDP, making it the defining econometric of the last century. While there are many aggregate and complicated calculations and different approaches that determine the final GDP figures, the most relevant for this book's purpose are not the ones that it includes but the nonmonetary exclusions and negative externalities that it does not measure.

> *The gross national product does not allow for the health of our children, the quality of their education, or the joy of their play. It does not include the beauty of our poetry or the strength of our marriages, the intelligence of our public debate or the integrity of our public officials. It measures neither our wit nor our courage, neither our wisdom nor our learning, neither our compassion nor our devotion to our country. It measures everything, in short, except that which makes life worthwhile.*
>
> —Robert F. Kennedy[5]

When I studied economics in the early 1980s, the world was consumed by the birth of Milton Friedman's monetarism. Like wild fire, it spread through Western universities, replacing Keynesian economics with ideologies that sought to commoditize everything on which a capitalist laid his eyes. This was the dawn of *sapiens 1.5* neoclassical economics that spread the ethos of *only money matters*, which transformed GDP in unimageable ways—and not necessarily for the better. Much of the old guard in academia, including my professors, had already been skeptical of the use of the GDP metric as a new measure of a nation's wealth and an indicator of prosperity, using terms such as *dismal* or *vulgar* for the way it left out everything that can't be measured monetarily. With monetarism becoming part of the academic curriculum, skepticism became criticism, which is now being validated after four decades of growth that externalized the cost of GDP maximization to society and the environment. Here are some of the main shortcomings that were true then and are now at the heart of what is wrong with our current economic models that uphold GDP—the largest metric for monetary quantification ever created—as the primary guide for world economies:

- While GDP proclaims to be the largest measure of a nation's prosperity, it does not include factors that are essential for human development such as education, gender equality, health, and happiness.
- GDP also excludes much of the productive activity that has not been quantified by economists who are more interested in preserving the predictability and the elegance of their models. Matters such as household production, bartering of goods and services, and volunteer or unpaid services are excluded.
- When applied to less developed countries, GDP does not consider the ecosystems of local economies and the gifting economy in which exchange involves not money but cultural norms that have been in place for centuries.
- By imposing GDP measures on developing countries, the pursuit of wealth has shifted from the traditional accumulation of capital gained through productive work to a culture driven by the accumulation of debt made available through the International Monetary Fund and the World Bank. This has enabled corruption and the rampant misuse of funds, saddling these countries and their citizens with generational debt on which they can barely make interest payments.
- One of the of the biggest misleading metrics inherent in GDP is the actual measure of wealth itself, described as per-capita income, which does not account for variances in incomes of various demographic groups. This mismeasurement enables economists to use a broad stroke to paint a false image of national prosperity while allowing economic inequality to fall through the cracks in the system.
- By far, the biggest flaw in GDP began to appear when systems thinking on a planetary scale first emerged in the mid-1970s. That

is when economic growth became the lightening rod, the enemy of a thriving planet.[6]

GDP champions a perpetual-growth paradigm that is often summarized by economists, financial analysts, and policy makers as a *grow-or-die* imperative. It is the biggest factor in the *Great Acceleration* that has moved some of Earth's systems past their tipping points. Today, the looming issues of climate change and ecological degradation call on us to limit that growth, or, at a minimum, couple it with what remains of our natural ecosystems' carrying capacities. These are the early warning signs from the Anthropocene life cycle that have been apparent for over five decades and represent the higher-order system that makes economic activity and all its associative metrics possible. But those who defend the use of GDP have cleverly argued against the adoption of such drastic changes, claiming that the metric was designed to measure only economic progress. It was never intended to include key externalities such as resource extraction and environmental impact.[7] Also, those defenders have made it clear that what is being measured is strictly quantitative. Qualitative constructs such as happiness, quality of life, the health of ecosystems, and the well-being of humanity as a whole are beyond what matters to their calculations and therefore are not part of the millions of data points that go into GDP.

The GDP is the single, most ubiquitous metric that defines modern success and prosperity in the hands of those who still hold CAPI in our *sapiens 1.5* global economy. It is the metric driven by our dualistic ontology that has externalized all nonmonetary matters. And it is the metric that has moved past its own carrying capacity, spreading toxicity in its *decline* and *entropy* phases and causing damage in nonlinear and chaotic ways for the next, higher-order system to deal with.

> *The world's leaders are correctly fixated on economic growth as the answer to virtually all problems, but they're pushing it with all their might in the wrong direction.*
>
> —Donella Meadows[8]

In looking to replace GDP, those who champion the ethos of the *sapiens 1.6* stage of development—such as Nobel Prize-winning economists

Joseph Stiglitz, Paul Krugman, and others—have inspired the creation of alternative metrics that are now informing some policymakers. *Sapiens 1.6* economists argue that GDP is too focused on material consumption and does not consider important factors such as environmental sustainability, social justice, and quality of life. This movement away from monetarism seeks to transcend the noncaring nature of the material world that *sapiens 1.5* established and replace it with economic models based on higher levels of consciousness that seek a more equitable distribution of resources and opportunity as well as care for the environment and for all humanity. It focuses on issues of economic diversity, community-based projects, quality of life, and the placement of human care and social cohesion above monetary goals. As it has grown in popularity, its most prevalent indices have been adopted by global institutions such as the Organisation for Economic Co-operation and Development (OECD) and the United Nations. The most inclusive alternatives to GDP could be summed up by these three indices: (1) the Human Development Index (HDI), which measures a country's development level based on life expectancy, education, and income per capita; (2) the Sustainable Economic Welfare Index (SEWI), which takes into account the long-term sustainability of an economy and includes factors such as investment in education and research, renewable energy use, and social cohesion; and (3) the Genuine Progress Indicator (GPI), which takes into account both economic and environmental factors and includes positive elements such as personal consumption, investment, and government services while subtracting negative elements such as pollution, crime, and natural resource depletion.[9]

These are the ethos that sought to make the *sapiens 1.6* stage an economic reality and at one point informed the UN's Sustainable Development Goals (SDGs). They are also the ethos that underly a green economy. During the Holocene era, the *sapiens 1.6* economic system could have provided the normal sequence of emergence that would have allowed the virtues of this stage to manifest worldwide. Unfortunately, as climate change and ecological disasters continue unabated, solutions from the *sapiens 1.6* system alone are proving insufficient in the face of our new existential reality. In Gravesian terms consistent with the rules of movement up the spiral, *sapiens 1.6* economic policies sought to fix the damage *sapiens 1.5* economic policies caused; and, while it might have brought awareness to economic inequality and fairness to a system built by *human intelligence*, it was sufficiently incapable of addressing issues emerging from the much higher-order system driven by *natural intelligence*.

Is Ecological Economics Enough?

Ecological economics differs greatly from mainstream economics in that it heavily reflects on the ecological footprint of human interactions in the economy. It focuses less on the incremental evolution of modern econometrics of both *sapiens 1.5* and *sapiens 1.6* and more on the impact human activities have on natural resources and the waste they generate in the process. As a field of study, it goes as far back as the days of Thomas Malthus. It is integrative, interdisciplinary, and transdisciplinary. It is a whole-systems approach that studies the coevolution of human economies and natural ecosystems and views the former as a subsystem of the latter. Its original concern was with the Malthusian catastrophe of overshooting resources that dealt with the limits of agricultural production in the face of exponential population growth. Over time, it has evolved to where we are today: facing an Anthropogenic catastrophe of limited resources of all kinds, coupled with the impending collapse of many of Earth's systems that have moved beyond their carrying capacity since we adopted the post-World War II ethos of *peace through commerce*.

The Romanian economist Nicholas Georgescu-Roegen is considered the modern-day father of ecological economics. Like so many visionaries of his generation, his work reached its zenith in the 1970s after we first saw Earth from outer space. Borrowing from advancements made in systems thinking, such as Ilya Prigogine's work on dissipative structures, Georgescu-Roegen introduced his most influential work in a 1971 book entitled *The Entropy Law and the Economic Process*. In it, he compares the entropic progressions—the irrevocable, qualitative degradation of order into chaos that is present at all the holonic levels within the natural world—to the entropic progression of the economic process. While the Earth moves naturally into different states of entropy, Georgescu-Roegen argued that economic activity is accelerating the process. He was among the first modern-day economists to argue that Earth's capacity to sustain human population and consumption levels is bound to decrease sometime in the future as the finite stock of mineral resources continues to be extracted and put to use. Consequently, the world economy will head toward an inevitable collapse, ultimately bringing about human extinction.[10]

Prigogine's research was conducted on chemical reactions in open, natural systems in which he had full control over the experiments ensuring their scientific integrity. There was no ulterior sinister motive to slander his work or challenge its findings. In Georgescu-Roegen's case, the application of Prigogine's principles extended beyond chemical reactions and warned of a dismal future for humanity, a sufficient reason for his work to be slandered and dismissed by both the physical sciences and economists. While his approach is considered groundbreaking today, when it was published it was attacked on several fronts. His book read more like a work in the fields of applied physics and mathematics than it did economics. Consequently, the scientific community heavily criticized it for misappropriating the laws of physics, including the second law of thermodynamics, which deals with the concept of entropy. Neoliberal economists and others criticized the book as well, labeling it as entropy pessimism.[11]

> *Will mankind listen to any program that implies a constriction of its addiction to exosomatic comfort? Perhaps, the destiny of man is to have a short but fiery, exciting, and extravagant life rather than a long, uneventful, and vegetative existence. Let other species—the amoebas, for example—which have no social ambitions whatever, inherit an Earth still bathed in plenty of sunshine.*
>
> —Nicholas Georgescu-Roegen[12]

Beyond Georgescu-Roegen's influence, today the field of ecological economics continues to grow and evolve as it seeks to preserve what is known as "natural capital" that concerns itself with all the resources nature provides to us. Natural capital is integrative in its approach as it factors in the air we breathe, the water we drink, the soil that grows our food, the forests that provide us with timber and clean air, and the minerals that we use to make everything from our smartphones to our automobiles. Ecological economists use the concept of natural capital to assess the economic value of ecosystem services such as water filtration, carbon storage, and pollination. They prioritize the addition of natural capital to the typical capital-asset analysis of land, labor, and financial capital and develop models and policies that support the sustainable management of natural capital. Additionally, they assess the environmental impacts of economic activity—such as climate change, resource depletion, and pollution—and develop new economic models that consider the biophysical constraints of the planet and the value of natural capital.[13]

The field of ecological economics continues to focus on Earth's carrying capacity, relentlessly questioning the fundamental assumption of mainstream-economic approaches. Matters such as cost-benefit analysis that exclude much of what the current system has externalized to the environment are being brought to the fore. Continuing to advance its whole-systems approach to economics, the field has brought forth the notion that the dominant economic narrative is decoupled from scientific research that points to the increasing fragility of Earth's systems coupled with resource scarcity. Sadly, this inclusive truth, instead of acting as a catalyst that propels the entire field of economics into the Anthropocene epoch, has had the opposite effect. The increasing evidence of Earth's system collapse has created a wedge between the field of ecological economics and the neoclassical economic narrative, and consequently the entire field of economics will remain topical and descriptive instead of integral and prescriptive.

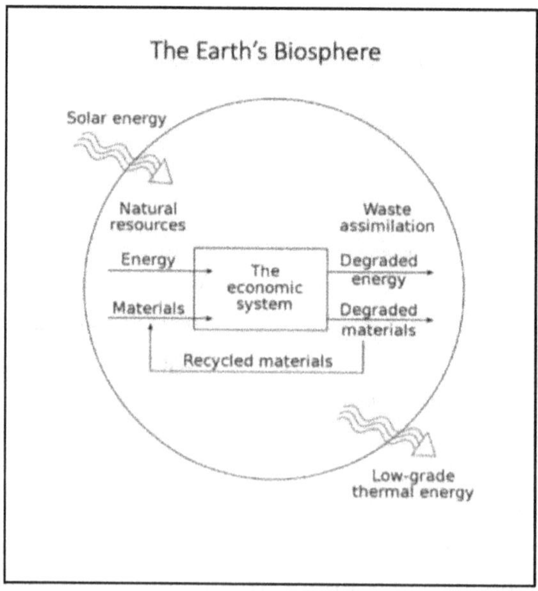

Figure 9.1. Ecological Economics. Humanity's economic system viewed as a subsystem of the global environment, wherein materials originally derived from natural resources are recycled back into the system. Used under the rules of Wikimedia Commons. https://commons.wikimedia.org/wiki/File:Diagram_of_natural_resource_flows-en.svg.

In ecological economics, the simple circular flow of income that is locked into the same fallacy as the reductive, circular-flow concept of consumer and producer is replaced with a more complex flow reflecting the input of solar energy, which sustains natural inputs and environmental services that are then used as units of production, as shown in figure 9.1. This schema shares several virtues with aspects present in other Gaiametry fractals discussed in earlier chapters, such as ecofeminism, the rights of nature, deep ecology, environmental philosophy, social ecology, Catton's new ecological paradigm, and the values of justice and care inherent in the Gaian archetype. It is yet another facet of the same diamond that seeks the preservation of all life on the planet. Still, this specialized field has unfairly remained on the margins of mainstream economics driven by the reductive thinking that still believes in the superiority of our species. But as our resources become scarcer and climate-related disasters increase in severity and frequency, we will find ourselves having to adopt the far more inclusive view of capital that recouples our economic activity with the finite resources of our planet. This is when the reign of *Homo colossus* comes to an end and we begin the long road of ending our separation from nature.

The New Metrics: From Macro Systems to Mega Systems

To address our ecological urgency effectively, we must move the field of ecological economics out of the worldview that sees it as a fringe practice and onto the center stage that recognizes it as a quintessential approach that will save us and millions of other species. Ecological economics must become the necessary replacement for the current economic ethos and hold a new form of CAPI that in many ways supports an ethos opposite to that which the current system upholds. It must be driven by a coevolutionary process in which the pace of economic growth slows to a point that does not cause further degradation of our ecosystems, made up of the air, the ground, and the water and the organisms they support.

Although no international body exists today to enforce these mandates, austerity measures that preserve the meager resources we have left must be put in place. In addition, a new economic system must—wherever ecologically and scientifically possible—stop or reverse the damage we have caused to various ecosystems before they reach their points of bifurcation and enter an unmanageable state of nonlinear chaos. To address both these existential mega issues, i.e., the preservative and the restorative, ecological economics must be redefined through a fully inclusive model that carries the new Anthropocene urgency to deal with the damage caused by first-tier economics. It must reverse the ethos of all the lower economic models that had little or no awareness of the planetary limits to growth and nest them in our new reality.

This is the quintessential manifestation of humanity overcoming its greatest challenge: the nesting of Promethean intelligence in Gaian intelligence. It is the *Second sapiens's* acknowledgment that the environmental stability we once enjoyed during the Holocene era is in danger of collapse. In order to mitigate the effects of that collapse, the new perspective examines the much larger, mega-system structures and puts in place measures to preserve what can still be preserved. It is less about the human-built infrastructure for economics and more about the preservation of nature's infrastructure in which all life, not just human life, is nested. As water is necessary for fish, the former cannot exist without the latter. In our blind pursuit of prosperity, we have slowly poisoned that water and must now focus on making it safe for the fish while we still can. We must heal and care for the most important and complex supply chain there is—made up of the biosphere, the atmosphere, the hydrosphere, and the pedosphere, all working together as one evolving system to ensure the optimum conditions for life.

Like all other Gaiametry fractals, economic activity in the Anthropocene is part of the complex adaptive system of life. It is a highly collaborative, resilient, self-organizing, nonlinear, emergent system driven by the *natural intelligence* of autopoiesis. It is grounded in the nonlinear qualities of nature's creativity, complexity, chaos, and interdependence that are present in the natural order from the smallest organisms to the entire biosphere. Most importantly, its feedback loops are taken fully into account at every holonic structure from the smallest to the largest. Anthropocene economics will no longer allow *Homo sapiens's* subordination of natural resources as ecosystem services. It puts an end to the *First sapiens's* dualistic ontology that carelessly externalized the byproducts his economic activities, forming the largest collective shadow that is now appearing to us as fate. Of all the Gaiametry fractals, none is more important than the one that will be tasked with designing a new economic system informed by our new reality. This is where an emerging form of *Second-sapiens* CAPI informed by Gaian intelligence must speak truth to those who hold current *First-sapiens* CAPI that rules our global economy. This is the sun in the sundial model, the North Star that aligns all other

Gaiametry fractals onto a new platform that will determine whether our species and millions of others survive.

If we are to think of the different Gaiametry attractors as pearls, economic activity in the Anthropocene epoch is simultaneously a pearl and the entire necklace that links all the other fractals together to create one powerful platform capable of prying our future from the hands of the *First sapiens.* It must reverse the reductive ethos of our current global economy and return us to a nonreductive state of mind that, first and foremost, sees the significant damage we have caused the planet in less than a century. It is based in the realization of how much of Earth's limited resources we have consumed and how that consumption is now triggering nonlinear and abrupt environmental change on a planetary scale.

Homo colossus has consumed far too much of the future and far too many of Earth's nonrenewable resources. If we plot the timeline of human history measured in years on the timeline of Earth's history measured in epochs, we begin to see things much more clearly. This vantage point reveals that, since life on Earth began around 3.5 billion years ago, modern human life has existed for *only thirty-seven minutes.* Yet in that brief time we have used one third of Earth's natural resources in the last 0.2 seconds; and in less than 0.05 seconds, or by 2032, we will need the resources of *two* planets the size of Earth to support our economic paradigm and our addiction to growth and consumption.[14]

> *There is no question whatsoever that, for the overall survival of mankind, his aspirations must lower. They must come down. You cannot possibly go on living in a setting in which one thinks that he is going to materially expand his existence forever. But no human being is going to accept that idea until the crisis becomes sufficiently severe for him to realize that it is this or else.*
>
> —Clare W. Graves, quoted by Tom Bayer[15]

The original ideas that gave birth to a possible new framework for economic activity occurred in 2009 when the Swedish scientist Johan Rockström, who is now the head of the Potsdam Institute for Climate Impact Research, and several of his colleagues articulated the concept of planetary boundaries. Their research incorporated the work of many renowned scientists and authors on the leading edge of this issue—from

Thomas Malthus to Donella Meadows and Georgescu-Roegen, James Lovelock, and everyone in between. It brought together three branches of scientific inquiry: ecological economics, sustainability science, and the study of resilience as it relates to the self-regulation of living systems.[16] The last two branches represent the new complexity that has been missing from ecological economics as a field in itself.

The planetary boundaries, as Rockström and his colleagues identify them, define the safe operating space for humanity with respect to the Earth's complex systems and are associated with the planet's biophysical processes that define the complex adaptive systems of life itself. They react in a nonlinear, often abrupt way around certain threshold levels uncovered in the research. The group identified nine, highly interlinked planetary boundaries, the crossing of which would have disastrous consequences for humanity. In figure 9.2, these boundaries

Planetary Boundaries 2009

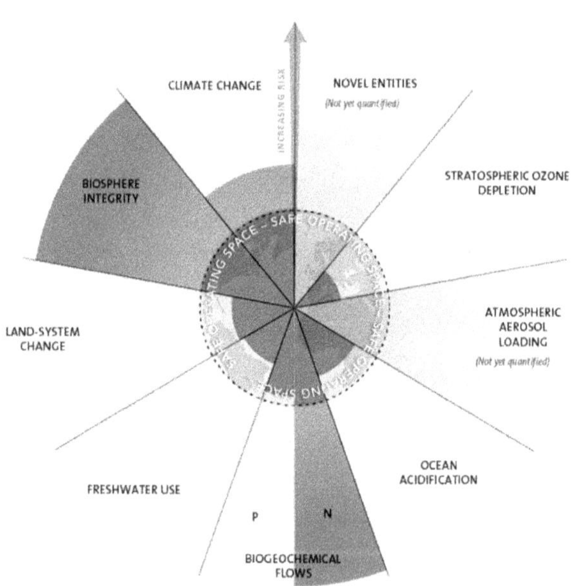

3 Boundaries Crossed

Figure 9.2. Planetary Boundaries Crossed in 2009. Azote for Stockholm Resilience Centre, Stockholm University. https:// www.stockholmresilience.org/research/planetary-boundaries.html. Used under the fair use rules.

are represented by the dotted circular line denoting the Earth. Climate change is only one of the nine systems. The others are novel entities, stratospheric ozone depletion, atmospheric aerosol loading, ocean acidification, biogeochemical flows, fresh water use, land system change, and biosphere integrity. Rockström and his colleagues have concluded that three of the nine boundaries—climate change, rate of biodiversity loss, and interference with the nitrogen cycle—have already been crossed (represented by the darkest segments on the graph) and that, if no action is taken, consequences will be detrimental if not catastrophic for large parts of the world.[17]

This seminal work has had a profound effect on how we view Earth-systems science. The long-held assumption has been that natural systems always reach homeostasis regardless of human activity. Accordingly, the prevailing 2009 scientific models suggest that factors affecting the systems relevant to global warming will likewise always stabilize in time. Rockström and his colleagues have challenged those models. According to Rockström, for instance, the old models suggest that "a doubling in atmospheric CO_2 concentration will lead to a global temperature rise of about 3°C… *once the climate has regained equilibrium* [my italics]."[18] However, and although the old models were complex in nature, they failed to consider the long-term feedback loops that further warm the climate, such as decreases in the surface area of ice cover or changes in the distribution of vegetation caused by human activity. Taking these feedback loops into account renders a much clearer—and more disturbing—picture. As Rockström's report puts it, "If these slow feedbacks are included, doubling CO_2 levels gives an eventual temperature increase of 6 °C… [which] would severely challenge the viability of contemporary human societies."[19]

That is, the study of the feedback loops is crucial for understanding the complex dynamics at work here. They clarify how the behavior of some Earth systems that have moved past their boundaries take on the characteristics of the exponential change described in the statistical model of entering the second half of the chessboard. Crossing these boundaries represents a complex system reaching the point of bifurcation and entering a state of chaos in which outcomes become far less predictable. In the Anthropogenic life-cycle model, which is the most complex of all models, we seem to be standing on the precipice of its nexus point where some of its subsystems have gone beyond the point of bifurcation one planetary boundary at a time. Because of the nature of complex systems of life at the mega-fractal level, going beyond planetary boundaries in one system can affect the stability of other systems in ways that remain unquantifiable through scientific methods that were adopted in pre-Anthropogenic times. Since 2009, the new scientific approach of the Potsdam Institute for Climate Impact Research has become the standard for many communities studying the science of the Anthropocene, from many of the UN's sustainable development programs to the Post Growth Institute and everything in between. It is at the heart of what is bringing urgency to the issue of addressing climate change. It has raised the stakes and expedited the time frame for our species to act; but, alas, we have utterly failed to keep the different Earth systems within safe limits. As figure 9.3 shows, by 2015, four of the nine Earth systems had moved past their planetary boundaries. By 2023, as shown in figure 9.4, six of the boundaries had been crossed.

Planetary Boundaries 2015

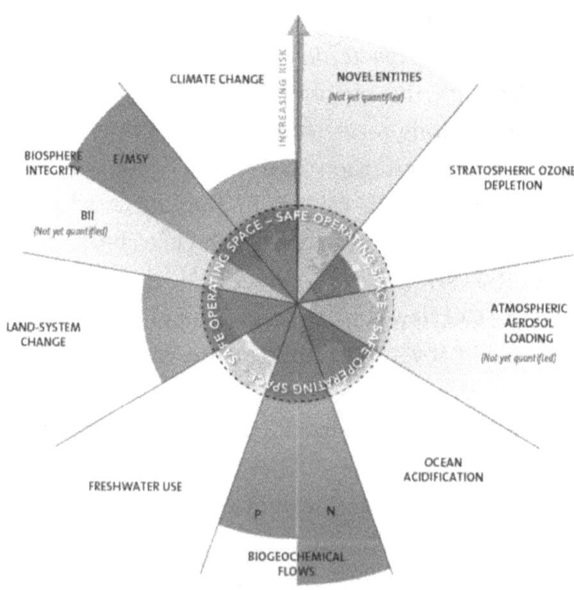

4 Boundaries Crossed

Figure 9.3. Planetary Boundaries Crossed in 2015. Azote for Stockholm Resilience Centre, Stockholm University. https:// www.stockholmresilience.org/research/planetary-boundaries.html. Used under the fair use rules.

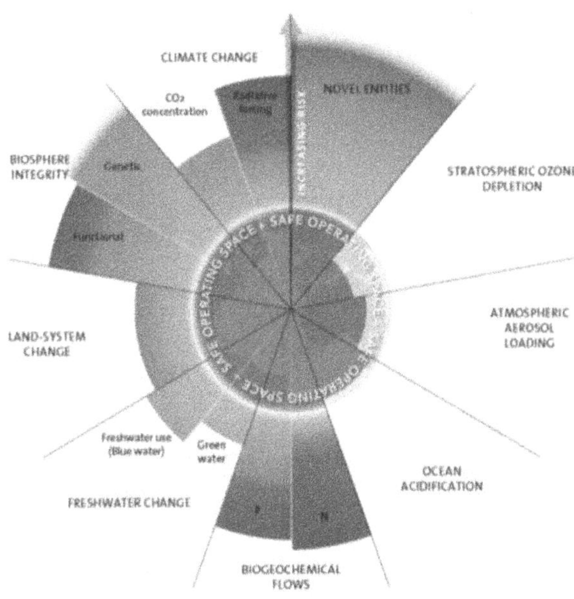

Figure 9.4. Planetary Boundaries Crossed in 2023. Azote for Stockholm Resilience Centre, Stockholm University. https:// www.stockholmresilience.org/research/planetary-boundaries.html. Used under the fair use rules.

These newest findings confirm that issues of planetary systems are a science of a much higher order, and while awareness of the problem has expanded and might now be attracting the attention of the *inner collective* in the *introduction* phase of the Anthropogenic life cycle, the tools and the degree of global cooperation required to address the issues effectively are grossly deficient. The findings, in a way, also confirm that certain subsystems within this new life cycle—which runs on *natural intelligence* that Rockström and his colleagues seem to have tapped into—might have been at their own nexus points for decades, but our reductive, Promethean intelligence has prevented us from seeing them. By challenging the established concept that human activity does not affect the invariable behavior of natural systems to reach homeostasis, the findings of Rockström's new model cited above predicts temperature rise to be more than double the current estimates by 2050, threatening many ecological life-support systems and the sustainability of human civilization.

Due to the tightly coupled relationship between the various planetary boundaries, we do not have the luxury of concentrating our efforts on any one of them in isolation from the others. If one boundary is crossed, then other boundaries are also under serious risk. If we keep cutting down the Amazon forest, changes in the atmosphere and the hydrosphere will be felt on other parts of the planet. If the polar ice melt continues at its current rate, tens of island nations from the Maldives to parts of the Philippines will be underwater in a few decades.[20] The overuse of nitrogen and phosphorus by industry and commercial agriculture has exceeded the rate at which animals, plants, and the environment can absorb these elements. The rest remains in the environment where it weakens the top soil or flows out into our waterways, affecting freshwater supply and adding to ocean acidification. Temperature rise and biogeochemical flows together are acting in an exponential way to erode the resilience of marine ecosystems and reduce their capacity to absorb CO_2 while contributing to the destabilization of other Earth systems. While it is crucial to keep temperature rise under 1.5°C, the model depends on staying on the safe side of all the subsystem boundaries—freshwater, land, aerosol, nitrogen–phosphorus, ocean, and stratospheric. The way these nonlinear changes are unfolding is the real proof of chaos theory: the effects of the fluttering butterfly wings that represent it are being multiplied many times over, and we are witnessing it in real time and on the grandest scale.

Beyond the reductive sciences that see these matters as separate issues, the newer view is quite simple: it takes an entirely different level of scientific rigor that is highly collaborative and a far greater degree of humility to understand Mother Nature's complexity and magnanimity. Both the science, in its Gaiametry form, and the necessary humility that accompanies it are still in their early *introduction* phase, fighting antibodies from the current system that refuses to subordinate human exceptionalism into our new reality. The more climate-driven disasters increase in frequency and intensity, the more we will realize that *Homo sapiens* cannot reverse the clock once certain Earth systems move past their nexus point. These mega-scale natural systems will not bow to human-built systems in their current exclusionary form. They may *not* reach equilibrium, contrary to the thought of the antiquated models of the Holocene imbedded in research that continues to resist higher-order science. Nor will they yield to the technology solutionists with their brilliant ideas who continue to use the current economic and financial infrastructure to mitigate climate collapse, while missing the bigger picture of the higher-order problems that have risen in our current reality.

The science of planetary boundaries remains in it embryonic stages and cannot claim to have all the answers. But being comfortable with not having all the answers is an essential part of the *human intelligence* that is nested in *natural intelligence.* Even now, Rockström and his colleagues acknowledge that many gaps still exist in their approach to understanding this higher-order science. Due to the complexity and size of the different Earth systems, there remains significant uncertainty over how long it will take to cause dangerous environmental change or to trigger other feedbacks that will drastically reduce the ability of those systems to return to safe levels.[21] We are on the second half of the chessboard, where change happens daily and the science about our Earth's systems that was true yesterday might become obsolete tomorrow. Awareness of this diminishing rate of predictability and our refusal to acknowledge it is what defines the new worldview of individuals who belong in that second school of thought of Gaian intelligence mentioned earlier in the chapter. Its members continue to grow in number with palpable unease with every passing day.

From GDP to GEP, the Gaiametry Economic Protocols

Until the framework for planetary boundaries was envisioned, ecological awareness as a branch of economic studies struggled to bring wider attention to the damage our human activity was causing the planet. It was as if two species of fish were involved: Mainstream economics was the dominant one, devouring its much smaller kin that was warning all creatures within the ecosystem of imminent danger. It wasn't until the water, the metaphor for the planet's ecosystems, began to show evidence of systemic poisoning that the smaller fish—ecological economics—moved slightly higher on the *introduction* phase of the Anthropogenic life cycle. It is at this stage that the field coalesced with the two new fields: sustainability science and Fritjof Capra's theory of the complex systems of life that outlines the evolution of systems thinking as articulated in chapter 3 and summarized in table 3.3. This coalescence gives us an early glimpse of what economic activity in the Anthropocene might look like. It is this type of coalescence that moves *human intelligence* in all its forms and expressions and nests it in the greater system of *natural intelligence* that will save our planet. In determining economic policies moving forward, a similar nesting process of all economic models must take place. When that happens, issues of economic activity will become synonymous with staying within the safe bounds of Earth's systems. That is the new superordinate goal for the *Second sapiens* who hold CAPI in the Anthropocene. It replaces the older *First-sapiens* superordinate goal that sought the blind pursuit of economic growth and the attainment of monetary wealth that transformed *Homo sapiens* into *Homo colossus.*

The idea for the GEP was born of the need to begin to frame economic activity in terms that acknowledge the Earth's limits to growth. It views the planet as one organism with *natural intelligence* and its full feedback loops and examines the long-term viability of the different economic models proposed for the Anthropocene. The externalization of all matters that defined *First-sapiens* deficiencies will be internalized and accounted for everywhere they appear and in whatever form they take. The GEP examine one of the most critical aspects of our global economy today—the supply chain and its ecological footprint in the production, distribution, and use of its goods from a whole-earth, cradle-to-grave sustainability perspective. The GEP also aim to assess the viability of some prevailing scientific and technological concepts that seem to be on the leading edge of sustainability practices but might fall short in providing the long-term ecosystems stability we need to prevent certain Earth systems from reaching or moving past their tipping points. If we were to view the planet through the lens of *natural intelligence* under the conditions that existed during the Holocene, we would see it as a healthy organism with its full physical resilience that allowed it to respond to all kinds of stressors that disrupt normal physiological homeostasis. In the Anthropocene, however, those conditions no longer exist, and it is up to us to determine whether our actions can restore the planet's homoeostasis.

To help answer the question of whether sustainable and regenerative practices at the local level can be scaled to planetary levels, I have borrowed a concept from monetary economics called the *velocity of money.* As the name implies, this metric measures the speed by which a single monetary unit like the US dollar moves through the economy. The faster it moves, the more robust the economic activity is. In the Gaiametry Economic Protocols, money is replaced by the rate of adoption of mitigative and restorative activities and becomes *velocity of Anthropogenic adoption.* Velocity in this case gauges how quickly these activities move from the smallest holon that applies them successfully to the largest, where they become standard planetary practices. In a system as complex as Gaia's, where exponential change on the second half of the chessboard has begun, we may never be able to gauge the velocity needed for us to avert ecological disasters. The metric, however, might serve as a way to identify barriers in our geopolitical landscape that are preventing the needed change from taking place. The velocity with which we resolve these barriers, whether they are geopolitical, environmental, or technological, become aggregate parts of the metric.

The GEP also require the transformation of our government institutions that must become part of the *sapiens 2.1* brain syndicate. The transition to *Second sapiens* cannot be left to the private sector alone. Historically, it has been government spending that helped the world rebuild after major existential disasters. The American government has intervened in massive reconstruction efforts in the aftermath of major wars such as the US Civil War and World War II. It has also played an essential role in creating new institutions that promote more evolved and equitable economic policies, as was the case during the Great Depression and FDR's New Deal. World governments played a crucial role in averting economic collapse by bailing out insolvent institutions during the 2008 financial crisis. The type of government intervention and the size of the investment needed to accommodate the shift to *Second-sapiens* virtues will eclipse previous efforts by several folds, and it cannot be achieved by governments that identify with the rigid and greatly diminished *sapiens 1.4* stage of development. To ensure a successful transition, governments in the Anthropocene epoch must possess *Second-sapiens* intelligence and play a leading role in the *sapiens 2.1* brain syndicate.

Compared to where we are today, the GEP require the reversal of government functions from being passive regulators with diminished capacities to becoming trailblazers with intelligence capacities that see beyond *sapiens 1.5* intelligence. They must fund research and development projects that are driven more by finding climate solutions and less by their economic scalability. This form of leadership was present in the United States in the 1960s under the presidency of John F. Kennedy when he declared a superordinate goal to develop the technologies needed for us to go to the moon. It was an inspirational call to greatness that forever transformed the world, but it couldn't have happened if research-and-development projects that were funded by the government had prioritized economic opportunities and market scalability. During that era, government spending on research and development accounted for roughly 12 percent of the government's budget, while today it stands at less than 4 percent.[22] Much of this decrease can be attributed to changes in the economic landscape under the *only-money-matters* ideological cycle, which greatly diminished the role of government, shifted research and development to the hands of the private sector, and lulled us into thinking that the R&D that's good for the economy is the only form of R&D we need.

From a Gravesian perspective, the Gaiametry Economic Protocols take their cues from the *life- conditions* half of the *sapiens 2.2* stage of development, the B^1 in the B^1–O^1 coupling of the double helix (see fig. 6.1). In other words, the protocols ask if the solutions proposed are coming from the O^1 station on the *complex-adaptive-intelligence* strand that is proprietary to the highly collaborative *sapiens 2.2* stage or if they are a clever masking of *sapiens 1.5* intelligence, the R in the E–R coupling, masquerading as a viable solution. It is the misalignment of the two strands that, in the past, has proven to be a primary cause of failure. B^1 represents the problems that are appearing in the Anthropocene life cycle, the stage's *life conditions* that appear in the planetary-boundaries model (see figs. 9.2, 9.3, and 9.4) showing the status of the nine Earth systems. In that same life cycle, the *complex adaptive intelligence* in both *sapiens 2.1* and *sapiens 2.2* is nested in the far-higher order of *natural intelligence.* The GEP attempt to assess the psychosocial resilience of the designers of planetary-scale solutions based on whether or not these solutions have mitigated some or any of the *life conditions* that appear in the B^1 half of the model. They are the same designers who possess capacities that form the *sapiens 2.1* brain syndicate, which is informed by the stage's *general thema* as Graves formulated it over five decades ago. This stage seeks the survival and the subsequent preservation of all life on the planet. In order for it to be fully effective, the GEP also ask if the solutions being offered hold CAPI in all the Gaiametry fractals detailed in earlier chapters. In an indirect way, the GEP also pay homage to much of Graves's research, quantitatively and qualitatively, and to his intuitive capabilities that are now being acknowledged due to the existential nature of what we're facing and the need to reverse much of what we have taken for granted under the reign of the *First sapiens.*

That reversal has become part of much of the new intelligence that today defines the mindsets and worldviews of those capable of thinking in

Second-sapiens ways. Below is a passage from Graves's 1974 piece, "Human Nature Prepares for a Momentous Leap," that summarizes those views. Note how he, like Rockström, exhibits a great degree of the humility that is common to those who have one foot in *human intelligence* and the other on the threshold of *natural intelligence*:

> According to my studies, it would be exceedingly presumptuous of the human race at this primitive stage of its development, approaching only the first step of the second ladder of existence, to imagine that the future could be predicted in precise detail. I say this because my studies indicate that something unique and unpredictable, something beyond the general form of the next system, has always emerged to characterize each new level.... From the standpoint of values, the future will be a reversal of the present. Technologically, the future will be a quantitative extension, but values and beliefs will represent a reversal, though in a higher-order form of those values and beliefs we have held most dear and in our institutional ways of living.... Take anything that *Homo sapiens* has strongly valued in the first ladder of existence, reverse it, put it in higher-order form, and you have the key to what this theory says.[23]

It is with that same humility, when we are just now approaching the first step into *natural intelligence*, that I offer my views on the values and beliefs that might come to shape *Homo sapiens's* future activities, including economics. Graves's uncertainty about understanding the human race has multiplied several times over since our entry into the Anthropocene epoch. His assessment of how *sapiens 2.2* sees the world as something beyond his/her ken and of our need to shift from a position of controlling to one of noninterfering acknowledges that we always have been and always will be part of nature's intelligence, not a species superior to or separate from it. It is this humility that replaces all the contrived *First Sapiens*-built systems with what Graves described as the "sheer fluid beauty and the fearless face-to-face awareness of now-naked life."[24] These words indicate how he viewed a significant aspect of individuals who exhibited quantitative, qualitative, and intuitive B^1–O^1 traits. Unlike his colleagues, and due to the open-ended nature of his framework, he couldn't dismiss qualitative and intuitive aspects since those traits might be proprietary to a future stage. He was often critical of other models that espoused an end stage of psychological growth, including Maslow's self-actualization stage, the apex in his *hierarchy-of-needs* model. Graves often referred to such models as man's greatest illusion: the illusion of psychological maturity.[25] The illusion is that the leading edge of human behavior is knowable and controllable, while in contrast the emerging reality is one of humility, observation, and noninterference.

Graves's own intuition might also be telling us that today we are the cusp of seeing that fluid beauty in its naked form being destroyed. We are seeing it in the collapse of the Earth's systems that can only be viewed from Jupiter and in the B[1] half of the *sapiens 2.2* stage. It is this collapse that, in James Lovelock's words, is forcing Gaia to evict us from her home. It is with this knowledge and uncertainty, combined with the humility of not knowing if our species has already been served the eviction notice, that I offer the following analyses of models that aim to define economic activity in the Anthropocene epoch.

Degrowth: The GEP's New North Star

Much of the science behind the setting of planetary boundaries can be translated in economics terms as matters of guarding the commons as those matters have evolved from their early agrarian origins. The *commons*, as the term implies, refers to social and natural resources that are accessible to all members of a community. The difference from the past is that now the community is the *planet*, not the local village and its grazing grounds. "Guarding the commons" now is about the collective benefit that comes from the proper management of the air, the land, the water, and other lifeforms—and, by extension, the nine Earth systems that are essential in preserving the viability of life. The concept is relevant to every holonic structure, and its implementation requires wise rationing of our remaining resources and ensuring that we stay within the Earth-systems' limits. These lofty goals face an uphill battle as much of the commons today is controlled by the private sector and free-market forces, not the collective of world societies that define humanity. Those who control the free markets are those who hold CAPI, and it is to their power that the truth of degrowth must be spoken.

Degrowth necessitates ending the economic policies of monetarism that pursue unbridled growth and replacing them with new ones that recognize our new Anthropogenic reality. In recognizing our planet as a living organism, we recognize its limits and the truth that continuous growth violates the natural order. The only way to preserve that natural order is to recognize that growth is only a phase and must always be seen as a temporary, or transitory, state. Accordingly, there is a new concept of a *nontransitory* state that is known to a new breed of academics as "steady-state economics," which couples economic activity with ecological limits.[26] From Malthus and Meadows and the work of Georgescu-Roegen that introduced the law of entropy to economics to the scientists who formulated the planetary- boundaries framework, degrowth is understood as the idea that must become the new guiding light for the Anthropocene epoch and should become synonymous with its economics.

> *We can't continue doing business in the Anthropocene the way we did in the Holocene. What's normal economic behavior today, can't be normal tomorrow. We need a "new economic normal" in which, at a minimum, the known tragic flaws of our current economic system are fixed.*
>
> —Peter Barnes[27]

The history of the degrowth movement can be traced back to the early 1970s, in that chaos crucible that gave birth to systems thinking and provided us with an early glimpse of the Anthropogenic life cycle. The concept was first introduced by French philosopher André Gorz, who argued that modern economic growth was unsustainable and that a transition to a new economic model based on ecological limits and social well-being was needed.[28] In the decades that followed and with the publication of books and articles by Georgescu-Roegen; his protégé, Herman Daly; E. F. Schumacher, and others, the movement gained traction in Europe and parts of North America.

However, for those who advocated for free-market capitalism, degrowth was the enemy. This divide took root immediately and only grew worse with time for two main reasons: (1) Gorz's affiliation with a movement that advocated for a new form of Marxism called the New Left allowed his detractors to project his views onto the greater polarizing dynamic between communism and capitalism that dominated world politics and the Cold War at the time; and (2) the term *degrowth* itself was stigmatized from the time it was coined and remains so to this day.

Our current, dominant economic narrative associates modernity, prosperity, and well-being with the growth paradigm, which continues to be measured by GDP. Psychologically, growth is associated with upward movement and positive experiences, while degrowth is associated with downward movement and negative experiences. This binary view has become integrated into our subconscious: degrowth is associated with bad economic times such as recessions that bring on austerity measures such as job cuts and lower salaries and provoke the fear of becoming poor. To lessen this effect, advocates of degrowth have developed a new framework that defines the field, along with alternatives to the neoclassical econometrics that have defined economic activity for the last five decades. The tenets of degrowth can be summarized in the following statement:

> Degrowth is part of a plan to achieve a rapid transition to renewable energy, restore soils and biodiversity, and reverse ecological breakdown. Its policies are designed to reduce ecological impact and inequality and to improve well-being. It seeks to scale down ecological destruction and less socially necessary production while expanding universal public goods and services such as health, education, transportation, and housing in order to decommodify the foundational goods that people need in order to lead flourishing lives. It introduces policies that prevent unemployment and guarantees jobs with a living wage. It reduces inequality and supports the sharing of national and global income more fairly while retraining people in industries that are becoming obsolete.[29]

Degrowth as a social movement has been critical of *First sapiens's* economic ideologies, whether it be the socialism that underpins the *sapiens 1.6* economic system or the capitalism that underpins the *sapiens 1.5* system. It is driven less by the ethos that seeks the redistribution of wealth and means of production and more by limiting the ecological damage caused by these two ideologies that focus on the well-being of humans to the detriment of our planet. All the subjects discussed earlier in this chapter—from income inequality and the human wellness indices that look to replace GDP, to the UN's different SDG programs—must be nested in the new degrowth paradigm that is our mandate for the Anthropocene. Degrowth takes a systemic view of matters that doesn't favor one ideology over another but puts all ideologies—economic and otherwise—through a different set of protocols informed by Gaian intelligence and the different Gaiametry fractals. Decoupling in this context is applied systemically to preserve and restore all nine Earth systems, not just the ones affecting climate change. It is a two-step process, involving first decoupling from human-built economic constructs and then a new coupling with the evolutionary pace of nature's different systems to achieve a global, steady-state economy. As we examine each model that has been proposed within the degrowth movement, the main GEP question becomes, Has this particular model helped us decouple from the old economic paradigm as viewed from the *life conditions* B^1 half in the *sapiens 2.2* stage that identifies with the *planetary-boundaries* framework? It might be difficult to answer the question conclusively due to its higher-order complexity and the brief time we've had to test the model. We remain in the early stages of the Anthropocene life cycle in which *sapiens 2.2* science has barely exited its *introduction* phase and has a learning curve that is exponentially longer and more difficult to climb than anything *First-sapiens* science has known.

Nevertheless, the answers we find to the decoupling question might themselves provide us with two important insights regarding (1) the likelihood that the model is an incremental translation of the *sapiens 1.5* intelligence masquerading as a solution to *sapiens 2.2* problems, and (2), the likelihood that the model is valid and feasible but will require structural changes so deep that we are unwilling to implement them as they will uproot the values and beliefs we have held most dear in our personal and institutional ways of living.

> *The first order system that contains the first six waves of adult psychological development tells the story of Homo sapiens living in a world of naturalistic abundance. The second order system tells the story of how psychological development will take place in a world of naturalistic scarcity.*
>
> —Clare W. Graves[30]

Degrowth and the Green Economy

Nowhere is the question of decoupling more important than in our movement away from fossil fuels and the adoption of new economic policies powered by renewable sources of energy. This issue is what has become known as the "green economy." Its overarching goal is to improve human well-being and social equity while significantly reducing environmental risks and ecological degradation. The concept of a green economy was first developed in the 1970s by German economist E. F. Schumacher, who argued that economic growth could not continue indefinitely without damaging the environment. Schumacher's ideas were influential in the development of the Brundtland Report, also known as Our Common Future, which was published by the World Commission on Environment and Development in 1987. The Brundtland Report introduced the concept of sustainable development, which is defined as "development that meets the needs of the present without compromising the ability of future generations to meet their own needs."[31]

A green economy is characterized by three main principles: environmental sustainability, resource efficiency, and social inclusivity. It holds the promise of revolutionizing global economic activity by creating high-paying green jobs without having to worry about an economic downturn resulting from job losses related to industries engaged in the extraction, processing, and distributions of fossil fuels and the infrastructure of related jobs. Many of its tenets represent an evolution of the *sapiens 1.6* ethos that sought to improve social equity and promote sustainable consumption while reducing waste and protecting the environment. What makes the green economy a possible model for the Anthropocene is the nesting of all those *sapiens 1.6* ambitions within a system capable of decoupling economic growth from environmental degradation. The idea that economic growth can continue in a green economy also attracts the attention of many who hold CAPI in the *sapiens 1.5* economic system, more specifically, the institutions that have the financial resources and the political power to effect change.

The idea that economic growth—a GDP measure—can be sustained within this new economy attracted many global institutions to pursue its adoption and facilitate its funding. From the International Monetary Fund, the World Bank, and the Organization for Economic Cooperation and Development to the UN's several development programs and the International Chamber of Commerce, change was afoot as the world began to adopt this more conscious approach toward economic activity. It became the leading narrative for a new economic model for a world that upheld sustainability practices. It has inspired our pursuit of ending our dependency on fossil fuels and put us on the path to reach the magic number of carbon neutrality by 2050. In the United States, it is behind the multi-trillion-dollar investment proposed in 2019 by progressive Democrats in their Green New Deal intended to accommodate the structural shifts we need to adapt in the Anthropocene. It is also behind the European Union's multi-billion-dollar European Green Deal proposed in 2021 with the aim of reducing emissions by 55 percent from their 1990 levels and to reach carbon neutrality by 2050.[32]

The shift to a green economy was first referred to as part of the Fourth Industrial Revolution that began with the new millennium. It gave us the Internet and made "renewal energy" part of our vernacular. It has since been reidentified as the Green Industrial Revolution, which preserves the *First sapiens's* historical view of the evolution of economic systems while adding the notion that it uses industrial principles and familiar econometrics to restore the damage previous industrial economies have caused. It calls on the development of industries that support the net-zero-by-2050 goals and for those industries to influence change at the macro levels needed to make the shift possible.

This turn of events appears to have the markings of systemic change that speaks in the economic language of *First sapiens* but is designed for *Second-sapiens* goals. For example, the International Energy Agency estimates that the global market for mass-manufactured, clean-energy technologies will be worth around $650 billion a year by 2030, which is more than three times today's levels, and that the related energy-manufacturing jobs could more than double in the same time period.[33] Other econometric research indicates that when the value of related activity—such as the industries involved in the supply chain of renewable power generation and the manufacturing of electric vehicles—is added to economic output, the numbers are also promising: in 2020, that figure stood at $1.3 trillion and was projected to increase tenfold by 2050.[34] It is estimated that the transition in the United States alone will provide $27 trillion of economic opportunity, which represents an enormous investment for the global green-banking community. The value of the most commonly used investment vehicle for the green economy was at $2.5 trillion at the end of 2022 and is expected to outpace investments in other funds for years to come.[35] This investment vehicle is known as ESG, which stands for three criteria that corporations must meet to become part of it: (1) the Environmental criterion, which evaluates a corporation's impact on climate change; (2) the Social criterion, which measures a corporation's diversity, equity, and inclusion; and (3) the Governance criterion, which covers corporate policies and stakeholder rights and responsibilities as well as how the corporation is managed and the way it measures success.

Other economic sectors have adopted the ethos of the green economy as well. The ecologically conscious part of the construction industry, for instance, is making sure that new construction and renovation projects lead to higher energy and resource efficiency. These measures enhance the quality of life for people living in and using the buildings while reducing greenhouse gas emissions and encouraging the recycling of construction material. And many entire industrialized countries have introduced measures that reduce bureaucratic layers in order to expedite the approval of net-zero projects to accommodate the transition. The green economy has also inspired a movement toward the restoration of nature that enables biodiversity to thrive while offering a cheap solution to absorb and store carbon. The EU, for example, has launched a continent-wide network to protect and restore sea and land areas to ensure the restoration of biodiversity and to guard against the degradation and pollution of soils.[36] The capturing and storing of carbon, along with the preservation of biodiversity, are two major attempts to mitigate the damage and to retore two of the nine Earth systems that have gone past their safe boundaries.

Degrowth and the Decoupling Question

The guidelines for a green economy, if implemented properly, can be seen as the operationalization of ecological economics since the two fields have so much in common. Like all Gaiametry fractals, a green economy guided by degrowth principles is considered a tightly coupled component of the ecosystem in which it resides. After all the sustainability measures have been deployed and some parts of the GEP have been met, the most important question remains: Have all these efforts proven to decouple economic activity from a corresponding increase of environmental pressure? The assumption is that if we can sustain economic growth while reducing the number of resources that negatively impact the environment, then the two are decoupled.[37] To achieve such a monumental task, decoupling requires significant changes in the government policies, corporate behavior, and consumption patterns that have defined the global economy since the start of the *Great Acceleration*. These changes will not be easy, as they represent the steep structural transition from *First-* to

Second-sapiens intelligence and will require a great degree of collaboration and cooperation among many competing economies that uphold GDP growth as their primary motivation.

The degrowth debate as it relates to the decoupling process has been muffled by neoclassical economists and technology solutionists who deceptively use one side of a concept developed by British economist William Stanley Jevons known as the "Jevons paradox." The concept states that when technological progress or government policies increase the efficiency of resource use, the falling cost of that use encourages increase in demand enough that the net resource use increases rather than decreases.[38] Since Jevons first articulated the concept in 1865, economists have used it to study matters such as increases in consumption as a result of increases in technological and resource efficiencies. What has become known as the "economies of scale" is a modern interpretation of Jevon's improved efficiency viewed through a reductive lens that focuses on lowering the relative cost of resource use while increasing the quantity demanded. Improved efficiency has become directly associated with prosperity measures such as increases in real incomes and the acceleration of economic growth. As with many models that are interpreted through the mind of *sapiens 1.5*, the consequences of increased demand and their feedback loops have been dismissed, ignoring the possibility of the paradox arising and affecting some planetary systems as they move toward their tipping points.

The question of how to measure a decoupled economy, and whether or not it can be achieved, has been the subject of much debate for more than a decade. In 2011, the International Resource Panel (IRP), an agency of the United Nations, began a series of periodic reports aimed at defining the decoupling process. The first was entitled *Decoupling Natural Resource Use and Environmental Impacts from Economic Growth.* It offered ample proof that the Jevons paradox is real and that efficiencies in resource use have caused more damage to our planet due to increased production and demand.[39] The report was complementary to the findings of the IPCC. It used the planetary-limits framework and other *sapiens 2.2* research to warn us of the causes of climate change and ecological degradation, but it also offered innovative insights on how a green economy can be guided and empowered by the decoupling process. The authors drew a clear distinction between two types of decoupling: (1) relative decoupling, which occurs when the rate of resources used is lower than

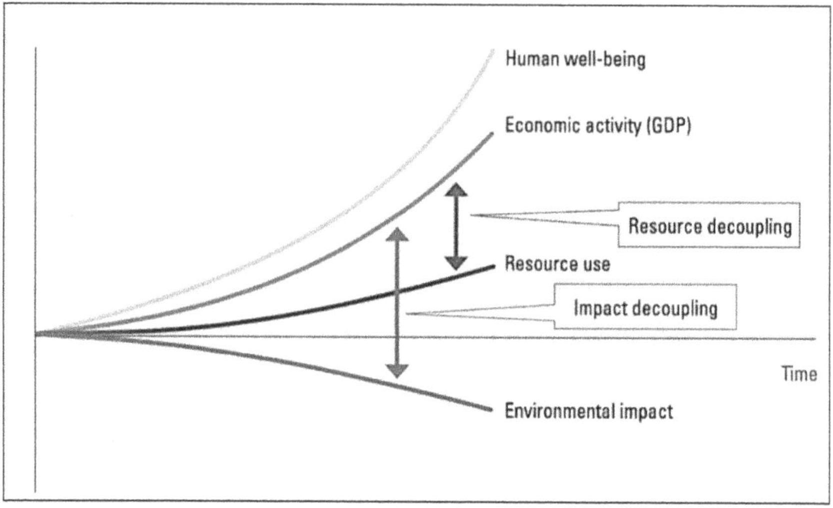

Figure 9.5. The Two Aspects of Decoupling: Resource and Impact. Note that, as natural-resource use and environmental impact are decoupled from economic growth, human well-being increases. M. Fischer-Kowalski, M. Swilling, E. U. von Weizsäcker et al, "Decoupling Natural Resource Use and Environmental Impacts from Economic Growth: A Report of the Working Group on Decoupling to the International Resource Panel," *UN environment programme: International Resource Panel* (2011), xiii; https://www.resourcepanel.org/reports/decoupling-natural-resource-use-and-environmental-impacts-economic-growth. Used with permission under fair-use rules.

the growth rate of GDP; and (2) absolute decoupling, which occurs when resource productivity grows faster than GDP.[40] Relative decoupling is also referred to as "resource decoupling," which is measured by the decrease in resources used per unit of economic output; and absolute decoupling is also referred to as "impact decoupling," which measures the decrease in environmental impact of overall economic activity. What matters most to the planetary mega system is impact decoupling since it addresses the most pertinent question: How effectively are we addressing the B[1] half—the *life conditions* part—of the *sapiens 2.2* stage?

Many entities around the world have adopted the decoupling approach as a way to contribute to climate mitigation and resource efficiency. The Global Carbon Project, for example, used the resource decoupling model to gauge the decoupling of economic activity from CO_2 emissions. The research used one main mechanism—the imposition of a carbon tax as a price for burning fossil fuels and emitting greenhouse gases—and found that from 2005 to 2019 more than twenty-five countries were successful in reducing carbon emissions while achieving economic growth.[41] The authors have advocated for similar taxation measures to be used on all extractive activities that define the global economy as we work our way toward impact decoupling. The extractive activities that are contributing to planetary degradation fall into four major types: construction materials, mineral and ore extraction, fossil-fuel extraction, and biomass use. It is the measure of the total reduction in these four areas, not just CO_2 emissions, that matters most to the GEP. Another, larger metric that has become a favorite of advocates for green growth is domestic material consumption (DMC). It is yet another gauge of resource decoupling that measures the total amount of raw materials extracted from within a country, plus that country's net physical trade. However, what it does not include are the "hidden" flows related to imports and exports of raw materials and products.[42]

Using the DMC, it was shown that some of the most advanced economies in the world, such as the United Kingdom, Japan, and the United States, have managed to decrease their material consumption since the 1990s while continuing to grow their GDP. But for those who think in whole-systems, noneconomic terms, the DMC remains a partial and unreliable measure for our planetary-scale issues when it comes to impact decoupling. The fact that these advanced countries have outsourced their manufacturing and material production to other counties only moves the environmental impact of these activities to other parts of the planet.

Other resource decoupling measures have been applied in different forms and at different country or regional levels, but when they are viewed as an aggregate measure of planetary-scale issues, they have proven to do little to decouple global GDP from the overall environmental impact our economic activities continue to have on the planet. In its 2016 report, the IRP acknowledged the short-sightedness of resource decoupling and concluded that, due to the shift of production from high-income countries to other parts of the world, global material productivity has declined since 2000 and that now the global economy needs more materials per unit of GDP than it did at the turn of the century.[43] Similarly, Gaya Herrington's quantitative work in 2020, which extended the findings of the authors of *Limits to Growth* using advanced research methods and new data, has proven that the predictions made in the original 1972 book were essentially correct and that unsustainable economic growth has continued. In similar findings that are critical of the entire decoupling approach, the European Environmental Bureau published a report in 2019 under the title *Decoupling Debunked* which makes the following conclusion:

> This report reviews the empirical and theoretical literature to assess the validity of the decoupling hypothesis. The conclusion is both overwhelmingly clear and sobering: not only is there no empirical evidence supporting the existence of a decoupling of economic growth from environmental pressures on anywhere near the scale needed to deal with environmental breakdown, but also, and perhaps more importantly, such decoupling appears unlikely to happen in the future.[44]

The principles of a green economy that seek environmental sustainability, resource efficiency, and social equity have been with us for several decades. These are the guiding principles of an ecologically aligned humanity that define the virtues of the *sapiens 2.2* stage of development. But so far, our implementation of these principles has been put through an infrastructure of existing global institutions created by the *First sapiens*—and those institutions still advocate for growth. They gave us the fallacy that green growth and the ideas behind the resource-decoupling concept are measures that can be used as part of the GEP. But in the end, they have proven to be nothing more than incremental translations of *sapiens 1.5* econometric protocols that have served the interests opposite to those of the planet. While a green economy promotes a transition to sustainable energy and the boom in jobs and economic growth that comes with it, we seem to be missing the mega-scale picture. Reductions in emissions from CO_2 and greenhouse gases are only part of what needs to be done to stabilize the planetary systems that are under threat. Once we have reached an economy run on renewables, the question will remain: how are we addressing the ever-increasing extraction of other materials that sustain the infrastructure of renewables and the continued economic growth which still champions the GDP above all other measures? The simple answer might lie in a different form of coupling: the coupling of the principles of a green economy with principles of degrowth.

Gaia's Supply Chain

As a better way to account for the shift in planetary resources that is not captured by any of the decoupling methods, another metric was proposed as a replacement to the DMC. In 2015, researchers with expertise in the sustainability sciences introduced the material-footprint (MF) metric. It is a wide-ranging metric intended to measure resource use from the beginning of a production chain to its end, or from when raw materials are extracted to when the product or service is consumed. As a representation of its planetary scale, researchers analyzed material flows related to both production and consumption networks of 186 countries. While other decoupling measures used in the aggregate indicate that wealthier countries have achieved resource decoupling and were capable of achieving impact decoupling, the 2015 MF analysis shows otherwise. Calculating raw-material equivalents of international trade proved that the global use of imported resources is, on average, three times higher than the physical quantity of traded goods.[45] That is, the amount of raw resources needed to create the traded goods is substantially greater than what is visible in the traded goods themselves. Further, say the researchers,

> As wealth grows, countries tend to reduce their domestic portion of materials extraction through international trade, whereas the overall mass of material consumption generally increases. With every 10 percent increase in gross domestic product, the average national MF increases by 6 percent. Our findings call into question the sole use of current resource-productivity indicators in policy making and suggest the necessity of an additional focus on consumption-based accounting for natural resource use.[46]

The MF framework is by far the single largest metric that gauges absolute decoupling of economic activity from material use. It has been adopted by many global and regional institutions and is now being used as one of the leading indicators for sustainable economic practices on a global scale. While it tells us how much more we need to reduce our global MF by in order to reach absolute decoupling, it provides no clarity on how or when the world's largest economies can fully decouple from their mandate to grow GDP.

While the MF covers all classes of material resources, it falls short of ensuring that the ecological impact of the entire life cycle of products being produced and the economic activities related to them is fully evaluated. In order for an indicator to meet the requirements of the GEP that run on *natural intelligence*, it must provide a complete picture of how material extraction—along with its processing, manufacturing, shipping, and ultimate disposal—affect other planetary boundaries that are tightly coupled as ecosystems. Unlike the current supply-chain models concerned with cost efficiency that externalizes all other costs to the environment, Gaia's supply chain is concerned with all ecosystems affected by global trade, from the ecosystem where raw material is extracted to the ecosystem to which it returns as waste. The MF metric also falls short of addressing a key driver of a green economy: the well-being of the people engaged in every phase of a product's life cycle, from those who work on the extraction of raw material and those who are part of its supply chain from beginning to end, to those who are engaged in its disposal and recycling. Regardless of how resilient or inclusive a human-built system for economics is, in order for it to become a viable tool in the GEP toolbox it must account for systemic feedback loops for every type of economic activity at every holonic level possible. In other words, ecological footprint must replace material footprint. These will be the mandates that help keep us within the necessary planetary boundaries.

Ecosystems and Renewable Energy

To examine economic models that keep us within the boundaries of the nine Earth systems, we must first look at the ecological footprint of the biggest driver of the green economy: renewable energy. It is by advancing a scalable platform of renewables that we will be able to reach our goal of net zero by 2050. However, if we are to use Gaia's supply-chain principles to evaluate this shift, many ecosystems issues that haven't been apparent to green-growth advocates come to the fore. In 2017, the World Bank set out to answer the question of how we get to net zero by 2050 and how many resources we need to get us there.[47] Based on their research models, the increase in material extraction required to build enough solar and wind power to electrify half of the world's economy would use an overwhelming amount of resources: 17 million metric tons of copper, 20 million tons of lead, 25 million tons of zinc, 80 million tons of aluminum, and at least 3 billion tons of iron. To move the entire world to 100 percent renewables would double these amounts. In addition, to make our energy alternatives as reliable as fossil fuels, the world will require batteries with enormous capacity for storage, and for that we need lithium. The World Bank estimates that the shift will require more than 40 million tons of it, an amount that is 27 times greater than the current levels of extraction.

In addition to concerns about adding to the crisis of resource overextraction, the mining process itself contributes considerably to the degradation of other planetary boundaries. This issue is not just a matter a materials footprint, it is one of an ecological footprint that affects all the planetary boundaries and is holonic in nature. Mining has become the primary driver of ecosystem collapse, deforestation, and loss of biodiversity. A look at the ecological footprint of just two key elements that go into building our renewable energy infrastructure serve as a small example of how Gaia's supply chain functions and the impact extractive activities have on the local ecosystems from which they are extracted. These two elements are silver, which is used in solar panels, and lithium, which is used in batteries.

The mining of silver, like all other mining activities, causes disruption to the local ecosystem due to the enormous open pits it creates. It also requires land clearing. A countless number of trees, and in some cases entire forests, are being cut down or destroyed to accommodate mining activities. This leads to deforestation, contamination of the water and the air, and other impacts on the surrounding ecosystem. Deforestation due to mining destroys natural habitats and contributes to the loss of biodiversity as it places many animal and plant species in danger of becoming extinct. Mining of any ore or mineral also consumes a massive amount of electricity and energy. The continual smelting and processing procedures for metals like silver emit harmful greenhouse gases into the atmosphere, adding to the carbon footprint. The process also causes acid runoff that can be damaging to all life forms and ecosystems that are downstream from the mine.[48] One of the largest silver mines in the world that carries an equally large ecological footprint is the Penasquito mine in Mexico. Based on the World Bank study, we need more than a hundred new silver mines the size of Penasquito to produce enough silver to accommodate the energy transition to renewables. If we continue to base our economic philosophy on the growth paradigm, the demand for *all* resources, not just silver, needed to support renewable energy will continue to double roughly every two-and-a-half decades.

The extraction of lithium, like all other extractive activities, also has an impact on the carbon footprint; but, due to its unique mining process called "brine mining," it has an ecological footprint that represents a toxic risk to local water resources and the ecosystems that depend on them. This reactive alkali metal not only powers batteries for energy storage, it also powers our phones, tablets, laptops, and electric cars. Brine mining is an energy-intensive process that involves pumping saltwater to the surface, where it is evaporated to remove the lithium and other minerals.[49]

It takes 500,000 gallons of water to produce one ton of lithium; and, at the current levels of demand, the production process is already wreaking havoc on local communities, affecting human lives and local biodiversity. In 2016, a chemical leak from the Ganzizhou Rongda lithium mine leaked toxic chemicals into the nearby Liqi river near the Tibetan Plateau, contaminating the water and killing a massive number of fish, cows, and yaks.

In the Americas, Argentina, Bolivia, and Chile hold more than half the world's supply of lithium, and the problem there is of a different nature. It is the limited supply of water in one of the driest places on Earth. Salar de Atacama, the largest salt flat in Chile, is the greatest source of lithium production in the world, but the region also has an extremely low level of annual rainfall, which places an uneven burden on the water supply for local communities. According to researchers, more than 65 percent of the region's water in 2018 was used to support lithium-mining activities, impacting the lives of farmers and the local ecosystem to the point that many communities were forced to import water from elsewhere.[50]

This exploration of a very small segment of Gaia's supply chain shows how complex the management of natural resources and their greater ecological footprint becomes when we incorporate all feedback loops into the design of a new global economy for the Anthropocene. Fresh water supply and loss of biodiversity in just the mining of lithium and silver alone have shown the nature of Gaia's tightly coupled systems and how these two activities have contributed to two planetary boundaries having already moved past their tipping points. If these two boundaries are indeed on the second half of the chessboard, then our pursuit of net zero by 2050 is in itself having a cascading effect on all other planetary boundaries. To explore the full ecological footprint of Gaia's supply chain for the energy transition alone, we would have to assess the full impact of every step from extraction to the end of life of a product, when it becomes part of a new and different type of landfill known today as "e-waste."

For a comprehensive view of the ecological footprint and the well-being of humans within the ecosystem of supply chains on a global scale, the Harvard Business Review published a comprehensive study in 2020 of three supply-chain networks of some of the world's largest corporations that consider themselves sustainability leaders: the auto, electronics, and pharmaceuticals industries. What they discovered was that along the entire supply chain, from top-tier to lower-tier suppliers, many were violating the standards these corporations were expecting them to uphold.[51]

From Mexico to China and Taiwan, procedures for handling issues of environmental safety, worker safety, and health were not being addressed effectively. The study attributes some of the blame to the corporations themselves for frequently placing orders that exceed suppliers' capacity or imposing unrealistic deadlines, leading supplier factories to demand heavy overtime from their workers. This is an example of the Jevons paradox applied to sustainability practices: the more we consider a product sustainable, the more of it we produce, which increases the total resources that go into it, resulting in less sustainable practices overall and a larger ecological footprint. And while these leading sustainability corporations might work on reducing the impact of these conditions with their suppliers, since their business model is still driven by a growth paradigm their activities will continue to affect the different planetary boundaries.

The Circular Economy

Ideas for creating an all-encompassing model that deals with lowering our material and ecological footprints have been around for decades. One of the first attempts to create such an inclusive design concept is known as cradle-to-cradle design (C2C), which was introduced in 2002. Taking a holistic approach toward the goals of a green economy, the model suggests that industry must protect and enrich ecosystems and nature's biological metabolism while maintaining a safe, productive *technical* metabolism for the high-quality use and circulation of organic and technical nutrients.[52] While many corporations have adopted this model into their corporate philosophy and production processes, it simply could not be used for the majority of the products that represent most of our material footprint today. This is due to its tight definition of technical nutrients as nontoxic material that does not harm the natural environment and can be used repeatedly throughout its life until eventually converting to waste.

The model, while establishing some initial parameters for a sustainable economic model for the world, has been harshly criticized. In 2009, Friedrich Schmidt-Bleek, the head of Germany's Wuppertal Institute for Climate, Environment, and Energy, called the C2C framework pseudo-psychological nonsense due to two factors: the scientific impossibility of closing the majority of the materials cycle used in today's global economy and the model's exclusion of 99 percent of materials that still impact the environment.[53] Closing the material cycle implies that 100 percent of any product's raw material can be recycled, resulting in zero waste.

Schmidt-Bleek speculates that to achieve such a goal would require an enormous amount of energy that would surpass any environmental gains made by using the model. He seems also to imply that as much as 99 percent of current products cannot meet the strict design requirements the model calls for. While it remains too restrictive for ubiquitous use, it has opened the door to other design considerations that not only deal with issues of organic and technical life cycles of products but also challenge the foundation on which the current linear-growth model is built. The alternative to this linear-growth model is known today as the "circular economy."

The circular economy represents the potential nesting of *human intelligence* in *natural intelligence* as much of its design is based on living systems. It replaces the current *sapiens 1.5* linear model that runs on the unsustainable ethos of take, make, and dispose with a circular-flow model that has the markings of a *sapiens 2.1* design. It brings the C2C principles out of their restrictive conditions and integrates them with industrial ecology and biomimicry, two fields of study that can be considered part of the *sapiens 2.1* brain syndicate. The former aims to restore our ecology, while the latter attempts to copy nature's design principles. The Ellen Mac Arthur Foundation, one of the strongest supporters of circular economies, describes it as follows:

> The circular economy refers to an industrial economy that is restorative by intention; aims to rely on renewable energy; minimizes, tracks, and eliminates the use of toxic chemicals; and eradicates waste through careful design. The term goes beyond the mechanics of production and consumption of goods and services. It rebuilds capital including social and natural and supports the shift from consumer to user. The concept of the circular economy is grounded in the study of non-linear, particular living systems. A major outcome of taking insights from living systems is the notion of optimizing systems rather than components.[54]

The concept of the circular economy requires a leap of faith into believing that human-created systems can behave in a cyclical manner similar to Gaia's ecological processes. It starts by examining the products we use in everyday life and redesigns them using material and production methods that follow biological life cycles, ensuring that the product, its component elements, and the packaging are compostable and nontoxic to the environment. Regarding products that don't biodegrade, the circular economy emphasizes recycling their component parts such as metals, polymers, and alloys that make up most of our consumer waste today. Circular economies are comprised of two cycles: the first is called the biological cycle and the second, the technical cycle. Together, they are designed to reduce or eliminate the high ecological costs of mining and industrial processing that are part of the current linear system. The ethos of take, make, and dispose is replaced with one of return and renew, in which products and components can be redesigned to be reassembled and regenerated.

One of the main principles in the biological cycle is regeneration. It plays an important role in restoring natural capital by employing regenerative farming practices that allow nature to rebuild soils and increase biodiversity. It seeks to redesign the food system itself by returning all

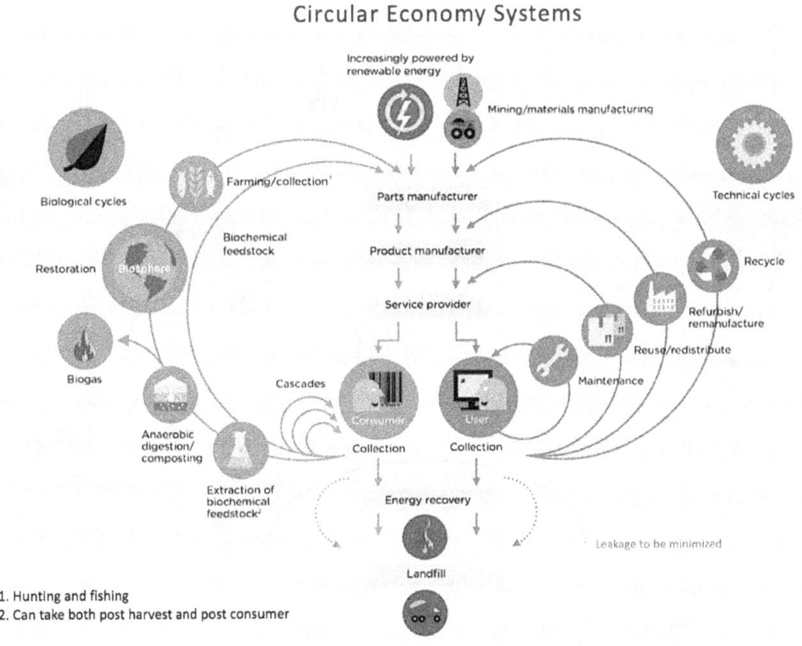

Figure 9.6. Circular Economy Systems. The two cycles that define the circular economy are biological and technical. Ellen MacArthur Foundation, February 2019; https://www.ellenmacarthurfoundation.org/circular-economy-diagram. Drawing based on Michael Braungart and William McDonough, *Cradle to Cradle*, 2002. Used with permission under fair-use rules.

biological materials to the Earth through composting and other methods that alleviate the reliance on fertilizers and chemicals and produce a natural biomass that can be used as fuel. Reversing modern industrial farming techniques, these practices restore nutrients to the top soil instead of eroding it and clean waterways instead of polluting them. There are several popular schools of thought that can help in the adoption of these practices.

In addition to regenerative agriculture, the biological cycle calls on the use of concepts such as restorative aquaculture, which seeks to restore ecosystems for fisheries, and agroforestry, which calls on active and regenerative ways to restore our forests.[55] The overarching goal of these practices is to increase local biodiversity, and improve air, soil, and water quality. The biological cycle also concerns itself with smaller loops, labeled as "cascades" in figure 9.5. The idea is to make use of products and organic materials that are already in the economy to ensure that their economic life is maximized, whether it involves, for instance, recycling food byproducts to make other products or using them as animal feed. Once these products reach the end of their useful economic cycle, they are returned to the soil as biodegradable material.

The technical cycle of the circular economy is far more intensive in design and engineering than the biological cycle and requires structural changes to how the current capitalist system works. Like the ideas expressed in *The Limits to Growth,* it is driven by the fact that the resources needed to manufacture products are of a finite nature. The cycle looks to utilize the shorter loops in figure 9.5 as a way to minimize the volume of materials that have to be recycled and therefore views the outermost loop as the stage of last resort.[56] This means that a greater emphasis is placed on the inner, smaller loops such as sharing, reusing, and refurbishing. The model underscores the idea that in order for these steps to work effectively, products must be designed to accommodate each loop. In the linear model of take, make, and dispose, the highest value is placed on the price of the newest, most innovative products, from the newest smartphone to the latest car model. Most of the associated costs of these products are externalized. The technical cycle seeks to reverse the situation by placing the highest value on the longevity and utility of products designed and produced specifically to account for all costs. It does so by greatly extending the useful life of a product, minimizing the need to recycle, and reducing the overall need to extract new material. It also requires the reworking of current production processes in order to extend the life of a product by making its parts modular, more durable, and easier to refurbish and to reuse. Designs call for products to be made from materials that can easily be separated when they reach the end of their useful life and must be recycled.

The smallest loop in the technical cycle concerns the idea of sharing, which emphasizes a shift away from ownership of things to community membership in them. This plan means to take advantage of the greatly underutilized use of household goods such as power tools and the bulk of products that fill our garage shelves and toolsheds. It replaces them with more durable products that provide the same utility but are owned by the community. It draws parallels with how modern libraries work and advances an evolved form of the concept of the commons. The digital age has made the sharing element of our economy a reality. We share our homes with guests through platforms such as Airbnb, and car sharing has become popular in major cities around the world. The digital economy has made possible the reselling of underutilized products of all types, from clothes to tools and everything in between. It has become a catalyst for spreading the ethos of sharing by shifting traditional economic models that require physical presence to online models, with the result that entire sectors such as higher education and the workplace are being disrupted. All these activities eliminate or reduce the need for certain physical products and the materials that go into making and maintaining them while also reducing the need to travel, which improves another Earth system by reducing our carbon footprint.

The sharing loop, along with all the other loops in the technical cycle of the circular economy—maintenance, reuse, and refurbishing and remanufacturing—is based on the idea that once a product is reengineered and a culture is committed to the ethos of return and renew, all loops become possible. They represent a cost saving to customers and businesses as they make use of products and materials already in circulation rather than investing in making new products. Maintenance of high-quality products with modular parts makes it easier to guard against their failure and decline. The maintenance loop is not limited to machines and highly engineered products; it can be extended to prolong the life of anything intended for consumer use—again from clothes to tools and everything in between. Similarly, the reuse loop keeps products in service in their original form and for their original purpose. It has gained acceptance across many sectors of our economy, from how we reuse cardboard packaging to the use of particular plastics to contain food, drink, and household cleaning products. The refurbishing-and-remanufacturing loop represents a higher-order form of the technical cycle and runs on the same ethos. Refurbishing includes repairing or replacing components, updating specifications, and improving cosmetic appearance. There's a growing right-to-repair movement around the world that aims to change regulations and make product design easier for users to repair and refurbish products themselves.[57]

The remanufacturing loop represents the last stage before a product and its components become waste and need to be recycled. Because of the high costs of recycling, this stage calls for reengineering products and components to the same, or improved, level of performance as a newly manufactured one would have. For that reason, the manufacturing loop requires more investment in plants and machinery than do the inner loops of the technical cycle, but the remanufactured items are typically provided with a warranty that is equivalent to, or better than, that of a newly manufactured product.[58] Although remanufacturing leaves a larger material footprint than the smaller loops, its footprint remains smaller than the one needed in the last loop: recycling. This is the final step in the technical cycle of the circular economy. The product at this stage cannot be refurbished or remanufactured, but the materials in it that still have value are retained and reprocessed into new material.

The adoption of circular economies is expected to have many economic and environmental benefits. Experts believe that it will make for a more equitable and innovative economy worldwide with higher rates of technological development, improved material efficiency, higher number of skilled jobs, energy efficiency, and more profit opportunities for companies.[59] Research by the same experts shows that, in addition to economic benefits, a circular economy has the potential to cut CO_2 emissions by half and material consumption by 32 percent by 2030. Further, by returning biological material to the soil, we revive land productivity and the health of the soil, which allows it to be 2.7 times more productive than current commercial farming methods using chemical fertilizers.

In order to be successful, circular economies need to empower worldwide cultural virtues that enable a radical rethinking of consumerism and the reshaping of the entire global-supply chain that slows its growth to a very slow pace in the face of climate disasters that continue to be in a state of exponential acceleration. This slow scaling will be happening in an economy that still relies on fossil fuels for 80 percent of its energy needs. Just as with any new idea, the more the world adopts the virtues of circular economies, the bigger the questions become. The most prominent question concerns the very nature of what circular economies call for, which is identified in their loops. Terms such as *sharing*, *reusing*, and *remanufacturing*—like the term *degrowth*—are stigmatized in today's economic reality, which associates prosperity with shiny new products. The values for which circular economies stand have to do battle with the values of the ubiquitous *sapiens 1.5* global economic system that has long been engrained in our culture and continues to grow and thrive on the externalization of costs, profit maximization, and product obsolescence; this engrained system has formed its own binary worldview that associates the power to purchase new things with well-being and prosperity and the users of recycled and reused items as less well-off and prosperous. Some elements of the circular-economies loops also identify with the virtues of a *sapiens 1.6* economic system, in that it is a communal stage of economic development that seeks the fair redistribution of wealth and requires a great degree of cooperation. These virtues are in direct contrast to the current dominant system that thrives on competition and is driven by meritocracy and the constant need to improve on scientific and technological discoveries, which don't necessarily favor circular economies.

Recent data on circular-economic activity indicate that only 8.6 percent of the world economy is circular; more than 90 percent of the resources extracted and consumed do not return to production cycles. Meanwhile recycling, due to the high cost of collection and sorting, is failing to measure at a rate that keeps up with growth.[60] While claiming to mimic living complex systems, circular economies are failing to commit to the high financial cost associated with the upshift in complexity. Like the leap into *Second-sapiens* intelligence, this shift is structural in nature, not an incremental translation that runs on the existing infrastructure of systems, values, and virtues. It requires massive capital investments in factories to change the way products are designed, produced, consumed, and discarded. Like our investment in renewable energy, an investment on this scale will have its own impact on our material and ecological footprint. Considering the pace of adoption and the obstacles facing circular economies, the OECD estimates that by 2060 the use of raw materials will nevertheless double compared to 2017 and that our greenhouse gases will increase by 49 percent compared to 2015, while the GDP is expected to quadruple in the same time period.[61]

Like many other pioneering ideas for the economics of Anthropocene, the *sapiens 2.1* brain syndicate is missing many elements in the circular economy that define the higher-order form of governance needed. Leadership in research and development in large is still driven by the *sapiens 1.5* ethos of scalability and market feasibility instead of the *Second-sapiens* ethos that seeks the preservation of life. Gauging the circular economy's effectiveness is further complicated by the obstacles mentioned earlier that make the *velocity of adoption* metric more difficult to implement. Regarding the question of who holds CAPI in the circular-economy model, a pattern seems to be emerging that can easily answer that question by answering a simpler one: Does the underlying motivation behind the model put GDP growth ahead of any other metric? Despite all the advantages of the circular economy, the answer to that question is *yes*, which defaults the model to one that is beholden to those who hold CAPI in the current economic and financial infrastructure. Based on research cited in this chapter, it seems that we're unable to decouple GDP growth from our growing material and ecological footprint, which makes it difficult to imagine that the circular economy in its current state will become the economic model for the Anthropocene.

Doughnut Economics

The ideas behind doughnut economics were envisioned by British economist Kate Raworth, a senior teaching associate at Oxford University's Environmental Change Institute and Professor of Practice at Amsterdam University of Applied Sciences. She introduced the concept in a 2012 paper and elaborated on it in her 2017 book, *Doughnut Economics: Seven Ways to Think Like a 21st Century Economist.* Hers was the first economic model to put the mega-scale, planetary-boundaries framework at the heart of its design, accompanied by a macro-scale, social-boundaries framework intended to keep us within the limits of all nine Earth systems. As depicted in figure 9.6, the model identifies twelve social boundaries that are nested within the planetary boundaries. In this model, an economy is considered prosperous when it meets all twelve social foundations without overshooting any of the nine ecological ceilings. This balance between the two boundaries is represented by the area between the two rings, the area which Raworth considers a safe and just space for humanity.[62]

Doughnut Economics

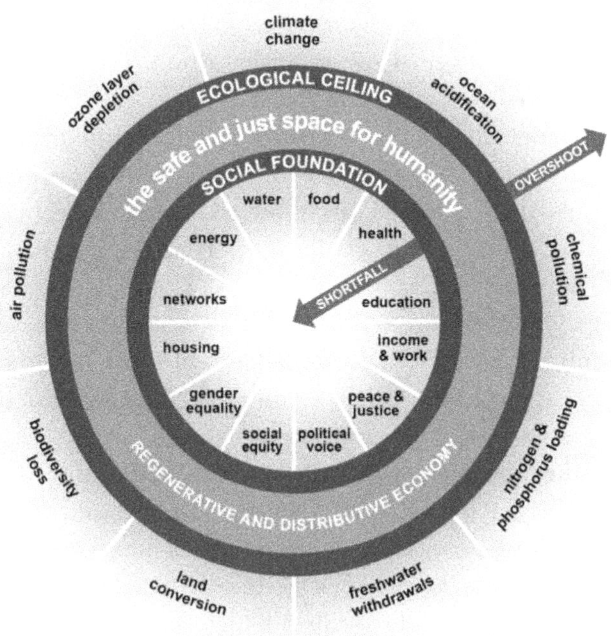

Figure 9.7. The Doughnut Economics Model. The twelve social boundaries are shown nested within the nine Earth-systems boundaries. "Overshoot" refers to human activity exceeding the Earth's capacity to handle it, and "shortfall" refers to people's lack of access to the basic necessities for a good life. Wikipedia public domain; https://upload.wikimedia.org/wikipedia/commons/1/12/Doughnut_%28economic_model%29.jpg. .

Much of the theme in Raworth's work, as in this book, is a critique of the current, unsustainable economic models that run the world. The twelve social boundaries she identifies—from fair income and renewable energy to social equity and political voice—have been covered in various and often overlapping ways throughout this book. She describes seven ways to make the model operational that can be summarized as follows: (1) Think in big-picture terms of the biosphere and its importance to economic and social systems. (2) Think in terms of systems and their feedback loops. (3) Abandon extractive activities and encourage regenerative design. (4) Advocate for policies that address wealth disparities and social justice issues. (5) Encourage economic policies that promote cooperation, fairness, and a sense of community. (6) Shift away from focusing on GDP and focus more on happiness, health, and equality. (7) Keep economic activity within this "sweet spot" where both people and the planet thrive.[63] In response to the international interest the book generated, Raworth cofounded the Doughnut Economics Action Lab (DEAL) to connect and collaborate with changemakers worldwide who are starting to put the ideas of doughnut economics into practice.

At its core, the model calls on us to abandon old thinking and develop new ways to improve our capacities to handle current and future challenges. It calls on us to create a new mindset that draws insights from areas that the reductive *sapiens 1.5* worldview has long dismissed and to bring forth complexity sciences that have been marginalized for the last five decades. These diverse schools of thought come from the fields of ecology, feminism, institutional knowledge, and behavioral and complexity economics and are intended to transform economies both locally and globally.[64] The two major phenomena that connect all the themes in the model also underpin many of the themes of this book: the abandonment of neoclassical economics driven by endless GDP growth, and the recognition that life in the Anthropocene and all its human constructs must be viewed in terms of the complex adaptive systems of life—the *natural intelligence* with all its complexity, its full feedback loops, and its interdependent nature.

While the doughnut-economics model is too new to determine its impact and potential, DEAL has developed training programs for corporations and local and regional governments in efforts to spread its adoption. Cities such as Amsterdam, Brussels, Copenhagen, Berlin, and Cambridge are experimenting with it as the newest tool to battle ecological collapse and climate change. It is no surprise that, as are all models critical of the status quo, this one has also been attacked by the antibodies of the current system that view GDP growth as the only way to meet the needs of the social boundaries. Criticism is also leveled by environmental activists who claim that social boundaries don't share the same dimensions or the same dynamics of environmental boundaries. They argue that social issues such as poverty rates and social equity are human constructs capable of evolving and adapting, whereas ecological boundaries are physical walls that cannot be negotiated.[65]

To get an idea of the *velocity of adoption*, one can draw parallels between this framework and the United Nations Sustainable Development Goals framework (UNSDG). It was adopted by member countries in 2015 and contains most if not all of Raworth's twelve social boundaries in addition to several planetary boundaries, as seen in table 9.1 below.

According to the UN, the sustainable development goals are the blueprint to achieve a better future for all. They address the global challenges we face, including those related to poverty, inequality, climate change, environmental degradation, peace, and justice.[66] All seventeen goals are interconnected, and the aim is to achieve them all by 2030. This remains the world's roadmap for ending poverty, protecting the planet, and tackling inequalities; it comprises a macro-systems representation of the doughnut-economies model used on a global scale. Like the doughnut-economies framework, many of these goals are addressed from different approaches and in different, overlapping parts of this book. And, just as have so many complex models that require the transcendence of *First-sapiens* intelligence, adoption of the SDG agenda has experienced enormous headwinds. 2023 marked the halfway point in its journey to 2030, and, based on data from that year's SDG summit, a mere 12 percent of the goals were on track. While the UN attributes much of the blame to Covid-19 and Russia's war in Ukraine and its aftermath, research shows

Table 9.1. The United Nations Sustainable-Development Goals (UNSDG). Image in public domain. https://www.un.org/sustainabledevelopment/sustainable-development-goals/.

that we wouldn't be on track even without these crises. Ending hunger has become a distant prospect, for instance, and guidance on transformative and accelerated actions is urgently needed.[67]

The bigger question that must still be asked might be viewed as unfair and discriminatory in nature: Would the pursuit of all twelve social boundaries to bring the world to a just state add to our material and ecological footprint, or can the two issues be decoupled? Another way to ask this question is, Can justice in human-built systems be reached without negatively impacting the planetary systems? Many of the goals in both models call for responsible consumption, sustainable economic growth, and the development of an innovative and sustainable industrialized infrastructure. The widest sustainability model in use today is that of the circular economy. Based on its trajectory, some if not most of the social boundaries could be reached as humanity's needs adjust and evolve and the model gains wider adoptability, but, as findings from the Stockholm Resilience Center show, planetary boundaries continue to follow a different order of complexity that operates on its own independent dynamics. Sustainable development in both the doughnut economies model and the UNSDG model also call on the use of renewable energy to help achieve their goals, but, as shown in the research by the World Bank and the OECD, the pursuit of a green and sustainable economy driven as it is by the incessant need for growth makes the goals in both models harder to achieve.

The graphic below from Raworth's 2017 book shows the deficiencies we have in each social boundary that make up the social foundation. The data is mapped along with the planetary-boundaries data from 2015 showing the four transgressed Earth systems. The darker areas in the inner circle represent the shortfall in reaching the social foundation. There is no new research from DEAL that points to the movement of the social boundaries in light of the two additional planetary boundaries that were transgressed in 2023.

When it comes to the question of who holds CAPI in both the doughnut economies and the UN's SDG models, it's clear that they both uphold the GDP growth paradigm as a way to achieve the social-boundaries goals. While the *velocity of adoption* in both models remains slow and riddled with obstacles, their ability to address issues of planetary boundaries remains questionable. Like the green economy and the circular economy, both models can easily default to an incremental translation of the *sapiens 1.5*

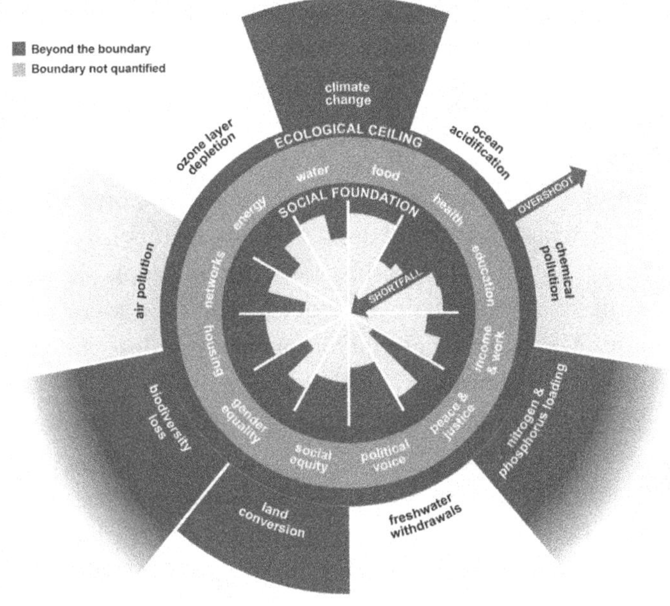

Figure 9.8. The Doughnut Economics Model Relative to Planetary Boundaries. Darker shaded segments from the ecological ceiling outward represent areas that have been transgressed beyond recommended boundaries. As explained for figure 9.7, "overshoot" refers to human activity exceeding the Earth's capacity to handle it, and "shortfall" refers to people's lack of access to the basic necessities for a good life. Wikipedia public domain; https://en.wikipedia.org/wiki/Doughnut_(economic_model)#/media/File:Doughnut-transgressing.jpg.

ethos that is bound to those who hold CAPI in the current economic and financial infrastructure. The slight difference is that the UN's SDG model has been adopted by its members as a global guide for sustainable development and relies on a high degree of cooperation and global coordination among its members. However, there is no enforcement mechanism that holds member countries accountable to their commitments. Accountability is an essential part of the *sapiens 2.1* brain syndicate that must be present in every model for Anthropocene economics. It is this higher order of governance that is endowed by enforcement mechanisms in a new form of Gaiacracy that transcends national borders. It also directs new research-and-development efforts toward the *Second-sapiens* ethos that seeks the preservation of life, away from the *sapiens 1.5* ethos that concerns itself with scalability, market feasibility, and the endless pursuit of profit.

Degrowth and Post Growth

Since the ideas behind the degrowth movement were born five decades ago, attempts to destigmatize them, or pursue their implementation, have failed as the world economy has grown by more than thirty times in that period, from $3.4 trillion to more than $104 trillion in 2022.[68] This is also the timeframe that has contributed most to the *Great Acceleration*. The development of a modern world is synonymous with growth and everything that comes with it, from job growth to infrastructure development that ensures the health, safety, and prosperity of people. Research has shown that these activities cannot be decoupled from a corresponding increase in our carbon and material footprint, regardless of how sustainability is measured; consequently, the actual reduction of economic and development activities becomes the sole pathway forward. The movement against growth-ism has seen a popular resurgence in the last few years, especially among younger generations concerned about their own future, and it takes a different yet simple approach to the implementation of many of the models examined so far. Much of this approach is summarized by Jason Hickel, an anthropologist specializing in economic anthropology. In his 2020 book, *Less is More: How Degrowth Will Save the World*, Hickel details five degrowth steps we should take toward saving our planet: (1) bring an end to planned obsolescence; (2) cut down on advertising; (3) switch from ownership to usership; (4) end food waste; and (5) scale down ecologically destructive industries such as the fossil-fuels industry.[69]

Hickel's recommendations appear in many of the models presented in this book. His arguments are well researched and come from a wider perspective that is rooted more in the planetary timeframe of an anthropologist than in a specific political or economic ideology rooted in the neoclassical worldview. What makes his views popular is this broad approach that places modern economics on the long arc of history. It can be likened to standing on Jupiter and viewing human behavior, its relationship with nature, and its biology, culture, and civilization going back in time from the dawn of the *sapiens 1.1* stage to where we are today. It is this kind of viewing of who we are and what we have been as a species, claiming superiority over nature and the resulting ecological destruction of that worldview, that brings our new reality into sharper focus. The appearance of modern economics in anthropological terms is an ephemeral, but dangerous, phenomenon that amounts to nothing more than a small blip over the course of time. But it is that very blip—the 0.2 seconds on the epochal timescale—that can usher in the extinction of millions of species, including our own, if we don't abandon the myopic neoclassical worldview and its obsession with economic growth.

Like the degrowth movement and other initiatives covered in this chapter, the post-growth movement is driven by the same overarching narrative that Earth's resources are finite and that continuous economic expansion based on the current neoclassical model and GDP growth is unsustainable. It also emphasizes staying within planetary boundaries and respecting ecological constraints and the mandates that come with them, from shrinking our material and ecological footprint to engaging in sustainability practices as outlined in circular and doughnut economies. Unlike the degrowth movement, however, post-growth acknowledges that economic growth *can* generate beneficial effects up to a point, beyond which other noneconomic indicators become necessary in order to increase human wellbeing.[70] This view is primarily based on a concept known as the Easterlin paradox, which was formulated in 1974 by the first economist to study happiness, Richard Easterlin, who was then a professor of economics at the University of Pennsylvania. The paradox states that, while at some point happiness correlates directly with income both within and among nations, over time, it does not trend upward as income continues to grow.[71] That is, more money doesn't lead to more happiness over time. Nevertheless, other factors—based primarily in behavioral economics and the keeping-up-with-the-Joneses phenomenon—play a role in maintaining us on a perpetual wheel of seeking higher incomes once happiness from the previous level of income has faded. Considering this issue alone, the post-growth movement has a steep hill to climb in order to decouple its intrinsic goals of happiness from our behavioral conditioning to pursuit higher income in perpetuity. A 2010 study on income equality shows that happiness and economic well-being can be achieved at a per capita income of $25,000.[72] But today, a family of four in the United States earning under $30,000 a year is considered to be below the poverty guidelines. In an economy that derives more than two-thirds of its economic output from consumer spending, happiness is directly tied to how much we spend and consume, even though the shift away from today's levels of consumption is critical not just to the post-growth movement but to all other movements concerned with planetary limits.

Aside from the debate on how to decouple happiness from the pursuit of higher income, the post-growth movement believes that economic growth has provided us with enough experience and data that we can now separate good growth from bad. According to the Post Growth Institute, good growth is associated with the development of human potential and happiness within in relation to a physically finite Earth. It aims to shift the current worldview from a consumption-driven economic system to one that offers a multitude of grassroot alternatives that can grow and allow the planet to thrive. It puts life and everything needed to sustain it at the center of economic and social activity, as opposed to the never-ending accumulation of money and the pursuit of growth of all kinds without regard for its consequences.[73] Like other sustainability models, post growth encourages community building and collaboration among academics, activists, policymakers, and businesses to share knowledge, develop practical solutions, and build momentum for systemic change toward a post-growth future.

Due to how new this model is, asking who holds CAPI in it is irrelevant. Like other models created by *Second-sapiens* intelligence, although it might attract early adopters in small communities around the world, it remains in its early *introduction* phase doing battle with antibodies from the current system. Its *velocity of adoption* is similar to other sustainability models, riddled with obstacles and facing the enormous challenges that come with decoupling our material and ecological footprint from economic growth. When it comes to the question of what it will take to shift economic paradigms at a global scale, whether it is the post-growth model or any other that has the planetary boundaries at its core, all questions are essentially reduced to one: Who holds CAPI over stopping the shift or causing it to become a reality? Sadly, the answer places our destiny and that of all life on the planet at the mercy of the *First sapiens* who still control most elements of the CAPI equation at most fractal levels in economics, geopolitics, and finance.

If there is a single metric responsible for the planet's ecological crisis, it is GDP and the *First sapiens's* obsession with it. Since climate change has become an issue, many well-meaning ideas and frameworks have come to the fore to help us mitigate the damage and adapt to changes in Earth's systems. In researching the models that are the subject of this chapter, two distinct patterns have emerged.

The first has shown that absolute decoupling of GDP growth from growth in the material and ecological footprint is not possible, even after we spend trillions on a transition to a green economy.

The second proves the Gravesian rule for the double-helix alignment: In this case, it concerns the *complex adaptive intelligence* present in the *sapiens 2.1* brain syndicate, the N^1 in the coupling on the double-helix station labeled A^1–N^1 (see fig. 6.1). It is this intelligence that creates the *Second-sapiens* models such as the ones for planetary boundaries, ecological economics, circular economies, and doughnut economies as well as the UNSDG framework. When these ideas are applied to our existential reality—the *life conditions* half of the model—they should address A^1 issues: the survival of all life on the planet. Once these tools are spread to the point that they hold CAPI in the *sapiens 2.1* stage, they can then effectively begin to address the B^1 *life conditions* that represent planetary collapse. This is the proper alignment and the sequence of emergence on the double helix. But, when the models are deployed through an infrastructure put in place by *First sapiens*, they take on a slightly evolved expression of *First-sapiens* economic systems that eventually prove to be insufficient. This is what is known today as "greenwashing," which is increasingly becoming part of our vernacular as climate-related events and ecological collapse increase in intensity and solutions claiming to hold the answer for a sustainable Earth fall by the wayside. Our obsession with GDP growth has also defaulted the CAPI metric on most of the Gaiametry fractals to individuals and institutions that hold power, authority, and influence in a world run by *First sapiens*.

Truth: The Spark that Ignites the Velocity of Anthropocene Adoption

At the core of speaking Gaian truth to economic power is the largest *velocity of adoption* metric; the one that aims to end all *First-sapiens* metrics. It is the speed with which we accept *the truth* about the state of our planet. That truth determines the *velocity of Anthropocene adoption* in all the Gaiametry fractals. The different economic models discussed in this chapter—ecological economics, degrowth, the green economy, decoupling, renewable energy, the circular economy, and the doughnut economy—all attempt to address the issue. Yet, we continue to breach the different Earth-systems boundaries in what seems to be a fraction of a second in geologic time. This is the *Second-sapiens* truth. On the Anthropocene life cycle that truth, like all the Gaiametry fractals, has remained in the early stages of the *introduction* phase, being attacked by the antibodies of a very clever and manipulative *First sapiens*, the Promethean trickster god who holds all the elements of CAPI at the macro and mega levels. The truth about the state of our planet only begins to gain the needed CAPI once its virtues become adopted by the outer collective in the second half of the *introduction* phase. It is a global constellation of *Second-sapiens* leaders who will put the world on notice that change, informed by the Anthropocene epoch, is afoot. It is at this critical phase that the current life cycle defined by neoliberal economics becomes subordinate to the emerging life cycle, that of the Anthropocene.

GEP represent the cutting edge of models on sustainable and regenerative economics, but in order to test whether or not they can move us from the early stages of the *introduction* phase and deliver our future to the hands of the outer collective in the Anthropocene life cycle, I created the chart below. Its series of questions are a natural outcropping of the *general thema* of *Second sapiens*: *the survival and the subsequent flourishing of all life on the planet.* They represent the criteria that determines the viability of economic models for the Anthropocene epoch.

Should *Second sapiens* win this uphill battle and move the needle in the Anthropocene life cycle past the *introduction* phase, the question becomes: Will Gaia be patient enough with our species and help us move to the cycle's *growth* and *maturity* phases? This is where all life on

Criteria for a Model to Qualify within Gaiametry Economic Protocols (GEP)	
1	Does the proposed model allow for full feedback loops inherent in Gaian intelligence, or is it an extension of the reductive nature of Promethean intelligence and its dualistic ontology?
2	Does the proposed model put GDP growth ahead of the limits of Earth's systems planetary boundaries?
3	Does the proposed model conflate green growth with other models driven by degrowth?
4	Does the proposed model integrate ecological economics with sustainability science and the autopoiesis of complex adaptive systems of life?
5	Is the proposed model created by *Sapiens 1.5* intelligence hiding behind technology solutionism, or is it Second Sapiens intelligence that factors in all the Gaiametry fractals of which technology is a small part?
6	Does the proposed model decouple GDP growth from the global material and ecological footprint?
7	Does the new model apply the *velocity of Anthropocene adoption* to determine the scalability of sustainable and regenerative practices, and can the barriers to doing so be identified?
8	Does the new model hold enough CAPI in the new system to make the old system obsolete?
9	Does the new model have wise government as part of its *Sapiens 2.1* brain syndicate, or are *Sapiens 1.5* free-market forces still in charge?
10	Does the new model have enough humility to recognize that our species is only at the threshold of understanding the complexity of the Anthropocene and that our future will be defined by chaos and significant uncertainly?

Table 9.2. Criteria for a Model to Qualify within Gaiametry Economic Protocols (GEP). Said E. Dawlabani.

the planet moves from survival mode to its long-term flourishing mode. Would Gaia's feedback loops that help her reach homeostasis wait for us to fully adopt all the fractals in the stage-attractor model that make up the entire Gaiametry framework? The totality of the framework is what ensures the steady state for all life to flourish in the long term.

The answer to many of these questions may lie in part in the abandonment of what Graves calls man's greatest illusion about psychological maturity and in the embrace of a reality that runs on a different form of intelligence—that of nature. It entails the shift from a perspective of actively controlling to a perspective of noninterference. The former is steeped in *human intelligence* that defines the *First sapiens*, the latter in *natural intelligence* that defines the second. It entails a shift from the arrogance of the all-knowing *sapiens 1. 5* to a position of humility, of observing and not knowing. It is the shift that acknowledges that we always have been and always will be part of Nature's intelligence, not a species superior to or separate from it. In this process, Promethean intelligence is nested in the Gaian intelligence that expands consciousness and the ineffably higher values of a world in a richer context and, to repeat Graves's words, the "sheer fluid beauty and the fearless face-to-face awareness of now-naked life."

Addiction to Growth

The year 2023 closed on several sobering planetary indicators coming from the B[1] *life conditions* half of the *sapiens 2.2* stage. That is also when *First-sapiens* world leaders gathered at the COP28 conference in Dubai, which concluded on December 13 with warm applause to the final remarks made by its president, Dr. Sultan Al Jaber. Dr. Al Jaber praised all attendees for reaching an agreement that signals the "beginning of the end" of the fossil-fuel era by laying the ground for a swift, just, and equitable transition, underpinned by deep emissions cuts and scaled-up finance.[74] On the surface, these words carried much promise, but a close look at past patterns for enforcing these commitments tell a different story. During the conference, activists and climate experts began to sound the alarm on the vagueness of the wording in the agreement and the absence of enforcement mechanisms.

US climate envoy John Kerry summed it best in this statement: "The language on fossil fuels in the text does not meet the test of keeping [1.5°C] alive. I, like most of you here, refuse to be part of a charade of not phasing out fossil fuels. This is a war for survival."[75] The final agreement was amended to include language on phasing out fossil fuels for the first time in the history of COP conferences, but it made no provisions for any enforcement mechanism or a timeframe for a phaseout.

For Dr. Jaber, this was a victory on his terms. In addition to being the president of COP28, he is also the president of the Abu Dhabi National Oil Company, one of the largest state-owned oil producers in the world. Earlier in the conference, he had made declarations to attendees that climate deniers often repeat: he claimed that there is "no science" indicating that a phaseout of fossil fuels is needed to restrict global heating to 1.5°C and that such a phaseout would not allow sustainable development "unless you want to take the world back into caves."[76] Ironically, the words *survival* and *caves* are part of the *general thema* of the *sapiens 1.1* stage that seems to be destined to repeat at the *sapiens 2.1* stage threatening all life forms. Yet, we seem to be caught up in the promise of sustainable development in a world that still relies on fossil fuels for 80 percent of its energy needs.

COP28 was held against the backdrop of one of the warmest years on record, the B[1] planetary problem in the *sapiens 2.2* coupling. During the conference, a working group of two hundred researchers and climate scientists released the Global Tipping Points Report, warning that the gravest threats to humanity are drawing closer as carbon emissions continue to heat the planet to ever more dangerous levels. The report warns of five critical natural thresholds that are at risk of being crossed: the collapse of big ice sheets in Greenland and the West Antarctic, the widespread thawing of permafrost, the death of coral reefs in warm waters, and the collapse of one oceanic current in the North Atlantic.[77] Like all other planetary warning signs coming from the IPCC, the Potsdam Institute for Climate Impact Research, and the Stockholm Resilience Center, this report is based in *Second-sapiens* science and is part of the *sapiens 2.1* brain syndicate. It is science of a much higher-order system that runs on *natural intelligence* with all its feedback loops fully intact. Unlike the dualistic ontology of the *First sapiens* that celebrates its deficient achievements at COP events while repressing negative feedback, these scientific sources are telling us we are witnessing mega-scale ecological collapse in real time. The critical thresholds we have crossed will lead to the loss of whole ecosystems and impact our ability to grow staple crops at some point in the near future. Should warnings like these go unheeded, they will have cascading effects that will cause mass displacement of people and trigger social unrest, political instability, and financial collapse. Acting on these matters underpins the very survival of our world, one in which the *First sapiens* hold all the cards that are preventing real change from taking place. This is the evidence that we are on the second half of the chessboard where domino effects can easily be triggered and change moving forward becomes more difficult to predict. Yet, like the proverbial ostrich, we stick out heads in the sand and choose to ignore the warning signs as we continue to grow our economy and pursue sustainable development through a veneer of humanitarian-sounding doublethink and moralistic rationalizations.

TEN
THE VIEW FROM JUPITER

What if we're wrong? Perversely, decades of climate denial and disinformation have made global warming not merely an ecological crisis but an incredibly high-stakes wager on the legitimacy and validity of science and the scientific method itself. It is a bet that science can win only by losing. And in this test of the climate, we have a sample size of one.

—David Wallace-Wells
The Uninhabitable Earth

I began my research for this book in 2016 but had to set it aside to care for my wife, Elza. In retrospect, I realize that the interruption had been a blessing in disguise, for it gave me time to gain perspective as I witnessed the rapid ecological change taking place in the world, with all its ensuing chaos and uncertainty. Much of what my research had revealed in 2016 has not withstood the test of time—not even for these few short years. So much of our understanding of the natural world and what we have taken for granted in it has changed or has altogether been rendered obsolete. The Earth has gotten warmer, the polar ice has melted faster, and the coral reefs have died more quickly. The permafrost that holds dangerous methane gases and ancient forms of bacteria has thawed sooner by decades than expected. The wet has gotten wetter, the hot has gotten hotter, and dry had gotten dryer. Climate-related disasters have increased in size and frequency, and the voices of both climate activists and climate deniers have gotten louder and more violent. Fossil-fuel producers have become the sponsors of the largest annual UN-backed climate summit, and the world's GDP has continued to grow unabated in spite of a crippling global pandemic. Further, our material and ecological footprints have continued to grow in spite of all the sustainable-development measures that have been introduced. Even our goal to keep temperature rise under 1.5° C by 2050 was shattered in 2023, declared unequivocally by such organizations as the National Oceanic and Atmospheric Administration (NOAA) the hottest year on record.[1] This limit was the most crucial one the scientific community has set to help us mitigate ecological and societal collapse, and we have overshot it twenty-seven years before the prescribed time, proving that unpredictability and chaos are the new norm. The three forces that are driving the *Great Obsolescence*—the post-war geopolitical framework and its ethos of *peace through commerce,* the digital disruption, and climate change—have coalesced much sooner and have moved societal and planetary boundaries past certain tipping points along the different holonic structures that ensure the continuity of life. From the smallest microscopic ecosystem to Earth's nine different systems, change is afoot, and it has remained exponential and chaotic, becoming less predictable with every passing day. This is how life will be defined in the Anthropocene, and the sooner we accept it the sooner we will find new ways to live with it.

This book takes a collective approach to identifying the challenges we face for this needed transition. Much of it has focused on mega- and macro-systems issues and the developmental limitations we must overcome at the various holonic structures. Its narrative is defined by the hierarchical and sequential nature of stage development and the uniqueness of each stage's life cycle. In terms of these dynamics, climate change and ecological collapse seem to violate that sequential order. They add an entirely new dimension for which we are utterly unprepared, one that requires the exponential expansion of our psychological capacities.

To add to the uncertainty, parts of that ecological dimension have entered states of chaos and exponential change that cannot be easily quantified. This has further expanded the gap between the problem itself and our capacity to deal with it effectively. It is in that gap that we must find the transformational tools to help us adapt to our new reality. It is a collective trauma we must go through, and we will likely have to do it without the help of our leaders, who seem unwilling or unable to enact the change our new reality requires. While this book examines different ways to process our grief and help us out of the darkness, psychologically there will be no return to the steady states of mental health that accompanied the so-called haven on Earth we enjoyed during the Holocene era.

Our new reality was not the way Graves and Beck envisioned the normal sequence of human emergence into the eighth stage of development wherein humanity is in harmony with the planet's ecology. The psychosocial evolution of *Homo sapiens* has been short circuited, and this last known stage in the model will not manifest as a natural progression of human values and states of consciousness. Instead, we are being dragged kicking and screaming into it in an effort to mitigate the damage, while those who hold power remain in denial about the severity of our new reality. It is dividing us as a species in ways we've never been divided before, and the denialists hold the competitive advantage in the fight. Should they win, they will find themselves on the losing side once ecological collapse leaves them on an inhospitable planet made so by their own shortsighted decisions. The pre-Anthropocene vision of this model will not become the leading edge of an ecologically aligned humanity with its own collective mind. We may never know what it is to experience the world as a single dynamic organism. We may never experience the wholeness of existence through mind and spirit the way Beck, Cowan, and Wilber defined it.

This short circuiting of our reality should not, however, be the reason we stop advocating for change and acting on what needs to be done. Doing so will be a rebellion that must be brought on by *Second sapiens.* It will amount to the long-awaited reversal of values and beliefs of which Graves spoke five decades ago; but it must now happen out of existential urgency, not out of the normal enfolding of stage development and human consciousness.

In conducting the research for this book and adapting it to the Gravesian model, I have become convinced that a breakdown in human civilization will happen within our lifetime, but the modern mind refuses to acknowledge this probability. Once we bypass the limitations of the *sapiens 1.5* stage with its deficient motivations and reductive ways of thinking—once we understand how it manipulated all the *First-sapiens* stages—we begin to see change and collapse from the higher-order systems of the *Second sapiens,* as if we're standing on Jupiter and looking back. It is from this vantage point that the changing trends in the Earth's systems will become irrefutable. It is from here that we will see the blue marble become arid and barren of hue in brown and beige.

My views will, without a doubt, be attacked by the antibodies of the current system and many who approach the study of the Anthropocene through different disciplines than mine. Therefore, I wish to make it clear that the inevitability of societal collapse is my personal conclusion and mine alone. It is based on an emergent form of science defined by the complex adaptive systems of life whose long-term feedback loops have been ignored and externalized for centuries and are now appearing to us as fate. The nature of that fate is in the acceleration of collapse of the mega systems that contain all other systems that ensure life and the coping structures that come with it, and that fate is our new normal. It will remain so until Gaia on her own timeline decides it has reached a new homeostasis. We are now at her mercy, and in case she has run out of compassion for our species, preparing for possible collapse becomes the prudent thing to do. We cannot continue placing our future in the hands of Newtonian scientists and *First-sapiens* politicians and technology solutionists. Instead, we must now live with a new paradox, the acceptance of collapse as an existential, yet resilient, state of being. What is required is the acceptance of collective suffering and inconsolable despair, of witnessing the collapse of civilization and coming face to face with our own mortality.

The idea of societal collapse, as unpopular as it may sound, has been around for decades. Its scientific basis was born in the chaos crucible of the 1970s when the authors of *The Limits to Growth* predicted its arrival by 2040. Recent findings by researchers such as Gaya Herrington and others using modern methods have confirmed that we are on track toward that collapse This threat to human-built systems is also what caused eco-sociologist William Catton to call for an ecological revolution on the behalf of our planet. Since the publication of Catton's 1980 book, *Overshoot,* research by the Stockholm Resilience Center has confirmed we have overshot six of our nine Earth-systems' boundaries. In the last four decades, the insatiable appetite of *Homo colossus* has grown by more than tenfold, and the powerful and unseen ways of encroaching on our planet that Catton spoke of are today fully visible and undeniably convincing.

What hasn't changed is the way mainstream society is viewing those who speak about collapse: They are being stigmatized and ostracized. They are being called *doomers* and *cultists* and a whole range of other negative and pejorative names. The modern mind is quick to dismiss them and to associate their behavior with religious fanatics warning of the end times and of religious prophecies that never materialize. Others seem to be more philosophical about collapse and claim that, based on history, civilizations always rise and fall. What these arguments are missing is that, this time, collapse is not coming from religious prophecy, and today's ecological conditions may not be conducive for new civilizations to rise.

This book has repeatedly acknowledged Clare W. Graves as among the systems thinkers who emerged in 1970s. Like the work of the authors of *The Limits to Growth* (Meadows, Randers, and Meadows), Catton, Lovelock, Margulis, and many others cited in this book, Graves's work has been tested and continues to be proven against institutional and academic headwinds that are steadfast in their old, *First-sapiens* ways. Its interdisciplinary, qualitative, and intuitive nature has proven to belong in *Second-sapiens* sciences, not the reductive sciences of *sapiens 1.5.* One of Graves's three scenarios about the future of humanity concerned the testing of its collective resilience through successive catastrophes as a way to determine its capacity to stabilize the world. Failing the test, he predicted, humanity will be forced to regress to as far back as *sapiens 1.1* and *sapiens 1.2* levels. At the time he made these predictions, the collective threat to humanity—the leading edge of the *life conditions* half of the model— was the specter of nuclear war. Today the collective threat is much bigger, but it has remained invisible and out of the conscious awareness of most people. It is the specter of ecological collapse and our continued failure to mitigate the instability it is causing. This book's narrative is based on Graves's *six-upon-six* hypothesis, which was slightly more optimistic than the above scenario in which collective resilience is tested. At the time he formulated the hypothesis, he and many of his generation held hope that our leaders would rise collectively and address all the issues that were pressing against the boundaries of Earth's systems. This hope and understanding is what gave birth to the concept of the Anthropocene life cycle, the earliest view of what exponential growth in psychosocial capacities on the other side of *First-sapiens* development would look like. It is what gave the early systems thinkers their guarded optimism. And it was that same guarded optimism—the kind that assumes that human civilization is worth saving—that drove me to write this book.

Hope is a human construct, a byproduct of the optimistic mind based on an expectation of positive outcomes in life. It is a source of creative energy that propels us to find practical pathways for an improved future. It might even require a person or a culture to advance to a higher stage of development in which the content of hope appears anew and in a higher-order form than it was in the earlier stages that repressed it. This sequential movement is an essential part of the Gravesian conditions for change, not only for the evolving meaning of hope but for the million other fractals that define stage development. *Sapiens 1.1,* for example, had hoped that someday he wouldn't have to live at the mercy of Nature's wrath and under the threat of her predators, so he sought safety in numbers and formed tribes. He developed better tools to kill the beast and better ways to domesticate plants and animals. It was his hope for a better life that moved our species to the *sapiens 1.2* stage. Similarly, the Dark Ages that Europe endured from the fifth to the tenth centuries engendered the hope for something better that propelled our species from the *sapiens 1.4* to the *sapiens 1.5* stage.

But what happens when the ethos representing hope at the *sapiens 1.5* stage in today's *life conditions* is in reality the killer of hope at the *sapiens 2.2* stage, and the longer we remain in denial of that truth the worse our new reality becomes? What is needed at our current threshold is an entirely new understanding of what having hope will mean in our necessary shift to a higher stage of development. Hope, when viewed from the O^1 half of the *sapiens 2.2* stage, becomes part of Nature's homeostasis. It is morally indifferent to *First sapiens's* activities and desires. It is also indifferent to the binary nature of Western civilization that asserted itself as the leading edge of evolutionary virtues. Hope in the Anthropocene life cycle lies in our transcendence of the current reductive and mechanical views of reality that have defined the *general thema* of the *sapiens 1.5* and its scientific mind. Hope in the Anthropocene epoch will manifest in ways that go beyond language and meaning. It will entail the transcendence of the physical and the material realms and the reembrace of our spiritual nature in which ancient wisdom brings us back to a state of reverence for the land and for the cosmos.

The *natural intelligence* that drives *sapiens 2.2* will expect all life forms to follow its autopoietic processes and the interdependent, natural order of life. No feedback loops will ever be ignored. Nature's hope is realized in her endless quest to reach new states of equilibrium and in the continuous evolutionary change that involves the death of some species, the rise of others, and the flourishing of the ones that can adapt and evolve. It cares not when *First sapiens* gets a better job or buys a bigger home or a newer-model Tesla. Homeostasis will not necessarily be reached when we find permanent peace in places of war and conflict. Peace among *Homo sapiens* constitutes a smaller, macro-scale holonic structure in the higher, mega-scale order of the Anthropocene. Like the efforts of the Center for Human Emergence for peace in the Middle East (see ch. 8), peace in the Anthropocene becomes a systems-design issue that seeks to level the developmental asymmetries that exist between how *First sapiens* views peace—harmony among people—to how *Second sapiens* views it: ecological alignment of all humanity with Earth's systems. Homeostasis will also not be reached when the world rejoices at the addition of the words "fossil-fuel phaseout" to an agreement that has no enforcement mechanisms. The approaching Anthropocene epoch will not comprise an incremental stage of development in which we can extend what we now know to its next logical iteration and extract its higher-order, binary meaning. It will be an entirely new epoch that will require a completely new form of philosophical inquiry. It heralds the death of the civilization given to us by the industrial world, and the sooner we acknowledge that truth, the quicker we will become *Second sapiens* capable of handling what is to come.

Collapse and the Darkness before the New Dawn

Our failure to stabilize the world would mean that our regression back to the stages of *sapiens 1.1* and *1.2* will become a distinct probability. And while this book offers the more optimistic perspective on what we need to do to reach a civilization organized under *Second sapiens*, a return to a world defined by haphazard bands of tribes and nomads seems increasingly likely. Based on how quickly we are breaching planetary boundaries and other supporting evidence of collapse, cascading global catastrophes seem almost inevitable.

Our current behavior is what evolutionary biologists describe as evolutionary suicide or Darwinian extinction, a phenomenon represented in Aesop's fable *The Goose that Laid the Golden Egg*. In the story, because the farmer's extraordinary goose lays a golden egg every day, he kills it, believing he will find even more gold inside the goose's body. But he doesn't, leaving him with the proscription against greed and the lesson that pursuing more than what is viable will bring loss.

Like the farmer, instead of being satisfied with a normal pace of consumption that couples economic growth with the planet's limited resources, *sapiens 1.5* has breached the planetary limits and killed the goose—the planet's resilience to maintain life. While we don't have the resources of two more planets to support human life, we *do* have enough resources to sustain it for a while if the world population were cut to 30 percent of what it is today.[2] But if that is required in order for Gaia to reach a new homeostasis, the outcome will be nothing short of a collective horror of unprecedented proportions. To put it in proper perspective, World War II, the Holocaust, and all other atrocities associated with it annihilated about 3 percent of the world's population. The perishing of 70 percent of the world's population would mean the death of 5.6 billion people, a percentage much higher than the 50 percent Graves estimated in 1980. Our probable descent to *sapiens 1.1* and *1.2* on an increasing unstable planet does not preclude the possibility that as a species we become extinct. Nor would this form of extinction be measured on a geologic timescale. It would be a near-term extinction event. Think of it in terms of the asteroid that wiped out the dinosaurs. Climate change is an asteroid of our own making that has already hit the Earth, but the aftershocks from multiple points of impact will ripple in slow motion over decades.

> *The greatest challenge the Anthropocene poses is a philosophical one: Understanding that this civilization is already dead. The sooner we confront our situation, and realize there is nothing we can do to save ourselves, the sooner we can get down to the difficult task of adapting with mortal humility to our new reality.*
>
> —Roy Scranton[3]

As successive natural disasters force our descent to lower stages, the mental-health models discussed in earlier chapters will alter greatly, if not become altogether obsolete. Kubler-Ross's stages-of-grief framework, like all the others, is a creation of the modern optimistic mind. These frameworks were designed to help us get past certain mental states, overcome sorrow, accept loss, adapt to change, and become more resilient as a result. They dealt mostly with the mental and psychological well-being of the individual with little attention to the collective, existential issues that affect all humanity.

But what guarantees life for that humanity is a healthy planet, and our planet's health is declining rapidly, making her outlook and ours anything but optimistic. We cannot continue to behave as if the future will be just like the past, and all we need is a few more sessions on a therapist's couch to make everything okay. To continue with that narrative will only make us less prepared for every new disaster and deepen our denial of the reality of the Anthropocene. During accelerated collapse, collective anger will not result in meaningful collective action. Issues of social justice, the presence of structural resources in financial and judiciary systems, and issues of identity and equity will all become meaningless.

Collectively and individually, we can longer bargain with ourselves. Internal dialogue will not bring us back to the way things were. The only relevant form of dialogue is in finding ways to accept the collapse of human civilization and our own mortality. Depression during collapse will become a collective and permanent state. The sense of sadness and hopelessness can no longer be restored by any sense of collective optimism. There is no planet B. Once we realize that our own past actions have made the planet into the biggest prison from which there will be no escape, we will begin to learn to live at the mercy of an unpredictable warden. This will be the metaphor for the gloomy and greatly altered reality of the fall of civilization, and the sooner we acknowledge it, the sooner we will begin to adapt. It will free those of us who survive from any attachment to the past and its material nature—from the panic, the denial, and the outrage. This acceptance will set us on a new course to rebuild what remains of us and our world, and we will do it with love, care, and temperance; more importantly, we will do it with reverence for what remains of Nature as we learn how to live with her again.

The Post-Collapse Gravesian Model

In the Gravesian sequence of development, our failure to adopt the changes called for in the Gaiametry framework is where the model crumbles and the further climb up the development ladder ends. This is where we acknowledge our collective inability to overcome the chasm between the *First sapiens* and the Second. This is where *darkness-before-the new-dawn* phase becomes much darker, and the collapse of civilization becomes a forgone conclusion. There is no more *momentous leap* to prepare for or the promise of exponential growth in psychological capacities. With *life conditions* collapsing down to A in the A–N coupling, maintaining any higher states of *complex adaptive intelligence* becomes a struggle. In the aftermath of collapse, all mental-health models default to various survival states within the *sapiens 1.1* stage, the kind we see in post-apocalyptic movies such as *The Hunger Games* and the *Mad Max* series. The only difference this time around is that, unlike the cavemen we were 100,000 years ago, we will take with us the activated brain capacities of the pre-collapse world, without the presence of the institutions and the infrastructure that created them and supported their propagation. They will become dormant, waiting for *life conditions* to stabilize before they can become activated again. We will also take with us some of the tools and the weapons we created. Post-collapse is also a post-human-civilization state of existence absent the collective progress our species has made and lacking in cultural and institutional fortitude that propagated our modern humanity. A post-collapse state of being will default us to the primal responses of fight or flight, and all our physical and psychological energy will go into that effort. The struggle for the survival of the fittest *Homo sapiens* will begin anew.

Should post-collapse *Homo sapiens* survive extinction and begin a repeat of *sapiens 1.1,* the dormant pre-collapse intelligence we bring with us will expedite our stabilization at this stage. This will constitute a new form of existence that holds the promise for our species' recovery. However, while our historic counterpart enjoyed an abundance of flora and fauna, and as Graves so prophetically observed, for post-collapse *sapiens 1.1* bounty will become scarcity. Naturalistic scarcity will shape the post-collapse nature of *Homo sapiens* for the rest of our existence. Regardless of how far up we move on the spiral of development, every station on the entire strand of its DNA helix labeled *life conditions* must be directed by this new existential reality from which there will be no escape (see fig. 6.1). Scarcity will define the *general thema* of every stage. It will entail the diligent guarding of the small number of species that remain and the limited resources they need to survive life after collapse. Every station along the entire *complex adaptive intelligence* half of the model will serve this new *general thema* through different strategies that are proprietary to every post-collapse stage.

For post-collapse *sapiens 1.1,* in addition to doing what we must to stay alive, we will have to find the few places on the planet where it is still possible to live. This might be difficult, since the places even in the far north once considered safe from the effects of temperature rise are now experiencing devastating consequences. In 2020, for instance, Siberia reported a record-breaking 100°F accompanied by a record number of wildfires that caused smoke to extend to the North Pole.[4] Ecological stability, even after Nature reaches a new homeostasis, may not resemble much of what we have known in the Holocene. We will become post-collapse nomads, faced with the frequent destruction of habitat and the constant need to move to safer spaces quickly and without any attachment to geography. Psychologically, post-collapse *sapiens 1.1* will possess an awareness of self, but out of our necessity to survive, our savagery will always reside within us. An ancient memory that defined our pre-collapse counterpart—the need to kill others and the beasts who come for us or our food—will be reactivated. Unlike our historic *sapiens 1.1* predecessor, the lucky few who survive the collapse will use their higher brain capacities to help us adapt much more quickly. They will also be the first-hand witnesses to Nature's wrath caused by human activity. This experience will become a generational memory that gets deeply imbedded in our consciousness. The thing that *won't* change on this return to history, however, is the inordinate amount of time we will spend on ensuring our physical safety, leaving little time to worry about our higher needs further up the hierarchy. Once we reach a relative sense of stability and become less nomadic, we will begin to shift our energy toward the next stage, a post-collapse, tribalistic form of existence.

The timeframe for this critical transition is impossible to predict. What kept *sapiens 1.1* in that stage for 100,000 years or more was the relative stability of *life conditions* made possible by Nature's abundance. There was no need or reason to move to higher states. In a post-collapse world, though, that form of stability will not exist overall, and we will have to discover new islands of it after observing Nature's behavior over long periods of time. This effort might take as long as it did historically, or we might get lucky and reach a new state of stability much sooner. Stability will free us from the constant threats to survival and enable us to transition to a new, post-collapse *sapiens 1.2* stage. Once again, we will begin to experience the relative safety and stability of tribal existence. Even though we will continue to be restricted by natural scarcity, as long as we stay within the necessary restrictions, we will begin to have some control over the destiny of our species again. While the stage's *general thema* remains *sacrifice self to the way of the elders*, the wisdom of those elders will be vastly different. Their dormant capacities that were present before collapse, along with the historic record that documents the history of human civilization, will coalesce with the scars left by ecological collapse to inform this new stage of existence.

Returning on a Road Less Traveled

The circle of wise elders at the post-collapse *sapiens 1.2* stage, as a substitute for the pre-collapse *sapiens 2.1* brain syndicate, will necessarily become the leading edge of *Homo sapiens* development on this new journey. The difference will be that we will have the benefit of hindsight and can dig deeper into history to discover how we went wrong. These elders will reexamine the entire Western concept of progress as an outer measure of an evolving humanity; they will attend to inner wisdom, care for what remains of the human race, and redirect their focus to our relationship with the land and the cosmos. The matter will not be one of just a brain syndicate; it will be of a brain-heart-soul syndicate that forms a new circle of wisdom and can act on its findings without the fear of higher-order stages thwarting its efforts.

With natural scarcity representing the *general thema* of post-collapse existence, CAPI defaults to this new circle as a condition for survival and ecological stability. Out of necessity, the global brain, which would have been fully reawakened at the *sapiens 2.2* stage, takes on a dual form in order to connect the disparate tribes that remain: The first will be its organic form that will transcend *human intelligence* and bring it back into the fold of Gaia's *natural intelligence*, of 3.5 billion years of autopoietic evolution. The second will be its synthetic form that represents the complexity of the pre-collapse digital world that removed physical borders and made us into one global community. A post-collapse global community will resemble a loosely connected network of tribal villages, but their ability to thrive beyond their new confines will greatly depend on how much of the digital infrastructure survives or on how much of it we can rebuild. Such an infrastructure will serve as a new distributed form of intelligence that allows the islands of tribes to share information on a variety of matters, ranging from emerging post-collapse ecological trends to what species of plants and animal can survive and where.

CAPI in a post-collapse world will be driven by entirely different metrics. It will question the merits of Western civilization, not for the purpose of demonizing it but to understand its virtues, its limitations, and its long-ignored feedback loops. It will require the somber and thoughtful form of mature transparency we need in order to create a new blueprint for sustaining life that is transcendent in nature. It will reexamine all the *First-sapiens* stages with a new, integrative lens. It will revisit the historical circumstances that birthed the *sapiens 1.3* stage and reexamine its motivation for conquest and greed. Historically, those were the characteristics that set our species on the course to ecological and societal collapse. *Sapiens 1.3* was also the stage that ushered in the age of empires and allowed colonialism and all its ugly peripheral expressions to dominate the world. It is the stage that tried to wipe out native and ancient wisdom and subjugate what remained of it to its will and way of life. It planted the seeds for slavery and much of the systemic inequality that has defined our struggles in a pre-collapse world.

This new form of CAPI will also revisit the *sapiens 1.4* stage and examine how monotheism— more specifically, the Abrahamic religions—came to dominate spiritual expression and, in the process, silence Gaia's voice and reduce our spiritual nature to a dualistic linearity ruled by the patriarchy. In doing so, we will rediscover how physical and spiritual phenomena were and remain dynamic processes that are part of the greater intelligence that is constantly evolving. These processes are not part of a fixed hierarchical institution that negates the individual's ability to experience the divinity inherent in everyday life and in the goodness of people and Nature. To the contrary, they are inherent in the way transcendental poets and philosophers have seen things; they are also present in the wisdom of Eastern philosophy and that of Native American tribes. Such perspectives are what will reconnect us to the wisdom of the past and extend our presence beyond the ephemeral blip of time that ended civilization. They are what will permanently pacify our past obsession with being superior to Nature and bring us back into her fold.

> *In the morning I bathe my intellect in the stupendous and cosmogonal philosophy of the Bhagavat Geeta, since whose composition years of the gods have elapsed, and in comparison with which our modern world and its literature seem puny and trivial; and I doubt if that philosophy is not to be referred to a previous state of existence, so remote is its sublimity from our conceptions. I lay down the book and go to my well for water, and lo! there I meet the servant of the Brahmin, priest of Brahma, and Vishnu and Indra, who still sits in his temple on the Ganges reading the Vedas, or dwells at the root of a tree with his crust and water-jug. I meet his servant come to draw water for his master, and our buckets as it were grate together in the same well. The pure Walden water is mingled with the sacred water of the Ganges.*
>
> —Henry David Thoreau[5]

A post-collapse *sapiens 1.2* circle of wisdom will also revisit the *sapiens 1.5* stage to figure out how its genius became so reductive and manipulative and how the dark side of its virtues became the leading cause in societal and ecological collapse. Many of these shortcomings have been discussed throughout the book, but in a post-collapse world understanding them will become an essential part of the narrative. The new brain-heart-soul circle will do all this exploration without allocating blame to any particular *First-sapiens* stages, knowing that the process that brought us to collapse was a cumulative one driven by deficient behavior along every stage.

The physical manifestation of matter and the material world is what has defined the *First sapiens*. It has also been a small part of our neurology and brain mass that has promoted our dualistic ontology, making us forget the nature of existence in terms of the pairs of opposites, one of them being the dichotomy between the human and the natural world that has held the universe in balance for billions of years, long before we emerged as a species. If it has been our separation from nature and the belief that we are superior to it that has brought us to where we are today, then this is what needs to be reversed.

The deficient behaviors of the *First sapiens* have been driven by our embrace primarily of one form of intelligence—logic. A post-collapse *Homo sapiens* will transcend the mind's attachment to logic, which after all represents just one facet of human consciousness. It will embrace higher states of awareness that reconnect us to the psychic and spiritual states that have long been sidelined. This is where the road to being one with Nature and cosmic wonder will begin anew. It is in these higher realms that natural and spiritual intelligence reside. Just as in the intelligence of Gaia that has existed since time immemorial, we will again identify with the binary nature of our world and live with the full conscious awareness of the pairs of opposites as a condition for our survival. This is the perspective and behavior that will define a world in balance in which we learn again to respect all feedback loops inherent in the natural and spiritual order. Unlike modern science that has dismissed the wholeness inherent in the pairs of opposites, we will reintegrate the two and recognize that together they are the holonic whole, the entire tapestry that defines the mystery of existence.

Much of the discussion of *natural intelligence* in this book has centered around the inclusive virtues of the *sapiens 2.2* stage. It is full of intuitive and qualitative practices shaped by the exponential increases in psychological capacities, the study of the complex systems of life, and the high degrees of collaboration and transdisciplinary virtues that make the whole more than the sum of its parts. It has brought back our need to understand and account for feedback loops as a way to avert ecological collapse and align humanity on a sustainable trajectory. The Gravesian model is one of many that represent this stage as the highest in human development. But what if this arduous climb up the ladder that has taken thousands of years has been only one of many ways for us to get to a higher state of consciousness? What if the aims of *sapiens 2.2* have been nothing more than a modern expression of ancient primal symbols and instincts that reside in our collective unconsciousness that holds different views on human progress? What if our ancestors in the tribes that dotted the world before Western conquest sidelined and subjugated them were driven by their own unique experiences and native intelligence? What if those tribes adopted their own primal symbols of archetypes and gods and goddesses to live in harmony with Nature? What if they treated Nature with such deep respect that the term *ecological collapse* caused by human activity would have meant the violation of every principle of cosmic and natural order that has ever existed since time immemorial?

The Wisdom of the Native Americans

The wisdom of the Native American tribes can serve as a source of inspiration that might save our species from extinction. I cannot possibly pay the native peoples of this land the proper respect and provide a deeper understanding of their vast and rich traditions in just a few lines. Nor do I wish to appropriate any part of their rich and storied culture in any way. I cannot claim to have spent time engaging with them, nor have I studied their traditions and virtues in ways that qualify me to speak on their behalf.

There are, however, certain patterns of behavior and thought that are common among the different tribes that populated the world prior to the brutality of the Western *sapiens 1.3*. Caring for the land and for one another is the undercurrent that permeated all tribes within the *sapiens 1.2* stage, and a look at how Native Americans view that care today gives us a glimpse of what we will need to do to survive in the future. In light of the continued scarcity that will define a post-collapse world, these are virtues that would need to remain with us for the rest of our species' presence on Earth.

Like the historic *general thema* of the *sapiens 1.2* stage that dominated human expression thousands of years ago, the wisdom in elders' stories that inspired their tribe's actions and the continuity of tradition are virtues that remain alive today among Native American nations. The Cherokee people living in the Southeastern woodlands place an immense value on storytelling as an oral tradition that has defined a large part of the historic educational process. Stories are passed down through generations in order to preserve history, values, and lessons learned; they connect current generations to their ancestors, the land, and the natural world. This tradition is also kept alive among the Lakota people who live on the Northern plains. Their elders are seen as the keepers of knowledge and tradition, passing on a wisdom that provides invaluable insights and lessons for younger generations. Viewed from a post-collapse perspective, this activity speaks to nothing less than the totality of an existence that has always remained in harmony with nature. The return to it in the long arc of history will express the single most important story that must be told to all future generation. This is the story of how we have ignored ancient wisdom, decoupled ourselves from Nature, and caused her collapse.

Native wisdom also knows that living in greater harmony with Nature cannot come unless people live in harmony among themselves. This understanding is common among all native nations, including the Cherokee, who emphasize cooperation and the mutual aid that reflects the interconnectedness of all things and the responsibility to act in ways that benefit the community and future generations.[6] The Lakota share a similar philosophy that fosters respect and compassion for all life forms, serving as a guiding principle for their interactions with the natural world and one another. That natural order and our place in it brings an understanding of the inherent value within all things. It serves as a new reminder for treating our ecology and everything in it, including plants and animals, with the respect and dignity they have deserved all along. Native cultures strive to be in balance with nature and respect its cycles and rhythms, an attitude reflected in their interaction with the land and in the way they approach their agricultural practices and management of water resources. Ceremonies play an important part in propagating cultural and spiritual life, and each ceremony has a specific meaning and tradition that is passed down through generations.

Issues of governance in a post-collapse world can also draw on Native American wisdom to understand how to live in peace with other tribes and stay in harmony with Nature. The Haudenosaunee Confederacy, also known as the Iroquois League, was an alliance among six Native American nations that were at war with each other but were brought together through a common desire to live in peace.[7] They are the founders of a concept known as the Great Law of Peace, from which our founding fathers drew inspiration. Its principles underscore a commitment to cooperation and peaceful conflict resolution based on consensus, mutual respect, and the inclusion of diverse voices. Guiding these principles are seven core teachings: honesty, respect, kindness, courage, wisdom, humility, and generosity. Just as these principles guided each native nation, they came to guide all seven nations by continuing to emphasize the importance of personal and interpersonal conduct, which led to the continued fostering of strong communities and social harmony. More importantly these principles preserved the importance of environmental stewardship by emphasizing the people's greater role as caretakers of the environment, respecting the land and its resources and practicing sustainable methods of food production.

> *Whatever befalls the earth befalls the sons of the earth. Humankind has not woven the web of life. We are but one thread within it. Whatever we do to the web, we do to ourselves. All things are bound together. All things connect.*
>
> —Chief Seattle[8]

These diverse Native American practices give form to much that is needed in the *sapiens 2.2* stage as we reintegrate what *sapiens 1.5* has excluded from its conscious awareness. But, in a post-collapse world, they will form a major part of the new circle of wisdom made up of the brain-heart-soul syndicate They will give a familiar face to the ecological alignment that we are struggling to achieve. It is the mind and spirit connection that bypasses all the destructive stages built on logic and the quantitative ways of the Western mind. Chief Seattle's above words from 1854 might as well have been spoken by any of the systems thinkers who emerged from the chaos crucible of the 1970s and intuitively warned us about our deficient ways of thinking. Living in harmony with others and with the land and all living creatures is in the holonic structure of things that has existed long before the modern mind articulated the scientific nature of holons. It is characteristic of the *natural intelligence* from which native American tribes have never separated, and it is what we so desperately need to return to in order for our species to have a chance at survival.

Before Everything Was Measured

Before Galileo, Descartes, and Newton reduced the universe to mechanical models and precise measurement, *Homo sapiens* lived in constant inquiry into the mystery of existence, of the cosmos, and of life and death. This state of mind has been true from the ancient Greeks and their complex pantheon of deities representing various aspects of nature, themes of morality, and the relationship between humans and the divine to the Egyptians who believed in the soul's ability to journey freely after death as it goes through the Underworld guided by the Book of the Dead. It has been true from the ancient Mayans who developed intricate calendars based on celestial cycles and planetary alignments and their elaborate temples that served as a connection to the Divine to the world of Indian deities, of Shiva and Shakti representing the cosmic dance of creation and destruction and the dual and cyclical nature of the universe. All such spiritual practices, with their varied and unique interpretations and expressions, comprise how our ancestors honored our presence in the physical world and its relationship to the cosmos. These practices reflected faith wrapped in esoteric, philosophical, and spiritual garb, presenting itself as an innate form of intelligence that still escapes the modern mind. This intelligence understands the binary nature of everything in the universe in all its varied forms without the necessity of scientific proof. It understands the complexity that existed before science simplified it and reduced it to a measurement. It grants faith in the immeasurable, the "void within" that existential philosopher Jean Paul Sartre defined as the eternal human condition. These are the things that, in many cases, still escape language and meaning. They make up what poets refer to as the symphony of existence and what spiritual teachers call cosmic consciousness. It is the tapestry of creation, the ground of being, and the holographic principle all wrapped up in one eternal dance.

In 2004 I had a transformational experience that brought to reality the meaning of that eternal dance: I was a student of the spiritual path Surat Shabd Yoga when in December of that year a tsunami in the Indian ocean claimed the lives of more than 200,000 people. A few days later at a spiritual gathering, when asked about the meaning of the tragedy, my *satguru* (*Skt.* true guru) stoically referred to the event as Shiva and Shakti playing soccer on higher planes. While that might have sounded cruel and heartless to the average person, envisioning what ecological and societal collapse look like from those higher spiritual planes might help us accept our collective fate. In the teachings of my guru, it is from those higher states of spiritual development that we come to understand the world of the mind as merely part of the lowest and densest form of existence, the physical realm. This realm is where time, space, and matter are made manifest.

Just as I cannot claim to have deep knowledge of the rich traditions of Native Americans, I cannot claim to know the deeper layers of Eastern spiritual practices. I am not a strict adherent to my guru's teachings, nor does my topical treatment of the knowledge of the soul and of karma represent an authoritative stance on any esoteric or philosophical subject. I offer these brief and personal views only as an invitation to consider a different approach to the care of the land and the treatment of others in a world ravaged by the limitations of the mind and the physical realms. Just as there is a hierarchy in psychosocial development, there is a hierarchy in spiritual development. While growth in the Gravesian model is driven by a never-ending quest to reach higher states of psychological health, many Eastern spiritual practices, including Surat Shabd Yoga, are driven by a never-ending quest to mitigate karma—the omnipotent law of action and reaction—in order to reach the highest plane in spiritual development known in Buddhism and Hinduism as *nirvana.* That is the desired state in which the soul reaches perfect freedom from attachment and worldly suffering and from the cycle of birth and rebirth.[9] The law of karma is Nature's stubborn and inexorable law from which there is no escape. It exacts a full accounting of all our actions and reactions and is the feedback that completes all loops. Karma ensures that we must eventually all face the consequences of our actions both collectively and individually. It is the supreme power that came into existence when the universe manifested as matter. It is present at every holonic structure in the vast configuration of the universe, from the microcosm to the macrocosm. It is said that we incur karma just by being born, and birth or rebirth represent cycles of imperfection in the soul that must return to the physical realms in order to learn what remains of the lessons before it can reach nirvana. To end the painful cycles of birth and rebirth, saints and sages have offered ways to mitigate our karmic footprint. Learning to meditate is one way to escape the trappings of the mind and access the higher realms of existence, the realms of the soul. Acts of truthfulness, purity, selflessness, and universal love become virtues along the path. Gandhi's teachings of nonviolence are part of the path as well. The Eastern spiritual perspective is also present in the fulfillment of benevolent desires and aspirations and acts of selfless service. It is present in the deeds that are of charitable and philanthropic nature. These acts discipline the mind and divert its powers toward the altruistic and self-purifying virtues that free the soul from its bondage.

> *Everything in the Universe is the fruit of a Just Law, the Law of Causality, the Law of Cause and Effect, the Law of Karma.*
>
> —Gautama Buddha

Karma can also be mitigated in how we treat other lifeforms on the planet. According to the moral, social, and spiritual codes of conduct of my teachings, we are not to interfere in the lives of any animals. Eating meat, foul, and fish adds points to our karmic footprint since these creatures are considered living entities working their way up the spiritual evolutionary ladder. But we must eat to survive, and thus the adoption of a vegetarian diet is recommended as the one that carries the smallest karmic footprint.

Ironically, these ancient views are now coalescing with the view of environmentalists. A plant-based diet has a carbon footprint 75 percent lower than that of a nonvegetarian diet and causes considerably less harm to the land and the water and to biodiversity—all factors in the forces that are now pressing against the boundaries of the Earth systems and pushing us closer to collapse. The ancient concept of karma, like the spirituality and wisdom of the Native American tribes, can show us how to live in harmony with Nature and the cosmos again. It can show us a different path that we could have taken to realize our full potential while remaining in awe of the mystery of the unknown.

It might be that our inquiry into planetary matters, whether it comes from *First sapiens* or *Second*, represents the peak of human intelligence. Maybe the idea that we are entering into the new Anthropocene epoch will prove to have been just a passing one as our planet takes a slightly longer period of time to adjust to all the changes caused by our activities and eventually return us to a state of ecological balance. It might be that it is possible for us to survive this new era of ecological change and preserve some elemental aspects of human civilization. Through her resilience, perhaps Gaia can return to the heaven on earth known as the Holocene, proving that the emergence of this new epoch has been an illusion created out of fear by those who don't fully understand her capacities, which lie beyond the comprehension of the mind. Perhaps Gaia can prove scientists wrong when they say that our business-as-usual scenario will cause irreversible and ubiquitous change and no ecosystem on Earth will be safe. It is possible that solutions called for by scientists—from our massive investment in a green-energy infrastructure and carbon capture to new approaches to agricultural practices and a shift away from a meat-based diet—can mitigate enough ecological damage so that all life can continue. It is also possible that global governing structures can evolve beyond the paper tiger known as the United Nations and that a new breed of world leaders can act as one to stem further degradation of our planetary systems. And it is possible for us to adopt the post-collapse virtues outlined in this chapter as pre-collapse aspirations and ways to avoid ecological collapse and reconnect with Nature. We might come to understand how, in the woven web of life, we are but one small thread. It is still possible for us to mingle the pure waters of Western thought with the sacred waters of Eastern transcendentalism and emerge fuller humans rising from the ashes of darkness. We can break the shackles of karmic debt, of death and rebirth, and overcome fear and the earthly desires of our egos, knowing that we are part of the cosmic mystery that sprang into being billions of years ago.

In the grand scheme of things, the question of survival is not up to us to answer. It is a matter that has already been decided by factors beyond the grasp of humankind, complex dynamics that transcend our quest for meaning in the cosmic unknown. The mystery of existence, human and otherwise, is but a whisper in a vast void, a melody played on the strings of fate. That fate was determined in a single burst of quantum energy over thirteen billion years ago. Its echoes ripple outward, forever stretching the fabric of time and space. With the tiniest variation in those ripples, nothing would have been the same. The fact that I'm writing this book and you are reading it is testament to the perfection of the universe. Not a single Milky Way, not a single planet, and not a single creature or molecule are out of place. There is no sin or mistake in calculation. There is no dualistic ontology or moral turpitude that can alter the trillions of interactions perfected over billions of years of cosmic existence. The cosmic joke lies in our tendency to search for significance in a potentially meaningless existence. We construct narratives, create values, and strive for goals, despite the possibility that the universe exists in a state of indifference to our struggles and aspirations. Maybe this is what our current ecological predicament is offering us: an invitation to laugh at ourselves and our existential woes. Accepting the absurdity of life can liberate us from our anthropocentric tendencies that often place us at the center of the universe. This is the nature of the mystery that remains beyond our grasp. It is a symphony both of stardust and of newly born stars, all orchestrated by a silent conductor. All we can do is give it meaning.

Notes

INTRODUCTION

Epigraph. Bird and Sherwin, *American Prometheus*, xiii.

1. Francis, *Light after Dark*, 187–99.
2. LitCharts, "Science and Morality."
3. Mattick, "Hotfoots of the Gods."
4. Harari, *Homo Deus*, 71–75.
5. Chaucer, *Canterbury Tales*, General Prologue, lines 1–12.
6. Wikipedia, "Ecopsychology."
7. Graves, "Levels of Existence," 10.
8. Beck and Cowan, *Spiral Dynamics*, 286–89.
9. Graves, *Never Ending Quest*, vi.
10. Tonkin, "Meme Distribution Data."
11. Beck and Cowan, *Spiral Dynamics*, 286–89.
12. Beck et al, *Spiral Dynamics in Action*, 18–20.
13. Graves, "Human Nature Prepares for a Momentous Leap," 84.

CHAPTER ONE

Epigraph. Friedman, *Thank You for Being Late*, 28.

1. The United Nations, "The United Nations Charter: Preamble."
2. Korten, *Post-Corporate World*, 1.
3. Wang, "Cold War and War on Terror."
4. Fritz and Sheesgreen, "Pay Freeze at the UN?"
5. Taylor, "Exclusive: US Slashed CDC Staff inside China."
6. Dawlabani, "Castles in the Sand."
7. Rankin, "Ex-NATO Head Says Putin Wanted to Join Alliance."
8. Zakaria, "Russian Invasion of Ukraine an Unequal Fight."
9. Killian and Plante, "The Russian Oil Supply Shock of 2022."
10. Coates, "A Century of Sanctions."
11. Maalouf, *Emerge!*, 64–68.

12. Hamid, "Middle Eastern Autocrats Embarrassed Biden at Will."
13. LNG Allies, "Joint Letter to President Biden on Energy Security."
14. Milman, "How the Gas Industry Capitalized on the Ukraine War."
15. Climate Action Tracker, "Global Reaction to Energy Crisis Risks Zero Carbon Transition."
16. Friedman and Friedman, *Free to Choose*, 215.
17. Richardson, "The Great Depression."
18. Federal Reserve Media Center, "Transcript of Chair Powell's Press Conference."
19. Krugman, "Inflation."
20. Northwest Bank, "Don't Let Your Buying Power Slip Away."
21. Pullokaran, "SVB News."
22. Wikipedia, "Obsolescence."
23. Boyd, "Human Reboot."
24. Scranton, *We're Doomed: Now What?*, 4.

CHAPTER TWO

Epigraph. Schumacher, *Small Is Beautiful*, 13.

1. Brecht, *Martin Luther*, 192–95.
2. Kricheldorf, *Getting It Right*, 63.
3. Graves, "Levels of Existence," 23.
4. Steed, "Every Once in a While," 24–28, 74.
5. Beck et al, *Spiral Dynamics in Action*, 49–50.
6. Ibid., 37–50.
7. Graves, *Never Ending Quest*, 6.
8. Wikipedia, "Complex System."
9. Koestler, *Ghosts in the Machine*, 55.
10. Graves, "Levels of Existence," 8.
11. Dawlabani, *Light of Ishtar*, 127–30.
12. Graves, *Never Ending* Quest, 176.
13. Wikipedia, "Kondratiev Wave."
14. Nitz, *Green Prophet.*
15. Wikipedia, "Resolution Trust Corporation."
16. Hera, "Forget about Housing."
17. Andrews, "Greenspan Concedes Error on Regulation."
18. Ong et al, *Patterns of Ownership of Single Family Rentals.*
19. Dayen, "Wall Street Is Dismantling Financial Reform Piece by Piece."
20. Federal Reserve Board, "Remarks by Governor Ben S. Bernanke."
21. Wikipedia, "William McChesney Martin, Jr."

CHAPTER 3

Epigraph. Capra and Luisi, *Systems View of Life,* 14.

1. Americans for Prosperity, "IPCC, The World's Unrivaled Authority."
2. Malthus, *Essay on the Principle of Population,* 18.
3. Ibid.
4. Harari, *Homo Deus,* 72.
5. Steffen et al, "The Anthropocene," 619.
6. Steffen et al, "The Trajectory of the Anthropocene," 14.
7. Watts, "Johan Rockström."
8. Stockholm Resilience Centre, "Planetary Boundaries."
9. Catton, *Overshoot,* 170.
10. Frogstuff, "Bracketing and Phenomenological Reduction."
11. Huber et al, "Emergent Complexity of the Cytoskeleton," 26.
12. Graves, "Levels of Existence," 21.
13. Bar-Yam, *General Features of Complex Systems.*
14. Ibid.
15. Spirkin, "Philosophy as a World View and a Methodology."
16. MacLennan, *Evolutionary Psychology.*
17. Capra and Luisi, *Systems View of Life,* 165.
18. Mingers, "Introduction to Autopoiesis," 159.
19. Lovelock, *Gaia,* 9.
20. Rantanen et al, "The Arctic Has Warmed Nearly Four Times Faster."
21. Lovelock, *Revenge of Gaia,* 32–34.
22. Wikipedia, "Paris Agreement."
23. Odendahl, Terry, "The Failures of the Paris Climate Change Agreement."
24. World Meteorological Organization, "Past Eight Years Confirmed to Be Warmest on Record."
25. United Nations, "Code Red."
26. United Nations, "Cooperate or Perish."
27. Thunberg, "If World Leaders Choose to Fail Us."
28. Faria, "UN Boss Thinks Socialism Will Fix the World's Problems."
29. Carmen, "Metacapital Framework."
30. Graves, "Levels of Existence," 18.
31. Graves, "Human Nature Prepares for a Momentous Leap," 84.
32. Tsanoff, *Moral Ideals of Our Civilization,* 125.
33. Wikipedia, "Ilya Prigogine."
34. Harris, *Thresholds of the Mind,* 41.
35. Hofstadter, *Metamagical Themas,* 365.
36. Prigogine and Stengers, *Order Out of Chaos,* xiv.

37. Ibid., 143.
38. Conte, "Perfect Game," 140–62.
39. Plutynski and LaPlane, "Cancer."
40. Graves, "An Emergent Theory of Ethical Behavior."
41. Tyson, *Starry Messenger*, 42–61.
42. Graves, "Levels of Existence," 8.
43. Ibid., 2.
44. Meadows et al, *Limits to Growth*, 23–24.
45. Passell et al, "Limits to Growth."
46. Meadows et al, *Limits to Growth*, 31.
47. Herrington, "Update to Limits to Growth."
48. Heinberg, "Limits to Growth at 50."
49. Wikipedia, "Systems Theory."
50. Murphy, "America's Largest Private Companies."
51. Noor, "Project 2025."
52. Lovelock, *Vanishing Face of Gaia*, 255.

CHAPTER FOUR

Epigraph. Graves, "Human Nature Prepares for a Momentous Leap," 72.

1. Beck et al, *Spiral Dynamics in Action*, 11.
2. Ibid, 14.
3. Ibid, 13.
4. Graves, "Human Nature Prepares for a Momentous Leap," 72.
5. Graves, *Never Ending* Quest, iv.
6. Wikipedia, "Abraham Maslow."
7. Graves, *Never Ending* Quest, iv.
8. Beck et al, *Spiral Dynamics in Action*, 17.
9. Ibid., 18.
10. Graves, *Never Ending Quest*, v.
11. Graves, "Levels of Existence," 3.
12. Beck, "Six Games to Glory."
13. Dawlabani, "Clare W. Graves Revisited."
14. Center for Human Emergence Middle East.
15. Graves, "Levels of Existence," 7.
16. Beck and Cowan, *Spiral Dynamics*, 31.
17. Ibid., 53.
18. Ibid., 55.
19. Ibid., 50.
20. Graves, "An Emergent Theory."
21. Beck and Cowan, *Spiral Dynamics*, 168.

22. Ibid., 76–80.
23. Ibid., 42.
24. Ibid., 34–47.
25. Beck, *In Quest of the Master Code.*
26. Graves, "Levels of Existence," 8.
27. Graves, "Human Nature Prepares for a Momentous Leap," 84.
28. Ibid., 82.
29. Loizos, "1,100+ Notable Signatories."
30. Graves, "Levels of Existence," 10.
31. Graves, *Never Ending Quest*, 163.
32. Ibid., 202.
33. Beck and Cowan, *Spiral Dynamics*, 203–14.
34. Beck and Dawlabani, "Economic Systems."
35. Beck and Cowan, *Spiral Dynamics*, 215–28.
36. Dawlabani, *MEMEnomics*, 105–8.
37. Beck and Dawlabani, "Economic Systems."
38. Beck and Cowan, *Spiral Dynamics*, 229–43.
39. Dawlabani, *MEMEnomics*, 108–123.
40. Beck and Dawlabani, "Economic Systems."
41. Beck and Cowan, *Spiral Dynamics*, 245–59.
42. Wilson, "What is Human Nature?"
43. Naess, "The Shallow and the Deep," 95.
44. Beck and Dawlabani, "Economic Systems."
45. Beck and Cowan, *Spiral Dynamics*, 260–65.
46. B Lab, "What is a Benefit Corporation?"
47. Beck and Dawlabani, "Economic Systems."
48. Dawlabani, "Bloody Dance."
49. Graves, "Human Nature Prepares for a Momentous Leap," 78.
50. Ibid., 83–84.
51. Graves, *Never Ending Quest*, 503.

CHAPTER FIVE

Epigraph. Graves, "Human Nature Prepares for a Momentous Leap," 75.

1. Ibid., 81–82.
2. Turnbull, *Mountain People.*
3. Beck, "Momentous Leap."
4. Graves, "Human Nature Prepares for a Momentous Leap," 81–82.
5. Tonkin, "Meme Distribution Data."
6. Beck and Cowan, *Spiral Dynamics*, 274–6.
7. Graves, "Levels of Existence," 10.

8. Dawlabani, "Introduction to Spiral Dynamics."
9. Basar, "Theory of the Whole-Brain-Work," 136.
10. Lipton, *Becoming the Superorganism.*
11. *Psychology Today*, "Howard Bloom."
12. Bloom, *Global Brain*, 223.
13. Graves, *Never Ending Quest*, 370.
14. Serwer, "Elon Musk's Free Speech Charade."
15. McArdle, "Wall Street Dems Threaten to Support Trump."
16. Wikipedia, "Paul Volker."
17. Hirsch, "Comprehensive Case against Larry Summers."
18. Beck, "Spiral Dynamics Perspective."
19. Beck and Cowan, *Spiral Dynamics*, 286–89.
20. Graves, *Never Ending Quest*, 398.
21. Beck and Cowan, *Spiral Dynamics*, 287.
22. Dewoody et al, "Pando Lives," 493.
23. United States Department of Agriculture, "Pando (I spread)."
24. Dawlabani, *MEMEnomics*, 66–67.

CHAPTER SIX

Epigraph. Crutzen and Schwägerl, "Living in the Anthropocene."
1. Jason, "Ken Wilber."
2. Integral European Conference, "Planetary Awakening 2.0."
3. Wittrock, "ITC 2015."
4. McElreath and Henrich, "Dual Inheritance Theory."
5. Lipton, *Biology of Belief*, 21.
6. Ibid., 57.
7. Gould, *Structure of Evolutionary Theory*, 187.
8. Lipton, quoted in Atkinson et al, *Our Moment of Choice*, 153.
9. Ibid., 154.
10. Lovelock, *Vanishing Face of Gaia*, 255.
11. Margulis, quoted in Royte, "Attack of the Microbiologists."
12. Gould, "Kropotkin Was No Crackpot."
13. Dawkins, *Extended Phenotype*, 235.
14. Varela, *AZ Quotes.*
15. Hickman, "James Lovelock."
16. Tyrrell, *On Gaia*, 209.
17. Lovelock, *Revenge of Gaia*, 47.
18. Sorkin, "BlackRock C.E.O. Larry Fink."
19. Carmen, "The Metacapital Framework."
20. Graves, "Levels of Existence," 2.

21. Wikipedia. "Ecopsychology."
22. Dunlap and Catton, "Struggling with Human Exceptionalism."
23. Catton, *Overshoot*, 84.
24. Lehto, review of Ostrom, *Governing the Commons.*
25. Hardin, "Tragedy of the Commons."
26. Wikipedia. "Environmental philosophy."
27. Wikipedia. "List of Environmental Philosophers."
28. Smith, Mick. "Deep Ecology," 141.
29. Jungian Confrerie, "The Mother Archetype."
30. Cattunar, "Gender Oppression."
31. Weisheipl, "Ockham and the Mertonians," 639.
32. Crosby, *Measure of Reality*, 9–19.
33. Graves, *Never Ending Quest*, 391.

CHAPTER SEVEN

Epigraph. Campbell, *Myths to Live By*, 104.

1. Collapse Psychology, "How Do We Respond to Ongoing Collapse?"
2. Abdurrachman et al, "Five Periods of Mass Extinction."
3. American Psychological Association, "APA Dictionary of Psychology: Collective Unconscious."
4. Perry, "The Shadow."
5. Jung, *The Undiscovered Self*, 68.
6. Academy of Ideas, "Carl Jung."
7. Kübler-Ross, quoted from the *EKR Foundation.*
8. Casabianca, "Mourning and the Five Stages of Grief."
9. Scudellari, "State of Denial."
10. Monbiot, "Denial Industry."
11. Casabianca, "Mourning and the Five Stages of Grief."
12. Van Zomeren et al, "Toward an Integrative Social Identity Model," 504.
13. Casabianca, "Mourning and the Five Stages of Grief."
14. Drwotzan, "Stranded Assets Could Exact Steep Costs."
15. Casabianca, "Mourning and the Five Stages of Grief."
16. Haase, "Climate Change and Mental Health Connections."
17. Stevens, "What are the Signs and Symptoms of Depression?"
18. Casabianca, "Mourning and the Five Stages of Grief."
19. Campbell, *Creative Mythology*, 4–6 passim.
20. Levi-Strauss, "Structural Study of Myth," 431.
21. Campbell, *Hero with a Thousand Faces*, 59.
22. Ibid., 64–68.

23. Ibid., 77.
24. Ibid., 90.
25. Ibid., 91.
26. Ibid., 107–10.
27. Ibid., 155.
28. Ibid., 204–05, 209. Campbell's quote, "Be sure there's nothing… renew its form," is from Ovid, *Metamorphoses* 15, 252–55.
29. Tolle, "Return of Aliveness."
30. O'Reilly, "True Battle for Fredericksburg."

CHAPTER 8

Epigraph. Gibran, "The Plutocrat."

1. Hickel, *Less is More,* 12.
2. Bascom, "Probing Question."
3. Sage, "Plant Seeds," iii.
4. Harari, *Homo Deus,* 395.
5. Graves, "Human Nature Prepares for a Momentous Leap," 79–81.
6. Livingston and Samenow, "In Hot Water."
7. United Nations, "Hottest July Ever."
8. Mead, quoted by National Museum of American History.
9. Adizes, *Managing Corporate Lifecycles,* 262.
10. Ibid., 264.
11. Ibid.
12. Storrow and E&E News, "Senate Passes Historic Climate Bill."
13. Adizes, *Managing Corporate Lifecycles,* 264.
14. Maalouf, *Emerge!,*180.
15. Pacifica Graduate Institute, "What Ecopsychology Is."
16. Kellert and Wilson, *Biophilia Hypothesis,* 416.
17. Roszak, "Nature of Sanity."
18. Rajalakshmi, "Does 'Climate Anxiety' Belong in the DSM?"
19. Woodbury, "Climate Trauma," 4.
20. Kotzé and Kim, "Earth System Law."
21. Wikipedia. "United Nations Conference on Sustainable Development."
22. Center for Democratic and Environmental Rights. "First US Rights of Nature Enforcement Case Filed."
23. Ibid.
24. Myers, "First Rights of Nature Enforcement Case Filed in the U.S."
25. Kolbert, "Lake in Florida Suing to Protect Itself."
26. Day, "Can a Waterway Sue You?"
27. Noor, "Game Changing."
28. Our Children's Trust, "Meet Our Team."

29. Gelles and Baker, "Judge Rules in Favor of Montana Youths."
30. Ibid.
31. Setzer and Higham, "Global Trends in Climate Change Litigation," 22.
32. Belshaw, *Environmental Philosophy*, 36.
33. Vogel, "Environmental Philosophy after the End of Nature," 1.
34. Warren, *Ecofeminist Philosophy*, 16.
35. Gaard and Gruen, "Ecofeminism," 24.
36. Mies and Shiva, *Ecofeminism*, 24.
37. Warren, "Feminist Environmental Philosophy."
38. Stokols, *Social Ecology in the Digital Age*, 33.
39. Bookchin, *Urbanization without Cities.*
40. Luke, "Deep Ecology," 183.
41. Naess, *Ecology, Community and Lifestyle*, 164–5.
42. Catton and Dunlap, "Environmental Sociology," 46.
43. Dunlap and Catton, "Struggling with Human Exceptionalism," 24.
44. Catton and Dunlap, "Environmental Sociology," 33.
45. Catton, "A Retrospective View," 475.
46. Ibid.
47. Greer, "As Night Closes In."
48. Dowd, "Overshoot."

CHAPTER NINE

Epigraph. Hickel, *Less Is More*, 78.

1. Fankhauser et al, "Meaning of Net Zero," 16.
2. Wikipedia, "How to Avoid a Climate Disaster."
3. Dawlabani, *MEMEnomics*, 125–51.
4. World Bank, "China's Transition to a Low-Carbon Economy."
5. Newfield, *Robert Kennedy*, 64, 234–25.
6. Dawlabani, *MEMEnomics*, 209–13.
7. Choi, "Gross Domestic Product."
8. Meadows, *Thinking in Systems*, 146.
9. Grittayaphong, "Beyond GDP."
10. Georgescu-Roegen, *The Entropy Law*, 304.
11. Ayres, "Practical Limits to Substitution," 116.
12. Georgescu-Roegen, "Energy and Economic Myth," 379.
13. Edwards and Abivardi, "Value of Biodiversity," 233.
14. World Counts, "Number of Planet Earths We Need."
15. Graves, quoted by Bayer, "Good Crisis Is Needed," 11.
16. Rockström et al, "Safe Operating Space for Humanity," 472.
17. Ibid, 473.

18. Ibid, 472.
19. Ibid.
20. Darrah, "Islands that Have Disappeared."
21. Rockström et al, "Safe Operating Space for Humanity," 473.
22. Dawlabani, *MEMEnomics*, 225.
23. Graves, "Human Nature Prepares for a Momentous Leap," 82.
24. Graves, *Never Ending Quest*, 398.
25. Ibid., 400.
26. Center for the Advancement of the Steady State Economy, "Definition of Steady State Economy."
27. Barnes, "Economics for the Anthropocene."
28. Duverger, "Degrowth."
29. Hickel, "What Does Degrowth Mean?" 1108.
30. Graves, "Levels of Existence," 8.
31. United Nations, "Our Common Future."
32. European Commission, "Delivering the European Green Deal."
33. European Commission, "Factsheet."
34. Lambert, "$10.3 Trillion."
35. CFA Institute, "ESG Investing and Analysis."
36. European Commission, "Delivering the European Green Deal."
37. UNEP International Resource Panel, "Decoupling," xv–xvii.
38. Bauer and Papp, "Book Review Perspectives."
39. UNEP International Resource Panel, "Decoupling," 76.
40. Ibid., xv.
41. Roser, "Argument for a Carbon Price."
42. Eurostat. "Glossary: Domestic Material Consumption (DMC)."
43. UNEP International Resource Panel, "Global Material Flow and Resource Productivity."
44. European Environmental Bureau, "Decoupling Debunked."
45. Wiedmann et al, "Material Footprint of Nations," 6271.
46. Ibid.
47. World Bank Group, "Growing Role of Minerals and Metals."
48. Wikipedia, "Silver Mining."
49. Zehng, "Environmental Impacts."
50. Katwala, "Spiralling Environmental Cost."
51. Villena and Gioia, "More Sustainable Supply Chain."
52. Lovins, "Rethinking Production," 39.
53. Unfried, "Der Umweltretter [Environmental Saviour] Michael Braungart."
54. Ellen MacArthur Foundation. "What Is a Circular Economy?"
55. Ibid.

56. Ibid.
57. Wikipedia, "Right to Repair."
58. Ellen MacArthur Foundation, "What Is a Circular Economy?"
59. European Parliament, "Circular Economy."
60. Parker, "Circular Economy Rhetoric."
61. OECD, "Global Material Resources Outlook for 2060."
62. O'Neill et al, "A Good Life for All," 6.
63. Doughnut Economics Action Lab, "Seven Ways to Think Like a 21st Century Economist."
64. Doughnut Economics Action Lab, "What Is Doughnut Economics?"
65. Lavilley, "Doughnut Economics."
66. United Nations, "Take Action."
67. Braun and Bohner, "Sustainable Development Goals' Current Status."
68. Mathisen, "Mapped."
69. Hickel, *Less Is More*, 207–19.
70. Jackson, *Prosperity without Growth*, 3–11.
71. Easterlin, "Does Economic Growth Improve the Human Lot?," 112.
72. Wilkinson and Pickett, *The Spirit Level*, 8.
73. Post Growth Institute, "Exploring a Just and Livable World."
74. United Nations, "UN Climate Change Conference."
75. Gambrell et al, "As COP28 Nears Finish."
76. Carrington and Stockton, "Cop28 President Says There Is 'No Science.'"
77. McKay and Loriani. "Earth System Tipping Points."

CHAPTER TEN

Epigraph. Wallace-Wells, *Uninhabitable Earth*, 219.

1. National Oceanic and Atmospheric Administration, "2023 Was the World's Warmest Year on Record."
2. World Counts. "Number of Planet Earths We Need."
3. Scranton, *Learning to Die in the Anthropocene*, 23.
4. Turner, "UN Confirms Hottest Temperature Ever Recorded."
5. Thoreau, *Walden*, 279.
6. Lowe et al, "Cherokee Self-Reliance," 3.
7. National Museum of the American Indian, *Haudenosaunee Guide for Educators.*
8. Perry, "Chief Seattle's Speech."
9. Singh, *Wheel of Life*, 2.

Bibliography

Abdurrachman, Mirzam, Aswan, and Yahdi Zaim. "Five Periods of Mass Extinction on Earth. Are We Entering the Sixth?" *The Conversation* (30 January 2018); https://theconversation.com/5-periods-of-mass-extinction-on-earth-are-we-entering-the-sixth-57575.

Academy of Ideas. "Carl Jung, The Shadow, and the Dangers of Psychological Projection." *Academy of Ideas* (February 28, 2018); https://academyofideas.com/2018/02/carl-jung-shadow-dangers-of-psychological-projection/.

Adizes, Ichak. *Managing Corporate Lifecycles.* Santa Barbara: Adizes Institute, 2004.

American Psychological Association. "APA Dictionary of Psychology: Collective Unconscious." *American Psychological Association* (updated April 19, 2018); https://dictionary.apa.org/collective-unconscious.

Americans for Prosperity. "IPCC, The World's Unrivaled Authority on Climate Science." *France 24* (August 9, 2021); https://www.france24.com/en/live-news/20210809-ipcc-the-world-s-unrivalled-authority-on-climate-science.

Andrews, Edmund L. "Greenspan Concedes Error on Regulation." *New York Times,* October 23, 2008; http://www.nytimes.com/2008/10/24/business/economy/24panel.html.

Atkinson, Robert, Kurt Johnson, and Deborah Moldow, eds. *Our Moment of Choice: Evolutionary Visions and Hope for the Future.* New York, NY: Atria Books, 2020.

Ayres, Robert U. "On the Practical Limits to Substitution." *Ecological Economics* 61 (2007): 115–128.

Barnes, Peter. "Economics for the Anthropocene." *Schumacher Center for a New Economics* (July 2014); https://centerforneweconomics.org/publications/economics-for-the-anthropocene/.

Bar-Yam, Yaneer. *General Features of Complex Systems* [PDF]. Cambridge, MA: *Encyclopedia of Life Support Systems* (2002); https:// www.eolss.net/Sample-Chapters/C15/E1-29-01-00.pdf.

Basar, Erol. "The Theory of the Whole-Brain-Work." *International Journal of Psychophysiology* 60, no. 2: 133–38; https://www.sciencedirect.com/science/article/abs/pii/S0167876006000080.

Bascom, Nick. "Probing Question: Why did Mammals Survive the K/T Extinction?" *Penn State Research* (January 18, 2010); https://www.psu.edu/news/research/story/probing-question-why-did-mammals-survive-k-t-extinction/#:~:text=%22Even%20if%20large%20herbivorous%20dinosaurs,were%20relatively%20abundant%20after%20the Retrieved June 30, 2023.

Bauer, Diana, and Kathryn Papp. "Book Review Perspectives: The Jevons Paradox and the Myth of Resource Efficiency Improvements." *Sustainability: Science, Practice, and Policy* 5, no. 1 (March 18, 2009).

Bayer, Tom. "Good Crisis is Needed." *The Dallas Morning* News, May 14, 1978.

Beck, Don E. *In Quest of the Master Code* [Video]. *Inside Edge Foundation* (December 7, 2011); https://www.youtube.com/watch?v=fBv819T4eBc.

________. "The Momentous Leap—From the League of Nations to the United Nations to the Global Meshworks: A 21st Century Transformation." *United Nations Values Caucus* (2013); http://www.humanemergencemiddleeast.org/docs/SDi_UN_Momentous_6_2013.pdf.

________. "Six Games to Glory: A Winning Strategy for the 1995 South African Springbok Team." *Spiral Dynamics Integral* (2015); spiraldynamics-integral.de/wp-content/uploads/2015/11/Beck-Don-Six-Games-To-Glory.pdf.

________. "A Spiral Dynamics Perspective on Cultural Emergence and Nation Building." World Future Society Annual Conference, July 8, 2011. See *The MEMEnomics Group*; http://www.memenomics.com/don-elza-wfs-2011-vancouver.

Beck, Don E. and Christopher C. Cowan. *Spiral Dynamics: Mastering Values, Leadership, and Change.* Malden, MA: Blackwell, 2005.

Beck, Don E. and Said E. Dawlabani. "Economic Systems and the Emerging Values of Humanity: Don Beck and Said Dawlabani [Video]." *Bretton Woods 75* (September 9, 2019); https://www.youtube.com/watch?v=RAfFvELptn0.

Beck, Don E., Teddy Hebo Larsen, Sergey Solonin, Rica Viljoen, and Thomas Q. Johns. *Spiral Dynamics in Action: Humanity's Master Code.* West Sussex, England: John Wiley & Son, Ltd., 2018.

Belshaw, Christopher (2001). *Environmental Philosophy: Reason, Nature, and Human Concern.* London: Routledge, 2001.

Bendell, Jem. *Deep Adaptation: A Map for Navigating Climate Tragedy.* Occasional Paper 2. Initiative for Leadership and Sustainability

(IFLAS), University of Cumbria, Ambleside, UK (July 27, 2018); https:// lifeworth.com/deepadaptation.pdf.

Bird, Kai and Martin J. Sherwin. *American Prometheus: The Triumph and Tragedy of J. Robert Oppenheimer.* New York, NY: Vintage Books, 2005.

B Lab. "What is a Benefit Corporation?" *B Lab: United States and Canada* (accessed May 23, 2022); http://benefitcorp.net.

Bloom, Howard. *Global Brain: The Evolution of Mass Mind from the Big Bang to the 21st Century.* New York, NY: John Wiley & Sons, 2000.

Bookchin, Murray. U*rbanization without Cities: The Rise and Fall of Citizenship.* Montreal: Black Rose Books, 1992.

Boyd, Olivia. "Human Reboot: The Rise of Artificial Intelligence." *The Art and Science of the Possible* (May 2018); https://www.the-possible.com/rise-of-artificial-intelligence-computers-robots-make-jobs-automated-obsolete/#:~:text=Artificial%20intelligence%20(AI)%20researchers%20believe,Yale%20Universities%20published%20in%20March.

Braun, Johanna and Frauke Bohner. "Sustainable Development Goals' Current Status." *Reliefweb; OCHA Services* (October 2023); https://reliefweb.int/report/world/sustainable-development-goals-current-status#:~:text=The%20Sustainable%20Development%20Goals%27%20current,the%20face%20of%20multiple%20crises%22.

Brecht, Martin. *Martin Luther: His Road to Reformation 1483–1521.* Translated from the German by James L. Schaff. Minneapolis: Fortress, 1985.

Campbell, Joseph. *Creative Mythology.* Vol. 4 of *The Masks of God* New York, NY: Viking, 1964.

________. *The Hero with a Thousand Faces.* 3rd ed. Novato, CA : New World Library, 2008.

________. *Myths to Live By.* New York, NY: Penguin Compass, 1993.

Capra, Fritjof and Pier Luigi Luisi. *The Systems View of Life: A Unifying Vision.* Cambridge, England: Cambridge University Press, 2014.

Carmen, Susanna. "The Metacapital Framework: A Design-Led Approach to Mapping Ecosystems." *Enlivening Edge* (November 3, 2016); https://enliveningedge.org/tools-practices/metacapital-framework-design-led-approach-mapping-ecosystems/.

Carrington, Damian, and Ben Stockton. "Cop28 President Says There Is 'No Science' behind Demands for Phase-Out of Fossil Fuels. *The Guardian* (December 3, 2023); https://www.theguardian.com/environment/2023/dec/03/back-into-caves-cop28-president-dismisses-phase-out-of-fossil-fuels

Casabianca, Sandra Silva. "Mourning and the Five Stages of Grief." *PsychCentral* (updated February 11, 2021); https://psychcentral.com/lib/the-5-stages-of-loss-and-grief.

Catton, William R. *Overshoot: The Ecological basis of Revolutionary Change.* Champaign: University of Illinois Press, 1980.

________. "A Retrospective View of My Development as an Environmental Sociologist" [PDF]. *Organization and Environment.* 21, no. 4 (October 30, 2008): 471–77; doi:10.1177/1086026608328870.

Catton, William R. and Riley E. Dunlap. "Environmental Sociology: A New Paradigm." *American Sociologist* 13, no. 1 (January 1978); 41–49; https://www.jstor.org/stable/27702311.

Cattunar, Barbara. "Gender Oppression in the Enlightenment Era" (July 13, 2014); http://www.hsnsw.asn.au/articles/WomenOfTheEnlightenment.pdf.

Center for the Advancement of the Steady State Economy. "Definition of Steady State Economy." *CASSE* (2024); https://steadystate.org/discover/definition-of-steady-state-economy.

Center for Democratic and Environmental Rights. "First US Rights of Nature Enforcement Case Filed— 04/27/2021." *Cder* (accessed July 23, 2023; https://www.centerforenvironmentalrights.org/news/first-us-rights-of-nature-enforcement-case-filed.

Center for Human Emergence Middle East (accessed March 22, 2023); http://www.humanemergencemiddleeast.org.

CFA Institute. "ESG Investing and Analysis." *CFA Institute* (accessed October 18, 2023); https://www.cfainstitute.org/en/rpc-overview/esg-investing.

Chaucer, Geoffrey. *The Canterbury Tales.* Translated from Middle to Modern English at Towson University (accessed April 5, 2024); https://tigerweb.towson.edu/duncan/chaucer/duallang1.htm.

Choi, Kwan. "Gross Domestic Product." *Internet Archive* (accessed September 27, 2023); https://web.archive.org/web/20200924144700/https://www2.econ.iastate.edu/classes/econ355/choi/gdp.htm.

Climate Action Tracker. "Global Reaction to Energy Crisis Risks Zero Carbon Transition." *Climate Action Tracker* (June 8, 2022); https://climateactiontracker.org/publications/global-reaction-to-energy-crisis-risks-zero-carbon-transition/.

Coates, Benjamin. "A Century of Sanctions." *OSU.EDU* (December 2019); https://origins.osu.edu/article/economic-sanctions-history-trump-global.

Collapse Psychology. "How Do We Respond to Ongoing Collapse?" *Collapse Psychology* (accessed June 1, 2024); https://collapsepsychology.org.

Conte, Joseph M. "The Perfect Game: Dynamic Equilibrium and the Bifurcation Point in Robert Coover's *The Universal Baseball Association.*" Chapter 6 in *Design and Debris: A Chaotics of Postmodern American Fiction.* Tuscaloosa: University of Alabama Press, 2002.

Crosby, Alfred W. *The Measure of Reality: Quantification and Western Society, 1250–1600.* Cambridge, England: Cambridge University Press, 1997.

Crutzen, Paul J. and Christian Schwägerl. "Living in the Anthropocene: Toward a New Global Ethos." *YaleEnvironment360* (January 24, 2011); https:// e360.yale.edu/features/living_in_the_anthropocene_toward_a_new_global_ethos.

Darrah, Petrina. "Islands that Have Disappeared: A Tragic Loss to the World." *Global Vision International* (March 16, 2023); https://www.gviusa.com/blog/smb-islands-that-have-disappeared-a-tragic-loss-to-the-world/#:~:text=The%20Kiribati%20Islands%2C%20a%20group,crops%20and%20access%20clean%20water.

Dawkins, Richard. *The Extended Phenotype: The Long Reach of the Gene.* Oxford: Oxford University Press, 1982.

Dawlabani, Said E. "The Bloody Dance of the Red and the Green: A Spiral Dynamics Perspective on Geopolitics." *The MEMEnomics Group* (December 19, 2016); https://www.academia.edu/40264133/The_Bloody_Dance_of_the_Red_and_the_Green_A_Spiral_Dynamics_Perspective_on_Geopolitics.

________. "Castles in the Sand, Part 3: Monetary Implosion." *Medium* (August 16, 2020); https://s-dawlabani.medium.com/castles-in-the-sand-part-iii-monetary-implosion-d9d9f31a8475.

________. "Clare W. Graves Revisited: Beyond Value Systems; Biocultural Coevolution and the Double Helix Nature of Existence." *Integral Leadership Review* (December 2020); http://integralleadershipreview.com/17759-12-21-clare-w-graves-revisited-beyond-value-systems-biocultural-co-evolution-and-the-double-helix-nature-of-existence/.

________. "Introduction to Spiral Dynamics in Large Scale Applications" [Video]. Presentation at the Center for Integrative Psychology. *YouTube* (October 2016); https://www.youtube.com/watch?v=7JW5xiZ7fjg&t=605s.

________. *The Light of Ishtar: A Story of Love, Loss and the Search for Meaning.* Cardiff, CA: Waterside Productions, 2021.

________. *MEMEnomics: The Next-Generation Economic System.* New York, NY: SelectBooks, 2013.

Day, April. "Can a Waterway Sue You?" *Save The Water* (February 9, 2023); https://savethewater.org/can-a-waterway-sue-you/.

Dayen, David. "Wall Street Is Dismantling Financial Reform Piece by Piece." *The New Republic* (December 19, 2014); https://newrepublic.com/article/120606/volcker-rule-delayed-how-wall-street-dismantling-financial-reform.

Dewoody, Jennifer, Carol A. Rowe, Valerie D. Hipkins, and Karen E. Mock. "Pando Lives: Molecular Genetic Evidence of a Giant Aspen Clone in Central Utah." *Western North American Naturalist* 68, no. 4 (2008), 493–97.

Doughnut Economics Action Lab. "Seven Ways to Think Like a 21st Century Economist" [chart]. *Doughnut Economics Action Lab* (accessed November 23, 2023); https://doughnuteconomics.org/about-doughnut-economics#introduction.

________. "What Is Doughnut Economics?" *Doughnut Economics Action Lab* (accessed November 23, 2023); https://doughnuteconomics.org/about-doughnut-economics#introduction.

Dowd, Michael. "Overshoot: Where We Stand Now." [Guest post on Dave Pollard's website]. *How to Save the World* (September 21, 2021); https://;howtosavetheworld.ca/2021/09/21/overshoot-where-we-stand-now-guest-post-by-michael-dowd/.

Drwotzan, Mark. "Stranded Assets Could Exact Steep Costs on Fossil Energy Producers and Investors." *MIT News* (August 19, 2022); https://news.mit.edu/2022/stranded-assets-could-exact-steep-costs-fossil-energy-producers-investors-0819#:~:text=The%20estimated%20global%20net%20present,from%20%241.3%20to%20%242.3%20trillion.

Dunlap, Riley E. and William R. Catton Jr. "Struggling with Human Exceptionalism: The Rise, Decline, and Revitalization of Environmental Sociology." *American Sociologist* 25 (Spring 1994): 5–30; https://www.thegreatstory.org/dunlap-catton-1994-struggling.pdf.

Duverger, Timothée. "Degrowth: The History of an Idea." *EHNE: Sorbonne University* (2020); https://ehne.fr/en/encyclopedia/themes/material-civilization/transnational-consumption-and-circulations/degrowth-history-idea.

Easterlin, Richard A. "Does Economic Growth Improve the Human Lot? Some Empirical Evidence" [PDF]. *New York Times* (1974; accessed November 28, 2023): 89–125; http://graphics8.nytimes.com/images/2008/04/16/business/Easterlin1974.pdf.

Edwards, Peter J., and Cyrus Abivardi. "The Value of Biodiversity: Where Ecology and Economy Blend." *Biological Conservation* 83, no. 2 (1998): 239–246.

Ellen MacArthur Foundation. "What Is a Circular Economy?" *Ellen MacArthur Foundation.* https://www.ellenmacarthurfoundation.org/topics/circular-economy-introduction/overview.

European Commission. "Delivering the European Green Deal: On the Path to a Climate-Neutral Europe by 2050." *European Commission* (July 14, 2021);

https://commission.europa.eu/strategy-and-policy/priorities-2019-2024/european-green-deal/delivering-european-green-deal_en.

________. "Factsheet: The Green Deal Industrial Plan." *European Commission* (February 1, 2023); https://ec.europa.eu/commission/presscorner/detail/en/FS_23_514.

European Environmental Bureau. "Decoupling Debunked—Evidence and Arguments against Green Growth as a Sole Strategy for Sustainability." *EEB* (July 8, 2019); https://eeb.org/library/decoupling-debunked/.

European Parliament. "Circular Economy: Definition, Importance, and Benefits." *Topics: European Parliament* (May 24, 2023); https://www.europarl.europa.eu/news/en/headlines/economy/20151201STO05603/circular-economy-definition-importance-and-benefits.

Eurostat. "Glossary: Domestic Material Consumption (DMC)." *Eurostat: Statistics Explained* (last edited August 10, 2023); https://ec.europa.eu/eurostat/statistics-explained/index.php?title=Glossary:Domestic_material_consumption_(DMC).

Fankhauser, Sam, Stephen M. Smith, Myles Allen, Kaya Axelsson, Thomas Hale, Cameron Hepburn, J. Michael Kendall, Radhika Khosla, Javier Lezaun, Eli Mitchell-Larson et al. "The Meaning of Net Zero and How to Get It Right." *Nature Climate Change* 12 (2022): 15–21; https://doi.org/10.1038/s41558-021-01245-w.

Faria, Zachary. "UN Boss Thinks Socialism Will Fix the World's Problems. He's Wrong." *The Washington Examiner* (July 20, 2020); https://www.washingtonexaminer.com/opinion/un-boss-thinks-socialism-will-fix-the-worlds-problems-hes-wrong.

Federal Reserve Board. "Remarks by Governor Ben S. Bernanke at the Conference to Honor Milton Friedman, University of Chicago, Chicago, Illinois, November 8, 2002." *Federal Reserve Board* (accessed October 23, 2022); https://www.federalreserve.gov/boarddocs/speeches/2002/20021108/default.htm.

Federal Reserve Media Center. "Transcript of Chair Powell's Press Conference." *Federal Reserve Media Center* (April 29, 2020); https://www.federalreserve.gov/mediacenter/files/FOMCpresconf20200429.pdf.

Francis, Charles. *Light after Dark*. Vol. 1, *Structures of the Sky*. Harborough, England: Troubador Publishing, Ltd., 2018.

Friedman, Milton and Rose Friedman. *Free to Choose: A Personal Statement*. New York, NY: Mariner Books,1990.

Friedman, Thomas L. *Thank You for Being Late: An Optimist's Guide to Thriving in the Age of Accelerations*. New York, NY: Farrar, Straus, and Giroux, 2016.

Fritze, John and Deirdre Sheesgreen. "Pay Freeze at the UN? Trump Administration Owes the United Nations $1 Billion." *USA Today* (October 9, 2019); https://www.usatoday.com/story/news/politics/2019/10/09/donald-trump-dismisses-united-nations-deficits-says-others-should-pay/3917554002/.

Frogstuff. "Bracketing and Phenomenological Reduction." *Phenomenology Research* (May 7, 2011); https://phenomenologyresearch.wordpress.com/2011/05/07/bracketing-and-phenomenological-reduction/.

Gaard, Greta and Lori Gruen. "Ecofeminism: Toward Global Justice and Planetary Health." *Society and Nature* 2 (1993): 1–35; https://www.academia.edu/32438639/Ecofeminism_Toward_Global_Justice_and_Planetary_Health.

Gambrell, Jonn, Jamey Keaten, Seth Borenstein, and Sibi Arasu. (11 December, 2023). "As COP28 Nears Finish, Critics Say Proposal 'Doesn't Even Come Close' to What's Needed on Climate." The Associated Press (December 11, 2023); https://apnews.com/article/cop28-climate-summit-negotiations-fossil-fuels-47dfd6dbf32d987e885acd6dbffc7954#.

Gelles, David and Mike Baker. "Judge Rules in Favor of Montana Youths in a Landmark Climate Case." *New York Times*, August 14, 2023; https://www.nytimes.com/2023/08/14/us/montana-youth-climate-ruling.html?campaign_id=54&emc=edit_clim_20230815&instance_id=100099&nl=climate-forward®i_id=171139812&segment_id=142079&te=1&user_id=a0dacb39ab1ec6e2dc3c181fba2d5d38.

Georgescu-Roegen, Nicholas. "Energy and Economic Myth." *Southern Economic Journal* 41, no. 3 (1975): 347–81.

________. *The Entropy Law and the Economic Process*. Cambridge, MA: Harvard University Press, 1971, 236–248.

Gibran, Kahlil. "The Plutocrat." In *The Forerunner: His Parables and Poems*. New York, NY: A. A. Knopf, 1920.

Gould, Stephen Jay. "Kropotkin Was No Crackpot." *Natural History* 106 (June1997):12-21.https://libcom.org/article/kropotkin-was-no-crackpot-stephen-jay-gould.

________. *The Structure of Evolutionary Theory*. Harvard: Belknap Harvard, 2002.

Graves, Clare W. "An Emergent Theory of Ethical Behavior Based upon an Epigenetic Model." *Dr. Clare W. Graves* (1959); https://www.clarewgraves.com/articles_content/1959/I.html.

________. "Human Nature Prepares for a Momentous Leap." *The Futurist* (April 1974): 72–87.

________. "Levels of Existence Conception of Adult Human Behavior." Transcript of speech originally entitled, "The Emergent-Cyclical

Phenomenological-Existential Double-Helix Level of Existence Conception of Adult Human Behavior." University of North Texas, April 17, 1978. Edited by Said Elias Dawlabani and available through the Spiral Dynamics Group, Inc. (2022); https://www.memenomics.com/wp-content/uploads/2022/12/Graves-1978-transcription-1-1.pdf.

________. *The Never Ending Quest.* Edited by Christopher Cowan and Natasha Todorovic. Santa Barbara, CA: ECLET, 2005.

Greer, John Michael. "As Night Closes In." *Resilience* (February 5, 2015); https:// www.resilience.org/stories/2015-02-05/as-night-closes-in/.

Grittayaphong, Praew. "Beyond GDP: Three Other Ways to Measure Economic Health." *Federal Reserve Bank of St. Louis* (April 19, 2023); https://www.stlouisfed.org/open-vault/2023/apr/three-other-ways-to-measure-economic-health-beyond-gdp.

Haase, Elizabeth. "Climate Change and Mental Health Connections." *American Psychiatric Association* (May 2023); https://www.psychiatry.org/patients-families/climate-change-and-mental-health-connections.

Hamid, Shadi. "Middle Eastern Autocrats Embarrassed Biden at Will." *Brookings* (July 22, 2022); https://www.brookings.edu/blog/order-from-chaos/2022/07/22/middle-eastern-autocrats-embarrassed-biden-at-will/.

Harari, Yuval Noah. *Homo Deus: A Brief History of Tomorrow.* New York, NY: Harper Collins, 2018.

Hardin, Garrett. "The Tragedy of the Commons." *Science* (December 13, 1968). See *The Garrett Hardin Society* (updated March 13, 2005); www.garretthardinsociety.org/articles/art_tragedy_of_the_commons.html.

Harris, Bill. *Thresholds of the Mind.* Beaverton, OR: Centerpointe Press, 2002.

Heinberg, Richard. "The Limits to Growth at 50: From Scenarios to Unfolding Reality." *Millennium Alliance for Humanity and the Biosphere* (February 24, 2022); https://mahb.stanford.edu/library-item/the-limits-to-growth-at-50-from-scenarios-to-unfolding-reality/.

Hera, Ron. "Forget about Housing, the Real Cause of the Crisis Was OTC Derivatives." *Business Insider* (May 11, 2010); https://www.businessinsider.com/bubble-derivatives-otc-2010-5.

Herrington, Gaya. "Update to Limits to Growth: Comparing the World3 Model with Empirical Data." *Journal of Industrial Ecology* (November 3, 2020); https://advisory.kpmg.us/content/dam/advisory/en/pdfs/2021/yale-publication.pdf.

Hickel, Jason. *Less Is More: How Degrowth Will Save the World.* New York, NY: Penguin, 2020.

________. "What Does Degrowth Mean? A Few Points of Clarification" [PDF]. *Globalizations* 18, no. 7, (2021): 1105–11; https://blogs.law.columbia.edu/utopia1313/files/2022/11/What-does-degrowth-mean-A-few-points-of-clarification.pdf.

Hickman, Leo. "James Lovelock: Humans Are Too Stupid to Prevent Climate Change." *The Guardian* (March 29, 2010); https://www.theguardian.com/science/2010/mar/29/james-lovelock-climate-change.

Hirsch, Michael. "The Comprehensive Case against Larry Summers." *The Atlantic* (September 13, 2013); https://www.theatlantic.com/business/archive/2013/09/the-comprehensive-case-against-larry-summers/279651/.

Hofstadter, Douglas R. *Metamagical Themas: Questing for the Essence of Mind and Pattern.* New York, NY: Basic Books, 1985.

Huber, F, J. Schnauss, S. Roenicke, P. Rauch, K. Mueller, C. Fuetterer, and J. Kaes. "Emergent Complexity of the Cytoskeleton: From Single Filaments to Tissue." *Advances in Physics* 62, no. 1: 1–112 (January 2013); https://pubmed.ncbi.nlm.nih.gov/24748680/.

Integral European Conference. "Planetary Awakening 2.0." *IEC 2023* (May 24–28, 2023); https://integraleuropeanconference.com/iec-2023-program/.

Jackson, Tim. *Prosperity without Growth: Economics for a Finite Planet.* Sustainable Development Commission. New York, NY: Routledge, 2009.

Jason, Todd. "Ken Wilber: Why I'm Hopeful about the Future" [Video Interview]. *YouTube* (September 2022); https://www.youtube.com/watch?v=H_jYzjJNSV4.

Jung, C. G. *The Undiscovered Self: The Dilemma of the Individual in Modern Society.* New York, NY: Berkley, 2023.

The Jungian Confrerie. "The Mother Archetype" (accessed May 6, 2023); https://www.jungian-confrerie.com/phdi/p1.nsf/supppages/8209?opendocument&part=24#:~:text=The%20mother%20archetype%20is%20a,wisdom%20of%20the%20divine%20feminine.

Katwala, Amit. "The Spiralling Environmental Cost of Our Lithium Battery Addiction." *Wired Magazine* (August 5, 2018); https://www.wired.co.uk/article/lithium-batteries-environment-impact.

Kellert, Stephen R. and Edward O. Wilson. *The Biophilia Hypothesis.* Cambridge MA: Harvard University Press, 1984.

Killian, Lutz and Michael D. Plante. "The Russian Oil Supply Shock of 2022." *Federal Reserve Bank of Dallas* (March 22, 2022); https://www.dallasfed.org/research/economics/2022/0322.

Koestler, Arthur. *Ghosts in the Machine.* London: Hutchinson & Co, 1967.

Kolbert, Elizabeth. "A Lake in Florida Suing to Protect Itself." *New Yorker* (April 11, 2022); https://www.newyorker.com/magazine/2022/04/18/a-lake-in-florida-suing-to-protect-itself.

Korten, David C. *The Post-Corporate World: Life after Capitalism.* Oakland, CA: Berrett-Koehler, 2000.

Kotzé, Louis J. and Rakhyun E. Kim. "Earth System Law: The Juridical Dimensions of Earth Systems Governance." In *Earth System Governance* 1 (January 2019). *ScienceDirect* (accessed July 3, 2023); https://www.sciencedirect.com/science/article/pii/S2589811619300023?via%3Dihub.

Kricheldorf, Hans R. *Getting It Right in Science and Medicine: Can Science Progress through Errors? Fallacies and Facts.* Switzerland: Springer International, 2016.

Krugman, Paul. "Inflation: A Revolution of Falling Expectations." *New York Times,* July 19, 2022; https://www.nytimes.com/2022/07/19/opinion/inflation-prices-fed.html?searchResultPosition=2.

Kübler-Ross, Elisabeth. *EKR Foundation* (accessed June 1, 2024); https://www.ekrfoundation.org/elisabeth-kubler-ross/quotes/.

Lambert, James. "$10.3 Trillion: The Value of the Green Economy Opportunity." *Oxford Economics* (November 8, 2022); https://www.oxfordeconomics.com/resource/the-value-of-the-green-opportunity/.

Lavilley, Vincent. "The Doughnut Economics: Definition and Critical Analysis." *Bonpote* (July 2022); https://bonpote.com/en/the-doughnut-economics-definition-and-critical-analysis/.

Lehto, Otto. Review of Elinor Ostrom. *Governing the Commons: The Evolution of Institutions for Collective Action. Goodreads* (accessed July 2, 2024); https://www.goodreads.com/en/book/show/1048424#CommunityReviews.

Levi-Strauss, Claude. "The Structural Study of Myth." *Journal of American Folklore* 68, no. 270 (October–November 1955): 428–44.

Lipton, Bruce. *Becoming the Superorganism of Humanity* [Video]. *Source of Synergy* (July 2014); https://www.youtube.com/watch?v=aZ0gNa2jDJI.

________. *The Biology of Belief: Unleashing the Power of Conciseness, Matter, and Miracles.* 10th anniversary ed. Carlsbad, CA: Hay House, 2016.

________. "An Introduction to Conscious Evolution: A Theory We Can Thrive With." *Spandau* 7, no. 1 (2017): 183–92.

LitCharts. "Science and Morality: Theme Analysis [of Kurt Vonnegut's Cat's Cradle]." *LitCharts* (accessed April 3, 2023); https://www.litcharts.com/lit/cat-s-cradle/themes/science-and-morality.

Livingston, Ian, and Jason Samenow. "In Hot Water: South Florida Ocean Tops 100 Degrees; Could be World Record." *Washington* Post, July 25, 2023; https://www.washingtonpost.com/weather/2023/07/25/florida-record-warm-ocean-climate/.

LNG Allies. "Joint Letter to President Biden on Energy Security." *LNG Allies: the USLNG Association* (February 25, 2022); https://lngallies.com/energy-security/.

Loizos, Connie. "1,100+ Notable Signatories Just Signed an Open Letter Asking All AI Labs to Immediately Pause for at Least 6 Months." *Tech Crunch* (March 28, 2023); https://techcrunch.com/2023/03/28/1100-notable-signatories-just-signed-an-open-letter-asking-all-ai-labs-to-immediately-pause-for-at-least-6-months/.

Lovelock, James. *Gaia: A New Look at Life on Earth.* Oxford: Oxford University Press, 1979.

________. *The Revenge of Gaia: Earth's Climate Crisis and the Faith of Humanity.* New York, NY: Basic Books, 2006.

________. *The Vanishing Face of Gaia.* New York, NY: Basic Books, 2009.

Lovins, L. Hunter. "Rethinking Production." In Worldwatch Institute. *2008 State of the World: Innovations for a Sustainable Economy.* New York, NY: W. W. Norton, 2008.

Lowe, John, Cheryl Riggs, Jim Henson, and Patricia Liehr. "Cherokee Self-Reliance and Word–Use in Stories of Stress." *Journal of Cultural Diversity* 16, no. 1 (Spring 2009): 5–9. See *National Library of Medicine* (accessed December 28, 2023); https://www.ncbi.nlm.nih.gov/pmc/articles/PMC2914319/.

Luke, Timothy W. "Deep Ecology: Living as if Nature Mattered." *Organization and Environment* 15, no. 2 (June 2002): 178–186; https://journals.sagepub.com/doi/10.1177/10826602015002005.

Maalouf, Elza S. *Emerge! The Rise of Functional Democracy and the Future of the Middle East.* New York, NY: Select Books, 2014.

MacLennan, Bruce. *Evolutionary Psychology, Complex Systems, and Social Theory.* Knoxville: Department of Electrical Engineering and Computer Science, University of Tennessee (accessed October 30, 2022); http://web.eecs.utk.edu/~bmaclenn/papers/EPCSST.pdf.

Malthus, Thomas. *An Essay on the Principle of Population.* London: J. Johnson, 1798.

Margulis, Lynn: see Royte, Elizabeth.

Mathisen, Rubin. "Mapped: The World's Largest Economies, Sized by GDP (1970–2022)." *Visual Capitalist* (April 22 2022); https://www.visualcapitalist.com.

Mattick, Paul. "Hotfoots of the Gods." *New York Times,* February 15, 1998; https://www.nytimes.com/books/98/02/15/reviews/980215.15mattict.html.

McArdle, Mairead. "Wall Street Dems Threaten to Support Trump if Warren Wins Nomination." *National Review* (September 26, 2019); https://

www.nationalreview.com/news/wall-street-democrats-threaten-to-support-trump-if-elizabeth-warren-wins-nomination/.

McElreath, Richard, and Joseph Henrich. "Dual Inheritance Theory: The Evolution of Human Cultural Capacities and Cultural Evolution." In Robin Dunbar and Louise Barrett, eds. *Oxford Handbook of Evolutionary Psychology*. Oxford: Oxford University Press, 2007.

McKay, David I. Armstrong, and Sina Loriani. "Earth System Tipping Points." *Global Tipping Points* (accessed December 19, 2023); https://global-tipping-points.org/section1/1-earth-system-tipping-points/.

Mead, Margaret. National Museum of American History. *Smithsonian* (accessed June 26, 2024); https://americanhistory.si.edu/collections/nmah_1285394

Meadows, Donella. *Thinking in Systems: A Primer.* Edited by Diana Wright. White River Junction, VT: Chelsea Green, 2008.

Meadows, Donella H., Dennis L Meadows, Jørgen Randers, and William Behrens III. *The Limits to Growth; A Report for the Club of Rome's Project on the Predicament of Mankind.* New York, NY: Universe Books, 1972.

Mies, Maria and Vandana Shiva. *Ecofeminism.* Halifax, NS: Fernwood Publications, 1993.

Milman, Oliver. "How the Gas Industry Capitalized on the Ukraine War to Change Biden Policy." *The Guardian* (September 22, 2022); https://www.theguardian.com/environment/2022/sep/22/gas-industry-ukraine-war-biden-policy.

Mingers, John. "An Introduction to Autopoiesis: Implications and Applications." *Systems Practice* 2, no. 2 (1989): 159–80; https://www.academia.edu/2521737.

Monbiot, George. "The Denial Industry." *The Guardian* (September 19, 2006); https://www.theguardian.com/environment/2006/sep/19/ethicalliving.g2.

Murphy, Andrea. "America's Largest Private Companies." *Forbes Magazine* (November 14, 2023); https://www.forbes.com/lists/largest-private-companies/.

Myers, Steve. "First Rights of Nature Enforcement Case Filed in the U.S.—Wilde Cypress Branch v. Beachline." *Center for Democratic and Environmental Rights* (January 27, 2022); https://www.centerforenvironmentalrights.org/blog-2/first-rights-of-nature-enforcement-case-filed-in-the-us-wilde-cypress-branch-v-beachline.

Naess, Arne. *Ecology, Community and Lifestyle: Outline of an Ecosophy.* Translated by David Rothenberg. Cambridge, England: Cambridge University Press, 1989.

________. "The Shallow and the Deep, Long-Range Ecology Movement: A Summary." *Inquiry* 16, no. 1–4 (1973): 95–100. *Taylor and Francis Online* (August 29, 2008); https://www.tandfonline.com/doi/abs/10.1080/00201747308601682.

National Museum of the American Indian. *Haudenosaunee Guide for Educators* (accessed December 28, 2023; https://americanindian.si.edu/sites/1/files/pdf/education/HaudenosauneeGuide.pdf

National Oceanic and Atmospheric Administration. "2023 Was the World's Warmest Year on Record, by Far." *NOAA* (January 12, 2024); www.noaa.gov/news/2023-was-worlds-warmest-year-on-record-by-far.

Newfield, Jack. *Robert Kennedy: A Memoir.* New York, NY: Penguin Group, 1988.

Nitz, Brian. *Green Prophet* (2014); https://www.greenprophet.com. Specific quote no longer available.

Noor, Dharna. "Game Changing: Spate of US Lawsuits Calls Big Oil to Account for Climate Crisis." *The Guardian* (June 7, 2023); https://www.theguardian.com/us-news/2023/jun/07/climate-crisis-big-oil-lawsuits-constitution.

________. "'Project 2025': Plan to Dismantle US Climate Policy for the Next Republican President." *The Guardian* (July, 27, 2023); https://www.theguardian.com/environment/2023/jul/27/project-2025-dismantle-us-climate-policy-next-republican-president Retrieved March 12, 2024.

Northwest Bank. "Don't Let Your Buying Power Slip Away." *Northwest Bank* (April 16, 2021); https://www.nw.bank/newsroom/realtor-news/how-higher-interest-rates-affect-your-buying-power#:~:text=Higher%20Rates%20%3D%20Less%20Purchasing%20Power,power%20decreases%20by%20about%2010%25.

Odendahl, Terry. "The Failures of the Paris Climate Change Agreement and How Philanthropy Can Fix Them." *Stanford Social Innovation Review* (January 22, 2016); https://ssir.org/articles/entry/the_failures_of_the_paris_climate_change_agreement_and_how_philanthropy_can.

OECD. "Global Material Resources Outlook for 2060: Economic Drivers and Environmental Consequences." *OECD* (October 2018); https://www.oecd.org/environment/waste/highlights-global-material-resources-outlook-to-2060.pdf.

O'Neill, Daniel W., Andrew L. Fanning, William F. Lamb, and Julia K. Steinberger "A Good Life for All within Planetary Boundaries" [PDF]. *University of Leeds* (2018); https://eprints.whiterose.ac.uk/127264/1/GoodLifeWithinPB_AuthorAcceptedVersion.pdf

Ong, Paul M., Anne Yoon, Silvia Gonzalez, and Chhandara Pech. *Patterns of Ownership of Single-Family Home Rentals: San Joaquin County. UCLA Center for Neighborhood Knowledge* (February 2022); https://knowledge.luskin.ucla.edu/wp-content/uploads/2022/03/SanJoaquin_SFR_Final.pdf.

O'Reilly, Frank A. "The True Battle for Fredericksburg, December 11–13, 1862." *American Battlefield Trust* (accessed June 30, 2023); https://www.battlefields.org/learn/articles/true-battle-fredericksburg.

Ostrom, Elinor. *Governing the Commons: The Evolution of Institutions for Community Action.* Cambridge, England: Cambridge University Press, 2015.

Our Children's Trust. "Meet Our Team." *Our Children's Trust: Youth v. Gov* (accessed July 23, 2023); www.ourchildrenstrust.org/our-team.

Pacifica Graduate Institute. "What Ecopsychology Is." *Pacifica Graduate Institute* (accessed September 3, 2023); https://www.pacifica.edu/degree-program/community-liberation-ecopsychology/ecopsychology/.

Parker, Gillian. "Circular Economy Rhetoric Needs a Reality Check." *Economist Impact* (February 19, 2023); https://impact.economist.com/sustainability/circular-economies/circular-economy-rhetoric-needs-a-reality-check.

Passell, Peter, Marc Roberts, and Leonard Ross. "The Limits to Growth." *New York Times Book Review,* April 2, 1972; https://www.nytimes.com/1972/04/02/archives/the-limits-to-growth-a-report-for-the-club-of-romes-project-on-the.html.

Perry, Christopher. "The Shadow." *Society of Analytical Psychology* (August 12, 2015); https://www.thesap.org.uk/articles-on-jungian-psychology-2/about-analysis-and-therapy/the-shadow/.

Perry, Ted. "Chief Seattle's Speech." *Center for the Study of the Pacific Northwest* (accessed December 28, 2023); https://www.washington.edu/uwired/outreach/cspn/Website/Classroom%20Materials/Reading%20the%20Region/Texts%20by%20and%20about%20Natives/Texts/8.html.

Plutynski, Anya and Lucie LaPlane. "Cancer." *Stanford Encyclopedia of Philosophy* (June 19, 2019, rev. October 23, 2023); https://plato.stanford.edu/entries/cancer/#MechPictCanc.

Post Growth Institute. "Exploring a Just and Livable World beyond Capitalism." *Post Growth Institute* (accessed November 28, 2023); https://postgrowth.org.

Prigogine, Ilya, and Isabelle Stengers. *Order out of Chaos: Man's New Dialog with Nature.* New York, NY: Verso Books, 2017.

Psychology Today. "Howard Bloom: About." *Psychology Today* (May 4, 2023); https://www.psychologytoday.com/us/contributors/howard-bloom.

Pullokaran, Jomy Jos. "SVB News: These Companies Have Deposits in the Crisis-Hit Bank. Check the list." *CNBC TV 18* (March 13, 2023); https://www.cnbctv18.com/business/companies/silicon-valley-bank-check-list-of-companies-having-deposits-16146121.htm.

Rajalakshmi, Niranjana. "Does 'Climate Anxiety' Belong in the DSM? Psychotherapists Have Different Opinions about Making Climate Anxiety a Diagnosis." *Science Line* (March 21, 2022); https://scienceline.org/2022/03/does-climate-anxiety-belong-in-the-dsm/.

Rankin, Jennifer. "Ex-NATO Head Says Putin Wanted to Join Alliance Early on in His Rule." *The Guardian* (November 4, 2021); https://www.theguardian.com/world/2021/nov/04/ex-nato-head-says-putin-wanted-to-join-alliance-early-on-in-his-rule.

Rantanen, Michael, Alexey Yu. Karpechko, Antti Lipponen, Kalle Nordling, Otto Hyvärinen, Kimmo Ruosteenoja, Timo Vihma, and Ari Laaksonen. "The Arctic Has Warmed Nearly Four Times Faster than the Globe since 1979." *Nature: Communications Earth & Environment* 3, no. 168 (August 11, 2022); https://www.nature.com/articles/s43247-022-00498-3.

Richardson, Gary. "The Great Depression." *Federal Reserve History* (November 22, 2013); https://www.federalreservehistory.org/essays/great-depression.

Rockström, Johan, Will Steffen, Kevin Noone, Asa Persson, F. Stuart Chapin III, Eric F. Lambin, Timothy M. Lenton, Marten Scheffer, Carl Folke, Hans Joachim Schellnhuber, Björn Nykvist et al. "A Safe Operating Space for Humanity." *Nature* 461 (September 23, 2009): 472–75; https://doi.org/10.1038/461472a.

Roser, Max. "The Argument for a Carbon Price." *Our World in Data* (June 1, 2021); https://ourworldindata.org/carbon-price.

Roszak, Theodore. "The Nature of Sanity: Psychiatrists Often Fail to Chart the Emotional Bond We Have with the Natural Habitat." *Psychology Today* (January 1, 1996, updated June 9 2016); https://www.psychologytoday.com/intl/articles/199601/the-nature-sanity.

Royte, Elizabeth. "Attack of the Microbiologists" [on Lynn Margulis]. *New York Times Magazine* (January 14, 1996); https//:www.nytimes.com/1996/01/14/magazine/attack-of-the-microbiologists.html.

Sage, Rowan F. "Plant Seeds and Floristic Preservation in the Anthropocene." *Annals of Botany* 129, no. 7 (June 18, 2022): i–v,; https://doi.org/10.1093/aob/mcac064.

Schumacher, Ernst F. *Small Is Beautiful: A Study of Economics as if People Matter.* New York, NY: HarperCollins, 2010.

Scranton, Roy. *Learning to Die in the Anthropocene: Reflections on the End of Civilization.* San Francisco: City Lights, 2015.

________. *We're Doomed: Now What? Essays on War and Climate Change.* New York, NY: Soho Press, 2018.

Scudellari, Megan. "State of Denial." *Nature Medicine* 16, no. 3 (March 2010): 248; https://doi.org/10.1038/nm0310-248a.

Serwer, Adam. "Elon Musk's Free Speech Charade Is Over." *The Atlantic* (April 12, 2023); https://www.theatlantic.com/ideas/archive/2023/04/elon-musk-twitter-free-speech-matt-taibbi-substack/673698/.

Setzer, Joana, and Catherine Higham. "Global Trends in Climate Change Litigation: 2022 Snapshot" [PDF]. *Grantham Research Institute on Climate Change and the Environment* (June 30, 2022); https://www.lse.ac.uk/granthaminstitute/publication/global-trends-in-climate-change-litigation-2022/.

Singh, Kirpal. *The Wheel of Life.* Anaheim, CA: Ruhani Satsang, 1980.

Smith, Mick. "Deep Ecology: What Is Said and (to Be) Done?" *The Trumpeter* 30, no. 2 (2014): 141–56; https://trumpeter.athabascau.ca/index.php/trumpet/article/view/1378.

Sorkin, Andrew Ross. "BlackRock C.E.O. Larry Fink: Climate Crisis Will Reshape Finance." *New York Times,* January 14, 2020; https://www.nytimes.com/2020/01/14/business/dealbook/larry-fink-blackrock-climate-change.html.

Spirkin, A. "Philosophy as a World View and a Methodology." Chapter 1 in *Dialectical Materialism. Marxist.org* (accessed May 26, 2024); https://www.marxists.org/reference/archive/spirkin/works/dialectical-materialism/ch01-s04.html.

Steed, Nicholas. "Every Once in a While, a Theory Comes along That Explains Everything." *Maclean's Magazine* 80, no. 19 (October 1967).

Steffen, Will, Paul J. Crutzen, and John R. McNeill. "The Anthropocene: Are Humans Now Overwhelming the Great Forces of Nature?" *AMBIO: A Journal of the Human Environment* 36, no. 8 (December 2007): 614–21; doi: 10.1579/0044-7447(2007)36[614:taahno]2.0.co;2.

Steffen, Will, Wendy Broadgate, Lisa Deutsch, Owen Gaffney, and Cornelia Ludwig. "The Trajectory of the Anthropocene: The Great Acceleration." *Sage Journals: Anthropocene Review* 2, no. 1 (March 2, 2015): 1–18; https://journals.sagepub.com/home/anr.

Stevens, Amanda. "What are the Signs and Symptoms of Depression?" *Heights Treatment* (February 15, 2021); https://www.theheightstreatment.com/2021/02/15/what-are-the-signs-and-symptoms-of-depression/.

Stockholm Resilience Centre. "Planetary Boundaries." *Stockholm University* (May 12, 2023); https://www.stockholmresilience.org/research/planetary-boundaries.html.

Stokols, Daniel. *Social Ecology in the Digital Age: Solving Complex Problems in a Globalized World.* San Diego: Elsevier, Inc., 2018.

Storrow, Benjamin, and E&E News. "Senate Passes Historic Climate Bill—Here's What Comes Next." *Scientific American* (August 8, 2022); https://www.scientificamerican.com/article/senate-passes-historic-climate-bill-heres-what-comes-next/?utm_source=google&utm_medium=paid&utm_campaign=tfd_dsa&gad_source=1&gclid=CjwKCAjww_iwBhApEiwAuG6ccM9LOnWy7bipbtCXWBEC4GH6DK2Sk_awiVtrTBQoPVZ4jdvzAGXTPxoCzDwQAvD_BwE.

Taylor, Marisa. "Exclusive: US Slashed CDC Staff inside China Prior to Coronavirus Outbreak." *Reuters* (March 25, 2020); https://www.reuters.com/article/us-health-coronavirus-china-cdc-exclusiv/exclusive-u-s-slashed-cdc-staff-inside-china-prior-to-coronavirus-outbreak-idUSKBN21C3N5.

Thoreau, Henry David. *Walden; or, Life in the Woods.* Boston: Ticknor and Fields, 1854.

Thunberg, Greta. "If World Leaders Choose to Fail Us, My Generation Will Never Forgive Them."

The Guardian (September 23, 2019); https://www.theguardian.com/commentisfree/2019/sep/23/world-leaders-generation-climate-breakdown-greta-thunberg.

Tolle, Eckhart. "The Return of Aliveness: The Dark Night of the Soul." In Thomas Moore. "A Dark Night of the Soul and the Discovery of Meaning." *Kosmos* (Spring/Summer 2015); https://www.kosmosjournal.org/kj_article/a-dark-night-of-the-soul-and-the-discovery-of-meaning/.

Tonkin, Alan. "Meme Distribution Data." *GRI Equity* (accessed May 20, 2024); https://www.griequity.com/resources/integraltech/GRIBusinessModel/spiraldynamics/meme-data.html.

Tsanoff, Radoslav. *The Moral Ideals of Our Civilization.* New York, NY: E. P. Dutton, 1942.

Turnbull, Colin M. *The Mountain People.* New York, NY: Simon & Schuster, 1972.

Turner, Ben. "UN Confirms Hottest Temperature Ever Recorded in the Arctic." *Live Science* (December 14, 2021); https://www.livescience.com/un-confirms-arctic-hottest-temperature.

Tyrrell, Toby. *On Gaia: A Critical Investigation of the Relationship between Life and Earth.* Princeton, NJ: University Press, 2013; https://press.princeton.edu/books/hardcover/9780691121581/on-gaia.

Tyson, Neil deGrasse. *Starry Messenger: Cosmic Perspectives on Civilization.* New York, NY: Henry Holt and Co., 2022.

UNEP International Resource Panel. "Decoupling Natural Resource Use and Environmental Impacts from Economic Growth." *UN Environment Programme* (2011); https://www.resourcepanel.org/reports/decoupling-natural-resource-use-and-environmental-impacts-economic-growth.

________. "Global Material Flow and Resource Productivity." *UN Environment Programme* (2016); https://www.resourcepanel.org/reports/global-material-flows-and-resource-productivity-database-link.

Unfried, Peter. "Der Umweltretter [Environmental Saviour] Michael Braungart." *Taz* (July 2009); https://taz.de/Oekologisch-industrielle-Revolution/!5166699/.

United Nations. '"Code Red' for Human-Driven Global Heating Warns UN Chief." *UN News* (November 15, 2022); https://news.un.org/en/story/2021/08/1097362.

________. "'Cooperate or Perish': At COP27 UN Chief Calls for Climate Solidarity Pact, Urges Tax on Oil Companies to Finance Loss and Damage." *UN News* (November 7, 2022); https://news.un.org/en/story/2022/11/1130247.

________. "Hottest July Ever Signals 'Era of Global Boiling Has Arrived,' Says UN Chief." *UN News* (July 27, 2023); news.un.org/en/story/2023/07/1139162.

________. "Our Common Future: Report of the World Commission on Environment and Development." *United Nations* (1987; accessed October 17, 2023); https://sustainabledevelopment.un.org/content/documents/5987our-common-future.pdf.

________. "Take Action for the Sustainable Development Goals." *Sustainable Development Goals* (accessed November 24, 2023); https://www.un.org/sustainabledevelopment/sustainable-development-goals/.

________. "UN Climate Change Conference—United Arab Emirates, November 30–December 12, 2023." *United Nations Climate Change* (accessed December 18, 2023); https://unfccc.int/cop28.

________. "The United Nations Charter: Preamble." *United Nations* (accessed June 1, 2022); https://www.un.org/en/about-us/un-charter/preamble.

United States Department of Agriculture. "Pando (I spread)." *USDA Forest Service* (accessed May 29, 2024); https://www.fs.usda.gov/detail/fishlake/home/?cid=STELPRDB5393641#:~:text=When%20the%20Pando%20clone%20was,from%20the%20expanding%20root%20system.

Valera, Francisco J. *AZ Quotes* (accessed June 26, 2024); https://www.azquotes.com/quote/1120779. Cited from Rudrauf, D. "From

Autopoiesis to Neurophenomenology: Francisco Varela's Exploration of the Biophysics of Being." *Biol Res* 36 (2003): 27–65.

________. "On Being Autonomous: The Lessons of Natural History for Systems Theory." In George Klir (ed.) *Applied Systems Research.* New York: Plenum Press, 1977, 77–85.

Van Zomeren, Martijn, Tom Postmes, and Russell Spears. "Toward an Integrative Social Identity Model of Collective Action: A Quantitative Research Synthesis of Three Socio-Psychological Perspectives." *Psychological Bulletin* 134, no. 4 (July 2008): 504–35; doi:10.1037/0033-2909.134.4.504.

Villena, Veronica, and Dennis A. Gioia. "A More Sustainable Supply Chain." *Harvard Business Review* (March–April 2020); https://hbr.org/2020/03/a-more-sustainable-supply-chain.

Vogel, Steven. "Environmental Philosophy after the End of Nature." *Environmental Ethics* 24, no. 1 (March 2002): 23–39; https://doi.org/10.5840/enviroethics200224139.

Wallace-Wells, David. *The Uninhabitable Earth: Life after Warming.* New York, NY: Tim Duggin Books, 2019.

Wang, Brian. "Cold War and War on Terror: Casualties and De-escalation." *Next Big Future* (September 16, 2017); https://www.nextbigfuture.com/2017/09/cold-war-and-war-on-terror-casualties-and-de-escalation.html.

Warren, Karen J. *Ecofeminist Philosophy: A Western Perspective on What It Is and Why It Matters.* Lanham, Maryland: Rowman & Littlefield, Inc., 2000.

________. "Feminist Environmental Philosophy." *Stanford Encyclopedia of Philosophy* (August 29, 2014; rev. April 27, 2015); https://plato.stanford.edu/entries/feminism-environmental/#LinPer.

Watts, Jonathan. "Johan Rockström: 'We Need Bankers as Well as Activists … We Have 10 Years to Cut Emissions by Half.'" *The Guardian* (May 29, 2021); https://www.theguardian.com/environment/2021/may/29/johan-rockstrom-interview-breaking-boundaries-attenborough-biden.

Weisheipl, J. "Ockham and the Mertonians." Edited by J. I. Catto. Vol. 1 of *The History of the University of Oxford.* Edited by T. H. Aston. Oxford: Clarendon Press, 1984.

Wiedmann, Thomas O., Heinz Schandl, Manfred Lenzen, Daniel Moran, Sangwon Suh, James West, and Keiichiro Kanemoto. "The Material Footprint of Nations." *Proceedings of the National Academy of Sciences of the United States of America* 112, no. 20 (2015): 6271–6, abstract.

Wikipedia. "Abraham Maslow." *Wikipedia* (last updated April 19, 2024); https://en.wikipedia.org/wiki/Abraham_Maslow.

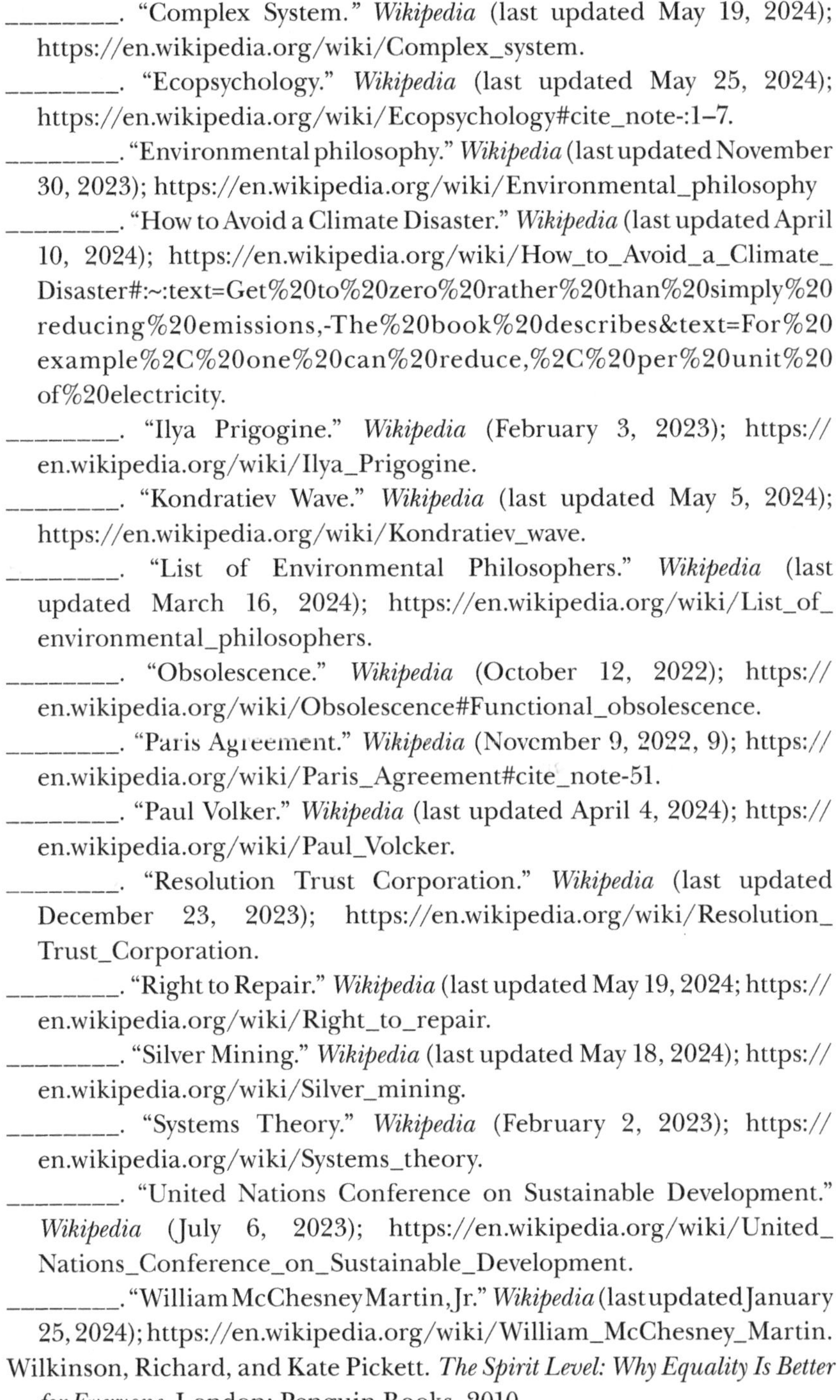

________. “Complex System.” *Wikipedia* (last updated May 19, 2024); https://en.wikipedia.org/wiki/Complex_system.

________. “Ecopsychology.” *Wikipedia* (last updated May 25, 2024); https://en.wikipedia.org/wiki/Ecopsychology#cite_note-:1–7.

________. “Environmental philosophy.” *Wikipedia* (last updated November 30, 2023); https://en.wikipedia.org/wiki/Environmental_philosophy

________. “How to Avoid a Climate Disaster.” *Wikipedia* (last updated April 10, 2024); https://en.wikipedia.org/wiki/How_to_Avoid_a_Climate_Disaster#:~:text=Get%20to%20zero%20rather%20than%20simply%20reducing%20emissions,-The%20book%20describes&text=For%20example%2C%20one%20can%20reduce,%2C%20per%20unit%20of%20electricity.

________. “Ilya Prigogine.” *Wikipedia* (February 3, 2023); https://en.wikipedia.org/wiki/Ilya_Prigogine.

________. “Kondratiev Wave.” *Wikipedia* (last updated May 5, 2024); https://en.wikipedia.org/wiki/Kondratiev_wave.

________. “List of Environmental Philosophers.” *Wikipedia* (last updated March 16, 2024); https://en.wikipedia.org/wiki/List_of_environmental_philosophers.

________. “Obsolescence.” *Wikipedia* (October 12, 2022); https://en.wikipedia.org/wiki/Obsolescence#Functional_obsolescence.

________. “Paris Agreement.” *Wikipedia* (November 9, 2022, 9); https://en.wikipedia.org/wiki/Paris_Agreement#cite_note-51.

________. “Paul Volker.” *Wikipedia* (last updated April 4, 2024); https://en.wikipedia.org/wiki/Paul_Volcker.

________. “Resolution Trust Corporation.” *Wikipedia* (last updated December 23, 2023); https://en.wikipedia.org/wiki/Resolution_Trust_Corporation.

________. “Right to Repair.” *Wikipedia* (last updated May 19, 2024; https://en.wikipedia.org/wiki/Right_to_repair.

________. “Silver Mining.” *Wikipedia* (last updated May 18, 2024); https://en.wikipedia.org/wiki/Silver_mining.

________. “Systems Theory.” *Wikipedia* (February 2, 2023); https://en.wikipedia.org/wiki/Systems_theory.

________. “United Nations Conference on Sustainable Development.” *Wikipedia* (July 6, 2023); https://en.wikipedia.org/wiki/United_Nations_Conference_on_Sustainable_Development.

________. “William McChesney Martin, Jr.” *Wikipedia* (last updated January 25, 2024); https://en.wikipedia.org/wiki/William_McChesney_Martin.

Wilkinson, Richard, and Kate Pickett. *The Spirit Level: Why Equality Is Better for Everyone*. London: Penguin Books, 2010.

Wilson, Edward O. "What is Human Nature? Paleolithic Emotions, Medieval Institutions, God-Like Technology." *Big Think* (accessed March 22, 2023); https://bigthink.com/hard-science/eo-wilson-what-makes-us-human-paleolithic-emotions-medieval-institutions-god-like-technology/.

Wittrock, Dennis. "ITC 2015—Notes from the Field" *Medium* (August 2015); https://medium.com/human-development-project/itc-2015-notes-from-the-field-e5e3eaf6d129.

Woodbury, Zhiwa. "Climate Trauma: Toward a New Taxonomy of Trauma." *Ecopsychology* 11, no. 1 (March 2019): 1–8; https:// www.researchgate.net/publication/330771918_Climate_Trauma_Toward_a_New_Taxonomy_of_Trauma.

The World Bank. "China's Transition to a Low-Carbon Economy and Climate Resilience Needs Shifts in Resources and Technologies." *World Bank* (October 12, 2022); https://www.worldbank.org/en/news/press-release/2022/10/12/china-s-transition-to-a-low-carbon-economy-and-climate-resilience-needs-shifts-in-resources-and-technologies#:~:text=China%20emits%2027%20percent%20of,of%20the%20world%27s%20greenhouse%20gases.

World Bank Group. "The Growing Role of Minerals and Metals for a Low Carbon Future." *Open Knowledge Repository* (June 30, 2017); https://openknowledge.worldbank.org/entities/publication/4cdae3a6-3244-56e5-9de3-8faa5b6c88da.

The World Counts. "Number of Planet Earths We Need." *The World Counts* (accessed September 26, 2023); https://www.theworldcounts.com/challenges/planet-earth/state-of-the-planet/overuse-of-resources-on-earth.

World Metrological Organization. "Past Eight Years Confirmed to Be Warmest on Record." *WMO* (January 12, 2023); https://wmo.int/news/media-centre/past-eight-years-confirmed-be-eight-warmest-record.

Zakaria, Fareed. "Russian Invasion of Ukraine an Unequal Fight, Putin's Priority Regime Change." *Business Today* (February 26, 2022); https://www.businesstoday.in/latest/world/story/russian-invasion-of-ukraine-an-unequal-fight-putins-priority-regime-change-fareed-zakaria-324043-2022-02-26.

Zehng, March. "The Environmental Impacts of Lithium and Cobalt Mining." *Earth.Org* (March 31, 2023); https://earth.org/lithium-and-cobalt-mining/.

INDEX

B

D

E

H

J

K

L

M

N

O

P

S

About the Author

SAID ELIAS DAWLABANI is a human evolution theorist and a leading authority on the application of stage development to large scale change. He is a writer and public speaker specializing in the Gravesian approach to psychosocial development and the evolution of societal systems. He was named one of the world's boldest thought leaders for his views on the future at a gathering of the world's leading economists marking the 75th anniversary of the Bretton Woods financial framework.

Dawlabani is the author of two other book. His first *MEMEnomics, The Next-Generation Economic System* (2013), brought recognition of his stage development model as a specialty in the field of cultural economics. His work has been translated to over 20 languages including Korean, Mandarin, German and Russian. He has given keynote speeches on sustainable and regenerative economics in many parts of the world. His second book, *The Light of Ishtar (2021),* is a personal memoir that chronicles his journey in life with his wife and soulmate Elza Maalouf through myth and psycho-spirituality.

Dawlabani founded of The MEMEnomics Group, a platform that is dedicated to *speaking Gaian truth to economic power* by uncovering the values of a regenerative future driven by a mandate for de-growth. He was a close associate of renowned geopolitical advisor, the late Don E. Beck. Dr. Beck was Graves' successor and one of the architects behind South Africa's transition from Apartheid and the author of Spiral Dynamics, the most authoritative theory on stage development and change. Before teaming up with Beck, Dawlabani had a prominent career in the real estate and building industries.

In 2005, he cofounded The Center for Human Emergence Middle East, with Beck and Maalouf. The center is a think tank that frames socio-political and economic issues of the region through the prism of cultural stage development. He is a contributor to *The Huffington Post, Medium, Integral Leadership Review, Kosmos Journal* and other publications. His work is featured in the *Leader-to-Leader Quarterly Journal, Newsweek* and *The Christian Science Monitor* and on NPR, PRN, and Voice of America. He's a past lecturer on the topic of transformational leadership at the Adizes Graduate School in Santa Barbara, and the University of Virginia. He can be reached at s.dawlabani@gmail.com

www.ingramcontent.com/pod-product-compliance
Lightning Source LLC
Chambersburg PA
CBHW050641270326
41927CB00012B/2827

* 9 7 8 1 9 6 2 9 8 4 6 2 1 *